SEVENTH EDITION

# Learning and Behavior

## PAUL CHANCE

WADSWORTH
CENGAGE Learning·

Australia · Brazil · Japan · Korea · Mexico · Singapore · Spain · United Kingdom · United States

*Learning and Behavior,* **Seventh Edition**
Paul Chance

Publisher: Jon-David Hague

Developmental Editor: Ken King

Assistant Editor: Jessica Alderman

Editorial Assistant: Amelia Blevins

Managing Media Editor: Mary Noel

Senior Brand Manager: Elisabeth Rhoden

Market Development Manager:
Christine Sosa

Art and Cover Direction, Production
Management, and Composition:
PreMediaGlobal

Manufacturing Planner: Karen Hunt

Senior Rights Acquisitions Specialist:
Dean Dauphinais

Cover Image: Tatyana Vychegzhanina

For product information and technology assistance, contact us at
**Cengage Learning Customer & Sales Support, 1-800-354-9706.**

For permission to use material from this text or product,
submit all requests online at **www.cengage.com/permissions.**
Further permissions questions can be e-mailed to
**permissionrequest@cengage.com.**

Library of Congress Control Number: 2012953850

Student Edition:

ISBN-13: 978-1-111-83277-3

ISBN-10: 1-111-83277-3

Loose-leaf Edition:

ISBN-13: 978-1-111-83496-8

ISBN-10: 1-111-83496-2

**Wadsworth**
20 Davis Drive
Belmont, CA 94002-3098
USA

Cengage Learning is a leading provider of customized learning solutions
with office locations around the globe, including Singapore, the United
Kingdom, Australia, Mexico, Brazil, and Japan. Locate your local office at
**www.cengage.com/global.**

Cengage Learning products are represented in Canada by
Nelson Education, Ltd.

To learn more about Wadsworth, visit **www.cengage.com/wadsworth**

Purchase any of our products at your local college store or at our
preferred online store **www.cengagebrain.com.**

Printed in the United States of America
1  2  3  4  5  6  7  17  16  15  14  13

# Brief Contents

# Contents

| **CHAPTER 4** | Pavlovian Applications | 95 |
| --- | --- | --- |

**CHAPTER 5**     Operant Learning: Reinforcement        126

**CHAPTER 8**    Operant Learning: Punishment    230

**CHAPTER 9**  Operant Applications   254

**CHAPTER 10**  Observational Learning   279

**CHAPTER 11** Generalization, Discrimination,
and Stimulus Control                                       313

---

**CHAPTER 12**   Forgetting   345

# Preface

A textbook is like a city: It is never finished. Go into any city and you see old buildings being torn down and new ones being built, trees being planted in vacant lots, jackhammers tearing up streets to install phone lines underground. The same is true of textbooks: Some topics are dropped, new ones added, chapters or sections moved from here to there. Here are some of the changes you'll see in *Learning and Behavior*, 7th edition:

- Updated content. The reference list includes over 100 items dated 2011 or later.
- New topics, including evaluative conditioning, asocial observational learning, computer-based VRET, progressive schedules, and constraint-induced movement therapy, among others.
- More studies are cited to document findings, especially those that are counterintuitive or controversial, such as that learning sometimes occurs without awareness of the contingencies involved.
- New applications, including the use of Pavlovian and operant procedures for diagnosis, assessment, and treatment of medical disorders.
- The Miller–Dollard theory of observational learning has been replaced with a generic operant learning model.
- Increased emphasis on the role of context in forgetting, and the idea that forgetting may be largely a matter of stimulus control, a view taken by increasing numbers of psychologists.
- Footnotes are replaced by brief marginal notes that students are more likely to read.
- An increased emphasis in the recommended reading lists on items students are likely to read, such as Hal Markowitz's *Enriching Animal Lives*, Susan Schneider's *The Science of Consequences*, and articles in *The New Yorker* and other popular periodicals.
- An increase in the number and variety of illustrations, including photographs and sketches.
- Increased coverage of research by evolutionary biologists, primatologists, ethologists, rehabilitation psychologists, developmental psychologists, and cognitive psychologists.

- An increase in coverage of research done outside the United States.
- Researcher affiliations are sometimes provided, mostly involving recent studies, to convey to students that not all noteworthy learning research comes out of Ivy League schools.
- A brief section near the end of each chapter called "A Final Word." My hope is that these will prompt the students to think about and discuss the implications of their reading.
- To make room for new material, I have deleted the workbook (students will find a study guide online); reduced chapter review questions from 20 to 10; shortened the discussion of memory; removed Edwin Twitmyer, the discussion of semantic conditioning, self-control, self-awareness, and mnemonic systems. Some of this material will be available on the book's website.

Although cities are constantly being "revised," some things remain the same for decades. The same is true of texts. The following key features of *Learning and Behavior* remain essentially unchanged:

- A readable style and a cordial tone that help make reading the text a welcome activity rather than a tedious chore, so that students get more out of their class sessions.
- Certain themes continue to run through the text: that learning is a biological mechanism (I call it evolved modifiability) by which individuals cope with change; that changes in behavior are the products of biological and environmental events; and that the natural science approach is the best way to study behavior.
- An abundance of examples and applications to help students "get" the principles, not merely memorize them.
- Though many of the experiments involve animal subjects, the emphasis is on what that research tells us about *human* behavior.
- Chapter 2 reviews the basic research methods used to study learning, including the single-subject designs that are unfamiliar to many students.
- Queries appear at irregular intervals to help keep students alert and help them monitor their progress.
- A practice quiz and review questions appear at the end of each chapter *without* answers. I believe the absence of answers prompts students to think about and discuss the questions and may result in interesting class discussions.
- Data graphs that represent findings in an easy-to-grasp form.

I hope you will find that this is the best edition yet of *Learning and Behavior*, but I'm already making notes for the next edition. As I said, textbooks, like cities, are never really finished.

## Acknowledgments

As always, many people contributed to the "renovation" of this book. Several instructors reviewed the 6th edition and suggested changes that were, as always, a great help. My thanks to:

Kim Andersen, Brigham Young University—Idaho
Shawn R. Charlton, University of Central Arkansas
W. Matthew Collins, Nova Southeastern University
Joanne Hash Converse, Rutgers, the State University of New Jersey
Runae Edwards-Wilson, Kean University
Yoshito Kawahara, San Diego Mesa College
Dennis K. Miller, University of Missouri
H. D. Schlinger, California State University—Los Angeles
David Widman, Juniata College

Other instructors and researchers who offered helpful comments or provided articles, images, or raw data include Willem-Paul Brinkman, Delft University of Technology; Adam Doughty, College of Charleston; Robert Epstein, American Institute for Behavioral Research and Technology; Susan Friedman, Utah State University; Chad Galuska, College of Charleston; Bryan Gibson, Central Michigan University; Reese Halter, Global Forest Science Institute; David Harrison, Bay Cove Human Services in Boston; William Heward, Ohio State University; Lydia Hopper, Georgia State University; Todd Huspeni, University of Wisconsin at Stevens Point; Marianne Jackson, California State University in Fresno; Kent Johnson, Morningside Academy, Seattle; Munsoo Kim, Chonnam National University, South Korea; Nobuo Masataka, Kyoto University, Japan; Koichi Ono, Komazawa University, Japan; David Palmer, Smith College; Thomas Parish, formerly of Kansas State University; James Pfister, Poisonous Plant Research Lab, Utah; Alan Poling, Western Michigan University; Albert Rizzo, University of Southern California; Erica Bree Rosenblum, now at the University of California at Berkeley; Barbara Rothbaum, Emory University; Carolyn Rovee-Collier, Rutgers University; Kurt Salzinger, Hofstra University; Stephen Scherer, San Diego Community College; Susan Schneider, Pacific University, Stockton; Satoru Shimamune, Hosei University, Japan; Edwin Taub, University of Alabama; and Andrew Whiten, University of St. Andrews, Scotland. I owe a special thanks to H. D. ("Hank") Schlinger, long a fan of *Learning and Behavior*, who sent me two dozen journal articles (most of them *not* by him), and with whom I exchanged numerous emails about this book.

I am also grateful to my editor, Ken King, who provided moral support and editing comments as I drafted the revision. I also want to thank Vernon Boes of Cengage Learning and Brenda Carmichael of PremediaGlobal and others who had a hand in producing what must be one of the best cover designs ever seen on a learning text. I also thank Gunjan Chandola and others at PreMediaGlobal for turning out the most aesthetically pleasing edition yet of *Learning and Behavior*.

Finally, I want to thank the students who emailed me with comments, mostly positive but always helpful, about the 6th edition. I cannot list them all, but Michael Allison, a student at San Diego Community College, and Kim Katsaros, a student at the University of Massachusetts in Lowell, seem representative. Michael thanked me for the occasional humor in the book and added, "I'm glad I don't have to read a stuffy and boring learning text." Kim also praised the book but criticized a passage she found offensive (and which, as a result, I deleted). When I hear from students, I often reply, "You made my day!" That is no exaggeration. Thank you, Michael and Kim, and thanks to all the students who took the time to share their thoughts, positive or negative, about *Learning and Behavior.*

As you can see, I am indebted to a lot of people, and I'm sure there are still more who deserve to be on my list. My apologies to you if you are among them. All of you, named and unnamed, have contributed in one way or another to *Learning and Behavior,* 7th edition. Any flaws in the text are my responsibility. Write to me about them at pc@paulchance.net.

Paul Chance

# Note to the Student: How to Get the Most from this Book

As always, I've done what I can to make this book interesting and easy to understand, but you've still got your work cut out for you: There's a lot to learn about learning. Here are some suggestions on how to get the most from this book:

- First, turn to Chapter 12 and study the section called "Learning to Remember." This information will help you learn any course content.
- Second, be sure to read the "Preview" and "In This Chapter . . ." sections at the start of each chapter. This material will help you see where the chapter is headed.
- Third, as you are reading through the text, answer the queries that appear. Write your answer on a slip of paper or say it aloud, then check your answer by reviewing the text above the query or by flipping to the query answers at the end of the chapter.
- Fourth, after you've read a chapter, read the review questions and consider how you would answer them if you were asked those questions in class or on an exam. This is a great thing to do in a study group, since many of these questions can be answered in various ways.
- Fifth, take the practice quiz provided at the end of the chapter. Be sure to *write* your answers as you would if you were taking a quiz in class, or say them to a study partner. These quizzes will help you learn the content *and* give you a rough idea of how well you have mastered it.
- Sixth, take a look at the book's Cengage website. The study guide there should help you master chapter content.

If you really want to get the most from a text or a course, you have to be an active learner. If you want to get the most out of a class, you can't just sit back and listen to the instructor. You have to be actively involved—ask questions, make comments, take notes. The same thing is true when learning from a text: Ask questions, answer queries, make notes, think about the implications and applications of what you read, discuss what you read with other students, and review, review, review. If you are an active learner, you will not only have a far better chance of acing the exams, you will be able to put more of what you learn to practical use for years to come.

If you have read the Preface, you know that I am eager to get feedback about the book from students as well as instructors. If you have thoughts about the book you'd like to share, email me at pc@paulchance.net.

# CHAPTER 1

# Introduction: Learning to Change

*Change is the only constant.*

—**Lucretius**

## PREVIEW

This chapter raises basic questions about the adaptation of humans and other living things to a changing environment. It looks at the adaptation of both species and individuals. The chapter devotes a good deal of space to topics usually covered in biology texts. The reason is that learning is a biological mechanism. Learning did not evolve so that you could learn to solve algebra word problems or program a computer. It is first and foremost a survival mechanism, a means of meeting the challenges that threaten our survival. One question I hope you will consider as your read this book is whether human learning ability is up to the challenges that threaten our survival today.

# THE CONSTANCY OF CHANGE

Keiko, a woman in her sixties, was walking in the underground boarding area in Shinjuku train station, one of the largest train stations in Tokyo, on a spring afternoon. Suddenly she felt very dizzy, so much so that she leaned on a nearby wall to keep from falling. When she looked around, she saw that other people were doing the same thing. It was not dizziness, then, but what was it? There were a few seconds of silence, then a woman nearby shouted, "Jishin da!" (Earthquake!). With that a couple of teenage girls standing nearby screamed.

Earthquakes are a common occurrence in Japan, so after a moment during which there were no signs the building was about to collapse, people continued on their way. Keiko boarded her train, but it did not move; instead there was an announcement: "All train traffic in Tokyo has been suspended."

No trains meant no subways. Keiko's apartment was miles away; how was she to get home? As she emerged from the station, another earthquake struck and someone shouted, "Mite!" ("Look!") and pointed toward the top of a skyscraper. Keiko looked up at Cocoon Tower, a building with a structure that fits its name, and saw it swaying back and forth, like the inverted pendulum of an old-fashioned clock. She wondered how it could sway so far without the upper part breaking off.

The area outside the station was packed with people, so Keiko knew there was little chance of getting a cab. Perhaps a bus? She got into a long line at a bus stop and waited. When a bus came, those at the front of the line boarded, but the bus went nowhere. Finally someone announced that bus transportation

*Cocoon Tower in Tokyo, Japan. The tower swayed back and forth during the March 11, 2011, earthquake, though it was 150 miles from the quake's epicenter.*

was suspended. The only way for Keiko to get home was to walk, but it was a long way from Shinjuku station and she had no map. She knew the way to her sister's home and it was closer, but there was no way to know what she might encounter along the way. Another quake might bring down buildings along her route. Her options were limited, however, so she set off on foot. It took her three hours, but she made it safely. Keiko had been lucky.

Many of the people who lived 150 miles to the northeast, nearer the earthquake's epicenter, were not so lucky. The Great East Japan Earthquake of March 11, 2011, at magnitude 9.0, was the strongest earthquake ever known to have hit Japan and one of the five most powerful earthquakes worldwide since 1900. The earthquake moved the northern part of Honshu, Japan's largest island, about *eight feet* to the east. A tsunami followed the quake, and a wall of water, in some places well over 100 feet high, crashed into the coast, washing away cars and trucks like leaves in a stream, destroying over 300,000 homes, schools, and factories, and killing over 15,000 people. The tsunami also inflicted severe damage on nuclear power plants, resulting in the release of radioactive material that poisoned dairy products, crops, and farmland within a 50-mile radius of the plants, and adding the threat of disease throughout much of Japan for weeks afterward.

Earthquakes, tsunamis, and other natural disasters are a part of life, but we tend to regard them as an aberration, a brief disruption in a normally constant world. When a great volcano erupts, as Mt. St. Helens in Washington State did in 1980, knocking over thousands of trees and covering the ground for miles around with a blanket of volcanic ash; when a gigantic tsunami hits land, as happened in the Indian Ocean in December 2004, killing over 200,000 people and destroying thousands of homes; when a heat wave kills over 50,000 people, as in Europe in the summer of 2003; when a drought rages across a continent, destroying crops and wiping out herds of sheep and cattle, as in Australia from 2006 until 2011, we think how strange it is that nature should misbehave so. It is, we tell ourselves, a momentary lapse, a kind of geological tantrum; soon our old planet will regain its composure, its constancy. But the truth is, as the Roman philosopher Lucretius said 2,000 years ago, "Change is the only constant." We live in a world that is ever-changing, like the varicolored patterns of a steadily rotating kaleidoscope.

Change is not the exception to the rule, it *is* the rule. Throughout nature, the struggle to survive is an effort to cope with change: The climate changes, prey animals become harder to see, predators become faster, diseases strike without warning, population increases put added stresses on the availability of food, water, habitable space, and other resources. Some changes, such as the movement of continents, take place over eons; others, such as the advance or retreat of glaciers, normally take hundreds or thousands of years; some, such as the changes in climate we are now seeing due to human use of fossil fuels, take decades; still others, such as the rise and fall of the sun or the abrupt lane change of an aggressive driver, occur on a daily basis. The one constant in our lives is change. Any individual or species must be able to cope with change if it is to survive. But how? By what mechanisms can we and other animals deal with such a fickle world? Charles Darwin offers one answer.

*To see a video of skyscrapers swaying during the Japan earthquake of 2011, go to youtube.com and search "Japan earthquake." If you think earthquakes are uncommon events, Google, "U. S. Geological Survey earthquake maps."*

*The earth's crust is constantly moving. To see a brief video on how whole continents have moved over millions of years, go to youtube.com and search "650 million years in under 2 minutes."*

CAPSULE **REVIEW** The world in which we live is not a stagnant place. It is constantly changing. Mountains rise and fall, forests become deserts, new diseases appear, countries rise and fall, famine is followed by abundance and visa versa. The history of humanity, and your own personal history, is about coping with change. One way species cope with change is through natural selection.

## NATURAL SELECTION

Charles Darwin was born in England in 1809. The son of a physician, he went to the University of Edinburgh in 1825 to study medicine. His heart was not in it, however, and when the blood and screams of a patient undergoing surgery without anesthesia sent him scurrying to the exit, he decided to pursue a degree in theology at Cambridge University. His heart wasn't in that field, either, and he spent much of his time pursuing his true love, natural history.

Shortly after graduating, Darwin accepted an offer to join an expedition on the British naval vessel HMS *Beagle* as the ship's naturalist. The *Beagle* was under the leadership of Captain Robert FitzRoy, a 23-year-old aristocrat who wanted a naturalist who would also serve as a suitable dinner companion. The chief purpose of the voyage was to map the shorelines of land areas around the world. It was a great success in this endeavor, but it is now remembered only because it gave Darwin the opportunity to gather hundreds of specimens of plants and animals in his effort to understand "that mystery of mysteries," the origin of species.

Darwin took a copy of Charles Lyell's *Principles of Geology* with him on the *Beagle*. Lyell, considered by many the father of geology, got many things wrong (he rejected the idea of ice ages, for example), but his view that the earth

*Portrait of Charles Darwin in the late 1830s when he was about 30 years old.*

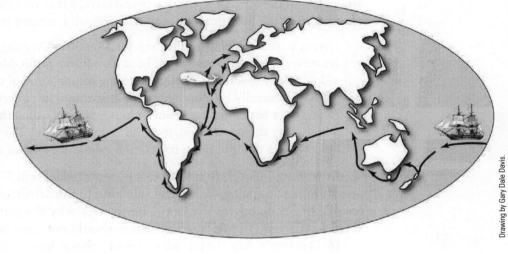

*The course of HMS* Beagle. *The* Beagle *left Plymouth, England, on December 27, 1831, and returned on October 2, 1836.*

changes gradually over eons gave Darwin a new perspective on where species came from. If the earth had been around for millions of years and changed slowly, as Lyell argued, there was no reason to think that the vast variety of life forms had appeared overnight in their current form.

Once back in England, Darwin focused attention on animal breeding as a source of insights into the variations in living things. He was himself a breeder of doves, and knew that breeders had long changed the characteristics of cows, horses, pigs, sheep, chickens, dogs, cats, and other domestic animals by selectively cross-breeding individuals with desirable characteristics. Such breeding seemed to provide a model for changes in species in the wild, but breeding was the result of deliberate, thoughtful intervention by the breeder. Who was nature's breeder?

*Work on selective breeding in foxes over a period of 40 years shows that behavioral characteristics can be selectively bred so that the descendants behave more like a different species than like their own ancestors. See Kukekova and Trut (2007); Trut (1999); also see Goldman (2010) for a nontechnical summary.*

The answer occurred to Darwin when he read a book by a fellow Englishman, Thomas Malthus (1798), called *An Essay on the Principle of Population*. Malthus was a clergyman who did not accept the then-popular idea that human population growth was the path to utopia. On the contrary, Malthus argued that it was the road to ruin. Resources are limited, and eventually an expanding population spells disaster. There are limits to all resources, and as populations increase, these resources prove inadequate to supply all individuals. "The power of population," he wrote, "is indefinitely greater than the power in the earth to produce subsistence for man."

Malthus focused on the effects of human population growth, but Darwin realized that all species of animals and plants produce far more offspring than the environment can possibly support, which inevitably leads to competition for resources. Some survive, but most do not. What determines which individuals and species will win out? Clearly the winners must have features that give them an advantage. Those of their offspring that share their parents' advantage will also tend to survive and reproduce. Over generations, these advantages, some of them very subtle, may accumulate and result in very different species. Darwin saw that the mechanism for change was analogous to the breeder's practice of selectively mating animals with desirable characteristics. The difference is that in the wild, *nature is the breeder:*

> Owing to this struggle for life, any variation, however slight and from whatever cause proceeding, if it be in any degree profitable to an individual of any species, . . . will tend to the preservation of that individual, and will generally be inherited by its offspring. The offspring, also, will thus have a better chance of surviving. . . . I have called this principle, by which each slight variation, if useful, is preserved, by the term of Natural Selection, in order to mark its relation to man's power of selection.

In writing "its relation to man's power of selection," Darwin is drawing attention to the analogy of **natural selection** to the *artificial* selection of breeders. "There is no obvious reason," he wrote, "why the principles which have acted so efficiently under domestication should not have acted under nature."

In Darwin's day, little was known about how characteristics were transmitted from one generation to the next. As Darwin noted, "The laws governing inheritance are quite unknown. . . ." The Austrian friar and founder of genetics, Gregor Mendel, did not publish his work on inheritance in peas until 1866, and it did not become widely known among scientists until the early 1900s. Nevertheless, it was clear that characteristics were somehow passed from one generation to another, and these characteristics were beneficial, detrimental, or of no significance in a particular environment.

It is important to note that natural selection depends on variations among the members of a species. If all members of a species were genetically identical, natural selection would be impossible. As Darwin wrote, "unless profitable variations do occur, natural selection can do nothing."

Darwin's critics have often said that even with variation, natural selection cannot possibly account for the sudden appearance of complex organs such as the human eye. You may be surprised to learn that Darwin agreed. But Darwin went on to say that complex organs do not normally appear suddenly. Far from it.

Evidence suggests that the human eye, for example, had its origin millions of years ago with the appearance of a few light-sensitive cells on the skin of some primitive animals. These light-sensitive cells would have proved helpful since anything that cast a shadow on them could, for example, warn of an approaching predator. Through additional variations and natural selection, more light cells appeared, and the light-detecting organ became more and more complicated until it gradually reached the sophisticated light-sensitive organ found in higher animals, including humans (Lamb, 2011; Schwab, 2011).

This may seem to be pure speculation, since we have no videotape of the evolution of the eye, but it is based on evidence suggesting increasing sophistication of organs, including the eye, as we go through the animal kingdom from the simplest to the more complex species. Consider, for example, the trematode *cercaria*, a parasitic flatworm that invades fish brains (Lafferty & Morris, 1996). Cercaria has two spots that, though they may look a bit like eyes, are nothing at all like any mammal's eye (see Figure 1-1). There is no

*Very few biologists question natural selection today, and it is widely accepted throughout Europe and Asia, but a Gallup poll found that four in ten Americans still believe that God created all forms of life in their present form about 10,000 years ago (Newport, 2010).*

*To see how the increasing complexity of the eye improves vision, go to youtube. com and search "Dawkins eye."*

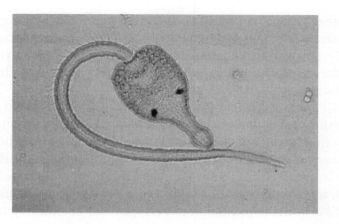

**Figure 1-1**  *The flatworm cercaria with two light-sensitive eye spots. (Image courtesy of Todd C.Huspeni, Curator of Parasites, Department of Biology and Museum of Natural History, University of Wisconsin—Stevens Point.)*

iris, no retina, no vitreous humor, nothing, really, except light-sensitive cells. (Light-sensitive cells form the retina of your more sophisticated eyes.) The cercaria's eyespots help it to find its way to a higher water level where it is more likely to encounter the killifish on which it depends. Go up the evolutionary scale and you see increasingly complex visual equipment. The eye of a reindeer, for example, not only sees more or less what you see, it also responds to ultraviolet light, which helps it to identify both predators and food in snow-covered areas (Hogg et al., 2011).

The human brain is another complex organ that did not appear overnight. The jellyfish has a simple network of neurons, but this primitive nervous system, which serves to coordinate its swimming movements, has no brain at all. The first true brains appear in worms. The brain of the earthworm is about the size of a mustard seed, but it is an advance over the jellyfish. Generally, the further up the evolutionary scale you go, the more complicated the brain and the greater its capacity for dealing with environmental changes.

The devices resulting from natural selection are rarely, if ever, as simple and efficient as they could be, but they generally work (Marcus, 2009; Olshansky, 2009). What natural selection demands is not perfection, but devices that are good enough to aid survival. Natural selection is a crude, inefficient mechanism, so it typically takes countless generations to develop sophisticated tools. You might compare it to carving the sculptures of Mt. Rushmore with a hammer and chisel while blindfolded. Nevertheless, it helps species meet the challenges of a changing environment.

All kinds of changes in the environment can affect the characteristics of a species. Climate change is perhaps the most important of these environmental changes, a point made by Darwin (1859). The west coast of Scotland is famous for its cold winters and its warm wool. Until recently the Soay sheep that produced that wool tended to be large, since smaller sheep often succumbed to the cold before reaching reproductive age. Over the past 25 years, however, the sheep of this area have been getting smaller and lighter (Ozgul et al., 2009; Maloney, Fuller, & Mitchell, 2010). This reduction in size parallels a change in climate due to global warming: Winters in Scotland have gotten shorter and milder in recent decades, so smaller sheep now are more likely to survive and reproduce.

Changes in terrain (due to a change in the course of a river or volcanic eruption, for example) can also induce changes in species through natural selection. Evolutionary biologist Erica Rosenblum and her colleagues at the University of Idaho (Rosenblum et al., 2010), studied three species of lizards in White Sands, New Mexico. All three species have dark skins in other geographic areas, but those that live in White Sands, an area with dunes composed of white gypsum, have developed lighter skins (Figure 1-2). The lizards evolved in areas where their dark skin made them difficult for predators to see, but when they moved into the white dunes, those dark skins made them vulnerable to predators. Those with lighter skins were more likely to survive and reproduce, and this selection process continued over generations until the lizards in the dunes were far lighter than their ancestors.

Pollution provides another example of how changes in the environment affect species characteristics. The classic example is the peppered moth, one

***Figure 1-2*** *The natural selection of skin color. Descendants of lizards that were dark-skinned elsewhere (bottom photo) became light in color when living among white sand dunes in New Mexico. (Photo courtesy of Erica Bree Rosenblum, Department of Biological Sciences, University of Idaho at Moscow.)*

of many large moths found in the British Isles. The peppered moth feeds at night and rests during the day on the trunks and limbs of trees. Its survival depends in large part on its ability to escape detection by the birds that find it an appetizing food. At one time, nearly all of these moths were a mottled light gray color, closely resembling the lichen-covered trees on which they rested. A rare black variation of the moth, first observed in 1848, stood out against this background like coal against snow, making it highly vulnerable. But when pollutants from burning coal killed the lichen and darkened the bark of trees, the light-colored moths increasingly fell prey to birds, whereas the dark moths tended to survive and reproduce. In forests near industrial centers, where pollution was common, the black moths increased in number, and the light-colored variety declined. In some areas, 90% of the moths were of the once-rare black variety (Kettlewell, 1959; see Figure 1-3). In recent years, improvement in local air quality has reversed this trend, so that the lighter variety of moth is once again dominant.

Predators are an important part of most animals' surroundings, and changes in predators play an important role in natural selection. Swanne Gordon of the University of California at Riverside and his colleagues (2009) did an experiment with guppies that demonstrates this. The researchers moved wild guppies in Trinidad from a stream that had no predators to a stream with guppy-eating fish. Eight years later Gordon transferred more guppies from the safer stream and compared the survival rate of their young with the young of guppies that had lived among the predators for many generations. The evolved guppies had a survival rate more than 50% higher than that of the newcomers.

Changes in the environment also affect human characteristics. Human skin color is largely due to the amount of melanin, a substance found in the

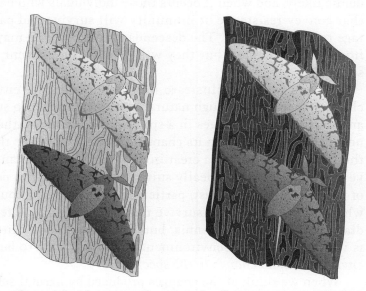

***Figure 1-3***  *The peppered moth and pollution. Prior to 1850, the gray peppered moth was hard to detect against the light trees on which it rested. After soot darkened the trees, the once-rare black variety became dominant. (Drawings by Diane Chance.)*

skin that screens out the sun's harmful rays. The more melanin, the darker the skin, and the more sunlight is screened out. The people of Scandinavia and northern Europe, where there is relatively little sunlight, are typically fair-skinned, a trait that allows them to absorb the sunlight they need to produce vitamin D. People who live near the equator, where there is an abundance of sunlight, are characteristically dark-skinned, a trait that protects them against the hazards of too much sun. Through natural selection, the human species acquires the coloration that survival in a given environment requires.

Many changes due to natural selection are not as obvious as those considered thus far. New diseases can result in widespread deaths, as happened with the bubonic plague that killed a third or more of the people living in Europe in the 14th century. The disease is caused by a bacterium, but the cause of the epidemic was garbage: People routinely threw garbage into the streets, rats fed on the garbage, and the fleas the rats carried infected people with the plague bacteria. Although the mortality rate of bubonic disease was high, some people were genetically resistant or immune to the disease. These people passed these advantages on to their young. This change no doubt proved helpful in subsequent epidemics of the same disease, which were generally less devastating. Not only that, but today this same genetic variation protects some people from the HIV virus that causes AIDS.

Today there is great concern among health professionals about global epidemics. The bacteria that causes bubonic plague is alive and well, as are any number of other microorganisms that pose a threat of pandemics. Increases in international travel and trade bring vectors (carriers of disease-causing organisms) into ports around the world (Smith et al., 2012). The failure of governments to monitor legal and illegal imports adequately makes a pandemic likely, and when it occurs those individuals who have genetic features that convey resistance or immunity will survive and pass on their advantage to their offspring. The descendants of survivors may look no different from those who died, but they will be slightly different, thanks to natural selection.

These examples illustrate how changes in the environment induce changes in species through natural selection. They also suggest that if there are no significant changes in a species' surroundings, there are likely to be no significant changes in its characteristics. We can see this, for example, in the American alligator, a creature that has scarcely changed in 200 million years. The alligator is ideally suited to its habitat, the ponds and wetlands of the American Southeast, particularly the states of Louisiana and Florida, where 2 million of them survive today. The alligator's territory has shrunk drastically over the millennia, but otherwise changed little. Once a species is well adapted to its environment, the rule seems to be: *no change in the environment, no change in the species.*

When we think of the changes produced by natural selection, we usually think of physical characteristics, such as size, shape, and color. In fact, the same pressures that select a physical feature, such as wings, can also select a behavior, such as wing flapping. For example, partridge tend to spend the bulk of their time on the ground, flying into trees only when in danger. In many instances they actually run up trees while flapping their wings. Biologist Kenneth Dial (reported in Wong, 2002) found that wing flapping while running up trees assists the partridge in getting out of reach of predators. Even partridge chicks with immature wings have an easier time reaching the branches as a result of flapping their stubby wings. Chicks that flap their wings when attempting to climb trees are more likely to escape predators than those that don't, so this behavioral tendency is as likely to be selected as are the wings.

Three kinds of behavior are largely the products of natural selection. What are these kinds of behavior? You're about to find out.

CAPSULE **REVIEW**    Charles Darwin was obsessed with the origin of the various life-forms. People had changed the characteristics of domestic animals for thousands of years through selective breeding, and it occurred to Darwin that nature might do much the same thing. Natural selection, he argued, helps species adapt to change over generations. Sophisticated organs do not appear abruptly, but over countless generations; evidence suggests that the human eye, for example, began as light-sensitive cells in primitive organisms. Natural selection changes not only physical characteristics, but certain kinds of behavior as well.

# EVOLVED BEHAVIOR

Natural selection produces a repertoire of largely innate, adaptive forms of behavior that help organisms cope with the demands of their particular environment. The behavior falls into three categories: reflexes, modal action patterns, and general behavior traits.

## Reflexes

A **reflex** is a relationship between a specific event and a simple response to that event. A reflex is not, as is often thought, a particular kind of behavior. Rather, it is a *relationship* between certain kinds of events, usually events in the immediate surroundings, and relatively simple forms of behavior (see Figure 1-4). An example is the tendency to blink when a speck of dirt hits your eye. The reflex is not the eyeblink itself, but the relation between the speck of dirt and the movement of your eyelid.

Reflexes are either present at birth or appear at predictable stages in development. Most reflexes are found in virtually all members of a species and are part of the adaptive equipment of the animal. All animals, from protozoa to college professors, have reflexes.

Many reflexes serve to protect the individual from injury. The amoeba is an irregularly shaped, one-celled animal that travels by extending a part of its perimeter forward and then pulling the rest along after. When the amoeba encounters a noxious substance, it immediately withdraws from it; this reflex

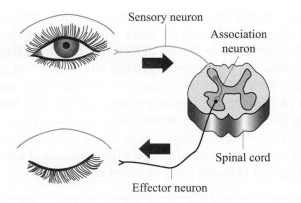

Sensory neuron

Association neuron

Spinal cord

Effector neuron

**Figure 1-4** *The reflex arc. In a typical reflex, an event excites sensory neurons that carry an impulse to the spinal cord, where the impulse is transmitted to an interneuron, which in turn transmits the impulse to effector neurons. The effector neurons carry the impulse to muscle tissues or glands, which then produce a simple response. (Drawing by Gary Dale Davis.)*

minimizes the harmful effects of the substance. Larger animals do much the same thing when they withdraw a limb from a painful object. The professor who picks up a very hot skillet will immediately release it and withdraw the injured hand. Other protective reflexes in humans include the the pupillary reflex, in which the iris contracts or relaxes in response to changes in light; the sneeze, by which irritants such as dust and pollen are expelled from the nose and lungs; and the vomit reflex, which removes toxic substances from the stomach in an efficient, if indelicate, manner.

**QUERY 1:** A reflex is a _____ between a _____ and a simple _____.

Other reflexes are important in food consumption. When an amoeba encounters some edible object, such as a dead bacterium, it immediately responds to the object by engulfing it and making a meal of it. Humans have a number of such consummatory reflexes: Touch a baby's face, and she will turn toward what touched her; this rooting reflex is useful in finding the mother's nipple. When the nipple touches the baby's lips, this evokes the sucking reflex, which brings milk into the baby's mouth. Food in the mouth elicits the salivary reflex, the flow of saliva that begins the process of digestion. The presence of saliva and food in the mouth triggers swallowing. Swallowing triggers peristalsis, the rhythmic motion of the lining of the esophagus that carries food to the stomach. Thus, the simple act of eating is, in large measure, a chain of reflexes.

We tend not to notice useful reflexes until they fail to function properly. Reflex failure is seen in people who have consumed excessive amounts of alcohol or other drugs that depress the central nervous system. Death from alcoholic intoxication can occur, for example, when the alcohol interferes with the respiratory reflex (inhaling and exhaling) or when the intoxicated person vomits inadequately and chokes to death on the vomit—a fact that ought to make people think twice about binge drinking. Fortunately, most of us are blissfully unaware that we even have reflexes until one of them malfunctions.

Not all reflexes are useful. Some people have life-threatening allergic reactions to certain foods, such as peanuts. In some people, epileptic seizures can be triggered by flickering lights, a loud noise, a certain kind of music, or a particular odor. Reflexes are subject to natural selection. Those that contribute to survival will appear more frequently in succeeding generations; those that hinder survival will literally tend to "die out."

Reflexes are highly stereotypic; that is, they are remarkably consistent in form, frequency, strength, and time of appearance during development. This is not to say, however, that they do not vary at all. The rooting reflex mentioned above may first appear in one infant at the age of seven days but may not show up in a second infant for another week. There is also some variation in the form a reflex takes. A tap below the knee may produce a barely detectable knee jerk in one person, whereas in another person of the same age and similar health, the same light blow may result in a kick that looks like an attempt to make a field goal. Reflexes also change across the life span. Motor reflexes tend to slow with age, which is probably one reason people are more likely to fall in their seventies than in their thirties.

## Modal Action Patterns

Another kind of naturally selected behavior is the **modal action pattern (MAP)**, a series of related acts found in all or nearly all members of a species (Tinbergen, 1951). They used to be called *instincts,* but this term fell out of favor, partly because it came to refer to any more or less automatic act (as in, "Martha *instinctively* slammed on the brakes"). Other terms seen in the literature include *fixed action patterns* and *species-specific behavior.*

Modal action patterns resemble reflexes in that they have a strong genetic basis; display relatively little variability from individual to individual or from day to day in the same individual; and often are reliably elicited by a particular kind of event, called a **releaser.** MAPs differ from reflexes in that they involve the entire organism rather than a few muscles or glands; are more complex, often consisting of long series of reflex-like acts; and are more variable than reflexes, though still rather stereotypic.

Because of their complexity and their utility, many modal action patterns appear to be thoughtful acts. In fact, they are probably no more thoughtful than is the behavior of a person who responds to a rap on the knee by jerking her leg. An illustration of the unthinking nature of modal action patterns is provided by the tropical army ant. Entire colonies of these ants charge across the forests in what appears to be a highly organized, intelligently directed campaign. However, the ants are merely following a chemical trail laid down by the ants ahead of them. T. C. Schneirla (1944) demonstrated that on a flat surface, such as a road, where no obstacles direct the course of the march, the lead ants tend to move toward the ants beside them. The column then turns in on itself, and the ants soon march round and round in a circle. This is not very intelligent behavior.

**? QUERY 2:**  Modal action patterns differ from reflexes in that MAPs involve the

_____ organism and are more _____ and

_____.

Various people (e.g., Carr, 1967; Dawkins, 1995; Skinner, 1966, 1975, 1984) have suggested that some modal action patterns are selected by gradual changes in the environment. Consider, for example, salmon that migrate upstream to breed. This act often requires the fish to ascend steep cliffs and swim against rushing currents. At one time, returning to the breeding area might have constituted a relatively easy swim up a gently rising stream. As geological changes gradually increased the steepness of the slope, those fish with the ability to make the trip bred successfully and reproduced their kind, whereas those not up to the challenge failed to reproduce. It seems likely that other modal action patterns (such as migration and mating rituals) are molded by the environment in much the same way.

MAPs evolve through natural selection because they contribute to the survival of the species. They do this chiefly by helping the individual find food, deal with threats to their safety, or pass their genes on to the next generation. The pine bark beetle burrows into pine trees to find a meal. Some spiders spin webs with which they capture prey, while others lie in wait and pounce on an unsuspecting meal as it passes by. The buck moth caterpillar climbs deciduous trees, particularly oaks, to feed on the leaves. Pigs root for worms, larvae, and truffles beneath the ground. Woodpeckers peck on trees to get at the insects that feed there, while the yellow-billed cuckoo and other birds feed on the caterpillars that feed on leaves.

Some apparently pointless aggressive behavior is actually part of food gathering. The cowbird lays its eggs in the nest of another, smaller species, such as a wren. The cowbird chick, being bigger than its nest mates, gets most of the daily menu and eventually pushes the smaller chicks from the nest. The mother wren ends up providing meals to a single chick that is twice her own size.

Many MAPs serve to protect the individual from environmental threats, such as predators. The rattlesnake shakes its rattle when approached by an animal, such as a Boy Scout, that may harm it. When confronted by a threatening dog, the house cat arches its back, hisses, growls, and flicks its tail. These acts make the cat appear larger and more formidable than it really is and may therefore serve to put off an attacker. The opossum responds quite differently to predators: It plays dead. Some of the opossum's predators eat only animals they themselves have killed; others will cover a dead animal they find and return to eat it later, so a "dead" opossum has a chance of surviving.

The beaver avoids predators by building a dam and then a lodge with an underwater entrance. It then packs mud on top of the lodge, which adds to the difficulty of getting at the beaver by tearing at the roof of the lodge.

Another kind of threat is posed by seasonal changes. Bears eat voraciously from spring to fall, thereby adding layers of fat. Then they seek shelter in a cave or in a cavity under a rock or fallen trees. There they spend most of the winter in a state of hibernation: They do not eat, drink, or eliminate wastes. A recent study of black bears in Alaska found that their metabolic rate fell by 75%, thus drastically reducing their consumption of calories (Tøien et al., 2011). This enables them to live off of the calories they stored as fat during the warmer months. Many birds and some mammals deal with cold by migrating to a warmer area in the fall. The Canada goose flies from its nesting grounds in the north to the much more temperate climate in the mid-Atlantic region.

Some of the most interesting modal action patterns have to do with reproduction. The male peacock attracts a female by spreading its flamboyantly decorated tail and causing it to tremble. (The tail, that is, not the female.) The male bighorn sheep wins a partner by bashing its head against that of its rival. The genital area of certain female primates becomes swollen and red when she is capable of being impregnated, and she displays these features to a potential partner, nonverbally saying, "I'm available!"

Modal action patterns also govern the care and rearing of the young. After mating, the female of a certain species of wasp builds a nest, places a paralyzed spider in it, lays an egg on top of the spider, closes the nest, and goes on its way, leaving the young wasp to fend for itself after it eats its first meal. The newborn of many higher species of animals require more nurturing, for which task their parents are genetically equipped. Most birds feed their young at least until they leave the nest. When the adult robin arrives at the nest, the chicks chirp loudly and then open their beaks wide; the parent responds to the gaping mouths by regurgitating a mix of worms and insects it has eaten. As the chicks get older the parent shoves undigested bits of prey between the chicks' gaping jaws.

Are there modal action patterns in human beings? It is hard to say. Darwin (1874) wrote of the instincts of self-preservation, lust, and vengeance, among others, in humans. Several decades ago, textbooks listed dozens of human instincts, including the sex instinct, the social instinct, the maternal instinct, and the territorial instinct (see, e.g., McDougall, 1908). But the list of human instincts has grown shorter over the years. Today, many researchers maintain that there are no true modal action patterns in people, that the "instincts" previously attributed to them lack the monotonous character of web spinning in spiders and nest building in birds. For instance, for thousands of years, people around the planet obtained food mainly by hunting and gathering, with men typically doing the hunting and women doing the gathering. But the hunting and gathering took different forms in different regions and at different times, and the gender roles were not absolute. And today people are more likely to obtain their food by sitting at a desk than by shooting deer or digging up roots.

Similarly, among humans the method of finding a sexual partner varies tremendously from culture to culture, from individual to individual, and even within the same individual from time to time. Humans have invented marriage, dating services, singles bars, personals columns, Internet chat rooms, massage parlors, and all sorts of rules and customs for defining how, when, where, and with whom sexual acts may be performed. The complexity and variability of mating rituals among humans is a far cry from the stereotypic mating behavior of most other animals.

The same sort of case can be made against the so-called maternal instinct. True, many women do desire to have children and to protect and nurture them, as do many men. But there is tremendous variation in how mothers perform these tasks. In some societies, young children are fondled and held constantly, and their slightest need is met immediately; in others, children are left largely to their own resources. Moreover, women in Western societies increasingly delay or forgo altogether the traditional maternal role. True modal action patterns are not so readily discarded.

There are, then, few if any modal action patterns in humans. The role of genetics in behavior is, however, seen in both nonhumans and humans in the form of general behavior traits.

## General Behavior Traits

Over the past few decades, a great deal of research has focused on the role of genes in determining what I will refer to here as **general behavior traits.** By this I mean the tendency to engage in a certain kind of behavior. Examples include the tendency to be shy (or outgoing), aggressive (or mild-mannered), adventurous (or cautious), anxious (or relaxed), and obsessive-compulsive (or impulsive).

Some behavior traits were once classified as modal action patterns, but they differ from the latter in important ways. As noted previously, modal action patterns are elicited by fairly specific kinds of environmental events, called releasers. The gaping mouth of a fledgling induces the parent bird to provide food; a closed beak does not have this effect. Behavior traits, on the other hand, occur in a wide variety of situations. For instance, under certain circumstances, unpleasant experiences will reliably produce aggressive behavior in many animals, including people (Berkowitz, 1983; Ulrich & Azrin, 1962). But *unpleasant experience* covers a lot of territory. It can include, among other things, an electric shock, a pinprick, a spray of cold water, a threatening stare, an insult, an air temperature above 90 degrees, and so on. All can increase the likelihood of aggressive behavior. Modal action patterns are not released by so many different kinds of events.

Another difference between modal action patterns and behavior traits concerns the plasticity of the behavior. Compare the modal action pattern of the web-spinning spider with the aggressiveness of a shocked rat. Each web-spinning spider spins a web with a specific pattern, and it goes about the task with a remarkable sameness, like someone living a recurrent dream. Moreover, the web

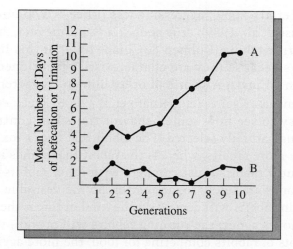

**Figure 1-5** *Fearfulness and heredity. A researcher put rats in an open enclosure, then bred the most fearful (as measured by urination and defecation) with one another (A), and the least fearful with one another (B). The graph shows the changes over ten generations. (Compiled from data in Hall, 1951.)*

spinning of one spider is remarkably like that of other members of the same species (Savory, 1974). But the rat that attacks its neighbor goes about it in a far less stereotypic manner, and there may be considerable difference between the attack of one rat and that of another of the same species.

Behavior traits are more variable than modal action patterns, but there is little doubt that heredity plays an important role in them. Selective breeding has, for example, produced strains of animals differing in fearfulness (Hall, 1951; Marks, 1986; see Figure 1-5), excitability (Viggiano et al., 2002), aggressiveness (Dierick & Greenspan, 2006), activity level (Garland et al., 2011), drug abuse (Matson & Grahame, 2011), and risk-taking (Jonas et al., 2010), among others.

Today, researchers can use genetic engineering to demonstrate the role of genes in behavior traits. Gleb Shumyatsky, a geneticist at Rutgers University, and his colleagues (Shumyatsky et al., 2005) removed a particular gene from mice and then bred a line of mice without the gene. Although these mice looked and generally behaved normally, the missing gene had a profound effect on one kind of behavior. When mice are placed on an unfamiliar white surface, they normally display caution. The engineered mice, however, were much bolder: They spent twice as much time exploring the area as the ordinary mice did. A similar study identified a genetic component in social dominance (Garfield et al., 2011).

Genes also play a significant role in the behavior traits of people. People have long recognized this with the expression *blood will tell*. Selective breeding and genetic engineering are not available as research tools where humans are concerned, but twin studies and studies of specific genes serve researchers well. Researchers have shown that, as in other animals, genes play an important role in fearfulness (Hettema et al., 2003), excitability

(Pellicciari et al., 2009), aggressiveness (Rhee & Waldman, 2002), activity level (Perusse et al., 1989), drug abuse (Li & Burmeister, 2009; Nielsen et al., 2008), and risk-taking (Kuhnen & Chiao, 2009). If this list of traits sounds familiar, it's because they are characteristics mentioned earlier that have been bred in animals. All sorts of other human characteristics have proven to be influenced by genes (e.g., Knafo et al., 2008; Kreek et al., 2005).

It is easy to see how some behavior traits can contribute to survival, thereby being naturally selected. The rabbit that flees a fox may escape and go on to create more rabbits, whereas the rabbit that stands its ground becomes fox food. But if rabbits must compete with other rabbits for food, the more aggressive ones are likely to fare better. So the desirable level of aggressive tendencies in rabbits will depend on the kind of threat they face. When there are lots of foxes about, the running rabbits will prevail; when there are few foxes but lots of rabbits competing for food, the more aggressive rabbits will dominate.

The same thing is undoubtedly true of people. For example, some people tend to be bold and adventurous, while others are cautious and reserved. Hunting gazelle with a spear requires walking into the grassy area where the gazelle feed, but these are often the same areas where lions prowl. Those people who lead the way are most likely to secure food for themselves and their group, but they are probably also the most likely to fall victim to lions. The more cautious people risk going hungry, but hungry people are more likely to reproduce than dead people. Even today we need people who "boldly go where no one has gone before," but we also need people who stay behind and balance their checkbooks.

Thanks to genetic variation and natural selection, then, adaptive forms of behavior (reflexes, modal action patterns, and general behavior traits) spread throughout a species and help it survive. As the environment changes, new adaptive forms of behavior appear and old ones that are no longer adaptive fade. Natural selection is a marvelous mechanism for producing both physical and behavioral characteristics suited to a changing environment, but it has its limits.

*Were you born straight? Or gay? The source of a person's sexual orientation is difficult to determine. One thing seems clear: Few people sit down one day, consider the options, and choose to be straight, gay, or bisexual.*

CAPSULE **REVIEW**   Natural selection produces three categories of behavior. Reflexive behavior is a simple response to a specific event. Examples include the blinking of an eye in response to a puff of air in the eye, and withdrawing a hand when it touches something hot. Modal action patterns are what used to be called instincts. They are far more complicated than reflexes, but like reflexes they are very stereotypical. Examples include the nest building of birds and the hibernation of bears. General behavior traits are behavioral tendencies with a strong genetic component. Examples include shyness, general anxiety, and compulsivity. Natural selection produces physical and behavioral characteristics that can be very helpful to species survival. However, it has its limitations.

## LIMITS OF NATURAL SELECTION

The chief problem with natural selection as a way of coping with change is that it is slow. It is slow because it occurs over generations.

Consider Gordon's study of guppies put into a stream where they were exposed to new predators. The guppies adapted, but it took between 13 and 26 generations. Guppies are short-lived, so those generations occurred over only eight years. Other species take longer to reach sexual maturity and have longer gestational periods, which makes adaptation through natural selection even slower. Humans, for example, reach sexual maturity in their teens and gestation is nine months, so it takes a minimum of about 13 years to produce a new generation. For us to get the kind of adaptive changes seen in Gordon's guppies would likely take more than 200 years, and that is assuming that women would routinely have children in their teens.

Natural selection is therefore of limited value in coping with abrupt changes. Hawaii, "the extinction capital of the world," provides an apt example. The Hawaiian islands were home to a great variety of wildlife when Captain Cook stumbled onto them in 1778. Unfortunately, Cook and other early visitors brought with them not only trinkets but rats. Other invasive species followed, including cats, dogs, and snakes. Some of the indigenous animals on the islands had little or no defenses against these new predators. In the 200 years since Cook's arrival, close to 200 species of animals that once lived on the islands have become extinct.

Another example is provided by the passenger pigeon. These North American birds, which resembled their cousin, the mourning dove, once numbered in the millions. Sometimes their flocks were so large that they blocked the sun and turned day into twilight. But natural selection was no help to the passenger pigeon against the shotgun and unregulated hunting, and the last passenger pigeon died in 1914.

 **QUERY 3:** The chief problem with natural selection is that it is _____.

A rapid change that threatens humans is infectious diseases. As mentioned earlier, bubonic plague killed millions of Europeans in the 14th century, and the flu pandemic of 1918 killed 27 million worldwide. Pandemics of similar magnitude are not only possible, but probable (Garrett, 1995). The Ebola virus, for instance, has no effective treatment, almost inevitably ends in a horrible death, and is highly contagious. The disease originated in and is currently limited to Africa, but this is the age of the jet plane and tourism, imports and exports, not to mention international terrorism, so it is quite possible that the Ebola virus will threaten people on every continent during this century. Natural selection is unlikely to work fast enough to prevent massive casualties from such a highly infectious and deadly disease.

A related problem with natural selection is that adaptations that served a species for thousands or even millions of years can become useless almost overnight. Lee Cronk (1992) provides several examples of this phenomenon in

*In 2009, an influenza virus spread around the globe. Vaccines were not available in time to block its spread. Had the virus been more lethal, the result would have been catastrophic (Peiris, Poon, & Guan, 2012).*

a delightful article called *Old Dogs, Old Tricks.* "Behavioral and physical adaptations that seem to make no sense in an organism's current environment," Cronk writes, "can be traced to the legacy of an earlier, different environment in which those traits were favored" (p. 13). He cites the example of the rabbit that dodges back and forth when pursued by foxes, bobcats, and coyotes. This practice is still helpful in eluding these predators, but it is less effective when the rabbit finds itself on a highway "pursued" by a truck. Similarly, Cronk notes, armadillos befuddled approaching predators for thousands of years by springing into the air. Once again, however, this behavior is not adaptive on modern highways. As Cronk puts it, "Leap two feet high in front of a Buick, and you're buzzard bait" (p. 13).

**? QUERY 4:** Natural selection helps the _____ to adapt to change, not the

_____.

Human beings also have become hostages to their genetic history. B. F. Skinner (1984) notes that humans evolved in a world in which salt and sugar were not readily available. Those individuals who had a natural preference for these foods were more likely to get the sodium and the calories needed for survival. We have, as a consequence, evolved into a species with strong preferences for both salty and sweet foods. But our world has changed. In industrial societies, salt and sugar are abundant, and many of us consume far too much of them, endangering our health in the process. Now, heart disease, stroke, and diabetes are major killers and are considered diseases of civilization. They could be called diseases of natural selection.

Sometimes abrupt changes in genes, called **mutations,** appear, and although most of them do not help in the struggle for survival, occasionally they prove useful. When the mutation provides a significant advantage, it may "sweep" through the population and could conceivably ensure the survival of the species. However, having desirable mutations sweep through the population is definitely *not* something we can count on (Hernandez et al., 2011).

**Hybridization,** the cross-breeding of closely related species, can also aid species adaptation. Mating between different species of animals sometimes occurs in the wild when the species share the same territory. A grizzly bear is known to have mated with a polar bear, for example, producing offspring with characteristics from each parent (Carroll, 2010). Your ancestors (and hence, you) may have profited from such hybridization: From 1% to 4% of the genes of people of European and Asian descent are those of *Homo neanderthalensis,* a species distinct from *Homo sapiens* (Carroll, 2010; Finlayson, 2010, Wong, 2000). Matings across species should increase the variabilty of genes in the next generation and thereby lead to useful adaptations, but hybrid animals are often sterile, so whether hybridization could speed up the adaptive process is uncertain.

There is also evidence that some genes "jump" from one area of a chromosome to another, changing the influence the genes would otherwise have

(Gage & Muotri, 2012). Like mutations and hybridization, this might increase the variability of features, including behavioral characteristics, but even if useful features appear, it takes multiple generations for natural selection to take advantage of them.

It seems clear that natural selection is not up to the challenge of rapid change. What is needed is the evolution of a characteristic that allows organisms to change, not over many generations, but *within the lifetime of the individual.* Fortunately, such a mechanism has evolved. I like to think of it as evolved modifiability, but most people call it learning.

CAPSULE **REVIEW**    The chief problem with natural selection is that it is slow. It typically takes place over many generations, so there is always a risk that the species will become extinct before adaptive changes appear. Abrupt changes in the environment, such as invasive species, new diseases, pollution, and changes in terrain due to powerful geological events such as earthquakes and volcanic eruptions, may not allow time for natural selection to work. Mutations and naturally occurring hybridization may help, but what is really needed is a mechanism for coping with change during the lifetime of the individual.

# LEARNING: EVOLVED MODIFIABILITY

Although **learning** has been defined in countless ways, among learning researchers it is often defined as *a change in behavior due to experience.* As you will soon see, this means *a change in behavior due to a change in the environment.* The definition is simple enough, but it deserves careful examination.

### Learning Means Change

Consider the word *change.* Why should learning be said to be a change in behavior? Why not say, for example, that learning is the acquisition of behavior?

The word *change* is preferred over *acquisition* because learning does not always involve acquiring something, but it does always involve some sort of change. Joan would like to *quit* smoking; Bill wants to *stop* biting his nails; and Mary and Harry would like to quarrel *less often.* All of these reductions in behavior, if they occur, are examples of learning, but nothing has been acquired—at least, not in the ordinary sense of that word. Learning means a change in some aspect of behavior such as its frequency, intensity, speed, or form (see Chapter 2).

Some authorities (e.g., Kimble, 1961) insist that only *durable* changes qualify as learning, but since there is no consensus about what *durable* means (a few milliseconds? a second? a minute? a week? a year?), adding durability to the definition does not seem to help. Besides, why should durability be a requirement? If you see your doctor because you had a severe pain in your chest that lasted six seconds, is your doctor going to say, "Six seconds? Oh, then it didn't happen"? She might say it's unimportant, but she isn't going to say it didn't happen. If an astronomer sees a star explode and disappear in three seconds, are other astronomers going to say, "Forget it. If it didn't last for at least a minute it didn't happen." The key issue in learning is whether a change in behavior occurred, not how long it lasted. The fact that you no longer remember all of those Spanish verbs you learned in high school doesn't mean that you didn't learn them.

### What Changes Is Behavior

What changes when learning occurs is behavior. **Behavior** may be defined as *anything a person or other animal does that can be measured* (Moore, 2011; Reber, 1995; Skinner, 1938). Actually, anything an animal does might qualify as behavior, whether measurable or not, but for scientific analysis we are necessarily limited to those things we can measure (Baum, 2011).

The concept of behavior seems simple enough, but it can get fuzzy when you examine it closely (e.g., see Angier, 2009). Is a heartbeat an example of behavior? What about the firing of a single neuron? How about the secretion of adrenaline into the bloodstream? Probably most people think of these as physiology, not behavior. But these are all things that people (and many other animals) do that can be measured, so they qualify as behavior. You have no doubt heard that dogs can learn to salivate at the sound of a bell. Salivation is the secretion of saliva by a gland, a topic for physiologists, but the dog produces the saliva and the amount of saliva can be measured, so it qualifies as behavior.

People think, so does thinking qualify as behavior? Most people would probably say No, arguing that behavior involves physical movement, whereas thoughts are mental. The word *mental* is usually defined as "of the mind," and the implication is that thoughts exist in a different dimension from the physical world (Descartes, 1637, 1641). That takes thoughts out of the reach of science. However, thinking is something people (and presumably some animals) do, so *if it can be measured*, it qualifies as behavior.

The chief difference between thinking and other forms of behavior is that one is private and the other is public. There is considerable evidence that much of what we call thinking is simply covert behavior. That is, what we do "in our head" is often merely a more subtle form of public behavior. For example, we can speak to others, or we can "think out loud" (mumble), or we can engage in "inner speech" (Huang et al., 2001; Schlinger, 2009; Watson, 1920). Schizophrenics often hear voices, for example, but research suggests that the voices they hear are actually their own—they are talking to themselves silently or softly (Lindsley, 1963; McGuigan, 1966; Slade, 1974; Stephane, Barton, & Boutros, 2001). Similarly, deaf people who use sign language in communicating with others seem to think with their fingers—signing subtly as they wrestle with a problem (Max, 1937; Watson, 1920).

Neurological evidence supports the idea that our covert speech is essentially a diminutive form of speech. In one experiment researchers found that a kind of magnetic stimulation of an area of the brain involved in language interfered with both overt and covert speech (Aziz-Zadeh, Cattaneo, & Rizzolatti, 2005). If thinking were fundamentally different from overt speech, it seems unlikely that stimulation that interferes with one would interfere with the other. Similarly, when the neuroanatomist Jill Bolte Taylor (2008) had a severe stroke, she lost the ability to speak both to others *and to herself.* We unwittingly acknowledge the shared nature of overt and covert speech when someone asks us what we are mumbling and we reply, "Oh, I was just thinking out loud."

What about unconscious thoughts—are they behavior? No, but they are not thoughts, either. The phrase *unconscious thoughts* is an oxymoron. True, your brain is routinely engaged in activities of which you are unaware, and some of these activities may affect your behavior (your covert and overt speech, for example). But the same thing can be said of your salivary glands, stomach, liver, intestines, and bone marrow; are the unconscious activities of these organs thoughts?

Yet thoughts are not identical to overt behavior. In particular, they often have different effects. If I'm in a stuffy room I can open a window and let in fresh air; *thinking* about opening a window will not have that effect. (Neither will talking about it.) Similarly, if you call someone an idiot, this behavior is likely to have consequences that will not follow if you merely think the person is an idiot. But these differences in effect do not justify assigning thoughts to a fundamentally different and mysterious realm. The effects of publicly performed behavior also can have different consequences. Shouting names at someone, for example, will have different effects than whispering the same words in their ear, and those whispered thoughts will have different effects than inaudible speech—that is, thoughts.

Like thoughts, feelings are often assumed to be excluded from behavior, but they need not be. Emotions are, after all, part of our response to events around us and sometimes in us—toothaches do not feel good, for example. Like thoughts, feelings pose special problems since much of what we call feelings are not normally publicly observable. However, feelings tend to "spill out" from the body in the form of readily observed behavior. When you feel happy you often have a smile on your face and a spring in your step; when you are sad, you are apt to "wear a frown" and may shed tears; when you have a toothache you may moan and hold your jaw. We can also "look in on" a person's feelings by recording physiological activity that is reliably correlated with expressed feelings. A person who reports feeling angry is likely to have an increase in heart rate and blood pressure; a person who is afraid is likely to have an increase in electrical conductivity of his skin; a person who is sexually aroused is likely . . . well, you get the idea.

Some people might argue that learning should be defined as a change in the nervous system that makes a change in behavior possible. In this view, behavior change is merely an indicator of learning. Great progress has been made in recent years in our understanding of the way learning experiences change the brain (e.g., Cohen et al., 2012; Holy, 2012; Kandel, 1970, 2007).

*Will we one day be able to "listen in" on a another person's thoughts by recording brain activity and translating it into words? There is now good reason to believe so (see Palmer et al., 2001; Silberman, 2006).*

No learning researcher denies that learning involves a change in the nervous system, but there are at least two problems with equating learning with neurological changes.

One problem is that we are just beginning to understand the biological mechanisms involved in learning. No one can point to changes in a rat's brain and say, "This animal can run a maze better today than it did yesterday." Nor can anyone point to features of a person's brain and say, "This person can play the piano." At present, the only reliable measure of learning is a change in behavior.

A second problem with defining learning as neurological change is that it denies the importance of behavior. It is, of course, very important to understand how experience changes the nervous system. But even if we were able to say, solely on the basis of physiological measures, "This rat can run a maze better today than it did yesterday" or "This person can play the piano," the changes in behavior would be paramount. When we go to a concert, we go to hear the pianist play, not to watch her neurons fire.

Thus, insofar as learning is concerned, behavior is literally "where it's at." The changes in behavior are not the *result* of learning; they *are* learning. They are the *result* of experience.

**?** **QUERY 5:** Behavior is anything an organism does that can be _____.

## What Changes Behavior Is Experience

Our definition says that learning is due to experience. **Experience** means changes in the environment, so our definition of learning is, in effect, *a change in behavior due to changes in the environment*. These changes in the environment are events that affect, or are capable of affecting, behavior. Such events are called **stimuli**.

Stimuli are physical changes in an organism's environment. They are the changes in air pressure we call sound, the light waves we call sights, the tactile pressures we call touch. The delicate fragrance of a rose derives from just so many molecules of "rose matter" arising from the flower. Even the gentle caress and softly whispered words of a lover are, in scientific terms, merely physical events. Stimuli often have significance beyond their physical properties (the fragrance of a rose may remind us of a friend), but it is their physical properties that define them.

Often in learning research the stimuli are very simple events such as a lightbulb coming on or going off or a buzzer sounding, but this does not mean that the experiences that change behavior are typically simple. A given stimulus is *always* part of a complex array of stimuli. A light that is illuminated in a small room may have different effects, for example, than the same light in a large room. Researchers typically define experience in terms of simple events in order to simplify the problem being studied.

In most studies of learning, the stimuli investigated occur outside the person or animal. However, physical events occur inside the body as well, and they, too, can affect behavior. We tend to define these internal events in terms of sensations—the pain of a toothache, the nausea of an upset stomach—but these sensations, like those from stimuli outside the body, have a physical basis. The toothache may be due to an inflamed root, the nausea caused by spoiled meat in the stomach.

This point raises an interesting philosophical question: Is it the physical event that affects behavior, or the sensation that is produced by the physical event? Some unfortunate people are incapable of experiencing pain, so if they pick up a hot skillet they do not immediately release it and their hand gets burned. Similarly, a deaf person does not respond to the sound of a telephone or the warning sound of a car horn. This issue, like most philosophical issues, is complicated and difficult to resolve. For practical reasons, however, scientists generally focus on readily observable physical features.

We saw earlier that changes in environment are largely responsible for the changes we see in natural selection. The rule of thumb is, no change in the environment, no change in the species. A parallel rule of thumb applies to learning: *no change in the environment, no change in behavior.*

Not all changes in behavior, even those resulting from changes in the environment, qualify as learning, however. A physician may give an emotionally distraught man a tranquilizer, but we do not then say that the patient learned to be calm. A woman who is usually very agreeable may, following a head injury, become very argumentative. If this change in behavior is due to brain damage, we do not say that she *learned* to be quarrelsome. Changes in behavior that are due to drugs, injury, aging, or disease do not qualify as learning.

There is a great deal more that might be said about the meaning of learning, but perhaps you now have a better understanding of why it is defined here as a change in behavior due to experience. To illustrate this definition, let's take a brief look at what is arguably the simplest example of learning, habituation.

 QUERY **6:** A stimulus is an environmental event that is capable of affecting

_____.

CAPSULE **REVIEW**   Learning is defined as a change in behavior due to experience. Change does not necessarily mean acquisition; it simply means that some feature of a given behavior is modified. What is modified is behavior, which means anything a person or other animal does that can be measured. The changes in behavior are products of experience—that is, changes in the environment. The general rule of thumb is, no change in the environment, no change in behavior. So two forces contribute to behavior: natural selection, which modifies characteristics of the species, including behavior; and learning, which modifies the behavior of the individual.

# HABITUATION: AN EXAMPLE OF LEARNING

**Habituation** is a reduction in the intensity or probability of a reflex response as a result of repeatedly evoking the response. Many versions of habituation have been demonstrated by researchers. Seth Sharpless and Herbert Jasper (1956), for example, noted the effects of loud noises on cats by recording their brain waves on an electroencephalograph (EEG). The EEG showed marked arousal at first, but the reaction declined steadily with each repetition of a given sound until the noise had hardly any effect. Wagner Bridger (1961) studied habituation in infants and found that when babies first heard a noise, they responded with an increase in heart rate. With repetition of the noise at regular intervals, however, the change in heart rate became less and less pronounced until, in some cases, the noise had no measurable effect. Habituation has even been demonstrated in the human fetus. A stimulus to the mother's abdomen during the last three months of pregnancy will produce movement in the fetus. If the stimulus is applied repeatedly in a regular way, the fetal response becomes steadily weaker (Leader, 1995). When the course of habituation is plotted on a graph, it usually reveals a fairly smooth, decelerating curve (see Figure 1-6).

Although habituation is a relatively simple phenomenon, it is not as simple as this discussion implies. Variations in the stimulus used to elicit the response affect the rate of habituation. For example, a sudden loud noise will typically elicit the startle reflex—the "jump" you experience when, for example, the wind causes a door to slam shut. But the rate at which habituation occurs depends on the loudness of the sound, variations in the quality of the sound, the number of times the sound occurs, the time interval between repeated exposures to the sound, and other variables. (For more on this, see Thompson, 2000, 2009.)

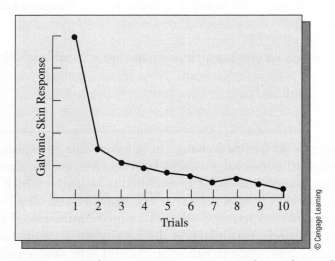

**Figure 1-6** *Habituation. Exposure to a novel stimulus produces a change in the electrical conductivity of the skin (the galvanic skin response, or GSR). Repeated exposure to the stimulus results in progressively weaker GSRs. (Hypothetical data.)*

**? QUERY 7:** Habituation involves a _____ in the probability or intensity of a response.

You can probably see how habituation would be helpful in survival. The world is a dangerous place, full of predators, venomous reptiles, stinging insects and plants, lightning, forest fires, hurricanes, not to mention drunk drivers and jealous boyfriends. The world also presents us with opportunities: An unsuspecting prey animal may come our way, for example, providing an easy meal. We and other animals need to be alert to events around us that might signal trouble or opportunity. However, events that occur repeatedly and do *not* signal trouble or opportunity can distract us from more important things, such as eating or sleeping. Habituation allows us to go on with whatever we are doing without interruption. If you live next to a train line, for example, at first the noise from passing trains prevents you from falling asleep, but with repeated exposure to the sounds you sleep like a rock, thanks to habituation.

Habituation isn't what most people think of when they think of learning, but it illustrates the essential nature of learning: a change in behavior due to experience. It also illustrates the survival value of learning. We have seen that changes in the environment produce both changes in the species (through natural selection) and changes in the individual (through learning). Which of those influences, nature and experience, is more important? That is our next topic.

CAPSULE **REVIEW**  Perhaps the simplest form of learning is habituation, a change in the frequency or strength of a reflex response due to repetition of an event. Like all forms of learning, it involves a change in behavior due to experience. In this case, the experience is the repeated presentation of a stimulus. Like all forms of learning, it evolved because it has survival value.

# NATURE VS. NURTURE

One of the longest-running arguments in the study of behavior—indeed, in all of science—concerns the relative importance of nature and nurture (basically, heredity and learning), in determining behavior. Do we, as individuals, behave a certain way because we were "born that way," or do we behave that way because our environment "taught" us to behave that way? The debate is evidenced in aphorisms people use every day, often without thinking about their larger significance. Is it true, for instance, that "blood will tell," or is it more accurate to say that "as the twig is bent, so the tree is inclined"? Are leaders born, or are they made? Can a person "turn over a new leaf," or is the leopard stuck with its spots?

Of course, no one denies that learning is important, at least in higher animals, and no one completely ignores the role of heredity. The most influential behavior scientist of the 20th century, B. F. Skinner, is often called an "extreme environmentalist," and has even been accused of denying that biology plays any role in behavior. Yet his earliest research interest was in biology, and throughout his career he wrote repeatedly of the role of biology in behavior (Morris, Lazo, & Smith, 2004; Skinner, 1969, 1975). In one passage, for example, Skinner (1953) writes that "behavior requires a behaving organism which is the product of a genetic process. Gross differences in the behavior of different species show that the genetic constitution . . . is important" (p. 26). Similarly, biologists such as E. O. Wilson (1978) who emphasize hereditary factors in behavior are often labeled "biological determinists," yet they acknowledge that experience plays an important role as well. Nevertheless, for centuries people have lined up on one side or the other of the nature–nurture debate, arguing that one or the other, heredity or learning, is the true determinant of behavior.

The trouble with the nature–nurture debate is that it creates an artificial division between the contributions of heredity and learning. The debate wrongly implies that the answer must be one or the other (Kuo, 1967; Midgley, 1987). In fact, nature and nurture are inextricably interwoven in a kind of Gordian knot; the two strands cannot be separated. As William Verplanck (1955) put it long ago, "learned behavior is innate, and vice versa" (see also Moore, 2001; Ridley, 2003; Schneider, 2003; see Figure 1-7).

Let's take, as an example, the question of aggression. Douglas Mock (2006), a zoologist at the University of Oklahoma, compared the aggression of great blue heron and great egret chicks toward their siblings. The egrets were much more likely to kill their siblings than were the herons. At first glance, it appears that egrets are innately more aggressive, but Mock performed an experiment to see if that is the case. He had egrets raise herons and herons raise egrets. If the difference in siblicide were solely determined by genetics, this switch should have made no difference. What Mock found, however, was that while egrets showed the same amount of aggression to their siblings, the

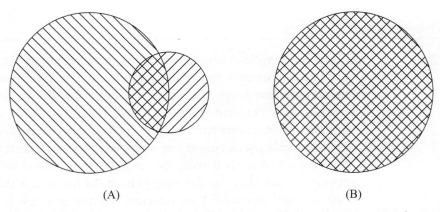

(A)                                    (B)

***Figure 1-7***   *Nature–nurture. The traditional view of the nature–nurture relationship (A) sees the two influences as overlapping but with one or the other dominating overall. The contemporary view (B) sees the two influences as inextricably intertwined in all areas, with neither dominating. (Drawing by Gary Dale Davis.)*

herons showed more. The difference was due to parental behavior: The herons bring their young large fish they can share; the egrets bring small fish the birds can swallow—*if* they get them before their nest mate does. The difference in environment influences the aggressiveness of the chicks.

Cats provided another example. It seems obvious that cats have a natural attraction to rats—as food, not as playmates. Zing Yang Kuo (1930) of China reared kittens under different conditions. Some grew up with their mothers and had the opportunity to see them kill rats. Others grew up away from their mothers and never saw rats killed. When the kittens matured, Kuo put them together with rats. He found that 86% of the cats that had been reared with their mothers killed rats, but only 45% of the others did. Thus, even something as basic as killing "natural" prey is strongly influenced by experience.

Aggression in humans also seems to be the product of a tangled mix of nature and nurture. Wilson (1978) reports that among the !Kung San, an aboriginal people of Africa, violence against their fellows was almost unknown. But Wilson points out that several decades earlier, when the population density among these people was greater and when there was less governmental control over their behavior, their per capita murder rate rivaled that of America's most dangerous cities. Wilson (1978) adds that the Semai of Malaya also demonstrated the capacity for both gentleness and violence. Murder is unknown among these people; they do not even have a word in their language for the concept. Yet when the British colonial government trained Semai men to fight against communist guerrillas in the 1950s, the Semai became fierce warriors. One anthropologist wrote that "they seem to have been swept up in a sort of insanity which they call 'blood drunkenness'" (Dentan, quoted in Wilson, 1978, p. 100). Wilson concludes from such evidence that "the more violent forms of human aggression are not the manifestations of inborn drives . . . [but are] based on the interaction of genetic potential and learning" (Wilson, 1978, p. 105).

**QUERY 8:**   Kuo's experiment showed that whether cats killed rats depended on whether they saw _____.

Even the ability to learn is itself the product of both heredity and experience. Numerous studies suggest that genes play a role in determining learning ability, but many other studies have shown that learning experiences are also important. For instance, Betty Hart and Todd Risley (1995; for a summary see Chance, 1997) did a longitudinal study of the verbal environment provided by parents with different educational backgrounds. They found huge differences in the amount and kinds of verbal exchanges between parents and their young children. Those children whose parents talked to them a lot (providing lengthy explanations and lots of positive feedback, for example) later scored higher on intelligence tests than those children whose parents were more reticent. The differences remained when race and socioeconomic level were held constant.

It is clear, then, that while we are biological organisms, we are also environmental organisms. Someone has said that asking, "Which is more important in determining behavior, heredity or environment?" is like asking, "Which is more important in determining the area of a rectangle, width or length?" All behavior reflects a blending of nature and nurture so complex and intricate that it is impossible to say where one begins and the other ends. Heredity and learning are merely different aspects of the same process, the effort to cope with life's one constant—change.

CAPSULE **REVIEW**    The nature–nurture debate has been going on for hundreds of years, perhaps longer. Many people still lean strongly toward the idea that genes or experience pretty much dictate our behavior. What science consistently reveals, however, is that the two are inextricably intertwined, so that it becomes difficult if not impossible to separate them. Experience can, for example, alter inherited tendencies, but genes play a major role in our ability to benefit from experience.

# A FINAL WORD

The apparent stability of the world is an illusion; the most constant feature of our environment is change.

One way of coping with change is through natural selection, but the changes take place across generations so natural selection is of no help to us in coping with new challenges, and it is of limited value in helping species cope with abrupt changes. These observations may seem of no immediate importance to you, but in fact they are, because some very substantial and abrupt changes are taking place in your environment.

For example, in 2012 atmospheric levels of carbon dioxide, a major source of global warming, reached 400 ppm in parts of Alaska, Canada, Iceland, Finland, Norway, and over the North Pacific, and sea levels are rising at the rate of 3.3 mm per year, about twice the rate they were rising in the second half of the 20th century (Thompson, in press). These facts are not merely of academic interest since they are directly related to changes in climate that are taking place worldwide. In the US, for example, in March of 2012 about 15,000 record temperatures were reported in the country; July was the hottest month in the lower 48 states since the government started keeping records in 1895; in August, over 60% of the contiguous states were in drought (Thompson, in press).

Some people will complain that these comments are inappropriate for a text on learning. What, they will demand, does climate change have to do with learning? My answer is, Everything! Learning is about changes in behavior due to experience, and experience means changes in our environment. Sooner or later we will change our behavior in response to changes in climate, but the rate of climate change is accelerating and many experts believe we are approaching a tipping point after which restoring a healthy climate will be impossible. This doesn't just mean life will be less comfortable; it means civilization as we know it will likely end, and our species may follow *Homo neanderthalensis* into extinction. Thus, we need to change our behavior *now*. That means not only consuming less energy and recycling more, it means moving toward a sustainable society, including a stable population and an economy that places less emphasis on consumption. Will we make these changes in behavior in time?

That question is for you to answer.

## RECOMMENDED **READING**

1. Angier, N. (2009, July 21). When "what animals do" doesn't seem to cover it. *New York Times*, p. D1. Download at www.nytimes.com/2009/07/21/science/21angier.html.

   Reports the efforts of Daniel Levitas, a student at the University of California at Berkeley, to determine the definition of the word *behavior*. He found little consensus among biologists specializing in behavior, and discovered the issue is more complicated than you might think.

2. Carroll, S. B. (2010, September 14). Hybrids may thrive where parents fear to tread. *New York Times*, p. D2.

   Interbreeding among similar species of animals (e.g., polar bear and grizzly bear) occurs in the wild. The mixing of genes can increase the variability in genes in a species and thereby aid adaptation. Humans may have benefited from hybridization: From 1% to 4% of the genetic material of Europeans and Asians appears to be from *Homo neanderthalensis*.

3. Heligman, D. (2009). *Charles and Emma: The Darwins' leap of faith.* New York: Holt & Co.

   This is the story of Charles Darwin and his wife, Emma. Emma was a religious fundamentalist, and believed that Charles might be condemned to hell for his blasphemous views. Charles found the literal interpretation of Genesis unacceptable because it conflicted with hard facts. The conflict posed a threat to their relationship, yet it survived.

4. Quammen, D. (2005, November). Was Darwin wrong? *National Geographic.* Available at http://magma.nationalgeographic.com/ngm/0411/feature1/fulltext.htm.

   Quammen's answer to his question is, No. He admits that Darwin was not always right—people doing groundbreaking work rarely are—but no one has yet offered a better explanation for the incredible diversity of life or the documented changes in species over time.

5. Ruse, M. (2000). *Can a Darwinian be a Christian?* Cambridge, UK: Cambridge University Press.

   Christian fundamentalists have a hard time accepting the concept of evolution. Ruse tackles the problem and concludes that, yes, it is possible to be a Darwinian and a Christian. If your religious beliefs conflict with evolution, you might find this book interesting.

## REVIEW **QUESTIONS**

*Note:* Many of the questions that appear here (and in subsequent chapters) cannot be answered merely by searching through the chapter and copying a line or two from the text. To answer the questions properly, you may have to apply information in the text in imaginative ways.

1. Define the following terms. Give an example or illustration of each that is *not* taken from the text.

   | | |
   |---|---|
   | modal action pattern | mutation |
   | behavior | natural selection |
   | general behavior trait | reflex |
   | habituation | releaser |
   | learning | stimulus |
   | hybridization | |

2. Are humans still evolving? How could you prove that they are or are not?

3. Why has the field mouse not evolved into an animal as large and ferocious as the grizzly bear?

4. In what sense is natural selection a product of the environment?

5. In what sense is what we learn the product of natural selection?

6. Invent a new reflex, one that would be helpful to humans.

7. Why is natural selection "behind the times"? Is learning behind the times?

8. How are reflexes, modal action patterns, and general behavior traits alike? How do they differ?

9. Learning is a mechanism for adapting to change. Are the changes ever *non*adaptive?

10. Captive animals often behave very differently from animals in the wild. In which circumstance is their true nature revealed? Where should one look to see true human nature?

## PRACTICE **QUIZ**

1. Learning is a _____ in _____ due to _____.

2. The human fondness for sugar and _____ illustrates that behavior that has survival value at one time may be harmful at another time.

3. The sight of a chick with an open mouth reliably results in an adult bird providing food. The chick's open mouth is an example of a _____.

4. Evolution is the product of _____ and _____.

5. A reflex is a _____ between a specific _____ and a simple response.

6. One example of a general behavior trait is _____.

7. _____ is a reduction in the intensity or probability of a reflex response due to repeated exposure to a stimulus that elicits that response.

8. Learning can be thought of as evolved _____.

9. The chief limitation of natural selection as a mechanism for coping with change is that it is _____.

10. Darwin likened natural selection to the _____ of animals.

## QUERY **ANSWERS**

Query 1: A reflex is a *relation/relationship* between a *specific event/stimulus* and a simple *behavior/response*.

Query 2: Modal action patterns differ from reflexes in that MAPs involve the *whole/entire* organism and are more *complex* and *variable*.

Query 3: The chief problem with natural selection is that it is *slow*.

Query 4: Natural selection helps the *species* to adapt to change, not the *individual*.

Query 5: Behavior is anything an organism does that can be *measured*.

Query 6: A stimulus is an environmental event that is capable of affecting *behavior*.

Query 7: Habituation involves a *decrease* in the probability or intensity of a response.

Query 8: Kuo's experiment showed that whether cats killed rats depended on whether they saw *their mothers kill rats.*

# CHAPTER

# 2 The Study of Learning and Behavior

*Sit down before fact as a little child, be prepared to give up every preconceived notion, follow humbly wherever and to whatever abysses nature leads, or you will learn nothing.*

**—T. H. Huxley**

## PREVIEW

One of the toughest things about the scientific study of behavior is that you have to go out of your mind. Nearly everyone, it seems, looks for explanations of behavior inside the mind, a mysterious and wispy entity that, in popular thought, resides between our ears and snuggles with, but is separate from, the brain. The scientific study of behavior requires adopting a very different, some will say downright alien, way of accounting for behavior, the natural science approach.

# THE NATURAL SCIENCE APPROACH

Poets, educators, and philosophers have long admired learning, sung its praises, and wondered at its power. But learning has been the subject of *scientific* analysis for little more than a hundred years.

What does scientific analysis mean when it comes to learning? Answers vary, but many learning researchers take the natural science approach. This approach maintains that learning is a natural phenomenon and can and must be accounted for like any other natural phenomenon. It is based on the following four assumptions:

*All natural phenomena are caused.* Things do not "just happen"; they are the result of other events. In the 1840s, Dr. Ignaz Semmelweis, a German-Hungarian physician, noticed that women who gave birth in a hospital were *more* likely to die of childbed fever than were women who gave birth at home, or even on the street. His attempt to find out why rested firmly on the assumption that the difference in death rates wasn't a random phenomenon, that there was something about the hospitals that made them more dangerous. This led to research that eventually changed medical practices and saved countless lives.

We can never prove that all events are caused, but the assumption is necessary to any science, including the science of behavior.

*Causes precede their effects.* Dr. Semmelweis assumed that whatever caused patients in a hospital to get childbed fever had to occur before they became ill. This is painfully obvious in most areas of science, yet many people never question the idea that future events can change behavior. People commonly say, for example, that a student studies hard because by doing so she *will get* a good grade. The future good grade is assumed to cause the current studying. Some will counter that it is not the future good grade, but the *expectation* that studying will result in a better grade that causes studying. One problem with this view is that our thoughts often coincide with or *follow*, rather than precede, the overt act they are assumed to cause (Bechara et al., 1997; Libet, 2005; Libet et al., 1983; Libet, Sinnott-Armstrong, & Nadel, 2010; Obhi & Haggard, 2004; Soon et al., 2008). Events (including thoughts) cannot reach into the past to change behavior.

*The causes of natural events include only natural phenomena.* Mind, spirits, psychic energy, and other mysterious forces have no place in the natural science approach. You cannot explain the movement of tectonic plates (and the earthquakes and tsunamis they cause) by attributing them to God's anger. Similarly, you cannot explain a person's overeating by attributing it to a lack of willpower or bad karma. A person may come up with an original idea, but we do not explain this creativity by attributing it to "the unconscious mind."

To explain behavior, which includes thoughts and feelings (see Chapter 1), we must identify the natural events that produce it. These events are either biological or environmental. Learning is the study of the changes in behavior produced by experience, so our main concern is with how events in the individual's environment change behavior.

*The simplest explanation that fits the data is best.* This is a fundamental tenet of all sciences known as *the law of parsimony*. It means, in part, that the fewer assumptions (unverified events) required by an explanation, the better.

For about 1,500 years, the dominant explanation of astronomical events, such as the position of the sun in the sky, was the geocentric theory offered by the Egyptian astronomer Claudius Ptolemy in the 2nd century A.D. This is the idea that the earth is the center of the universe. According to this model, the sun revolves around the earth once every 24 hours, creating day and night. But as astronomers gathered facts about the stellar bodies, the geocentric theory had to be modified again and again to accommodate facts that didn't fit it. The result was a complicated and inelegant theory. In 1543, the Polish astronomer Nicolaus Copernicus put forward a radically different explanation of astronomical events. His heliocentric theory proposed that the earth rotates on its axis (thereby creating periods of day and night every 24 hours), and revolves around the sun once every year. Both the geocentric and heliocentric theories provided an explanation of the known facts about the universe, but the heliocentric theory was simpler and far more elegant. As a result, all astronomers eventually accepted the heliocentric theory.

Today, many people, including many psychologists, accept explanations of behavior that rely on hypothetical events that are said to take place in the mind. One example is Freud's Thanatos, the idea that there is an unconscious drive toward self-destruction. This drive is said to explain risky behavior, such as abusing drugs, picking fights, and driving recklessly. The law of parsimony suggests that if such behavior can be accounted for by observable natural phenomena, such as heredity and environmental events, then there is nothing to be gained by speculations about mysterious and unobservable forces in a conscious or unconscious mind (Moore, 2010; Palmer, 2003; Schall, 2005).

*For many people, applying the assumptions of natural science to behavior requires a major shift in their view of human nature. Fear not: The shift will not turn you into a robot.*

The four assumptions just described are fundamental to the natural science approach. However, studying learning requires more than those assumptions. It also includes methods consistent with those assumptions. Let us begin with ways of measuring learning.

CAPSULE **REVIEW**    This text takes the natural science approach to behavior. It assumes that all natural phenomena are caused; that causes are natural phenomena and precede their effects; and that the simplest explanation with the fewest assumptions is the best. These assumptions cause most people no problem when applied to fields such as physics, chemistry, and biology, but when applied to behavior, particularly human behavior, they are often difficult to accept—even by physicists, chemists, and biologists.

## MEASURES OF LEARNING

To measure learning is to measure changes in behavior. There are many ways of doing this that are consistent with the natural science approach; we will consider the most basic ones here.

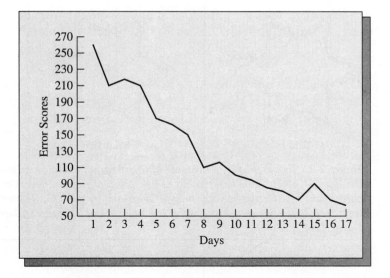

**Figure 2-1** *Errors as a measure of learning. A decline in the number of errors (such as entering the wrong alleys of a maze) is a measure of learning. (Adapted from Tolman and Honzik, 1930.)*

*Errors.* A common way of measuring learning is to look for a reduction in errors. A rat can be said to have learned to run a maze to the extent that it goes from start to finish without taking a wrong turn. As training progresses, the rat will make fewer and fewer errors (see Figure 2-1). Similarly, a student is said to have learned a spelling list when she can spell all the words without error. One way to measure progress in reading is to record the number of times the student stumbles over a word, with each such stumble counting as one error.

*Topography.* Learning may be measured as a change in the topography of a behavior, which refers to the form a behavior takes. (You might think of a topographic map, which shows the form of earth's surface.) Topography may be used as a measure of learning in mirror tracing. The task is to trace a form while looking at its reflection in a mirror. It is harder than it seems, and at first the pencil line meanders wildly. With practice, however, a person can trace the shape rather neatly (see Figure 2-2). The change in topography is a measure of learning. Computers are now being used to track topographical changes in three-dimensional space. For example, the movements of a fish through an aquarium can be tracked (Pear & Chan, 2001).

*Intensity.* We can also measure learning by noting changes in the intensity of a behavior. When a laboratory rat learns to press a lever, the resistance of the lever may be increased so that greater force is required to depress it. The increase in pressure exerted by the rat is a measure of learning (see Figure 2-3). The same sort of phenomenon occurs outside the laboratory. Having taught a child to sing a song, we can then teach her to sing it more softly. I once impressed my neighbors to no end by teaching my mixed-breed dog, Sunny, to "speak" (bark loudly) and to "whisper" (bark softly) on command.

*There is some overlap in the various measures of learning. In the tracing task in Figure 2-2, for example, we might count the number of times the pencil marks fall outside the star. If we count each such point as an error, we can measure learning as a reduction in errors rather than a change in topography.*

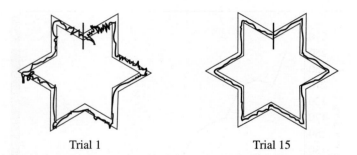

Trial 1                    Trial 15

**Figure 2-2**   *Topography as a measure of learning. A person attempted to trace between the lines of a star while looking at the figure's image in a mirror. On the first trial the participant's performance was shaky and erratic; by trial 15, the performance was much improved. The change in topography is a measure of learning. (Adapted from Kingsley and Garry, 1962, p. 304.)*

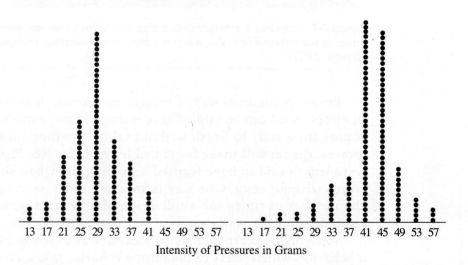

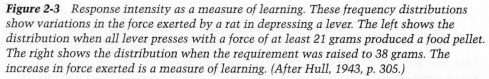

Intensity of Pressures in Grams

**Figure 2-3**   *Response intensity as a measure of learning. These frequency distributions show variations in the force exerted by a rat in depressing a lever. The left shows the distribution when all lever presses with a force of at least 21 grams produced a food pellet. The right shows the distribution when the requirement was raised to 38 grams. The increase in force exerted is a measure of learning. (After Hull, 1943, p. 305.)*

*Speed.* A change in the speed with which a behavior is performed is another measure of learning. The rat that learns to run a maze reaches the goal faster than an untrained rat (see Figure 2-4). In the same way, a first grader takes a long time to recite the alphabet at the beginning of the year but later runs through it with the speed of an auctioneer. Likewise, a surgeon usually gets faster at operations the more he performs them. A surgeon once told me that when he first started doing a particular operation, it took him nearly an hour, but after having done the procedure a hundred times it took him only about ten minutes. (He told me this while I was on the operating table.) As these examples illustrate, learning often means doing something more

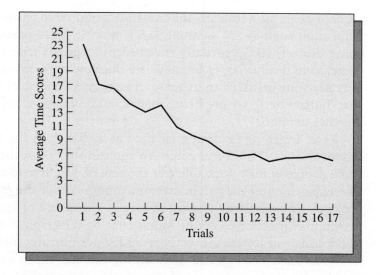

**Figure 2-4**   *Speed as a measure of learning. The decline in the average time it takes rats to run a maze indicates learning. (Adapted from Tolman and Honzik, 1930.)*

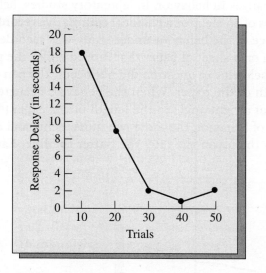

**Figure 2-5**   *Latency as a measure of learning. There is a long delay before the response (in this case, salivating) appears, but this latency gets shorter with more trials. (Compiled from data in Anrep, 1920.)*

quickly. However, learning can also mean a reduction in speed. When children are hungry, they tend to eat quickly; learning good table manners means learning to eat more slowly.

*Latency.* A similar measure of learning is a change in latency, the time that passes before a behavior occurs. We will see in the next chapter that a dog can be taught to salivate at the sound of a ticking metronome. As the training proceeds, the interval between the ticking and the first drop of saliva gets shorter; this change in latency is a measure of learning (see Figure 2-5). Similarly, a student beginning to learn the multiplication table pauses before answering a question such as "How much is 5 times 7?" With practice, the pauses become shorter, and eventually the student responds without hesitation. This decrease in hesitation, or latency, is a measure of learning. Sometimes, however, learning involves an increase in latency. When we are told, "Don't make snap judgments!" we are being instructed to delay before judging; that is an increase in latency.

*Rate.* Learning is often measured as a change in the rate at which a behavior occurs. This term refers to the number of occurrences per unit of time. A pigeon may peck a disc at the rate of, say, five to ten times a minute. The experimenter may then attempt to increase or decrease the rate of disc pecking. The resulting change in rate is a measure of learning. Similarly, a person may practice receiving Morse code by telegraph. If the rate of decoding (the number of letters correctly recorded per minute) increases, we say that he has learned (see Figure 2-6). Learning can also mean a decrease in the rate of behavior. A musician may learn to play the notes of a composition more slowly, for example.

*Rate and speed are related, but not identical, measures of learning.*

Rate is an especially useful measure of learning, partly because it allows us to see subtle changes in behavior. In laboratory studies, behavior rate was once tallied by means of an electromechanical **cumulative recorder.** With this device, every occurrence of the behavior under study was recorded by the movement of an inked pen on a sheet of paper that moved under the pen at a steady pace. So long as the behavior in question did not occur, the pen made a straight line along the length of the paper. When the behavior occurred, the pen moved a short distance at a right angle to the length of the paper (see Figure 2-7a). The higher the rate of behavior, the more pen movements and the steeper the slope of the ink line; the lower the rate, the flatter the line. Each point on the line

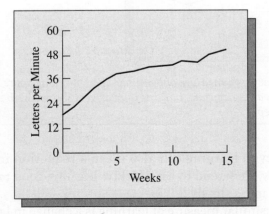

**Figure 2-6** *Rate as a measure of learning. Number of Morse code letters correctly received. The increase in rate of decoding is a measure of learning. (Adapted from Bryan and Harter, 1899.)*

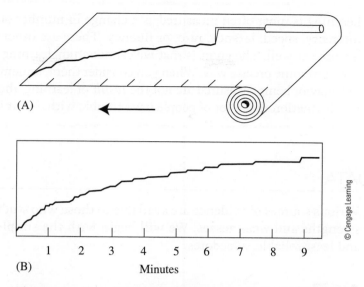

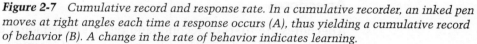

(B)                 Minutes

**Figure 2-7** *Cumulative record and response rate. In a cumulative recorder, an inked pen moves at right angles each time a response occurs (A), thus yielding a cumulative record of behavior (B). A change in the rate of behavior indicates learning.*

indicates the total number of times the behavior has occurred as of that moment, so the graph provides a **cumulative record** (see Figure 2-7b). Because the data line is cumulative, it can never fall below the horizontal. Today, cumulative recorders are gathering dust in storage rooms, replaced by computer software. The cumulative record produced by the computer is, however, essentially the same as the one produced by the older electromechanical devices.

**QUERY 1:** If the rate of a behavior is increasing, the slope of the cumulative record

_____. A flat record indicates that the behavior is

_____.

*Fluency.* Fluency is a measure of learning that combines errors and rate; it is the number of correct responses per minute. For example, a student who calls out the answers to single-digit addition problems (such as 9 + 4, 7 + 3, and 5 + 9) provided by a teacher, may call out 12 answers in one minute. If 10 of those answers are correct, then his fluency measure is 10 correct per minute. If, after instruction or practice, his fluency rate is 22 correct per minute, that provides a clear measure of learning.

These seven measures of learning are the most commonly used by researchers. Having reliable ways of measuring learning is essential to the study of behavior, but it is not sufficient. There must also be trustworthy ways of obtaining data.

*B. F. Skinner was the first to devise a cumulative recorder, but he was not the first to record behavior cumulatively. That honor goes to biologist James Slonaker, who used it to measure lifelong activity in the white rat (Todd, pers. comm., 2001; see Slonaker, 1912).*

Learning is most often measured as a change in number of errors, topography, intensity, speed, latency, rate, or fluency. There are other ways of measuring learning as well. The point is that we cannot study learning unless we can measure it in some precise way. When you consider them, remember that the changes in behavior being measured are not the *result* of learning; they *are* learning. That is a distinction that a lot of people have trouble with, but it is important.

# SOURCES OF DATA

Various sources of evidence are available to those who study learning. Each has strengths and weaknesses. We will begin with the simplest, most common, and least reliable: anecdotes.

### Anecdotes

**Anecdotes** are first- or secondhand reports of personal experiences. They can include specific information about measures of learning, such as the number of errors made, but they are more often less specific. They are often identified by phrases such as "In my experience . . ." and "I've found that. . . ." Sometimes anecdotal evidence takes on the character of common wisdom: "They say that . . ."; "It's common knowledge that . . ."; and "Everybody knows that. . . ."

Unfortunately, what "everybody knows" is not always correct. Bloodletting persisted as a treatment for medical disorders for about 2,000 years because "everybody knew" that it worked. Actually, it almost certainly killed many more people than it helped; one of its more famous victims may have been George Washington, the first president of the United States. People can point to anecdotal evidence to support all kinds of principles and practices, but sorting out which anecdotes to believe is often difficult.

Perhaps the best way to demonstrate the trouble with anecdotes is with an anecdote. I once spoke to a psychologist who complained about the school his daughter attended. "You won't believe this," he said, "but they don't teach the kids how to read." He was talking about Whole Language, a method of reading instruction in which students are read to and exposed to books but aren't taught to sound out words. The assumption is that the students will pick up reading skills through a kind of osmosis, without any formal instruction. Unfortunately, the psychologist's child, whom I will call Samantha, was *not* learning to read. I asked her father what he did. "We got a how-to book," he said, "and taught her to read."

Although Whole Language has been discredited as a way of teaching beginning reading skills (Chall, 1995; Treiman, 2000), this anecdote does not qualify as hard evidence against it: The psychologist may have exaggerated his child's failure to read; the problem may have been due to a poor teacher, an unnoticed illness, or some other variable besides the method of instruction. We simply cannot say *from such anecdotes* that Whole Language is ineffective.

Positive anecdotes are equally untrustworthy. Let us suppose, for example, that you meet a teacher who is a devoted practitioner of Whole Language. You ask the teacher if the method works. She replies, "Absolutely! I've seen it work. I had one student who picked up reading easily without any formal instruction at all. Her name was Samantha. . . ." You see the problem: The teacher who "sees" an instructional method working may be unaware of other important variables, such as instruction in the home.

Despite their limitations, anecdotes cannot to be summarily dismissed. They can provide useful leads, and they keep us in contact with "popular wisdom," which, after all, is not always wrong. Still, better evidence is required for a science of learning (Spence, 2001).

## Case Studies

We get a slightly better grade of data with the **case study.** Whereas anecdotal evidence consists of casual observations, a case study examines a particular individual in considerable detail.

The case study method is often used in medicine. A patient with a mysterious symptom may be studied with great care as doctors attempt to understand his illness. Economists also do case studies. They may study a company to find out why it failed or succeeded. Similarly, educational researchers might do a detailed study of a teacher or school that gets particularly good results. And case studies are often used in attempting to understand abnormal behavior, such as delusions.

There are, however, serious problems with case study evidence. One problem is that doing a case study takes a good deal of time. Because of this, generalizations are often based on very few cases. If those few cases are not representative of the larger group, conclusions about that group may be in error.

Another problem is that the case study cannot answer certain questions about behavior. We cannot, for example, use the case study to determine whether falling off a ladder is likely to produce a fear of heights. We may interview a person who fell off a ladder and who subsequently developed a fear of heights, but this does not establish that the fall caused the fear. For years, many clinical psychologists and psychiatrists insisted that homosexuality was a neurotic disorder because their homosexual clients were all neurotic. Then, in the 1950s, Evelyn Hooker pointed out that the *heterosexual* clients of clinicians were also neurotic, but no one concluded that heterosexuality was a form of neurosis (see Chance, 1975).

Case study evidence is also flawed in that much of the data obtained comes not by direct observation of the participant's behavior, but from what the participant or other people report about the participant's behavior. Such reports are notoriously unreliable.

When appropriate, the case study is a step above the anecdote because at least the data are obtained in a fairly systematic way. But a stable science of behavior cannot be built on the sandy soil of the case study. Better control is required. One way of getting better control is with descriptive studies.

 **QUERY 2:** The chief difference between anecdotal and case study evidence is that

anecdotal evidence is based on casual _____, whereas case

studies _____.

## Descriptive Studies

In a **descriptive study,** the researcher attempts to describe a group by obtaining data from its members—often by conducting interviews or administering questionnaires. To devoted advocates of the case study, the descriptive study seems superficial. But by gathering data from many cases and analyzing the data statistically, the descriptive study reduces the risk that a few unrepresentative participants will lead to false conclusions.

In a typical descriptive study, we might ask people (in interviews or by means of a questionnaire) about their fears and their childhood experiences. We might then compare the childhood experiences of those who have phobias with those who do not. Statistical analysis might then suggest whether there were any reliable differences between the two groups. We might find, for example, that people with phobias are more likely to have overprotective parents than people without phobias.

Descriptive studies represent a vast improvement over case studies, but they have their limitations. One is that although descriptive studies can suggest hypotheses to explain a phenomenon, they cannot test those hypotheses. We might find that phobia victims are twice as likely as others to describe their parents as overprotective, yet overprotective parenting may not be important in producing phobias. It could be, for example, that overprotective parenting is associated with some other variable, such as a genetically based high level of anxiety, and this other variable is what accounts for the higher incidence of phobias. The only way to determine that is to perform an experiment.

## Experimental Studies

An **experiment** is a study in which a researcher manipulates one or more variables (literally, things that vary) and measures the effects of this manipulation on one or more other variables. The variables the researcher manipulates are called **independent variables;** those that are allowed to vary freely are called **dependent variables.** In learning experiments, the independent variable is typically some sort of experience (an environmental event), and the dependent variable is some kind of change in behavior. There are many different kinds of experiments, but all fall into one of two types: between-subjects designs and within-subject designs.

In **between-subjects experiments,** the researcher typically identifies two or more groups of participants. (These experiments are also called *between-group* or *group* designs.) The independent variable is then made to differ across these groups. Suppose you wish to study the role of certain experiences on aggressive behavior. You might assign people to one of two groups and expose those in one group to the experiences you think will produce aggression. The participants who are exposed to the aggression-inducing experience are called the **experimental group;** those who are not exposed to it are called the **control group.** (The participants need not actually appear in groups; here, the term *group* refers only to assignment to experimental or control conditions.) Next you compare the tendency of participants in the two groups to behave in an aggressive manner. If the experimental participants behave more aggressively than the control participants, then the experiences provided may have been responsible.

Although experiments involving two groups are common, it is quite possible to conduct between-subjects experiments with many groups. In an experiment on aggression, you might have several experimental groups, each of which is exposed to a different kind or a different amount of aggression-inducing experiences. You would then compare the performance of each group not only with the control group but with every other experimental group (see Figure 2-8).

The essential element of a between-subjects design is that an independent variable differs across participants. Any differences in the dependent variable are assumed to be the result of differences in exposure to the independent variable. The validity of this assumption rests on the extent to which the participants being compared are alike. It would not do if one group were appreciably older than the other, for example, because any differences in the results might be due to differences in age rather than to the independent variable. Likewise, the two groups should not differ in health, gender, education, or a host of other variables.

 QUERY 3:   The essential element of a between-subjects design is that the independent

variable varies _____ participants.

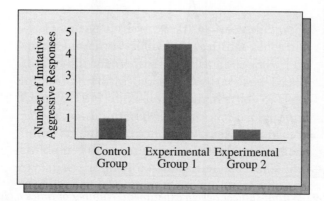

***Figure 2-8***   *Between-subjects design experiment. Data are compared from different individuals in different conditions. (Compiled from data in Rosenkrans and Hartup, 1967.)*

To minimize such differences, participants are usually assigned at random to one of the groups. This may be done, for example, by flipping a coin: If the coin comes up heads, the participant goes into the experimental condition; tails, the participant is in the control group. Through such random assignment, any differences among the participants should be distributed more or less equally among the groups. However, with small groups even random assignment leaves open the possibility of differences among the groups, so the more participants in each group, the better.

Another way to reduce pretreatment differences among groups is through matched sampling. In **matched sampling,** participants with identical features are identified. Animals may be matched for age and sex quite easily. Human participants can be matched for these variables, and also for IQ, educational level, socioeconomic background, and so on. After participants have been matched, one member of each pair is assigned at random to the experimental group, the other to the control group. After the results of a between-subjects experiment are in, they are usually subjected to statistical analysis in an attempt to estimate the likelihood that differences in results are due to the independent variable.

The alternative to the between-subjects design is the **within-subject experiment** (Kazdin, 1982; Morgan & Morgan, 2008). (These experiments are also called *single-subject* designs.) In these experiments, a participant's behavior is observed before the experimental treatment and then during or after it. The initial period during which a participant's behavior is observed is known as the **baseline period** because it provides a basis for comparison. In figures depicting within-subject data, this period is usually labeled "A." The treatment period follows the baseline and is labeled "B." If the A and B periods yield different results (e.g., different latencies or different rates of behavior), this should be apparent in the data graph (see Figure 2-9).

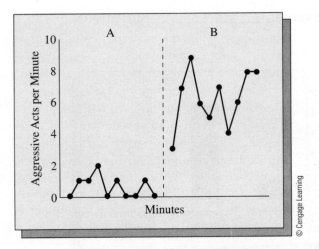

**Figure 2-9** *Within-subject design experiment. Number of times a child hit a stuffed animal each minute during a ten-minute baseline (A) and during an experimental intervention (B). (Hypothetical data.)*

The essential element of a within-subject design is that the independent variable varies within the participants. In other words, each participant is in the experimental "group" *and* in the control "group" at different times. Any differences in the dependent variable are presumed to be the result of differences in experiences at different times.

Because the independent variable varies within the same person or animal, concern that the results might be due to differences among participants is greatly reduced. However, it is possible that some extraneous variable is responsible for the results. An animal could become ill during an experiment, for example, and this could give the illusion that the experimental treatment had changed the participant's behavior when, in fact, it had not. To rule out such possibilities, the experimenter may return to the baseline (A) condition in what is known as an **ABA reversal design** (Sidman, 1960/1988). The experimenter may then reinstate the experimental (B) condition (Figure 2-10). In a sense, the researcher repeats the experiment within the same study.

QUERY 4: The essential element of a within-subject design is that the independent

variable varies _____ participants.

Using an ABA reversal design is a little like turning a light switch on and off to see whether it controls a given light. By switching back and forth between A and B conditions, the researcher is able to demonstrate the extent to which a behavior is influenced by the independent variable. The data are all the more convincing if they are replicated with additional participants, but large numbers of participants are unnecessary. Statistical analysis is also not usually required: You don't need statistics to tell you that a light goes on and off when you throw a particular switch.

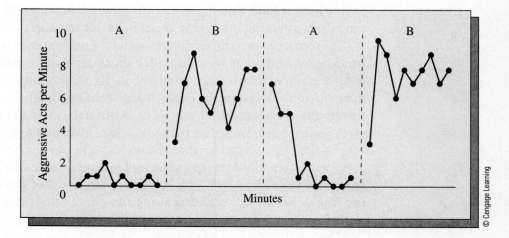

***Figure 2-10*** *Within-subject design with reversal. A and B conditions can be repeated to verify the effect of the intervention. (Hypothetical data.)*

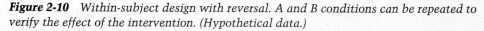

*Although the single-subject reversal design is thought of as a recent development, the first use of it may date back to the Greek physician Galen. He used it to make a diagnosis 1,700 years ago! (See Brown, 2007.)*

Although within-subject experiments and between-subjects experiments differ in the number of participants and in the use of statistics, these are not the most important differences between them. A far more important difference has to do with the way in which extraneous differences among participants are controlled. In between-subjects experiments, these differences are controlled chiefly through random assignment and matching. The assumption is that important differences among participants will "even out" across the groups. In within-subject experiments, extraneous differences among participants are controlled by comparing participants against themselves. The assumption is that if the *same* participant is observed under experimental and control conditions, extraneous differences *among* participants are largely irrelevant.

Both between-subjects and within-subject experiments allow us, within limits, to see the effects of independent variables on dependent variables. They are a substantial advance over descriptive studies. Not even experimental studies are perfect, however.

## Limitations of Experiments

The great power of the experiment comes from the control it provides over variables. However, this very control has led to the criticism that experiments create an artificial world from which the researcher derives an artificial view of behavior (Schwartz & Lacey, 1982).

In many learning experiments, the dependent variable is an extremely simple behavior: A rat presses a lever, a pigeon pecks a disc, a person presses a button. The independent variable is also likely to be simple: A light goes on or off, a few grains of food fall into a tray, a person hears the word *correct*. The experiment may also occur in an extremely sterile, artificial environment: a small experimental chamber, for example, or (in the case of human participants) a room with only a table, a chair, and a box with a toggle switch. Some people have a hard time believing that the artificial world of the experiment can tell us anything important about behavior in natural environments.

To some extent the criticism is fair. Experiments do create artificial conditions, and what we find under those artificial conditions may not always correspond with what would occur under more natural conditions. But the control that makes the experiment seem artificial is necessary to isolate the effects of independent variables. Although no one is particularly interested in lever pressing, disc pecking, and button pushing, using such simple acts as the dependent variable allows us to better see the impact of the independent variable. More complicated behavior would be more realistic but less revealing. Understanding lever pressing and disc pecking, *per se*, is not the researcher's goal; understanding the effect of environment on behavior is. (For more on this point, see Berkowitz & Donnerstein, 1982.)

The artificiality of experiments is largely the result of control. When researchers create more realistic experiments and study more complicated behavior, they almost inevitably reduce control over important variables and produce data that are harder to interpret. One way around the problem is to do two kinds of experiments: laboratory experiments and field experiments.

Laboratory experiments offer the control that allows the researcher to derive clear-cut principles. Field experiments—those done in natural settings—allow the researcher to test laboratory-derived principles in more realistic ways. For instance, we might study learning in the laboratory by having rats run mazes and then test the principles derived in field experiments of rats foraging in the wild. Or we might test the effects of different lecture rates on student learning in carefully controlled laboratory experiments and then perform an analogous experiment in a classroom.

Despite their limitations, experiments provide a degree of power that is not available through other means. Consequently, most of the evidence we will consider in the pages that follow will be from experimental research. Much of that research involves animals. Can we really learn about human behavior from experiments with rats, pigeons, and other furry and feathered creatures?

CAPSULE **REVIEW**   Learning may be studied in various ways. Anecdotal and case study evidence is unreliable, though a good source of hypotheses. Descriptive studies can provide useful and reliable information but cannot account for why a phenomenon occurs. Because of these limitations, learning is usually studied by means of between-subjects and within-subject experiments. Experiments have their limits as well, but they are the best tool available for investigating natural phenomena.

## ANIMAL RESEARCH AND HUMAN LEARNING

Animals have been called "furry and feathered test tubes" (Donahoe & Palmer, 1994, p. 71). Most people, including most learning researchers, are far more interested in human behavior than they are in animal behavior. If the goal is to understand *human* learning and behavior, why study rats and pigeons? There are several reasons.

Researchers generally believe that animal research is essential to improving our understanding of human behavior. Richard McCarty (1998) writes that "many of the most important developments in psychology over the past century have been linked to or informed by research with animals" (p. 18; see also Miller, 1985). Why are animals so important?

First, animals make it possible to get control over the influence of heredity. Because experimental animals are purchased from research supply companies, their genetic histories are fairly well known. This means that genetic differences from one participant to another, an important source of variability in behavior, are substantially reduced. We cannot, of course, have breeding programs to produce people with uniform genetic backgrounds. Theoretically, researchers can reduce genetic variability in humans by studying learning in identical twins, but identical twins are not as identical as people think (Moore, 2001). Moreover, they are uncommon; relying on them for all research on behavior is impossible.

Second, with animals it is possible to control a participant's learning history. Animals can be housed from birth in environments that are far less variable than their natural environments, thus greatly reducing the influence of unintended learning experiences. This sort of control cannot be achieved with human participants. Humans, particularly adult humans, come to experiments with very different learning histories.

Third, it is possible to do research with animals that, for ethical reasons, cannot be done with people. It might be interesting and useful to know whether a certain kind of experience would make people depressed or induce them to attack their neighbors, but doing such research with people raises serious ethical problems.

**? QUERY 5:**   One advantage of animal research is that it provides better control of

_____ and _____.

Despite the obvious advantages of animals as research participants, their use has been criticized. Perhaps the objection heard most often is that the results obtained tell us nothing about people (Kazdin & Rotella, 2009). Critics complain, "People are not rats!" or "Just because pigeons behave that way, doesn't mean that *I* behave that way."

Researchers are, of course, well aware of the differences among species; indeed, it is through animal experimentation that some of these differences have come to light (e.g., Breland & Breland, 1961). One needs to be cautious in generalizing research on one species to another. If researchers establish that a particular kind of experience affects rat behavior in a certain way, the assumption is that human behavior will be affected in a similar manner, but that assumption must be bolstered by other evidence, such as data from descriptive or experimental studies with people. In most instances such evidence corroborates the findings of animal research.

A second objection to animal research is that it has no practical value. Unlike the biomedical research that uses animals to determine the health risks of smoking, this argument goes, animal research on behavior merely provides facts that only a theoretician could find useful. It is true that animal research is sometimes aimed at answering esoteric theoretical questions, but the findings of this research often have great practical value. Principles derived from animal research have been put to good use in numerous areas, including child rearing (Becker, 1971; Sloane, 1979), education (Chance, 2008; Dermer, Lopez, & Messling, 2009; Layng, Twyman, & Strikeleather, 2004), business (Agnew & Daniels, 2010; Carter et al., 1988), and sports (Boyer et al., 2009; Luiselli & Reed, 2011; Martins & Collier, 2011; Ward, 2011).

The beneficiaries of animal research include not only people, but animals. In the past, the training of pets, saddle horses, farm animals, and circus animals relied heavily on harsh measures. The expression, "Don't beat a dead horse" derives from the widespread physical abuse of horses in the days of horse-powered transportation. Today animal training is much more likely to be done in a more humane and effective manner, thanks largely to procedures discovered or perfected through animal research (see, e.g., Skinner, 1951; Pryor, 1999). These same procedures resulted in improvements in veterinary care and in the quality of life for animals in zoos and similar facilities (Markowitz, 1982; Stewart, Ernstam, & Farmer-Dougan, 2001; also see Chapters 4 and 9).

A third objection to animal research is that it is intrinsically unethical. This "animal rights" view maintains that people have no more right to experiment on rats than rats have to experiment on people. The issue is controversial (Balster, 1992; Burdick, 1991; Miller, 1985; Shapiro, 1991a, 1991b) and deserves to be treated seriously.

Ethical problems do arise in the use of animals in experiments, and researchers are not indifferent to them. In 2011, the National Research Council (2011) concluded that while the genetic similarity of chimpanzees to humans (we share 98% of our genes) makes them an ideal subject for behavioral and biomedical research, it also raises ethical concerns. While the NRC stopped short of ending all funding of research on chimpanzees, it severely limited their use to problems that cannot be answered in other ways (Altevogt et al., 2011; National Research Council, 2011).

**QUERY 6:** The beneficiaries of behavioral research with animals include both

_____ and _____.

But critics of animal research ignore the fact that ethical issues arise when we use animals for other purposes besides research. If it is unethical to use animals for research, is it ethical to eat them? Do people have the right to conscript animals for farm work, such as hauling heavy loads and plowing fields? (In some parts of the world, people and animals alike would starve if such practices were forbidden.) Do equestrians have the right to ride horses and to force them to risk injury by jumping barriers? Thousands of dogs have spent their lives assisting people who are blind, deaf, or confined to wheelchairs. Do people have the right to require animals to spend their lives this way? Millions of animals are kept as pets; by what right do people keep animals in captivity for their own amusement? Probably most people believe that at least some of these uses of animals are ethical. If they are, then why is it unethical to use animals in research?

Some people might answer that research animals are not as well treated as those that serve humans in other ways. It is true that laboratory animals are typically confined to relatively small and uninteresting spaces. On the other hand, they are not beaten, teased, left to bake in a hot car, subjected to inclement weather or foul living quarters, denied veterinary care, or abandoned—as is often the case with working animals and pets. Conditions for the care of laboratory animals are set by various state and federal laws and by ethical review boards. Indeed, one assumption in interpreting data from animal research is that the animals have received good treatment. It is for this reason that one group of researchers (Balster, 1992) writes that "the scientific community goes to great lengths to ensure the welfare of their animals; to do otherwise *is bad scientific method*" (p. 3; emphasis added).

In an effort to prevent unnecessary suffering, the American Psychological Association (2010) and other organizations have established guidelines for the conduct of animal research. These require that certain standards be met in the care and handling of animals. Animals may, for instance, be made to "work" for their food; but the amount of work is typically far less than that required of animals in domestic service or living wild. The guidelines also set standards for the use of **aversives** (stimuli the animal would avoid, given the option). If a question can be answered without the use of aversives, they are not to be used. When aversives are deemed necessary, they must be no more severe than is required by the nature of the research. The use of aversives must also be justified by the probable benefits to be gained from the research. Inspections by health departments and humane societies help to ensure that researchers meet these standards.

Some critics maintain that animal research is unethical because computer simulations can replace animals in research: We need no longer run rats through mazes or train pigeons to peck a disc for food, they argue; silicon animals can replace those with fur and feathers. Computers can be programmed to simulate the behavior of animals. A good example of this is *Sniffy the Virtual Rat* (Alloway, Wilson, & Graham, 2011). This program provides an image of a laboratory rat in an experimental chamber on the computer screen. The simulated rat moves about doing rat-like things: exploring its surroundings, scratching and licking itself, drinking water, eating food it finds in a food tray, and learning to press a lever. Sniffy is a useful instructional tool, but it is a mistake to think that simulated animals (or people, for that matter) can replace living research participants. We cannot program a computer to simulate the effects of a variable on behavior *until we know what those effects are.* That is precisely what research is designed to discover.

The point of this discussion is not that there are no valid grounds for objecting to animal research. It is that we should keep in mind that we use animals in a variety of ways for our benefit—and for theirs. Some animals serve by helping the blind find their way, by detecting explosives or illegal drugs, by pulling a plow through a field, or by providing companionship. Others serve by providing answers to questions about learning and behavior that may greatly improve the lives of both animals and people.

 QUERY 7:   Computer _____ cannot replace animal research because they

are programmed based on findings from animal research.

CAPSULE **REVIEW**   Both humans and other animals may serve as participants for experiments on learning. Animals make greater control possible but leave open the possibility that the results do not apply to humans. Often, basic research is done with animals, and the principles derived from this research are then tested on humans in applied settings. Animal research raises ethical questions, but so do other common uses of animals, and animals as well as people benefit from animal research. Both animal and human research are essential to an understanding of learning and behavior.

# A FINAL WORD

A major theme of this text is that *all* behavior, including all human behavior, can be viewed as a natural phenomenon, and therefore subject to study with the methods of natural science. This means that we can account for behavior with empirically derived principles and without recourse to vague and unverifiable hypothetical concepts. Not all behavior has been satisfactorily analyzed in terms of natural phenomena, but considerable progress has been made toward that goal. It is for you to decide whether the successes thus far achieved justify adopting the natural science approach to learning and behavior.

## RECOMMENDED **READING**

1. Bachrach, A. J. (1962). *Psychological research: An introduction.* New York: Random House.

   A highly readable little book on research methods, this provides an insider's view of behavioral research and despite its age should be required reading for all psychology and behavior science majors.

2. Fernald, D. (1984). *The Hans legacy: A story of science.* Hillsdale, NJ: Erlbaum.

   This is a very readable account of the case of Clever Hans, a horse known far and wide for his great intelligence, and of the effort of scientists to determine if Hans was as smart as he seemed.

3. Sagan, C. (1997). *The demon-haunted world: Science as a candle in the dark.* Baltimore, MD: Penguin.

   The famous astronomer Carl Sagan shows how easily people who don't accept the natural science approach can be led astray.

4. Shapin, S. (November 6, 2006). Sick city. *The New Yorker,* 110–115.

   This short history of the efforts of Dr. John Snow identifies the means by which cholera spread in the epidemics of 19th-century London. This is far afield from learning, but it illustrates the effectiveness of the natural science approach and shows how it contrasts with so-called commonsense analysis.

5. Shermer, M. (2002, June). The shamans of scientism. *Scientific American*, p. 35. Michael Shermer could be called a professional skeptic. He is the editor of *Skeptic* magazine and author of a column for *Scientific American* in which he regularly ponders the line between science and pseudoscience. This article advocates scientism, "a worldview that encompasses natural explanations for all phenomena."

## REVIEW **QUESTIONS**

1. Define the following terms. Give an example or illustration of each that is not provided in the text.

ABA reversal design
anecdotal evidence
aversives
baseline period
between-subjects experiment
case study
control group
cumulative record
fluency

dependent variable
descriptive study
experiment
experimental group
independent variable
matched sampling
within-subject experiment
topography

2. What are the principal *similarities* between within-subject and between-subjects designs?

3. Distinguish among speed, rate, and latency.

4. How could you quantify the changes in topography associated with learning to speak a foreign language?

5. Explain how the rate of behavior is reflected in a cumulative record.

6. What is the chief virtue of matched sampling?

7. In what kind of experiment is statistical analysis least likely to be necessary?

8. You are studying cocaine addiction in rats. An animal rights activist accuses you of animal cruelty. How can you defend your work?

9. You are attempting to discover learning principles by studying the effects of experience on the eyeblink. A friend says that eyeblinking is a trivial kind of behavior, not worth studying. Defend your work.

10. Some researchers argue that learning is a change in the brain produced by experience. Discuss the virtues and weaknesses of this definition.

## PRACTICE **QUIZ**

1. This text takes the _____ approach to behavior.

2. One reason that many learning studies use animals is that with animals it is possible to get greater _____ over variables.

3. T. H. Huxley wrote, "Sit down before fact as a _____ _____."

4. The law of _____ says that the simplest explanation that fits the data is best.

5. The kind of experiment that can be likened to turning a light switch on and off is an _____ design.

6. _____ design experiments assume that there are no important differences among participants.

7. A change in _____ means a change in the form a behavior takes.

8. _____ is a measure of learning that combines errors and rate.

9. If there is a reduction in the time that passes before a behavior occurs, we say that learning is measured in terms of _____.

10. A cumulative record measures learning as a change in the _____ of behavior.

## QUERY **ANSWERS**

Query 1. If the rate of a behavior is increasing, the slope of the cumulative record *rises/goes up.* A flat record indicates that the behavior is *not occurring.*

Query 2. The chief difference between anecdotal and case study evidence is that anecdotal evidence is based on casual *observation,* whereas case studies *examine an individual in detail.*

Query 3. The essential element of a between-subjects design is that the independent variable varies *across* participants.

Query 4. The essential element of a within-subject design is that the independent variable varies *within* participants.

Query 5. One advantage of animal research is that it provides better control of *heredity/genetics* and *learning history/previous learning.*

Query 6. The beneficiaries of behavioral research with animals include both *humans* and *animals.*

Query 7. Computer *simulations* cannot replace animal research because they are programmed based on findings from animal research.

# CHAPTER 3

# Pavlovian Conditioning

*The normal animal must respond not only to stimuli which themselves bring immediate benefit or harm, but also to [those that] only signal the approach of these stimuli; though it is not the sight and sound of the beast of prey which is in itself harmful . . . but its teeth and claws.*

**—Ivan Pavlov**

## PREVIEW

Years ago an instructor who used an earlier edition of this text criticized the chapter on Pavlovian conditioning for being too long. "After all," he said, "Pavlovian conditioning is merely of historical interest." I suspect that view is shared by a lot of people, including more than a few psychologists. I emphatically disagree. I do not think it is possible to understand human nature without understanding the basic principles that Pavlov discovered and others have elaborated. Pavlovian conditioning is not about teaching dogs to slobber at the sound of a bell, nor is it about learning that one event predicts another. It is about one of the major ways that events change our behavior, including the behavior we call thoughts and feelings. Understanding it is central to understanding people, including ourselves.

# BEGINNINGS

Around the end of the 19th century, a Russian physiologist reached a turning point in his career. He had spent several years doing research on the physiology of digestion, work that would soon win him a Nobel Prize. But in middle age, still relatively unknown, he wrestled with one of the most difficult decisions of his career: Should he continue his present line of work or take up a new problem, one that could lead nowhere and that some of his colleagues might regard as an unfit subject for a respectable scientist? The safe thing to do, the easy thing to do, would have been to continue the work he had started. But if he had, psychology would have suffered an immeasurable loss, and the chances are that neither you nor I would ever have heard of Ivan Petrovich Pavlov.

Pavlov started his career with research on the circulatory system and then moved on to the physiology of digestion. He developed special surgical procedures that enabled him to study the digestive processes of animals over long periods of time by redirecting an animal's digestive fluids outside the body, where they could be measured. He used this technique to study the salivary glands, stomach, liver, pancreas, and parts of the intestine. In the case of the salivary glands, the procedure was a relatively simple operation. The salivary duct of a dog was detached from its usual place inside the mouth and directed through an incision in the cheek. When the dog salivated, the saliva would flow through the duct and be collected in a glass tube. With animals prepared in this way, Pavlov could make precise observations of the actions of the glands under various conditions (see Figure 3-1).

One of Pavlov's goals was to understand how the body breaks food down into chemicals that can be absorbed into the blood. This process starts with the salivary reflex: When food is taken into the mouth, it triggers the flow of saliva. The saliva dilutes the food and starts breaking it down chemically. In a typical experiment on the salivary reflex, Pavlov would bring a dog into the laboratory, put food into its mouth, and observe the result.

© Cengage Learning

***Figure 3-1*** *Surgical preparation for studying the salivary reflex. When the dog salivated, the saliva drained into a tube attached to the dog's cheek. This way the salivary response could be precisely measured.*

## IVAN PAVLOV: AN EXPERIMENTER FROM HEAD TO FOOT

George Bernard Shaw said he was the biggest fool he knew. H. G. Wells thought he was one of the greatest geniuses of all time. But Ivan Pavlov described himself as "an experimenter from head to foot" (in Wells, 1956).

Of the three characterizations, Pavlov's was probably the most accurate. His discoveries were much more important, and much less commonsensical, than Shaw believed, but they also failed to bring the utopia that Wells anticipated. There is, however, no denying that Pavlov was a brilliant experimenter and a zealot fiercely committed to science.

Pavlov was born in Ryazan, a small peasant village in Russia, in September 1849, a decade before the publication of Darwin's *On the Origin of Species*. His father was a poor priest who had to keep a garden to ensure that his family would eat.

As a boy, Pavlov showed little promise of later greatness. His academic performance was mediocre, and probably few people in his village expected him to become a famous scientist—or a famous anything, for that matter. He grew up to be slim, agile, athletic, and incredibly energetic, with blue eyes, curly hair, a long beard, and the fire of genius.

As Professor Pavlov, he was sometimes an impatient, stubborn, and eccentric man who waved his hands excitedly when he spoke. If one of his assistants botched an experiment, he might explode in anger; half an hour later, he would have forgotten all about it. But of all the things one might say about Pavlov, surely the most important is this: He was an experimenter. Nothing was so important, nothing so precious, as his experiments. "Remember," he once wrote, "science requires your whole life. And even if you had two lives they would not be enough. Science demands . . . the utmost effort and supreme passion" (in Cuny, 1962, p. 160).

Pavlov's passion for science stayed with him throughout his long life. Age slowed him, of course, but not the way it slows most of us. Ever the experimenter, he observed the toll that time had taken and noted it with objective interest. On his deathbed, he was the observer, as well as the subject, of a final experiment. As life slowly left him, he described his sensations to a neuropathologist so that these data might be recorded for the benefit of science. Somehow he kept this up almost until the end. One report of Pavlov's death (in Gantt, 1941) relates that in those last moments he slept a bit, then awoke, raised himself on his elbows, and said, "It is time to get up! Help me, I must get dressed!"

The effort was understandable. He had been away from his laboratory, from his science, for nearly six whole days.

*Ivan Pavlov, one of the giants in the field of learning. (Drawing by Steve Campbell. Image © 2000 by Funfaces. Reprinted with permission of Funfaces.)*

Pavlov was fascinated by the adaptability of the glands. He found, for instance, that if he gave a dog dry, hard food, there was a heavy flow of saliva; if he gave the animal watery food, there was very little saliva. And if he put an inedible substance into the dog's mouth, the amount of saliva depended on the amount needed to eject the substance: A marble evoked very little saliva, while sand resulted in a large supply. So the reflex action of the gland depended on the nature of the stimulus. Each time, the gland responded according to the need. "It is as if," said Pavlov, "the glands possessed a 'kind of intelligence'" (quoted in Cuny, 1962, p. 26).

The cleverness of the glands did not end there, however. When a dog had been fed a number of times, it began to salivate *before* anything was put into its mouth. In fact, it might start salivating as soon as it entered the laboratory. Pavlov, like others of his day, assumed that these "psychic secretions" were caused by the thoughts, memories, or wishes of the animal. The ancient Greeks had noticed that merely talking about food often made a person's mouth water. What fascinated Pavlov was that the dogs did not salivate when they were first brought into the laboratory, but only after they had been fed there repeatedly. How could this be? How could experience alter the action of a gland?

This question preoccupied Pavlov to the point of making him shift his attention to psychic reflexes. It was not an easy decision. It was extremely important to Pavlov that he retain his identity as a physiologist. If psychic reflexes really were the products of the mind, then they were not a fit subject for a physiologist. On the other hand, if psychic reflexes involved glands, then why should a physiologist not study them? Pavlov argued with himself along these lines, back and forth; finally, he could no longer resist the challenge. He had to understand these psychic reflexes.

## BASIC PROCEDURES

Pavlov began by observing: "I started to record all the external stimuli falling on the animal at the time its reflex reaction was manifested . . . at the same time recording all changes in the reaction of the animal" (1927, p. 6).[1] At first, the only reaction was the ordinary salivary reflex: When an experimenter put food into a dog's mouth, it salivated. But after a while, the animal would salivate before receiving food. By observing the "external stimuli falling on the animal," Pavlov was able to see what triggered these psychic secretions (see Figure 3-2). He noticed, for instance, that after a while the sight or smell of food would cause the dog to salivate. "Even the vessel from which the food has been given is sufficient . . . and, further, the secretions may be provoked

---

[1]Unless otherwise noted, all references to Pavlov refer to *Conditioned Reflexes*, first published in English in 1927.

**Figure 3-2** *Pavlov's conditioning stand. With a dog strapped into a stand as shown, an experimenter could test the effects of various procedures on the salivary response. Saliva drained into a glass tube at the fistula (as shown in Figure 3-1), or into a graduated vial. In addition, a kymograph provided a record of the saliva produced during an experiment. See Pavlov, 1927, pp. 18–19. (From Yerkes and Morgulis, 1909.)*

*When an experimenter provides learning experiences, they are often called procedures. But keep in mind that these procedures, at least in their basic forms, mimic experiences that occur in natural settings.*

*Many text authors and instructors use the terms* conditioned *and* unconditioned, *the terms used in Pavlov's 1927 book. However, this seems to be a translation error; the words* conditional *and* unconditional *are closer to Pavlov's meaning, so they are used here (Gantt, 1966).*

even by the sight of the person who brought the vessel, or by the sound of his footsteps" (p. 13).

There are, Pavlov concluded, two distinct kinds of reflexes. One kind is the largely inborn and usually permanent reflex found in virtually all members of a species and that varies little from individual to individual. The dog that salivates when food is put into its mouth manifests this type of reflex. Pavlov called these **unconditional reflexes** because they occur more or less unconditionally.

The second type of reflex is not present at birth; it must be acquired through experience and is, compared to innate reflexes, relatively impermanent. Because these psychic reflexes depend on experience, they vary considerably from individual to individual. The dog that salivates at the sound of a particular person's footsteps is an example of this type of reflex. Pavlov called these **conditional reflexes** because they "depend on very many conditions" (p. 25).

Pavlov admitted that other terms would have served as well: Unconditional reflexes might have been referred to as inborn, unlearned, or species reflexes; conditional reflexes could have been called acquired, learned, or individual reflexes. But the terms *conditional* and *unconditional* caught on and are still used today.

An unconditional reflex consists of an **unconditional stimulus (US)** and the behavior it evokes, the **unconditional response (UR)**. Unconditional stimuli are typically events that are important to survival. For example, Karin Wallace and Jeffrey Rosen (2000) demonstrated that rats show a strong unconditional fear response to an odorous chemical derived from fox feces. As the authors note, "In the wild, when a rat is attacked by a predator, it is usually . . . too late for defensive maneuvers" (p. 912). Thus the rat that has an innate tendency to freeze or run away when it detects odors associated with its enemies has a better chance of avoiding those enemies.

Meat powder is an unconditional stimulus that reliably evokes the unconditional response of salivation:

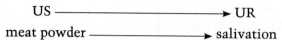

US ⟶ UR
meat powder ⟶ salivation

A conditional reflex consists of a **conditional stimulus (CS)** and the behavior it reliably evokes, the **conditional response (CR)**. When the sight of a food dish regularly evokes salivation, the food dish is a CS and salivating is a CR:

CS ⟶ CR
food dish ⟶ salivation

Pavlov's next question was, How does a neutral stimulus (one that does not naturally evoke a reflex response) come to do so? How, for example, does a food dish become a CS for salivating?

Pavlov noticed that stimuli associated with food, such as the food dish and the handler who fed the dog, became conditional stimuli for salivating. He began conducting experiments to understand better how this association led to salivating. In some experiments, Pavlov set a metronome to ticking and then put meat powder in a dog's mouth. At first, the ticking had no effect on salivation; but after the sound of the metronome had been repeatedly paired with food, the ticking began to elicit salivating. Pavlov found that virtually any stimulus could become a conditional stimulus if it regularly preceded an unconditional stimulus.

**QUERY 1:** Pavlov identified two kinds of reflexes, _____ and

_____.

*Nearly everyone thinks Pavlov routinely paired a bell with food. He used lots of different stimuli as CS, but I'm not sure he ever used a bell.*

An example will illustrate the point. If you were to clap your hands near a dog, it might respond in a number of ways, but salivating is not likely to be one of them. As far as the salivary reflex is concerned, clapping is a neutral stimulus. Now suppose you clap your hands and then immediately give the dog a bit of food:

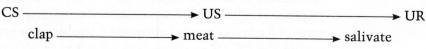

CS ⟶ US ⟶ UR
clap ⟶ meat ⟶ salivate

## WHAT'S WHAT IN PAVLOVIAN CONDITIONING?

Students sometimes have difficulty identifying the components of a conditioning procedure (the CS, US, CR, and UR), especially when given an unfamiliar example of conditioning. The following questions (adapted from Hummel, Abercrombie, & Koepsel, 1991) may help you identify the elements of any conditioning procedure:

1.  What reflex response occurs before conditioning?

    _____. This is the UR.

2.  What stimulus elicits the UR before conditioning?

    _____. This is the US.

3.  What reflex response occurs as a result of conditioning?

    _____. This is the CR.

4.  What stimulus elicits the CR?

    _____. This is the CS.

If you were to repeat this procedure several times, the dog might begin salivating when you clap your hands:

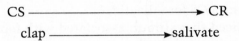

CS ⟶ CR

clap ⟶ salivate

Each pairing of CS and US is one trial, and the procedure (or experience) is best known as **Pavlovian** or **classical conditioning**. However, it also goes by a variety of other names, including sign learning, signal learning, stimulus learning, S-S learning, respondent learning, and probably one or two others.

There are two defining elements of Pavlovian conditioning. First, the behavior elicited by the US is a reflex response, such as salivating, eye blinking, sweating, or jumping in response to a loud noise. Second, the appearance of the two stimuli is independent of behavior; the CS and the US are presented *regardless of what the animal or person does.* For example, a dog did not have to salivate, or do anything else, to get food.

You have just learned the most basic form of Pavlovian conditioning. Next we will take up higher-order conditioning.

*To watch a man undergo eyeblink conditioning, go to YouTube and search "eyeblink conditioning." The one by Moorcook and Reynolds is excellent.*

CAPSULE **REVIEW**    Pavlov showed that there are two kinds of reflexes, unconditional and conditional. An unconditional reflex consists of an unconditional stimulus and an unconditional response; a conditional reflex consists of a conditional stimulus and a conditional response. Unconditional reflexes are largely innate; conditional reflexes are products of experience. The procedure that establishes a conditional response is called Pavlovian or classical conditioning. There are two critical features of Pavlovian conditioning: First, the behavior involved is a reflex response; second, the CS–US pairing occurs regardless of what the individual does.

# HIGHER-ORDER CONDITIONING

The basic Pavlovian procedure, as you have seen, consists of presenting a neutral stimulus followed by an unconditional stimulus. Suppose, however, that a neutral stimulus precedes a well-established CS. The CS is not a US, yet thanks to conditioning it does elicit a CR. So, if you paired a neutral stimulus with the CS, would the neutral stimulus become another CS?

G. P. Frolov, who worked in Pavlov's lab, decided to find out. First he trained a dog to salivate at the sound of a ticking metronome by following the ticking with food. When the metronome was well established as a CS for salivating, Frolov held up a black square and then activated the metronome:

$$CS_2 \longrightarrow CS_1 \longrightarrow CR$$
$$\text{black square} \longrightarrow \text{metronome} \longrightarrow \text{salivation}$$

At first the dog salivated at the sound of the metronome but not at the sight of the black square. After several pairings of the two stimuli, however, the dog began salivating when it saw the square. The black square had become a CS for salivating *even though it had never been followed by food:*

$$CS \longrightarrow CR$$
$$\text{black square} \longrightarrow \text{salivation}$$

The procedure of pairing a neutral stimulus with a well-established CS is called **higher-order conditioning**.

Higher-order conditioning greatly increases the importance of Pavlovian conditioning because it means that many more stimuli can come to elicit conditional responses. For example, physiologists J. M. Graham and Claude Desjardins (1980) demonstrated that a male rat that responds to a sexually receptive female by increasing the level of certain hormones will respond in a similar manner to an odor that has been paired with a receptive female. Thanks to higher-order conditioning, a neutral stimulus became a CS by being paired with the odor, without its ever having been paired with a receptive female. This might give the rat a reproductive advantage in the wild: The rat that responds to a stimulus associated with the female's scent has an advantage over the rat that responds only to her scent.

Higher-order conditioning may be even more important to humans than it is to rats. Among people, words are particularly likely to become conditional stimuli by being paired with conditional stimuli—including other words. In one classic experiment, Carolyn and Arthur Staats (1957) asked college students to look at nonsense syllables such as *YOF*, *LAJ*, and *QUG* as they were flashed on a screen. At the same time, the students repeated words spoken by the experimenters. For some students, the experimenters paired the syllable *YOF* with positive words such as *beauty, gift,* and *win,* and the syllable *XEH* with negative words such as *thief, sad,* and *enemy.* For

*Some psychologists, particularly social psychologists, speak of evaluative conditioning. This often refers to higher-order Pavlovian conditioning in which the CR is a change in feelings about the CS.*

other students, the associations were reversed: *XEH* was paired with positive words, *YOF* with negative ones. (Notice that no US was ever presented.) After this, the students rated each nonsense syllable on a seven-point scale ranging from unpleasant to pleasant. The results indicated that the nonsense syllables came to elicit emotional responses similar to the emotional value of the words with which they had been paired. When a nonsense syllable was regularly associated with pleasant words, it became pleasant; when it was paired with unpleasant words, it became unpleasant. In other words, *YOF* came to elicit good feelings in some students and bad feelings in others, depending on the words with which it had been associated. Higher-order conditioning, then, appears to play an important role in the emotional meaning of words.

**?** QUERY **2:** In higher-order conditioning, a neutral stimulus is paired with a well-

established _____ stimulus.

These examples of higher-order conditioning illustrate what is called second-order conditioning since the CS is one step away from the US (Rescorla, 1980). Second-order conditioning has been documented in a number of species, including rats (Bond & Di Giusto, 1976) and flies (Tabone & de Belle, 2011). Third-order conditioning, in which a neutral stimulus is paired with a $CS_2$, has also been demonstrated in animals (Foursikoc, in Pavlov, 1927). Remember that in higher-order conditioning, the neutral stimulus is paired only with an established CS, not the US. So how far can we go with this? Could we get conditioning by presenting a neutral stimulus before a $CS_3$ or a $CS_4$? There is evidence that if the US is a shock, it is possible to get fifth-order conditioning (Finch & Culler, 1934). This means that if a neutral stimulus is paired with a CS that was paired with a CS that was paired with a CS, that was paired with a CS that had previously been paired with a shock, the neutral stimulus will become a $CS_5$! However, the further away you get from a pairing with the US, the weaker the CR is likely to be (Pavlov, 1927; Brogden, 1939a).

Pavlovian procedures are effective in producing conditional responses. Measuring the course of conditioning, however, is more difficult than it might appear.

CAPSULE **REVIEW** In most conditioning experiments, a neutral stimulus is paired with a US, such as food. In higher-order conditioning, a neutral stimulus is paired with a well-established CS. This procedure may be less effective in establishing a CR than CS–US pairings, but it is very important in the lives of humans. Many of our emotional reactions (our likes, dislikes, fears, and loves, for example) appear to be acquired at least partly through higher-order conditioning.

# MEASURING PAVLOVIAN LEARNING

In most studies of Pavlovian conditioning, the CS and US are presented close together. Given that the US is by definition capable of evoking the UR, how is it possible to tell when learning occurs? Suppose, for example, that you sound a tone and then, 2 seconds after the tone stops, you put food into a dog's mouth. How can you tell when the dog is salivating to the tone as well as to the food?

One answer is to note when salivation begins. If the dog begins salivating after the CS begins but *before* the presentation of the US, conditioning has occurred. In this case, you can measure the amount of learning in terms of the latency of the response—the interval between the onset of the CS and the first appearance of saliva. As the number of CS–US pairings increases, the response latency diminishes; the dog may begin salivating even before the tone stops sounding.

In some conditioning studies, the interval between CS onset and the appearance of the US is so short that using response latency as a measure of learning is difficult. One way to test for conditioning in these situations is to use **test trials** (also called probe trials). This involves presenting the CS alone (i.e., without the US) periodically, perhaps on every fifth trial. If the dog salivates even when it gets no food, the salivation is clearly a conditional response to the tone. Sometimes, test trials are presented at random intervals, with the conditional stimulus presented alone, perhaps on the third trial, then on the seventh, the twelfth, the thirteenth, the twentieth, and so on (Rescorla, 1967; but see Gormezano, 2000). When test trials are used, the number of CRs in a block of, say, ten test trials is plotted on a curve. Learning is thus represented as an increase in the frequency of the conditional response.

Another way to measure Pavlovian learning is to measure the intensity or strength (sometimes called amplitude) of the CR. Pavlov found that the first CRs are apt to be very weak (a drop or two of saliva), but with repeated trials, the saliva flow in response to the CS increases rapidly. The increase in the number of drops of saliva is a measure of learning.

One problem in attempting to measure Pavlovian learning is a phenomenon known as **pseudoconditioning** (Grether, 1938). Pseudoconditioning is the tendency of a neutral stimulus to elicit a CR after a US has elicited a reflex response. For example, suppose a nurse coughs just as he gives you a painful injection. When you receive the injection, you wince. Now suppose that after the injection, the nurse coughs again. Very likely you will wince again, just as you did when you received the injection. You might think conditioning has occurred—the cough appears to have become a conditional stimulus for wincing. But you might be mistaken. A strong stimulus, such as a needle jab, can sensitize you to other stimuli so that you react to them more or less as you would react to the strong stimulus. If a nurse jabs you with a needle, you may then wince when he coughs, even if he did not cough before jabbing you. You wince, not because conditioning has occurred, but because the needle jab has sensitized you to other stimuli.

Obviously, if a stimulus has not been paired with a US, any effect it produces cannot be the result of conditioning. A problem arises, however, when a stimulus *has* been paired with a strong US. Is the behavior that occurs a conditional response, or is it the result of the earlier exposure to a strong stimulus? We can determine the answer by presenting the CS and US to control group subjects in a random manner so that the stimuli sometimes appear alone and sometimes appear together (Rescorla, 1967; but see also Rescorla, 1972). After this we can compare the performance of these control subjects with experimental subjects for which the CS and US always (or at least usually) appear together. If subjects in the experimental group perform differently from subjects in the control group, the difference in behavior may be attributed to conditioning.

Pavlovian conditioning is considered a simple form of learning. You are about to discover that it is complicated by a number of variables.

CAPSULE **REVIEW**    Researchers use various techniques to measure the effectiveness of Pavlovian procedures. One method is to continue pairing CS and US and observe whether the reflex response occurs before the presentation of the US. Another technique is to present the CS alone on certain trials and see whether a CR occurs. In testing for learning, it is important to control for the phenomenon of pseudoconditioning, in which a stimulus may elicit a CR even though it has not become an effective CS. The difficulty of measuring Pavlovian learning is one thing that complicates its study; another is that it is sensitive to a number of variables. This is what Pavlov meant when he said that the CR depends on many conditions.

## VARIABLES AFFECTING PAVLOVIAN CONDITIONING

The course of Pavlovian conditioning depends on a number of variables. Let us consider what seem to be the most important.

### How the CS and US Are Paired

Pavlovian conditioning involves the pairing of stimuli. The amount of learning that occurs depends to a large extent on how the stimuli are presented. There are four basic ways of pairing stimuli (see Figure 3-3).

In **trace conditioning**, the CS begins and ends before the US appears. There is, then, a gap between the two stimuli. Trace conditioning gets its name from the assumption that the CS leaves some sort of neural trace. In the laboratory, trace conditioning is used to study eyelid conditioning in people. Typically, a buzzer sounds for, say, 5 seconds, and then, perhaps a half second later, a puff of air is blown into the person's eye, causing him to blink. After several such pairings of the buzzer and air, the person blinks at the sound of the buzzer. The trace procedure has been used with a variety of reflex responses in a variety of species, including the honeybee (Szyszka et al., 2011).

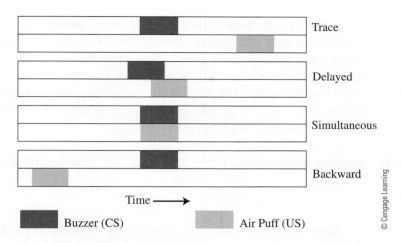

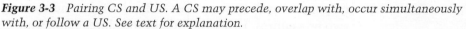

*Figure 3-3*  *Pairing CS and US. A CS may precede, overlap with, occur simultaneously with, or follow a US. See text for explanation.*

Trace conditioning often occurs outside the laboratory: We see the flash of lightning and a moment later we hear the crash of thunder; we hear the dog growl and then feel its teeth; the mother sings to her baby and then offers her nipple.

**QUERY 3:** In trace conditioning, the _____ begins and ends before the

_____ appears.

In **delay conditioning**, the CS and US overlap. That is, the US appears before the CS disappears. To apply the delay procedure to eyelid conditioning, we might sound a buzzer for 5 seconds and sometime during this period, we might send a puff of air into the person's eye.

Like trace conditioning, delay conditioning often occurs outside the laboratory: We often hear the thunder before the lightning has faded from view; the dog may continue to growl even as it bites; the mother may continue to sing softly as she nurses her baby. As in trace conditioning, the CS appears before the US; the difference is that in the delay procedure the CS and US overlap.

Some researchers distinguish between short-delay and long-delay procedures (Lavond & Steinmetz, 2003). The difference refers to the length of time the CS is present before the US appears. In the short-delay procedure, the CS may be present from several milliseconds (a millisecond is 0.001 second) to a few seconds before the US appears. For instance, a light may be on for a tenth of a second before an electric current is applied to the grid floor of a rat's experimental chamber. In the long-delay procedure, the CS may persist for several seconds or even minutes before the US appears. A light may come on and remain on for 5 minutes before an electric current is applied to the chamber floor.

Initially, short- and long-delay procedures produce similar results: A conditional response begins to appear soon after the CS appears. But in the case of long-delay conditioning, the CR latency (the interval between the onset of the CS and the CR) gradually increases. Eventually, the CR does not appear until just before the US. Apparently, what happens in long-delay conditioning is that the CS is not merely the stimulus presented by the experimenter, but also the passage of a given period of time.

**?** QUERY 4:   In delay conditioning, the _____ ends only after the

_____ begins.

Both trace and delay procedures are capable of producing conditional responses, and most studies of Pavlovian conditioning involve one of these two procedures. However, other procedures for pairing CS and US are possible.

In **simultaneous conditioning**, the CS and US coincide exactly. We might, for instance, ring a bell and blow a puff of air into a person's eye at the same moment. Both stimuli begin and end at the same time. The simultaneous appearance of CS and US is probably rare in the natural environment, but something approximating it may occur: Thunder and lightning sometimes occur together if the storm is nearby; the dog may snarl and bite at the same instant and stop snarling the moment it releases your leg; the mother may provide the nipple at the very same time she sings to her baby, and she may stop singing the instant she withdraws the nipple.

Simultaneous conditioning is a weak procedure for establishing a conditional response (Bitterman, 1964; Heth, 1976). In fact, if lightning always accompanied thunder but never preceded it, a sudden flash of lightning might not make us flinch in the least.

In **backward conditioning**, the CS *follows* the US. For instance, a puff of air directed at a person's eye could be followed by the sound of a buzzer. This US–CS sequence can occur outside the laboratory, as when a person sits on a splinter and then (having jumped up from the uncomfortable resting spot) sees the offending object.

It is very difficult to produce a CR with the backward procedure. Pavlov described some attempts made at backward conditioning in his laboratory. In one experiment, one of his assistants exposed a dog to the odor of vanilla after putting a mild acid into the dog's mouth. (The acid, possibly vinegar, was a US for salivation.) The assistant presented acid and vanilla, in that order, 427 times, yet the odor of vanilla did not become a CS for salivating. However, when another odor *preceded* the acid, it became a CS after only 20 pairings. These results are typical of those obtained by others who have attempted backward conditioning (Gormezano & Moore, 1969). There is evidence that backward conditioning is sometimes effective (e.g., Albert & Ayres, 1997; Ayres, Haddad, & Albert, 1987; Keith-Lucas & Guttman, 1975; Spetch, Wilkie, & Pinel, 1981), but the procedure is, at best, inefficient (for reviews, see Hall, 1984; Wilson & Blackledge, 1999).

Because of the relative ineffectiveness of simultaneous and backward procedures, they are seldom used in studies of Pavlovian conditioning, but it's interesting to note that ad agencies often use simultaneous and backward conditioning (see Chapter 4).

## CS–US Contingency

A **contingency** is an if–then statement. One event, X, is contingent on another event, Y, to the extent that X occurs if and only if Y occurs.

Various experiments have suggested that the effectiveness of Pavlovian procedures varies with the degree of contingency between CS and US. In one study, Robert Rescorla (1968) exposed rats to a tone followed by a mild shock. Although all the rats received the same number of CS–US pairings, in additional trials the US sometimes appeared alone. In one group, the shock occurred without the CS in 10% of the additional trials; in a second group, the US appeared alone in 20% of the trials; and in a third group, the US appeared alone in 40% of the trials. The results showed that the amount of learning depended on how reliably the CS predicted shock. When the CS was nearly always followed by the US, conditioning occurred. When a shock was about as likely to occur in the absence of a CS as in its presence (the 40% group), little or no learning took place.

Rescorla concluded that contingency was essential to Pavlovian learning, but later work raised doubts about this. Some researchers found evidence of Pavlovian conditioning even when there was *no* contingency between CS and US (Durlach, 1982; see Papini & Bitterman, 1990, and Wasserman, 1989, for discussions of this issue). Nevertheless, we can say that, other things being equal, the rate of Pavlovian conditioning will vary with the degree of CS–US contingency.

In the laboratory, it is a simple matter to ensure rapid learning by creating a high degree of contingency between the CS and US. Pavlov was able to pair a ticking metronome with food so that if the metronome was ticking, the dog always got food, and if it was not ticking, the dog never got food. Outside the laboratory, however, life is more complicated. A stimulus will sometimes precede a particular US and other times will appear alone—or, to be more precise, it will appear with stimuli other than the US. For example, you may meet someone new and have a short, pleasant exchange, but the next meeting may be neutral or unpleasant. This second experience will tend to undermine the positive effects of the first pleasant meeting. The lack of perfect contingency between a CS and a given US (or a well-established CS) not only makes for less than ideal learning conditions but may also account to some extent for the ambivalent reactions we often have toward people or things in our environment, as when we find ourselves saying, "I can't decide if I like that guy or not."

## CS–US Contiguity

Contiguity refers to the closeness in time or space between two events. In Pavlovian conditioning, contiguity usually refers to the interval between the CS and US. This interval is called the **interstimulus interval (ISI)**. In

## PAVLOVIAN FLOWCHART

Students are often confused by the various methods of pairing conditional and unconditional stimuli. When presented with a new example of conditioning, they may have difficulty deciding whether the procedure used was trace, delay, simultaneous, or backward. The following flowchart, a modified version of one provided by John Hummel and his colleagues (1991), may help.

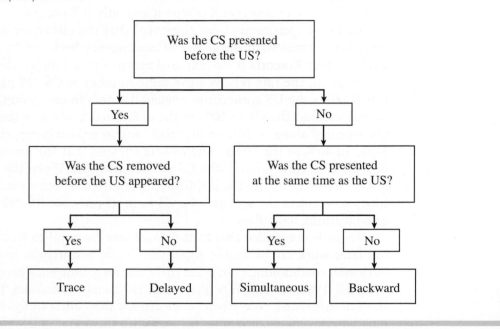

trace conditioning, the ISI is the interval between the termination of the CS and the onset of the US; in delay conditioning, where the two stimuli overlap, it refers to the interval between the onset of the CS and the onset of the US. In general, the shorter the ISI, the more quickly conditioning occurs (Mackintosh, 1974; Wasserman, 1989). However, the simultaneous procedure, with no interval at all, is ineffective. The optimum interval depends on a number of variables.

One important variable is the kind of response being learned. For instance, in establishing a conditional eyeblink response, the ideal CS–US interval is usually less than one-half second (Lavond & Steinmetz, 2003). In fear conditioning, in which a stimulus is paired with a stimulus that arouses fear, the ISI may be much longer, perhaps several minutes. And it is possible to obtain very good results with long CS–US intervals in studies of **taste aversion**. Taste aversion conditioning usually consists of pairing a distinctive taste with a substance that induces nausea. Some researchers have produced taste aversions with CS–US intervals of several hours (Revusky & Garcia, 1970; Wallace, 1976; for more on taste aversions, see Chapter 4).

Other research shows that the ideal CS–US interval varies with the level of stress (Servatius et al., 2001).

**QUERY 5:** In Pavlovian conditioning, _____ usually refers to the interval between CS and US.

The optimum CS–US interval also varies according to the type of conditioning procedure used, with short intervals generally being less important in delay conditioning than in trace conditioning. However, even in trace conditioning, extremely short intervals may not work well, as a study by Gregory Kimble (1947) demonstrates. Kimble trained college students to blink in response to a light. The gap between the light and a puff of air to the eye was short, from 0.1 to 0.4 second. On every tenth trial, Kimble withheld the US to see whether the students would blink. At the end of the experiment, he compared the response rates and found that the group with the longest CS–US intervals produced conditional responses on 95% of the test trials. Groups with shorter intervals responded less frequently; the shortest intervals produced CRs on an average of only 45% of test trials (see Figure 3-4).

It is difficult to generalize about the role of contiguity in Pavlovian conditioning. Although shorter intervals are generally preferable to longer ones, the ideal interval varies in complex ways from situation to situation. For example, while longer CS–US gaps are ineffective in trace conditioning, this varies with learning history. In one study, honeybees with experience at short-interval trace conditioning then learned with gaps that normally would have been too long (Szyszka et al., 2011). Contiguity is complicated, but it cannot be ignored because it affects the success of any given conditioning procedure one way or another.

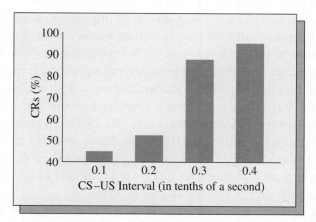

**Figure 3-4**  *CS–US interval. The average percentage of conditional responses on test trials revealed improved conditioning with longer CS–US intervals up to 0.4 second. (Compiled from data in Kimble, 1947.)*

## Stimulus Features

Researchers have used all sorts of stimuli in conditioning experiments, but not all are highly effective. The physical characteristics of the CS and US affect the pace of conditioning.

It might seem that, given several neutral stimuli, one would serve as a CS as well as another. But although nearly any stimulus can become a CS, some serve the purpose far more readily than others. This is illustrated by experiments in which the CS consists of two or more stimuli (e.g., a red light and a buzzer) presented simultaneously. Such a **compound stimulus** is paired with a US for one or more trials, after which the experimenter tests for conditioning by presenting the compound stimulus and each component of the CS alone. In one of the first studies of compound stimuli, one of Pavlov's assistants simultaneously presented cold and tactile stimulation to a dog, followed by a few drops of mild acid in the mouth (a US for salivation). Then the experimenter tested the dog with the cold stimulus alone, the tactile stimulus alone, and the compound stimulus. The results revealed that although both the tactile stimulus and the compound stimulus were effective conditional stimuli, the cold stimulus alone was utterly ineffective.

This phenomenon is known as **overshadowing** because, as Pavlov noted, "The effect of one [stimulus] was found very commonly to overshadow the effect of the others almost completely" (1927, p. 141). The overshadowed stimulus does not go entirely unnoticed; it simply does not become an effective CS (Rescorla, 1973).

Perhaps the chief distinguishing characteristic of an effective CS is its intensity: Strong stimuli overshadow weak ones. Leon Kamin (1969) used a compound stimulus consisting of a strong light and a weak tone and found that when he presented each stimulus alone, the light produced a stronger CR than the tone. Other studies demonstrate that a loud noise makes a better CS than a soft noise, that a bright light is more effective than a soft light, that a strong flavor or odor works better than a mild one, and so on.

The intensity of the US is also very important, with stronger stimuli producing better results, in general, than weaker ones. Kenneth Spence (1953) demonstrated this in a study of eyelid conditioning. The US was a puff of air exerting either 0.25 pound of pressure per square inch (psi) or 5 pounds psi. In a 20-trial test period, college students trained with the weak US gave an average of fewer than six conditional responses to the CS, whereas those trained with the stronger US gave an average of 13 CRs. In another experiment, Brett Polenchar and his colleagues (1984) used four levels of mild shock (from 1 to 4 milliamps) as the US. They sounded a tone and then delivered a shock to the hind leg of a cat, causing it to flex its leg. The rate of CR acquisition increased with the intensity of the shock (see Figure 3-5).

It is possible, however, for either a CS or a US to be too intense. In eyelid conditioning, a bright light may make a better CS than a dim one, but if the light is very strong, it may be an unconditional stimulus for blinking and will therefore interfere with learning. Likewise, a very weak electric current makes a poor US, but so may a very strong one.

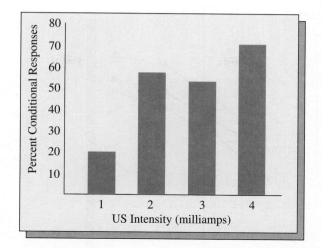

**Figure 3-5** *Conditioning and US intensity. Average percentage of CRs on seventh day of training for cats exposed to four levels of shock. Generally, the more intense the US, the more effective the training. (Compiled from data in Polenchar et al., 1984.)*

**QUERY 6:** If one part of a compound stimulus fails to become a CS, _____

has occurred.

Some stimuli are inherently more likely to become conditional stimuli than others. One example is offered by Petra Kirsch and Wolfram Boucsein (1994) of the University of Wuppertal in Germany. In their study, some people saw slides of spiders or snakes followed by an electric shock; other people saw neutral items followed by shock. Both groups of volunteers acquired a conditional fear response to the pictures, but the conditioning was more effective with spider and snake images. (Whether the conditionability of snake and spider images is innate or due to previous conditioning is up for discussion; for more on this, see the next section and Chapters 4 and 12.)

The ability of a stimulus to become a CS also depends on the nature of the US. In general, conditioning proceeds best when both the CS and the US affect internal receptors or when both affect external receptors. In experiments with rats, for example, a distinctive taste is likely to become a CS when the US causes sickness, but a combination of sight and sound is more likely to become a CS when the US is shock (Garcia & Koelling, 1966; see Chapter 13). This finding seems quite sensible from an evolutionary standpoint: Sickness is likely to be the result of eating tainted food, and such food is likely to have a distinctive taste; painful external stimuli—such as the bite of a predator—are likely to be preceded by a distinctive sight or sound.

## Prior Experience with CS and US

The effects of a conditioning procedure depend partly on the individual's previous exposure to the stimuli that will serve as CS and US. Suppose, for example, that a dog hears a bell that is sounded repeatedly but is never paired

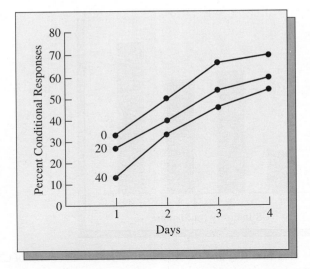

**Figure 3-6**   *Latent inhibition. Percentage of CRs (leg flexion) in sheep and goats on four days following 0, 20, or 40 preexposures to the CS. (From "Latent Inhibition: Effects of Frequency of Nonreinforced Preexposure of the CS," by R. E. Lubow, 1965,* Journal of Comparative and Physiological Psychology, *60, p. 456, Figure 2. Copyright © 1965 by the American Psychological Association. Reprinted by permission.)*

with food. If an experimenter then begins pairing the bell with food, how will the dog's previous experience with the bell affect learning?

Research shows that the appearance of a stimulus without the US interferes with the ability of that stimulus to become a CS later (see Figure 3-6). This phenomenon is called **latent inhibition** (Lubow & Moore, 1959). It probably occurs at least partly because prior exposure undermines the contingency between the CS and US during training. (See Rescorla's 1968 experiment on contingency, above.) If a CS sometimes appears alone during training, conditioning proceeds more slowly, so it is hardly surprising that exposure to the CS alone before training interferes with conditioning. Janice McPhee and colleagues (2001) added a 28-day interval between the CS preexposure and the conditioning session, yet the preexposure still interfered with conditioning.

Latent inhibition suggests that novel stimuli (stimuli with which the individual has had little or no experience) are more likely to become conditional stimuli than are stimuli that have appeared many times in the absence of the US. But what if the novel stimulus is part of a compound stimulus that includes an effective CS? Suppose, for example, that a researcher conducts an experiment on Pavlovian learning in rats, first by repeatedly pairing a tone and an electric shock, then by repeatedly pairing a compound stimulus consisting of the tone and a novel stimulus (light) with the shock. What will happen if the researcher now presents the light alone? Leon Kamin (1969) performed this experiment and found that the light did not become a CS. This phenomenon, called **blocking**, resembles overshadowing in that one stimulus interferes with the ability of another to become a CS. In overshadowing, however, the effect is the result of differences between the stimuli in characteristics such as intensity; in blocking, the effect is due to prior experience with one part of a compound stimulus.

Blocking would seem to be a useful phenomenon. Exposure to a stimulus that signals an important event, such as the availability of food or a danger such as a predator, helps us prepare for that event and thereby survive. But there is little additional benefit from duplicate signals; in blocking, we are merely ignoring duplicate signals.

Blocking might, however, work against us. When we eat foods that make us sick to our stomach, we tend to feel nauseated when we taste those foods again. We therefore avoid those foods, and that can help us survive. But suppose you eat a mango, a tropical fruit with a distinctive flavor, for the first time and later become slightly nauseated. Months later, you eat a bowl of fresh fruits that includes slices of mango and cranberry, a fruit that's new to you. If you then become sick, thanks to blocking you are likely to develop an aversion to mango—even though it may have been the cranberries that made you ill.

There is another way in which experience with a neutral stimulus can affect later conditioning. Suppose two neutral stimuli, such as a bell and a light, are repeatedly presented together but are not paired with a US. Then one of these stimuli, perhaps the bell, is repeatedly paired with an unconditional stimulus so that it becomes a CS. What effect will this procedure have on the capacity of the light to become a CS? Wilfred Brogden (1939b), using dogs as subjects, paired a light and a bell for 2 seconds 20 times a day for ten days. Then, for some of the dogs, he repeatedly paired the bell with a mild shock to one of the animal's front legs to elicit a reflex movement. Next, Brogden presented the light to see what would happen. He found that this stimulus often elicited a CR even though it had never been paired with the US. Brogden called this phenomenon **sensory preconditioning**. Dogs that had not been exposed to the bell–light pairing did not respond to the light in this way. In general, then, a stimulus will become a CS more rapidly if it has been paired with another stimulus that has since become a CS.

## Number of CS–US Pairings

Because conditioning requires the pairing of stimuli, it seems logical that the more often the CS and US appear together, the more likely a conditional response is to occur. In general, nature accepts this logic. However, the relationship between the number of stimulus pairings and the amount of learning is not linear: The first several pairings are more important than later ones. Thus, conditioning usually follows a decelerating curve (see Figure 3-7).

From a survival standpoint, the curvilinear relationship between CS–US pairings and learning makes excellent sense. If important events reliably occur together, the sooner the individual adapts, the better. If, for example, you see a black widow spider and then receive a painful bite, it is important that you acquire a healthy fear of those spiders. People who require several CS–US pairings for learning in this kind of situation are obviously at a serious disadvantage.

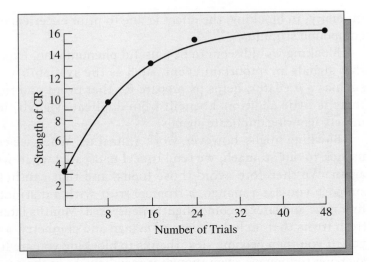

**Figure 3-7** *Number of CS–US pairings and conditioning. The more times a shock to the wrist followed a tone, the stronger the response to the tone alone. (After Hull, 1943, from data in Hovland, 1937.)*

The number of CS–US pairings required to produce a CR varies greatly. In some cases a hundred or more pairings produce only a weak CR; in others, a single pairing is effective (Fanselow, 1990; Sugai, Azami, Shiga et al., 2007).

### Intertrial Interval

We saw earlier that the CS–US interval is important to learning. Another interval that affects the rate of conditioning is the gap between successive trials. (Recall that each pairing of the CS and US is one trial.) The **intertrial interval** can vary from about a second to several years. Suppose you want to train a dog to salivate when you clap your hands. You decide that you will pair the hand clap with food ten times. How much time should you allow between each of the ten trials?

In general, experiments comparing various intertrial intervals find that longer intervals are more effective than shorter ones. While the optimum interval between CS and US is often a second or less, the best intertrial interval may be 20 seconds or more (Lavond & Steinmetz, 2003; Prokasy & Whaley, 1963).

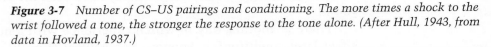

QUERY 7: Four variables that affect the rate of conditioning are _____,

_____, _____, and _____.

### Other Variables

The variables discussed thus far are perhaps the most important, but many others affect the course of Pavlovian conditioning. For instance, Harry Braun and Richard Geiselhart (1959) compared eyelid conditioning in children, young

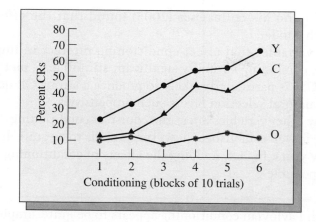

**Figure 3-8** *Conditioning and age. Eyelid conditioning for the first 60 trials proceeded more rapidly among children (C) and young adults (Y) than among older adults (O). (After Braun and Geiselhart, 1959.)*

adults, and senior citizens. As Figure 3-8 shows, learning was closely related to age; in fact, the procedure was not effective in establishing a conditional eyeblink in the oldest subjects. (See also Woodruff-Pak, 2001.)

Temperament can also affect conditioning. Pavlov noticed that some dogs are highly excitable, whereas others are much more sedate. He found that these differences, which may be largely due to heredity, affect the rate of learning: the more excitable dogs learned faster.

Stress also affects conditioning. Janet Taylor (1951) found that anxious students acquired conditional responses more quickly than those who were more relaxed (see Figure 3-9). Richard Servatius and colleagues (2001) also found that, in general, stress facilitated Pavlovian learning, but Michael

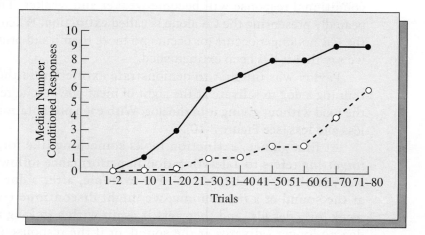

**Figure 3-9** *Conditioning and anxiety. Eyelid conditioning proceeded more rapidly among anxious college students (solid line) than among relaxed ones (broken line). (From Taylor, 1951.)*

Zorawski and his colleagues (2005) found that the effects of stress may vary with gender.

The variables that affect conditioning interact in important ways. For example, combining naturally significant stimuli (e.g., pictures of snakes) and intense USs is particularly likely to produce a strong CR quickly. It is easy to see how natural selection favors such propensities.

Many other variables affect the course of conditioning. Once a conditional response is well established, however, it tends to be quite durable and may last for many years. In fact, undoing the effects of conditioning can be difficult, or even impossible.

CAPSULE **REVIEW**    Although Pavlovian conditioning appears to be quite simple, it is complicated by the effects of a number of variables. Chief among these is the manner in which a researcher (or nature) pairs the CS and US; these include trace, delay, simultaneous, and backward procedures. The length of the CS–US interval and the degree to which the US is contingent on the CS also affect the rate of learning. Characteristics of the stimuli involved can be important as well. Prior experience with either the CS or the US can affect learning; exposure to a stimulus before conditioning can cause latent inhibition and blocking. Other important variables include the number of CS–US pairings and the length of intertrial intervals.

# EXTINCTION OF CONDITIONAL RESPONSES

Once a conditional response is established, it can be maintained indefinitely so long as the conditional stimulus is sometimes followed by the unconditional stimulus. If, however, the CS is repeatedly presented without the US, the conditional response will become weaker and weaker. The procedure of repeatedly presenting the CS alone is called **extinction.** When, as a result of this, the CR no longer occurs (or occurs no more than it did prior to conditioning), we say that it has been extinguished.

Pavlov was the first to demonstrate extinction in the laboratory. After training a dog to salivate at the sight of meat powder, he repeatedly presented the food without giving it to the dog. With each presentation, the dog salivated less and less (see Figure 3-10).

At first glance, extinction looks something like forgetting. However, *forgetting* refers to a deterioration in performance following a period without practice (see Chapter 12). For example, after a dog learns to salivate at the sound of a metronome, we might discontinue training for a day, a week, or a decade, and then test it again with a ticking metronome. If the dog no longer salivates at the sound, or if the response is weaker, we may say that forgetting has occurred. Extinction is a very different procedure: The practice sessions continue, but the sound of the metronome is not paired with food. The CS–US contingency is dissolved. Thus, we can view

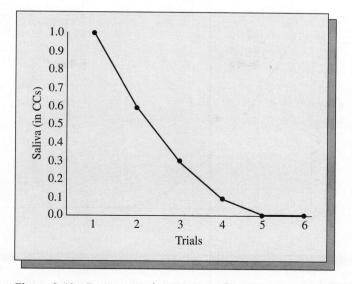

**Figure 3-10** *Extinction of a CR. A conditional response will extinguish if the CS (in this case, the sight of food) is repeatedly presented alone. (Compiled from data in Pavlov, 1927.)*

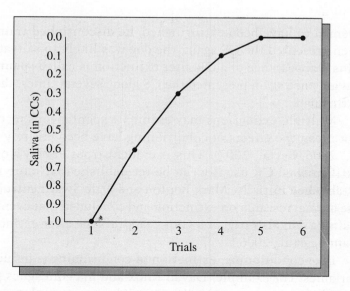

**Figure 3-11** *Extinction as learning. The extinction of the salivary response may be plotted as the increase in the "not-salivating response." (Compiled from data in Pavlov, 1927.)*

extinction as a form of conditioning in which the CS is paired with the *absence* of the US. During extinction, Pavlov's dogs are learning the "not salivating" response (see Figure 3-11).

The extinction curve shown in Figure 3-10, which is fairly typical, suggests that the CR steadily approaches zero and stabilizes at some very low level. This is not quite the case. Pavlov discovered that if, after a response

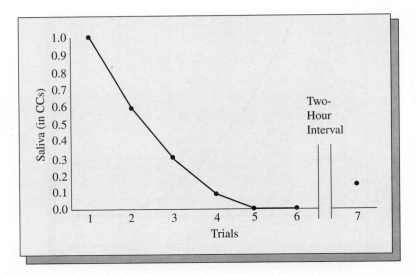

**Figure 3-12** *Spontaneous recovery. A conditional response will extinguish if the CS is repeatedly presented alone. Following a rest period, the CR spontaneously reappears. (Compiled from data in Pavlov, 1927.)*

seemed to have been extinguished, he discontinued training for a time and then presented the CS again, the dog was likely to salivate (see Figure 3-12). This reappearance of a CR after extinction is called **spontaneous recovery.** If Pavlov once again presented the CS alone several times, the CR would rapidly extinguish.

Multiple extinctions may eliminate spontaneous recovery, but this does not mean the effects of conditioning have been entirely undone (Bouton et al., 2006; Lattal, 2007). This is evident from Pavlov's observation that an extinguished CR usually can be reestablished far more readily than it was established initially. Mark Bouton and Dale Swartzentruber (1991) reviewed the animal research on extinction and concluded that events that occur during training can also trigger a CR's reappearance after extinction. (See also Van Damme et al., 2006.)

Like conditioning, extinction of conditioning is influenced by numerous variables. For example, Dayan Knox and his colleagues (2012) found that a period of stress prior to conditioning did not prevent the acquisition of a fearful response, but did interfere with its extinction. In another experiment, researchers found that methylphenidate, better known as Ritalin, a drug used to treat hyperactivity, improved the extinction of fear (Abraham, Cunningham, & Lattal, 2012). The extinction of conditional responses is, like conditioning itself, far more complicated than it seems.

Despite many experiments conducted over a period of about a hundred years, we still do not thoroughly understand Pavlovian conditioning. A number of experts have, however, attempted to construct theories to account for various Pavlovian phenomena.

CAPSULE **REVIEW**    Conditional responses can be weakened by repeatedly presenting the CS alone, a procedure known as extinction. This procedure is often confused with forgetting, but the two are quite different. Following extinction, the CS may elicit the CR again, a phenomenon known as spontaneous recovery. Multiple extinctions reduce the likelihood that a CR will reappear, but they do not eliminate it.

# THEORIES OF CONDITIONING

*One way to think about theories of learning is to consider learning a kind of Rubic's Cube. The challenge is to figure out how to make the facts fit into an elegant pattern.*

There is no unified theory of Pavlovian conditioning, no set of propositions that together account for all of the findings in the conditioning literature. However, a number of theories have been proposed, and each has its supporters. We will begin with theories that focus on the nature of the CR, starting with Pavlov's.

## Stimulus Substitution Theory

Pavlov's attempt to understand conditioning focused on the nature of the conditional response. What exactly is the CR? His answer: The CR is the UR.

Remember that Pavlov was a physiologist, so his approach was to think about the physiological mechanisms involved in reflexes. He assumed that in an innate reflex, the US stimulates nerve fibers, which in turn stimulate other nerve fibers that evoke the UR (see Figure 3-13). These neural links are what would now be called hard wired; that is, part of the innate structure of the organism.

Now the question becomes, What happens during conditioning? Pavlov proposed that conditioning involves the formation of a new neurological connection between the CS neurons and the US neurons. By repeatedly pairing a bell with food, Pavlov said, a new neural link is formed from the CS neurons to the US neurons so that the bell comes to stimulate the US area of the brain, which then triggers the UR. A US and a well-established CS both stimulate the area of the brain that evokes the UR. Thus, the CR and the UR are the same; the difference is that in one case the neural link to the US area is innate, and in the other it is acquired. "The path of the inborn reflex," wrote Pavlov, "is already completed at birth; but the path of the signalizing reflex [i.e., the CS–US connection] has still to be completed in the higher nervous centers" (p. 25). Pavlov used the telephone as a convenient analogy. "My residence," he wrote, "may be connected directly with the laboratory by a private line, and I may call up the laboratory whenever it pleases me to do so; or on the other hand, a connection may have to be made through the central exchange. But the result in both cases is the same" (p. 25).

According to Pavlov, then, conditioning does not involve the acquisition of any new behavior, but rather the tendency to respond in old ways to new

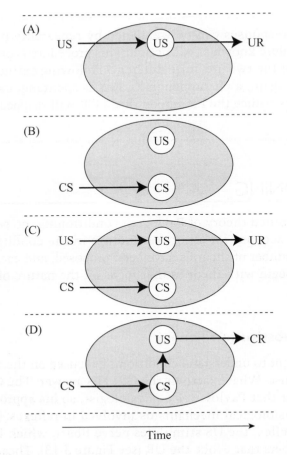

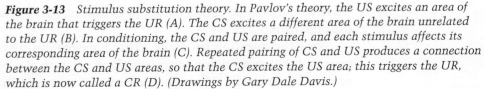

**Figure 3-13**  *Stimulus substitution theory. In Pavlov's theory, the US excites an area of the brain that triggers the UR (A). The CS excites a different area of the brain unrelated to the UR (B). In conditioning, the CS and US are paired, and each stimulus affects its corresponding area of the brain (C). Repeated pairing of CS and US produces a connection between the CS and US areas, so that the CS excites the US area; this triggers the UR, which is now called a CR (D). (Drawings by Gary Dale Davis.)*

stimuli. The CS merely substitutes for the US in evoking the reflex response, hence the name **stimulus substitution theory**.

Pavlov's research generally supported his theory, since the CS and US both elicited salivation. Other observations also support Pavlov's theory. In one of his experiments, Pavlov repeatedly turned on a lamp before providing food. As expected, the light became a CS for salivating. However, something else happened as well. When the dog was able to move about freely, it licked the lightbulb! Why should a dog lick a lightbulb that had been paired with food? One possibility is that the lightbulb had become a substitute for food, which is, in Pavlov's theory, what happens neurologically.

Later research involving another unexpected effect from conditioning also supports this interpretation. Jenkins and colleagues (Brown & Jenkins, 1968; Jenkins & Moore, 1973) illuminated a disc on the wall of a chamber and then followed this with food grain in a tray. After a number of these light–food pairings, the pigeon in the chamber began pecking the key whenever the disc was illuminated. Note that pecking the disc had no effect on the arrival of food; food appeared in the tray regardless of what the bird did. Once again, Pavlov might say, "See, the disc is a substitute for the US, so the bird responds to it as it would to the US!"

Higher-order conditioning might also be accounted for by stimulus substitution theory: A $CS_2$ presumably stimulates the $CS_2$ region of the brain, which stimulates the $CS_1$ region, which stimulates the US region, which evokes the CR (see Figure 3-14). "Why else," Pavlov might ask, "would a stimulus that has never been paired with a US evoke a CR?"

But not all of the facts from conditioning research support stimulus substitution. A critical problem is that there is evidence that the

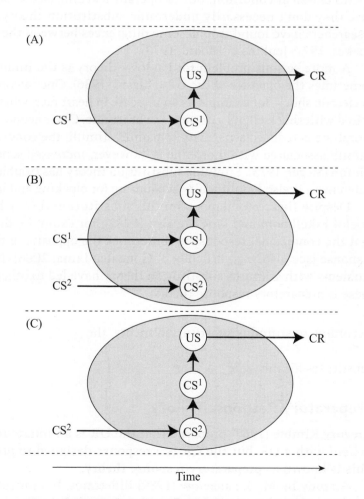

**Figure 3-14** *Higher-order conditioning. Pavlov's explanation parallels his explanation of basic conditioning: There is a connection between the $CS_1$ and US areas of the brain (A). Conditioning pairs $CS_2$ with $CS_1$ (B). This creates a connection between those neural areas; the result is that $CS_2$ triggers the CR (C). (Drawings by Gary Dale Davis.)*

CR and UR are *not* the same. As a rule, the conditional response is weaker than, occurs less reliably than, and appears more slowly than the UR. These differences are not too troublesome, however. The CS may simply be said to provide weaker stimulation of the US area of the brain; hence, the CR is weaker than the UR.

But there are often qualitative differences between conditional and unconditional responses. For instance, Karl Zener (1937) trained dogs to salivate to the sound of a bell and then watched their spontaneous responses to food and to the CS. Like Pavlov, Zener found that both the CS and the US elicited salivation, but Zener noticed that the two stimuli also elicited other behavior as well. When the dog received food, it made chewing movements but otherwise remained still; when the CS appeared, the dog became active but did not chew. Gregory Kimble (1967) pointed out that these differences might not be due to classical condition, but to operant learning (see Chapter 5), in which case they don't necessarily undermine substitution theory. However, other researchers have found troublesome differences between the CR and UR (e.g., Boakes, 1977; Jenkins & Moore, 1973).

A more serious problem for Pavlov's theory is the finding that the CR is sometimes the *opposite* of the UR (Hilgard, 1936). One unconditional response to electric shock, for example, is an increase in heart rate, whereas a CS that was paired with shock elicits a *decrease* in heart rate. One unconditional response to morphine is reduced sensitivity to painful stimuli; the conditional response to stimuli associated with morphine is, however, *increased* sensitivity to painful stimuli (Siegel, 1975). Stimulus substitution theory has trouble explaining these differences; it also has difficulty accounting for blocking and latent inhibition.

Despite these problems, stimulus substitution theory has its defenders. Roelof Eikelboom and Jane Stewart (1982), for example, dispute the notion that the conditional response is sometimes the opposite of the unconditional response (see also, e.g., Bruchey & Gonzalez-Lima, 2006). Nevertheless, the problems with stimulus substitution theory have led to other theories. One of these is preparatory response theory.

**? QUERY 8:** According to stimulus substitution theory, the _____ substitutes for the _____.

## Preparatory Response Theory

Gregory Kimble (1967) proposed that the UR is an innate response designed to *deal* with a US, but the CR is a response designed to *prepare* for the US. This is known as **preparatory response theory**.

A study by M. S. Fanselow (1989) illustrates. If a rat receives an electric shock, it responds by jumping. Fanselow preceded the shock with a tone. The rats soon responded to the tone, but not by jumping; instead they "froze." One interpretation of this result is that the rats innately respond to painful stimuli by jumping, but respond to events that precede pain by freezing. In the wild, rats do not often get electrical shocks, but they do get attacked by animals—snakes, cats, dogs, foxes, and people, among others. (Rats do not have a lot of friends.) If a rat is quietly snacking on some grain in a barn and suddenly a house cat sinks its teeth into the rat's neck, the rat might break free and survive if it suddenly leaps into the air. However, if the rat leaps into the air when it merely sees a cat or hears it meow, this could lead to a fatal attack. By freezing, the rat improves the odds that it will go unnoticed, and prepares it to jump or run if the cat attacks.

## Compensatory Response Theory

Shepard Siegel (1972) of McMasters University in Canada offers a variation of the preparatory theory called **compensatory response theory**. Siegel argues that the CR prepares the animal for the US by compensating for its effects. The unconditional response to morphine, for instance, includes decreased sensitivity to pain, but the CR to stimuli associated with morphine is increased sensitivity to pain (Siegel, 1975). In this case, the person prepares for the drug by suppressing the body's response to it.

This means that when people repeatedly take a drug in a particular setting, aspects of the setting may become CS for reduced responses to the drug. L. O. Lightfoot (1980), then a graduate student at Waterloo University in Canada, demonstrated this in a study with male college students. First he had the students drink a substantial amount of beer in a 30-minute period on each of five consecutive days. The first four drinking sessions took place in the same location. On the fifth day, some students drank beer in the familiar setting, whereas others imbibed in a new place. All the students then took tests of intellectual and perceptual-motor skills after drinking. Those who drank in the familiar setting scored higher on the tests, indicating they were less inebriated, even though they had had the same amount of alcohol. Stimuli previously associated with drinking had muted the effects of the alcohol. The novel setting lacked these CSs, so there was no compensatory CR and the alcohol hit with greater force.

Siegel's theory may also account for certain cases of sudden death following drug use. Such deaths are commonly attributed to accidental overdose, but sometimes they occur following a dose that, given the person's history of drug use, should not have been fatal (Reed, 1980; Siegel, 1984). Anecdotal evidence suggests that the deaths are sometimes due to the absence of stimuli normally present when people take the drug. Siegel (1984) asked ten former heroin addicts who had nearly died following drug use about the circumstances surrounding their close call. In seven cases, there was something unusual about the near-fatal event. Two addicts had used different injection procedures; two had taken the drug in unusual locations. A woman who usually required two or more attempts at penetrating a vein nearly died after she injected herself successfully on the first try. Apparently, the unsuccessful attempts had become a CS that evoked a compensatory response. The absence of the CS meant a stronger, nearly fatal, reaction to the drug. Laboratory research with animals supports this anecdotal evidence (e.g., Siegel, 2005; Siegel et al., 1982).

The CR theories described here are among the most influential, but others have made important contributions. Among them are opponent process theory (Solomon & Corbit, 1974) and sometimes opponent process theory, or SOP (Wagner, 1981; Mazur & Wagner, 1982). We must move on, however, to theories that focus on the CS.

## CONDITIONAL AWARENESS

Many students who know about Pavlovian conditioning will, if asked to explain it, say something like this: "Pavlov rang a bell and then gave a dog food. After doing this several times, the dog associated the bell with food. When the bell rang, the dog knew food was coming, so it salivated." This view of conditioning assumes that a conditional response is the *result* of an awareness of the CS–US connection. "After all," the student is likely to say, "why would the dog salivate unless it knew food was coming?"

The awareness theory is popular not only with students but with some psychologists (Allen & Janiszewski, 1989; Lovibond & Shanks, 2002). Nevertheless, it faces serious difficulties. For instance, research with human participants has demonstrated that conditioning sometimes occurs without awareness that the CS and US are related. In one study, Kenneth Diven (1937) asked people to take a word association test. He presented them with a series of words and after each one they were to say whatever words occurred to them. One of the test words was *barn*. While the person was responding to this word, he always received a shock. All of the participants showed a conditional response (the galvanic skin response, a measure of fear) to the word *barn*, yet half of them were unable to say what word preceded shock. Numerous studies have gotten similar results (e.g., Bechara et al., 1995; Clark & Squire, 1998; De Houwer et al., 1997; Dickinson & Brown, 2007; Esteves et al., 1994; Öhman et al., 1995; Öhman & Mineka, 2001; Öhman & Soares, 1994, 1998; Papka, Ivry, & Woodruff-Pak, 1997; Schiffman & Furedy, 1977; Soares & Öhman, 1993; Walther & Nagengast, 2006). If conditioning sometimes occurs without awareness, then awareness cannot be said to cause, or even to be essential to, conditioning.

Another problem for the awareness model arises when very simple animals undergo conditioning. Roundworms and flatworms, for example, condition very well, yet it is hard to believe they have an awareness of the CS–US relationship. Worms do not have brains, in the usual sense of the word, so what are they supposed to use to recognize, for example, that a light precedes a shock? Worse still for the awareness model, one-celled animals can learn through Pavlovian procedures. It seems absurd to suggest that an amoeba can be aware of a CS–US association.

Despite these and other problems, the awareness view endures. Why? Perhaps because rejecting a causal role for awareness conflicts with the traditional view that behavior is the product of an autonomous mind (see, e.g., Furedy & Kristjansson, 1996; Shanks & St. Johns, 1994).

Those who believe in the autonomous mind accuse their opponents of treating the person as an "empty organism." But giving up the mind as an agent of change does not mean that people are empty. People and some other animals may become aware at some point that one stimulus regularly precedes another, and this can be useful knowledge. The point is that this knowledge, the awareness of a link between CS and US, is, like the CR itself, conditional. It is not a *cause* of learning, but *one of the things that is sometimes learned.*

The theories considered so far attempt to explain the nature of the CR. Other theories focus on the CS. What determines how and why a given stimulus becomes a CS? There are, once again, a number of answers to the question. However, I will concentrate on the most influential of these theories, the Rescorla-Wagner model. (It has a lot of formulas, so many students find it intimidating, but bear with me; it's not so bad.)

## Rescorla-Wagner Model

In Pavlov's stimulus substitution theory, a stimulus becomes a CS simply by being paired with a US repeatedly. But contiguity alone, while desirable, is not sufficient. As you may recall, Robert Rescorla (1968; see p. 69) paired a tone and a mild shock with various groups of rats. All rats received the same number of CS–US pairings, but in some groups the CS also appeared alone on some trials. The chief finding was that the more often the tone appeared without a shock, the less learning occurred. Rescorla concluded that there needed to be a contingent relationship between CS and US for conditioning to occur.

This conclusion, however, was undermined by Kamin's (1969) blocking experiment described earlier. Kamin paired a tone with electric shock until the tone became a CS, and then presented the tone and a light simultaneously, followed by a shock. The question was, Would the light then act as a CS when presented alone? It did not. The CS blocked the new stimulus from becoming a CS. Pavlov's theory, with its focus on contiguity of CS and US, could not account for this finding because the new stimulus was paired with the US. But Rescorla's idea that contingency was the critical factor in learning was also unable to explain blocking because, once the tone and light were combined, their appearance reliably predicted shock. In other words, shock was contingent on the appearance of light. The light had both contiguity and contingency working for it, yet it did not become a CS.

Rescorla went back to the proverbial drawing board and, with his colleague Allan Wagner (Rescorla & Wagner, 1972; Wagner & Rescorla, 1972), came up with a new theory of Pavlovian conditioning, arguably the most influential theory of conditioning in the past 40 years.

The Rescorla-Wagner model argues that there is a limit to the amount of conditioning that can occur in the pairing of two stimuli. One determinant of this limit is the nature of the US. Pairing a bell with a bit of juicy steak, for example, is more likely to produce strong conditioned salivation than pairing a bell with a piece of dry bread, and dry bread is likely to work better than a piece of cardboard. Nor are the characteristics of the US the only variables affecting learning. Certain stimuli become CS in a few pairings, while other stimuli can be paired with a US hundreds of times without much effect.

There is a limit to how much a dog can salivate, and this means that there is a limit to the amount of conditioning that can occur, even with the most effective CS and US. Further, each time a CS and US are paired and some learning occurs, the individual gets closer to reaching the maximum amount of conditioning possible. Suppose, for example, that you see a bee and are then stung by it. Chances are this pairing of bee and pain will make you fearful of bees. If the next time you see a bee you are once again stung, your fear will increase. However, there is probably a limit to how fearful bee sting pain can make you become. If you were to see bees five times and were stung on all five occasions, you would probably be about as afraid of bees as you could get. Being stung after seeing bees on a hundred more occasions probably wouldn't make much difference.

The rate at which conditioning proceeds is not, however, uniform. The first pairing of CS and US usually produces more learning than the second pairing, and the second produces more learning than the third, and so on. This results in the familiar decelerating learning curve seen in Figure 3-7. Rescorla and Wagner realized that these ideas—that there is a limit to the amount of conditioning that can occur, that the limit depends on characteristics of the CS and US, and that each successive pairing produces less learning—can be stated mathematically in a formula:

$$\Delta V_n = c(\lambda - V_{n-1})$$

The formula looks complicated, but it merely expresses in mathematical form the ideas just covered. The amount of learning on any given trial is indicated as a change ($\Delta$, delta, the symbol for change) in the strength of the association ($V$, for value) on that trial ($n$). This number is determined by a constant ($c$, a number falling between 0 and 1) based on the characteristics of the CS and US being paired; the total amount of learning that can occur (lambda, $\lambda$, a number equal to or greater than 0) with the US being used; and the amount of learning that has occurred as of the previous trial. The formula means that if you want to predict the amount of learning on a given trial, you subtract the amount of learning that has occurred as of the previous trial from the maximum amount of learning that can occur and multiply that number by a constant representing the conditionability of the stimuli paired.

**?  QUERY 9:**  The Rescorla-Wagner model recognizes that the greatest amount of learning

occurs in the _____ pairings of CS and US.

The best way to come to grips with the formula is to work through it using some hypothetical numbers. Suppose we are pairing the sight of a bee and its sting. Let's arbitrarily set $\lambda$ at 100. Initially $V$ is 0 because there have been no pairings of CS and US. Now let's assume that the sight of a bee and its sting are both salient stimuli, so we set $c$ at 0.5. (Salient means having features that make conditioning likely to be successful.) On the very first trial, we get the following:

$$\Delta V_1 = 0.5(100 - 0) = 50$$

Multiplying 0.5 times 100, we get 50. This can be interpreted to mean that 50% of all the learning that will occur from all pairings of CS and US (symbolized by $\lambda$) will occur on the first trial. If we continue the calculations for subsequent trials, we see that the rate of learning necessarily diminishes:

$$\Delta V_2 = 0.5(100 - 50) = 25$$
$$\Delta V_3 = 0.5(100 - 75) = 12.5$$
$$\Delta V_4 = 0.5(100 - 87.5) = 6.3$$
$$\Delta V_5 = 0.5(100 - 93.8) = 3.1$$

As you can see, after five trials, almost 97% of all learning that *can* occur from pairing these two stimuli *has* occurred. If the stimuli being paired are even more effective, then *c* would be higher, and conditioning would proceed more quickly. Suppose that you are stung by a bee and you have an allergic reaction to the bee's venom. You are in great pain and cannot breathe, and you fall to the ground gasping for breath. As you lie there, you are terrified that you are about to die. It seems likely that such an experience would produce considerably more conditioned fear at the sight of a bee and that conditioning would proceed more rapidly. The CS (sight of a bee) is the same, but the US is more potent, so we'll put the value of *c* at 0.8, and see what happens:

$$\Delta V_1 = 0.8(100 - 0) = 80$$
$$\Delta V_2 = 0.8(100 - 80) = 16$$
$$\Delta V_3 = 0.8(100 - 96) = 3.2$$
$$\Delta V_4 = 0.8(100 - 99.2) = 0.64$$

The first thing you are likely to notice is that increasing the potency of the stimuli used (going from a *c* of 0.5 to 0.8) results in a huge increase in the amount of learning on the first trial. The second thing you might notice is that more learning occurs in three trials than occurred in five trials with a weaker US.

Blocking occurs because by the time $CS_1$ is combined with $CS_2$, nearly all the learning that can occur has already occurred. In a sense, the first CS "uses up" what the US has to offer, and there just is not much conditioning available. If we look at Kamin's blocking experiment using the Rescorla-Wagner formula, we can see this. Let's assume that *c* totals 0.5. If we pair the tone and shock five times, we get the numbers shown earlier:

$$\Delta V_1 = 0.5(100 - 0) = 50$$
$$\Delta V_2 = 0.5(100 - 50) = 25$$
$$\Delta V_3 = 0.5(100 - 75) = 12.5$$
$$\Delta V_4 = 0.5(100 - 87.5) = 6.3$$
$$\Delta V_5 = 0.5(100 - 93.8) = 3.1$$

Now let's suppose that we present the compound stimulus consisting of tone and light, and let's assume that the light has the same salience (that it is just as suitable as a CS) as the tone, so that *c* remains 0.5. (The tone and light are each half as conditionable as the tone alone, because there is only so much conditioning to go around. This does not, however, change the value of *c*.) If we now continue conditioning trials with the compound stimulus, the conditioning proceeds as follows:

$$\Delta V_6 = 0.5(100 - 96.9) = 1.6$$

Thus, the increase in learning available is only 1.6, and this must now be divided equally between the tone and light, assuming they are equally conditionable. So the amount of learning in trial six is only 0.8 (1.6 divided by 2) for each CS. In other words, neither the light nor the tone changed much as a result of this pairing.

Blocking occurs, then, because there's very little learning left to occur. In a sense, the US has "taught" nearly everything it can. Whether Kamin's experiment demonstrates blocking can be questioned because (according to Rescorla-Wagner) there is not much learning to be blocked. In addition to blocking, the Rescorla-Wagner theory accounts for the negatively accelerating slope of the typical conditioning curve, the fact that salient stimuli produce more learning in less time, and the reduction of the CR during extinction.

The theory does not account for all aspects of conditioning, however (Miller, Barnet, & Grahame, 1995). It does not explain latent inhibition, for example. And, while the Rescorla-Wagner equation neatly expresses the essence of conditioning, the formula cannot actually be used to predict the specific findings of a particular experiment because we cannot specify in advance the value of *c*. Thus, while the Rescorla-Wagner theory has dominated efforts to explain why stimuli become CSs, there are others.

## Other CS Theories

The British psychologist Nicholas Mackintosh (1974) offers one. His theory suggests that learning depends on which events in the environment we attend to, and that depends largely on how well that event predicts the US. Thus, if a tone is followed by a shock 90% of the time, it is likely to be noticed and so will become a CS; if it is followed by shock 10% of the time, it is far less likely to attract attention and therefore unlikely to become a CS. Unfortunately, sometimes an event reliably predicts the US yet does not become a CS as readily as one that is less predictive (Hall & Pearce, 1979).

Two other Britishers, John Pearce and Geoffrey Hall (Pearce & Hall, 1980), also assume that attention to the CS is of critical importance in conditioning. According to their theory, organisms pay attention to novel events, not familiar ones. So, if the appearance of a US is surprising, we will pay attention to the events that precede it. Thus, if a CS occurs alone on one trial, and then the US follows it on the next, this is a surprise and draws attention to the CS, so learning occurs. This theory also has its critics, however (Rodriguez, Alonso, & Lombas, 2006).

Despite their limitations, all the theories described here have stimulated research. This heuristic effect is one of the most important benefits of a good theory: It raises questions that lead to more facts, which in turn lead to new theories, which lead to new facts. Pavlov's theory led to a great deal of research, including Kamin's experiment on blocking, which provided the impetus for the Rescorla-Wagner model, and the failures of that theory gave rise to the Mackintosh theory, and problems with that theory led to the Pearce-Hall theory, which has stimulated additional research and new theories (e.g., Gallistel & Gibbon, 2000). It is through this process, a zigzag and sometimes confusing course, that science pursues understanding.

CAPSULE **REVIEW**   Pavlov believed that the CR and UR were the same and that the CS merely substituted for the US; hence the name stimulus substitution theory. Subsequent research showed that the CR and UR are often quite different, sometimes even the opposite of one another. Other theories account for this by proposing that the CR prepares the organism for the US or helps it compensate for its effects. The Rescorla-Wagner model suggests that whether a particular stimulus becomes a CS depends on the salience of the stimulus and the US and on the total amount of conditioning that can occur. None of the theories of Pavlovian conditioning has provided a satisfactory explanation of all conditioning phenomena. However, each has generated a great deal of research, which has, in turn, enriched our understanding of conditioning and may one day lead to a more successful theory.

# A FINAL WORD

Many students come away from their study of Pavlovian conditioning convinced that Pavlov taught us little more than how to make dogs drool at the sound of a bell. Sadly, even some psychologists take this view. They are mistaken. Pavlovian conditioning has proved immensely useful in explaining a wide range of human and animal behavior (Turkkan, 1989).

It seems clear that the ability to develop conditional reflexes would give any animal a much improved chance of surviving in a changing world. As Pavlov suggested, a deer that reacts with fear to the sight, sound, or odor of a tiger is more likely to live long enough to pass on its genes than one that responds only to the feel of the tiger's teeth in its neck. The same thing is true, of course, for another of the tiger's prey, *Homo sapiens*.

Our ability to learn from the association of events plays an important role in our survival, but it also enriches our lives. Pavlovian conditioning modifies reflexive acts—the contraction of muscles and the secretion of glands—but we experience many of these acts as emotions. Years ago I had a dog, Ginger, who drooled when I tapped a spoon on the rim of a sour cream carton. But Ginger not only salivated, she also showed every sign of being excited and happy. In the same way, we acquire positive and negative feelings toward all sorts of things in our environment: We detest one kind of music and love another; we can't stand one kind of food and can't turn down another. We go on a first date with someone and are later asked how it went. We say, "No sparks" or "We connected." The language is vague but emotionally descriptive. When we talk about these emotional reactions, we are talking mainly about the effects of Pavlovian conditioning.

As our understanding of Pavlovian conditioning has improved, we have found myriad ways of putting it to practical use. Many of them greatly enrich our lives. We will consider some of those applications in the next chapter.

## RECOMMENDED **READING**

1. Cuny, H. (1962). *Ivan Pavlov: The man and his theories.* (P. Evans, Trans.). New York: Fawcett.

   This book includes an excellent review of Pavlov's work, along with a number of selected writings by Pavlov.

2. Hollis, K. L. (1997). Contemporary research on Pavlovian conditioning: A "new" functional analysis. *American Psychologist, 52,* 956–965.

   This review of research makes it clear that Pavlovian conditioning is a very dynamic and important field.

3. Pavlov, I. P. (1906). The scientific investigation of the psychical faculties or processes in the higher animals. *Science, 24,* 613–619.

   This article is perhaps the earliest English language report by Pavlov on his conditioning experiments.

4. Todes, D. P. (1997). From the machine to the ghost within: Pavlov's transition from digestive physiology to conditional reflexes. *American Psychologist, 52,* 947–955.

   Todes describes Pavlov's transition from physiologist to behavior scientist.

5. Windholz, G. (1997). Ivan P. Pavlov: An overview of his life and psychological work. *American Psychologist, 52,* 941–946.

   Provides a brief review of Pavlov's life and work.

## REVIEW **QUESTIONS**

1. Define the following terms:

   | | |
   |---|---|
   | backward conditioning | preparatory response theory |
   | blocking | latent inhibition |
   | classical conditioning | overshadowing |
   | compensatory response theory | Pavlovian conditioning |
   | compound stimulus | pseudoconditioning |
   | conditional reflex | Rescorla-Wagner model |
   | conditional response (CR) | sensory preconditioning |
   | conditional stimulus (CS) | simultaneous conditioning |
   | contiguity | spontaneous recovery |

| | |
|---|---|
| contingency | stimulus substitution theory |
| delay conditioning | test trial |
| extinction | trace conditioning |
| higher-order conditioning | unconditional reflex |
| interstimulus interval (ISI) | unconditional response (UR) |
| intertrial interval | unconditional stimulus (US) |

2. What did Pavlov mean when he said that glands seemed to possess intelligence?

3. One of Pavlov's most important discoveries was that salivation could be attributed to events occurring in the dog's environment. Why is this important?

4. Why is pseudoconditioning a problem for researchers?

5. Give an example of higher-order conditioning from your own experience.

6. How is overshadowing different from blocking?

7. Explain the differences among trace, delay, simultaneous, and backward conditioning procedures. Illustrate each procedure with an example not given in the text.

8. How would you determine the optimum intensity of a CS for eyelid conditioning?

9. Peggy Noonan, a political speechwriter, reported that soon after she had a baby she returned to the campaign trail. One day she saw something in a crowd and began lactating. What did she see?

10. How has the study of Pavlovian conditioning altered your view of human nature?

## PRACTICE **QUIZ**

1. The conditional response is so named because it depends on many _____.

2. In higher-order conditioning, a neutral stimulus is paired with a well-established _____.

3. _____ thought Pavlov was one of the greatest geniuses who ever lived.

4. Pavlovian conditioning usually involves _____ behavior.

5. In Pavlovian conditioning, the appearance of the US is normally _____ on the appearance of the CS.

6. Generally speaking, the shorter the CS–US interval, the _____ (faster/slower) the rate of learning; the shorter the intertrial interval, the _____ (faster/slower) the rate of learning.

7. Braun and Geiselhart found that older subjects acquired conditional responses _____ (more/less) rapidly than younger subjects.

8. The Rescorla-Wagner theory of conditioning assumes that there is a _____ to the amount of conditioning that can occur in the pairing of two stimuli.

9. The least effective form of Pavlovian conditioning is probably the _____ procedure.

10. Latent _____ is the result of the CS having appeared alone before conditioning trials.

## QUERY **ANSWERS**

Query 1. Pavlov identified two kinds of reflexes, *unconditional* and *conditional*.

Query 2. In higher-order conditioning, a neutral stimulus is paired with a well-established *conditional* stimulus.

Query 3. In trace conditioning, the *CS* begins and ends before the *US* appears.

Query 4. In delay conditioning, the *CS* ends only after the *US* begins.

Query 5. In Pavlovian conditioning, *contiguity* usually refers to the interval between CS and US.

Query 6. If one part of a compound stimulus fails to become a CS, *overshadowing* has occurred.

Query 7. Four variables that affect the rate of conditioning are (any four of these): *how the CS and US are paired; CS–US contingency; CS–US contiguity; stimulus features; prior experience with CS and US; number of CS–US pairings; intertrial interval; age; temperament; emotional state/stress.*

Query 8. According to stimulus substitution theory, the *CS* substitutes for the *US*.

Query 9. The Rescorla-Wagner model recognizes that the greatest amount of learning occurs in the *first/earliest* pairings of CS and US.

# Pavlovian Applications

*These are our facts. I do not know what the psychiatrists will say, but we shall see who is right!*

**—Ivan Pavlov**

## PREVIEW

Because Pavlovian conditioning involves simple reflexive behavior, many people find it hard to believe that it has any practical value. Nothing could be further from the truth. In this chapter we will take a brief look at the way Pavlovian research has helped us deal with problems in seven areas: fear, prejudice, paraphilia, taste aversion, advertising, drug addiction, and health care. We begin with fear.

## FEAR

The first person to study human emotions systematically was John B. Watson. In Watson's day, fear was commonly thought to be either the result of faulty reasoning or a kind of instinctual reaction (Valentine, 1930).

The work of Watson and his students changed all that. They found that relatively few stimuli innately arouse fear or other strong emotional reactions, but objects that are paired with those items will come to elicit those emotions as well. We now know that our emotional reactions, including not only fear but love, hate, and disgust, are largely learned, and they are learned mainly through Pavlovian conditioning. Watson called them **conditioned emotional responses**. His work vastly improved our understanding and treatment of emotional disorders, particularly the unreasonable fears called phobias.

Phobias are among the most common behavior problems (see Figure 4-1). One survey found, for example, that out of every 1,000 people interviewed, 198 were afraid of their dentist and 390 were afraid of snakes (Agras, Sylvestor, & Oliveau, 1969). (No doubt dentists are comforted to know that they are preferred over snakes.)

Watson and graduate student Rosalie Rayner (Watson & Rayner, 1920; Watson & Watson, 1921) began their study of fear by testing a number of infants to see their reactions to fire, dogs, cats, laboratory rats, and other stimuli then thought to be innately frightening. They found no evidence of innate

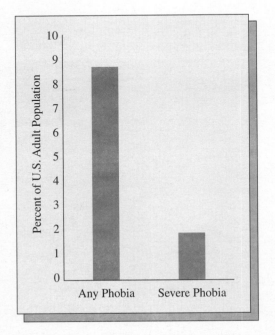

**Figure 4-1**   *Incidence of fear. Percentage of American adults with specific phobias during a 12-month period. (Compiled from data in Kessler et al., 2005.)*

fear of these objects. They did find, however, that a sudden loud noise is an unconditional stimulus for crying and other fearful reactions.

Next, the researchers attempted to establish a fear reaction through classical conditioning. Their subject was Albert B., a healthy, 11-month-old boy who showed no signs of fearing a white rat, a pigeon, a rabbit, a dog, a monkey, cotton wool, or a burning newspaper. He appeared to be a happy, normal baby who rarely cried. The researchers established that a loud noise was a US for fear. When they struck a steel bar with a hammer, Albert would jump suddenly. Using this loud noise as an unconditional stimulus, it took little time to establish a conditional fear response to a white rat. Watson and Rayner presented Albert with the rat, and then one of the experimenters hit the steel bar with a hammer. After a few pairings of this sort, Albert began to cry and show other signs of fear as soon as he saw the rat. He had learned, through Pavlovian conditioning, to fear white rats.

Other studies have verified that Pavlovian procedures can establish fears in people and other animals. For example, Arne Öhman and colleagues (1976) had college students look at pictures of snakes until they had habituated—that is, until the pictures had no emotional effect as measured by the galvanic skin response (GSR; see habituation in Chapter 1). Then the researchers followed the pictures with an electric shock to the hand. There was, of course, a fear response to the shock, and soon the pictures alone evoked fear.

*The Little Albert study violates today's ethical standards, but keep in mind that the standards in Watson's day were very different.*

**?** QUERY 1: Albert became fearful of the rat because the arrival of the rat regularly

preceded _____.

We can readily come up with examples of fearful reactions that very likely were established through Pavlovian conditioning. Most people, for example, are made uneasy by visits to the dentist. This is hardly surprising when one considers that dental visits frequently entail some discomfort. The whine of the dentist's drill is all too often accompanied by pain, so the sound of the drill soon arouses anxiety. We may even come to fear anything associated with the painful drill, such as the dentist and the dentist's assistant (Ost & Hugdahl, 1985).

Very likely, the same sort of process accounts for the fear many people experience in a doctor's examining room, the school principal's office, or a mathematics classroom. A person who struggles with a math course, for example, may feel ill at ease in the classroom even when class is not in session.

Watson's work not only improved our understanding of fears but also led to effective forms of treatment. Mary Cover Jones (1924a, 1924b), another of Watson's students, was the first to show that Pavlovian conditioning could help people overcome fears as well as acquire them. Jones's subject was Peter, a 3-year-old with a fear of rabbits. Peter's fear was "home grown," as Watson phrased it, not the result of deliberate conditioning. The experiment with Albert showed how Peter's fear may have been acquired; more important, it suggested how it might be removed.

*Albert and Peter are famous in behavior science, but they are often confused with one another, even in psychology texts. To keep these two studies straight, think of the story of Peter Rabbit, and you will remember that it was Peter and the rabbit and Albert and the rat.*

Jones started by bringing a rabbit in view, but she kept it far enough away that it did not disturb Peter as he ate a snack of crackers and milk. In this way, Jones paired a CS for fear (the sight of the rabbit) with a positive US (crackers and milk). The next day, Jones brought the rabbit closer to Peter, but not close enough to make him uneasy. On each succeeding day the experimenter brought the rabbit closer, always pairing it with crackers and milk, until Peter showed no fear even when Jones put the rabbit into his lap. Finally, Peter would eat with one hand and play with the rabbit with the other. Jones called this use of Pavlovian conditioning to reverse the unwanted effects of previous conditioning **counterconditioning**. Because the person is gradually exposed to the fear-evoking stimulus while feeling relaxed, this kind of therapy is now often called **exposure therapy**.

Jones's treatment is called in vivo (roughly translated, "in the flesh") exposure therapy because the person is directly exposed to the frightening stimulus. Other forms of exposure therapy have been developed since Jones's work with Peter. Probably the best known of these is **systematic desensitization**, developed by the psychiatrist Joseph Wolpe (1973; McGlynn, 2010). In this case the therapist works with the client to arrange a list of scary scenes. For example, suppose you are afraid of speaking before a group of people. You and the therapist work up a list of situations related to public speaking and arranged from those that arouse little or no discomfort to those that you find terrifying (see *Fear of Public Speaking*). After this the therapist asks you to imagine the first scene, perhaps describing it for you in detail, and then instructing you in ways to relax. Thus the scene (a CS for fear) is paired with a positive US (relaxation). When the initial scene no longer causes any discomfort, the therapist will move on to the next scene. This process

## FEAR OF PUBLIC SPEAKING

A person afraid of public speaking who undergoes systematic desensitization would imagine scenes such as the following (but longer and more detailed), arranged according to their initial level of fearfulness:

Chatting with a friend in a relaxed setting

Answering a personal question from the friend

Meeting your friend and someone you don't know in a relaxed setting

Giving brief answers to questions asked by your friend and the stranger

Giving more expanded answers to questions asked by the stranger

Meeting with two friends and three of their friends to discuss a school or work project

Answering questions asked at the meeting

Offering your opinions on an issue raised at the meeting

Reporting facts to the group while seated at a table

Reporting to the group on an issue that needs to be decided

And so on, ending with . . .

Standing on a stage before an audience of 1,000 people giving a speech from notes you have prepared.

continues until you feel at ease imagining yourself speaking to a large audience. Note that you never experience terrifying fear during this process; instead, desensitization to one scene prepares you for the next.

A recent variation of exposure therapy involves the technology called virtual reality. Virtual reality technology uses computer software, a helmet, and goggles to create a highly realistic electronic simulation of an environment. A person afraid of heights and wearing the helmet and goggles may, for example, see a bridge to her left, and turn toward it so that the bridge now appears to be in front of her. She may then approach the bridge, then step onto it and look over the side at the river far below. This form of treatment, called **virtual reality exposure therapy (VRET)**, falls somewhere between Mary Cover Jones's in vivo treatment and Wolpe's imaginary treatment. With VRET the person interacts in an environment that is neither imaginary nor real!

Barbara Rothbaum and her colleagues (1995) conducted the first controlled experiment involving VRET. In their study, people with a fear of heights walked on nonexistent footbridges and outdoor balconies of varying heights and went up a glass elevator that could ascend 50 floors. The treatment involved exposing the subjects to realistic but low-level fearful stimuli. When the person felt comfortable walking on a low virtual bridge, he or she would walk on a higher bridge. The result of the procedure was a marked reduction in fear of heights. In fact, most people who completed treatment later exposed themselves to situations that had once been frightening, even though they were not asked to do so.

In another study, Rothbaum and her colleagues (2000) applied VRET to treat a fear of flying. They compared virtual reality treatment with in vivo exposure therapy using real airplanes. They found little difference in effectiveness between the two treatments; people in both treatment groups fared substantially better than those in a no-treatment control group. Treated participants reported less anxiety about flying, and far more of them actually flew after treatment than did those in the control group (see Figure 4-2). By six months following the end of treatment, 93% of those who had received exposure therapy had flown in a plane.

Hunter Hoffman (Carlin, Hoffman, & Weghorst, 1997; Hoffman, 2004) and his colleagues at the University of Washington in Seattle used VRET to treat a woman with a severe spider phobia. The woman, referred to by the code name Miss Muffet, saw her fear of spiders increase over a 20-year period. In that time she also developed compulsive rituals to deal with her fear. For example, after washing clothes, she sealed them in plastic bags to ensure there would be no spiders on them when she put them on; she routinely fumigated her car to kill any spiders that might have taken up residence there; and every night before retiring she searched her bedroom for spiders and then sealed the windows with duct tape to prevent spiders from coming in during the night. When she began to be afraid to leave the house, she finally sought help.

**? QUERY 2:** VRET stands for _____ _____ _____

_____.

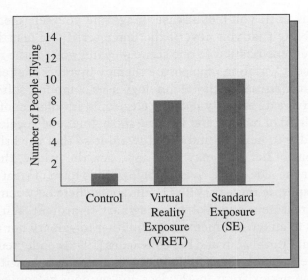

**Figure 4-2** *Fear of flying. People with a fear of flying received no treatment (controls), VRET, or in vivo exposure therapy. After treatment, all had the opportunity to fly on a plane. Of the 15 people in each group, only one that received no treatment flew, 8 who received VRET flew, and 10 who received in vivo therapy flew. (Compiled from data in Rothbaum et al., 2000.)*

Help came in the form of *SpiderWorld*, a virtual environment in which the client explores a kitchen with cabinet doors that he or she can open and close. In the kitchen there is a large virtual spider, a tarantula. Miss Muffet's treatment required her to complete a series of increasingly difficult tasks. She repeated each task until she could do it without discomfort, then moved on to the next, slightly more difficult task. After ten one-hour sessions, Miss Muffet showed a sharp reduction in her fear of spiders. She was even able to hold a *live* tarantula in her hand. There was also a sharp reduction in her spider rituals. No treatment is highly effective with everyone, but of 23 phobia clients Hoffman and his colleagues treated, 19 reported a significant reduction in fear (see also Garcia-Palacios et al., 2002).

VRET has also been used to treat post traumatic stress disorder (PTSD), an anxiety disorder associated with trauma (Rothbaum et al., 2012). One VRET program was specifically designed to treat PTSD in survivors of the Twin Towers attack in New York on September 11, 2001 (Difede & Hoffman, 2002); another treats Vietnam veterans (Rothbaum et al., 2001); and another treats veterans of Iraq and Afghanistan (Reger et al., 2011). The U.S. military has not only embraced VRET in the treatment of PTSD in combat veterans (Reger & Gahm, 2008; Rizzo et al., 2011), but in preparing inexperienced troops for the stresses of war in hopes of reducing future PTSD (Rizzo et al., 2012).

The various forms of exposure therapy have been used to treat all sorts of fears, including fear of public speaking (Anderson et al., 2000; Paul, 1969), mathematics (Zettle, 2003), water (Egan, 1981), heights (Williams, Turner, & Peer, 1985), claustrophobia (Booth & Rachman, 1992), and social phobia (Anderson et al., 2003; ter Heijden & Brinkman, 2011), among others. Reviews

*For a brief look at a program designed to help people with PTSD anonymously, go to youtube.com and search "Rizzo PTSD."*

***Figure 4-3*** *The Delft Remote VRET System. Dutch researchers developed a program that lets a therapist in one location provide VRET to a patient in another location via the Internet. A person with a fear of public speaking, for example, interacts with a group of avatars, such as those depicted here, while a therapist monitors her behavior and provides real-time guidance. (Image courtesy of Willem-Paul Brinkman, Department of Intelligent Systems/Interactive Intelligence Group, Delft University of Technology, The Netherlands.)*

of research literature reveal that VRET is as effective as traditional forms of exposure therapy in treating anxiety disorders (Gregg & Tarrier, 2007; Parsons & Rizzo, 2008; Powers & Emmelkamp, 2008). It appears that the next wave of exposure therapy will be Internet-based VRET (Kang et al., 2011; see Figure 4-3; also see references to the work of Rosenthal and Culbertson in the Addiction section of this chapter).

Although VRET and even Wolpe's systematic desensitization look very different from the in vivo exposure therapy Mary Cover Jones devised to treat Peter in the 1920s, in fact all three are merely different ways of implementing Pavlovian conditioning. They are, in essence, the same procedure Pavlov used to train dogs to salivate at the sound of a metronome.

CAPSULE **REVIEW**     Watson demonstrated that human fears and other emotions are largely due to conditioning. Fortunately, the same conditioning procedures that create unwanted fears can help people overcome them. These procedures are collectively called exposure therapy. Examples include systematic desensitization and virtual reality exposure therapy. Although VRET is definitely "high tech," it and other forms of exposure therapy rest on conditioning principles established by Pavlov more than a hundred years ago.

# PREJUDICE

To be prejudiced is, in its most general sense, to prejudge, to judge before one has the relevant facts. The word is most often used, however, to refer to negative views about a person or group; in its extreme form, prejudice is roughly synonymous with hate.

Hatred is another of those conditioned emotional responses Watson identified. We seem to learn to dislike people and things in much the same way that we learn to fear them. This notion is supported by some brilliant experiments by Arthur and Carolyn Staats. Their basic strategy was to pair a neutral word with one that was presumably a CS for a positive or negative emotional response. In one study (Staats & Staats, 1958), college students watched as ethnic words, such as *German, Italian,* and *French,* flashed on a screen. At the same time, the students repeated words spoken by the experimenter. The experimenters paired most of the nationalities with unemotional words such as *chair, with,* and *twelve,* but they paired the words *Swedish* and *Dutch* with more potent words. For some students, they paired *Dutch* with *gift, sacred, happy,* and other positive words, while they paired *Swedish* with negative words such as *bitter, ugly,* and *failure.* For other students, this procedure was reversed: *Swedish* appeared with positive words and *Dutch* with negative ones. Afterward, the students rated each nationality on a scale. These ratings showed that the feelings aroused by the words *Swedish* and *Dutch* depended on the emotional value of the words with which they had been paired. When the word *Dutch* had appeared with positive words, it got a more positive rating than when it had appeared with negative words (see Figure 4-4).

*Note the similarity of this study with the one described in Chapter 3 in which Staats and Staats paired nonsense syllables, such as YOF, with positive and negative words. You may have thought that study was silly; basic research often seems silly until you see the implications.*

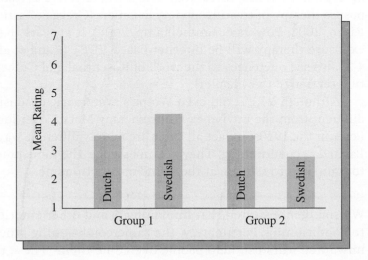

***Figure 4-4*** *Conditioned prejudice. For participants in Group 1, Dutch appeared with positive words, while Swedish appeared with negative ones. In Group 2, the procedure was reversed. After training, participants rated the words Dutch and Swedish from pleasant (1) to unpleasant (7). The ratings reflect the words with which Dutch and Swedish appeared. (Compiled from data in Staats and Staats, 1958.)*

It seems likely that much of the prejudice directed toward certain ethnic, racial, and religious groups is a result of naturally occurring conditioning resembling the Staats and Staats experiment. Even factually accurate statements such as "On September 11, 2001, Muslim extremists hijacked two planes and flew them into the World Trade Center, killing thousands of people" pair emotionally charged words (*extremists, hijacked, killing*) with the words designating a particular group (*Muslim*) and are likely to affect our feelings toward members of that group. This is so even though the Muslim terrorists were not representative of Muslims in general.

You could argue that the Staatses established certain *words* as conditional stimuli, not the people those words represent. But there is evidence (e.g., Williams, 1966; Williams & Edwards, 1969) that the two are connected—that if the word *Arab* is paired with words like *terrorists* and *killing*, this will affect how we react toward Arabs as well as toward the word *Arab*. It is probably not a coincidence that assaults against Arabs in the United States increased markedly after the attacks on September 11, 2001. Similarly, if the words *Negro, Republican, black, Irish*, and *communist* are paired with words that arouse hostility, we can expect those words, and the people they represent, to arouse hostility.

Information is often offered as a cure for prejudice. People hate, it is said, because they are ignorant of the facts; provide them with the facts, and their hatred will die. But if prejudice is largely the product of conditioning (and the evidence suggests it is), facts alone are unlikely to be an effective antidote. A related tactic is to put the prejudiced person in contact with people in the groups he hates. But this tactic may be weak against a prejudice that is the result of decades of conditioning (Horowitz, 1936).

**QUERY 3:** Prejudice is an example of a CER, or _____.

Yet we may be able to counter "hate training" with "love training." If the word *Arab* (or *Muslim*) is often paired with negative words, such as *fanatic* and *murderer*, and with negative images, such as videos of Arabs burning American flags, then hatred for Arabs is likely to result. If, however, *Arab* is sometimes paired with positive words, such as *charitable* and *peace-loving*, and with positive images, such as videos of Arabs condemning violence, then the influence of the negative associations will be weakened.

This idea is supported by research. For example, Thomas Parish, then at Kansas State University, and colleagues (Parish, Shirazi, & Lambert, 1976) changed the negative feelings of white American children toward Vietnamese people by pairing images of Vietnamese with positive words. The same tactic was *not* successful in changing feelings toward African Americans. The difference in results is not particularly surprising, given that the Vietnamese were relatively new to the area, so the children had received far less "hate training" toward them than they had toward African Americans. The implication was that more training aimed at undermining bias against African Americans would work, and this is supported by other research.

For example, Michael Olsson of the University of Tennessee and Russell Fazio of Ohio State University (2006) paired images of people engaged in various kinds of activities with positive or negative words. One part of the study involved pairing images of African Americans with positive words. For example, a photograph of an African American working as a cashier might be paired with the word *outstanding*. The researchers paired other images (e.g., farm equipment, umbrellas) with neutral words (e.g., *waffles, electrical outlet*). Altogether the study participants (nearly a hundred female college students) viewed hundreds of images. The procedure shifted their feelings about African Americans toward the positive, but it took a good many conditioning trials to get this result.

It might have occurred to you that the participants in this study noticed the systematic pairing of African Americans with positive words and responded differently to avoid accusations of racism. But only two participants showed any sign of awareness of the conditioning procedure or the purpose of the study, and their data were eliminated from the analysis. Thus, it seems that the same sort of experiences that lead to negative feelings toward a group can lead to positive feelings toward that group.

None of these or similar studies suggest that turning a hardcore racist into a true egalitarian will be as easy as training a dog to salivate at the sight of a food bowl (see Parish & Fleetwood, 1975). But the research on changing feelings through what some call "evaluative conditioning" (Davey, 1994; De Houwer, 2011; Gawronski & Walther, 2012; Hofmann et al., 2010) does suggest that there are things parents, teachers, and others can do to counteract the effects of racist teaching. As the lyricist Oscar Hammerstein reminds us in the play, South Pacific, *You've Got to Be Carefully Taught.* Whether we feel love or hate toward certain groups is largely a matter of the kind of teaching, mostly in the form of classical conditioning, that we receive, particularly in childhood (Olsson & Fazio, 2002).

CAPSULE **REVIEW**   Prejudice, like fear, is mostly the product of classical conditioning. It is acquired largely through the association of a particular group (or words and images representing or resembling that group) with negative words or images. Thus, prejudice can be acquired with little or no personal contact with members of a group. Research also shows that the same kinds of experiences that produce prejudice can reverse it, though the more "training" in hate a person has had, the more difficult it is to change their feelings.

# THE PARAPHILIAS

Sigmund Freud said that people are "polymorphously perverse," meaning that they can achieve sexual pleasure in a great many ways. Society approves of some of these activities and disapproves of others. Items on the disapproved list are widely considered perverse or unnatural and are called paraphilias. (*Paraphilia* literally means "incorrect love.") They include voyeurism

## THE BOY NEXT DOOR

Templeman and Stinnett (1991) surveyed 60 male college students to determine what sexual activities they had engaged in. Their findings included the following:

2% exhibitionism

3% sexual contact with girls under age 12

5% coercive sex (i.e., forcing someone to engage in a sexual act; in some cases this includes rape)

8% making obscene phone calls

Altogether, 65% of the men admitted to having engaged in some form of sexual activity that most people would probably call inappropriate, if not outrageous.

*What is considered a paraphilia varies from time to time and place to place. In the Greece of Plato's day, homosexuality was quite acceptable. By contrast, until a few decades ago most people in the United States considered homosexuality a sin or a psychiatric disorder. Now it is increasingly acceptable.*

(viewing a person who is nude or partially clothed or who is engaging in sexual activity), exhibitionism (displaying one's genitals to another person without his or her consent), fetishism (an attraction to certain objects or body parts, such as the feet), transvestism (wearing the clothes of the opposite sex; also called cross-dressing), sadism (inflicting pain on a sexual partner), masochism (being humiliated or hurt by a sexual partner), pedophilia (sexual activity with a prepubescent child), and rape (having intercourse with a person without the person's consent). Various studies, many involving college students, have shown that the paraphilias are more common among males than many people would like to think (see *The Boy Next Door*). The paraphilias are uncommon in females (Feierman & Feierman, 2000).

Thanks to Freud, many people believe that the tendency to become sexually aroused in unconventional ways is due to mysterious unconscious forces. The masochist's behavior, for example, is often said to be driven by a death wish or a need to suffer degradation and pain as penance for oedipal urges. Although different paraphilias may have different origins, there is no scientific evidence for the Freudian explanations. There is evidence, however, that conditioning plays a key role.

Consider masochism, for example. The masochist is sexually aroused by being subjected to painful or degrading experiences. One masochistic man wrote in his diary, "Debbie spanked me so hard I was burning. My skin was blistered in certain parts. . . . *I need Debbie*" (Pipitone, 1985; emphasis added). How does a person come to experience sexual pleasure when exposed to what are normally painful or humiliating events?

Pavlov described an experiment that suggests an answer. In this experiment, Pavlov followed an electric shock with food. Incredibly, the dog soon salivated in response to the shock, just as it might have salivated in response to a bell. In other words, the shock became a CS for salivating. Other dogs learned to salivate in response to other painful stimuli, such as pinpricks. What is even more astonishing is that these stimuli seemed to lose their aversive qualities. Pavlov (1927) wrote that not even the tiniest and most subtle objective phenomenon usually exhibited by animals under the influence of strong injurious stimuli can be observed in these dogs. No appreciable changes in the pulse or in the respiration occur in these animals, whereas such changes are always most prominent when the noxious stimulus has not been converted into [a CS for salivating]. (p. 30)

Pavlov's dogs behaved as if they actually enjoyed what were once painful stimuli! It is possible that masochism has a similar origin. If painful or degrading experiences repeatedly precede pleasurable sexual stimulation, the aversive stimuli might themselves become sexually arousing. The late John Money (1987), then a sex researcher at Johns Hopkins University, received a letter from Bombay, India, following a conference at which he spoke:

> I read with keen interest your recent interview in *Debonair* during your visit to India. Especially I read about the man who wanted his behind smacked for achieving orgasm. During my early schoolhood . . . in Calcutta we were (all boys) often caned on our upturned, upraised buttocks by the headmaster (with his attractive wife sometimes looking on and passing humiliating, sarcastic comments). Needless to say, this brutalized our love-maps and in certain cases brought about orgasms and a sickening addiction to the rod and a good whipping.
>
> I was nine when the canings began, and seventeen when I left school. . . . I got sexual feelings from around the age of twelve, especially if she [the headmaster's wife] was watching. (p. 273)

This is anecdotal evidence, so it has little scientific value. However, this and similar reports fit Pavlov's finding that dogs tolerated, and possibly enjoyed, pain after it had been repeatedly paired with food. It is easy to see how analogous experiences might contribute to the development of masochism and other unconventional sexual activities. (O'Donohue & Plaud, 1994, question the role of learning in human sexuality, but see also Pfaus, Kippin, & Centeno, 2001, and Hoffman, 2011, for discussions of this question.)

Pavlovian conditioning not only suggests a basis for paraphilias, it also suggests treatments. One such treatment is **aversion therapy** (Holmes, 1991; Lockhart, Saunders, & Cleveland, 1989; Marshall & Eccles, 1991). In aversion therapy a CS that elicits inappropriate sexual arousal is followed by a noxious US. When such therapy is effective, the stimuli that once elicited sexual arousal no longer do so and may even elicit feelings of anxiety and discomfort.

A fairly typical example of aversion therapy is provided in a case study reported by N. I. Lavin and colleagues (1961). They used aversion therapy to treat a married man who was sexually aroused by dressing in women's clothing. His interest in cross-dressing began when he was 8 years old; in adolescence, his masturbation always accompanied cross-dressing fantasies. Even after marrying, he continued to seek sexual stimulation by dressing in women's clothing. He sought treatment at age 22 after his wife discovered his idiosyncrasy and urged him to get help. He was also worried that others might discover his secret.

His therapists began by taking photographs of him in female dress. Next they gave him an emetic drug, and just as it began to make him nauseated, they showed him slides of himself in women's clothing. He also heard a tape of himself, recorded earlier, in which he described what the slide showed. As the training sessions proceeded, cross-dressing had less and less appeal. After six days of very intensive treatment, the young man showed no further interest in cross-dressing. A follow-up several years later found no evidence of a recurrence of the problem.

In a variation of this procedure, Barry Maletzky (1980) treated ten exhibitionists. Just as a patient imagined that he was about to expose himself, Maletzky held a bottle of a foul-smelling acid under the patient's nose. (The odor was described by patients as a cross between rancid butter and dirty gym socks.) The patients went through these sessions twice a month for an average of about three months. Not only did the patients report fewer instances of exhibitionistic fantasies and dreams, but claims of improved behavior were corroborated by police reports and field observations. The men also expressed increased self-confidence and self-esteem. Some of them had been referred for treatment by legal authorities and may have been in therapy involuntarily, but this made no difference in the results. A follow-up 12 months after treatment revealed no occurrences of exhibitionism.

The successes described here do not mean that the paraphilias always respond well to aversion therapy. In fact, some paraphilias are resistant to all forms of treatment, and relapse is common (Hall, 1995; Hanson et al., 2002). Even when treatment is helpful, "booster" sessions (periodic re-treatment) are often required to maintain the initial gains (Becker & Hunter, 1992; Kilmann et al., 1982).

Because aversion therapy involves the use of noxious stimuli, such as emetic drugs and foul-smelling solutions, it is often depicted as an abomination, like something from the pages of Orwell's science fiction novel *1984*. It is important to realize, however, that clients typically volunteer for aversion therapy, often after other treatments have failed.

*The question arises, Who decides whether a person is to be treated for a paraphilia? In most cases the decision is made by the individual himself, although this may be under pressure from family, friends, an employer, or the courts. In any case it is not normally the therapist's decision.*

Other treatments of paraphilias, some based on conditioning (Laws & Marshall, 1991; Pithers, 1994) and some involving drugs or surgery (Perkins et al., 1998), are available, but they have their own problems. For example, according to Jay and Lisa Feierman (2000), surgical castration is far more effective than aversion therapy in treating certain paraphilias. But castration is obviously an irreversible and highly invasive procedure, and it may have other drawbacks (Perkins et al., 1998). Despite its effectiveness, it is even more controversial than aversion therapy and is rarely used in the United States. The use of drugs to suppress testosterone levels, a procedure called chemical castration, also can be effective in reducing sexual offenses (Cordoba & Chapel, 1983), but ensuring that the offender takes the drug presents problems.

CAPSULE **REVIEW**   Conditioning can help us understand how various forms of sexual behavior, including those generally considered aberrant, are established. It has also suggested certain treatments, the most researched being aversion therapy. Some of the paraphilias are particularly difficult to treat, perhaps because the behavior involved is itself partly the product of numerous trials of classical conditioning.

## WHO ARE THE VICTIMS?

Whether sexual offenders, including pedophiles and rapists, should be compelled to undergo aversion therapy, or any other treatment, is an important question. Opponents often cite the use of aversion therapy in the film, *A Clockwork Orange,* in which a psychopathic rapist is treated with a harsh and unrealistic form of aversion therapy.

Some people disapprove of mandatory aversion therapy on the grounds that if we become accustomed to using it to treat sexual offenses, we might gradually embrace it to suppress the activities of people who are merely idiosyncratic or unusually creative. Should Salvador Dali have been treated for painting melting clocks? What about therapy for people who burn the national flag to protest a war?

Certainly aversion therapy has the potential for abuse. So has morphine, an excellent means of relieving pain, but we do not ordinarily reject treatments merely because they can be misused. And while it is appropriate to worry about the rights of sexual offenders, we might, in debating this issue, also consider the rights of potential victims.

## TASTE AVERSION

Eating is essential to survival, but it is also dangerous. Some attractive substances are tasty and quite nutritious; others can kill. It would be very helpful if we had an innate tendency to avoid eating dangerous substances, but for the most part such behavior is learned. How?

Much of the groundbreaking research on this problem was done by John Garcia and his colleagues. His interest in the topic may have stemmed from a personal experience: When Garcia was 10 years old, he had his first taste of licorice. Several hours later, he came down with the flu. After he recovered, he found he could no longer tolerate licorice (see Nisbett, 1990). He knew that the licorice had not made him sick, but he had an aversion to licorice all the same.

In one of his first experiments, Garcia and his colleagues (1955) gave rats a choice between ordinary tap water and saccharin-flavored water. The rats preferred the sweet-tasting water. Then Garcia exposed some of the rats to gamma radiation while they drank the sweet-tasting water. (Gamma radiation causes nausea.) These rats later avoided saccharin-flavored water. Moreover, the higher the radiation level, the stronger the aversion to sweet water (see Figure 4-5). Sweet water had become a CS for nausea; in other words, its taste made the animals sick. The rats had acquired a **conditioned taste aversion,** now sometimes called **conditioned food avoidance**.

**? QUERY 4:** In the Garcia experiment just described, the CS is _____, and

the US is _____.

Garcia's study differs from Pavlov's work, and from most other research on conditioning, in two important ways. First, the CS and US occurred together

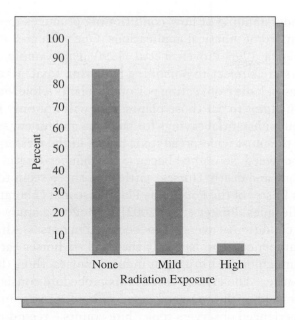

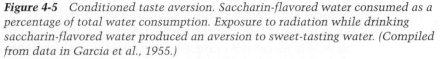

**Figure 4-5** *Conditioned taste aversion. Saccharin-flavored water consumed as a percentage of total water consumption. Exposure to radiation while drinking saccharin-flavored water produced an aversion to sweet-tasting water. (Compiled from data in Garcia et al., 1955.)*

only once, whereas most studies of conditioning involve many pairings. Second, the interval between the CS and US was several minutes; in most studies successful conditioning requires an interval of no more than several seconds. The situation was, however, analogous to Garcia's boyhood experience with licorice: One exposure to licorice followed much later by illness resulted in an aversion to licorice.

Foods that can make an animal ill might also kill it or make it vulnerable to attack or disease, so one-trial learning can mean the difference between life and death. The person who has a narrow escape and thereafter avoids eating that food is more likely to survive than one who must have 10 or 15 narrow escapes before learning the lesson. Further, the effects of poisonous foods are often delayed, sometimes for several hours. The animal (including the human animal) that acquires an aversion to a toxic food despite such delayed effects has a distinct advantage over one that learns only if he or she becomes ill immediately after eating.

Numerous studies support this view. Lincoln Brower (1971) studied taste aversion in the blue jay, which feeds on all sorts of insects, including butterflies. In the larval stage, the monarch butterfly sometimes feeds on a kind of milkweed that is harmless to the monarch but renders it poisonous to other animals; it retains its poison in the butterfly stage. Blue jays generally refuse to eat monarch butterflies, but this tendency is not innate; it is the result of conditioning. Sometimes jays with this conditioned taste aversion vomit at the sight of a monarch butterfly.

Our understanding of how conditioning produces food aversions has led to some important practical applications. One such area is livestock management (Provenza, 1996; Provenza et al., 1990). For example, livestock that graze in meadows are subject to poisoning by eating toxic plants. About 2–3% of grazing livestock die from eating poisonous plants (Holechek, 2002). If animals can be trained *not* to eat those plants, this will not only mean less suffering for them, but substantial savings for ranchers and for consumers.

One of the most widespread toxic plants in the western part of the United States is locoweed, so named because it produces erratic behavior, nervousness, tremors, and death. Horses, cattle, and sheep seem to find it quite palatable. James Pfister of the Poisonous Plant Research Laboratory in Logan, Utah, and his colleagues (Pfister et al., 2002) conducted a study to see if they could establish a conditioned aversion to locoweed in horses. Although the study involved a number of steps, basically they had six horses eat locoweed and gave them lithium chloride, a drug that induces nausea; thus, the taste of locoweed preceded nausea. The critical test of this procedure consisted of tethering the horses in a field with locoweed twice a day for ten minutes. During these periods experienced observers took "bite counts," recording how many times a horse ate various plants, including locoweed. Five of the six treated horses ate *no* locoweed; the remaining horse ate locoweed on only one of the test days. These results contrast dramatically with the consumption of locoweed by four horses in the untreated control group (see Figure 4-6).

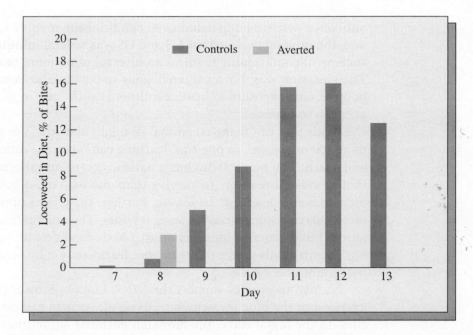

*Figure 4-6* Conditioned aversion to locoweed. Proportion of locoweed eaten by horses that had conditioned taste aversion treatment (light bar) and untreated controls (dark bars). All consumption for the treated group on day 8 was by one horse. (Adapted from Pfister et al., 2002, Conditioned taste aversions to locoweed [Oxytropis sericea] in horses. Journal of Animal Science, 80, Figure 2, p. 82. Reprinted with permission.)

In Brazil and other South American countries, cattle eat a highly toxic plant called mio-mio. Milton Almeida and colleagues (Almeida et al., unpubl. MS, 2011), most of them Brazilians, fed cattle enough mio-mio to make them sick. Some time after this the researchers put the animals in a paddock that included mio-mio. A control group went to the paddock with no prior exposure to the toxic plant. None of the treated animals that went into the paddock 23 or more hours after treatment showed any sign of sickness, whereas more than half of the untreated animals became seriously ill and some died. The effectiveness of the conditioning procedure varied with the interval between the conditioning trial and the move to the paddock. Evidently it takes time for mio-mio to produce sickness, and it is sickness that produces the taste aversion.

Other studies confirm the benefits of conditioned food avoidance with cattle (Pfister, 2000; Ralphs, 1997), goats (Provenza et al., 1990), and sheep (Almeida et al., 2009; Provenza, Lynch, & Nolan, 1993). It even appears that mice and rats can acquire an aversion to a farmer's food grains (Ralphs & Provenza, 1999). How long the effects of conditioned food avoidance last is hard to say, but there is evidence that they can last for at least three years (Ralphs & Provenza, 1999). Even if additional conditioning is required, the benefits are likely to outweigh the time and expense. Conditioning holds out promise of other applications on farms and ranches (see *Nature's Weed Whackers*).

CAPSULE **REVIEW**   Conditioned taste aversions result from the pairing of distinctive flavors and aversive (especially nausea-inducing) stimuli. While the CS and US must normally appear close together for conditioning to be effective, taste aversions often occur even when the US is delayed for an hour or more. Research in this field has not only helped us understand taste preferences but has established procedures that can prevent suffering in range animals and save ranchers and consumers a good deal of money. It can even help farmers by turning some grazing animals into weed eaters.

## ADVERTISING

Pavlov's laboratory is a long way from Madison Avenue, but advertising agencies are very interested in the emotional reactions people have to products. They are particularly interested in making products arouse feelings of fondness, on the reasonable assumption that people are apt to buy things they like.

Advertisers attempt to do this by pairing products with stimuli that reliably elicit positive emotions (Schachtman, Walker, & Fowler, 2011; Zane, 2012). In television commercials, for example, a particular brand of beer will be associated with attractive people having a good time. There will be no mention of alcoholism or fetal damage caused by alcohol consumption, no scenes of fatal car accidents, no photographs of battered women who, after drinking, fell victim to

## NATURE'S WEED WHACKERS

We are all increasingly concerned about the use of toxic chemicals on our food, but finding economical alternatives is difficult. What else can the farmer do to keep down weeds except spray them with poison? One answer: Hire sheep.

Morgan Doran and his colleagues at the University of California in Davis trained sheep to avoid eating grape plants while grazing (Trained Sheep Graze, 2007). Using procedures developed by Fred Provenza of Utah State University (e.g., Provenza, Lynch, & Nolan, 1993), Doran used Pavlovian conditioning to enlist the help of sheep in controlling vineyard weeds without damaging the grape vines themselves.

First the researchers let sheep eat grape leaves. Then they gave the animals a small dose of lithium chloride, a drug that causes nausea. After this, they turned the sheep loose in a vineyard. The animals were free to eat whatever they wanted, but they avoided eating the grape vines and filled up on weeds. They had acquired an aversion to grape plants.

With sheep as weed eaters, farmers avoid the cost and health risks of herbicides and produce a safer product for consumers. Sheepherders with trained animals can get free food for their animals and might even receive a fee from the grape farmer for weeding their orchard. The same four-legged technology might serve as well in other kinds of orchards and even on crop farms.

Sheep, nature's weed whackers. Efficient and so much quieter than the mechanical variety.

---

date rape. We see only young, healthy, attractive people holding beer bottles and having a good time.

Marketers do the same sort of thing when they pair a new product with one of their popular products, a practice they call co-branding (Grossman, 1997). Another technique is to pair competing products with items that arouse negative emotions. A competitor's trash bag, for example, may be shown falling apart, leaving garbage all over the kitchen floor, or a cat may be shown turning its back on a competitor's cat food.

**QUERY 5:** Advertisers pair their products with items that arouse _____.

Do such techniques really induce us to like the advertised item? The millions of dollars spent by manufacturers on advertising certainly suggest that they think so, and research suggests that they are right. For instance, in one experiment (reported in Kiviat, 2007), people tasted peanut butter from three different jars. Seventy-five percent of them preferred the peanut butter from the jar with the brand name label on it, even though all three jars had the same kind of peanut butter. In a similar experiment, children preferred the french fries and chicken nuggets from a McDonald's package over those from other packages, though the food was the same. Such experiments suggest that the pairing of popular names and images with a product affects the way people respond to the product.

Note the similarity of this study to those of Staats and Staats earlier in this chapter and in Chapter 3.

Gerald Gorn (1982) conducted the first experiment on the role of conditioning in marketing. He had American college students listen either to a tune from the film *Grease* or to classical Indian music. Gorn assumed that the students would enjoy the popular American music more than the unfamiliar Eastern variety. While listening to the music, the students viewed a slide showing either a beige or a blue pen. Later, the students were allowed to have one of the pens. Of the students who heard the popular music, 79% chose a pen of the same color they had seen while listening to the music; of those who heard the Indian music, 70% chose a pen *different in color* from the one they saw on the slide.

Gorn came in for criticism because of problems with his methodology, but his basic findings have been confirmed by a number of other studies. For example, two Dutch researchers, Edward Groenland and Jan Schoormans (1994), paired pens with music that people either liked or didn't like. Their liking for the pens afterward reflected their liking for the music that accompanied the pens (see also Bierley et al., 1985; Redker & Gibson, 2009).

In another experiment, Elnora Stuart and her colleagues (Stuart, Shimp, & Engle, 1987) had college students view a number of slides. Some of the slides depicted various fictitious products (e.g., Brand V candy, Brand R cola); others depicted a variety of scenes that were either neutral (e.g., a radar dish, a license plate) or aroused positive feelings (e.g., a mountain waterfall). For some students (the conditioning group), scenes that aroused good feelings regularly followed Brand L toothpaste; for the other students, the scenes that followed Brand L toothpaste were almost always neutral. The researchers evaluated the students' feelings about Brand L toothpaste with four rating scales. The result was that students in the conditioning group rated Brand L toothpaste more positively than did students in the control group. Moreover, the more times the toothpaste and pleasant scenes appeared together, the more positively the students felt about the product (see Figure 4-7). Students in the conditioning

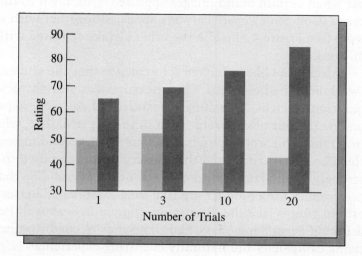

**Figure 4-7** *Conditioning and brand appeal. Mean ratings of Brand L toothpaste as a function of number of trials for control group (light bars) and conditioning group (dark bars). Higher ratings indicate more positive feelings. (Compiled from data in Stuart et al., 1987.)*

**Figure 4-8** *Can conditioning subvert brand loyalty? Research aimed at undermining the commitment of dedicated Coke™ and Pepsi™ drinkers paired images of the products (here identified as Brand A and Brand B) with positive words and images, such as those shown here, or with negative words and images. The most loyal fans were not moved. (The brand images were drawn by Deborah Underwood based on images provided by Bryan Gibson, Department of Psychology, Central Michigan University, Mount Pleasant, Michigan. The mountain scene is courtesy of Bas Meelker/Shutterstock.com)*

group were also much more likely than controls to indicate a willingness to buy Brand L toothpaste, should it become available.

Studies have been done with actual brands, with similar results, at least when the participants were initially rather neutral toward the brands (e.g., Redker & Gibson, 2009). But can conditioning change people's preferences when they are already strongly attached to a product? Some people, for example, have a strong preference for Coke™, while others are equally committed to Pepsi™. Could an advertising campaign shift people from one brand to the other through conditioning? Bryan Gibson (2008) of Central Michigan University looked into this question. He asked college students to participate in a study ostensibly on vigilance. He showed them a large number of images and words on a computer, and their task was to hit the space bar when certain brand images appeared. Unknown to the participants, one brand (Coke™ or Pepsi™) always appeared together with a positive image or word (see Figure 4-8) while the other always appeared with a negative image or word.

After this Gibson looked for evidence that the students' feelings for the two brands had changed. One measure was straightforward and included questions such as, "All things considered, if you were to purchase soft drinks on one of your next several trips to the supermarket, what are the chances in 10 that you would purchase Coke™?" A second measure was more subtle. The results indicated that the conditioning failed to move people who strongly favored one brand over the other. It could be that long-established preferences for a product are like long-established biases toward racial and ethnic groups (see the discussion of prejudice, above). People who grew up drinking Pepsi™ may have had thousands of conditioning trials from advertising campaigns and naturally occurring experiences (e.g., drinking Pepsi™ at a birthday party or while resting following exercise). It is unlikely that so much conditioning can be undone with a few ads for a competing product.

It's also possible that the conditioning procedure used in the study was at fault. Like most ads, the brand name and the positive word or image coincided. You may recall that such simultaneous conditioning is one of the less effective procedures. Had the brand name *preceded* the words and images, perhaps there would have been more change.

Many ads are based on simultaneous conditioning, and some are based on what amounts to backward conditioning since the brand name follows the positive stimuli. Presenting the brand name (the CS) first works better (Baker, Honea, & Russell, 2004; Macklin, 1996; Stuart, Shimp, & Engle, 1987). Advertisers also need to understand the blocking and overshadowing phenomena (see Chapter 3) or their efforts can be counterproductive.

Of course, the use of conditioning procedures to sell products began long before Pavlov began his studies on salivating dogs. In the 1800s, for example, the manufacturers of a medicine for gonorrhea called their product Listerine™, thereby pairing it with Joseph Lister, a highly regarded physician at the time (Marschall, 1993). What conditioning researchers have contributed is not so much new marketing techniques as a better understanding of the role conditioning plays in consumer behavior. This understanding is valuable not only to advertisers, but to the consumers the advertisers are trying to influence.

---

CAPSULE **REVIEW**    Advertising can be viewed as the business of creating conditioned emotional responses toward products. One way marketing experts do this is by pairing products they want to sell with items that already arouse positive emotions. Advertising is not so much about providing information about a product as it is about creating conditioned emotional responses to those products.

---

# DRUG ADDICTION

Drug addiction is a major clinical and societal problem throughout much of the world. In the United States, for example, the cost of drug addiction in 2005 was about $468 billion (National Center on Addiction and Substance Abuse, 2009). The personal costs are also heavy: Thousands of people suffer debilitating illnesses or die prematurely as a result of drug use, their family members suffer abuse and loss of income, and people die because of intoxicated drivers.

Drug abuse has proven difficult to deal with. One problem is reaching an understanding of the fundamental nature of the behavior involved. Many people still think of it as the result of character flaws, but this is a circular explanation: Why doesn't Jerry stop using cocaine? "Because he's weak." How do you know he's weak? "Because he keeps using cocaine!" Such "explanations" do nothing to advance our understanding of addiction or move us toward more effective treatments.

Many drug abuse researchers view addiction as a brain disease (Hanson, Leshner, & Tai, 2002; Leshner, 1997). There is no question that addiction to drugs involves the brain, but the effects of a drug on the brain do not fully explain addictive behavior. Classical conditioning goes a long way in helping us understand it (McCarthy et al., 2011).

Let's begin with some basics: Addictive drugs have in common that they produce a pleasurable experience; in many addictive drugs this is called a *high*. After a period of repeated drug use, the level of drug required to produce a high increases; this is known as drug *tolerance*. Once a person is addicted to a drug, failure to take the drug produces strong cravings for the drug and other feelings of discomfort called *withdrawal*. When people remain off the drug for an extended period, the cravings and other withdrawal symptoms typically fade away; yet despite prolonged abstinence and the lack of any trace of the drug in the body, withdrawal symptoms reappear in certain situations and the person resumes use of the drug, a phenomenon called *relapse*. All of these phenomena—high, tolerance, withdrawal, and relapse—seem to be fairly well explained by Pavlovian conditioning.

The drug a person takes is an unconditional stimulus, and the high it produces is the unconditional response. Just about anything associated with the drug—drug paraphernalia, the furniture and people present, music from a radio, the sound of machinery, the odor of the drug, the room temperature, the feel of the floor, the taste of food eaten before taking the drug—can become conditional stimuli. The conditional response elicited by these stimuli is not a version of the UR, but physiological changes that prepare the person for the drug by reducing its effects (Siegel, 2005; see the related discussion in the theories section of Chapter 3).

Research supports the idea that the CR suppresses the effects of the drug, thereby producing tolerance. For example, Canadian researcher Shepard Siegel and his colleagues (1982) gave three groups of rats, some of which had never received heroin before, a strong dose of the drug. Some of the heroin-experienced rats received the test dose in the same place they had received previous doses; others received the same dose in a novel setting. The results were clear-cut. The dose was lethal for 96% of the inexperienced rats, but for experienced rats mortality depended on where they received the drug. Of those injected in a familiar environment, 32% died; of those injected in a new environment, 64% died. In the novel environment, the CSs that normally would evoke the conditional response (the physiological changes that suppress the body's reaction to the drug) were absent, so the drug hit with far greater force. This shows the role of conditioning in drug tolerance.

If the drug does not follow the CS, Siegel (2005) argues, these physiological changes (the CR) are experienced as drug cravings and other withdrawal symptoms. In the case of humans addicted to heroin and other opioids, these other symptoms typically include anxiety, sweating, muscle aches, tremor, nausea, vomiting, and diarrhea. The idea that withdrawal symptoms are a response to cues previously associated with the drug is supported by research. In one experiment, a rat received a morphine infusion each time it pressed a lever (MacRae & Siegel, 1997). With each lever press another rat in a different chamber also received an infusion of the drug *without* pressing a lever. (A third group of rats also received an infusion, but not of an addictive drug; they served as a control group.) Every seven days of the study the researchers stopped the infusions and looked for withdrawal symptoms. They found that the lever-pressing rats showed far more withdrawal than the rats that received the drug without lever pressing (see Figure 4-9).

The rats that received morphine received the same amount of drug, and were in basically the same kind of environment, except for one thing. During the periods without drugs, the lever-pressing rats had the cues from the lever, the stimulus that was most reliably associated with the drug. The rats that received the drug without pressing the lever did not have that strong signal for the CR. (See also Mello & Mendelson, 1970.)

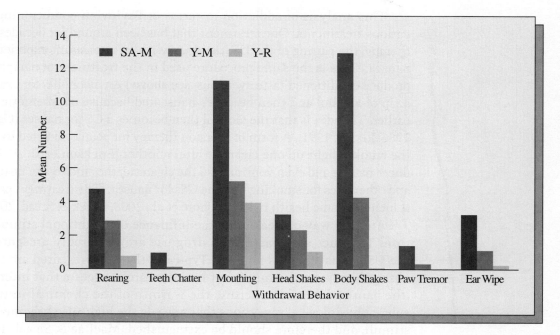

**Figure 4-9** *Withdrawal as a CR. Mean frequency of withdrawal symptoms in rats that self-administered morphine by pressing a lever (SA-M), by yoked controls that received morphine without pressing a lever (Y-M), and by yoked controls that received a saline solution (Y-R). (From The role of self-administration in morphine withdrawal in rats, by James MacRae and Shepard Siegel, 1997, Psychobiology, 25[1], Figure 2, p. 80. Reprinted with permission.)*

But what about relapse? Why should relapse occur after a prolonged period of abstinence? An addict goes into treatment, his body is cleansed of the addictive drug, he feels cured and is convinced he will never go back to using the drug. Then he leaves the treatment center, returns to his home, and in a matter of days is on drugs again; why? Once again conditioning seems to play a major role. The former drug addict returns to the same environment where he became addicted to the drug—the same neighborhood with the same drug suppliers, the same friends and acquaintances, the same parks. Many of these people and places were associated with drug use. The supplier provided the drugs, and some of the friends and neighbors took drugs with him in the same back alleys, rooms, and parks. These conditional stimuli elicit the conditional response, including cravings for the drug and other withdrawal symptoms. Even if his former drug supplier doesn't approach him and offer him a free "hit," the other cues make abstinence difficult.

**QUERY 6:** Classical conditioning provides explanations for the basic phenomena

of drug addiction, the high, _____, _____, and

_____.

This analysis of addiction in terms of Pavlovian conditioning has led to various treatments. One treatment that has been around for decades is aversion therapy, the pairing of the US (the drug) with an unpleasant experience, such as nausea. (This is the same procedure used in the treatment of paraphilias and to produce conditioned taste aversions; see above.) An alcoholic, for example, takes a sip of alcohol and then becomes nauseated because of an emetic drug taken earlier. The idea is that the alcohol then becomes a CS for nausea (Cannon et al., 1986; Elkins, 1991). A form of aversion therapy for people addicted to tobacco has the smoker light up one cigarette after another (Erickson et al., 1983). This induces nausea and even vomiting, so the cigarette, the smoke, the taste of tobacco, and other cues for smoking become CSs for nausea. (The treatment can work, but it includes some health risks; see Fiore et al., 2008; Hajek & Stead, 2001).

Another way of weakening the influence of conditional stimuli is extinction: The cues associated with drug use are repeatedly presented without the US so that there is no high. Typically the CSs presented are the publicly observable external stimuli, but basic research suggests that internal stimuli (the pain of a needle puncture, the warmth of the chemical in the arm, the subtle physiological sensations that precede the high) also become conditional stimuli, and therefore should be extinguished (MacRae & Siegel, 1997; Siegel, 2005). As a result, therapists are now looking for ways to present internal stimuli associated with the drug as well as external stimuli (McCarthy et al., 2011). As you know, extinguishing a CR can be difficult even in the lab, and the durability of a CR poses serious problems in a natural environment (Conklin & Tiffany, 2002).

Traditionally, the extinction therapy occurs in a clinic or therapist's office, which is very different from the settings in which drugs are typically taken. One thing that might improve the extinction procedure is to present the CSs alone in the same sort of environment where the drug is typically taken. Ideally this would mean taking a client into a drug area where he would be exposed to conditional stimuli without their being followed by the drug. This makes sense in theory, but it would be a risky thing for both the therapist and the client. However, experimental research is now being done using the virtual reality world used to treat anxiety disorders (see the discussion of fear, above).

For example, Zachary Rosenthal, a psychologist at Duke University, has created a virtual reality world that resembles the kind of situations drug addicts find irresistible (see Rosenthal et al., 2010). The client "walks into" various virtual environments (e.g., a room where people are snorting cocaine) while the therapist is at his side. In each setting the client rates the level of craving he experiences. Since no high follows, the craving level declines. This should make the extinction procedure more effective.

But Rosenthal has taken the procedure a step further: When the craving level is low, he sounds a tone. The idea is that the tone then becomes a CS for *not* craving the addictive drug. When the client leaves the treatment area, he takes a cell phone with him. Whenever he finds himself feeling a craving for drugs, he dials a number and hears the tone, the CS for *not* craving, and the cravings subside. Whether Rosenthal's program will prove effective is unclear, but it seems promising. (For other examples of VR treatment of drug addiction, see Bauman et al., 2003; Bordnick et al., 2009.)

Another interesting approach to addiction treatment is suggested by the work of Christopher Culbertson and others at UCLA (see Stix, 2010). They created a virtual "meth house" on Second Life, a web-based virtual community. Methamphetamine users went through the simulated house while Culbertson collected data on their cravings. It proved to be a useful way of assessing the levels of cravings induced by drug-related items, and might one day be the basis for effective treatment.

There are other approaches to treating drug addiction—12-step programs, individual and family counseling, drug replacement therapy (e.g., taking methadone as a substitute for heroin), antagonistic drug therapy (drugs that block the targeted drug from producing a high). But although these treatments may seem unrelated to Pavlovian conditioning, in at least some cases there is a connection. The use of antagonistic drugs, for example, although often thought of as a medicinal treatment, is a way of extinguishing conditional stimuli: The addict takes a whiff of cocaine, for example, but gets nothing from it, thus weakening the cues for cravings.

Drug addiction is a complex problem, and it is likely that effective treatment will require multiple treatment approaches. However, it is clear that classical conditioning is involved in the origin and maintenance of addiction, and it will almost certainly play a part in its treatment.

CAPSULE **REVIEW**    Drug addiction is a major social problem throughout much of the world. Its analysis in terms of classical conditioning helps us understand the basic phenomena: the high, tolerance, withdrawal symptoms, and relapse. It has also led to treatments, including aversion therapy and extinction. There is as yet no cure for drug addiction, though treatment can help, and it is likely that classical conditioning will be part of any effective treatment that is devised.

## HEALTH CARE

Classical conditioning is beginning to prove surprisingly useful in the diagnosis and treatment of medical disorders.

Consider diagnosis. Usually doctors diagnose a disorder on the basis of physiological measures, such as blood levels of certain chemicals, changes in anatomy such as those caused by growths, or by behavioral phenomena such as an erratic heartbeat or uncoordinated movements. But there is now evidence that classical conditioning procedures may help in the diagnosis of a variety of diseases. For example, if an apparently healthy infant does not respond normally to environmental events, what is the problem? Is he retarded? Autistic? Deaf? An obvious way to test for deafness is to make a noise (clap one's hands) and see if the baby looks toward the sound. But if he fails to respond, is the reason deafness or a neurological problem such as autism? Research suggests that deafness can be ruled out through eyeblink conditioning (Lancioni & Hoogland, 1980). If you pair a sound with a puff of air to the eye, for example, and no conditional eyeblink occurs, this suggests that the child is deaf.

Similarly, if an adult is showing signs of intellectual decline, is it normal aging or is the patient in the early stages of dementia? Diana Woodruff-Pak and colleagues (1996) found that adults who learned poorly through conditioning were much more likely than others to develop dementia later. The ability to diagnose dementia before it becomes apparent will be very important when early-stage treatments are developed. Research has also shown that conditioning proceeds differently in patients with Alzheimer's disease (AD) than in normal people of the same age (Solomon et al., 1991), so conditioning might not only identify patients with dementia, it may distinguish between AD and other kinds of dementia. Other work suggests that people with autism and obsessive-compulsive disorder condition *more* rapidly, under certain circumstances, than other people (Tracy et al., 1999), so conditioning might be useful in identifying people with these disorders. Pavlovian conditioning is also used as a way of studying neurological functions (e.g., Kandel, 1970, 2007) and neurological problems (e.g., Marenco, Weinberger, & Schreurs, 2003; Stanton & Gallagher, 1998).

Let's now take a look at how classical conditioning may help in understanding and treating one kind of medical problem, immune disorders.

**?** QUERY 7: Classical conditioning appears to be a way of helping to diagnose several

medical disorders, one of which is _____.

The body's efforts to heal injuries, remove toxins, destroy harmful viruses and bacteria, and generally fight to restore good health are collectively referred to as the immune system. Recent research has suggested that the immune system is susceptible to influence (both positive and negative) by Pavlovian conditioning. One example is allergic reactions.

An allergic reaction involves the release of histamines by the immune system in response to certain kinds of substances known as allergens. The histamines serve to rid the body of allergens by attacking them at the molecular level and by expelling them from the body by, among other things, sneezing and coughing. Researchers have long known that allergic reactions are not always due entirely to genetically based reactions to allergens. A hundred years ago, J. MacKinzie (reported in Russell et al., 1984) described the case of a patient who had an allergic reaction when presented with an artificial rose.

As a result of such reports, some scientists have wondered whether certain allergic reactions might be partly the result of conditioning. Michael Russell and his colleagues (1984) exposed guinea pigs to the protein BSA so they would be allergic to it. Next, the researchers paired BSA (now a US for an allergic response) with the odor of fish or sulfur. After several pairings, the guinea pigs were tested with the odors alone. The animals reacted with an immediate rise in blood histamine, a sure sign of allergic reaction. The odors had become conditional stimuli that elicited a conditional allergic response. In other words, the animals became allergic to certain odors through Pavlovian conditioning. Russell suggests that, in the same way, a person who is allergic to a substance may become allergic to things frequently associated with it. The person who is allergic to tomatoes may break out in hives when eating something that has the taste, smell, or look of tomatoes, even though there are no tomatoes in it. Similarly, a person who is allergic to rose pollen may sneeze at the sight of a rose—even an artificial one.

Conditioned allergic reactions might be assumed to be merely faint imitations of "the real thing," but Russell and his colleagues found that the histamine levels produced in response to conditional stimuli were nearly as high as those from BSA. Thus, the person whose sneezing, wheezing, and headache are due to a CS is not necessarily less miserable than the person whose symptoms are caused by exposure to an allergen.

The immune system doesn't just produce allergic reactions; it defends us against major diseases, such as cancer. Ironically, the same chemotherapy used to combat cancer has also been found to suppress the immune system. This is a very unfortunate side effect because it not only reduces the body's efforts to destroy the cancer but also makes the person vulnerable to other illnesses, particularly infectious diseases.

Pavlovian conditioning suggests that stimuli associated with chemotherapy would, in time, suppress the immune system. There is evidence that this is the

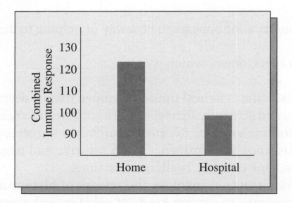

**Figure 4-10** *Conditioning and immune response. Combined measures of three immune responses at home and in the hospital where patients had received nausea-inducing chemotherapy. (Compiled from data in Bovbjerg et al., 1990.)*

case. Dana Bovbjerg and his colleagues (1990) at the Mount Sinai School of Medicine in New York City found that women receiving chemotherapy for ovarian cancer showed decreased immune functioning when they returned to the hospital for treatment (see Figure 4-10). Apparently, the hospital itself had become a CS for conditioned immunosuppression (i.e., suppression of the immune system). This could mean that, because of conditioning, the treatment that is meant to help patients also hurts them (see also Ader & Cohen, 1975, 1993).

Such findings also raise the possibility that Pavlovian procedures can be used to *boost* the immune system. If a neutral stimulus is paired with a drug or procedure that facilitates immune functioning, that stimulus might become a CS for a stronger response from the immune system.

Research on the application of Pavlovian conditioning in medicine is still in its early stages, but there is every reason to believe that its usefulness will expand in the years ahead (see Spector, 2009; Szcytkowski & Lysle, 2011).

CAPSULE **REVIEW**   Pavlovian conditioning shows promise as a means of diagnosing and studying medical problems, including deafness, autism, and dementia. It also may prove useful in the treatment of some health problems. In the past, medical treatment of serious illness tended to ignore the immune system; today, the emphasis is increasingly on facilitating the immune system. Through conditioning, we may soon be able to enhance the immune response to help people fight off diseases such as cancer.

## A FINAL WORD

We have seen that Pavlovian conditioning provides insights into fear, prejudice, the paraphilias, taste aversion, advertising, drug addiction, and health care. These applications of Pavlovian conditioning are representative, but there are many others, and more are being explored all the time.

The variety of applications of Pavlovian conditioning also suggests how important naturally occurring conditioning is in our daily lives. Do you, for example, prefer jazz to classical music? Are you more comfortable alone than in large crowds? Does your blood boil when you see Ku Klux Klansmen marching in a parade? Do you feel a shiver up your spine when you hear the national anthem? Does reading *Romeo and Juliet* move you to tears (or put you to sleep)? When you hear rap music, do you sway in rhythm with the beat, or do you plug up your ears with cotton? All such reactions, and thousands of others that we think of as embedded in the very fiber of our being, are not purely products of our genes; they are to a large extent due to learning, particularly Pavlovian conditioning.

Those who dismiss Pavlovian conditioning as a procedure for getting dogs to salivate at the sound of a bell clearly have a lot to learn.

## RECOMMENDED **READING**

1. Ledoux, J. (1996). *The emotional brain*. New York: Touchstone.

   This is a discussion of the neural mechanisms involved in emotional conditioning.

2. Packard, V. (1957/2007). *The hidden persuaders*. Brooklyn, NY: Ig Publishing.

   Originally published in 1957, this is a classic on the ways that businesses try to persuade consumers to buy their products. Packard was a journalist, so this best seller is an easy read.

3. Pavlov, I. P. (1941). *Conditioned reflexes and psychiatry* (W. H. Grant, Trans.). New York: International Publishers.

   This is Volume 2 of *Lectures on Conditioned Reflexes*. In it, Pavlov attempts to apply conditioning principles to the interpretation of neurotic disorders.

4. Spiegler, M. D., & Guevremont, D. D. (2009). *Contemporary behavior therapy*. Belmont, CA: Wadsworth Publishing.

   Many of the treatments under the heading of behavior therapy are based on classical conditioning. This textbook provides a thorough review of these and other treatments, and is well worth studying if you are considering a career in clinical psychology.

5. Wolpe, J. (1973). *The practice of behavior therapy* (2nd ed.). New York: Pergamon Press.

   This is an old but excellent look at the therapeutic use of conditioning procedures provided by one of the world's leading experts.

## REVIEW **QUESTIONS**

1. Define the following terms and provide an example of each:

   aversion therapy
   conditioned emotional response
   conditioned taste aversion

counterconditioning
exposure therapy
systematic desensitization
virtual reality exposure therapy (VRET)

2. Suppose your doctor advises you to eat liver, which you despise. How might you overcome your aversion to liver?

3. Pavlovian learning usually requires CS–US intervals of no more than a few seconds. Taste aversion conditioning is an exception. Why does this exception exist?

4. How can you increase the likelihood that your child will share your devotion to jazz music?

5. You are in charge of rehabilitating criminals convicted of various hate crimes. Can Pavlovian conditioning help?

6. What does the work of Staats and Staats lead you to predict about the backgrounds of Ku Klux Klan members?

7. Invent a better term for the disorders known as psychosomatic illnesses.

8. Why are people more likely to develop aversions to foods they have not often eaten?

9. Many people hate groups of people with whom they have had no direct experience. How can Pavlovian conditioning account for these emotions?

10. How has reading this chapter altered your view of Pavlovian conditioning?

## PRACTICE **QUIZ**

1. The phenomenon of latent _____ suggests that we are more likely to develop aversions to novel foods than to familiar ones.

2. People used to believe that children were instinctively afraid of fire, animals, and many other things. John Watson and Rosalie _____ found that many such fears were not innate but were acquired through conditioning.

3. The first person to use counterconditioning to treat a phobia was probably _____.

4. The work of Staats and Staats suggests that prejudice may be partly the result of _____-order conditioning.

5. Dana Bovbjerg and his colleagues found that women receiving chemotherapy in a hospital later showed decreased functioning of their _____ system when they returned to the hospital.

6. Gorn influenced product choice by pairing pens of a certain color with certain kinds of _____.

7. In _____ therapy, a stimulus that elicits an inappropriate response is paired with an aversive stimulus such as shock or an emetic drug.

8. The pairing of a particular food with nausea-inducing stimuli often results in a conditioned _____.

9. Morgan Doran used conditioning to train sheep not to eat _____.

10. Masochism may be the result of pairing stimuli that cause pain or humiliation with those that cause _____.

## QUERY **ANSWERS**

Query 1. Albert became fearful of the rat because the arrival of the rat regularly preceded *a loud noise*.

Query 2. VRET stands for *virtual reality exposure therapy*.

Query 3. Prejudice is an example of a CER, or *conditioned emotional response*.

Query 4. In the Garcia experiment just described, the CS is *saccharin*, and the US is *radiation*.

Query 5. Advertisers pair their products with items that arouse *positive emotions*.

Query 6. Classical conditioning provides explanations for the basic phenomena of drug addiction, the high, *tolerance, withdrawal symptoms*, and *relapse*.

Query 7. Classical conditioning appears to be a way of helping to diagnose several medical disorders, one of which is *dementia/Alzheimer's disease/ deafness/autism/obsessive-compulsive disorder*.

# CHAPTER

# 5 Operant Learning: Reinforcement

*Nothing succeeds like success.*

**—French Proverb**

## PREVIEW

Pavlovian conditioning plays an important role in our lives, and in the lives of all animals. But we are not passive beings that respond only in reflexive ways to events around us. We act on our surroundings and change them, sometimes in ways that favor us, sometimes in ways that work against us. Our success and happiness, and our survival as individuals and as a species, depends a great deal on how we affect the world, and how those effects change our behavior.

# BEGINNINGS

About the same time Pavlov was trying to solve the riddle of the psychic reflex, a young American graduate student named Edward Lee Thorndike was tackling another problem: animal intelligence. In the 19th century, most people believed that higher animals learned through reasoning. Anyone who owned a dog or cat could "see" the animal think through a problem and come to a logical conclusion, and stories of the incredible talents of animals abounded. Taken together, these stories painted a picture of animal abilities that made some pets little less than furry Albert Einsteins. Thorndike recognized the impossibility of estimating animal abilities from this sort of anecdotal evidence: "Such testimony is by no means on a par with testimony about the size of a fish or the migration of birds," he wrote, "for here one has to deal not merely with ignorant or inaccurate testimony, but also with prejudiced testimony. Human folk are as a matter of fact eager to find intelligence in animals" (1898, p. 4).[1]

This bias led people to report remarkable feats but not more ordinary, unintelligent acts. "Dogs get lost hundreds of times and no one ever notices it or sends an account of it to a scientific magazine," wrote Thorndike, "but let one find his way from Brooklyn to Yonkers and the fact immediately becomes a circulating anecdote. Thousands of cats on thousands of occasions sit helplessly yowling, and no one takes thought of it or writes to his friend, the professor; but let one cat claw at the knob of a door supposedly as a signal to be let out, and straightway this cat becomes the representative of the cat-mind in all the books. . . . In short, the anecdotes give really the . . . *supernormal* psychology of animals" (pp. 4–5).

But how could one go about studying the *normal*, or ordinary, psychology of animals? How could one study animal intelligence scientifically? Thorndike's answer was to present an animal with a problem. Then he would give the animal the problem again and see whether its performance improved, test it again, and so on. He would, in other words, study animal intelligence by studying animal learning.

In one series of experiments, Thorndike put a chick into a maze. If the chick took the correct route, it found its way to a pen containing food and other chicks. When Thorndike first put a chick into a maze, it tried to jump out of the enclosure and then wandered down one blind alley after another, peeping loudly all the while, until it finally found its way out. With succeeding trials, the chick became more and more efficient; finally, when placed in the maze it would go directly down the appropriate path.

Thorndike's most famous experiments involved cats. He would place a hungry cat in a "puzzle box" and put food in plain view but out of reach (see Figure 5-1; Chance, 1999). The box had a door that could be opened by some simple act, such as pulling a wire loop or stepping on a treadle. Like the chicks, the cat began by performing a number of ineffective acts. Thorndike wrote that the cat typically

---

[1]Unless otherwise noted, all references to Thorndike are to his 1898 dissertation.

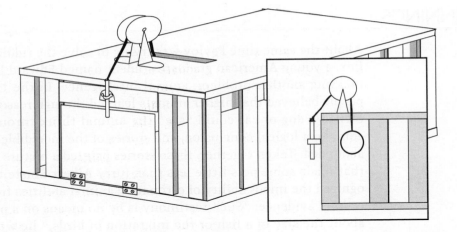

**Figure 5-1** *Box A, one of Thorndike's puzzle boxes. Pulling on the loop (see side view, inset) released a bolt, and the door fell open. (Drawn from description in Thorndike, 1898, by Diane Chance.)*

tries to squeeze through any opening; it claws and bites at the bars or wire; it thrusts its paws out through any opening and claws at everything it reaches; it continues its efforts when it strikes anything loose and shaky; it may claw at things within the box. (p. 13)

Eventually, the cat would pull on the loop or step on the treadle, the door would fall open, and the cat would make its way to freedom and food. When Thorndike returned the cat to the box for another trial, it went through the same sort of activity until it again did what was required to open the door. With each succeeding trial, the animal made fewer ineffective movements until, after many trials, it would immediately pull on the loop or step on the treadle and escape. Thorndike recorded the time it took the animal to escape on each trial and plotted these data on a graph, producing what are probably the first learning curves (see Figure 5-2).

**? QUERY 1:** Thorndike studied animal learning as a way of measuring animal

_____.

Thorndike concluded that a given behavior typically has one of two kinds of consequences or effects. He called one kind of consequence a "satisfying state of affairs," the other an "annoying state of affairs." If, for instance, a chick goes down a wrong alley, this behavior is followed by continued hunger and separation from other chicks—an annoying state of affairs. If the chick goes down the correct alley, this behavior leads to food and contact with other chicks—a satisfying state of affairs. When a cat tries to squeeze through the bars of its cage, it remains confined and hungry—an annoying consequence;

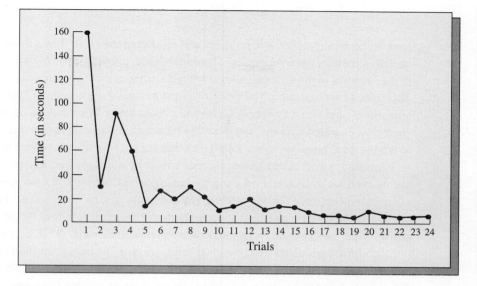

***Figure 5-2*** *Puzzle box learning curve. The time cat 12 took to escape from box A (see Figure 5-1) on succeeding trials. (Compiled from data in Thorndike, 1898.)*

## E. L. THORNDIKE: WHAT THE OCCASION DEMANDED

*E. L. Thorndike, whose law of effect created the foundation for operant learning. (Photo courtesy of Humanities and Social Science Library/New York Public Library/Science Photo Library.)*

E. L. Thorndike started life on August 31, 1874, the son of an itinerant Methodist minister. His parents, who were bright and idealistic, ran a tight ship—so tight, in fact, that someone once said of the family, "There is no music in the Thorndikes." Thorndike's biographer, Geraldine Joncich (1968), wrote that there was "a smothering of lightheartedness and carefree gaiety . . . with Victorian culture" (p. 39). This home life produced a boy who was well mannered, industrious, and studious, but also shy, serious, and moderate to excess. Thorndike himself hinted that he lacked spontaneity and humor when he said, "I think I was always grown-up" (in Joncich, 1968, p. 31).

In 1893, the young grown-up went off to Wesleyan University, where he developed an interest in literature. As a graduate student at Harvard, he shifted from English to psychology and took up the problem of animal intelligence. As there was no laboratory space for his

*(Continued)*

subjects, he kept the animals in his room and conducted the experiments there "until the landlady's protests were imperative" (Thorndike, 1936, p. 264). Finally, William James (one of the founders of modern psychology) offered him the use of his cellar, and that became Thorndike's new laboratory. The work in James's basement went well, but Thorndike had little money, and when Columbia University offered him a fellowship, he packed up his "two most educated chickens" and moved to New York. It was at Columbia that Thorndike wrote the dissertation on animal intelligence that started him off on a brilliant career.

Toward the end of that career, Thorndike must have thought about these and other events in his life as he prepared a short autobiographical article. In it he argued that his accomplishments were not the result of any deliberate plan or "inner needs." Instead, he seemed to compare his own behavior with the trial-and-success activity of his experimental animals. "I did," he explained, "what the occasion seemed to demand" (1936, p. 266).

Thorndike's bibliography lists over 500 items, including 78 books. In addition to his work in learning, he made important contributions to educational psychology (a field he practically invented) and to psychological testing. We are lucky indeed that Thorndike had such a demanding environment.

---

when it pulls at a wire loop, the door opens and it escapes and finds food—a satisfying consequence.

Thorndike (1911) later called this relationship between behavior and its consequences the **law of effect** and offered this definition:

> Of several responses made to the same situation, those which are accompanied or closely followed by satisfaction to the animal will, other things being equal, be more firmly connected with the situation, so that, when it recurs, they will be more likely to recur; those which are accompanied or closely followed by discomfort to the animal will, other things being equal, have their connections with that situation weakened, so that, when it recurs, they will be less likely to occur. (p. 244)

Thorndike's law identifies four key elements: the environment (situation or context) in which a behavior occurs, the behavior that occurs, the change in the environment following the behavior, and the change in the behavior produced by this consequence. Another way of expressing the essence of the law in fewer words is:

Behavior is a function of its consequences.

*The law of effect means that our environment is constantly "talking" to us, constantly providing feedback about our behavior. "Yes," it tells us, "do that again." "No," it says, "don't do that."*

This easy-to-remember expression of the law (the most important law in all of behavior science) is, like most easy-to-remember expressions of principles, cryptic. Nevertheless, it conveys the idea that the consequences of behavior are a major factor in what we and other species do.

Thorndike was not, of course, the first person to notice that consequences influence behavior. Philosophers had long debated the role of hedonism (the tendency to seek out pleasure and avoid pain) in behavior. But Thorndike was the first person to show that behavior is systematically strengthened or weakened by its consequences. The basic idea may seem obvious to you now, but in 1898 it was no more obvious than Isaac Newton's law of gravity was in 1687.

**?** QUERY 2: According to Thorndike's law of _____, the strength of a behavior

depends on its _____.

It is fairly obvious that the capacity to benefit from the consequences of our own actions contributes to the survival of an individual and, hence, a species. Anyone who is skeptical will find demonstrations of its value in the research literature. For instance, some years ago Lee Metzgar (1967) released several white-footed mice in a laboratory environment that resembled the animals' natural habitat. After several days, he released more mice and then after several minutes released a screech owl into the area. The owl caught five of the newcomers for every one of the long-term residents. The latter had had time to explore their surroundings; the new arrivals had not. Exploring the surroundings, testing whether they could squeeze between those two rocks, or crawl under that bit of log, or burrow under that pile of leaves, is useful. As real estate agents are wont to say, "It pays to know the neighborhood." And it pays to be able to learn from the consequences of our actions.

## TYPES OF OPERANT LEARNING

Building on the foundation provided by Thorndike, B. F. Skinner began a series of studies in the 1930s that greatly advanced our understanding of learning and behavior. Skinner (1938) built an experimental chamber designed so that an electrically operated food magazine dropped a few pellets of food into a tray (see Figure 5-3). Clark Hull, a prominent psychologist at the time, dubbed the chamber the "Skinner box," and the name quickly caught on and is still heard today. After a rat became accustomed to the noise from the food magazine and readily ate from the tray, Skinner installed a lever; thereafter, food fell into the tray only when the rat pressed the lever. Under these conditions, the rate of lever pressing increased dramatically (see Figure 5-4).

Skinner called experiences whereby behavior is strengthened or weakened by its consequences **operant learning** because the behavior operates on the environment. The behavior is typically instrumental in producing the events that follow it, so this type of learning is also called **instrumental learning.** It goes by other names as well, including response learning, consequence learning, and R-S learning.

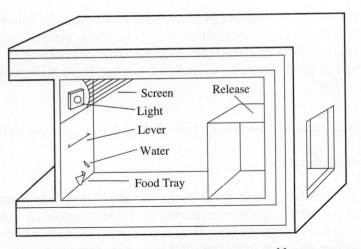

**Figure 5-3** *One of Skinner's original experimental boxes, now generally referred to as a Skinner box. One wall has been cut away to show the inside of the box. The food magazine and other apparatuses were contained in the space outside the left panel. Each time a rat pressed the lever, it activated the food magazine, which dropped a few pellets of food into the tray. (From* The Behavior of Organisms: An Experimental Analysis *[p. 49], by B. F. Skinner, 1938, New York: Appleton-Century-Crofts. Copyright © 1938, renewed 1966. Reprinted by permission of B. F. Skinner.)*

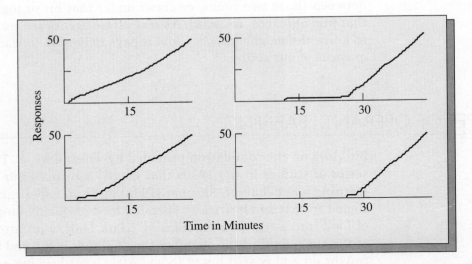

**Figure 5-4** *Lever pressing and reinforcement in four rats. The cumulative records above show that when each lever press was followed by food, the rate of pressing increased rapidly. (For help in interpreting these records, see Figure 2-7.) (Adapted from* The Behavior of Organisms: An Experimental Analysis *[p. 68], by B. F. Skinner, 1938, New York: Appleton-Century-Crofts. Copyright © 1938, renewed 1966. Reprinted by permission.)*

Deviating slightly from Thorndike, Skinner identified four types of operant procedures or experiences: two that strengthen behavior and two that weaken it (see Figure 5-5). In this chapter we will focus on those that strengthen behavior. (We will take up those that weaken behavior in Chapter 8.)

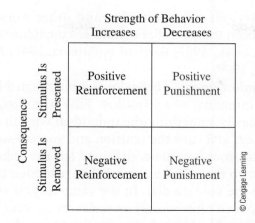

Strength of Behavior
Increases   Decreases

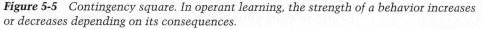

**Figure 5-5**  *Contingency square. In operant learning, the strength of a behavior increases or decreases depending on its consequences.*

In ordinary parlance, *reinforcement* means an increase in strength, as when we reinforce a ceiling by adding columns. In learning, **reinforcement** means an increase in the strength of behavior due to its consequence. Charles Catania (2006) maintains that an experience must have three characteristics to qualify as reinforcement: First, a behavior must have a consequence. Second, the behavior must increase in strength (e.g., occur more often). Third, the increase in strength must be the result of the consequence.

There are, Skinner said, two kinds of reinforcement. In **positive reinforcement,** the consequence of a behavior is the appearance of, or an increase in the intensity of, a stimulus. This stimulus, called a **positive reinforcer,** is ordinarily something the individual seeks out. If you put money into a vending machine and you get the food you want, you are likely to put money into that machine in the future, given the opportunity. And if you play the saxophone and the sound produced is distinctly better than the last time you played it, you may continue playing even if, to other ears, the result is remarkably unmelodic.

Because the consequences involved in positive reinforcement are usually things most people consider rewarding (e.g., success, improved performance, praise, food, recognition, approval, money, special privileges), positive reinforcement is sometimes called **reward learning.** Skinner (1987) objected to the term. "The strengthening effect is missed when reinforcers are called rewards," he wrote. "*People* are rewarded, but *behavior* is reinforced" (p. 19).

Some argue that Skinner is being a bit picky in this, and *reward learning* is seen in the learning literature and even more in the neuroscience and biological literature. But whether you use the term or not, it is important to remember that events that we routinely recognize as rewards often fail to strengthen the behavior they follow. Attention is typically reinforcing, for example, especially with children, but not always (Sy et al., 2010). Even more perversely, some things that would seem to be distinctly *un*rewarding can strengthen the behavior they follow. Strange as it may seem, reprimands,

*If causes must precede their effects, how can an event that follows a behavior strengthen that behavior? The answer is that it doesn't. What is strengthened is not the act the reinforcer follows, but the tendency to engage in that kind of behavior in the future.*

restraint, captivity, electrical shocks, and other normally unpleasant experiences have been found, under certain circumstances, to be reinforcing (e.g., Abramowitz et al., 1987; Bernard & Gilbert, 1941; Morse & Kelleher, 1977; Piazza et al., 1999).

In **negative reinforcement,** a behavior is strengthened by the removal, or a decrease in the intensity, of a stimulus. This stimulus, called a **negative reinforcer,** is ordinarily something the individual tries to escape or avoid. If you get into your car and turn the ignition and you are suddenly blasted by loud music (because your boyfriend/girlfriend left the radio volume at maximum), you turn down the volume control. The reduction in sound reinforces the act of turning the volume dial. In the same way, if your efforts to play the saxophone produce only sounds as welcome to your ears as the scraping of fingernails on a blackboard, you are apt to put the instrument aside. Doing so ends your torture, and this reinforces the act of discontinuing your performance.

What reinforces behavior in negative reinforcement is escaping from an aversive (unpleasant) situation. Once you have learned to do this, you often learn to avoid it entirely. For example, after escaping from the loud noise of your car radio, you may in the future turn down the volume control *before* you turn on the ignition. And instead of escaping from the screeching noise of your saxophone playing, you may "forget" to practice. For this reason, negative reinforcement is sometimes called **escape learning** or **escape-avoidance learning.**

As with positive reinforcement, identifying consequences that will strengthen behavior when they are reduced or removed is not always easy. What *you* find aversive, another person may find rewarding. The only way to be sure if an event is negatively reinforcing is to determine its effect on behavior. If the removal or reduction of a stimulus strengthens behavior, then it is a negative reinforcer.

Note that both positive and negative reinforcement increase the strength of behavior. The difference is that in positive reinforcement, something is added to the situation, while in negative reinforcement something is removed. The terms *positive* and *negative* do not describe the nature of the consequence; they indicate only that something has been added or subtracted.

Although positive and negative reinforcement are often discussed as though they were independent of one another, in reality they often occur together. Thorndike's puzzle box experiments illustrate this. Confinement to a small space is often aversive to cats. If the cat pulled a string and the door fell open, the cat was able to escape from the box. Escape from the box negatively reinforced pulling the string. Once the cat was out of the box, it could eat the food that had been out of reach. Reaching the food positively reinforced pulling the string. So what Thorndike called a satisfying state of affairs was most likely a combination of positive and negative reinforcement.

Another problem with the distinction between positive and negative reinforcement is that what is positively reinforcing at one time can be negatively reinforcing at another. Alan Hundt and David Premack (1963) demonstrated this in a very clever experiment. They put rats in a chamber with a motorized exercise wheel that could be turned on by pressing a lever and turned off by licking water from a dispenser. Once a rat turned the wheel on, it continued to spin (which meant the rat had to run) until the rat licked water (which it had to do while running). The rats pressed the lever and ran for a while, then licked water and stopped exercising. Thus, spinning of the wheel positively reinforced lever pressing, and stopping of the wheel negatively reinforced licking.

Sometimes the distinction between positive and negative reinforcement is impossible to make. Brian Iwata (1987) gives the example of a person in a cold room who turns up the heat. Is the reinforcer an increase in warmth (a positive reinforcer) or a decrease in cold (a negative reinforcer)?

Because of the confusion the positive–negative distinction causes, some experts suggest doing away with it (e.g., Michael, 1975). The question is disputed in journals (see, e.g., Baron & Galizio, 2005, 2006; Chase, 2006; Iwata, 2006; Michael, 2006; Nakajima, 2006; Staats, 2006). Unfortunately, the distinction, the terms, and the confusion persist.

**?** QUERY 3: Positive and negative reinforcement have this in common: Both

_____ behavior.

I have said that reinforcement is an increase in the strength of a behavior due to its consequences. What exactly does *strength* mean? Thorndike and Skinner equated strength with the frequency or probability of the behavior. The emphasis on frequency is understandable because one of the things we most want to know about behavior is how likely it is to occur. However, as John Nevin (1992; Nevin & Grace, 2000) of the University of New Hampshire points out, reinforcement has other strengthening effects besides rate increase: It increases the tendency of the behavior to persist after reinforcement is discontinued; the tendency to occur despite other, aversive consequences (e.g., punishment); the tendency to persist even when more effort is required; and the tendency to persist despite the availability of reinforcers for other behavior. Nevin, who studied engineering before focusing on behavior science, likens the effects of reinforcement to the physicist's concept of momentum. Just as a heavy ball rolling down a hill is less likely than a light ball to be stopped by an obstruction in its path, behavior that has been reinforced many times is more likely to persist when "obstructed" in some way, as (for example) when one confronts a series of failures. Nevin calls this **behavioral momentum** (Mace et al., 1997; Nevin, 1992; Nevin & Grace, 2000).

Allen Neuringer (1986, 2002) notes that *any* feature of a behavior (e.g., its frequency, intensity, duration, persistence, form, etc.) can be strengthened so long as a reinforcer can be made contingent on that particular feature. He notes that even the randomness of behavior can be strengthened with reinforcement (Neuringer,

2002). This may sound like no great trick, but behaving in a truly random fashion is not easy. In one study, Neuringer and his colleague Suzanne Page (Page & Neuringer, 1985) provided reinforcers to pigeons for a series of eight disc pecks, but only when the series of pecks was different from the previous 50 sequences. Under these circumstances, the pecking patterns became almost truly random.

So, while many studies and applications of reinforcement target the frequency of behavior, it's important to keep in mind that reinforcing consequences can modify just about any feature of behavior, not just its frequency. Let's now take a look at the kinds of events that strengthen the behavior they follow.

CAPSULE **REVIEW** The term operant learning indicates that the individual operates on the environment, and the effects of this action strengthen or weaken the behavior. There are four types of operant learning: positive and negative reinforcement and positive and negative punishment. The terms positive and negative have to do with whether something is added or removed following a behavior. Reinforcement of either type strengthens behavior. Reinforcing events cannot be identified a priori; the only proof that a consequence is reinforcing is that it strengthens the behavior it follows.

## B. F. SKINNER: THE DARWIN OF BEHAVIOR SCIENCE

*Of all contemporary psychologists, B. F. Skinner is the most honored and the most maligned, the most widely recognized and the most misrepresented, the most cited and the most misunderstood.*

**—A. Charles Catania**

Burrhus Frederic Skinner was born in Susquehanna, Pennsylvania, in 1904. His mother kept house while his father earned a living as a lawyer.

After high school, he went off to Hamilton College in New York State, where he received a classical education. He continued to enjoy literature, history, music, and the arts throughout his life. After Hamilton, he lived in New York's Greenwich Village for a time and tried to become a novelist. The attempt failed, and, after reading the work of Pavlov and Watson, he went to graduate school at Harvard to study behavior.

After Harvard, Skinner began the research that would eventually be published, in 1938, as *The Behavior of Organisms*. His views on behavior offended many, and Skinner was thereafter attacked and misrepresented. It was the misrepresentation that bothered him more. People erroneously and repeatedly said that he denied the existence of thoughts and feelings; that he denied a role for biology in behavior; that he believed people were robotic machines; that he rejected freedom and dignity. What Skinner actually said and wrote can scarcely be recognized from the writings of his critics (Morris, 2001; Morris, Lazo, & Smith, 2004; Palmer, 2007; Todd & Morris, 1992).

*B. F. Skinner, the Darwin of behavior science, in 1942. (Photograph Courtesy of University Archives, University of Minnesota, Twin Cities.)*

Even Skinner's critics acknowledge, however, that he made many important contributions to our understanding of behavior. He made changes in the rate of behavior a standard measure of learning; made the individual, rather than the group, the object of experimental study; practically invented the ABA research design; replaced Thorndike's subjective terminology with the more precise language we use today; and suggested ways that a natural science of behavior could be applied to medicine, work, child rearing, education, and other fields. Along the way he won practically every award ever given to a psychologist, including the American Humanist of the Year award and the National Medal of Science.

In January 1990, Skinner was diagnosed as having leukemia. It was, he said, not a bad way to go. There would not be much suffering, just an increasing vulnerability to infectious diseases, one of which would, sooner or later, carry him off.

On August 10, 1990, at its annual convention, the American Psychological Association awarded Skinner a special citation for a lifetime of outstanding contributions, the first such award ever granted by the association. Skinner was quite frail, but he approached the podium unassisted, and spoke for 15 minutes without notes. His thesis was a familiar one: Psychologists should embrace the natural science approach to behavior.

It was Skinner's last public appearance. He left the auditorium to return to his home, where he continued rising early in the morning to write in his private study, answer his mail, and greet visitors. Five days later he was admitted to the hospital. On August 19, while in the hospital, he worked on the final draft of an article. The next day he slipped into a coma and died.

It is now more than a hundred years since the death of Charles Darwin, and creationism is still taught in some schools. Yet the basic principles of evolution are understood and taken for granted by most educated people. A hundred years from now traditional ideas about behavior may still prevail, but perhaps the basic principles of behavior will be understood and taken for granted by educated people. If so, much of the credit will have to be given to the Darwin of behavior science, B. F. Skinner.

# KINDS OF REINFORCERS

Some people have attempted to compile lists of reinforcing consequences (see, e.g., Reiss, 2000). These lists, which can be of practical value, are really lists of events that are *typically* reinforcing. The only *defining* feature of a reinforcing event is its effect on behavior. If an event strengthens the behavior it follows, it is a reinforcer; if it doesn't have that effect, it is not a reinforcer. There are many different kinds of reinforcing events. However, most can be classified as primary or secondary and as either natural or contrived.

## Primary and Secondary

**Primary reinforcers** are those that appear to be innately effective, what William Baum (2007) refers to as "phylogenetically significant events." This is typically true, but the defining feature of primary reinforcers is that they are not dependent on learning experiences. Since they are not the product of learning, they are often called **unconditioned reinforcers.** The most obvious primary reinforcers, and the ones most often used in research, are food, water, and sexual stimulation. Others that are readily recognized as innate are sleep, activity (i.e., the opportunity to move about), drugs that produce a high or relieve discomfort, electrical stimulation of certain areas of the brain (see neuromechanics, below), and relief from heat and cold.

There appear to be several other, less obvious, primary reinforcers. Social contact seems to be innately reinforcing among many mammals, including the rat. Mycroft Evans and others (1994) at Reed College found that female rats would press a lever to get access to a male rat. The male rat was not capable of mating, so sexual contact was not the reinforcer. Other female rats got access to food and water by pressing a lever, but these consequences were no more reinforcing than contact with another rat. Humans also find social contact reinforcing, so much so that they have been called the social animal (Aristotle, 1985; Aronson, 2011). Even the loners among us seek company from time to time. The word *hermit* exists in our dictionaries, but hermits seem to be extremely rare.

Another reinforcer that seems to be innate in many species, especially humans, is exerting control over the environment. The developmental psychologist Carolyn Rovee-Collier (1999; Rovee & Rovee, 1969) provides an example of the reinforcing power of control. She loosely tied one end of a soft ribbon to a baby's ankle and the other end to a mobile above the infant's head so that when the baby moved her foot, the mobile moved. The result was that the baby started kicking like a soccer player. Infants as young as eight weeks kicked their foot to make the mobile move. There was no apparent reinforcer for kicking other than seeing the mobile move. Environmental control is reinforcing throughout a person's life.

**?** QUERY **4**: The defining feature of primary reinforcers is that they are *not* dependent on

_____ .

Sociologist John Baldwin (2007) adds sensory stimulation to the list of primary reinforcers. He calls it "the unknown reinforcer" because we seldom recognize its reinforcing qualities. He argues that one reason people become overweight is because of the sensations food provides—the fragrance and texture of the food as well as the taste and the sense of fullness.

In some cases it's difficult to say precisely what it is about a primary reinforcer that makes it effective. Ilze Kalnins and Jerome Bruner, developmental psychologists, showed a film to infants aged 5 to 12 weeks (Kalnins & Bruner, 1973; see also Siqueland & Delucia, 1969). The clarity of the images the babies saw depended on their sucking on an artificial nipple. In one condition, if the baby sucked at a certain rate, the images came into focus; in another condition, sucking at that rate resulted in the images becoming blurred. In each case the infants sucked at the rate required to make the images clear. The study definitely demonstrated reinforcement, but what was reinforcing? Are clear images innately reinforcing, or was the reinforcer the control that the child exerted over the images?

Some of the most powerful primary reinforcers (food, water, and sex, in particular) no doubt played an extremely important role in our survival. Had your ancestors not done the things necessary to produce these reinforcers, it's likely you would not be here. Some primary reinforcers lose their effectiveness rather quickly, however, a phenomenon known as **satiation.** If you have not eaten for some time, food can be a powerful reinforcer, but with each bite the reinforcing power of food is diminished until finally it is ineffective; that is the point of satiation.

**Secondary reinforcers** are those that are *not* innate, but the result of learning experiences. Everyday examples include praise, recognition, smiles, and applause. Because secondary reinforcers normally acquire their reinforcing power by being paired with other reinforcers, including secondary reinforcers, they are also called **conditioned reinforcers.** A demonstration is provided by Donald Zimmerman (1957), who sounded a buzzer for two seconds before giving water to thirsty rats. After pairing the buzzer and water in this way several times, Zimmerman put a lever into the rat's chamber. Each time the rat pressed the lever, the buzzer sounded. The rat soon learned to press the lever, even though lever pressing never produced water. The buzzer had become a conditioned reinforcer.

In another study, W. M. Davis and S. G. Smith (1976) paired a buzzer with intravenous injections of morphine. The researchers then used the buzzer as a reinforcer for lever pressing. Not only was the buzzer an effective reinforcer, but its effectiveness was directly related to the amount of morphine with which it had been paired (see also Goldberg, Spealman, & Goldberg, 1981). It is easy to see how other secondary reinforcers might acquire their powers in essentially the same way. Food reduces hunger, and because one needs money to buy food, money is regularly associated with food. Thus, money acquires its reinforcing properties by being paired with the things it buys.

Even subtle changes in the environment will act as reinforcers if they are regularly paired with other reinforcers. A rat that learns to press a lever for food when a white light is on will, for example, press a lever when a red light is on if doing so causes the red light to become white. With proper training, a rat will press a lever to produce a series of changes in light color, from green to blue to red to white, even though the only time the rat receives food for pressing is when the white light is on. Each change in the light is a secondary reinforcer for pressing. Stop providing food for presses when the white light is on, however, and pressing in the presence of all lights will stop. In other words, the reinforcing power of the various light colors depends on food, a primary reinforcer.

Secondary reinforcers are generally somewhat weaker than primary reinforcers, at least when the organism has been deprived of both for a period, but secondary reinforcers have certain advantages. For one thing, they usually satiate much more slowly than primary reinforcers. Food "wears out" quickly; positive feedback ("That's right," "That's better") does not.

A second advantage of conditioned reinforcers is that it is often much easier to reinforce behavior immediately with them than with primary reinforcers. If you are training a horse to walk with its head held high, you might offer the animal a few grains of oats—a primary reinforcer—each time it does so. But this would require walking to the horse and that would mean a delay in reinforcement and might result in some other behavior being reinforced. If you repeatedly pair the sound made by a clicker (originally, a small metallic toy called a cricket) with oats, you can then reinforce behavior with clicks (Pryor, 1999; Skinner, 1951). The sounds provide immediate reinforcement. If the clicks are sometimes followed by food, they will remain reinforcing. Porpoise trainers use a whistle in the same way (Pryor, 1991).

Another advantage of conditioned reinforcers is that they are often less disruptive than primary reinforcers. Eating and drinking take time. A clicking sound or a word of praise can reinforce behavior without interrupting it.

Conditioned reinforcers also have the advantage that they can be used in many different situations. Food and water are very effective reinforcers when the animal or person is hungry or thirsty but not so much at other times. A stimulus that has been paired with food, however, may be reinforcing even when the animal or person is not at all hungry. Reinforcers that have been paired with many different kinds of reinforcers can be used in a wide variety of situations. Such reinforcers are called **generalized reinforcers** (Skinner, 1953). The most obvious example of a generalized reinforcer may be money.

Although secondary reinforcers have several advantages over primary reinforcers, they have an important disadvantage: Their effectiveness depends on their association with primary reinforcers. Money, for example, is powerfully reinforcing, but money loses its reinforcing capacity once it is no longer "backed up" by other reinforcers. Money printed by the Confederate States of America began to lose its value even before the end of the American Civil War because it could not be exchanged for food, clothing, or other reinforcers. Once the war was over, Confederate money became worthless—except as fuel or mattress stuffing. Primary reinforcers are more resilient: A hungry person will work for food even if the food cannot be exchanged for anything else.

## Natural and Contrived

**Natural reinforcers** are events that follow spontaneously from a behavior: When you get up in the morning you brush your teeth and, as a result, your mouth no longer tastes like a garbage pail; you pedal your bike and the pedaling moves the bike forward; you climb some stairs and reach the floor where your class meets. Each reinforcing event is an automatic consequence of an action, so natural reinforcers are sometimes called **automatic reinforcers.**

**Contrived reinforcers** are events that are provided by someone for the purpose of modifying behavior. For example, a parent may give a child a piece of cookie when the child says "Cook-ee" with the idea of getting her to try to say words. A boss may provide bonuses to highly productive workers to maintain their efforts. And a rehabilitation therapist might show a patient a graph depicting her progress to reinforce her persistence.

The distinction between natural and contrived reinforcers seems clear enough, but sometimes it is blurred. When you put money into a vending machine and receive the drink you want, this seems to be a natural reinforcer: The drink is an automatic consequence of putting coins into a slot. But the vending company arranged the consequence of putting money into a vending machine so that you will put more money into their machines. Similarly, a teacher may compliment the question you ask in class. Is this a spontaneous response to the quality of your question, or is the instructor trying to get you to participate more?

As with primary and secondary reinforcers, the distinction is further confused by the fact that both kinds of consequences often occur together. Consider the child who brushes his teeth. One consequence of brushing is that the mouth feels cleaner, and if this strengthens the tendency to brush, it is a natural reinforcer. Another possible consequence of brushing is that a parent praises the child for doing so. The praise is a consequence arranged by the parent to strengthen the tendency to brush, so it is a contrived reinforcer. The same behavior produces both natural and contrived reinforcers.

Regardless of the kind of reinforcers used, reinforcement can have a powerful effect on behavior. But the power is not uniform; it depends on a number of variables, some of which we will now examine.

---

CAPSULE **REVIEW**    Reinforcers are classified as primary or secondary, contrived or natural. Primary reinforcers are largely innate; secondary (or conditioned) reinforcers are the products of learning. Secondary reinforcers that are effective in a wide variety of situations are called generalized reinforcers. Contrived reinforcers are arranged by someone to change behavior; natural reinforcers are the natural consequence of the behavior they follow.

---

## OPERANT AND PAVLOVIAN LEARNING COMPARED

Operant and Pavlovian learning are often confused, so let's consider the differences between them. The most important difference concerns the role of behavior. In operant learning, an important environmental event normally depends on the performance of behavior: You must *do* something to get food from a vending machine or music from a saxophone. In Pavlovian conditioning, an important event occurs, but it is independent of behavior: First you see the

*(Continued)*

lightning, then you hear the scary thunder. To put it another way, in operant learning an event (the reinforcing or punishing consequence) is contingent on a behavior, whereas in Pavlovian conditioning an event (the US) is contingent on another event (the CS).

Pavlovian and operant learning also involve different kinds of behavior. Pavlovian conditioning typically involves reflexive behavior, such as the blink of an eye or the secretion of digestive juices; operant learning usually involves behavior that is not reflexive, such as the wink of an eye or the purchase of food. The difference in behavior is somewhat problematic, however. It is sometimes difficult, for example, to distinguish between a reflexive eyeblink and an eyewink. Also, behavior that is normally reflexive, such as vomiting, can sometimes be modified by operant procedures (Wolf et al., 1965).

The situation is further complicated by the fact that Pavlovian and operant learning often occur together (Allan, 1998; Davis & Hurwitz, 1977). Consider the case of Little Albert, discussed in Chapter 4. Albert learned to fear a white rat when sight of the rat was followed by a loud noise. This appears to be a simple case of Pavlovian conditioning, and so it is. But read Rayner and Watson's laboratory notes about the experiment:

> White rat which he had played with for weeks was suddenly taken from the basket (the usual routine) and presented to Albert. He began to reach for rat with left hand. Just as his hand touched the animal the bar was struck immediately behind his head. (quoted in Watson, 1930/1970, p. 160)

Note that the loud noise occurred just as Albert *reached for* the rat. Thus, the loud noise followed a nonreflexive (operant) behavior, reaching. Pavlovian conditioning was involved because the rat and the noise occurred together regardless of what Albert did; but operant learning may also have occurred because the loud noise followed reaching for the rat.

Similarly, consider the dog trainer who reinforces the appropriate response to various commands, such as *sit, stay, come, and fetch*. Each appropriate act is followed by a bit of food. Described in this way, this seems to be a simple case of operant learning. But notice that the commands are sometimes followed by food; this pairing of stimuli (command and food) is the essence of Pavlovian conditioning. We may expect, therefore, that the dog will not only learn to respond appropriately to the commands but will also come to enjoy hearing the commands and may even salivate when it hears them.

Operant and Pavlovian learning are like buddies. They are not identical, but they spend a lot of time together.

# VARIABLES AFFECTING OPERANT LEARNING

### Contingency

Where operant learning is concerned, the word *contingency* refers to the degree of correlation between a behavior and its consequence. The stronger this correlation is, the more effective the reinforcer is likely to be. Put another way, the more reliably a reinforcer follows a behavior, the more it strengthens the behavior.

Lynn Hammond (1980) performed an experiment reminiscent of Rescorla's (1968) study on contingency in Pavlovian conditioning (see Chapter 3). Hammond

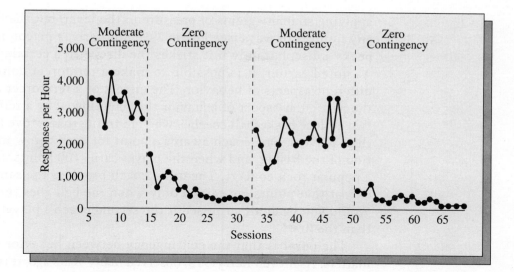

**Figure 5-6**   *Contingency and reinforcement. The mean response rate of lever pressing for ten rats when food was contingent and noncontingent. (Adapted from "The Effect of Contingency upon the Appetitive Conditioning of Free-Operant Behavior," by L. J. Hammond, 1980,* Journal of the Experimental Analysis of Behavior, 34[3], *p. 300. Copyright © 1980 by the Society for the Experimental Analysis of Behavior, Inc. Reprinted with permission.)*

manipulated the probability that food would come after a lever press and in its absence. He found that if rats were as likely to get food by not pressing a lever as they were by pressing it, they did not continue to press the lever (see Figure 5-6).

**QUERY 5:**  _____ refers to the likelihood that a reinforcer will follow a

behavior.

It is easy to see why contingency is important to learning. Learning to touch-type is difficult, even though there is a perfect correlation between the key pressed and the letter that appears on the page or computer monitor. Now imagine learning to type using a keyboard that is defective: Sometimes when you press the letter *a* you get *a*, but sometimes you get *c* or *d* or some other letter. When you press the *c* key, you may get a *c*, but sometimes you get something else. And so on, with each of the 26 letters of the alphabet. Even if you get the appropriate letter 90% of the time (i.e., correct actions are reinforced 9 out of 10 times), learning to touch-type is almost certain to take much longer than with a properly functioning keyboard.

Reinforcers are contingent on various aspects of a behavior, but these are not always obvious. Consider a rat that receives food when it presses a lever. There is a contingency between lever pressing and food, but what does lever pressing mean? Typically, if the rat touches a lever with its paw, nothing happens; if it pushes on the lever slightly, nothing happens; only when the rat depresses the lever far enough to close an electrical circuit that operates the food magazine does it receive food. Thus, food is contingent on applying so many grams of pressure to the lever, but the rat can do that in any number of ways (see Figure 2-3). Similarly, a pigeon receives food if it pecks a disc, but only if it strikes the disc with a certain amount of force. As noted earlier, it is possible to make a reinforcer contingent on many different aspects of behavior. The effects of a reinforcer depend, then, on the particular aspect of behavior that is followed by a reinforcer. Consider two college basketball coaches who are trying to improve the free throws of their players. One coach awards a point for each throw made in the direction of the basket, and when the player earns 100 points, he gets a ticket to a popular rock concert. The other coach provides the same consequences, except that points are earned only when the ball goes through the basket. Would you be at all surprised if the second coach's players improved more than the first?

The point is that the contingency between behavior and consequence matters. As Steven Kerr (1975) observed many years ago, it is folly to reward A and expect to get B.

## Contiguity

Contiguity refers to the gap in time between a behavior and its reinforcing consequence. In general, the shorter this interval is, the faster learning occurs (Escobar & Bruner, 2007; Hunter, 1913; Okouchi, 2009; Schlinger & Blakely, 1994; Thorndike, 1911; see Figure 5-7).

One reason that immediate consequences produce better results is that a delay allows time for other behavior to occur. This behavior, and not the

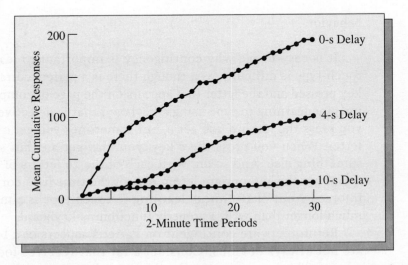

**Figure 5-7** *Contiguity and reinforcement. Mean cumulative responses when reinforcement was immediate, delayed 4 seconds, and delayed 10 seconds. (Adapted from "The Effects of Delayed Reinforcement and a Response-Produced Auditory Stimulus on the Acquisition of Operant Behavior in Rats," by H. D. Schlinger, Jr., and E. Blakely, 1994, The Psychological Record, 44, p. 396, Figure 1. Copyright © 1994 The Psychological Record. Reprinted with permission.)*

contingent behavior, is reinforced. Imagine, for example, that you are learning to pilot an oil tanker. Big ships change direction slowly, so there is a delay between turning the ship's wheel and a change in the ship's direction. You may turn the wheel appropriately, but by the time the ship finally responds, you may have taken some other, inappropriate, action. This inappropriate behavior is then reinforced by the desired change in direction. This delay is no doubt one thing that makes learning to steer great ships difficult.

Even though immediate reinforcement clearly produces faster learning, a number of studies have shown that learning can occur despite reinforcement delays (Dickinson, Watt, & Griffiths, 1992; Lattal & Gleeson, 1990; Wilkenfield et al., 1992). For example, the effects of delaying reinforcement can be muted if the delay is regularly preceded by a particular stimulus. Henry Schlinger and Elbert Blakely (1994) conducted an experiment that compared the effects of signaled and unsignaled delay of reinforcement. They set up a photoelectric beam near the ceiling of an experimental chamber. When a rat broke the beam by rising up on its hind legs, food fell into a dish. For some rats, breaking the beam resulted in immediate food delivery; for others, food came after a four-second or ten-second delay. For some rats receiving delayed reinforcement, a tone sounded immediately after the rat broke the beam. As expected, the results showed very clearly the superiority of immediate reinforcement over delayed reinforcement. They also showed that a four-second delay was less detrimental than a ten-second delay. However, the effects of delay were not so great when the delays were preceded by a tone (see Figure 5-8).

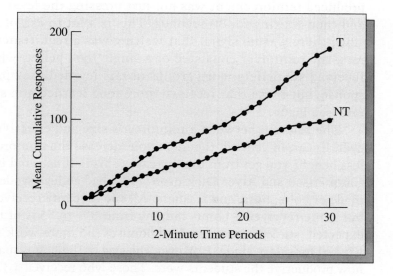

**Figure 5-8**  *Effects of signaled delayed reinforcement. Mean cumulative responses when delayed reinforcement was preceded by a tone (T) and when there was no tone (NT). Reinforcement was delayed 4 seconds in each case. (Adapted from "The Effects of Delayed Reinforcement and a Response-Produced Auditory Stimulus on the Acquisition of Operant Behavior in Rats," by H. D. Schlinger, Jr., and E. Blakely, 1994,* The Psychological Record, 44, *p. 396, Figure 1. Copyright © 1994 The Psychological Record. Reprinted with permission.).*

The effects of delay on reinforcement depend on a number of variables besides signals and is therefore far more complicated than this brief discussion suggests (see, e.g., Doughty et al, 2012; Ito, Saeki, & Green, 2011; Lattal, 2010; Odum, 2011). The bottom line, however, is that Thorndike was right when he suggested that behavior is more likely to be strengthened if "satisfaction" accompanies or closely follows the behavior.

## Reinforcer Characteristics

Reinforcers are not all alike; some work better than others. One important characteristic is size or strength (sometimes referred to as magnitude). Although small reinforcers given frequently usually produce faster learning than large reinforcers given infrequently (Schneider, 1973; Todorov et al., 1984), the size of the reinforcer does matter. Other things being equal, a large reinforcer is generally more effective than a small one (Christopher, 1988; Ludvig et al., 2007; Wolfe, 1936). If you happen to look down while walking along a sidewalk and see a dollar bill, the chances are you will continue looking in that area and may continue looking down even when you go on your way. But the reinforcing effect is apt to be much stronger if what you see is a $100 bill.

A large reinforcer can even counteract the negative effects of reinforcer delay (Lattal & Gleeson, 1990). In a recent study, Adam Doughty, Chad Galuska, and their students (2012) at College of Charleston reinforced lever pressing in rats after a 30-second delay, but only if the rat did not respond again during that 30-second period. In other words, the behavior that produced reinforcement was not just pressing the lever, but pressing *once* and then waiting for 30 seconds. This is a lot to ask of a rat, particularly since there was no signal that waiting was a requirement. For half of the rats, the reinforcer consisted of a single food pellet, while the other rats received six pellets. Both groups of rats learned the "press and wait" response, but those that received more food learned at a significantly faster rate (see Figure 5-9).

The relation between a reinforcer's size and effectiveness is not, however, linear. In general, the more you increase the reinforcer magnitude, the less benefit you get from the increase. This is illustrated in a study in which Carol Frisch and Alyce Dickinson (1990) had college students assemble parts made of bolts, nuts, and washers. All the students received an hourly wage, but some received a bonus ranging from 3% to 55% of the hourly pay. As expected, students who received bonuses did more work than students who worked for salary alone. However, the size of the bonus made no difference in how productive the students were. Those who received a 3% bonus did just as much work as those who received 25% or 55%.

**?** QUERY 6: In general, the more you increase the amount of a reinforcer, the

_____ benefit you get from the increase.

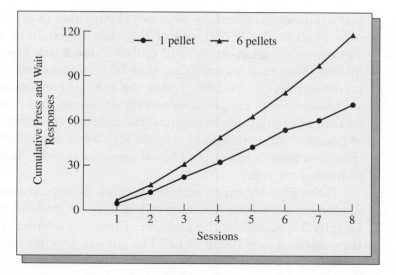

**Figure 5-9** *Reinforcer magnitude combats reinforcer delay. Rats learned to press a lever and then wait 30 seconds without pressing, but those that received six food pellets learned faster than those that received one pellet. (Adapted by Adam Doughty from Figure 2 B in "Effects of Reinforcer Magnitude on Response Acquisition with Unsignaled Delayed Reinforcement" by A. H. Doughty, C. M. Galuska, A. E. Dawson, & K. P. Brierley, Behavioural Processes, 2012, 90, 287–290. Reprinted with permission of the publisher and author.)*

In addition to magnitude, there are qualitative differences in reinforcers. You might think that to a rat, food is food, but in fact rats have rather discriminating tastes. Rietta Simmons (1924) repeatedly ran rats through a maze. Some rats found a bit of bread and milk at the end of the maze; others found a sunflower seed. Rats receiving bread and milk outperformed those that received sunflower seed. M. H. Elliott (1928) performed a similar experiment comparing sunflower seeds with bran mash. Again the group fed sunflower seeds came in second. It would appear that, to the rat, the sunflower seed is a rather inferior food. In other studies, animals and people given a choice between performing a task for either of two reinforcers often show strong preferences (Killeen, Cate, & Tran, 1993; Parsons & Reid, 1990). Identifying preferred reinforcers can improve the effectiveness of a reinforcement procedure in applied settings (Mace et al., 1997).

## Behavior Characteristics

Certain qualities of the behavior being reinforced affect the ease with which it can be strengthened. Obviously, learning to walk a balance beam is easier than learning to walk a tightrope. Less obviously, behavior that depends on smooth muscles and glands is harder to reinforce than behavior that depends on skeletal muscles.

At one time it appeared that reinforcement could increase or decrease the heart rates of rats by 20% (Miller & DiCara, 1967). These astonishing results led people to envision the treatment of medical problems such as high blood pressure and irregular heartbeat through reinforcement.

Unfortunately, researchers were not always able to replicate the early findings. Neal Miller (1978), one of the early researchers in this field, began to express doubts, and he and collaborator Barry Dworkin (Dworkin & Miller, 1986) finally concluded that "the existence of visceral learning remains unproven" (p. 299). Today the general consensus seems to be that such biofeedback can work in certain situations, but (with the exception of treatment of migraine headaches) the benefits are generally too small to be of practical value (Hugdahl, 1995/2001). Even with the best of reinforcers, then, learning to lower your blood pressure is more difficult than learning to lower your voice.

Task difficulty varies with the species. Evolved tendencies can make the reinforcement of behavior more or less difficult (Breland & Breland, 1961; see Chapter 13). Consider the problem of training a bird to peck a lighted disc. How difficult is it likely to be? The answer depends on the kind of bird. It seems likely that it would be considerably easier to train a pigeon to peck a lighted disc than to train a hawk to do so. Pigeons are seed eaters, so pecking is part of their repertoire almost from the moment they crack through their shell. Hawks do not peck; they use their beaks to tear prey apart.

## Motivating Operations

A **motivating operation** is anything that changes the effectiveness of a consequence (Keller & Schoenfeld, 1950; Laraway et al., 2003; Michael, 1982, 1983, 1993). There are two kinds of motivating operations: those that increase the effectiveness of a consequence, and those that decrease its effectiveness. Today these two kinds of procedures are called **establishing operations** and **abolishing operations,** respectively (Iwata, Smith, & Michael, 2000; Laraway et al., 2003).

A good example of an establishing operation is depriving an animal of food; this makes food a more potent reinforcer. For instance, E. C. Tolman and C. H. Honzik (1930) gave rats food on reaching the end of a maze; some rats had been deprived of food, others had not. As Figure 5-10 shows, the former showed greater change than the latter. In general, the greater the level of deprivation (e.g., the longer the interval since eating), the more effective the reinforcer (Cotton, 1953; Reynolds & Pavlik, 1960). Similarly, attention is likely to be more reinforcing after a period without attention (Sy et al., 2010).

Deprivation is not the only kind of establishing operation. If a drug lowers your blood sugar level, sweet foods might become more reinforcing than usual. A rat in a chamber will learn to press a lever if the floor of the chamber provides an electric shock and lever pressing turns off the power for a time. Thus, pain can be an establishing operation. So can fear (Miller, 1948a). Under ordinary circumstances you might not be willing to turn a crank to generate power for a radio, but if a nearby nuclear power plant has shut down, it's likely you would gladly turn the crank to find out whether you are about to be nuked.

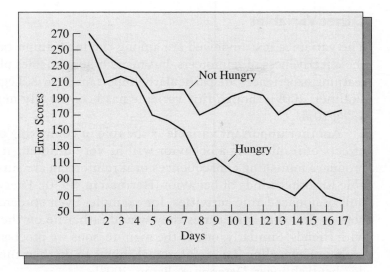

**Figure 5-10** *Food deprivation and learning. Rats that had been deprived of food learned to run a maze (at the end of which they found food) more efficiently than rats that had not been deprived of food. (Adapted from Tolman and Honzik, 1930.)*

? QUERY 7: A motivating operation is anything that changes the effectiveness of a

_____.

In the same way, rest is more reinforcing to someone who has been exercising; physical activity is more reinforcing to a person who has been sitting in classrooms all day; warmth is apt to be reinforcing to someone in a cold room; quiet is often reinforcing in a noisy setting; a computer game is more reinforcing in an environment with little to do; if you are rebuked by an instructor for your work on a project, this is likely to make compliments from other instructors more reinforcing, and so on.

Most establishing operations seem quite predictable, but some are counterintuitive. For example, having to work hard for a reinforcer or having to wait a long time for its delivery seems to make it *more* effective in the future (Zentall & Singer, 2007). Intuitive or not, it is impossible to guarantee that a given consequence will reinforce behavior, but establishing operations can improve the odds.

Most discussions of motivating operations (including this one) focus on establishing operations, but abolishing operations (those that undermine the power of a reinforcer) are also important. Some drugs, for example, reduce the reinforcing effects of food (Northrop et al., 1997, cited in Laraway et al, 2003). This fact can have practical implications. For example, if a drug makes food less reinforcing, it may help people lose weight. Similarly, if a drug reduces the reinforcing power of nicotine or heroin, this may help people end their addiction.

### Other Variables

The variables just reviewed are among the most important in determining the effectiveness of reinforcers, but many other variables play a part. Previous learning experiences are particularly important (Pear & Legris, 1987; Pipkin & Vollmer, 2009), though this variable has been largely neglected (Salzinger, 1996, 2011).

Another important variable is the role of competing contingencies: The effects of reinforcing a behavior will be very different if the behavior also produces punishing consequences or if reinforcers are simultaneously available for other kinds of behavior (Herrnstein, 1970). Every student feels the pull of nonacademic activities, for example. Even students who enjoy their classes find that sometimes they would rather lie on the grass or hang out with friends. Similarly, one of the main reasons we procrastinate is that there are more appealing (i.e., reinforcing) things to do than the things on our "to do" list (Schlinger, Derenne, & Baron, 2008).

The variables discussed here, and others, interact with one another in complex ways, so reinforcement learning is far more complicated than is usually supposed by those who incorrectly refer to it as trial-and-error learning.

CAPSULE **REVIEW**   Reinforcement effects depend on a number of variables. These include the degree of contingency and contiguity, reinforcer characteristics, task characteristics, motivating operations, learning history, competing contingencies, and other variables, all of which interact with one another in complex ways.

## NEUROMECHANICS OF REINFORCEMENT

It seems obvious that there must be a physiological mechanism underlying reinforcement. To put it another way, there must be something in the brain that tells us, when behavior produces a reinforcing consequence, "Hey! That was good. Do it again" (Flora, 2004). What is it, physiologically speaking, that tells us to "do it again"?

Perhaps the first major breakthrough in answering this question came with a brilliant experiment conducted in the 1950s by James Olds, an American psychologist then doing postdoctoral work at McGill University in Canada, and a Canadian graduate student named Peter Milner (Olds & Milner, 1954). Together they implanted an electrode in a rat's brain and connected the electrode by a wire to a weak electrical source. Though tethered by its thin cable, the rat was free to wander around in its experimental area (see Figure 5-11). There was a lever available to the rat, and if it pressed it this completed an electrical circuit between the electrode and the power source. In other words, if the rat pressed the lever, its brain got a mild electric jolt. Sooner or later the rat was bound to press the lever. The question was, would it do so again?

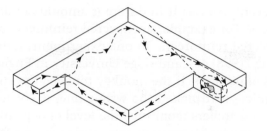

**Figure 5-11** *Brain stimulation as reinforcement. A rat exploring a tabletop enclosure received electrical stimulation of its brain whenever it wandered into a certain area. It repeatedly returned to this area. The dotted line pointing upward represents the connection to the source of electrical stimulation. (From James Olds, "CNS and Reinforcement of Behavior,"* American Psychologist, *1969, 24, p. 115, fi gure 1. Copyright 1969 by the American Psychological Association. Reprinted by permission.)*

It did. Again and again. And again. And again. It wandered about a bit between jolts, but it kept returning to the lever and pressing it. The electrical stimulation of its brain was clearly reinforcing. Olds and Milner had demonstrated the reinforcing potential of electrical stimulation of the brain (ESB). Researchers since then have used ESB to reinforce behavior in a variety of animals including fish, rabbits, dogs, monkeys—and humans (see, e.g., Bishop, Elder, & Heath, 1963). Sanjiv Talwar and his colleagues (2002) at the State University of New York in New York City attached remotely controlled electrodes to the brains of rats. This made it possible for the researchers to deliver ESB from a distance and to reinforce forward movement, right turns, and left turns and thereby direct the rat's course in much the same way that a hobbyist directs the course of a remotely controlled model airplane. Although the rats were free to move about as they wished, the researchers effectively controlled their movement with ESB reinforcement. In fact, their control over the rats was so effective that some journalists called them robo-rats.

*The Talwar study raises ethical concerns that have not escaped the attention of researchers, including Talwar.*

The work of Olds and Milner and others suggested that the implanted electrodes stimulated the brain's "reward center," and the implication was that ordinary reinforcers might be reinforcing because they, too, had the power to stimulate this center. The reward center is now more often called the **reward pathway.** In humans, it is thought to be an area in the septal region (the area separating the two cerebral hemispheres) and running from the middle of the brain to the frontal cortex. Picture a bus line running from a point midway between your ear canals to your forehead, and you'll have a rough idea of where the reward pathway is located. This region is rich in cells that, when stimulated, produce dopamine. **Dopamine** is one of the brain's major neurotransmitters (a chemical that transmits an impulse from one neuron to another) and, more importantly for our purposes, one source of a natural "high."

Just about anything good that happens to us seems to produce an increase in dopamine. How much dopamine is released by a particular event varies. All addictive drugs induce a dopamine release, but cocaine has a stronger effect than, say, alcohol.

The same event can result in different amounts of dopamine depending on circumstances. For example, unexpected reinforcers produce more dopamine than expected reinforcers. In one experiment, Jeffrey Hollerman and Wolfram Schultz (1998) of Cambridge University in England presented monkeys with pairs of pictures. If the monkey touched the correct picture, it got a bit of apple juice; if it picked the wrong one, it got nothing. During the experiment the researchers monitored the level of dopamine in the monkey's brain. Dopamine-producing neurons were active during the early trials, when the monkey was beginning to learn the task, but became less active as it became more skilled. Periodically, however, the researchers gave the monkey an extra, unexpected shot of juice, and this produced an increase in dopamine production.

**? QUERY 8:** Positive reinforcement is associated with the release of _____ in the brain.

It is interesting to note that this and similar findings correspond to behavioral data showing large gains in learning in the early stages of training, followed by steadily smaller gains. This produces the familiar decelerating learning curve. It is possible that one reason for the decline in the rate of learning is that the consequence is less and less surprising and therefore produces less and less dopamine.

Dopamine is a precursor for (i.e., it is converted into) epinephrine, better known as adrenaline, another important neurotransmitter. Adrenaline also provides a rush. An adrenaline high seems to be the chief reason some people participate in (i.e., find reinforcing) certain forms of dangerous activities, such as rock climbing, bungee jumping, and skydiving. I recall a successful lawyer who went skydiving every weekend he could. After a jump, apparently in a state of something approaching euphoria, he waxed enthusiastic about his sport and ended, "I want to do it again and again and again and again and again!" As Flora (2004) points out, that is almost a definition of reinforcement: a consequence that makes us want to do something again.

The point is that it looks as though some neurotransmitters may be at the core of what makes certain experiences reinforcing. No doubt many more discoveries will be forthcoming about the neurological mechanisms of reinforcement. But it is a mistake to assume, as so many people now do, that brain research will one day make studies of the role of experience obsolete. Many people seem to think that if we know what is going on in the brain, we don't need to bother about what is going on in the environment. It is important to remember that what triggers the release of dopamine is usually something happening *outside* the body.

The situation is analogous to the relationship between environment and the genes. Many people still think of genes as dictating physical features and even much of our behavior. But as you saw in Chapter 1, that view has fallen by the wayside, at least among biologists. They now see genes as responding to environmental events, events that have the power to turn them "on" or "off." This does not mean that genes are unimportant, or even that they are less important than the environment; it just means that genes do not themselves dictate behavior. The same thing is true of the relationship between neurophysiology and behavior. What goes on in the brain during reinforcement is important, but what goes on there is usually triggered by events that occur in the environment. In a sense, it is the consequences of behavior that "turn on" or "turn off" the cells that release dopamine.

Consider this analogy: If we wish to understand how a person rides a bicycle, an understanding of the mechanics of the bicycle itself (the way the steering works, the way the pedals move the wheels, and so on) will help. But we would not say that once we have mastered the mechanics of the bicycle we have explained bicycle riding. We must also consider the behavior of the rider. The bicycle does not, after all, ride itself. In the same way, an understanding of the neuromechanics of reinforcement is important, but it cannot, by itself, provide a complete understanding of behavior change. The brain does not ride itself.

To understand reinforcement, we must also consider the "behavior" of the environment. That is what theories of reinforcement attempt to do.

CAPSULE **REVIEW**    Reinforcement must be mediated by anatomical structures and physiological processes. Research to date suggests that the structures are neurons in the septal region of the brain. The neurons most intimately involved seem to be those that produce dopamine and adrenaline, both of which produce generally positive sensations. A complete understanding of reinforcement will require an understanding of the effects of reinforcers in the brain, but neurophysiology cannot, in itself, provide a complete understanding of reinforcement.

## THEORIES OF POSITIVE REINFORCEMENT

We often hear that "practice makes perfect," as if merely performing a skill repeatedly leads inevitably to mastery. Thorndike showed, however, that this idea is in error.

Thorndike (1931/1968) conducted several experiments intended to separate the influence of practice from that of reinforcement. In one experiment, he tried to draw a 4-inch line with his eyes closed. He drew the line over and over again for a total of 3,000 attempts, yet there was no improvement. On the first day of practice, the lines varied from 4.5 to 6.2 inches; on the last day, they varied from 4.1 to 5.7 inches. The medians for each day also revealed no evidence of learning (see Figure 5-12). In a similar experiment, Thorndike

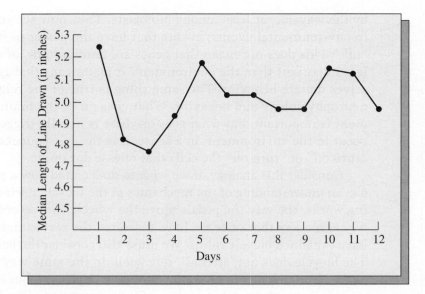

***Figure 5-12*** *The effect of practice without reinforcement. Attempts to draw a 4-inch line while blindfolded showed little improvement. (Compiled from data in Thorndike, 1931/1968.)*

(1927) had students draw a 4-inch line 400 times without feedback; again there was no improvement. After this he had the students draw the line 25 more times, but this time he allowed them to open their eyes after each attempt to see the results of their effort; this time there was marked improvement. Thorndike concluded that practice is important only insofar as it provides the opportunity for reinforcement.

But why do reinforcers strengthen behavior? Many psychologists have attempted to solve the riddle; we will consider the efforts of Hull, Premack, and Timberlake and Allison.

## Hull's Drive-Reduction Theory

Clark Hull (1943, 1951, 1952) believed that animals and people behave because of motivational states called **drives.** For him, all behavior is literally driven. An animal deprived of food, for example, is driven to obtain food. Other drives are associated with deprivation of water, sleep, oxygen, and sexual stimulation. A reinforcer, then, is an event that reduces one or more drives.

Hull's **drive-reduction theory** works reasonably well with primary reinforcers such as food and water because these reinforcers alter a physiological state. But there are many reinforcers that do not seem to reduce physiological needs. Teachers more often reinforce behavior with positive feedback ("OK," "That's right") and praise than with food and water. Employers are more likely to strengthen desirable employee behavior with bonuses and commendations than with sleep. Yet there is no evidence that positive feedback,

*People who don't understand reinforcement claim it is a circular explanation of behavior. But reinforcement doesn't explain anything; it is the name for the increase in behavior strength due to its consequences.*

praise, money, and commendations reduce physiological drives. How, then, can reinforcement be explained in terms of drive reduction? Hull answered this question by suggesting that such secondary reinforcers derive their reinforcing powers from, and are therefore dependent on, their association with drive-reducing primary reinforcers.

The distinction between primary and secondary reinforcers is widely accepted today, but Hull's critics were not satisfied that this distinction saved his theory. They pointed out that some reinforcers are hard to classify as primary or secondary. For instance, we saw earlier that a baby will suck on a pacifier to bring an image into focus (Kalnin & Bruner, 1973; Siqueland & Delucia, 1969). But why does a focused image reinforce behavior? Is there a physiological drive that focused images satisfy? Have focused images been paired with other reinforcers, such as food?

Even reinforcers that normally seem related to a physiological condition may not depend on drive reduction. For instance, male rats find the opportunity to copulate with a sexually receptive female reinforcing, a fact that seems consistent with Hull's theory. But Frederick Sheffield and his colleagues (1951, 1954) found that rats would work for such an opportunity even when the rats were interrupted before the male ejaculated. Copulation without ejaculation would not seem to reduce a drive, yet it was reinforcing. Is it reinforcing because copulation has been associated with other reinforcers? How likely is that in a rat? Moreover, edible substances such as saccharin that have no nutritional value, and therefore no drive-reducing value, nevertheless are reinforcing.

Because of such problems, most psychologists today find Hull's drive-reduction theory an unsatisfactory explanation of why reinforcers work. There are just too many reinforcers that neither reduce drives nor acquire their reinforcing properties from their association with primary reinforcers. Hull is not without his defenders (see Smith, 1984), but most researchers find other theories of reinforcement more attractive.

## Relative Value Theory and the Premack Principle

David Premack (1959, 1965) took an altogether different approach to the problem of reinforcement. Whereas reinforcers are ordinarily viewed as stimuli, Premack noticed that they can be thought of as behavior. Take the case of reinforcing lever pressing with food. The reinforcer is usually said to be the delivery of food, but it can just as easily be considered the act of eating the food. This idea sets the stage for Premack's theory.

It is clear, said Premack, that in any given situation some kinds of behavior have a greater likelihood of occurrence than others. A rat is typically more likely to eat, given the opportunity to do so, than it is to press a lever. Thus, different kinds of behavior have different values, relative to one another, at any given moment. It is these relative values, said Premack, that determine the reinforcing properties of behavior. This theory, which may be called the **relative value theory,** makes no use of assumed physiological drives. Nor does it depend on the distinction between primary and secondary reinforcers. To determine whether a given activity will reinforce another, we need know only the relative values of the activities.

As a measure of the relative values of two activities, Premack suggested measuring the amount of time a participant engages in both activities, given a choice between them. According to Premack, reinforcement involves a relation, typically between two behaviors, one of which is reinforcing the other. This leads to the following generalization: Of any two responses, the more probable response will reinforce the less probable one. This generalization, known as the **Premack principle,** is usually stated somewhat more simply: *High-probability behavior reinforces low-probability behavior.*

The Premack principle suggests that if a rat shows a stronger inclination to drink than to run in an exercise wheel, drinking can be used to reinforce running. Premack (1962) tested this idea by conducting an experiment in which he deprived rats of water so that they were inclined to drink and then made drinking contingent on running: To get a drink, the rats had to run. The result was that the time spent running increased; in other words, drinking reinforced running.

**QUERY 9:** According to the Premack principle, _____ behavior reinforces

_____ behavior.

Premack's theory says that it is the relative value of activities that determines their reinforcement value. This theory implies that the relationship between drinking and running could be reversed, that running could reinforce drinking if the relative value of running could be made greater than that of drinking. Premack tested this idea by providing rats with free access to water but restricting their access to the exercise wheel. He then made running contingent on drinking: To get to the exercise wheel, the rats had to drink. Under these circumstances, drinking increased; in other words, running reinforced drinking (see Figure 5-13).

In another experiment, Premack (1959) gave first graders the opportunity to eat candy dispensed from a machine or to play a pinball machine. The children could stick with one activity or alternate between the two. Some children spent more time at the pinball machine; others preferred to eat candy. After identifying these relative values, Premack made access to each child's more probable behavior contingent on performance of that child's less probable behavior. For instance, a child who preferred playing pinball now had to eat candy to get access to the pinball machine. The result was that the less probable behavior increased.

Premack's theory of reinforcement has the advantage of being strictly empirical; no hypothetical concepts, such as drive, are required. An event is reinforcing simply because it provides the opportunity to engage in

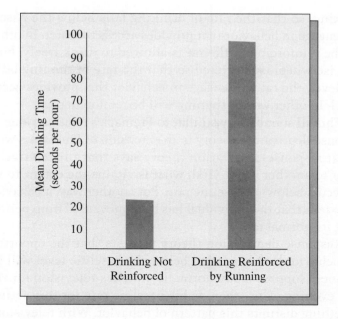

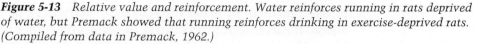

**Figure 5-13**  *Relative value and reinforcement. Water reinforces running in rats deprived of water, but Premack showed that running reinforces drinking in exercise-deprived rats. (Compiled from data in Premack, 1962.)*

preferred behavior. The theory is not without its problems, however. One problem concerns those troublesome secondary reinforcers. As Premack (1965) himself notes, his theory does not explain why the word *yes* (for example) is often reinforcing. Another problem with the theory is that low-probability behavior will reinforce high-probability behavior if the participant has been prevented from performing the low-probability behavior for some time (Eisenberger, Karpman, & Trattner, 1967; Timberlake, 1980). The latter problem has led some researchers to turn to response-deprivation theory.

## Response-Deprivation Theory

Because of the problems with Premack's relative value theory, William Timberlake and James Allison (1974; Timberlake, 1980) proposed a variation of it called **response-deprivation theory** (also sometimes called equilibrium theory or response-restriction theory). The central idea of this theory is that behavior becomes reinforcing when the individual is prevented from engaging in the behavior at its normal frequency.

Any behavior that occurs with some frequency has a baseline level. For instance, if a rat is given the opportunity to drink or run in an exercise wheel whenever it likes, it will, over a period of time, establish steady rates for each behavior. Response-deprivation theory predicts that if we restrict access to drinking, so that the rate of drinking falls below the baseline level, the rat will engage in behavior that provides access to water. In other words, drinking will be reinforcing. If the rat is allowed to drink freely, but its access to the exercise wheel is restricted so that the rate of running falls below the baseline level, the rat will engage in behavior that provides access to the exercise wheel. In other words, running will be reinforcing.

This all sounds very similar to Premack's relative value theory, and indeed response-deprivation theory is an extension of Premack's work. The difference is that response-deprivation theory says that the relative value of one reinforcer to another is not vital; what is vital is the extent to which each behavior occurs below its baseline rate. Put another way, a behavior is reinforcing to the extent that the individual has been prevented from performing that behavior at its normal rate.

Response-deprivation theory predicts that the opportunity to engage in any behavior that has fallen below the baseline level will be reinforcing. For instance, suppose a boy normally watches television for three or four hours each evening. This, then, is his baseline rate for this activity. Now suppose something disrupts this pattern of behavior. With television viewing reduced to, say, one hour, he is likely to engage in activities that provide access to television. If carrying out the garbage or performing other household chores earns him a chance to watch television, the frequency of such activities is likely to increase.

**? QUERY 10:** According to response-deprivation theory, schoolchildren are eager

to go to recess because they have been deprived of the opportunity to

_____.

Response-deprivation theory works well enough for many reinforcers, but like the theories of Hull and Premack, it has trouble explaining the reinforcing power of *yes*. Words such as *yes, right,* and *correct* can be powerfully reinforcing. Recall that when Thorndike provided such feedback to students attempting to draw a 4-inch line while blindfolded, they improved rapidly (Thorndike, 1927). How are we to fit such findings into response-deprivation theory? Still, response-deprivation theory provides an intriguing way of looking at the problem of reinforcement.

The theories of reinforcement considered so far concentrate on positive reinforcement. Some researchers have focused their attention on explaining avoidance, and it is to these theories that we now turn.

CAPSULE **REVIEW**    Many theorists have wondered what it is about reinforcers that makes them reinforcing. Hull proposed the drive-reduction theory, based on the idea that reinforcers reduce a drive caused by physiological deprivation. Premack's relative value theory discards the drive concept and argues that reinforcers are effective because they provide access to preferred kinds of behavior. The response-deprivation theory of Timberlake and Allison suggests that reinforcement depends on the discrepancy between the baseline rate of a behavior and the present opportunity to perform the behavior.

## THEORIES OF AVOIDANCE

In negative reinforcement, a behavior is strengthened when it is followed by the removal of a stimulus. This stimulus is an aversive event—that is, something the animal or person will normally escape or avoid, given the opportunity. Richard Solomon did research on negative reinforcement with shuttle boxes. In one study, Solomon and Lyman Wynne (1953) put a dog in one compartment of a shuttle box. After a time the light in the compartment went off, and 10 seconds later the dog received a shock through the floor. Typically the dog whimpered and moved about in an agitated manner for a time and then jumped over the hurdle to the second compartment. The light in this compartment was on, and there was no shock. Some time later the light went out and, 10 seconds later, the floor would again provide a shock. The dog again escaped the shock by jumping to the other compartment. With each trial the dog endured the shock for a shorter period before jumping. Soon it jumped the instant the shock began. Eventually the dog began jumping when the light went off and thereby avoided shock entirely. After once avoiding shock, most dogs received few additional shocks.

Researchers have conducted the same sort of experiment many times with rats and other creatures, including (in modified form) humans, with similar results.

The fact that an animal jumps a hurdle when shocked is not particularly puzzling: Escape from an aversive stimulus is reinforcing. But why does it perform an act that avoids shock? As Murray Sidman (1989a) noted, "Successful avoidance meant that something—the shock—did not happen, but how could something that did not happen be a reinforcer?" (p. 191). After all, Sidman adds, things are not happening all the time! It seems illogical to say that things that do not happen can explain things that do happen, so explaining avoidance became a major theoretical problem. Two main accounts of avoidance have been offered: two-process theory and one-process theory.

### Two-Process Theory

**Two-process theory** says that two kinds of learning experiences are involved in avoidance learning: Pavlovian and operant (Mowrer, 1947). Consider the dog that learns to jump a hurdle to escape a shock. A light goes off, and shortly afterward the dog receives a shock. Soon after that the dog jumps over the hurdle to a shock-free compartment. Escaping shock is negatively reinforcing, so the dog soon jumps the hurdle as soon as the shock begins.

But wait: If the trials continue, the dog begins to jump the hurdle before it is shocked. It learns not only to escape shock but also to avoid it. Why? What reinforces jumping when there is no shock to escape?

This is where Pavlovian conditioning comes in. Recall that before the shock begins, a light goes out. Shock is a US for fear. Any stimulus that reliably precedes a US for fear becomes a CS for fear. So, through Pavlovian conditioning, the extinguished light becomes a CS for fear. The dog can escape this aversive stimulus (the dark chamber) by jumping the hurdle, and this is what it does. Thus, jumping before receiving a shock is reinforced by escape from the dark compartment.

According to two-process theory, then, there really is no such thing as avoidance, there is only escape: First the dog escapes the shock, and then it escapes the dark chamber.

**QUERY 11:** The two processes in two-process theory are _____ and

_____.

Two-process theory fits all the essential facts. In addition, the theory leads to logical predictions that can be tested. In one experiment, Neal Miller (1948a) demonstrated that escape from an aversive situation can reinforce behavior. He put rats into a white compartment and shocked them. They soon learned to jump through a door to a neighboring black compartment where they did not receive shocks. Miller put the rats in the white compartment again, but this time he did not shock them. Once again the rats went to the black compartment, even though there were no shocks to escape. The rats, it seems, were escaping from the white compartment. Miller put the rats into the white compartment again, but this time he closed the door. The rats could escape to the black compartment by turning a wheel that opened the door, and they soon learned to do so even though, once again, there were no shocks in the white compartment (see Figure 5-14a). Miller put the rats into the white compartment and again closed the door, but this time turning the wheel did nothing; to escape to the black compartment, the rats had to press a lever. The rats soon gave up on the wheel and learned to press the lever even though, as before, there were no shocks (see Figure 5-14b). These experiments suggest that pairing the white compartment with shock caused it to affect behavior in much the same way as the shock. Through association with shock, the white compartment had become a CS for fear, and escaping from it was reinforcing.

Unfortunately, not all tests of two-process theory have produced supportive evidence (Herrnstein, 1969). The idea that the avoidance behavior is reinforced by escape from an aversive CS leads logically to the prediction that if the CS were to lose its aversiveness, the avoidance behavior would cease to

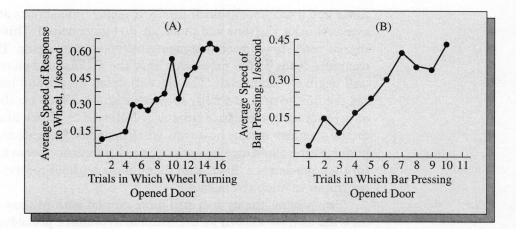

**Figure 5-14**  *Two-process theory and escape. After a white compartment was paired with shock, a rat learned to turn a wheel (A) and press a lever (B) when these acts enabled it to escape the compartment. (Adapted from Miller, 1948, Figures 2 and 4, pp. 94 and 96.)*

occur. There is evidence that the signal for shock does lose its aversiveness, yet the avoidance response persists!

Solomon and Wynne (1953; see description above) noticed that the dogs in their study showed considerable evidence of fear of the CS in the early stages of learning, but once they had learned to avoid shock, the CS no longer seemed to trouble them. Leon Kamin and his colleagues (1963) conducted an experiment to see whether Solomon and Wynne were right. In their experiment, they first trained rats to press a lever for food. Then they trained the animals to escape shock in a shuttle box, with the shock preceded by a tone. Training continued until the rats had avoided shock from 1 to 27 times. Then the researchers returned the rats to the original training chamber where they could press a lever for food. An aversive CS will reduce the rate of ongoing behavior (such as lever pressing), a phenomenon called conditioned suppression. Kamin and his coworkers used conditioned suppression as a measure of the aversiveness of the sound that signaled shock. While the rats were in the chamber with the lever, the researchers sounded the tone to see whether it would suppress the rate of lever pressing. They found that the rats that had avoided shock 27 times showed less fear (i.e., conditioned suppression) than those that had avoided shock fewer times. This is consistent with what Solomon and Wynne noticed: Fear of the CS decreases as the animal learns to avoid shock. This finding poses a problem for two-process theory, for if the CS becomes less frightening as avoidance training continues, what reinforces the avoidance behavior?

A related problem for two-process theory has to do with the·failure of avoidance behaviors to extinguish. Consider the rat that can avoid shock by jumping a hurdle when a tone sounds. As learning proceeds, the rat receives fewer and fewer shocks until finally it receives no shocks at all. When the rat avoids shocks, the tone and shock are no longer paired. This means that escaping the tone should become progressively less reinforcing. Two-process theory therefore leads to the prediction that the avoidance behavior, once learned, will begin to extinguish: The rat will delay longer and longer before jumping the hurdle until it finally receives a shock. Thus, we should see a pattern of deteriorating avoidance behaviors followed by shock and escape. The predicted scenario is not, however, what happens. Instead, the animal steadily performs the avoidance behavior. Indeed, avoidance behaviors are remarkable for their persistence. Even after many trials without receiving a shock, the rat continues to jump the hurdle.

Two-process theory lost still more ground with Murray Sidman's research on what is now known as the **Sidman avoidance procedure** (Sidman, 1953, 1966). In this procedure, the shock is not preceded by a tone or other signal. A rat receives shocks at regular intervals through a grid floor, but it can delay the shocks for 15 seconds by pressing a lever. If it presses the lever again before the end of this delay period, it earns another 15-second delay. Thus, by pressing the lever regularly, the rat can completely avoid shock. The important aspect of the Sidman procedure is that there is no signal (no light going off, no tone sounding) correlated with impending shock. Sidman found that not much happened at first: The rat received shocks periodically and, between shocks, it explored the chamber. But after several minutes, the rat began to press the lever and delay some shocks, therefore receiving fewer shocks each minute. This was bad news for two-process theory because no signal means no aversive stimulus to escape, and escape from an aversive stimulus is what is supposed to reinforce avoidance behavior.

Douglas Anger (1963) proposed that there is a signal in the Sidman procedure: time. The shocks, said Anger, occur at regular intervals. The passage of time therefore signals the approach of shock. The animal does not escape the CS in the same way it might by jumping a hurdle, but it is allowed to get "further away" from the shocks—further away in terms of time, not distance.

Anger's proposal raised a new dilemma: How could one rule out the possibility that time became a CS in escape-avoidance situations? Richard Herrnstein and Phillip Hineline (1966) provided an elegant solution to this problem. In their experiment, rats had a choice: If they pressed a lever at a steady rate, they would receive shocks an average of once every 20 seconds; if they did not press the lever, they would receive shocks an average of about once every 7 seconds. Note that these shock intervals are merely averages: A rat might press the lever and get an immediate shock, or it might not press the lever and receive no shock for several seconds. Still, the rat was better off, in the long run, if it pressed the lever. What Herrnstein and Hineline had done was to render time useless as a possible signal for shock. According to two-process theory, no signal means no avoidance behavior, yet 17 of the 18 rats in the Herrnstein and Hineline experiment learned to press the lever and avoid shocks. The problems with two-process theory have led many researches to embrace one-process theory.

### One-Process theory

One-process theory proposes that avoidance involves only one process: operant learning (Herrnstein, 1969; Sidman, 1962). Both escape and avoidance behaviors are reinforced by a reduction in aversive stimulation. Consider, once again, the dog in the shuttle box. A light goes off, and a few seconds later it receives a shock. Jumping a hurdle is reinforced by the termination of shock. So far, so good. But what is the reinforcer for avoiding shock? Two-process theorists said that the absence of shock could not reinforce behavior: How can something that does not happen be a reinforcer? But one-process theory says that something does happen: There is a reduction in exposure to shock, and this is reinforcing.

The Herrnstein and Hineline (1966) study described above supports one-process theory, and so do other experiments. But what about the extreme resistance of avoidance behaviors to extinction? Can one-process theory explain this? One-process theory says that the animal that has learned to avoid shocks by jumping a barrier continues to do so because by doing so it continues to avoid shock. If this is the case, one way to get the animal to stop jumping the hurdle would be to prevent it from jumping after you have disconnected the shock apparatus. The animal would try unsuccessfully to jump the hurdle, and—nothing would happen. No shock! After several such trials, when the animal is again free to jump the hurdle, it should decline to do so. And this is just what happens. In fact, the best way to get an animal (or person) to stop performing an unnecessary avoidance behavior is to prevent the behavior from occurring.

One-process theory of avoidance has an elegant simplicity, but it cannot be said to have won the day. In 2001, a prestigious journal devoted a special section to an article making the case for two-factor theory (Dinsmoor, 2001) and to commentaries by other experts. The debate rages on.

---

CAPSULE **REVIEW**    Avoidance learning has generated its own distinct theories. Two-process theory assumes that both Pavlovian and operant learning are involved. One-process theory explains avoidance entirely in terms of operant procedures.

---

## A FINAL WORD

Operant learning, like Pavlovian conditioning, is often dismissed as trivial. It is, some argue, the means by which pets and circus animals learn tricks and people acquire habits. In fact, operant learning is about as important to human survival as oxygen. It is also arguably the chief means by which we pursue happiness.

The process of learning from consequences is analogous to the process by which species change through natural selection. Thorndike wrote, for example, that a cat in a puzzle box does many different things to escape, and "from among these movements one is *selected by success*" (p. 14; emphasis added). Just as the environment selects certain genetic features of a species, such as skin color and innate behavior, it also selects certain kinds of behavior of an individual, such as stepping on treadles and reading textbooks.

But operant learning is not merely a means of establishing or breaking simple habits. In the chapters that follow you will see not only how various patterns of consequences affect behavior, but also that operant learning accounts for some of the most sophisticated forms of human behavior and has generated more practical applications than any other approach to behavior. Studying these chapters may prove difficult, but I can (almost!) guarantee that the consequences of doing so will make the effort well worthwhile.

## RECOMMENDED **READING**

1. Bjork, D. W. (1993). *B. F. Skinner: A life*. New York: Basic Books.

   This is a readable and authoritative look at the life and work of the most important figure in the history of learning. I found Skinner's autobiography more interesting, but it is three volumes.

2. Lattal, K. A. (1998). A century of effect: Legacies of E. L. Thorndike's *Animal Intelligence* monograph. *Journal of the Experimental Analysis of Behavior, 70*, 325–336.

   Lattal reviews Thorndike's work and the profound effect it has had on psychology in general and on learning in particular.

3. Schneider, S. (2012). *The science of consequences: How they affect genes, change the brain, and impact our world*. New York: Prometheus Books.

   This is a highly readable and entertaining exploration of the ways that the consequences of our behavior change us. It is a "must read" for all psychology majors.

4. Skinner, B. F. (1953). *Science and human behavior*. New York: Free Press.

   Skinner's views are often misrepresented, even in college texts. In this book, you find that what Skinner believed is quite different from what many people say he believed. See especially Chapters 5 and 6, which bear directly on the subject matter of the present chapter.

5. Thorndike, E. L. (1898). Animal intelligence. *Psychological Review Monographs, 2*(8).

   This is one of the seminal works in learning and, indeed, in all of behavior science, and for behavior scientists to not read it is, in my view, comparable to a biologist not reading Darwin's *Origins*. More than a hundred years after its publication, it is frequently cited not only in psychology but in biology and neuroscience. It is a doctoral dissertation that reads more like a trade book. If your library doesn't have it, look for his 1911 book, *Animal Intelligence*.

## REVIEW **QUESTIONS**

1. Define the following terms in your own words:

| | |
|---|---|
| automatic reinforcer | one-process theory |
| behavioral momentum | operant learning |
| conditioned reinforcer | positive reinforcement |
| contrived reinforcer | positive reinforcer |
| dopamine | Premack principle |
| drive-reduction theory | primary reinforcer |
| establishing operation | reinforcement |
| escape-avoidance learning | relative value theory |
| generalized reinforcer | response-deprivation theory |
| instrumental learning | reward learning |
| law of effect | reward pathway |
| motivating operation | satiation |
| natural reinforcer | secondary reinforcer |
| negative reinforcement | Sidman avoidance procedure |
| negative reinforcer | two-process theory |

2. One of Skinner's chief contributions to behavior science is said to be the use of the rate of behavior as a dependent variable. How does this approach differ from Thorndike's studies of chicks running mazes?

3. If a pain stops after taking medicine, this is usually considered a positive thing, so why is it called negative reinforcement if the tendency to take the drug is strengthened?

4. What is the single most important difference between Pavlovian and operant learning?

5. Why does a delay in a reinforcer reduce its strengthening power?

6. A classmate argues that ESB is both a primary and a contrived reinforcer. Do you agree? Why or why not?

7. Some people argue that neuroscience will explain all of behavior, including learning. Why is this view mistaken?

8. Why is the Premack principle sometimes called Grandmother's Rule?

9. What are the problems with the drive-reduction theory of reinforcement?

10. What is the chief difference between Premack's relative value theory and Timberlake and Allison's response-deprivation theory?

## PRACTICE **QUIZ**

1. The relationship between behavior and consequences is called the law of _____.

2. Reinforcement occurs when the consequences of a behavior _____ the behavior.

3. Negative reinforcement is sometimes called _____ learning.

4. John Nevin suggests that the increase in strength due to reinforced can be considered behavioral _____.

5. The most important difference between Pavlovian and operant learning concerns the role of _____.

6. An important variable in operant learning that has been largely neglected is _____.

7. There are two kinds of motivating operations. Those that increase the effectiveness of a reinforcer are called _____.

8. According to David Premack, reinforcement involves a relation between a high-_____ behavior and a low-_____ behavior.

9. According to _____ theory, an activity becomes reinforcing when an individual is prevented from engaging in it at the baseline rate.

10. The two processes of the two-process theory of avoidance are _____ and _____.

## QUERY **ANSWERS**

Query 1. Thorndike studied animal learning as a way of measuring animal *intelligence*.

Query 2. According to Thorndike's law of *effect*, the strength of a behavior depends on *its consequences*.

Query 3. Positive and negative reinforcement have this in common: Both *strengthen* behavior.

Query 4: The defining feature of primary reinforcers is that they are *not* dependent on *learning*.

Query 5. *Contingency* refers to the likelihood that a reinforcer will follow a behavior.

Query 6. In general, the more you increase the amount of a reinforcer, the *less* benefit you get from the increase.

Query 7. A motivating operation is anything that changes the effectiveness of a *reinforcer*.

Query 8. Positive reinforcement is associated with the release of *dopamine* in the brain.

Query 9. According to the Premack principle, *high-probability/likely/strong* behavior reinforces *low-probability/unlikely/weak* behavior.

Query 10. According to response-deprivation theory, schoolchildren are eager to go to recess because they have been deprived of the opportunity to *move about/exercise*.

Query 11. The two processes in two-process theory are *Pavlovian conditioning* and *operant learning*.

# 6 Reinforcement: Beyond Habit

*Established scientific principles are sufficient to account for puzzling phenomena.*

**—David Palmer**

## PREVIEW

You have seen that much of our behavior operates on our environment, affecting it in ways that then make us more or less likely to persist in that behavior. While it is impossible to deny the reality of such operant learning, some people underestimate its importance, dismissing it as merely the means by which habits are established or broken. New forms of behavior, especially the sudden solution of a problem (the "Aha!" experience of insight) and creative acts, it is claimed, are the products of a mysterious, unpredictable, and ultimately unknowable mind. And other kinds of human behavior are, it is said, too complicated to be accounted for by something as simple as the law of effect. The natural science approach to learning rejects this view. In this chapter, we will consider how reinforcement takes us beyond habit.

# SHAPING NEW BEHAVIOR

We saw earlier that if lever pressing results in food falling into a tray, the rate of lever pressing typically increases (see Figure 5-4). But what if the rat never presses the lever? *You cannot reinforce a behavior that does not occur.*

One answer is to reinforce any behavior that resembles lever pressing. Suppose a hungry rat is sitting in a corner, away from the lever, scratching and grooming. You watch carefully, and when the rat turns its head toward the lever, you press a button that causes a few food pellets to fall into the food tray. This operation causes a sound that has been paired with food several times in the past. As a result, the rat immediately goes to the food tray and eats. After eating, the rat wanders around a bit but eventually turns again toward the lever. You press the button again, and the rat immediately runs to the food dish and eats. After a few more reinforcements, the rat is spending most of its time in the vicinity of the food tray. Now you begin reinforcing any movement toward the lever until the rat is next to it. When the rat touches the lever in any way, you reinforce that behavior. Soon the rat presses the lever, and you provide reinforcement. Now you provide reinforcement only when the rat presses the lever, and soon it presses the lever steadily, stopping only to go to the food tray and eat.

This training procedure, the reinforcement of successive approximations of a desired behavior, is called **shaping** (Skinner, 1951). Shaping makes it possible to establish behavior in a few minutes that rarely or never occurs spontaneously (see Figure 6-1). Had Thorndike known about the reinforcement of successive approximations, he very likely would have had the dog going to the corner on command in a very short time.

**QUERY 1:** Shaping is the reinforcement of successive _____ of a desired

behavior.

Skinner (1977) describes how he shaped the behavior of his daughter, Deborah, when she was less than a year old. Skinner held Deborah on his

***Figure 6-1*** *Shaping clockwise turns. As viewed from above, a pigeon is shown at points at which its behavior was reinforced. At first (extreme left figure), any turn to the right produced food. After this, reinforcement required successively closer approximations of a complete circle. The first complete circle appeared after about 15 minutes of shaping. (Figures drawn by Diane Chance from photographs by Paul Chance.)*

lap, and when the room grew dark he turned on a nearby table lamp. Deborah smiled at this, so Skinner decided to see if the light would reinforce her behavior. He turned off the light and waited until Deborah lifted her left hand slightly, then turned the light on and off quickly. She moved her hand again, and Skinner turned the light on and off. Gradually, Skinner required bigger and bigger arm movements for reinforcement until Deborah was moving her arm in a wide arc "to turn on the light" (p. 179).

*Shaping comes from science, but its practical application is an art.*

The shaping procedure can be put to more practical use. A teacher can praise a student's first efforts at printing the alphabet even though the letters are barely recognizable. Once the student can easily make these crude approximations, the teacher can require something better for reinforcement. In this way, the teacher gradually "ups the ante" until the student prints the letters clearly. Similarly, a rehabilitation therapist may place relatively mild demands on a patient at first and congratulate the patient for achieving them. When the patient becomes comfortable with the required task, the therapist can raise the standard slightly and proceed as before.

## THE SHAPING OF SHAPING

Once you have learned about shaping, it may seem an obvious way to generate new behavior. It wasn't obvious to E. L. Thorndike. Here is how he describes his attempts to teach a dog to go to the corner of a large pen on command:

> I would pound with a stick and say, "Go over to the corner." After an interval (10 seconds for 35 trials, 5 seconds for 60 trials) I would go over to the corner (12 feet off) and drop a piece of meat there. He, of course, followed and secured it. On the 6th, 7th, 16th, 17th, 18th and 19th trials he did perform the act before the 10 seconds were up, then for several times went during the two-minute intervals without regarding the signal, and finally abandoned the habit altogether. (1898, p. 77)

Shaping was not obvious to B. F. Skinner, either. In 1943 he and two of his graduate students, Keller Breland and Norman Guttman, decided to teach a pigeon to bowl. The goal was to get the bird to hit a ball with a sideward sweep of its beak, sending the ball toward some tiny pins. The plan was to reinforce each swipe with food. They put a ball on the floor of the experimental chamber and waited for the first swipe, but the behavior didn't occur. Skinner (1958a) describes what followed:

> Though we had all the time in the world, we grew tired of waiting. We decided to reinforce any response which had the slightest resemblance to a swipe—perhaps, at first, merely the behavior of looking at the ball—and then to select responses which more closely approximated the final form. The result amazed us. In a few minutes, the ball was caroming off the walls of the box as if the pigeon had been a champion squash player. (p. 94)

Skinner and his students had molded a new behavior—something the bird did not naturally do—by reinforcing any behavior that remotely resembled it and then reinforcing closer and closer approximations of it. This was the first scientific demonstration of shaping.

Once people learn about a scientific breakthrough, it often seems obvious: Harvey's discovery of the circulation of the blood; Benjamin Franklin's discovery that lightning is electricity; Louis Pasteur's discovery that bacteria cause disease. But if you think shaping is obvious, ask someone who hasn't heard about it or seen it used how he or she would train a dog to walk to the corner of a pen on command.

Shaping is not just an instructional tool; it is also a naturally occurring phenomenon. For example, people often unwittingly shape *undesirable* behavior in others. Tantrums, for example, are often the product of shaping. A tired parent may give in to a child's repeated requests "to shut him up." On the next occasion, the parent may resist giving in to the child's demands. The child responds by becoming louder or by crying, and the parent yields to avoid causing a scene. On a subsequent occasion, determined to regain control, the parent may refuse to comply when the child cries or shouts, but gives in when the child produces bugle-like wails. And so it goes: The parent gradually demands more and more outrageous behavior for reinforcement, and the child obliges, eventually engaging in full-fledged tantrums. The fact that the parent does not *intend* to shape tantrums is irrelevant; what matters is consequences, not intentions.

Some animals seem to use a kind of shaping procedure in the training of their young. Observations in the wild suggest that otters first feed their young on dead prey (mostly fish), but as the pups mature their parents bring prey that are more and more challenging. The prey may be injured but thrashing about, so the young otters must finish the job to eat. This process continues until finally the adults take their young to the hunting area and bring them uninjured prey. Thus, the young otters build on past skills until they master the art of hunting and killing prey on their own.

The use of shaping by animals seems to have been documented in meerkats, a carnivorous mammal related to the mongoose. Meerkat pups accompany adults on foraging trips during which the older animals pass on lizards or other prey to the young. Alex Thornton and K. McAuliffe (2006) observed meerkat groups as they foraged and found that the youngest pups received live prey from adults 65% of the time, while older pups received live prey 90% of the time. Apparently, the adults make things easy for the youngest pups, but as the pups gain experience the adults require more of them, a crude form of shaping.

It's tempting to think that the adult animals are deliberately shaping the behavior of their young, but it's more likely that they are simply responding to the consequences of their own behavior. If you are an adult meerkat and you give a live lizard to an inept, young pup, the lizard is likely to get away. Then you have to recapture it or find another. With practice, the pups should get better at hanging on to prey, so the parents can risk giving them livelier meals. Thornton and McAuliffe performed an experiment that supports this interpretation. They gave some meerkat pups live (but stingless) scorpions, and they gave others hard-boiled eggs. They did this for three days and then gave each of the pups a live scorpion. Meerkats that had eaten eggs for three days let two-thirds of the scorpions get away, but none of the scorpions escaped from meerkats that had had practice with live scorpions.

Shaping goes a long way toward explaining the appearance of new forms of behavior. It parallels the process by which natural selection shapes species: The way a person or animal behaves in a given situation varies, just as species characteristics do (Kinloch, Foster, & McEwan, 2009; Neuringer, 2002; Page & Neuringer, 1985; Skinner, 1981). Some variations of behavior are more useful than others, and they tend to be selected by the environment, while others "die out." In both natural selection and shaping, new forms evolve through variation and selection. In each case, the rule is the same: From the old comes the new.

Sometimes the new behavior that emerges is not one act, but a series of connected acts called a behavior chain, our next topic.

CAPSULE **REVIEW**   Shaping is the reinforcement of successive approximations of a desired behavior. It is also a naturally occurring phenomenon that generates new forms of behavior. It is the means by which new forms of behavior are drawn from old forms of behavior.

## TIPS FOR SHAPERS

The rate at which shaping proceeds depends primarily on the skill of the trainer. Instructors often have students practice shaping by training a rat to press a lever or a pigeon to peck a disc. There is always a good deal of variability in the rate at which the animals progress. The students usually attribute these differences to the intelligence of the animals. Sooner or later a student whose animal has made no progress will complain, "My rat is too stupid to learn to press a lever!" At this, the instructor often turns the animal over to a student who has already succeeded at the task. Within a few minutes, the "stupid" rat is pounding on the lever like a drummer boy.

You may conclude from this that it is not the rat that is stupid, but the student who failed to train it. But in doing so, you are making precisely the same mistake the student made. Learning failures have less to do with the instructor's or trainer's intelligence than they do with his or her skill at shaping (see Todd et al., 1995).

What distinguishes good shapers from poor ones? First, good shapers reinforce small steps. Trainers who get poor results often require too much at once. After reinforcing the rat's turning toward the lever, the poor trainer may wait for the rat to walk over to the lever; the more successful trainer waits only for the rat to take a single step in the direction of the lever.

Second, good trainers provide immediate reinforcement. Poor trainers often hesitate slightly before reinforcing an approximation—often explaining, "I wanted to see if he'd do more." The successful trainer reinforces the instant the desired approximation occurs.

Third, good shapers provide small reinforcers. Shaping laboratory animals usually involves the mechanical delivery of a uniform amount of food, one or two food pellets for a rat, a few pieces of grain for a pigeon. However, if food delivery is done by hand, some trainers will give larger amounts of food. This necessarily slows the course of training because the animal takes longer to consume a larger amount of food. Similarly, people attempting to shape behavior in humans sometimes slow learning by providing too much in the way of reinforcers. If you give a child candy or toys to reinforce each approximation, these reinforcers are apt to become the focus of attention. A simple "Well done!" or even "That's better" is usually more effective.

Fourth, good shapers reinforce the best approximation available. The trainer may work out a shaping plan in advance that includes five or ten distinct approximations of lever pressing that are to be reinforced. The poor trainer will stick to that plan no matter what, reinforcing approximation D only after approximations A, B, and C have been reinforced. The more successful trainer will use the plan as nothing more than a rough guide. If the rat skips a few intermediate steps, fine; the good trainer will reinforce any progress toward the goal. If you get lucky, take advantage of it.

Fifth, good trainers back up when necessary. Learning doesn't always progress smoothly. The rat that has been spending a good deal of time near the lever may move away from it and groom or explore other parts of the chamber. At this point, the trainer may need to take a step back—to reinforce an earlier approximation, such as turning in the direction of the lever. The trainer who is willing to lower the standard when necessary will progress more rapidly than the one who insists on waiting for something better.

# CHAINING

Women gymnasts compete on something called a balance beam. Basically this competition requires them to walk across a 4-inch-wide beam and, along the way, do somersaults, handstands, back flips, and other impossible stunts without landing on their heads. Competing on the balance beam consists of performing a number of these acts in a particular sequence. Such a connected sequence of behavior is called a **behavior chain.**

Among the more ordinary (and less hazardous) behavior chains is making a call with an antique (landline) phone: You pick up the receiver, listen for a dial tone, dial or punch a set of numbers, and hold the receiver to your ear. Dining in a restaurant consists of sitting at a table, studying the menu, placing an order with a waiter, eating the meal, paying the bill, and leaving. A good deal of animal behavior consists of partly learned behavior chains. Predators, for example, search for prey, stalk it, pursue it, kill it, and eat it.

Usually the segments of a chain must be completed in a particular order. In using an old telephone, if you dial the number before you pick up the receiver, the call will not go through. Similarly, dining out may not go well if you attempt to order a meal before being seated.

**QUERY 2:** What are the parts of the chain known as brushing one's teeth?

Teaching an animal or person to perform a behavior chain is called **chaining.** Skinner (Skinner, 1938; This Smart University, 1937) trained a rat named Plyny to pull a string that released a marble from a rack, pick up the marble with its forepaws, carry it to a tube projecting two inches above the floor of the experimental chamber, lift the marble to the top of the tube, and drop it inside.

Other researchers and animal trainers have trained laboratory animals to perform even more complex chains. Carl Cheney (pers. comm., August 21, 1978) trained a rat to climb a ramp, cross a drawbridge, climb a ladder, walk across a tightrope, climb another ladder, crawl through a tunnel, step into an elevator that carried it back down to its starting point, press a lever, and finally receive a few pellets of food (see Figure 6-2).

The first step in chaining is to break the task down into its component elements, a procedure called **task analysis.** Once the individual links of the chain have been identified, it is possible to reinforce the performance of the links in the correct sequence. There are two basic ways of doing this.

In **forward chaining,** the trainer begins by reinforcing performance of the first link in the chain. This is repeated until the task is performed without hesitation. At this point, the trainer requires performance of the first two

*Chaining, like shaping, is both a tool for changing behavior and a naturally occurring phenomenon. Our environment (with or without people) "trains" us to perform a set of acts in a particular sequence.*

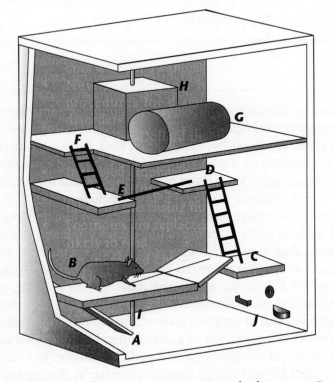

***Figure 6-2*** *Chaining. Starting at A, rat climbs ramp to B, crosses drawbridge to C, climbs ladder to D, crosses tightrope to E, climbs ladder to F, crawls through tunnel to G, enters elevator at H, descends to I, presses lever at J, and receives food. (Drawn by Diane Chance.)*

links, and this short chain is reinforced until it is performed smoothly. Then the trainer requires performance of the first three links, and so on.

If one of the links does not readily occur, the trainer uses shaping to build it. For example, rats do not readily pull on strings or pick up marbles. If you wanted to train a rat to replicate Plyny's performance, you might begin by shaping string pulling, perhaps by providing a bit of food whenever the rat touches the string, then when it bites it, then when it holds the string in its mouth, then when it pulls it. Similarly, in teaching a student to recite a poem (a linguistic chain), you might need to shape the proper pronunciation of a word or the expression of a particular phrase.

Forward chaining is a logical, commonsense approach, but it is not always the most efficient way of developing a chain. Often the better way is to begin with the *last* link in the chain and work backward toward the first element. This variation is called **backward chaining.** In Plyny's case, you might first train the rat to drop a marble down a tube. Next you would train the animal to carry the marble to the tube and drop it. When the rat readily performs the last two tasks, you can require performance of the last three links, and so on. As in forward chaining, any behavior that does not occur spontaneously must first be shaped.

Note that in backward chaining, the chain is never performed backward. Plyny does not drop a marble down a tube, then carry the marble to the tube, and so on; the parts of the chain are always performed in their proper sequence. Training is backward only in the sense that links in the chain are added from "back to front." So, once a rat has learned to perform the last link in a chain, it then learns to perform the last two links in the chain, then the last three, and so on.

*The effectiveness of backward chaining teaches us that doing things backward sometimes qualifies as "forward thinking."*

 QUERY 3: How would you use backward chaining to train a rat to run a maze?

An interesting thing about chaining is that each link in the chain is reinforced, at least in part, by the opportunity to perform the next step in the chain. Each step in making a cake, for example, is reinforced by access to the next step in the cooking process: Getting the ingredients together is reinforced by being able to mix them; mixing the ingredients is reinforced by being able to put the batter into the cake pans; filling the cake pans is reinforced by being able to put the pans into the oven; putting the pans in the oven is reinforced by seeing the batter rise and turn golden brown, and so on. Similarly, each link in the predator's chain is reinforced by the subsequent link: Searching for prey is reinforced by the opportunity to stalk it; stalking prey is reinforced by the opportunity to chase it; chasing prey is reinforced by the opportunity to attack it, and so on.

Only the last act in a chain typically produces a reinforcer that is not part of the chain. In the laboratory this is usually a primary reinforcer. This is sometimes the case outside the laboratory as well: The predator gets to eat the prey it has hunted, stalked, chased, and killed, and we get to eat the cake we labored so long in making. This last reinforcer is crucial; without it, the chain is not likely to be performed. Even a well-established chain eventually breaks down if the final link in the chain does not produce a reinforcer.

 **QUERY 4:** The two forms of chaining are _____ and _____.

Chaining occurs naturally and accounts for many of the routines that people develop, from brushing our teeth and getting dressed to performing a surgical procedure or flying an airplane. Shaping and chaining are essential to an understanding of the development of new, complex forms of behavior. We will now consider some examples, beginning with insightful problem solving.

CAPSULE **REVIEW**

Chaining is the process of reinforcing each of a series of related behaviors to form a behavior chain. As a training procedure it can take either of two forms: forward chaining and backward chaining. Often the links in a behavior chain do not occur spontaneously and so must be established through shaping. Chaining, like shaping, can occur naturally.

## INSIGHTFUL PROBLEM SOLVING

Problem solving is an area shrouded in mystery. It is often spoken of in conjunction with references to "the mysteries of mind" and is said to be one of those subjects that defy scientific analysis. Researchers who have approached problem solving from the standpoint of operant learning have given the lie to that view.

A **problem** is a situation in which reinforcement is available but the behavior necessary to produce it is not. Often, the necessary behavior is not currently in the person's or animal's repertoire. Consider Thorndike's cats: To get out of the boxes, the cats sometimes had to do something they had never done before. Thorndike noticed that the cats solved the problem by walking around the cage and scratching and pawing at things until they happened to trigger the mechanism that opened the cage door. Thorndike said they learned to solve the problem through "trial and accidental success."

 **QUERY 5:** A problem is a situation in which _____ is available, but the

behavior necessary to produce it is not.

When people attempt to solve problems, they often try one thing and then another, like Thorndike's cats, until they hit on a solution. But there are times when the solution seems to appear suddenly, like Athena springing from the head of Zeus. In these instances, problems are said to be solved not by learning, but "by insight." In fact, Jerome Bruner (1983), a major figure in the area of cognitive psychology, suggests that insight is by definition a solution that occurs *without benefit of learning.*

The best-known experiments on insightful problem solving are those described in *The Mentality of Apes* by the German researcher Wolfgang Kohler (1927/1973). In one of the most famous experiments, Kohler gave a chimpanzee named Sultan two hollow bamboo rods. The end of one rod could be inserted into the end of the other to make one long rod. Outside Sultan's cage lay a bit of fruit, just far enough from the bars that it could not be reached with either short stick alone. After an hour of unproductive work, Sultan sat down on a box and examined the sticks. His keeper wrote that

> while doing this, it happens that [Sultan] finds himself holding one rod in either hand in such a way that they lie in a straight line; he pushes the thinner one a little way into the opening of the thicker, jumps up and is already on the run towards the railings . . . and begins to draw a banana towards him with the double stick. (p. 127)

Sultan, Kohler said, solved the problem through insight: Sitting there on the box, looking at the two sticks, he had a sudden flash of understanding. Such insightful problem solving, it was said, could not be accounted for by operant learning, because the correct solution appeared suddenly, without benefit of reinforcement. But did it?

Some years after Kohler's work, Louis Peckstein and Forrest Brown (1939) performed experiments similar to Kohler's and found no evidence of solutions emerging suddenly without benefit of reinforcement. In a replication of Kohler's two-stick problem, for example, they found that it took a chimpanzee 11 trials over a period of four days to learn to put two sticks together to retrieve food. Their chimpanzee first learned to retrieve food with a single stick and then learned to combine two sticks while playing with them. It then *gradually* learned to use the combined sticks to retrieve food.

Other evidence adds doubt about the apparent suddenness of insight into problems. Darwin's theory of evolution, for example, was not due to a sudden burst of insight. It was, ironically, the product of a slow evolution (Gruber, 1981; Weiner, 1994). As Verlyn Klinkenborg (2005) observed concerning Darwin's theory:

> We can say, with Thomas Huxley, "How extremely stupid not to have thought of that!" But, of course, Darwin did not simply think of it. He prepared for years to be ready to think of it when he did. (p. A14)

*The apparent suddenness of insight is comparable to the boiling over of a pot of soup on your stove. The overflow is abrupt, but it took time for the soup to get to that point.*

A classic study by Harry Harlow (1949) demonstrates the "evolution" of insight. Harlow provided monkeys with a problem in which a bit of food could be found under one of two lids that varied in some way, such as color, size, or shape. In one series of trials, the prize would always be under the larger lid; in another series, it would always be under the square lid, and so on. Success on the first trial of any series was necessarily a matter of chance; there was no way of telling which lid covered food on the first trial. Success on the second and subsequent trials could be successful if the monkeys selected the same kind of lid that hid food on the first trial.

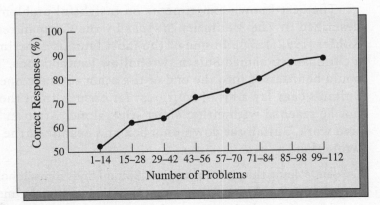

**Figure 6-3** *The "evolution" of insight. The percent of correct solutions on trial 2 of a series increased gradually with training. (After Harlow, 1949.)*

In any given series, the monkeys would slowly learn to pick the correct lid. Gradually, over many series of learning trials, their learning rate improved (see Figure 6-3). Eventually, they would get the second problem in a new series right about 90% of the time. This change emerged slowly, however, and was clearly the result of the animal's reinforcement history. Harlow repeated the same experiment with children between the ages of 2 and 7 and got the same result: no sudden burst of insight, but a gradual improvement in performance due, apparently, to the reinforcement of correct choices.

**QUERY 6:** Harlow's data show that "insightful" solutions may be arrived at

_____ as a result of a number of learning experiences.

Nevertheless, people and animals *do* sometimes struggle with a problem for some time and then abruptly produce a solution. If, however, the sudden appearance of a solution can be shown to be dependent on learning history, the notion that insightful problem solving is fundamentally different from other instances of operant learning is seriously challenged.

One of the most frequently cited demonstrations of insightful problem solving is Kohler's suspended fruit problem. In this experiment, Kohler suspended a banana or other piece of fruit from the ceiling of a cage and placed large boxes nearby. The chimpanzees under study attempted to reach the fruit by jumping, but the fruit was too high. Sultan

soon relinquished this attempt, paced restlessly up and down, suddenly stood still in front of the box, seized it, tipped it hastily straight towards the objective, but began to climb on it at a (horizontal) distance of half a metre, and springing upwards with all his force, tore down the banana. (1927/1973, p. 40; see Figure 6-4).

In such instances of problem solving, the solution's abrupt appearance is often said to be a spontaneous and inexplicable act of mind, impossible to

**Figure 6-4**    *Insight in the chimpanzee. Kohler presented a chimp with a situation similar to that shown here: a bunch of bananas that were out of reach. See text for explanation. (© SuperStock/SuperStock)*

account for in terms of the reinforcement of previous behavior. The claim is that such insight is different from the gradual selection of correct actions seen, for example, in Thorndike's cats and Harlow's monkeys. But is insight really independent of prior reinforcement? Unfortunately, Kohler's records of the experiences of the animals prior to testing are spotty. In the case just cited, it is not clear what kinds of experiences Sultan had with the use of boxes or the retrieval of fruit from high places. However, if the same sort of insight occurred in animals with a particular reinforcement history, but not in animals that lacked that history, this would demonstrate that the insight was the result *of those experiences*, not of some mysterious hocus-pocus of the mind.

In a brilliant experiment, Robert Epstein and his colleagues (1984) taught pigeons (a) to push a small box toward a green spot that was placed at various points in the chamber and (b) to climb on a box that was already beneath a toy banana and peck the banana. In addition, each bird spent time with the banana until the bird neither jumped nor flew toward the banana. Once this was accomplished, the researchers hung the toy banana from the ceiling out of reach of the pigeon and placed the box elsewhere in the chamber. Note that the researchers did *not* train the bird to push the box toward the banana. In fact, the situation was quite similar to that confronted by Sultan. The bird's behavior was also remarkably like that of the chimp:

> It paced and looked perplexed, stretched toward the banana, glanced back and forth from box to banana and then energetically pushed the box toward it, looking up at it repeatedly as it did so, then stopped just short of it, climbed, and pecked. The solution appeared in about a minute for each of three birds. (Epstein, 1984, p. 48f; see Figure 6-5.)

**(?) QUERY 7:**    The experiment by Epstein and colleagues demonstrates that insightful

problem solving is largely the product of _____.

**Figure 6-5**   *Insight in the pigeon. In (A), the bird looks back and forth from banana to box. In (B) it pushes the box toward the banana. Then in (C) it climbs on the box and pecks the banana. Compare to Figure 8-9. (Photographs courtesy of Dr. Robert Epstein; reprinted by permission.)*

Note that, in this experiment, the solution appeared suddenly after a period of "contemplation," as is supposed to happen in insightful problem solving. The point is that this "sudden insight" depended on the previous reinforcement of the separate behaviors required for a solution. Birds that had been trained to climb the box and to peck the banana, but not to push the box, did not solve the problem. It would appear that achieving insight into a problem depends largely on past reinforcement of behavior related to the solution (Epstein, 1999).

One could still argue that the birds had solved the problem through some mysterious process (e.g., the workings of the avian unconscious), but it is more parsimonious to attribute the solution to the animal's learning history. We humans are far better at solving problems than other animals, but this does not mean that our reinforcement history is less important. Indeed, our greater success at achieving insight seems to be largely due to our being more adept at learning from the consequences of our behavior.

CAPSULE **REVIEW**   Insightful problem solving, once thought to be an unfathomable mystery, is now understood to be largely the product of learning history. Experiments suggest that the "sudden" appearance of insightful solutions is typically not sudden and that the appearance of a solution depends *directly* on the individual's history of reinforcement.

# CREATIVITY

If insightful problem solving has been shrouded in mystery, it is nothing compared to that surrounding creativity. This realm of behavior is often said to defy scientific analysis. But is creativity really unfathomable?

Let us begin with a definition. Creativity has been defined in many ways, but one feature that is always mentioned is novelty. For a drawing, sculpture, story, invention, dance, idea, or anything else to be judged creative, it must be novel; that is, it must be relatively unlike other drawings, sculptures, stories, inventions, dances, or ideas.

Novelty is seldom sufficient, in and of itself, for a product to be judged creative. A 2-year-old child scribbling on the wall with a crayon may produce a composition unlike any the world has ever seen, but it is not likely to be called art. A biologist may theorize that plant life evolved out of animal life. That may be a novel idea, but it is unlikely to be embraced by other biologists simply because it's new. However, nothing (regardless of its merits) is judged creative unless it is different from other products of its type. To be creative, then, means above all else to behave in original ways.

Where does original behavior come from? In ancient Greece, people believed that the muses (spirits that specialized in art, music, or literature) visited a person. If one wanted to write poetry, one waited for Erato, the muse of poetry; the poet was merely an instrument for Erato's work. This theory is still expressed by people in the arts and even by some psychologists and psychiatrists. They typically move the muses into the person, usually lodging them in the "unconscious mind" (Andreasen, 2010; Freud, 1958/2009). Psychiatrist Nancy Andreasen (2010) writes, for example, "The creative process is characterized by flashes of insight that arise in the unconscious reservoirs of the mind and brain" (p. 9).

**QUERY 8:** The idea of increasing creativity by means of reinforcement seems illogical at

first because reinforcement _____.

An analysis of creativity in terms of operant learning looks chiefly to the history of reinforcement. In the 1960s, Karen Pryor (1991) was an animal trainer at the Ocean Science Theater in Hawaii. The theater was a kind of aquarium at which people could watch porpoises and other sea animals perform tricks. One day Pryor and the other trainers realized that the show they put on for the public was getting stale. The animals were getting "a little too good, a little too slick, a little too polished" (p. 234). To liven things up a bit, the trainers decided to demonstrate how the animals were trained by waiting for Malia, one of their star performers, to do something and then reinforcing that behavior. The audience would actually see learning take place as the reinforced behavior increased rapidly in frequency. The plan worked extraordinarily well, and the trainers made it a regular part of the show. In the next few days, Malia received reinforcement for all sorts of typical porpoise behavior: tail slapping, swimming upside down, rising out of the water, and so on. After only 14 shows, however, the trainers had a new problem: They were running out of behaviors to reinforce.

Malia solved the problem for them. One day Malia "got up a good head of steam, rolled over on her back, stuck her tail in the air, and coasted about 15 feet with her tail out" (p. 236). It was a delightful sight, and everyone, including the trainers, roared with laughter. Malia received a fish and repeated the stunt a dozen times. Pryor gradually realized that all a trainer had to do to get novel behavior was to reinforce novel behavior. Malia was soon producing novel behaviors on a regular basis; she had learned to be creative.

*Note that Pryor gradually realized that reinforcers could strengthen novel behavior. If that doesn't sound familiar, you need to reread the previous section. ;-)*

Pryor (Pryor, Haag, & O'Reilly, 1969) repeated the experiment in a more formal fashion with a porpoise named Hou. The new pupil was not as fast a learner as Malia had been, but Hou eventually produced four novel stunts in one training session. After this, Hou "came up with novelty after novelty, sinking head downwards, spitting water at the trainer, jumping upside down" (p. 242). By the thirteenth training session, Hou had produced a novel behavior in six out of seven consecutive sessions. Note that Pryor did not decide beforehand what Hou should do, nor did she shape creative behavior; she simply reinforced any new behavior that appeared.

Even some small-brained species can show remarkable creativity if originality is systematically reinforced. Pryor and her group (1969) reinforced novel behavior in pigeons. As a result, some of the birds engaged in such unusual behavior as lying on their backs, standing with both feet on one wing, and hovering two inches above the cage floor.

A number of studies have shown that the same basic technique, reinforcing novel behavior, can increase the creativity of people. In one study, John Glover and A. L. Gary (1976) asked fourth and fifth graders to think of uses for various objects such as a can, brick, or pencil. The students worked in teams and earned points by coming up with uses for a particular object. At various times, different kinds of criteria had to be met to earn points. The result was that reinforcement affected the kinds of behavior produced. When unusual uses earned points, the number of unusual uses rose sharply. For instance, during the baseline period, students asked to come up with uses for a box might suggest variations on the idea that a box is used to store things in (e.g., "hold books in," "hold leaves in," etc.). But when originality earned points, some very unusual uses appeared. Asked for uses of a brick, for example, one student suggested attaching a brick to each foot as a way to develop leg strength. Another, asked to come up with an original use for blackboard erasers, proposed that they could be stuffed into his shirt "to make my shoulders look bigger." Originality and other measures of creativity showed a strong increase as a result of reinforcement for creative ideas.

Kathy Chambers and her colleagues (1977) obtained similar results when they reinforced originality in block building. In this study, one of the experimenters asked first and second graders to build things with blocks. Each time a child in the experimental group produced a new form of construction, the experimenter praised him or her. The experimenter watched children in the control group work but made no comment about their constructions. Praise resulted in nearly twice as many different constructional forms being produced by children in the experimental group.

**QUERY 9:** How could an auto manufacturer increase the creativity of its designers?

Other studies of the effects of reinforcement on creative behavior have produced similar results (Glover, 1979; Goetz, 1982; Goetz & Baer, 1973; Sloane, Endo, & Della-Piana, 1980; Winston & Baker, 1985). Despite such evidence, some psychologists have suggested that reinforcement actually makes people *less* creative. For example, numerous studies have found that promised rewards have a negative effect on creativity (Amabile, 1983; Deci & Ryan, 1985; Hennessey & Amabile, 1998). In a typical study a child draws a picture, and after this the researcher offers a reward for drawing additional pictures. The child complies, and then these pictures are compared with the child's original effort. The usual result is that the rewarded pictures are *less* original than the unrewarded work. In some studies, the performance of those who are promised a reward is compared with those who are not. In one experiment, Teresa Amabile (1982) offered children a reward for constructing a collage, and their efforts were less creative than those of children who performed the task without expecting to receive anything. Not all of the studies involve children. Arie Kruglanski and colleagues (1971) asked college students to invent titles for paragraphs and found that those who were promised a reward produced less novel titles than those who were not.

Some people conclude from such research that rewards undermine creativity. There are a number of problems with this research and the conclusion drawn from it. For one, *promising* a reward in advance of a behavior is not the same thing as *providing* a reward *after* the behavior. Another flaw concerns the contingency between behavior and reward: In studies that show reduced creativity, the reward is simply for performing an act (drawing any picture, for example), not for *creative* performance. In studies that show increased creativity, rewards are contingent on *creative* behavior. Robert Eisenberger, a social psychologist at the University of Delaware, and Stephen Armeli, now at Fairly Dickinson University (1997), found, for example, that if they rewarded conventional performance on a task, they got more conventional performance, but if they rewarded creative performance, they got more creativity. Other studies have produced similar results (Eisenberger, Armeli, & Pretz, 1998; Eisenberger & Rhoades, 2001; Eisenberger & Selbst, 1994). Increasing creativity seems to be no great trick; all you need to do is reinforce creative acts whenever they occur. So creativity is a characteristic of behavior that can be reinforced.

But why are people inclined to be less creative when promised a reward for merely performing a task? The question is more complicated than it seems (see Neuringer, 2003; 2004), but Eisenberger and Linda Rhoades (2001) suggest that part of the answer is that creativity is not always appreciated. When offered a reward for performing a task, the surest way of receiving the promised reward is to perform the task in a conventional (i.e., not original) way. If there is no reward at stake, then you can afford to be creative. Suppose, for example, that you are hired to paint the exterior of a person's house white with blue trim. Usually this means painting the walls white and the shutters blue. You could paint not only the shutters blue, but the rain gutters, spouts, window frames, and door jambs. This would be rather creative, but if you wanted to be sure of getting paid you would probably do the job in the more conventional manner. If the house you are painting is your own, however, and you live in a neighborhood where eccentricity is reliably admired, you can paint in an unconventional way.

The clear implication of creativity research, taken as a whole, is that creative behavior, like any other operant behavior, is a function of its consequences. When original behavior has positive consequences, people are more likely to be creative. When original behavior has negative consequences, they are less likely to be creative. You could still argue that the creative acts originate in the mind or in some crevice of the brain, but there is little evidence for these hypotheses and they add little to the understanding provided by learning.

Now let us turn to an excellent example of creativity in science: Skinner's very original explanation of superstition.

CAPSULE **REVIEW**

Like insightful problem solving, creativity now seems less mysterious than it once did. Instead of attributing the creative act to a muse or some dark, hidden recess of the mind, we can see that creativity is a function of learning, particularly the history of reinforcement. This new understanding brings with it the realization that creativity is not the domain of the chosen few; we can all learn to be more creative.

## SUPERSTITION

Hart Seely (2007) is a journalist and humor writer who freely admits to magical thinking. In a tongue-in-cheek article he explains how his behavior as a baseball fan helps win ball games:

As a child, I personally led the Yanks to several world championships. When the team needed help, I ran out back and pitched a tennis ball against the garage. I served up home runs to Mickie Mantle and blew fast balls past the hapless Willie Mays. The garage fell apart, but the Yankees always won.

Unless they lost. That happened because my sister hid the ball, or I just didn't concentrate hard enough.

Mr. Seely's behavior may seem more than a little strange, but if you are a sports fan you may have engaged in similar activities to influence the outcomes of sporting events. Mr. Seely would admit that his behavior is superstitious.

**Superstitious behavior** is any behavior that occurs repeatedly even though it does not produce the reinforcers that maintain it. Many things can influence whether the Yankees defeat the Orioles, but throwing tennis balls at your garage is not one of them. In most instances of reinforcement, there is a causal connection between a behavior and the reinforcer that maintains it. But in the case of behavior such as Mr. Seely describes, there is no such connection. Why, then, does the behavior persist?

Many answers have been offered (see Shermer, 2002; Vyse, 2000). One that has experimental support comes from B. F. Skinner (1948). He put a pigeon into an experimental chamber and modified the feeding mechanism so that grain became available every 15 seconds, *regardless* of what the bird happened to be doing at the time. In other words, the reinforcer was *not* contingent on any behavior. What Skinner wanted to know was, Would the delivery of food in this way affect the pigeon's behavior?

He found that six out of eight pigeons developed some clear-cut behavior: One bird turned in counterclockwise circles, another raised its head toward one of the corners of the cage, one pigeon bobbed its head up and down, two birds swung their heads to and fro, and the sixth pigeon made brushing movements toward the floor, as if trying to peck it. The birds appeared to have learned to perform strange rituals, even though the reinforcer came regardless of whether the birds engaged in the behavior. Skinner called these acts superstitious because the birds behaved as if their rituals produced reinforcement, when in fact they did not.

Skinner's explanation of this phenomenon is quite simple. When the first reinforcer arrived, the bird had to be doing *something*. If it happened to be bobbing its head up and down (something that pigeons are inclined to do occasionally), then head bobbing was accidentally reinforced. This meant that head bobbing was likely to occur again, which meant it was still more likely to be reinforced, and so on. Thus, superstitious behavior is the product of coincidental reinforcement.

**QUERY 10:** Superstitious behavior by definition does not produce _____.

Superstitious behavior is not restricted to pigeons. Gregory Wagner and Edward Morris (1987) of the University of Kansas conducted a study of superstitious behavior in children. They began by introducing preschool children to a mechanical clown named Bobo that periodically dispensed marbles from its mouth. Bobo spit out marbles at fixed intervals regardless of what the children did. The researchers told the children that "sometimes Bobo will give marbles" and that they should take any marbles Bobo might provide and put them in a box. When they had collected enough marbles, they would be able to trade them for a toy. The researchers worked with one child at a time and, after explaining about the marbles and the toys, left the child alone with Bobo. They found that seven of the 12 children developed superstitions. Some children sucked their thumbs, some swung their hips back and forth, some touched Bobo or kissed him on the nose.

Koichi Ono (1987) of Komazawa University in Tokyo established superstition in university students. The students sat at a table with three levers. At the back of the table was a partition with a signal light and a counter that recorded points earned. Ono told the students they were to earn as many points as they could. In fact, nothing the student did had any effect on the accumulation of points. Periodically the light would come on and the counter would register one point—regardless of what the student did.

Most of the students engaged in superstitious behavior, at least for brief periods. Mostly the superstitions involved pulling the levers, with five of the 20 students pulling the levers over 1,000 times, and two more pulling them over 2,000 times—though lever pulling had nothing to do with receiving points. One student's superstitious behavior went well beyond pulling levers. At one point, she stopped pulling the levers momentarily and happened to put her right hand on the lever frame. Ono writes:

> This behavior was followed by a point delivery, after which she climbed on the table and put her right hand to the counter. Just as she did so, another point was delivered. Thereafter she began to touch many things in turn, such as the signal light, the screen, a nail on the screen, and the wall. About 10 minutes later, a point was delivered just as she jumped to the floor, and touching was replaced by jumping. After five jumps, a point was delivered when she jumped and touched the ceiling with her slipper in her hand. Jumping to touch the ceiling continued repeatedly and was followed by points until she stopped about 25 minutes into the session, perhaps because of fatigue. (p. 265)

Many human superstitions seem too complex and durable to be explained solely by coincidental reinforcement. Richard Herrnstein (1966) proposes that if a person can be induced to perform a superstitious act (e.g., if a parent gives a child a rabbit's foot to carry "for good luck"), the behavior might then be maintained by coincidental reinforcement. (For more on this, see Neuringer, 1970; Gleeson, Lattal, & Williams, 1989.)

Not everyone is happy with the reinforcement explanation of superstition. In studies with pigeons, John Staddon and Virginia Simmelhag (1971) and W. Timberlake and G. A. Lucas (1985) failed to obtain the rituals Skinner reported. They suggest that coincidental reinforcement merely increases the rate at which naturally dominant behaviors, such as pecking and wing flapping, occur (see the discussion in Staddon, 2001). Other studies have, however, produced results similar to Skinner's (e.g., Justice & Looney, 1990). Moreover, as you have seen, there is the evidence that coincidental reinforcement has produced clearly superstitious behavior in people. Did Koichi Ono's university student jump toward the ceiling because she had a natural tendency to jump?

*If superstitious behavior is learned, does this mean that faster learners should be more superstitious than slower learners?*

Superstitions can be harmful (e.g., some folk remedies can kill rather than cure), but they are usually fairly innocuous. As Stuart Vyse (1997) points out, Skinner's pigeons risked little by turning in circles or engaging in other superstitious acts. "There is a strong tendency," Vyse writes, "to repeat any response that is coincident with reinforcement. In the long run, this tendency serves the species well: If turning in a circle really does operate the feeder, the bird eats and survives another day; if not, little is lost" (p. 76). Humans also "turn in circles" when this behavior is coincidentally reinforced. Most of the time, little is lost.

## QUICK! GET SOME MUD!

What would you do if, while camping miles from a hospital, a venomous snake bit you?

There seems to be no end of ideas about how to cure snakebite. Some advocate covering the wound with mud. Others believe the cure is to drink whiskey. Some think the answer is to fast, while others are convinced you need to kill and eat the snake that bit you. Some people believe it's possible to save yourself by casting a spell. Others will scoff at that idea—and urge you to cauterize the wound with a red-hot knife.

Why are there so many superstitious cures for snakebite? I believe the answer probably has to do with the fact that the victim is likely to survive no matter what you do. This means, of course, that whatever you do is likely to be coincidentally reinforced.

It has been reported that when venomous snakes bite humans, only about half of the victims actually are injected with venom. This means that in half the cases of venomous snakebite, whatever treatment is tried will appear to be helpful. Additionally, many harmless snakes are commonly mistaken for venomous ones. And even if the snake is venomous and does inject venom, many victims will survive without any treatment. All of which means that the odds are very good that no matter what steps a person takes to treat snakebite, the person will survive—and application of the treatment, however useless, will be reinforced.

You cannot, of course, persuade the person who has "seen it work" that his particular cure is superstitious. So if you are ever out camping with friends and are bitten by a snake, don't be surprised if someone shouts, "Quick! Get some mud!"

CAPSULE **REVIEW**    When people or animals behave as if their behavior produces reinforcement, when in fact it does not, the behavior is called superstitious. Evidence suggests that superstitious behavior is shaped and maintained at least partly by coincidental reinforcement. Reinforcement alone does not entirely account for all superstitious behavior, but it seems clear that coincidental reinforcement does play an important role in superstition.

## HELPLESSNESS

Faced with a series of difficult challenges, some people make a feeble effort to cope and then, if denied success, they "throw in the towel." Others in the same situation take it on the chin and keep on fighting. Many people attribute such differences to internal traits due to genes. Genes are a factor in all behavior, but seldom if ever offer a complete explanation.

Some years ago, Martin Seligman and his colleagues (Overmier & Seligman, 1967; Seligman & Maier, 1967) were interested in the effects of Pavlovian fear conditioning on operant escape learning. In their experiments, they strapped a dog into a harness and paired a tone with shock. Then they put the dog into one side of a shuttle box, sounded the tone, and delivered a shock to the dog's side of the box.

Normally when a dog is put into a shuttle box and shocked, it quickly jumps over the barrier to the other compartment. If that area is shock-free, then each time the dog receives a shock it escapes over the hurdle more quickly. If shocks are preceded by a tone, the dog learns to jump the hurdle when the tone sounds and thereby avoids shock entirely. Seligman and his coworkers were interested in observing what effect the tone would have on escape learning if the tone had been paired with shock. For example, if the tone that sounded were already a CS for fear, might the dog jump the barrier and avoid shock on the very first trial?

What actually happened astonished the researchers and the research community. Seligman (1975) writes that the

> dog's first reactions to shock in the shuttle box were much the same as those of a naive dog: it ran around frantically for about thirty seconds. But then it stopped moving; to our surprise, it lay down and quietly whined. After one minute of this we turned the shock off; the dog had failed to cross the barrier and had not escaped from shock. On the next trial, the dog did it again; at first it struggled a bit and then, after a few seconds, it seemed to give up and to accept the shock passively. On all succeeding trials, the dog failed to escape. (p. 22)

The degree of passivity in these dogs was impressive. Seligman removed the barrier from the shuttle box so that the dog need only walk to the other side, yet the dog remained where it was, passively enduring the shock. Then Seligman got into the safe side of the box and called to the dog; the dog made no effort to move. Then he put salami on the safe side of the box; the dog continued to lie there, enduring shock.

Seligman called this phenomenon **learned helplessness** because the inescapable shock seemed to teach the dogs to do nothing; they had learned to be helpless. Further research demonstrated that it was not the prior exposure to shock, *per se*, that produced helplessness but the inescapability of the shock. Researchers have demonstrated helplessness repeatedly in other species, including fish (Padilla et al., 1970), rats (Maier, Albin, & Testa, 1973), cats (Masserman, 1943), and people (Hiroto, 1974; Hiroto & Seligman, 1974).

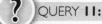 QUERY 11:    Exposure to _____ aversives leads to learned helplessness.

If helplessness is learned, can learning experiences prevent helplessness? There is some evidence that they can. For instance, Seligman and Steven Maier (1967) gave one group of dogs ten escape trials in the shuttle box *before* exposing them to inescapable shock. When they tested these dogs in the shuttle box again, they readily jumped the hurdle.

Other research demonstrates that "immunization training" may produce amazing resilience in the face of adversity. For example, Joseph Volpicelli and others (1983) trained some rats to press levers to escape shock and exposed others to the same amount of inescapable shock. After this the researchers put the rats in a shuttle box. In this study, unlike those described above, shuttling from one side of the box to the other did not allow the rats to escape shock. The reason for this change in procedure was to see whether the animals would continue trying to escape shock even though their efforts did not pay off. The result was that naïve rats—those that had no shocks beforehand—at first jumped readily from compartment to compartment, but their rate of shuttling declined sharply as testing continued. Rats that had been exposed to inescapable shock showed far less inclination to shuttle, and their rate of shuttling declined further with continued testing. Rats that had been able to escape shock by pressing a lever, however, behaved very differently. These rats shuttled at a constant high rate, showing almost no decline over the course of 200 trials. After once learning to escape shocks, these rats refused to give up!

Robert Eisenberger has demonstrated much the same thing in people. He reasons that if people can learn to give up easily, they can also learn to be indefatigable. He and his colleagues (Eisenberger, 1992; Eisenberger & Cameron, 1996; Eisenberger, Masterson, & McDermott, 1982) found that reinforcing a high level of effort and persistence despite difficulties increases the tendency to work hard at difficult tasks for a prolonged period. You could say that he trains people *not* to quit. Eisenberger calls this **learned industriousness.**

The difference between those who become discouraged easily and those who don't seem to know how to give up and who tackle every problem like a linebacker sacking a quarterback appears to be largely a matter of reinforcement history. Experience (mainly our history of reinforcement) teaches us to quit or to strive, to roll over or to fight on.

**? QUERY 12:** Learned industriousness is the opposite of _____.

CAPSULE **REVIEW** Learned helplessness has given us a new way to look at the failure of some people (previously dismissed as shiftless, lazy, or irresponsible) to deal effectively with life's challenges. It may also help us understand how the Unsinkable Molly Browns among us become "unsinkable." There is reason to believe that there are things we can do to immunize ourselves and others against helplessness.

## A FINAL WORD

One of my goals in this chapter was to show that operant principles can provide credible scientific accounts of complex behavior, that, as David Palmer has written, "established scientific principles are sufficient to account for puzzling phenomena" (2003, p. 174).

But some people are apt to object, not because the scientific account isn't believable but because it *is*. Many of us are romantics: We *like* the puzzling nature of behavior; we *like* believing that ideas bubble up from our unconscious mind or from our brain largely or entirely independently of previous experience; we *like* believing that we are somehow beyond understanding. We fear that if we can explain human behavior in scientific terms, it will take the romance out of the human experience.

The best reply I can give is to point out that people said the same thing when Neil Armstrong and Buzz Aldrin walked on the moon. The moon had been a mysterious and romantic object, some people said, but the footprints of science had taken that away. That was about 40 years ago. Those footprints are still there, yet I still look up at the moon with wonder. Don't you?

## RECOMMENDED **READING**

1. Donahoe, J. W., & Palmer, D. C. (1994). *Learning and complex behavior.* Boston: Allyn & Bacon.

   This text, devoted to the analysis of complex human behavior, will be heavy going for many undergraduates, but it will be worth the effort for those who are contemplating graduate work in psychology. See in particular the chapter on problem solving.

2. Eisenberger, R. (2000). Learned industriousness. In R. Eisenberger (Ed.), *Blue Monday: The loss of the work ethic in America* (pp. 150–170). New York: iUniverse.

   Eisenberger makes the case for the role of learning in determining why one person is indefatigable in the face of great challenges while another resigns to "fate."

3. Epstein, R. (1996). *Cognition, creativity and behavior.* New York: Praeger.

   Epstein discusses a variety of topics in this book, but I particularly recommend the chapters on creativity.

4. Peterson, G. B. (2004). A day of great illumination: B. F. Skinner's discovery of shaping. *Journal of the Experimental Analysis of Behavior, 82,* 317–328.

   This very readable account of the discovery of shaping is not only an important footnote in the history of science, it is a fascinating description of the process of discovery. This process more often resembles a climb up a rocky slope than a jump from a trampoline.

5. Vyse, S. (2000). *Believing in magic: The psychology of superstition.* New York: Oxford University Press.

   Stuart Vyse offers a fascinating review of superstitious behaviors and the attempts to explain them.

## REVIEW **QUESTIONS**

1. Does the children's game "Hot and Cold" make good use of shaping?

2. Describe the procedure you would use to train a dog to retrieve the morning newspaper from your front lawn.

3. How is chaining a form of shaping?

4. Occasionally the solution to a problem comes to a person in a dream. Can you account for this in terms of operant learning?

5. Why is insight not an adequate *explanation* of problem solving?

6. You head the product development division of a major corporation. How can you get the people in your division to come up with ideas for new products?

7. Explain why people within the same family often share the same superstitious beliefs.

8. Professional athletes and fishermen seem to be particularly likely to engage in superstition behavior. Why do you suppose this is the case?

9. If you wanted to "immunize" your child against helplessness, how would you do it?

10. How has your study of operant learning changed your views of human nature?

## PRACTICE **QUIZ**

1. Shaping is the reinforcement of _____ of a desired behavior.

2. The first demonstration of shaping in an animal involveS teaching a pigeon to _____.

3. The first step in building a behavior chain is to do a _____ analysis.

4. The experiment in which pigeons pecked a simulated banana hanging from the ceiling demonstrated that insight is the product of the history of _____.

5. Gregory Wagner and Edward Morris studied _____ behavior with the help of a mechanical clown named Bobo.

6. In some experiments, promised rewards tend to reduce creativity. This is because the rewards are not _____ on creative behavior.

7. _____ behavior does not produce the reinforcers that maintain it.

8. Robert Eisenberger found that reinforcing effort in the face of difficulties can establish what he calls learned _____.

9. There are two forms of chaining, _____ and _____.

10. Karen Pryor demonstrated that creative behavior could be reinforced in _____ (kind of animal).

## QUERY **ANSWERS**

Query 1. Shaping is the reinforcement of successive *approximations* of a desired behavior.

Query 2. Answers will vary. A typical chain might include picking up a toothbrush, dampening the brush under the spigot, putting toothpaste on it, moving the brush against the teeth, rinsing the mouth, rinsing the brush, and returning the brush to its container. Obviously, the chain could be extended considerably. *The Odd Couple*'s Felix Unger would specify the precise manner in which each tooth is to be brushed.

Query 3. Put food in the goal box (the end of the maze), put the rat just outside the goal box, and release the rat. On the next trial, put food in the goal box but put the rat farther away from the goal box. Keep backing the rat up in this way until it is starting at the beginning.

Query 4. The two forms of chaining are *forward* and *backward*.

Query 5. A problem is a situation in which *reinforcement* is available, but the behavior necessary to produce it is not.

Query 6. Harlow's data show that "insightful" solutions may be arrived at *gradually/slowly* as a result of a number of learning experiences.

Query 7. The experiment by Epstein and colleagues demonstrates that insightful problem solving is largely the product of *reinforcement/reinforcement history*.

Query 8. The idea of increasing creativity by means of reinforcement seems illogical at first because reinforcement *strengthens a behavior that occurs/ makes a behavior that occurred likely to be repeated.*

Query 9. Answers will vary, but should emphasize a contingency between innovative designs and reinforcing consequences. For example, the company might offer time off and/or bonuses for original designs, or it might provide designers with a small royalty based on the price of the designed product.

Query 10. Superstitious behavior by definition does not produce *the reinforcers that maintain it.*

Query 11. Exposure to *inescapable* aversives leads to learned helplessness.

Query 12. Learned industriousness is the opposite of *learned helplessness.*

# CHAPTER

# 7 Schedules of Reinforcement

*The tendencies to respond eventually correspond to the probabilities of reinforcement.*

—**B. F. Skinner**

## PREVIEW

By now you realize that reinforcement plays a vital role in learning and, hence, in our everyday lives. The *pattern* of reinforcement over time—whether each occurrence or every other occurrence or every fifteenth occurrence of an act is reinforced, or whether the act is reinforced only if it occurs after a given interval or only when a given signal is present, and so on—affects behavior in important ways. Students (and some psychologists) do not always appreciate the importance of these patterns. In this chapter I will try to convince you that schedules research is not just a Rubik's Cube® for the entertainment of obsessive-compulsive academicians.

# BEGINNINGS

In the early days of his research on reinforcement, Skinner devised a machine that delivered pellets automatically each time a rat pressed a lever, but he had to make the pellets by hand, a tedious and time-consuming process. One pleasant Saturday afternoon, he calculated that unless he spent the rest of the day at the "pill machine," the pellets would run out by Monday morning. This led him to ask a fateful question: Does every press of a lever have to be reinforced?

The answer was no, and this opened up a whole new area of learning research. Several years later, Skinner and postdoctoral student Charles B. Ferster experimented on numerous ways of arranging reinforcement contingencies and noted the distinctive effects of these variations on behavior (Ferster & Skinner, 1957). Each variation followed a certain rule describing the contingency between a behavior and reinforcement; they called these distinctive rules **schedules of reinforcement.**

The various reinforcement schedules produce distinctive patterns of behavior. To many people, these **schedule effects** do not have anything to do with learning. They think of learning as the acquisition of behavior: A pigeon that never turned in counterclockwise circles now does so reliably and efficiently. A child who could not ride a bicycle at all now rides with skill and ease. A college student for whom the equation $F = ma$ once meant nothing now uses the formula to solve physics problems.

But learning also includes changes in which no new behavior appears. A pigeon that turns in counterclockwise circles at the rate of three or four a minute now makes ten turns a minute. A child who previously rode a bicycle once a week now does so every day. A physics student who used to solve textbook problems involving force and mass at the rate of one every 15 minutes now solves two or three of the problems in that time. Such changes in behavior are often the result of changes in the reinforcement schedule in effect.

Or consider a factory worker who is employed at two factories. In one plant he is paid an hourly wage for spray-painting lawn chairs; in the other, he is paid so much per chair for the same work. The employee turns out more chairs per day in the factory where he is paid so much per chair. The difference in productivity is likely the result of the different schedules of reinforcement.

Learning can also mean a change in the pattern of behavior. If a pan of cookies must bake for ten minutes, it is pointless to check the cookies during the first five minutes or so, but it is essential to check on them before the ten minutes have elapsed. The cook learns to avoid opening the oven in the first several minutes but to check on the cookies during the last few minutes of baking time.

Just as acquisition of new behavior is partly the product of reinforcement contingencies, so changes in the rate and pattern of performance are partly due to reinforcement contingencies. The changes in the cook's behavior reflect the fact that reinforcement (e.g., seeing cookies that are done or nearly done) is available near the end of baking time but not earlier. Similarly, the factory worker on piecework paints more chairs because his earnings reflect the number of chairs painted, not the number of hours he spends in the factory.

We shall see that a particular kind of reinforcement schedule tends to produce a particular rate and pattern of performance. And if a behavior is occurring at a steady rate and pattern and the reinforcement schedule changes, usually the rate and pattern of behavior change in predictable ways. The changes in behavior that result from changes in a reinforcement schedule are examples of learning. They are, like all other examples of learning, changes in behavior due to experience.

# SIMPLE SCHEDULES

### Continuous Reinforcement

The simplest of simple schedules is called **continuous reinforcement (CRF).** In continuous reinforcement, a behavior is reinforced every time it occurs. If, for example, a rat receives food every time it presses a lever, then lever pressing is on a continuous reinforcement schedule. Likewise, a child's behavior is on CRF if she is praised every time she hangs up her coat, and your behavior is on CRF when you operate a vending machine if, each time you insert the requisite amount of money, you receive the item selected.

Each reinforcement strengthens behavior, so continuous reinforcement leads to very rapid increases in the rate of behavior. It is especially useful, then, when the task is to shape up some new behavior or establish a behavior chain. You can see that it would be much easier to teach a pigeon to make counterclockwise turns by reinforcing each successive approximation of the desired behavior than it would be if you were to reinforce successive approximations only occasionally.

Although continuous reinforcement typically leads to the most rapid learning of new behavior, it is probably rare in the natural environment. Most behavior is reinforced on some occasions but not others. A parent is not able to praise a child every time she hangs up her coat, and vending machines sometimes take our money and give us nothing in return. When reinforcement occurs on some occasions but not others, the behavior is said to be on an **intermittent schedule.** There are many kinds of intermittent schedules (see Ferster & Skinner, 1957), but the most important ones fall into four groups (see Figure 7-1). We begin with those called fixed ratio schedules.

### Fixed Ratio

In a **fixed ratio (FR) schedule,** a behavior is reinforced when it has occurred a fixed number of times. For instance, a rat may be trained to press a lever for

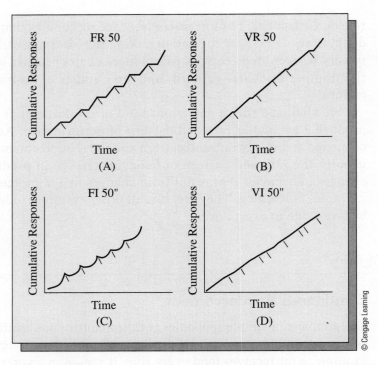

***Figure 7-1*** *Intermittent schedules of reinforcement. In an FR 50 schedule (A), every 50th response is reinforced; in a VR 50 schedule (B), an average of 50 responses is required for each reinforcement; in an FI 50" schedule (C), a response is reinforced when it occurs after a 50-second interval; in a VI 50" schedule (D), a response is reinforced after an average interval of 50 seconds. Short diagonal lines indicate delivery of a reinforcer. (Hypothetical data.)*

food. After shaping the behavior, the experimenter may switch to a schedule in which every third lever press is reinforced. In other words, there is a ratio of three lever presses to each reinforcement. The schedule is usually indicated by the letters FR, followed by the number of times the behavior must occur for each reinforcement. The lever pressing of our hypothetical rat, for example, is on an FR 3 schedule. (Continuous reinforcement is actually a kind of fixed ratio schedule, then, and may be designated FR 1.)

Animals on fixed ratio schedules perform at a high rate, often punctuated by short pauses after reinforcement (for a review, see Schlinger, 2008). A rat that lever presses on an FR schedule for food will press the lever quickly and steadily until food drops into the tray. It will then eat the food, pause for a short time, and then return to work at the lever. The pauses that follow reinforcement have traditionally been called **post-reinforcement pauses,** and they have generated considerable interest among researchers (see Figure 7-1a). They are not required by the schedule, and in fact they reduce the total amount of reinforcement the animal gets, so why do they occur?

**QUERY 1:** An FR1 schedule is also called _____.

It is tempting to dismiss post-reinforcement pauses as the result of fatigue. The animal performs a behavior a number of times and then pauses to "catch its breath" before returning to work. But animals on other types of schedules often work even harder without pauses, so fatigue is not the whole answer.

One variable that seems to be important is the ratio of responses to reinforcement. The more work required for each reinforcement, the longer the post-reinforcement pause (Baron & Derenne, 2000; Ferster & Skinner, 1957). Thus, pauses are longer in an FR 100 schedule than in an FR 20 schedule. Because of this, post-reinforcement pauses are now often called **pre-ratio pauses** (Derenne & Baron, 2002; Derenne, Richardson, & Baron, 2006) and Schlinger, Derenne, and Baron (2008) have even suggested the more neutral term **between-ratio pause**.

Michael Perone (2003) suggests that pauses are a way of escaping, momentarily at least, the "aversive aspects of the schedule" (p. 10). In other words, working for long periods "without pay" is aversive, and we escape by not working for a while. Henry Schlinger (pers. comm.) has suggested that procrastination, which is basically a pause before working, may be a pre-ratio pause: When we procrastinate, we take a "break" before setting to work. Adam Derenne and Alan Baron (2002) of the University of Wisconsin in Milwaukee provide evidence that another reason for pauses could be the availability of other reinforcers. Rats, for example, regularly groom themselves, scratch itches, have a drink, and look around. They cannot very well do these things and press a lever steadily at the same time. They are not pausing, then; they are working for other reinforcers. Similarly, after you've translated your messy notes from your history class, you may check your email and make yourself a snack before translating your messy notes from your literature class. These activities produce a pause in your work on note translations.

Variables that affect post-reinforcement (or pre-ratio or between-ratio) pauses do not ordinarily affect **run rate**—the rate at which behavior occurs once it has resumed following reinforcement. Thus, increasing the ratio of lever presses to reinforcers from, say, 5:1 to 10:1 (i.e., from FR 5 to FR 10) does not change how rapidly a rat presses once it has begun lever pressing. What it does is increase the length of the breaks the rat takes after each reinforcement. However, anything that increases the length of post-reinforcement pauses will necessarily reduce the overall rate of performance—that is, the total number of lever presses per minute or hour.

Fixed ratio schedules are fairly common outside the laboratory. Some games make use of fixed ratio schedules. Each time you get a ping-pong ball past your opponent, for example, you win a point. Perhaps the best examples of FR schedules involve work. Some employees are paid on a fixed ratio schedule, though it is usually called piecework. The garment worker, for instance, is paid so much for each shirt sewn. In some cases the ratio is higher than FR-1; the field hand is not paid for each apple picked, but rather for a basket full of apples.

**?** QUERY 2:    The rate at which a behavior occurs once it has begun is called the

_____ rate.

## Variable Ratio

Instead of providing a reinforcer when a behavior has occurred a fixed number of times, it is possible to vary the requirement around some average. For example, instead of reinforcing every fifth lever press, we might reinforce after the second, the eighth, the sixth, the fourth, and so on. This is called a **variable ratio** or **VR schedule.** In a VR 5 schedule, reinforcement might occur after one to ten lever presses, but the overall average will be one reinforcement for every five presses.

Variable ratio schedules typically produce steady performance at run rates similar to comparable FR schedules (see Figure 7-1b). If post-reinforcement pauses occur, they usually appear less often and are shorter than in a similar FR schedule. In VR schedules, the pauses are strongly influenced by the size of the _average_ ratio and by the _lowest_ ratio (Blakely & Schlinger, 1988; Schlinger, Blakely, & Kaczor, 1990). In a VR 50 schedule, for example, the number of lever presses required for reinforcement averages 50, but the number required on any one run might vary from 10 to 100, or it might vary from 40 to 60. A VR 50 schedule that requires a minimum of 40 lever presses per reinforcement will produce longer pauses than a VR 50 schedule that requires a minimum of 10. A VR 50 schedule that sometimes reinforces after a single response may produce no pauses at all. Thus, a VR schedule can be thought of as a series of different FR schedules, and the length of the pauses tends to reflect the lowest ratio (e.g., FR 1) more than the average for the overall schedule (e.g., VR 50).

Because VR schedules typically produce fewer and shorter pauses than FR schedules, a VR schedule usually produces more behavior in an hour than a comparable FR schedule. This is so even though the actual payoff is the same. That is, the animal on an FR 50 schedule earns as much food for its 50 lever presses as the animal on a VR 50 schedule does (on average) for its 50.

Variable ratio schedules are common in natural environments. As fast as the cheetah is, it does not bring down a victim every time it gives chase, nor can it depend on being successful on the second, third, or fourth try. There is no predicting which particular effort will be successful. The cheetah may succeed on two attempts, and then fail on the next ten tries. All that can be said is that, on average, one in every two of its hunting attempts will pay off (O'Brien, Wildt, & Bush, 1986). (For many predators, the ratio is much higher than that.)

Probably most predatory behavior is reinforced on VR schedules, although the exact schedule varies depending on many factors. For instance, if the elk in a particular area are heavily infested by parasites, they will be easier for wolves to bring down, so the average ratio of attacks to reinforcement will be low. As the wolves remove the sicker animals from the herd, however, the remaining elk will be harder to kill, and the ratio of attempts to reinforcement will be higher.

Variable ratio schedules are important in human society as well. The classic example of a VR schedule is the salesperson working on commission: He or she is paid for each sale, but not every effort to sell something is successful. One reinforcer for attempting to sell a product is the pay the salesperson receives if successful. But because the salesperson is probably not paid at the moment of the sale, the immediate reinforcer may be the sale receipt because this signals that a commission will be forthcoming. Another example of the VR schedule among humans is gambling, particularly casino gambling.

## LIFE IS A GAMBLE

Slot machines, roulette wheels, and other forms of casino gambling are designed so that most of the time, people lose. The average return on $1 "invested" in a slot machine, for example, is about 90%. That means that for every $1 gambled, the person wins, on average, $.90. Why would anyone agree to give someone $1 in exchange for $.90?

Gamblers themselves often say that they gamble for the fun of winning. And there is evidence that gambling produces physiological changes associated with reinforcement (Krueger, Schedlowski, & Meyer, 2005). But this explanation is unsatisfactory because, in the long run, gamblers lose. Most people look for an explanation of gambling, especially compulsive gambling, in the gamblers themselves: They are morally weak, stupid, have a "gambling gene," are depressed or anxious, or have an unconscious need to punish themselves (Dixon, 2006).

Another possibility is that the source of the problem is in the gambler's experience—in particular the schedule of reinforcement provided by games of chance (Kassinove & Schare, 2001; Skinner, 1953; Weatherly & Dannewitz, 2005). The payoff in most games of chance resembles variable ratio schedules of reinforcement, and such schedules can produce high rates of behavior that are very resistant to change.

But many people gamble without getting hooked. Why do some become compulsive gamblers while others do not? The most likely explanation seems to be the momentary variations in schedules. The fact that a slot machine pays off on a given schedule, for example, does not mean that everyone playing it has precisely the same experience. One person may have a series of three or four wins in his first 20 tries, while another may win nothing. Or one person may hit a small jackpot of $50 on her tenth bet, while the other wins no more than $2 in 50 tries. If both gamblers persist for a prolonged period, their fates are likely to be similar: They will lose money. Yet variations in the schedule, especially early on, may produce differences in the tendency to continue gambling.

In an experiment with pigeons, Alan Christopher (1988) tested the effects of early wins on willingness to gamble. First, he trained two pigeons to obtain their daily food by pecking at an illuminated disc. Pecking at the disc paid off at a steady rate: Fifty pecks earned three seconds at a food tray. This schedule allowed the birds to maintain normal body weight by working only about a half hour a day.

*(Continued)*

Next Christopher gave the birds a choice between working and gambling. He illuminated a disc that, like a slot machine, paid off in an unpredictable way. But Christopher arranged things so that novice gamblers got "lucky": During the first three days, the pigeons could earn far more food by gambling than they could by working. And Christopher made sure that now and then the birds had a big win—up to 15 seconds at the food tray. After the third day, however, the birds were better off working than gambling. The question was, Would they go back to work, or were they hooked on gambling?

They were hooked. The birds pounded relentlessly at the less rewarding gambling disc, so much so that they began to lose weight. Christopher prevented them from gambling for fear that they would starve themselves. Unable to gamble, the birds went back to work and began gaining weight.

Christopher provided the gambling disc again to see if the birds had learned their lesson. They had not. Once again they gambled and began losing weight, so Christopher ended the experiment. He did not want them to gamble their lives away.

## VR HARASSMENT

An example of the power of VR schedules to maintain behavior at a high rate may be seen in the case of a man accused of making harassing phone calls (30,000 Obscene Calls Traced, 1991). Apparently the man would call a woman and tell her he was holding members of her family hostage and would kill them if she did not stand naked outside her home. The ruse worked an average of about once in every 100 attempts—a VR 100 schedule. Such a schedule could be expected to produce a high rate of behavior. Apparently it did: The man made some 30,000 calls. On one day alone he called 130 women.

Not to be outdone, a woman spurned by her former lover called him more than 1,000 times a day for three years (Woman Pesters Ex-Lover with 1,000 Calls a Day, 2000). To escape the harassment, the man changed jobs and his phone and pager numbers, but the woman discovered the new numbers and resumed the calls—and added 500 faxes a day.

We cannot know for sure that these episodes were due to reinforcement schedules. However, it seems the most likely explanation, and animal studies suggest that people can become very persistent if reinforced intermittently.

### Fixed Interval

Reinforcement need not be based on the number of times a behavior occurs. In interval schedules, reinforcement is dispensed following a behavior, but only when the behavior occurs after a given period of time. In **fixed interval (FI) schedules,** the behavior under study is reinforced the first time it occurs after a constant interval. For example, a pigeon that has learned to peck a disk may be put on an FI 5″ (read, FI 5-second) schedule. The first time the bird pecks the disc, food is delivered into its food tray, but for the next five seconds, disc pecking produces no reinforcement. Then, at the end of the five-second interval, the very next disc peck is reinforced. Note that the reinforcer is not delivered merely because a given period of time has elapsed; a disc peck is still required.

Like fixed ratio schedules, fixed interval schedules produce post-reinforcement pauses. Typically, the bird on an FI schedule seldom pecks immediately after reinforcement, and then steadily increases the rate of pecking. By the time the interval has elapsed, the pecking rate is quite high. Thus, FI schedules produce a scallop-shaped cumulative record (see Figure 7-1c).

Why should FI schedules produce a scallop-shaped curve while FR schedules produce a steady run rate between pauses? Possibly because the FR schedule reinforces steady performance, whereas the FI schedule does not. Consider the case of a rat pressing a lever on an FR 50 schedule. The animal has a lot of work to do before it receives its next reinforcement, and any pause delays the reinforcer's arrival. Now consider the rat on an FI 50" schedule. No lever presses will produce reinforcement until 50 seconds have passed, so pressing during this period is pointless. Gradually the rat increases its rate of lever pressing until, near the end of the interval, it is pressing rapidly and steadily.We might expect that after some experience with this schedule the rat would become more efficient, delaying until, say, 40 seconds had elapsed. Surprisingly, this does not happen. No matter how long an animal is on an FI schedule, it begins pressing the lever long before doing so pays off, producing the familiar scallop-shaped curve.

Good examples of FI schedules in the natural environment are hard to come by. In many animal species, the females become sexually receptive at fairly regular intervals, and attempts by males to mate with them at other times are seldom reinforced. This therefore looks like an FI schedule. But estrus (sexual receptivity) is indicated by specific odors and other stimuli, and male sexual behavior is more likely to be under the influence of these cues than under the influence of the schedule.

Examples of FI schedules in humans are easier to think of, perhaps because we more often live by the clock. Your behavior is on an FI schedule when you bake bread because looking in the oven will be reinforced only when it occurs after a certain period. The first time you bake bread, you may open the oven door repeatedly to see how it's doing, but with experience you learn to wait until the required baking time has nearly elapsed before peeking inside the oven. The closer you get to the end of the required cooking time, the more often you open the oven door. Stephen Ceci and Uri Bronfenbrenner (1985) performed an experiment much like this example and got a scalloped curve, except that there was more checking at the beginning of the baking process than expected.

Edward Crossman (1991) suggests that waiting for a bus meets the criterion for an FI schedule. Suppose you approach a bus stop just as the bus leaves. The buses on this route are normally 15 minutes apart, so you have about 15 minutes to wait. Seeing your bus approach is likely to be reinforcing, but looking in the direction from which the bus will come is unlikely to be reinforced for several minutes. Thus, the behavior of looking for a bus is likely to occur infrequently in the early part of the 15-minute interval and much more frequently as the interval nears its end. When 15 minutes have elapsed, you are likely to be staring fairly steadily in the direction of the bus. Plot this behavior on a cumulative record, and the result will be a scalloped curve.

Studying provides another example. Many students show little inclination to study during the early days of the semester but spend increasing amounts of time studying as midterm exams approach. After midterms, their study time falls off sharply until shortly before finals. Plotted on a curve, studying would then show the familiar scalloped curve of FI schedules (but see Michael, 1991). We see exactly the same thing in members of Congress. Very few bills are passed during the first three or four months of a legislative session, but the rate of bill passing increases steadily after that, ending with a frenzy of bill-passing near the close of the session. The result is the same sort of scalloped curve we see in laboratory animals. Paul Weisberg and Phillip Waldrop (1972) found this scalloped pattern in all sessions of Congress from 1947 to 1968 (see Figure 7-2). Thomas Critchfield and colleagues at Illinois State University (2003) got similar congressional scallops over a 52-year period.

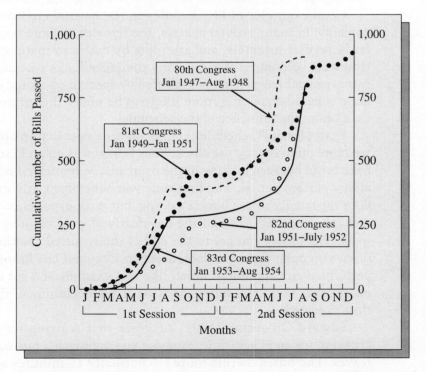

**Figure 7-2** *Fixed interval legislating. Cumulative number of bills passed during legislative sessions of Congress from January 1947 to August 1954. (From "Fixed-Interval Work Habits of Congress," by P. Weisberg, and P. B. Waldrop. 1972, Journal of Applied Behavior Analysis, 5[1], Figure 1, p. 94. Copyright © 1972 by the Society for the Experimental Analysis of Behavior, Inc. Reprinted with permission of the publisher and author.)*

## Variable Interval

Instead of reinforcing a behavior after a fixed interval, it is possible to vary the interval around some average. For example, instead of always reinforcing disc pecking after an interval of 5 seconds, we might reinforce a peck after 2 seconds, then after 8 seconds, 6 seconds, 4 seconds, and so forth. On such **variable interval (VI) schedules,** the length of the interval during which performing is not reinforced varies around some average. In a VI 5" schedule, the average interval between reinforced pecks is 5 seconds. Variable interval schedules produce high, steady run rates, higher than FI schedules, but usually not as high as comparable FR and VR schedules.

We can find VI schedules in natural environments as well as in the lab. Leopards often lie in wait for their prey rather than stalk it. Sometimes the wait may be short, sometimes long, but remaining alert and waiting quietly are eventually reinforced by the appearance of prey. The same sort of thing may be seen in spiders, snakes, and many other species. Human hunters also lie in wait for game. Deer hunters typically take a position in a tree or other high point and wait for a deer to appear within range. Sometimes they wait for hours; sometimes a deer appears almost immediately. Similarly, the nature photographer is on a VI schedule because he or she must wait for varying lengths of time before having the opportunity to get a good picture. Air traffic controllers who watch a radar screen are also on a VI schedule because the signals for which they watch occur at irregular intervals. We also find ourselves on VI schedules when we must wait in line at the bank. Each time a customer is served, we get closer to the teller, which is likely reinforcing, but one person ahead of us may take less than a minute to conduct his business and the next may take ten minutes. We experience the same sort of VI schedule when we wait "in line" on an Internet site.

**QUERY 3:** In a _____ schedule, reinforcement is contingent on the number

of times a behavior occurs; in an _____ schedule, reinforcement

is contingent on the behavior occurring after a given period since the last

reinforcement.

Interestingly, animals have preferences among the simple schedules just described. It is not surprising that a pigeon or a person will prefer a VR 10 schedule over an FR 100 schedule, but certain types of schedules are preferred over others even when, in the long run, the rate of reinforcement is the same. For example, pigeons sometimes prefer to work on a VR schedule rather than an FR schedule that pays off just as well. One factor is the length of the interval between reinforcements. If the interval is very short, the birds prefer a VR schedule; if it is long, they prefer FR. (The efforts to explain these preferences are interesting but beyond the scope of this text. See Field et al., 1996; Hall-Johnson & Poling, 1984; King, Schaeffer, & Pierson, 1974.)

## Extinction

B. F. Skinner was very good at designing and constructing gadgets to use in research. One device was a mechanism for automatically dispensing food into a tray each time a rat pressed a lever. One day while Skinner was out of the lab the mechanism jammed, so the rat that was lever pressing no longer got food. When Skinner returned to the lab he saw what had happened and looked at the cumulative record, which showed a steady decline in the rate of lever pressing. Skinner was looking at the first extinction curve of operant behavior.

You will recall that in classical conditioning, extinction means the CS is never followed by the US. In operant learning, **extinction** means that a previously reinforced behavior is never followed by reinforcers. Since no reinforcer is provided, extinction is not truly a reinforcement schedule; however, we might think of it as an FR schedule requiring an infinite number of responses for reinforcement. In an early study of extinction, Skinner (1938) trained rats to press a lever and then, after reinforcing about a hundred lever presses, disconnected the feeding mechanism. Everything was as it had been during training, except that now lever pressing no longer produced food. The result was a gradual decline in the rate of lever pressing (see Figure 7-3).

Although the overall effect of extinction is to reduce the frequency of the behavior, the immediate effect is often an abrupt increase. This is called an **extinction burst.** When extinction is used to treat practical behavior problems, the extinction burst gives the impression that the procedure has made the problem worse, rather than better. Tell a mother that she should ignore her child's demands for a treat, and the demands are likely to turn into screams and the parent will say, "I tried that; it didn't work." If extinction is continued, however, the extinction burst is typically followed by a fairly steady decline in the behavior.

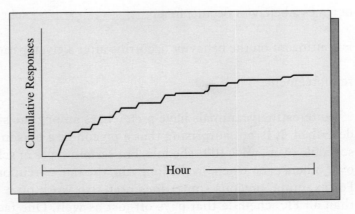

**Figure 7-3** *Extinction curve. This cumulative record shows the decrease in response rate of one rat when lever pressing no longer produced food. (Compare Figure 5-4.) (Adapted from* The Behavior of Organisms: An Experimental Analysis *[p. 68], by B. F. Skinner, 1938, New York: Appleton-Century-Crofts. Copyright © 1938, renewed 1966. Reprinted by permission.)*

Another effect of extinction is an increase in the variability of behavior. The individual seems to operate on the principle, "If at first you don't succeed, try something else!" Often the something else will be a variation of the previously reinforced behavior. We can make use of this phenomenon during shaping: After repeatedly reinforcing an approximation of the desired behavior, we can withhold reinforcement. This increases the variability of the behavior, which makes it likely that a better approximation of the desired behavior will appear. When it does, it can be reinforced. This use of extinction during shaping is a delicate procedure, however, because if one waits too long for a better approximation, the behavior may deteriorate.

Extinction often increases the frequency of emotional behavior, particularly aggression. Rats that receive food for pressing a lever sometimes bite the lever when pressing it no longer produces reinforcement. The aggression will be directed at another animal if one is nearby, even though the other animal was in no way responsible for the failure of the reinforcer to arrive (Azrin, Hutchinson, & Hake, 1966; Rilling & Caplan, 1973). Research also provides evidence that extinction can produce an increase in aggressive behavior in humans (e.g., Todd, Besko, & Pear, 1995). The tendency of extinction to provoke aggressive behavior will be familiar to anyone who has ever kicked a stuck door, slammed down a telephone receiver when a call did not go through, or slapped a recalcitrant computer.

Another effect of extinction is the reappearance of previously reinforced behavior, a phenomenon called **resurgence** (Epstein, 1983, 1985; Mowrer, 1940). Suppose a pigeon is trained to peck at a disc, and then this behavior is extinguished. Now suppose some new behavior, such as wing flapping, is reinforced. When the bird flaps steadily, this behavior is put on extinction. What does the bird do? Wing flapping declines, as expected, but something unexpected also occurs: The bird begins to peck at the disc again. As the rate of wing flapping declines, the rate of disc pecking increases (see Figure 7-4). Animal trainer Karen Pryor (1991) describes an instance of resurgence in a porpoise. An animal named Hou received reinforcement for performing a behavior learned in the previous training session. If this behavior were not reinforced, Hou would then run through its entire repertoire of previously learned stunts: breaching, porpoising, beaching, and swimming upside down.

The notion of resurgence can help us understand what some clinicians call regression, the tendency to return to more primitive, infantile modes of behavior (Epstein, 1985; Mowrer, 1940). The man who is unable to get his wife to behave as he would like by asking her nicely may shout and throw things, a form of behavior that got good results with his mother when he was a boy. The behavior "asking nicely" is on extinction, and the man reverts to a form of behavior that used to be effective. The behavior may very well be unconscious, meaning that he cannot specify the learning history that produced it. However, Robert Epstein (1985) notes that there is no need to assume, as Freud did, that the behavior that resurges will be more primitive than the behavior it replaces. It is simply behavior that used to produce reinforcement.

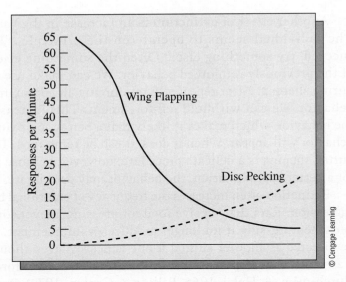

**Figure 7-4** *Resurgence. When a response (wing flapping) is put on extinction, a previously reinforced response (disk pecking) reappears. (Hypothetical data.)*

**? QUERY 4:** The reappearance, during extinction, of previously effective behavior is called

_____.

One extinction session is often not enough to extinguish behavior. This is often so even when the extinction session lasts for several hours and involves hundreds or even thousands of unreinforced acts. What usually happens is that the rate of the previously reinforced behavior declines and finally stabilizes at or near its baseline (pre-reinforcement) level. Extinction appears to be complete. If, however, the animal or person is later put back into the training situation, the extinguished behavior often occurs again, almost as though it had not been on extinction. You may recall that this reappearance of a previously extinguished behavior occurs during Pavlovian extinction and is called spontaneous recovery (see Chapter 3). In general, the longer the interval between the two extinction sessions, the greater the recovery.

We can see spontaneous recovery in everyday situations. A person who makes a number of unsuccessful attempts to get food from a vending machine may give up but may try again later in the day. This reappearance of the behavior is spontaneous recovery. Likewise, the teacher who finds that he has been reinforcing silly comments from students by smiling at them may put the behavior on extinction by not smiling. The frequency of silly remarks will fall off but may then reappear unexpectedly. In the absence of reinforcement, behavior that has spontaneously recovered soon drops off again. However, if behavior that reappears after extinction is reinforced, the rate jumps. The person who tries the vending machine after numerous failures may find that it now works, and may resume using the machine almost as if it had never

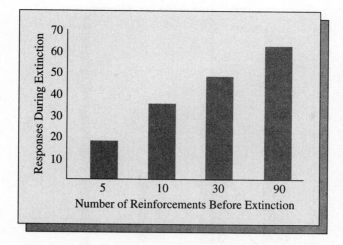

**Figure 7-5** *Extinction and number of reinforcements. The average number of responses made during extinction increased with the number of reinforced responses prior to extinction. (Compiled from data in Williams, 1938.)*

broken down. The teacher who extinguishes silly remarks, but then laughs when one occurs is apt to see a sharp increase in silly comments.

If a behavior is kept continuously on extinction, it will continue to decline in frequency. The rate at which extinction occurs depends on many factors, including the number of times the behavior was reinforced before extinction (Thompson, Heistad, & Palermo, 1963; Williams, 1938; see Figure 7-5), the effort the behavior requires (Capehart, Viney, & Hulicka, 1958; see Figure 7-6), the type (Shahan & Podlesnik, 2005) and size (Reed, 1991) of the reinforcer provided during training, and the reinforcement schedule in force prior to extinction (Grace, Bedell, & Nevin, 2002; Weisberg & Fink, 1966).

Extinction and reinforcement are parallel procedures, but they do not have equal effects: One non-reinforcement does not "cancel out" one reinforcement. Skinner (1938) noticed that dozens of unreinforced lever presses might follow a single reinforcement. On one occasion he provided one reinforcement, consisting of three food pellets, and the rat then pressed the lever 60 more times even though it received no more food. Thus, behavior is usually acquired rapidly and extinguished slowly (Morse, 1966; Skinner, 1953).

Although the rate at which a behavior declines during extinction will vary, the eventual result is the same. It is not possible to say, however, that extinction entirely erases the effects of previous reinforcement. Even after performing an act thousands of times without reinforcement, the behavior may occur with a frequency that slightly exceeds its baseline level. There is considerable doubt, in fact, that a well-established behavior can ever be truly extinguished, in the sense that it is no more likely to occur than it was before training (see, for example, Razran, 1956). To paraphrase Shakespeare: What's done can ne'er be (entirely) undone.

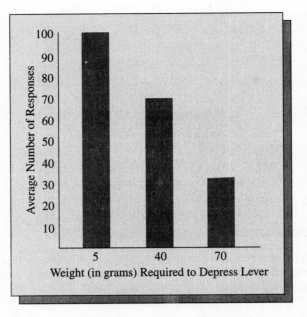

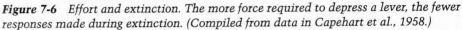

**Figure 7-6** *Effort and extinction. The more force required to depress a lever, the fewer responses made during extinction. (Compiled from data in Capehart et al., 1958.)*

## Other Simple Schedules

The reinforcement schedules just described are the bedrock of schedules research: Quite possibly more research has been done involving these schedules than with all other schedules combined. Yet there are other simple schedules that have received a good deal of attention. Let's consider a few of them briefly.

In a **fixed duration (FD) schedule,** reinforcement is contingent on the continuous performance of a behavior for some period of time. A typical example of an FD schedule is the child who is required to practice playing a piano for half an hour. At the end of the practice period, and provided the child has practiced the entire time, he receives a reinforcer. For example, a parent may provide milk and cookies or some other treat after a piano practice.

In a **variable duration (VD) schedule,** the required period of performance varies around some average. In the case of a child practicing the piano, any given session might end after 30 minutes, 45 minutes, 20 minutes, or 10 minutes. On average, the student will practice for half an hour before receiving the milk and cookies, but there is no telling when the reinforcers will appear.

Unfortunately, parents using duration schedules often provide insufficient reinforcement. The assumption is that the improvement that comes with practice will reinforce the student's work, but often this "intrinsic" reinforcer is too weak to be effective. Providing some treat at the end of the session should help. The Premack principle (see Chapter 5) suggests that if eating cookies and drinking milk are reinforcing, and if this behavior is contingent on practicing the piano continuously for some period, then playing the piano should itself become reinforcing. And indeed, this does seem to be the case.

In all of the schedules considered thus far, a reinforcer is contingent on behavior. It is possible, however, to create a schedule in which reinforcers are delivered independently of behavior (Lachter, Cole, & Schoenfeld, 1971; Zeiler, 1968). There are two kinds of such **noncontingent reinforcement (NCR) schedules.**

In a **fixed time (FT) schedule,** a reinforcer is delivered after a given period of time regardless of what behavior occurs. Fixed time schedules resemble fixed interval schedules except that in an FT schedule no behavior is required for reinforcement. In an FI 10″ schedule, a pigeon may receive food after a ten-second interval *but only if it pecks a disc;* in an FT 10″ schedule, the pigeon receives food every ten seconds *whether it pecks the disc or not.*

Fixed time schedules are not common outside the laboratory. Unemployment compensation and welfare payments do not precisely meet the definition of fixed time schedules, but they come close. Although certain behaviors are ostensibly required (e.g., people receiving unemployment compensation are supposed to look for work), in fact money is provided after a fixed period more or less independently of what the person does. The only true performance requirements are standing in line for the check and *saying* that one has tried to find work. Social critics who would replace welfare with "workfare" suggest that money should be contingent on behavior rather than time.

In **variable time (VT) schedules,** a reinforcer is delivered periodically at irregular intervals regardless of what behavior occurs. The only difference between VT schedules and FT schedules is that in VT schedules the reinforcer is delivered at intervals that vary about some average, whereas in FT schedules they arrive after a fixed period.

Genuine VT schedules are even harder to identify outside the lab than FT schedules. If you have a lot of aunts and uncles and periodically one of them dies and leaves you some money, that could be considered a VT schedule. This assumes, however, that you weren't required to be nice to them when they were alive.

 QUERY 5: In FT and VT schedules, reinforcement is contingent on _____

rather than _____.

**Progressive schedules** stand out from other schedules in that the rules describing the contingencies change systematically (Stewart, 1975). In fact, this feature makes me wonder if they can be considered simple schedules. There are theoretically four different types of progressive schedule (see Figure, 7-7), but I will focus on the most commonly studied, the **progressive ratio (PR) schedule** (Hodos, 1961; Killeen et al., 2009). In a PR schedule, the requirement for reinforcement typically increases in a predetermined way, often immediately following each reinforcement. The progression in the ratio is either arithmetic or geometric. For example, a rat might receive food after

*You might recognize that the reinforcement schedule Skinner used in his superstition experiment (see Chapter 6) was an FT schedule. Koichi Ono got superstitious behavior with VT schedules.*

| | Ratio | Interval | Duration | Time |
|---|---|---|---|---|
| Fixed | Fixed Ratio | Fixed Interval | Fixed Duration | Fixed Time |
| Variable | Variable Ratio | Variable Interval | Variable Duration | Variable Time |
| Progressive | Progressive Ratio | Progressive Interval | Progressive Duration | Progressive Time |

© Cengage Learning

**Figure 7-7**  *Simple schedules. Figure 7-1 displayed typical performance of the four most-studied schedules (FR, VR, FI, and VI), but other simple schedules are possible, as this table shows.*

pressing a lever twice. After this it might have to press the lever four times to receive food, then 6 times, 8 times, 10 times, and so on. In a geometric progression, the rat might have to press two times, then 4, then 8, 16, 32, 64, and so on. In some PR schedules what changes is not the number of responses required for reinforcement, but the reinforcer. The amount of food provided might get smaller and smaller, or its quality might diminish, or it might be delivered after a longer and longer delay. Whatever form the progression takes, it continues until the rate of the behavior falls off sharply or stops entirely. This is called the **break point**.

Whether progressive schedules occur naturally is debatable. When you start a new job, at first the workload may be relatively light, but then it gets heavier and heavier until you cannot keep up and you start looking for another job. If you apply for the Navy SEALs unit, you will find that the demands increase more and more until most of those who started the program have dropped out. Your health insurance company might announce that your monthly premium will increase by 50% in January, then it might increase another 30% in August, and so on; assuming you have to work to pay the premiums, this means more work for the same amount of coverage. These examples do not precisely fit the PR definition, since the progression is not usually predetermined and is not necessarily dependent on behavior. The reason researchers are interested in progressive schedules has less to do with their natural occurrence than with their value as a research and therapeutic tool (e.g., Dougherty et al., 1994; Lattal & Neef, 1996; Rickard et al., 2009; Roane, 2008).

## Stretching the Ratio

Rats will press levers and pigeons will peck discs hundreds of times for a single reinforcer, even if that reinforcer is a small amount of food. People have also worked steadily on very "thin" schedules—schedules that require many responses for each reinforcement. How is this possible? Why should a rat, much less a person, press a lever hundreds of times for some trivial amount of reinforcement?

The answer is a kind of shaping. An experimenter does not train a rat to press a lever and then put the behavior on an FR 100 schedule. Instead, he or she starts with a CRF schedule and, when the animal is working at a steady rate, increases the ratio to FR 3; when this schedule has been in force a while, the experimenter may go to FR 5, then FR 8, FR 12, FR 20, FR 30, and so on. Researchers call this procedure **stretching the ratio**, although a better term might be *stretching the contingency*, since the same procedure can be applied to interval, duration, and time schedules. It is essentially the same process used to shape new behavior, except that in this case what is being shaped is persistence.

 **QUERY 6:** The thinner of two schedules, FR 3 and VR 4, is _____.

Stretching the ratio almost certainly occurs in nature. Earlier we considered the wolves that prey on elk. When parasitic infection weakens the elk herd, hunting is relatively easy; as the wolves remove the sicker animals, hunting requires more effort. The shift from a low-ratio schedule to a high-ratio schedule (one in which most efforts are not reinforced) is probably a gradual one.

We may see stretching of the ratio among human "predators" by visiting a gambling establishment. Card sharks and pool hustlers sometimes let their competitors win frequently during the early stages of play and then gradually win more and more of the games. They stretch the ratio gradually because they do not want to "lose their pigeon." Stretching the ratio can be put to more benevolent purposes. Parents, for example, may praise their children each time they see them studying; gradually, however, they may reinforce the behavior less often.

**QUERY 7:** How could you "stretch the ratio" when a behavior is on an interval schedule?

Stretching the ratio must be done with some care; stretch too rapidly or too far and the tendency to perform will break down, a phenomenon called **ratio strain.** (Progressive schedules inevitably produce ratio strain and, as noted above, reach a break point.) Workers who grumble about being "overworked and underpaid" and who shirk their responsibilities may be suffering from ratio strain. However, Skinner (1953) noted that it is possible to stretch the ratio to the point at which an animal receiving food reinforcement expends more energy than it receives. Christopher (1988) demonstrated this in a study of gambling pigeons (see *Life Is a Gamble,* on page 199).

The simple schedules just described are, as the term implies, relatively uncomplicated, but they get a bit more challenging when combined to form compound schedules, our next topic.

CAPSULE **REVIEW** Simple schedules include continuous reinforcement, in which a behavior is reinforced each time it occurs, and various kinds of intermittent schedules, in which the behavior is reinforced on some occasions and not others. Intermittent schedules include FR, VR, FI, VI, EXT, NCR, FT, VT, FD, VD, and PR. (And if you don't know what those abbreviations stand for, you need to reread this section.) Stretching the ratio can thin a simple reinforcement schedule.

## COMPOUND SCHEDULES

Compound schedules consist of various combinations of simple schedules. We will consider only a few of the more important compound schedules.

In a **multiple** schedule, a behavior is under the influence of two or more simple schedules, each associated with a particular stimulus. A pigeon that has learned to peck a disc for grain may be put on a multiple schedule in which pecking is reinforced on an FI 10″ schedule when a red light is on but on a VR 10 schedule when a yellow light is on. The two reinforcement schedules alternate, with the changes indicated by changes in the color of the light. The experimenter refers to this as a MULT FI 10″ VR 10 schedule. The bird's cumulative record shows the familiar scalloped curve of FI schedules when the red light is on, followed by the rapid, steady behavior associated with VR schedules when the yellow light is on (see Figure 7-8).

A **mixed schedule** is the same as a multiple schedule except that there are no stimuli (such as red and yellow lights) associated with the change in reinforcement contingencies. In a MIX FI 10″ VR 10 schedule, disc pecking might be reinforced on an FI 10″ schedule for, say, 30 seconds and then on

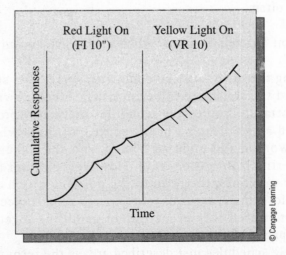

**Figure 7-8** *Multiple schedule. A pigeon's rate and pattern of responding change when a stimulus indicates a change in the reinforcement schedule in force. (Hypothetical data.)*

a VR 10 schedule for 60 seconds, but there is no clear indication that the schedule has changed.

**QUERY 8:** The difference between multiple and mixed schedules is that in

_____ schedules there is a signal that the schedule has changed.

In a **chain schedule,** reinforcement is delivered only on completion of the last in a series of schedules. Consider a pigeon on a CHAIN FR 10 FI 15″ VR 20 schedule: The bird pecks a red disc; after the tenth peck the disc changes from red to yellow. The yellow disc signals that an FI 15″ schedule is in effect; after 15 seconds, pecking the disc changes it from yellow to green. Working at the green disc results, after an average of 20 pecks, in food. The disc also becomes red again, indicating that the FR 10 schedule is once again in force. Note that the bird receives food only after completing the requirement of the last schedule. Despite this, the bird typically behaves as though food were provided on each of the separate schedules. When it is on the FI 15″ schedule, for example, the cumulative record shows the typical scalloped curve associated with FI schedules.

A **tandem schedule** is identical to a chain schedule except that there is no distinctive event (e.g., a light or buzzer) that signals the end of one schedule and the beginning of the next.

Chain and tandem schedules give rise to an interesting question: What reinforces the behavior during the schedules that _don't_ produce food? In the case of chain schedules, distinctive stimuli, such as the disc colors, indicate not only that a new schedule is in force but also that reinforcement is nearer. These stimuli may therefore act as secondary reinforcers. But what is the reinforcer in the case of the tandem schedule, where such stimuli are not provided? In this case, it may be that the changes in schedules themselves serve as cues because they do in fact signal that reinforcement is closer.

The schedules described thus far, both simple and compound, involve an individual. It is possible, however, to arrange schedules that make reinforcement dependent on the behavior of two or more individuals. Such arrangements are called **cooperative schedules.** For instance, we might arrange for two pigeons to receive food by pecking a disc when the two of them have pecked a total of 20 times. One might peck the disc at the rate of 10 times a minute while the other pecks 40 times a minute. As soon as the total number of pecks reaches 20, they each receive a few pieces of grain. Or we might arrange the schedule so that both birds receive food following a total of 20 pecks, but only if each of them has pecked 10 times. In a cooperative schedule, the reinforcement that one subject gets is partly dependent on the behavior of the other subject.

Cooperative schedules involving two individuals are the easiest to manage, but it is possible to arrange cooperative schedules with larger groups. For instance, a group of five birds might receive food when the group as a whole produces 100 disc pecks, provided that each bird pecks the disc at least 10 times.

Cooperative schedules are often used with people, though typically in an inefficient manner. For example, a group of students may be required to work together on a project. Each student in the group receives the same grade for the project, regardless of what each contributes. The students are supposed to share the work equally. However, reinforcement is not contingent on how the work is shared but on what the group as a whole produces. A common result is that some members of the group do more than their fair share while others do less. We can often see the same phenomenon in the workplace when employees are asked to work as a group on some project. This inequality of labor might be avoided or reduced by altering the cooperative schedule so that individual contributions are reinforced as well as the group effort. This is often the case in team sports. Winning or losing depends on the collective effort, but the performance of each player produces individual consequences, such as cheers and boos.

In the schedules discussed thus far, only one schedule is available to a person or animal at any given moment. In **concurrent schedules,** two or more schedules are available at once. A pigeon may have the option of pecking a red disc on a VR 50 schedule or pecking a yellow disc on a VR 20 schedule. In other words, concurrent schedules involve a choice. In the example just given, the animal would soon choose the yellow disc and the VR 20 schedule. Because a great deal of behavior involves choices, we will consider this problem in greater detail later.

---

CAPSULE **REVIEW**   Two or more simple schedules can be combined to form various kinds of compound schedules. When the schedules alternate and each is identified by a particular stimulus, a multiple schedule is said to be in force. When the schedules alternate but there is no signal, a mixed schedule is in force. In a chain schedule, reinforcement occurs only on completion of the last in a series of reinforcement schedules, with each schedule change signaled by a change in stimulus. Tandem schedules resemble chain schedules except that there is no signal. A cooperative schedule makes reinforcement contingent on the behavior of two or more individuals. In concurrent schedules, two or more schedules are available simultaneously, so that the individual must choose among them.

---

# THE PARTIAL REINFORCEMENT EFFECT

One peculiar schedule effect is the tendency of behavior that has been maintained on an intermittent schedule to be more resistant to extinction than behavior that has been on continuous reinforcement. This phenomenon is known as the **partial reinforcement effect (PRE).** (It is also referred to as the partial reinforcement extinction effect [PREE].)

The PRE was clearly demonstrated in a classic experiment by O. Hobart Mowrer and Helen Jones (1945). These researchers first trained rats to press a

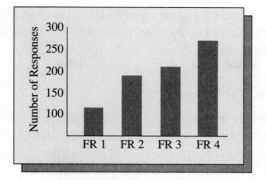

**Figure 7-9** *Partial reinforcement effect. Average number of lever presses by rats during extinction following four fixed ratio schedules of reinforcement. The thinner the schedule, the greater the number of responses during nonreinforcement. (Compiled from data in Mowrer and Jones, 1945.)*

lever for food. After this preliminary training, Mowrer and Jones randomly assigned the rats to one of five groups, four of which are of interest to us. In each group, lever pressing was on a different reinforcement schedule: CRF, FR 2, FR 3, and FR 4. After this the rats had a training session each day that lasted until lever pressing had been reinforced 20 times. After seven days and a total of 140 reinforcements, the researchers put lever pressing on extinction. The total number of presses during extinction showed a clear, counterintuitive pattern: The thinner the reinforcement schedule, the greater the number of lever presses during extinction (see Figure 7-9).

Human beings also sometimes show remarkable resistance to extinction following intermittent reinforcement (Pittenger & Pavlik, 1989; Poon & Halpern, 1971). In one study, Harlan Lane and Paul Shinkman (1963) put a college student's behavior on extinction after reinforcing it on a VI 100″ schedule. Although other variables besides the reinforcement schedule may have affected the student's behavior, it is interesting that the student worked for 11 hours and performed the behavior over 8,000 times without reinforcement!

PRE has been put to practical use in applied settings (e.g., Hanley, Iwata, & Thompson, 2001). Once a behavior is well established, a therapist may begin thinning the reinforcement schedule (stretching the ratio). This makes the behavior more resistant to extinction and therefore more likely to persist outside the therapeutic setting. Teachers can also make good use of the PRE by first establishing a behavior and then stretching the ratio of reinforcement.

 QUERY **9:**  PRE stands for _____.

The PRE, which has been demonstrated many times, is paradoxical because the law of effect implies that the unreinforced responses that occur during an intermittent schedule should *weaken* the tendency to press, not make it stronger. Because of this paradox, researchers have devoted considerable time and effort to accounting for the effect. We will consider four hypotheses for explaining the phenomenon.

## Discrimination Hypothesis

The **discrimination hypothesis** says that extinction takes longer after intermittent reinforcement because it is harder to distinguish (or discriminate) between extinction and an intermittent schedule than between extinction and continuous reinforcement (Mowrer & Jones, 1945).

Imagine that you are vacationing in Las Vegas, and you decide to try your luck at the slot machines. As it happens, the machine you approach is defective. Some gizmo in its works has gone temporarily awry so that it always pays off. You approach the machine, put in a quarter, and push the button. (It's one of the newer machines that use buttons rather than handles.) You win a dollar. You put in another quarter and win a few more dollars. Each time you put in a quarter and push the button, you win. After you deposit perhaps 100 quarters, and win 200 dollars, the machine suffers another breakdown, and now the machine never pays off. (Of course, you have no way of knowing this.) You put in a quarter, press the button, and much to your surprise, you win nothing. You put in another quarter, then another, and another, and so on, but you never receive anything. You can see that if you were in this situation, it would probably not be long before you would stop gambling at that machine.

You move on to try another machine. As in the first example, the slot machine you try is defective, but this time it does not pay off every time. Instead, it pays off on every 30th attempt. When you have inserted 100 coins—and won 200 dollars—the machine suffers another breakdown that prevents it from ever paying off. You are unaware of the defect and continue inserting coins. Now, how many coins must you insert before you have any clue that the reinforcement schedule has changed? The answer is 30 coins. In other words, there is nothing amiss about putting in 29 quarters without winning. You will eventually stop throwing quarters away, but you will probably persist longer than you did at the machine that switched from continuous reinforcement to extinction. The reason, according to the discrimination hypothesis, is that it takes longer to distinguish between extinction and an FR 30 schedule than it does to distinguish between extinction and an FR 1 schedule. You can probably see that it would take even longer to distinguish between extinction and an FR 100 schedule. Discriminating between extinction and a VR 100 schedule would take still longer because in that schedule a behavior may sometimes occur 150 or more times before producing reinforcement. Thus, the discrimination explanation of the PRE proposes that behavior extinguishes more slowly after intermittent reinforcement than after continuous reinforcement because the difference between CRF and extinction is greater than the difference between an intermittent schedule and extinction.

As appealing as the discrimination hypothesis is, it has not proved entirely satisfactory at predicting behavior (Jenkins, 1962). Other explanations have attempted to build on the discrimination hypothesis in one way or another. One of these theories is the frustration hypothesis.

## Frustration Hypothesis

Abram Amsel (1958, 1962) has proposed the **frustration hypothesis** to explain the PRE. Amsel argues that nonreinforcement of previously reinforced behavior is frustrating. Frustration is an aversive emotional state, Amsel says, so anything that reduces frustration will be reinforcing. In continuous reinforcement, there is no frustration because there is no nonreinforcement, but when the behavior is placed on extinction, there is plenty of frustration. With each nonreinforced act, frustration builds. (Anyone who has repeatedly lost coins in a pay phone or a vending machine is familiar with the aversive state created by nonreinforcement of a behavior that is normally reinforced.) Any behavior that reduces an aversive state is likely to be negatively reinforced, so during extinction, frustration may be reduced by *not* performing the behavior. (In the same way, you will quickly abandon a pay phone that cheats you, thereby reducing your annoyance.)

When a behavior is reinforced intermittently, there are periods of nonreinforcement—and frustration. The individual continues to perform during these periods of frustration and eventually receives reinforcement. Thus, lever pressing *while frustrated* is reinforced. Put another way, the emotional state called frustration becomes a cue or signal for pressing the lever. Now when the behavior is placed on extinction, the animal becomes frustrated, but the frustration is a signal for lever pressing, so responding continues. This increases the frustration, and increased frustration is a signal for responding, so the behavior continues, which causes even *more* frustration, which is a signal for lever pressing, and so on.

The thinner the reinforcement schedule during training, the higher the level of frustration when the rat finally receives food. For the rat on a thin schedule, then, high-level frustration becomes a cue for lever pressing. With continued responding during extinction, the individual becomes increasingly frustrated, but because high-level frustration is a signal for lever pressing (the more frustrated the rat gets, the closer it gets to food), extinction proceeds slowly.

Frustration is one way of accounting for the PRE; another focuses on the sequence of cues.

## Sequential Hypothesis

E. J. Capaldi's (1966, 1967) **sequential hypothesis** attributes the PRE to differences in the sequence of cues during training. He notes that during training, each performance of a behavior is followed by one of two events, reinforcement or nonreinforcement. In continuous reinforcement, all lever presses are reinforced, which means that reinforcement is a signal for lever pressing. During extinction, no lever presses are reinforced, so an important cue for lever pressing (the presence of reinforcement) is absent. Therefore, extinction proceeds rapidly after continuous reinforcement because an important cue for performing is missing.

During intermittent reinforcement, some lever presses are followed by reinforcement, some by nonreinforcement. The *sequence* of reinforcement and nonreinforcement therefore becomes a signal for pressing the lever. A rat on an FR 10 schedule, for example, must press nine times without reinforcement before it presses the tenth time and receives reinforcement. The nine nonreinforced lever presses are a signal for lever pressing. The thinner the reinforcement schedule, the more resistant the rat will be to extinction because a long stretch of nonreinforced lever pressing has become the cue for continued pressing. In other words, the rat performs in the absence of reinforcement because, in the past, long strings of nonreinforced presses have reliably preceded reinforcement.

The frustration and sequential hypotheses have much in common. For instance, both assume that extinction is an active learning process, and both Amsel and Capaldi also assume that stimuli present during training become cues for behavior. The chief difference seems to be that Amsel finds the cues inside the organism (the physiological reaction called frustration), whereas Capaldi finds the cues in the environment (the sequence of reinforcement and nonreinforcement). We now consider a very different approach to the PRE, the response unit hypothesis.

**QUERY 10:** The frustration and sequential hypotheses are both variations of the

_____ hypothesis.

## Response Unit Hypothesis

Mowrer and Jones (1945) offer another explanation for the PRE called the **response unit hypothesis.** This approach says that to understand the PRE we must think differently about the behavior on intermittent reinforcement.

In lever pressing studies, for example, lever pressing is usually thought of as one depression of the lever sufficient to produce some measurable effect on the environment, such as activating a recording device. But, say Mowrer and Jones, lever pressing can also be defined in terms of what produces reinforcement.

In the case of a CRF schedule, the two definitions coincide exactly: Each time the rat presses the lever far enough to activate the recorder, it receives a bit of food. But consider what happens if we switch to an FR 2 schedule: One lever press produces nothing, but two presses produce food. If an animal receives food only after pressing the lever two times, "we should not think of this as press-failure, press-reward," write Mowrer and Jones (1945), "but rather as press-press-reward" (p. 301). In other words, if lever pressing is on an FR 2 schedule, then the unit of behavior being reinforced is *two* lever presses; if the schedule is FR 3, then the unit of behavior being reinforced is *three* lever presses; and so on. VR schedules are more complicated because the response unit is defined not only by the average number of acts required for reinforcement but also by the range of units. In a VR 4 schedule, for instance, producing reinforcement may sometimes require only one lever press and sometimes eight lever presses. Nevertheless, the idea that the behavior is defined by the number of times it must occur to produce reinforcement still applies.

Now consider again the Mowrer and Jones experiment described earlier. In the CRF group, the response unit was one lever press; rats in this group produced an average of 128 response units (lever presses) during extinction. In the FR 2 group, the response unit was two lever presses; rats in this group produced an average of 94 responses (188 lever presses divided by 2). In the FR 3 group, the response unit was three lever presses and the rats produced 71.8 responses (215.5 ÷ 3). In the FR 4 group, the response unit was four presses, and the rats produced 68.1 responses (272.3 ÷ 4). Notice that when responses are defined in terms of the units required for reinforcement, the total number of responses during extinction declines as the reinforcement schedule gets thinner (see Figure 7-10).

Mowrer and Jones note that when we define responses in terms of the units required for reinforcement, we find that "the apparent advantage of so-called intermittent reinforcement disappears" (p. 301). In other words, the PRE is an illusion. Behavior on intermittent reinforcement only *seems* to be more resistant to extinction because we have failed to take into account the response units required for reinforcement.

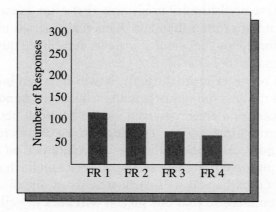

**Figure 7-10** *Partial reinforcement effect? Average number of responses by rats during extinction following four fixed ratio schedules of reinforcement. In this case, a response is defined as the number of lever presses required for reinforcement. The thinner the reinforcement schedule, the fewer responses during extinction. (Cf. Figure 6-2.) (Compiled from data in Mowrer and Jones, 1945.)*

Of the four main explanations of the PRE, the response unit hypothesis is easily the most elegant, but the PRE is a very complex problem, and no theory about it can yet claim to have won the day. However, other promising theories are being pursued (Nevin, 2012).

CAPSULE **REVIEW**

The number of times a behavior occurs during extinction varies with the schedule in effect before extinction. A behavior typically occurs many more times following intermittent reinforcement than following continuous reinforcement. This is known as the partial reinforcement effect. Attempts to explain the PRE include the discrimination, frustration, sequential, and response unit hypotheses.

## CHOICE AND THE MATCHING LAW

As you saw earlier, a concurrent schedule represents a choice. A pigeon on such a schedule may, for example, peck a red disc or a yellow disc, but it cannot do both simultaneously.

Making a choice may involve a great deal of thought. Human beings faced with a choice often verbalize silently, and sometimes aloud, about the relative merits of the various options. (We say that we are "weighing the alternatives.") It is possible that some other species engage in analogous behavior when faced with a choice. However, our interest is not in these cogitations but in the effect that the reinforcement schedules have on the choices made. The task is to predict, from the reinforcement schedules in force, how the person or animal will behave when faced with a given choice. Sometimes this is easily done. Imagine a rat in a T-maze arranged so that if the rat enters the arm on the right, it will receive food, but if it enters the arm on the left, it will receive nothing. We have no difficulty predicting that after a few trials, the rat will most often turn right rather than left. A choice situation in which behavior *A* is always reinforced and behavior *B* is never reinforced quickly results in the reliable performance of behavior *A*.

*People sometimes agonize over choices, but the agonizing doesn't explain the choice made. The cogitating is part of the behavior of choosing, and behavior cannot explain itself.*

Prediction becomes more difficult, however, when both alternatives are reinforced, and the only difference is in the relative frequency of reinforcement. Consider the case of a pigeon given a choice between pecking either of two discs, one red, the other yellow. Pecking the red disc is reinforced on an FR 50 schedule, and pecking the yellow disc is reinforced on an FR 75 schedule. What will the pigeon do? Perhaps it will go back and forth repeatedly between the two discs. Or perhaps it will work steadily at one disc, but the disc will be selected at random, so that one pigeon will peck at yellow, another at red. In fact, what happens is that the pigeon initially spends time at each disc, moving back and forth between them, but eventually settles on the disc with the richer reinforcement schedule. In fact, some animals have an uncanny knack for selecting the "better-paying" work. Humans are also quite good at identifying better-paying reinforcement schedules (Pierce & Epling, 1983).

Richard Herrnstein (1961, 1970, 2000; Herrnstein & Mazur, 1987) led the way in the study of choice. He showed that the effort devoted to each of two reinforcement schedules can be expressed by the formula

$$\frac{B_1}{B_2} = \frac{r_1}{r_2}$$

This formula means that given two behaviors, $B_1$ and $B_2$, each on its own reinforcement schedule, $r_1$ and $r_2$, respectively, the relative frequency of each behavior equals the relative frequency of reinforcement available.[1] This statement is called the **matching law** because the distribution of behaviors matches the availability of reinforcement (Herrnstein, 1961, 1970, 2000; for reviews of the literature, see Davison & McCarthy, 1988; Pierce & Epling, 1983; Poling et al., 2011).

In the case of two ratio schedules, such as FR 30 and FR 40, the subject samples each and then settles on the denser schedule. In concurrent ratio schedules, it makes sense to identify the more reinforcing schedule as quickly as possible and remain loyal to it. In the same way, if you can pick beans for Farmer Able for $5 a bushel, or for Farmer Baker for $4 a bushel, it makes little sense to switch back and forth. Other things being equal, your behavior will follow the matching law: You will pick steadily for Farmer Able.

**QUERY 11:** State the matching law in your own words.

Switching makes more sense when concurrent interval schedules are involved. Consider the case of a rat lever pressing on a concurrent FI 10″ FI 30″ schedule. Clearly, the payoff is better on the FI 10″ schedule, so it makes sense for the animal to spend most of its time working on that lever. But even on that schedule, there are periods during which lever pressing is useless. Some of this time could be spent pressing the lever on the FI 30″ schedule. And the longer the animal works on the FI 10″ schedule, the more likely it is that pressing the lever on the FI 30″ schedule will produce food. It therefore pays for the animal to devote most of its effort to the FI 10″ schedule but occasionally press the lever on the FI 30″ schedule. But does a rat actually do this? In fact, this is exactly what it does.

What about concurrent VI schedules? Suppose a rat has a choice between VI 10″ and VI 30″ schedules. Once again it makes sense for the animal to devote most of its time to the VI 10″ schedule, but occasional lever presses on the VI 30″ schedule are also likely to be reinforced. This is so even though delivery of reinforcement is variable and therefore unpredictable. Once again, animals behave in the most efficient manner: They focus on the VI 10″ schedule but periodically abandon this schedule to work on the VI 30″ schedule. In this way, they receive more reinforcement than they would if they worked solely on the better-paying VI 10″ schedule. Even when the

---

[1] I have changed Herrnstein's notation slightly in hopes of making the formula less confusing.

differences in schedules are fairly subtle, animals usually behave in a manner that is in their best interests.

We have seen that, given a choice between two interval schedules, an animal will alternate between them. Is it possible to predict, on the basis of the schedules in force, how much an animal will work on each schedule? Herrnstein (1961, 1970, 2000) found that it is indeed possible. He reports that in a two-choice situation, the choice may be predicted according to the mathematical expression

$$\frac{B_A}{B_A + B_B} = \frac{r_A}{r_A + r_B}$$

where $B_A$ and $B_B$ represent two behaviors, behavior $A$ and behavior $B$, and $r_A$ and $r_B$ represent the reinforcement rates for behaviors $A$ and $B$, respectively. This equation is merely a reformulation of the matching law.

Take the case of a rat trained to press a lever for food. Presses on lever A are reinforced on a VI 10″ schedule; presses on lever B are reinforced on a VI 30″ schedule. If the rat were to work solely on the VI 10″ schedule, it would receive a maximum of six reinforcers per minute. If it occasionally works on the VI 30″ schedule, it could obtain a maximum of two more reinforcers. Thus, of the total reinforcers obtainable, 75% (six out of eight) are available on the VI 10″ schedule, and 25% are available on the VI 30″ schedule. The value of $r_A$ is therefore about 0.75; that of $r_B$ is about 0.25. The formula predicts that the rat will devote approximately three-fourths of its effort to schedule $A$ (the VI 10″ schedule) and one-fourth to schedule $B$ (VI 30″). Experimental tests show that such predictions are surprisingly accurate.

In an early study, Herrnstein (1961) put pigeons on a concurrent VI schedule that was basically like the hypothetical rat study just described, but more complicated. He plotted the data to show the relationship between the proportion of responses on one key to the proportion of reinforcement on that key (Herrnstein, 1970). As you can see from Figure 7-11, the match between the two was nearly perfect.

Herrnstein extended the matching law beyond the two-choice situation, suggesting that *every* situation represents a kind of choice. Consider the pigeon that receives food when it pecks a disc. There are many things the pigeon can do besides peck the disc. It may groom itself, wander around the cage, peck at objects on the floor or on the walls, sleep, and so on. In pecking the disc, it is therefore choosing to engage in that behavior rather than various others. Indeed, even when the pigeon pecks the disc at a high rate, it continues to engage in other kinds of behavior, such as bobbing its head and turning to the left and right. Theoretically, it is possible to identify all of these actions and the reinforcers that maintain them and to predict the relative frequency of any one of them. This idea can be expressed by the formula

$$\frac{B_A}{B_A + B_o} = \frac{r_A}{r_A + r_o}$$

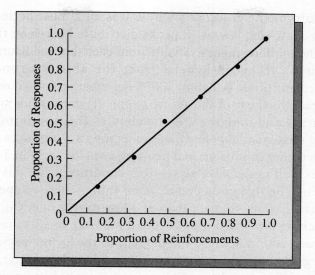

**Figure 7-11** *Matching. The diagonal line shows perfect matching between the proportion of responses and the proportion of available reinforcements. The pigeons came very close to perfect matching. (From "On the Law of Effect," by R. J. Herrnstein, 1970,* Journal of the Experimental Analysis of Behavior, 13, *Figure 4, p. 247. Copyright © 1970 by the Society for the Experimental Analysis of Behavior, Inc. Reprinted with permission of the publisher.)*

where $B_A$ represents the particular behavior we are studying, $B_o$ represents all *other* behaviors, $r_A$ represents the reinforcers available for $B_A$, and $r_o$ represents the reinforcers available for all other behaviors (Herrnstein, 1970). This formula has less predictive value than the formula for the two-choice situation because it is not possible to specify all the behaviors that may occur nor all the reinforcers those acts may produce. Some behaviors may, for example, be reinforced by events not readily subject to observation, as in the case of the reinforcement a rat receives when it scratches an itch. Still, the formula reminds us that behavior is a function of the reinforcers available for any behavior that might occur, not merely the reinforcers available for the behavior that interests us at the moment.

William Baum (1974) provides evidence that the matching law describes the foraging of free-ranging pigeons. He set up an apparatus for studying disc pecking in an attic space accessible to wild pigeons. Baum had no control over which birds pecked at a disc, but the apparatus was arranged so that only one bird could work at a time. After the birds had learned to receive food by pecking a disc, Baum gave them a choice between two discs. Pecking now paid off on VI schedules, with the disc on the right always providing food more frequently than the one on the left. Because the birds were wild and could come and go as they pleased, it is impossible to say just how many birds participated in the experiment, but Baum estimates the number at between 10 and 20.

The result for the group as a whole was an almost perfect correspondence with the matching law, with pecks distributed between the discs in proportion to the reinforcement available from each (but see Baum & Kraft, 1998).

Humans likewise benefit from the ability to match behavior to reinforcement (Kraft & Baum, 2001). For most of human existence, people no doubt made good use of the ability to apportion behavior appropriately among the hunting and foraging areas available. Today, a farmer may do this by devoting most available farmland to a crop that produces a nice profit under typical weather conditions and planting a smaller area in a less profitable crop that does well under adverse weather conditions. (This is known as hedging one's bet.) The rest of us do the same thing when we spend more time and energy at a high-paying job than at a low-paying one. College students obey the matching law when they devote more time to a five-credit course than to a one-credit course because a high grade in the former pays better (contributes more to grade point average) than a high grade in the latter.

Choice is a complicated topic, and it would be an exaggeration to say that the matching law always predicts the distribution of behavior accurately (Binmore, 1991; Staddon, 1991; Sy, Borrero, & Borrero, 2010). Nevertheless, the matching law does often hold for a wide variety of species, behaviors, reinforcers, and reinforcement schedules (see deVilliers, 1977, for a review). It holds, for example, whether we are considering different rates of reinforcement (Herrnstein, 1970), different amounts of reinforcement (Todorov et al., 1984), or different reinforcement delays (Catania, 1966). And it holds for punishment schedules as well as reinforcement schedules (Baum, 1975). It has accurately described behavior in some natural settings (Reed, Critchfield, & Martens, 2006; Romanowich, Bourret, & Vollmer, 2007; Vollmer & Bourret, 2000) and has been put to use in treating behavior problems (Borerro & Vollmer, 2002; McDowell, 1982). Its formulation is a milestone in the history of behavior science.

This introduction to choice and the matching law is (believe it or not) very elementary. If you feel you are ready for a more sophisticated discussion of these topics, a great place to start is an article by Alan Poling of Western Michigan University and his colleagues (2011). If you are a graduate student, you might also tackle William Baum's tutorial (Baum, 2010). Whether you read these articles or engage in behavior that produces reinforcers with less effort is, of course, a matter of choice.

---

CAPSULE **REVIEW**

People and many animals have a remarkable ability to distinguish between more and less reinforcing schedules. The tendency to work in proportion to the reinforcement available is so reliable that it is called the matching law. In the case of a choice among ratio schedules, the matching law correctly predicts choosing the schedule with the highest reinforcement frequency. In the case of a choice among interval schedules, the matching law predicts working on each schedule in proportion to the amount of reinforcers available on each.

---

## GHETTO CHOICE

A police officer in a small town arrested a suspected drug dealer. In the ten-minute ride to the police station, the suspect's beeper went off at least seven times, each time displaying only codes. In a single night's work, a dealer that busy probably makes $5,000 in drug sales. What are the dealer's alternatives? What other levers can he press? Typically, the only legal alternative available to the drug dealer is some sort of unskilled work paying something near minimum wage. If you were poor, with no realistic hope of getting the training that would lead to a well-paid job, and you had a choice between selling drugs for $5,000 a night or flipping burgers for $300 a week, which lever would you press?

## A FINAL WORD

A great deal of research has been done on schedules of reinforcement and their differential effects, but some psychologists have raised doubts about the value of this work (Schwartz & Lacey, 1982; Schwartz, Schuldenfrei, & Lacey, 1978).

Some critics argue that the schedules of reinforcement studied in the laboratory are artificial constructions not found in the real world. It is true that schedules found outside the laboratory are seldom as simple as those created by researchers. But this is true of all laboratory science: Researchers take a problem into the lab precisely because the lab allows them to simplify it.

Other critics complain that schedules research generally produces trivial findings. Who cares how long a pigeon pauses after reinforcement before pecking away at a disc again? But it is not trivial to note that personality (i.e., the characteristic behavior of an individual) is a function of the individual's history of reinforcement. Identifying the kinds of learning history that help produce behavioral tendencies is a considerable advance. Schedules research is one way to do this (see, for example, Doughty et al., 2005; Okouchi, 2007; Skaggs, Dickinson, & O'Connor, 1992).

Reinforcement schedules also have value as a research tool for answering all sorts of questions that have nothing to do with identifying schedule effects. For instance, schedules are now commonly used as a way of measuring the effects of drugs. Terry Belke and M. J. Dunbar (2001) trained rats to press a lever to get access to an exercise wheel. The reinforcement schedule was FI 60″, and the reinforcer was 60 seconds in the exercise wheel. This schedule produced a low rate of behavior, usually fewer than six lever presses a minute. Nevertheless, the familiar FI scallop pattern appeared (see Figure 7-12a). At this point the researchers administered cocaine in varying amounts ten minutes before running the rats. The cocaine had no detectable influence on the pattern of behavior until the researchers reached a dosage of 16 milligrams per kilogram of body weight. At that level, the scalloped pattern deteriorated (see Figure 7-12b). In much the same way, researchers used schedules as a basis for comparing the effects of alcohol and cocaine on

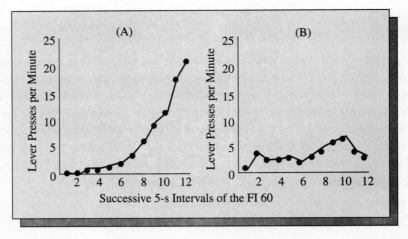

**Figure 7-12**  *Cocaine effects revealed in schedule performance. Lever pressing reinforced on an FI schedule showed the familiar scallop pattern (A). Cocaine administration had a pronounced effect on performance (B). (Adapted from an unpublished figure provided by T. Belke, based on data from Belke and Dunbar, 2001.)*

human performance (Higgins et al., 1992). Thus, schedule performance can provide a basis for evaluating the effects of psychoactive drugs, toxins, diet, sleep deprivation, exercise, brain stimulation, medicines, and many other variables.

Reinforcement schedules were once called the "sleeping giant" of behavioral research (Zeiler, 1984). The giant appears to have awakened (Morgan, 2010). I hope you now realize that it's a friendly giant.

# RECOMMENDED **READING**

1. Ferster, C. B., & Skinner, B. F. (1957). *Schedules of reinforcement.* New York: Appleton-Century-Crofts.

   This classic describes the basic kinds of reinforcement schedules and provides many graphs illustrating the rates and patterns of behavior associated with each. It is mandatory reading for anyone who plans to do research on learning, pharmacology, or neuroscience.

2. Hursh, S. R. (1984). Behavioral economics. *Journal of the Experimental Analysis of Behavior, 42,* 435–452.

   This discussion of economics framed in terms of reinforcement schedules should be read by anyone interested in economics.

3. Morgan, D. L. (2010). Schedules of reinforcement at 50: A retrospective appreciation. *The Psychological Record, 60,* 151–158.

   This is a short overview of the origins and major developments in schedules research.

4. Poling, A., Edwards, T. L., Weeden, M., & Foster, T. M. (2011). The matching law. *The Psychological Record, 61,* 313–322.

This is a good place to start if you want to learn more about the matching law, an important topic not only in behavior science but also in economics.

5. Rachlin, H. (1989). *Judgment, decision and choice: A cognitive/behavioral synthesis*. New York: W. H. Freeman.

In this short book, Rachlin attempts to show that choice and schedules can account for both overt behavior and rational thought. This book is for advanced students only.

## REVIEW **QUESTIONS**

1. Define the following terms:

   | | |
   |---|---|
   | between-ratio pause | post-reinforcement pause |
   | chain schedule | pre-ratio pause |
   | concurrent schedule | ratio strain |
   | continuous reinforcement | response unit hypothesis |
   | cooperative schedule | run rate |
   | discrimination hypothesis | schedule effects |
   | fixed duration (FD) schedule | schedule of reinforcement |
   | fixed interval (FI) schedule | sequential hypothesis |
   | fixed ratio (FR) schedule | stretching the ratio |
   | fixed time (FT) schedule | tandem schedule |
   | frustration hypothesis | variable duration (VD) schedule |
   | intermittent schedule | variable interval (VI) schedule |
   | matching law | variable ratio (VR) schedule |
   | mixed schedule | variable time (VT) schedule |
   | multiple schedule | progressive ratio schedule |
   | noncontingent reinforce-<br>ment (NCR) | |
   | partial reinforcement effect<br>(PRE) | |

2. John wants to teach Cindy, age 5, the alphabet. He plans to reinforce correct performances with praise and small pieces of candy. What sort of schedule should he use?

3. Mary complains that her dog jumps up on her when she gets home from school. You explain that she reinforces this behavior by petting and talking to the dog when it jumps up, but Mary replies that you must be wrong because she hardly ever does this. How would you respond to Mary's comment?

4. Fifteen-year-old David gives up easily in the face of frustration. How could you develop his persistence?

5. Joyce is annoyed because some of her employees fail to take the periodic rest breaks required by the union and the state's safety regulations. Why do you suppose this happens, and what can Joyce do to correct the problem?

6. Is gambling a form of superstitious behavior? (See the discussion of superstition in Chapter 6.)

7. In the days of public telephones, many people regularly checked the coin return after making a call. Explain this behavior.

8. How might you use what you know about reinforcement schedules to study the effects of the presence of observers on human performance?

9. A teacher reinforces longer and longer periods of quiet behavior in her students. How can she avoid creating ratio strain?

10. Pretend you are an economist who wishes to know the effect of inflation on purchasing. Describe an experiment that will shed light on the problem.

## PRACTICE **QUIZ**

1. In CRF, the ratio of responses to reinforcement is _____ to _____.

2. After a reinforcement, the rate of the reinforced behavior may fall to or near zero before increasing again. The period during which the behavior occurs infrequently is called a _____ pause.

3. One difference between FT and FI schedules is that in the _____ schedule, reinforcement is not contingent on a behavior.

4. Extinction is the opposite of _____.

5. Thinning a reinforcement schedule too rapidly or too much can produce _____.

6. Of the four explanations of the PRE, the one that essentially says there is no such thing is the _____ hypothesis.

7. If reinforcement is contingent on the behavior of more than one individual, a _____ schedule is in effect.

8. Choice involves _____ schedules.

9. The tendencies to respond eventually correspond to the probabilities of _____.

10. The _____ law means that, given a choice of activities, the proportion of responses to each activity will reflect the availability of reinforcement for each.

## QUERY **ANSWERS**

Query 1. An FR1 schedule is also called *CRF/continuous reinforcement.*

Query 2. The rate at which a behavior occurs once it has begun is called the *run* rate.

Query 3. In a *ratio* schedule, reinforcement is contingent on the number of times a behavior occurs; in an *interval* schedule, reinforcement is contingent on the behavior occurring after a given period since the last reinforcement.

Query 4. The reappearance, during extinction, of previously effective behavior is called *resurgence.*

Query 5. In FT and VT schedules, reinforcement is contingent on *time* rather than *behavior.*

Query 6. The thinner of two schedules, FR 3 and VR 4, is *VR 4.*

Query 7. You could do something analogous to stretching the ratio by "stretching the interval."

Query 8. The difference between multiple and mixed schedules is that in *multiple* schedules there is a signal that the schedule has changed.

Query 9. PRE stands for *partial reinforcement effect.*

Query 10. The frustration and sequential hypotheses are both variations of the *discrimination* hypothesis.

Query 11. Your answer should be something like this: The rate of behavior matches (or is proportional to) the rate of reinforcement.

# 8 Operant Learning: Punishment

*The world runs on fear.*

—**Jack Michael**

## PREVIEW

Reinforcement is essential to our survival: We learn to do those things that have, in the past, led to food, water, shelter, approval, and safety. Reinforcement is also essential to a good quality of life: We learn to do those things that provide companionship, relief from stress, and entertainment. But not all behavior has reinforcing consequences. Our survival and happiness also depend on learning *not* to do things that have, in the past, had negative consequences. Punishment, like reinforcement, is a teacher to which we must attend.

# BEGINNINGS

E. L. Thorndike`s classic research on learning (see Chapter 5) clearly demonstrated that behavior depends on its consequences. If pulling on a string or stepping on a treadle results in escape from a box, a cat will pull on the string or step on the treadle the next time it is in that box. Thorndike summarized this tendency in his law of effect, which you will recall can be expressed as *behavior is a function of its consequences.* This law implies that the nature of a consequence is the principal determinant of the strength of a behavior. If a behavior results in a "satisfying state of affairs," it is likely to become stronger; if it results in an "annoying state of affairs," it is likely to become weaker. These two kinds of consequences are what we now call reinforcers and punishers.

Thorndike initially assumed that positive and negative consequences have parallel effects: Negative consequences weaken behavior just as readily as positive consequences strengthen it. Later, when he looked again at punishment, he changed his views about it. In one experiment Thorndike (1932) presented college students with Spanish words or uncommon English words and asked them to choose a synonym from an array of five alternatives. If they guessed correctly, the experimenter said, "Right"; if incorrectly, the experimenter said, "Wrong." Thorndike then looked at the tendency of students to repeat right and wrong answers. He found that "Right" increased the tendency to repeat an answer, but "Wrong" did not decrease it. He did other experiments and got comparable results. This ran counter to his original view of the parallel nature of positive and negative consequences, and he concluded that punishment has little effect. We learn from success, not from failure.

B. F. Skinner (1938), best known for his research on reinforcement, also did research on the effects of punishment. In one experiment he trained rats to press a lever for food and then put the behavior on extinction. During the first ten minutes of extinction, some rats received a "slap" from the lever each time they pressed it. When Skinner compared the cumulative records of these rats, he found that punishment markedly reduced the rate of lever pressing, but the rate increased quickly once punishment ended. The end result was that punished rats pressed the lever about as often as those that had not been punished. As a result of such findings, Skinner came to the conclusion that punishment suppresses behavior, but only temporarily.

Further research revealed that Thorndike and Skinner greatly underestimated the power of punishment.

# TYPES OF PUNISHMENT

In everyday conversation, the word *punishment* usually refers to retribution or "payback." Someone commits an offense, and he "pays the price." This sort of language may be satisfactory in ordinary discourse, but it is useless in science, where terms must be defined in measurable ways. Punishment, like reinforcement, is defined by its measurable effects on behavior. Reinforcement means an increase in the strength of behavior due to its consequences.

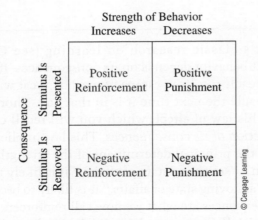

**Figure 8-1**   *Contingency square. In operant procedures, the strength of a behavior increases or decreases depending on its consequences.*

**Punishment** means a *decrease* in the strength of behavior due to its consequences. Following Charles Catania's (2006; see Chapter 5) observations on reinforcement, we can say that an experience must have three characteristics to qualify as punishment: First, a behavior must have a consequence. Second, the behavior must decrease in strength (e.g., occur less often). Third, the reduction in strength must be the result of the consequence.

There are two types of punishment (see Figure 8-1). In **positive punishment,** the consequence of a behavior is the appearance of, or an increase in the intensity of, a stimulus. Typical punishers in positive punishment include reprimands, electric shock, and physical blows, such as those delivered in a spanking. If you go for a walk in the park and are mugged, you may be less likely to walk in that park in the future; if so, walking in that park was positively punished.

In **negative punishment,** a behavior is weakened by the removal of, or a decrease in the intensity of, a stimulus. This stimulus is ordinarily something the individual seeks out. Fines are a good example because something we typically seek (money) is taken away. Parents and teachers try to use this sort of punishment when they take away privileges, such as eating dessert, watching television, playing a game, or using a computer. Because negative punishment means the removal or reduction of something, it is also called **penalty training** (Woods, 1974).

A popular form of penalty training is Time Out (TO), short for *Time Out from Positive Reinforcement.* It is used mainly with children, and consists of removing a misbehaving child from an area where he obtains reinforcement (Bean & Roberts, 1981; Cipani, 1999, 2004; Roberts & Powers, 1990). Although the child is removed from a reinforcing area, in effect the reinforcers are taken away from the child. Consider the case of a five-year-old boy who is bullying other children—pushing them to the floor, taking away their toys, disrupting their games. The teacher moves the child from the play area to a corner with a screen, thus preventing him from participating with or even seeing the other

*In reading about punishment, keep in mind that in the field of learning, punishment has nothing to do with retribution; it has to do only with reducing the strength of behavior.*

*One way that people misuse TO is by spending time with the child in the TO area—explaining why he is there, chatting with him, and otherwise giving him lots of attention. This can reinforce the inappropriate behavior rather than punish it.*

children. The boy is required to stay in the corner for two minutes, and must be quiet for at least the last 30 seconds of that period, before returning to the play area. Time Out is widely used in homes and elementary schools, but unfortunately it is often misused. Teachers and parents, for example, sometimes chat with the child during the time out period or provide toys "to keep him quiet," thereby rendering the procedure ineffective.

**(?)  QUERY I:**  Positive and negative punishment are similar in that both _____

a behavior.

The terms *positive* and *negative punishment* are at least as troublesome as the terms *positive* and *negative reinforcement*. How can punishment be positive? As in the case of reinforcement, the terms *positive* and *negative* do not refer to the nature of the events involved. They refer to the fact that something is added or subtracted from the situation. If something is added, we speak of positive punishment; if something is removed, we speak of negative punishment. The two variations of punishment have also been called type 1 and type 2, respectively.

## AVERSIVE CONFUSION: POSITIVE PUNISHMENT AND NEGATIVE REINFORCEMENT

Positive punishment and negative reinforcement are often confused. This is partly because both procedures involve aversive events such as shocks, spankings, pinches, and criticism. The difference is that in positive punishment an aversive is *added* following a behavior, and as a result the behavior occurs *less* often, whereas in negative reinforcement, an aversive is *removed* following a behavior, and as a result the behavior occurs *more* often.

Consider a laboratory example of positive punishment: A rat is in an experimental chamber. It has previously learned to obtain food by pressing a lever. It goes to the lever and presses it—and receives a brief shock to its feet. It presses the lever again and receives another shock. The consequence of pressing the lever is *delivery* of a shock. As a result, the rate of lever pressing *decreases*. Lever pressing has been positively punished.

Now consider a laboratory example of negative reinforcement: A rat is in an experimental chamber. The floor of the chamber delivers a mild, constant shock to the rat's feet. If the rat presses a lever, the shock ceases for five seconds. In other words, the consequence of pressing the lever is the *removal* of shock. As a result, the rate of lever pressing *increases*. Lever pressing has been negatively reinforced.

Positive punishment and negative reinforcement are very unfortunate terms, but we are stuck with them for the present. To keep the concepts straight, remember that both use aversives, but one adds them and the other takes them away. The key is to remember that positive means add, and negative means subtract. Then it all adds up.

 **QUERY 2:** In positive punishment, something is _____; in negative

punishment, something is _____.

CAPSULE **REVIEW**   Punishment in everyday use means retribution, but in the field of learning it means providing consequences that reduce the strength of behavior. There are two forms of punishment, positive and negative. In the first, something is added after a behavior; in the second, something is removed. The procedures, like those in reinforcement, are basically simple, but the effects of numerous variables complicate their effects.

## VARIABLES AFFECTING PUNISHMENT

Punishment, like reinforcement, is basically a simple phenomenon. However, the effects of a punishing experience depend on the complex interactions of many variables. Many of the same variables that are important in reinforcement are also important in punishment.

### Contingency

The degree to which punishment weakens a behavior (i.e., reduces its frequency) varies with the degree to which a punishing event is dependent on that behavior. If a rat receives a shock each time it presses a lever, but not otherwise, then there is a clear contingency between lever pressing and shock. If, on the other hand, the rat is as likely to get a shock when it doesn't press the lever as when it does, then there is no contingency. The greater the degree of contingency between a behavior and a punishing event, the faster the behavior changes.

An experiment by Erling Boe and Russel Church (1967) illustrates. After first training rats to press a lever for food, Boe and Church put lever pressing on extinction for 20 minutes. During 15 minutes of this period, some rats received shocks occasionally, regardless of what they did; other rats received shocks, but only when they pressed the lever; and the remaining rats never received shocks. After this, all the rats underwent an hour-long extinction session each day for the next nine days; none of the rats received shocks during these sessions. The result was that the amount of lever pressing during extinction varied with exposure to shock (see Figure 8-2). Rats that never received shocks showed a gradual decline in the rate of lever pressing, as is expected during extinction. The performance of rats that received noncontingent shocks was almost the same as that of rats that received no shocks. But rats that received shocks only when they pressed the lever showed a marked reduction in lever pressing during extinction.

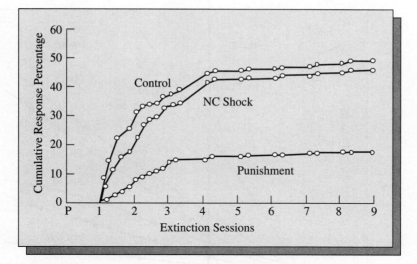

**Figure 8-2**  *Contingency and punishment. Cumulative record of the median number of responses (as a percentage of responses before punishment) following no shocks (control), noncontingent shocks, and response-contingent shocks (punishment). (Adapted from "Permanent Effects of Punishment During Extinction," by E. E. Boe and R. M. Church, 1967,* Journal of Comparative and Physiological Psychology, 63, *pp. 486–492. Copyright © 1967 by the American Psychological Association. Reprinted by permission.)*

Another way of looking at the role of contingency is to look at the probability of punishment. Nathan Azrin, W. C. Holz, and Donald Hake (1963) looked at this question with pigeons. First they established disc pecking on a VI schedule. Then they changed the contingencies so that all birds continued to receive food on the VI schedule but some also received a strong electric shock. For some of these birds, every disk peck resulted in shock; for others, every 100th peck produced shock; for still others, every 200th peck produced shock, and so on. As you can see from Figure 8-3, birds that received no shocks at all pecked at a high, steady rate. The rate of pecking for the other birds depended on how often pecking produced shock (see also Azrin, 1959).

There is evidence that inconsistent punishment can sometimes be effective if the probability of a punisher is made very high and is then *gradually* reduced (Lerman et al., 1997). As a practical matter, however, if you use punishment you would do well to remember that the more consistently a behavior is followed by a punishing event, the less likely the behavior is to occur in the future.

## Contiguity

The interval between a behavior and a punishing consequence is also very important: The longer the delay, the less effective the punisher is.

The importance of contiguity in punishment is nicely illustrated in an experiment by David Camp and his colleagues (1967). In this experiment, rats periodically received food for pressing a lever. They also sometimes received

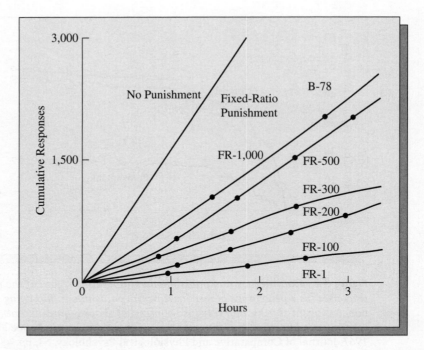

**Figure 8-3** *Effect of probability of punishment. All birds received food on a VI 3' schedule, but most also received severe shocks on an FR schedule. The frequency of disc pecking varied with the frequency of punishment. (From "Fixed-Ratio Punishment," by N. H. Azrin et al., 1963,* Journal of the Experimental Analysis of Behavior, 6(2), Figure 3, p. 144. *Copyright © 1963 by the Society for the Experimental Analysis of Behavior, Inc. Reprinted with permission of the publisher and author.)*

## TEXTING WHILE DRIVING—PUNISHABLE BY DEATH

By now you have surely heard that texting while driving increases the risk of traffic accidents. You cannot look at the text or the keyboard on your cell phone and simultaneously look at the road ahead of you, the traffic signals and signs, the pedestrians and animals crossing the road, and the vehicles around you. The same thing is true of chatting on a cell phone, playing video games, or programming your CD player while driving. The risks of such activities are supported not only by casual observation (such as the texting woman I saw almost drift into an oil tanker and then drift into the dividing lane) but also by research: In 2008, 16% of fatal traffic accidents involved inattentive drivers, up from 12% in 2004 (National Highway Traffic Safety Administration, 2009). Those who talk on phones while driving are *four times* as likely to be involved in a collision (Redelmeier & Tibshirani, 1997.

So, if engaging in irrelevant activities while driving is so risky, why do people do it? The most likely answer seems to be: because they get away with it. People who engage in distracting activities while driving are more likely to be in a crash, but this does not mean that crashing is a routine consequence of such behavior.

But, you say, the intensity of the punisher (injuries to oneself or others, criminal charges and fines, jail time, costly damage to one's vehicle) can be far worse than the reinforcer for the distracting behavior. After all, can sending a text message ("On way ETA 20 min") be reinforcing enough to merit the risk of being paralyzed for life? Can talking on a cell phone result in enough business income to justify the risk of killing a mother and her two children?

Logically, engaging in behavior that incurs such risks is absurd. But behavior has far more to do with contingencies than with logic. If people crashed into someone every time they read or sent a text message or talked on a cell phone while driving, chances are these practices would be as rare as sightings of the Dodo bird. But that isn't the schedule in effect. Put another way, high-frequency, low-intensity reinforcers generally seem to outweigh low-frequency, high-intensity punishers (look again at Figure 8-3).

If you think this means that we must simply accept the suffering as inevitable, you are very much mistaken. What it means is that we must recognize that the source of the problem is the contingencies in force, and to fix the problem we must devise ways of changing those contingencies.

shocks for lever pressing. For some rats, the shocks came immediately after pressing the lever; for others, the shocks were delayed by two seconds; for still other rats, there was a delay of 30 seconds. The researchers measured the effectiveness of shock in terms of a suppression ratio—basically the percentage of the responses that would have been expected without shocks. The results showed that immediate shocks suppressed lever pressing very effectively. When shocks followed lever presses by two seconds, they were far less effective in suppressing the behavior; a shock delayed by 30 seconds had even less value (see Figure 8-4).

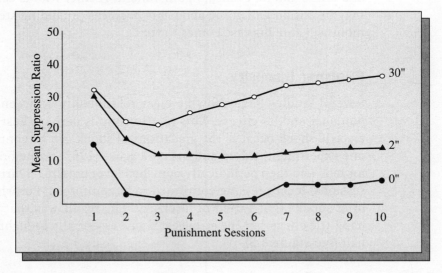

***Figure 8-4*** *Contiguity and punishment. Average suppression ratios for rats receiving response-contingent shocks that were immediate or delayed 2 or 30 seconds. The lower the suppression ratio, the more effective the procedure. (From "Temporal Relationship Between Response and Punishment," by D. S. Camp, G. A. Raymond, and R. M. Church, 1967,* Journal of Experimental Psychology, *74, Figure 3, p. 119. Copyright © 1967 by the American Psychological Association. Adapted with permission.)*

The importance of contiguity has also been demonstrated in experiments with people. In one study, Ann Abramowitz and Susan O'Leary (1990) studied the effects of immediate and delayed reprimands on the "off-task" behavior of hyperactive first and second graders. (Being off-task means doing things other than the assigned work.) In this study, teachers reprimanded the students either immediately or two minutes after the off-task behavior began. Reprimands were effective in suppressing off-task behavior in which the child interacted with another student, but only when the reprimands were immediate; delayed reprimands were useless.

Perhaps delays reduce the effectiveness of punishment because during the delay interval, other behaviors occur, and these may be suppressed rather than the intended behavior. Thus, a delayed punisher may suppress the same amount of behavior, but immediate punishment is more likely to act on the targeted behavior. In any case, the rule of thumb is clear: Those who would use punishment effectively must find ways of reducing the gap between the deed and the consequence.

Unfortunately, outside the laboratory this rule is known more for its neglect than for its observance. A mother on a shopping trip tells her mischievous child, "Just wait 'til we get home!" Such threats are normally not very effective because the threatened punishment comes (if at all) long after the offense. Teachers make the same error when they tell a youngster at nine o'clock in the morning that she will have to stay after school at the end of the day—six hours after the offense! It also seems likely that one reason our criminal justice system is ineffective is the delay between the commission of a crime and its eventual punishment. A thief who is caught "red-handed" may be out on bail going about his business (including stealing·property) for months before his case comes to trial.

## Punisher Intensity

Several studies have shown a clear relationship between the intensity of a punisher and its effects. This relationship is perhaps best seen in the use of electric shock because the gradations of shock can be controlled precisely. In one experiment, Camp and his colleagues (1967) trained rats to press a lever for food and then periodically punished lever pressing. During the punishment sessions, lever pressing continued to be reinforced. Punishment consisted of brief shocks that varied in intensity. The result was that the mildest shock had little effect, but the strongest shock essentially brought lever pressing to a halt (see Figure 8-5).

QUERY 3:    Figure 8-5 shows that the more _____ a punisher, the more it

_____ the rate of a behavior.

Other research has yielded similar findings (Azrin, 1960; Azrin, Holz, & Hake, 1963). After reviewing research on this problem, Nathan Azrin and

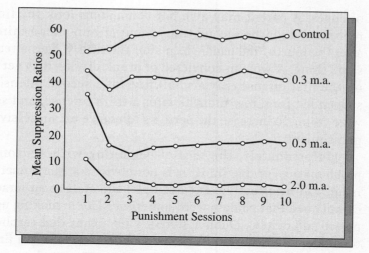

**Figure 8-5** *Punisher intensity. Average suppression ratios for rats receiving no shocks (control) or occasional response-contingent shocks of three intensities. The lower the suppression ratio, the more effective the procedure. (From "Temporal Relationship Between Response and Punishment," by D. S. Camp, G. A. Raymond, and R. M. Church, 1967, Journal of Experimental Psychology, 74, Figure 1, p. 117. Copyright © 1967 by the American Psychological Association. Adapted with permission.)*

W. C. Holz (1966) concluded, "All studies of the intensity of punishment have found that the greater the intensity of the punishing stimulus, the greater is the reduction of the punished responses" (p. 396). That conclusion still stands today.

## Introductory Level of Punisher

In using punishment, one may begin with a strong aversive that is almost certain to suppress the behavior, or one may begin with a weaker aversive and gradually increase its intensity until an effective level is found. Which is better?

Azrin and Holz (1966) argue that using an effective level of punishment from the very beginning is extremely important. The problem with beginning with a weak punisher and gradually increasing its intensity is that the punished behavior will tend to persist during these increases, and in the end a far greater level of punisher may be required to suppress the behavior. Research psychiatrist Jules Masserman (1946) found, for example, that cats would continue to respond despite strong levels of punishment if the punisher was initially weak and gradually increased. A punisher that might have suppressed a behavior entirely had it been used at the beginning became ineffective when it followed a series of weaker punishers (see also Miller, 1960; Azrin, Holz, & Hake, 1963). If punishment is to be used, then, the goal should be to begin with a punisher that is intense enough to suppress the behavior at the outset.

This point is by no means obvious. It is common practice for parents, teachers, employers, and judges to follow an initial offense with a mild aversive and then gradually increase the intensity of the aversive for subsequent offenses. A parent may give her son a stern look the first time he curses, reprimand him the second time, shout at him after a third offense, slap him after the fourth, and paddle him after the fifth. Judges often do essentially the same thing. A woman convicted of drunk driving may get off with a warning on the first offense, pay a small fine for a second offense, have her license suspended for a few months after a third offense, and so on. It is as if we were trying to increase the person's tolerance for successively higher levels of punishment.

*Why would a small fine make people more likely to be late? Review the section on concurrent schedules in Chapter 7, and you may come up with an answer.*

Unfortunately, the idea of beginning with a strong aversive is also problematic. For one thing, it is not obvious at the outset what level of punisher will be effective. For example, the staff at an Israeli day care center complained that parents were sometimes late in picking up their children (reported in Levitt & Dubner, 2005). This meant that teachers had to stay late to look after the children. The school decided to levy a fine of $3 per child if a parent were more than ten minutes late. The result was that parental tardiness *increased!* Soon there were twice as many late arrivals as there had been. The initial punisher was simply too weak. Would a $10 fine have worked? A $20 fine? $50? It's impossible to say for sure in advance.

## Reinforcement of the Punished Behavior

In considering punishment, remember that the unwanted behavior almost certainly is reinforced. If this were not the case, the behavior would not occur or would occur very infrequently. It follows that the effectiveness of a punishment procedure depends on the frequency, amount, and quality of reinforcers the behavior produces.

Consider a rat that receives food when it presses a lever. If pressing ceases to produce food, it is sure to decline. Similarly, an employee who frequently leaves work early does so because there are more rewarding things to do than stay at work. The success of efforts to punish behavior will depend, then, on the reinforcing consequences of the behavior (Azrin & Holz, 1961; Camp et al., 1967). In one study, Phil Reed and Toshihiko Yoshino (2001) used a noise to punish lever pressing in rats. When lever pressing was likely to produce food, rats pressed the lever even though doing so also caused a loud noise. When lever pressing did not "pay" well (when they got less food), even a half-second tone reduced lever pressing.

## Alternative Sources of Reinforcement

A related factor in the effectiveness of punishment is the availability of alternative ways of obtaining reinforcement. Consider a hungry rat that receives food when it presses a lever. Now suppose we begin shocking the rat when it presses the lever. You can see that if the lever is the rat's only means of obtaining food, it is likely to continue pressing despite the shocks unless they are very intense (see Figure 8-3). On the other hand, if the rat has another way of obtaining food, the shocks will likely suppress lever pressing quickly.

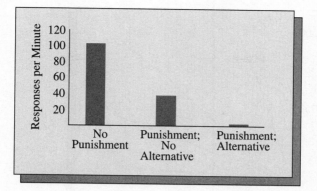

**Figure 8-6**  *Punishment and alternative source of reinforcement. Average number of responses per minute when the response was periodically reinforced, but never punished; when it was punished but there was no alternative means of obtaining reinforcement; and when it was punished but there was an alternative means of obtaining reinforcement. (Compiled from data in Herman and Azrin, 1964.)*

In a study by R. L. Herman and Azrin (1964), male psychiatric patients continued to perform a behavior that periodically produced reinforcers, even though the behavior also produced a loud, annoying sound. However, when the patients had an alternative way of obtaining reinforcers (one that did not produce noise), they readily did that. Punishment completely suppressed the original behavior when there was an alternative way of obtaining reinforcement (see Figure 8-6).

This finding has an obvious implication for the practical use of punishment: When punishing an unwanted behavior, be sure to provide an alternative means of obtaining the reinforcers that maintain that behavior. For instance, if a child receives adult attention by playing with his food at the dinner table, make sure that she can obtain attention in more acceptable ways. If you do that, punishment will be more effective—and, more importantly, may not be necessary.

## Motivating Operations

You will recall that the effectiveness of a reinforcer can be increased by performing an establishing operation, a kind of motivating operation (see Chapter 5). The same is true of punishment.

For example, food is more reinforcing when an animal is hungry, so if an unwanted behavior is maintained by food reinforcement, reducing the level of food deprivation is likely to make punishment more effective. Researchers demonstrated this by comparing the effects of punishment on disc pecking when birds were under different levels of food deprivation (Azrin, Holz, & Hake, 1963). Punishment had little effect when the birds were very hungry, but it suppressed disc pecking almost completely when the birds were only slightly hungry (see Figure 8-7).

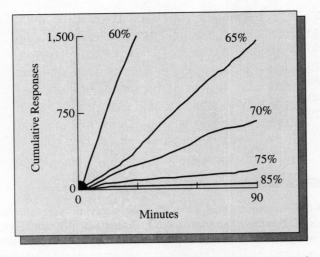

*Figure 8-7*   *Reinforcer deprivation and effects of punishment. Rate of behavior of bird 76 at various levels of food deprivation. Responses were periodically reinforced with food; every 100th response produced a strong shock. At the lowest level of food deprivation (85% of free-feeding weight), punishment was very effective; at higher levels of depriva-tion, it was less effective. (From "Fixed-Ratio Punishment," by N. H. Azrin et al., 1963,* Journal of the Experimental Analysis of Behavior, *6[3], p. 146. Copyright © 1963 by the Society for the Experimental Analysis of Behavior, Inc. Reprinted with permission of the publisher and author.)*

In the same way, social isolation is likely to be more effective as a punisher if a person has not spent much time with others recently. He is "hungry" for social contact, so withdrawing social contact should be a more effective punisher.

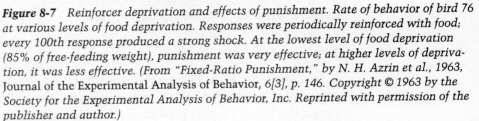

**QUERY 4:**   In general, the _____ the level of reinforcer deprivation, the

_____ effective a punisher is.

## Other Variables

The variables just reviewed are among the most important in determining the effectiveness of punishment, but other variables play a role. Qualitative fea-tures of the punisher, for example, can be important. A high-pitched sound may be a more effective punisher than a low-pitched sound. The different variables also interact in complex ways. Punishment, like reinforcement, is more complicated than it appears on first inspection.

**QUERY 5:**   Name four variables affecting punishment.

CAPSULE **REVIEW**  Although punishment is basically a simple procedure, it is complicated by the many variables that affect it. These include contingency, contiguity, punisher intensity, the introductory level of punishment, the availability of reinforcement for the punished behavior and for alternative behaviors, and motivating operations, among other things.

# THEORIES OF PUNISHMENT

Early theories of punishment (Estes, 1944; Guthrie, 1952; Skinner, 1953) proposed that response suppression was due to the disruptive effects of aversive stimuli. They pointed out that when a rat is shocked it might jump, then freeze or run hurriedly about. This behavior is clearly incompatible with, say, pressing a lever, so the rate of lever pressing is bound to decline. Skinner (1953) gives the example of a child who giggles in church. If the parent pinches the child, this arouses emotional behavior that is incompatible with giggling, so the giggling stops or declines. The punished behavior, said Skinner, "is merely temporarily suppressed, more or less effectively, by an emotional reaction" (p. 188).

Research on punishment undermined this explanation by producing two key findings: First, as we have seen, the effects of punishment are not as transient as Skinner thought if sufficiently strong aversives are used. Second, punishment has a greater suppressive effect on behavior than does aversive stimulation that is independent of behavior. This last point takes a bit of explaining.

If punishment reduces behavior rates merely because it evokes incompatible behavior, then it should make no difference whether the aversive stimuli used are contingent on behavior, but in fact it makes a great deal of difference. Recall the study by Boe and Church (1967), described earlier, in which some rats received noncontingent shocks. The experimenters also ran a group of rats that received occasional shocks, but in this group the shocks were contingent on lever pressing. Thus, some rats received shocks contingent on lever pressing, others received the same number of shocks independent of their behavior, and a control group received no shocks at all. As noted earlier, the noncontingent shocks did suppress lever pressing, but this effect was nothing compared to that of contingent shocks (look again at Figure 8-2).

The disruption theory of punishment could not explain this discrepancy between contingent and noncontingent aversives. Today, the two leading explanations of punishment are the two-process and one-process theories we encountered in considering avoidance learning (see Chapter 5).

## Two-Process Theory

Two-process theory says that punishment involves both Pavlovian and operant procedures (Dinsmoor, 1954, 1955; Mowrer, 1947). The theory is applied to punishment in much the same way it is applied to avoidance (see Chapter 5). If a rat presses a lever and receives a shock, the lever is paired with the shock. Through Pavlovian conditioning, the lever then becomes a CS for the same behavior aroused by the shock, including fear. Put another way, if shock is aversive, then the lever becomes aversive. The rat may escape the lever by moving away from it. Moving away from the lever is reinforced by a reduction of fear. Of course, moving away from the lever necessarily reduces the rate of lever pressing.

Critics of the two-process theory charge that the theory has the same flaws when applied to punishment as it does when explaining avoidance. For instance, the theory predicts that punishment would reduce responding in proportion to its proximity to the punished behavior. A rat that has been shocked when it pressed a lever should be less inclined to press the lever than to touch it, less inclined to touch it than to stand near it, less inclined to stand near it than to approach it, and so on. But this may not be the case. In one study, R. Mansfield and Howard Rachlin (1970) trained pigeons to peck two discs for food. The birds received food only if they pecked both discs in the proper sequence, first the right disc, then the left. Next the experimenters began shocking the birds each time they pecked the discs in the proper right–left sequence. They began with mild shocks and each day increased their intensity. They reasoned that if the two-process theory were correct, at some point the birds would peck the right disc but not the left. The right disc, being further removed from punishment, would be less aversive than the left and therefore would be more likely to be pecked. It is as if a student were punished for calling out answers instead of waiting to be called on by the teacher. After being punished, he might *start* to call out an answer and "catch himself." Similarly, the birds might start the key peck sequence but catch themselves and stop. It turned out, however, that behavior rates on the two keys declined together. If the birds pecked the right disc, they nearly always went on to peck the left. Because of such findings, the two-process theory has lost ground to the one-process theory of punishment.

**QUERY 6:** The two processes of the two-process theory are _____ and

_____.

## One-Process Theory

The one-process theory of punishment is similar to the one-process theory of avoidance (see Chapter 5). It says that only one process, operant learning, is involved. Punishment, this theory argues, weakens behavior in the same manner that reinforcement strengthens it.

The idea goes back to Thorndike (1911), who originally thought that punishment was the mirror image of reinforcement. He later abandoned the idea when he found that mild punishment (such as saying "wrong" after an answer) did not reduce the likelihood that the behavior would occur (Thorndike, 1932). Other researchers later showed, however, that Thorndike's punishers were just too weak to be effective and that stronger punishers produced effects parallel to reinforcement (Azrin & Holz, 1966; Premack, 1971; Rachlin & Herrnstein, 1969).

There is other evidence in favor of the one-process theory. As you know, the Premack principle states that high-probability behavior reinforces low-probability behavior. If the one-process theory is correct, then the opposite of Premack's reinforcement rule should apply to punishment: Low-probability behavior should punish high-probability behavior (Premack, 1971). This is, in fact, what happens (Mazur, 1975). If, for example, a hungry rat is made to run following eating, it will eat less. The low-probability behavior (running) suppresses the high-probability behavior (eating). One-process theorists conclude that Thorndike was right in the first place: Punishment and reinforcement have essentially symmetrical effects on behavior.

Reinforcement and punishment show a certain symmetry, but this does not mean that they are equally desirable ways of changing behavior. Indeed, punishment leaves much to be desired as an agent of change. It works, but it can also create problems.

CAPSULE **REVIEW**  The main attempts to explain how punishment works are two-process theory, which relies on Pavlovian and operant procedures, and one-process theory, which accounts for punishment entirely in terms of operant procedures.

# PROBLEMS WITH PUNISHMENT

Parents, teachers, employers, supervisors, spouses, kids on playgrounds, and, well, everyone at one time or another routinely uses punishment. The reason it is so widely used is that it works—at least in the short run. In other words, we use punishment because doing so is reinforced. Sometimes the reinforcement is positive, as when a teacher is praised by a principal for "running a tight ship." More often the reinforcement is negative, as when a teacher reprimands a student for talking, and the student becomes quiet.

Punishment can be a very powerful procedure. If the punisher regularly follows a behavior and is delivered immediately in sufficient strength from the outset, it typically produces a very rapid and substantial reduction in the behavior. If reinforcement of the unwanted behavior is discontinued and an alternative way of providing the same reinforcer is provided, the punished behavior may disappear entirely.

Punishment is also fast; there is no need to continue the practice for days or weeks to determine whether it will work. If a given consequence is going to reduce the frequency of a behavior, it will begin to do so immediately. Proper use of punishment can also produce a permanent suppression of the behavior, which is especially important if the behavior is potentially injurious.

And punishment has beneficial side effects. In a review of studies using shock in the treatment of autistic children, K. L. Lichstein and Laura Schreibman (1976) found that the children became more sociable, more cooperative, more affectionate, more likely to make eye contact, and more likely to smile. After reviewing the literature on the effects of punishment, Saul Axelrod (1983) wrote, "the vast majority of studies have reported positive side effects" (p. 8; see also Newsom, Flavall, & Rincover, 1983; Perone, 2003; Van Houten, 1983).

Unfortunately, there are certain potential problems with punishment of which everyone should be aware (Sidman, 1989b). While these problems may occur with any form of punishment, they are especially likely to occur with physical forms of positive punishment. The problems include escape, aggression, apathy, abuse, and imitation of the punisher.

A typical (and quite sensible) reaction to punishment is to try to escape or avoid the source of punishment. The child struggles to free herself from the parent who is spanking her; the failing student plays hooky from school; the employee who has botched an assignment "hides out" until the boss cools down. Sometimes it is possible to escape without actually fleeing. In one study, a rat received both food and shock when it pressed a lever (Azrin & Holz, 1966). The shock came through a grid floor, and the rat learned to lie on its back and press the lever while lying on its back. Presumably the rat's fur insulated it somewhat from the shocks.

We can also escape or avoid punishment by cheating and lying. The student who did not do his homework avoids punishment by copying someone else's work or by saying, "My dog ate it." Making excuses, fawning, crying, and showing remorse are other tactics that are often reinforced by escape from or avoidance of punishment. Indeed, one common result of frequent punishment is that people become quite good at these escape tactics.

The "ultimate escape," as Sidman (1989b) terms it, is suicide. Prisoners under torture will sometimes kill themselves to escape the pain. People who live in abusive relationships or who are victims of harassment by government sometimes escape these situations by removing themselves irrevocably from them. Suicide is an extreme measure to take, and better options are almost always available, but it illustrates the lengths to which people will sometimes go to escape or avoid intense punishment.

An alternative to escaping punishment is to attack those who punish. We criticize our critics, disparage those who disparage us, and answer each blow in kind. Aggression is particularly likely when escape is impossible. Like escape, aggression is often an effective way of exerting control over those who punish. An employee who is routinely badgered on the job or a student who is bullied or humiliated at school may retaliate with aggression. Employees who are mistreated sometimes steal materials, sabotage products, or deliberately slow production rates. Students who are miserable in school and cannot withdraw may vandalize school property or assault teachers. Religious and ethnic groups and governments attack those who have injured them, and those they attack reply in kind.

The aggression is not always directed at the source of injury. If two animals are put into the same chamber and one of them is shocked, the shocked animal may attack its neighbor (Ulrich & Azrin, 1962; Ulrich, Hutchinson, & Azrin, 1965). This is so even though the other animal had nothing to do with the attacker's pain. Shocked animals will even attack much larger neighbors: A mouse will attack a rat, a rat will attack a cat. If no other animal is present, shocked animals will attack inanimate objects. If no suitable object is available, a rat will work to obtain an object to bite (Azrin, Hutchinson, & McLaughlin, 1965). We can see much the same phenomenon, called *displaced aggression*, in people: A husband strikes his wife, the wife strikes a child, the child strikes a younger sibling, the sibling strikes the family dog (Marcus-Newhall et al., 2000). Like other animals, we also attack inanimate objects: Many people have thrown an object or slammed a door after being insulted.

A third problem with punishment, particularly when escape and aggression are not possible, is a general suppression of behavior. If aversives are a common consequence of many kinds of behavior, the result may be suppression not only of the punished behavior but also of behavior in general. A kind of malaise, or apathy, is a by-product of situations in which punishment is commonplace. Unless strong positive reinforcers provide a counterweight to punishment, the best thing to do may be nothing. When Carl Warden and Mercy Aylesworth (1927) punished rats for entering one of two passageways, they found that the rats tended to avoid entering either. Instead, they stayed in the release chamber. We may see a similar phenomenon in the classroom when a teacher regularly ridicules children for asking "stupid" questions. Those children not only become less likely to ask questions; they may be reluctant to answer questions or participate in other classroom activities.

Another difficulty with punishment, especially physical punishment, is the potential for abuse by the punisher. The use of corporal punishment in schools has resulted in broken bones, ruptured blood vessels, hematomas, muscle and nerve damage, whiplash, spinal injuries, and even death. (For more on this, see www.stophitting.com.) Child abuse in the home is often punishment that got out of hand. A parent slaps a child harder than intended and breaks a jaw, boxes the child's ears and breaks an eardrum, shakes a crying baby and causes brain damage. Sometimes parents inadvertently reinforce increasingly objectionable behavior (see the discussion of shaping in Chapter 6) and then resort to extreme forms of punishment to suppress it. Parents sometimes begin with a very mild form of punishment and gradually use stronger and stronger consequences, sometimes ending up causing bodily injury.

Another problem with punishment is that those who are punished tend to imitate those who punish them. When parents rely heavily on punishment in rearing their children, the children rely heavily on punishment in dealing with siblings and peers (Bandura & Walters, 1959; Sears, Maccoby, & Levin, 1957). As they become spouse, friend, coworker, and parent, they use punishment to deal with the troublesome behavior of others. Similarly, the boss who relies on punishment to keep her managers "in line" may find that those managers use similar methods in dealing with their subordinates.

*Nevin (2003, 2004) analyzed cases of retaliation by governments following terrorist attacks. He found no evidence that retaliating had any effect on terrorist behavior.*

*A man convicted of child abuse punished his children, ages 4, 11, and 13, by holding them under water, forcing them to take cold showers, and giving them electric shocks. He defended his actions by saying he was just trying to be "a loving father" (Sung, 2009).*

Of course, not all forms of punishment are equally troublesome. There is a great deal of difference between slapping a child and denying the child television viewing privileges. And, as noted earlier, *when properly used*, punishment can have beneficial side effects. Nevertheless, the potential for problems exists, particularly when physical punishment is involved, so experts now rely on, and advocate the use of, alternative procedures.

 QUERY 7:  The five problems that can arise with punishment are

_____, _____, _____,

_____, and _____.

CAPSULE **REVIEW**    Although punishment is often very effective in reducing the frequency of a behavior, it can give rise to certain problems, including escape, aggression, apathy, abuse, and imitation. Because of these problems, it is wise to consider alternatives.

## ALTERNATIVES TO PUNISHMENT

Because of the problems with punishment, researchers have sought alternative ways of modifying troublesome behavior (Lavigna & Donnellan, 1986). One alternative is to prevent the behavior from occurring by altering the environment in some way, a procedure called **response prevention** (Mills et al., 1973). Instead of punishing a child for playing with the family's precious china, we might put the china out of reach. A telephone lock may curb a child's tendency to make telephone calls to people on the other side of the globe. Poisons and firearms can be put under lock and key. A child who bites his hands may be required to wear gloves.

Another alternative to punishment is extinction. You saw in Chapter 7 that withholding *all* reinforcement for a given behavior will reduce the frequency of that behavior. Using extinction to reduce the frequency of unwanted behavior requires first of all identifying the reinforcers that maintain it. For example, adult attention is frequently the reinforcer that maintains misbehavior in children (Hart et al., 1964). One problem with extinction, as noted in Chapter 7, is the extinction burst, an increase in the behavior on extinction. Extinction also often provokes emotional outbursts, especially aggression and angry displays. Extinction is also hard to implement outside the laboratory since we often do not have control over all of the reinforcers available for an unwanted behavior. So, while extinction is an alternative to punishment, it is often problematic.

A much more effective alternative to punishment is **differential reinforcement,** a procedure that combines (when possible) nonreinforcement of an unwanted behavior and reinforcement of some other behavior (Ferster & Skinner, 1957). There are several forms of differential reinforcement; we will consider three of them.

In **differential reinforcement of alternative behavior (DRA)** reinforcement is made available for a specified alternative to the unwanted behavior (Athens & Vollmer, 2010; Petscher, Rey, & Bailey, 2009). In the lab, if a rat regularly presses lever A for food, you might put the behavior on extinction, but the decline in lever presses is apt to be slow. If, however, you also provide food for pressing lever B, the rate of pressing lever A will drop off much more rapidly. DRA gives the animal another way of obtaining the same reinforcement.

**QUERY 8:** In differential reinforcement, an unwanted behavior (or rate of behavior) is

placed on _____, and a more desirable behavior (or rate of

behavior) is _____.

The same procedure can be put to use outside the lab. If your 3-year-old has discovered that beating on objects with a spoon creates a fascinating variety of loud sounds and your ears are beginning to ache, you might ignore her musical efforts but lavish attention on her when she picks up a coloring book and starts scribbling in it. If coloring figures is reinforced, but banging on objects is not, she is apt to devote more time to art and less to music. And your ears are apt to be relieved.

A similar form of differential reinforcement is called **differential reinforcement of incompatible behavior (DRI).** In DRI, you reinforce a behavior that is incompatible with the unwanted behavior (Smith, 1987). By increasing the rate of a behavior that is incompatible with an unwanted behavior, you necessarily reduce the rate of the unwanted behavior. In the case of our lever-pressing rat, instead of reinforcing presses on lever B, we might reinforce the behavior of standing away from lever A. A rat cannot press a lever and simultaneously take a position out of reach of the lever.

Incompatible behaviors are usually easily identified. Moving rapidly is incompatible with moving slowly; smiling is incompatible with frowning; standing is incompatible with sitting. One of the best ways teachers can reduce the amount of time children spend wandering around a classroom is to praise students who are sitting in their seats. If you are sitting in your seat, you cannot be wandering around.

Sometimes the goal is not to eliminate a behavior entirely, but to bring down the rate to a reasonable level. In this case, **differential reinforcement of low rate (DRL)** is perhaps the ideal alternative to punishment. The behavior is reinforced, but only if it occurs at a low rate. In a DRL 5" schedule, a pigeon that pecks a disc receives reinforcement only if five seconds have elapsed since the last disc peck. Each disc peck in essence resets the clock, so that pecking before the interval has elapsed further delays reinforcement. The longer the interval required between disc pecks, the lower the rate of pecking. A DRL 5" schedule would reinforce a maximum of 12 pecks per minute. Pecking before the prescribed interval ends further reduces the number of reinforcements received per minute. The length of the interval between occurrences of the behavior can be increased gradually. DRL can produce extremely low rates of behavior in a relatively short time.

DRL is often very useful in applied settings. A child might repeat a rhyme ("Hickory, dickory, dock/ the mouse ran up the clock . . .") an average of once every five minutes until the parents have to plug up their ears with cotton. Praising the child's performance when it occurs after a period of ten minutes, and then after 12 minutes, then 15, and so on should reduce the rate to a tolerable frequency. Another option is to set a limit on the number of times the behavior is permitted during a larger block of time, such as a class period (Deitz & Repp, 1973; Austin & Bevan, 2011). DRL is different from the other forms of differential reinforcement considered here in that the problem behavior is not on extinction; what is on extinction is an undesirable *rate* of the behavior.

 **QUERY 9:** In a DRL 10" schedule, the effect of pressing a lever after eight seconds is to

_____.

One advantage of differential reinforcement is that it focuses attention on strengthening desirable behavior (or desirable rates of behavior) rather than on suppressing undesirable behavior. It thereby avoids the problems associated with punishment (Carr, Robinson, & Palumbo, 1990a: Carr et al., 1990b; Goldiamond, 1975b). Keep in mind, however, that differential reinforcement works best if you limit reinforcement of unwanted behavior as much as possible. Differential reinforcement may be of limited value if the troublesome behavior continues to be reinforced at its usual rate.

CAPSULE **REVIEW**   Fortunately, there are effective alternatives to punishment. These include response prevention, extinction, and various forms of differential reinforcement, including DRA, DRI, and DRL. These procedures are effective and are less likely to have adverse side effects than some forms of punishment.

# A FINAL WORD

Some people argue that punishment as a means of changing behavior is a good and necessary thing, and that there is too little of it. They argue that children are not well behaved because parents and schools don't paddle them often enough, that outrageous behavior by airline passengers and mall shootings are the result of a permissive society. They claim that we need to "knock some sense into people" who misbehave.

Go to a grocery store, a bus station, or other public area and watch parents interact with their kids. You are likely to see adults who regularly ignore their children when they behave well, but reprimand, threaten, shake, or slap them when they misbehave. All too often, good behavior gets the child nothing. You can see the same tendency in the workplace, at sporting events, in restaurants, in homes, and in international affairs. All too often the rule seems to be, punish bad behavior and ignore good behavior.

I have never heard a good argument for this imbalance.

## RECOMMENDED **READING**

1. Carey, J. (1988). *Eyewitness to history.* Cambridge, MA: Harvard University Press.

   Anyone who thinks that the problems with punishment are obvious should peruse this book for examples of the horrific use of aversives throughout human history.

2. Cipani, E. (2004). *Punishment on trial.* The author has made the book available without charge at www.ecipani.com/PoT.pdf.

   This highly readable book is a well-developed defense of punishment, aimed mainly at parents and teachers. Cipani, a therapist, identifies principles for the effective use of punishment and illustrates each with numerous examples and studies. Anyone who expects to be a parent or teacher should read this book, and probably so should those who expect to be managers.

3. Perone, M. (2003). Negative effects of positive reinforcement. *The Behavior Analyst, 26,* 1–14.

   Perone argues that positive reinforcement is not entirely above reproach, and punishment is not altogether bad.

4. Sidman, M. (1989). *Coercion and its fallout.* Boston: Authors Cooperative.

   This harsh critique of aversive control, including punishment, is by an expert on the subject.

5. Skinner, B. F. (1953). Punishment. Chapter 12 in *Science and human behavior* (pp. 182–193). New York: Free Press.

   Skinner stubbornly opposed punishment; here he makes his case against it.

## REVIEW **QUESTIONS**

1. Define the following terms:

   | | |
   |---|---|
   | differential reinforcement | negative punishment |
   | DRA | response prevention |
   | DRI | penalty training |
   | DRL | positive punishment |

punisher                    Time Out
punishment

2. Why do people rely so much on punishment?

3. What is the key difference between positive and negative punishment?

4. What is the key difference between negative reinforcement and punishment?

5. Why is it important to use extinction in conjunction with differential reinforcement?

6. How might David Premack define a punisher?

7. People often say they seek "open, honest relationships." Why are such relationships so rare?

8. What is the key difference between the two-process and one-process theories of punishment?

9. Why do you suppose it took researchers so long to appreciate the power of punishment?

10. Five-year-old Mary has misbehaved. Her father spanks her and sends her to her room. Has Mary been punished?

## PRACTICE **QUIZ**

1. The first formal studies of punishment were probably done by _____ around the turn of the century.

2. Positive punishment and _____ are often mistakenly thought to refer to the same procedure.

3. In a DRL 10" schedule, the effect of pressing a lever after eight seconds is to _____.

4. According to the two-process theory, punishment involves two procedures, _____ and _____.

5. Punishment is more likely to be effective if the individual has alternative means of obtaining the _____ that maintains the punished behavior.

6. David Camp and his colleagues found that a delay of 30 seconds greatly reduced the effects of contingent shock. They found that even a delay of _____ seconds made shocks less effective.

7. In using punishment, it is best to begin with a punisher that is _____ (slightly stronger/slightly weaker) than the minimum required to suppress the behavior.

8. The fact that an annoying behavior occurs implies that it has _____ consequences.

9. Five problems are associated with punishment. Three of these problems are _____.

10. One way of reducing the frequency of an unwanted behavior is to use DRI, which stands for _____.

## QUERY **ANSWERS**

Query 1. Positive and negative punishment are similar in that both *weaken/ suppress/reduce the strength of* a behavior.

Query 2. In positive punishment, something is *added/presented*; in negative punishment, something is *subtracted/removed*.

Query 3. Figure 8-5 shows that the more *intense* a punisher, the more it *reduces* the rate of a behavior.

Query 4. In general, the *higher/greater* the level of reinforcer deprivation, the *less* effective a punisher is.

Query 5. Any four of the variables covered may be named: contingency, contiguity, punisher intensity, beginning level of punishment, availability of reinforcement for the punished behavior, alternative sources of reinforcement, deprivation level, and qualitative features of the punisher.

Query 6. The two processes of the two-process theory are *Pavlovian conditioning* and *operant learning*.

Query 7. The five problems that can arise with punishment are *escape, aggression, apathy, abuse,* and *imitative use of punishment*.

Query 8. In differential reinforcement, an unwanted behavior (or rate of behavior) is placed on *extinction*, and a more desirable behavior (or rate of behavior) is *reinforced*.

Query 9: In a DRL 10" schedule, the effect of pressing a lever after eight seconds is to *delay reinforcement*.

# Operant Applications

*The great end of life is not knowledge, but action.*

—T. H. Huxley

## PREVIEW

It is generally granted that operant procedures are useful in teaching animals to do tricks and helping kids memorize the multiplication tables. However, many people are unaware of their value in, for example, rearing children, teaching kids and adults sophisticated skills, treating health problems, improving productivity, reducing accidents in the workplace, and improving the lives of animals. This chapter provides a small sampling of applications of operant learning. The chief goal is to demonstrate that procedures based on operant learning have found many useful applications, including those that involve complex behavior problems. We will consider examples of applications in the home, school, clinics, the workplace, and at the zoo, but the same principles and procedures can be applied in just about any setting.

# HOME

The importance of operant learning is perhaps most clearly conveyed in poor-quality orphanages. There the children typically fail to develop in anything like a normal way behaviorally (Nelson et al., 2009; Quinton, Rutter, & Liddle, 1984; Tizard & Hodges, 1978). These results are characteristically attributed to neglect, but what does neglect mean? As infants they are not picked up and coddled as often as babies are in most homes, but this lack of physical contact is a small part of what is missing. What neglect means is that their environment is largely unresponsive to them. As infants they cry when hungry or uncomfortable, but no one reliably comes to pick them up, to change their diapers, to feed them. Their crying has little effect. Even as they get older they have very little impact on their surroundings. People seldom talk to them, seldom instruct them in any way, and seldom provide praise or recognition or smiles in response to their behavior. If one's behavior has little or no effect on the environment, there can be little operant learning, and operant learning is absolutely essential to normal development.

The environment of a typical home is much more responsive than that of a poorly run orphanage. When children are taken from such orphanages and placed in high-quality foster care, they can show marked improvement (Nelson et al., 2009). But even children in "normal" homes often do not get the operant learning experiences needed for optimal development. Language development provides an excellent example.

Some psychologists believe that learning a first language is almost effortless and that "All it takes is exposure" (Roediger & Meade, 2000, p. 9; see also Trout, 2001). How likely do you think it is that, if you played a radio ten hours a day but never spoke to a baby or responded to the sounds she made, she would learn to speak? In fact, children expend a good deal of time and effort learning to communicate, and their parents typically do a good deal of teaching. How rapidly they learn depends on the amount of instruction and practice they receive (Hart & Risley, 1995).

Babies begin making sounds that, while perhaps not random, do not resemble any known language. (Baby vocalization is not called babbling for nothing.) Parents respond to these sounds by smiling at, touching, and talking to the baby. Thus, the baby's vocal behavior *has an impact on her environment.* This kind of natural reinforcement is very powerful. Parents later select certain sounds for reinforcement, and the more those sounds resemble words in the parents' language, the more reinforcement the parent provides. When the baby's efforts approximate *Ma-ma* or *Da-da* all sorts of wonderful things are apt to happen: Adults smile, tickle the child, laugh, clap, and repeat what the child has said. Through such shaping, parents teach their children the rudiments of language. Very likely, correct pronunciations are automatically reinforced by the similarity of the baby's utterances to those of the parent. (The music student experiences the same sort of automatic reinforcement when he plays a melody and notices that it resembles a professional recording.) After a time, *Ma-ma* no longer results in reinforcement; the child must say *Mommy.*

In the same way, *cook* must give way to *cookie* or no treat is forthcoming. Later the child may be required to use complete, grammatically correct sentences, such as "May I have a cookie, please?" Betty Hart and Todd Risley (1995) showed that parents who provided the most instruction and practice in language later had the children with the best-developed verbal skills.

Parents don't just teach their children language. They have a profound influence, positive or negative, on all sorts of behavior, mainly through the consequences they provide. For example, young children characteristically have poor impulse control (Goleman, 2006). Given a choice between receiving a small prize immediately and a bigger prize later, young children typically opt for the immediate reward, whereas older children will wait for the bigger one (Bandura & Mischel, 1965; Ito & Nakamura, 1998). The change is not an automatic result of aging, however. With time, children learn to distract themselves and use other techniques to make better choices (Patterson & Mischel, 1976). Research also shows that instruction in self-control procedures can increase their use. In one study, James Larson and colleagues (1998) found that aggressive adolescent boys could be taught to use self-control techniques to reduce their disruptive behavior. People who do not have good self-control do not lack willpower or character; they lack instruction. Reinforcement is a key part of that instruction.

The families studied by Hart and Risley ranged from welfare recipients to professionals. The key factor in a child's progress was not income level, but the kind of linguistic environment the parents provided.

Similarly, children vary tremendously in their diligence. The difference between those who become discouraged easily and those who don't know how to give up appears to be largely a matter of learning history. Experience (mainly the history of reinforcement) teaches them to quit or to strive, to roll over or fight on. You may recall from Chapter 6 that reinforcing a high level of effort and persistence results in dogged determination (e.g., Eisenberger & Cameron, 1996). If parents reinforce persistence in the face of difficulties, they are apt to end up with children who persevere despite life's challenges.

Of course, all parents are faced with problem behavior in children from time to time, and you have already seen that reinforcement and punishment can be used to cope with these problems. Reinforcing the kinds of behavior you *want* tends to reduce the frequency of *unwanted* behavior, but if unwanted behavior does occur it can usually be dealt with by means of differential reinforcement, especially DRI and DRL (see Chapter 8). Punishment is usually unnecessary, but when it is, Time Out, if properly used, works well with elementary school–aged children (Bean & Roberts, 1981; Cipani, 1999, 2004; Kazdin, 1980; Roberts & Powers, 1990).

Not everyone has children and even those who do have to deal with problems at home that have little or nothing to do with children. Operant learning principles can be put to good use in these areas as well. For example, they can help spouses or cohabitants get along (Eisler, Hersen, & Agras, 1973; Sosa, 1982), and they can help us deal with problems of aging partners and parents (Remoser & Fisher, 2009; Green et al., 1986; Haley, 1983). But for most people, and for society at large, rearing children to be well-behaved, productive citizens is the most important function of a family. How children "turned out" used to be viewed as largely a matter of genes and time; that is still perhaps the prevailing view, butmore and more people realize that, as Wesley Becker (1971) observed long ago, parents are teachers, and operant procedures, especially reinforcement, are the optimal way of teaching.

Parents are arguably the most important teachers children have, but classroom teachers also have a powerful influence on the next generation.

CAPSULE **REVIEW** The greatest influence of operant applications in the home concerns child rearing. The way that parents interact with their kids has a profound influence on their behavior, including the behaviors typically referred to as personality and character. Operant procedures also can help adults live together in harmony and cope with ill partners and aging parents.

# SCHOOL

Each issue of the prestigious educational journal *Phi Delta Kappan* includes numerous cartoons. If you examine a few issues, you will see that a lot of the cartoons depict students with low test scores, bad report cards, disapproving teachers, and various forms of punishment. The unstated message of this educational journal seems to be that school is a place where kids are frustrated, fail, and get into trouble. How sad—particularly when you consider that we know how to make school a place where students are challenged, succeed, and enjoy themselves (Chance, 2008). Making use of learning principles, particularly shaping and positive reinforcement, is one key to this transformation.

The reinforcing effects of approval and attention on student behavior were clearly demonstrated long ago (Hall, Lund, & Jackson, 1968; Thomas, Becker, & Armstrong, 1968; for a review see Beaman & Wheldall, 2000). In one early study, Charles Madsen, Wesley Becker, and Don Thomas (1968) asked two second-grade teachers to alter the way they responded to appropriate and inappropriate student behavior. One of these teachers, Mrs. A, generally ignored good behavior and dealt with misbehavior by scolding the offending child or making loud, critical comments. There were frequent periods of something approximating chaos in her class, which Mrs. A dealt with by making threats.

The researchers asked Mrs. A to make a simple, but fundamental, change in her behavior. Instead of ignoring the kids when they were good and criticizing them when they were bad, they asked that she generally ignore the kids when they were bad and make approving comments when they were good. The transition was difficult. Mrs. A had a long history of reprimanding, criticizing, and threatening students (she made comments of this sort at the rate of one a minute at the start of the study), and it was difficult for her to stop doing that. Nevertheless she did manage to reduce the number of negative comments and greatly increase the number of positives. For example, during the initial baseline period, Mrs. A praised student behavior an average of about once every 15 minutes; by the end of the study, she was praising about once

*Mrs. A is not unusual. Although teachers often report that they make frequent use of positive reinforcement, in fact most rely far more on reprimands and other forms of punishment (Beaman & Wheldall, 2000; Goodlad, 1984; Latham, 1997).*

every two minutes. Her tendency to criticize fell sharply, from about once a minute to about once every six minutes.

Although the researchers asked Mrs. A to recognize good behavior in any student, they suggested that she pay special attention to two students, Cliff and Frank. Cliff was a very bright boy who showed no interest in school. Mrs. A observed that "he would sit throughout entire work periods fiddling with objects in his desk, talking, doing nothing, or misbehaving by bothering others and walking around the room. Lately he has started hitting others for no apparent reason" (p. 140). Frank was a likeable boy of average intelligence. In the classroom he was often out of his seat and talking to other children and did not respond to his teacher's efforts to correct him.

**?** QUERY 1:    Madsen and colleagues asked teachers to shift their attention from

_____ behavior to _____ behavior.

The change in Mrs. A's behavior resulted in a marked change in her students, especially Cliff and Frank. As Figure 9-1 shows, the two boys were initially misbehaving in about half of the 20-minute intervals during which the researchers observed their behavior. When Mrs. A began recognizing good behavior, the boys responded. When she went back to ignoring good behavior (baseline 2), their old behavior patterns returned. At the conclusion of the study, the boys were misbehaving less than a third as often as they had at the beginning.

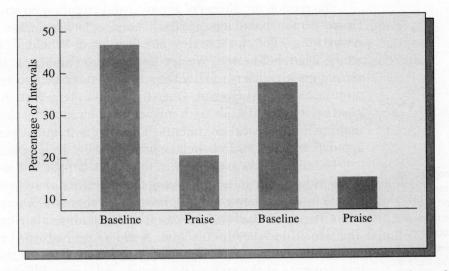

**Figure 9-1**   *Praise and disruptive behavior. Average percentage of intervals in which Cliff or Frank behaved inappropriately (talking, making noise, disturbing others, etc.) decreased when the teacher praised appropriate behavior. (Compiled from data in Madsen et al., 1968.)*

The researchers note that it wasn't easy for Mrs. A to catch Cliff being good, because he so seldom was. But as "the use of praise continued, Cliff worked harder on his assigned tasks, learned to ignore other children who were misbehaving and would raise his hand to get teacher attention. He was moved up to the fastest arithmetic group" (p. 149). Frank also responded well. He did his work, asked for extra assignments, and volunteered to do things to help his teacher.

The researchers recorded data only on Cliff and Frank, but it was clear the entire class responded well to the new Mrs. A. "I was amazed," she later wrote, "at the difference the procedure made in the atmosphere of the classroom and even my own personal feelings. I realized that in praising the well-behaved children and ignoring the bad, I was finding myself looking for the good in the children" (p. 149). School had become a more pleasant and productive place for both students and teacher.

Small children love attention, so it is not too surprising that the approval of a teacher is reinforcing, but adolescents are a different sort of beast, right? Apparently not. Studies find that adolescents and adults typically respond in much the same way to approval as the kiddies do. British school psychologist Eddie McNamara (1987) did a study with a group of disruptive teenagers. The students would call out, talk while the teacher was talking, ignore teacher requests, and ignore assigned work. McNamara asked the teacher to praise individuals, groups, and the class as a whole when they were "on task." The result was that time on task rose from 67% to 84% (see Figure 9-2).

These studies (and countless others) demonstrate that when appropriate behavior produces positive consequences such as praise, recognition, and approval, and minor misbehavior is ignored, the usual result is an increase in appropriate behavior and a simultaneous decrease in inappropriate behavior.

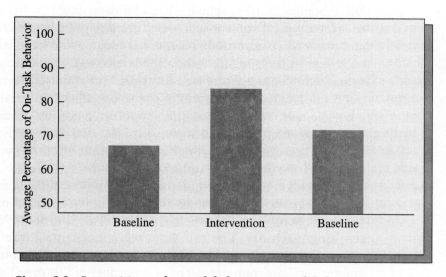

**Figure 9-2** *Recognition and on-task behavior. On-task behavior increased when the teacher praised students for being on task (intervention) and decreased when he stopped doing so. (Compiled from data in McNamara, 1987.)*

Approving good behavior and ignoring bad behavior is not *always* effective in reducing unwanted behavior, but these instances can be handled effectively in a number of ways. One approach is to use differential reinforcement of low rate (see Chapter 8). Two British researchers at the University of Glamorgan, Jennifer Austin and Deborah Bevan (2011), helped a teacher use DRL to reduce the excessive attention-seeking of three girls aged 7 and 8. The result was a sharp decline in the unwanted behavior (see Figure 9-3).

When students are on task and behaving appropriately, the classroom not only becomes a more pleasant environment for both teachers and students, the students typically learn a good deal more. This is illustrated in a study by Bill Hopkins and Robert Conard (1975). They asked elementary school teachers to make a few simple changes in the way they taught, all of them based on operant learning principles. The changes included moving about the room when students were doing seat work, deemphasizing reprimands and other forms of punishment, providing immediate feedback about performance whenever possible, and recognizing and praising students when they were on task. The principal results were a sharp reduction in discipline problems and a sharp increase in the rate of academic learning. Testing showed that the students, who ranged in ability from slow learners to gifted, advanced at the usual rate in spelling, at nearly double the normal rate in mathematics, and at more than twice the usual rate in reading. In addition to these changes, both students and teachers enjoyed their time together more.

Hopkins and Conard did not ask the teachers to change how they taught (except as noted), but the most effective instructional programs make explicit use of operant learning principles (e.g., Binder, 1988; Binder & Watkins, 1990; Bloom, 1986; Heward, 2012). One example is Morningside Academy in Seattle, Washington. Morningside is a private school that caters to students who have fallen behind in other schools. Kent Johnson and T. V. Joe Layng (1992) report that their typical student scores two or more years below grade level in reading and math when admitted. Yet these students, who have fallen further behind each year in their regular schools, advance two academic years in one school year. Such results require an educational program with a number of features, but reinforcement in the form of positive feedback and praise for good work is a key element. Morningside offers to return a portion of tuition to the parents of any student who fails to advance at least two years in the student's weakest area (e.g., reading). The school has made that offer for over 30 years and has refunded less than 1% of tuition (Johnson, pers. comm.).

Probably no classroom instructional approach has been developed that is more effective than an expert tutor, but individualized instruction was impractical except for the wealthy. Then B. F. Skinner (1958b) built the first teaching machines. The machines were mechanical (there were no desktop computers at the time) but could be used with a number of instructional programs. Each program consisted of a number of "frames," short presentations of information followed by questions for the student to answer. For example, in learning to spell the word *manufacture,* the student read a definition and a

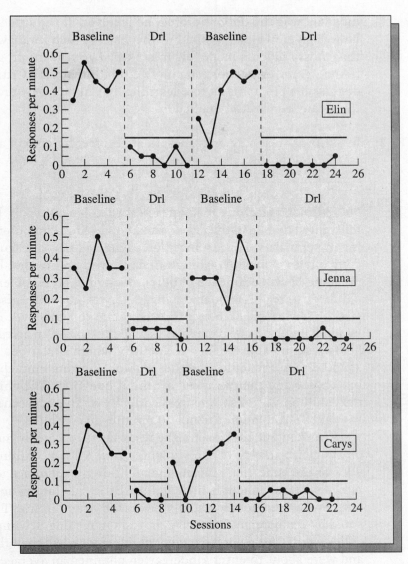

***Figure 9-3*** *Attention seeking. Requests for attention declined when a teacher reinforced infrequent requests. The horizontal lines during DRL indicate the maximum frequency allowed for reinforcement. (From "Using Differential Reinforcement of Low Rates to Reduce Children's Requests for Teacher Attention," by J. L. Austin and D. Bevan, 2011,* Journal of Applied Behavior Analysis, *44, p. 456. Copyright © 2011 by the Society for the Experimental Analysis of Behavior Inc. Reprinted with permission of the publisher and author.*

sentence that used the word and then copied the word. The next two frames provided a little information about the word's origin and asked the student to copy part of the word. The fourth and fifth frames showed the word with some missing letters and asked the student to fill them in. Finally, in the sixth frame, the student wrote the entire word. Each time the student completed a frame correctly, he was able to go on to the next frame. The opportunity to move on was the only reinforcer he received. If the student made a mistake, he was given the task again, but the tasks of each frame were easy enough so that most students made few mistakes. The student progressed through the frames, going on to more and more difficult material. Critics of Skinner often dismiss his programs as rote learning, but in fact they did the same kinds of things any good tutor would do.

**QUERY 2:** In Skinner's teaching machines, the reinforcer for correct answers was

_____.

Skinner's teaching machines never really caught on, but they have been reinvented thanks to the development of desktop computers and are now gaining in popularity. For instance, Joe Layng and his colleagues at Headsprout, a company in Seattle, Washington, developed an Internet-based instructional program designed to teach children, including preschoolers and kindergarten children, to read (Twyman, Layng, & Layng, 2011). Headsprout Reading consists of 80 lessons, each requiring the child to make over 180 responses. Each lesson focuses on one particular skill. For example, in an early lesson the child hears a sound and is asked to identify which of various letters makes that sound. When the child gives her answer, she gets immediate feedback about her choice and then is asked a similar question. The child advances to the next skill only after she answers correctly on five consecutive trials. Each lesson takes most children about 20 minutes to complete.

In developing the lessons, the researchers repeatedly modified them, based on the performance of the students, until 90% of children were successful 90% of the time. This means most children experience a very high success rate. As a result, there is little failure, little frustration, and very steady progress. Steady progress is usually powerfully reinforcing. The results, as measured by standardized achievement tests in reading, are impressive. Layng and colleagues (2003) report that eight children who had been through the program and were about to enter kindergarten obtained an average grade-equivalency score of 1.6 in reading on the Iowa Test of Basic Skills. Eight children who completed the program and were about to start first grade had an average grade-equivalent score of 2.3. Although grade-equivalency scores can be misleading (see Angoff, 1984), it is clear that these children were reading as well as many kids who were far ahead of them in school.

**QUERY 3:** The Headsprout reading program was designed so that most students will be

_____ most of the time.

Headsprout is an instructional program that makes the most of modern technology, but at heart it is based on basic operant learning principles. It is now absolutely clear that by applying such principles, school can be a place where students learn a great deal and have fun doing it. Today we laugh at cartoons about the idea that school is a place where students are frustrated, fail, and get into mischief. One day, we may wonder why we thought those cartoons were funny.

CAPSULE **REVIEW**

When implemented on a regular basis, operant procedures have a profound effect on both the social maturity of students and their academic growth. Simply providing positive consequences for appropriate behavior not only reduces disruptive behavior, but improves academic learning. Applying operant procedures to instruction adds to academic growth. The saying, "Teachers affect eternity; we can never tell where their influence stops," may be a bit of an exaggeration, but it is definitely *not* an exaggeration to say that a teacher has a major influence on the lives of students and, hence, on the nature of society.

# CLINIC

Perhaps the greatest impact of operant procedures so far has been in clinical settings. If so, it is probably because there are many health disorders that involve behavior problems for which the medical community has little or no effective treatment. Most of these are organic disorders. That is, the underlying problem is due to faulty genes, injury, exposure to toxins, microbial infection, and the like. Our focus here is not on medical disorders, as such, but on the use of operant learning in the treatment of three kinds of problems often associated with such disorders: self-injurious behavior, delusions, and paralysis.

## Self-Injurious Behavior

Children with developmental disorders such as autism and mental retardation sometimes seem bent on self-destruction. Some of these children will repeatedly bang their heads on the edge of a table or cabinet, sometimes causing retinal detachment or brain damage. They have been known to blind themselves by repeatedly poking themselves in the eye with a finger or fist. Some have chewed their flesh down to the bone or chewed off fingers.

*Some apparently healthy people, including college students (Whitlock & Eckenrode, 2006) and gifted students (Wood & Craegan, 2011), engage in self-injurious behavior.*

Not so very long ago, such behavior was considered involuntary, the direct result of the same brain disorder that caused the child's autism or retardation. The problem was dealt with by putting the child in restraints. This might take the form of a straitjacket or straps that fastened the hands to the sides. Sometimes patients were tied to their bed, spread-eagle, so they could not hurt themselves. This practice is far less common today thanks to the development of effective treatments based on operant learning. These treatments are available largely because of research in the 1960s.

One day Ivar Lovaas at UCLA was working with an autistic boy (see Chance, 1974). During the session the phone rang, and as Lovaas was talking on the phone, the boy began banging his head against the wall. The noise was annoying, and Lovaas absentmindedly reached over and slapped the child on the buttocks. At first he was horrified at his action—a therapist hitting a patient was unthinkable!—but then Lovaas noticed that something important had happened: The boy momentarily stopped banging his head. In that instance, Lovaas knew that the self-injurious behavior could be affected by its consequences.

Lovaas had been trained in traditional psychodynamic therapy, but after this experience he began experimenting with punishment. He found that a painful but completely harmless consequence could quickly suppress long-standing injurious behavior. In one study, Lovaas and J. Q. Simmons (1969) worked with a boy who hit himself as many as 300 times in a ten-minute period. (That is one blow every two seconds!) This behavior ended abruptly when the experimenters provided a painful but noninjurious electric shock to the boy's leg when he hit himself. Incredibly, a single shock practically ended the self-injurious behavior. After a total of only *four* contingent shocks, the self-injurious behavior stopped. An extremely high rate of self-injurious behavior had been terminated with just a few harmless (though not painless) shocks to the leg.

 QUERY 4: Once self-injurious behavior was thought to be due to an unconscious need

to suffer, but if that were the case, the shocks given by Lovaas and Simmons

should have _____ self-injurious acts.

Other experiments demonstrated that long-standing self-injurious behavior in children with developmental disorders could be ended or greatly reduced in short order with physical punishment. The aversives used were often painful but not harmful (Corte, Wolf, & Locke, 1971; Lovaas, Schaeffer, & Simmons, 1965; Risley, 1968; Tanner & Zeiler, 1975; Tate, 1972; Tate & Baroff, 1966). Ending self-injurious behavior meant that other therapeutic and instructional efforts could move forward. Still, no therapist liked the idea of using physical punishment, so a good deal of attention went into developing alternative treatments. Could reinforcement, for example, somehow reduce self-injurious behavior?

Research showed that it could (Foxx, 2001). Hughes Tarpley and Stephen Schroeder (1979), for example, found that differential reinforcement of incompatible behavior (DRI; see Chapter 8) can reduce self-injurious behavior. In one case, they periodically provided food to an 8-year-old boy if he played steadily with a ball. Playing with a ball is incompatible with hitting yourself in the face—if you are doing one, it is difficult or impossible to do the other. Within 40 minutes, the rate of face punching fell by over 90%. This was accomplished without punishment of any sort.

Reinforcement procedures such as DRI have proved so successful in controlling self-injurious behavior that aversives are now rarely used, and then only after reinforcement procedures have failed. And because self-injurious behavior and other kinds of behavior that interfere with normal development are now usually eliminated quickly with reinforcement, the children are able to benefit from efforts to improve their social and academic skills. The result has been that many children, who not so long ago would have spent their lives in restraint in institutions, are now able to go to school and lead fairly normal lives (Lovaas, 1987, 1993).

The efforts to treat self-injurious behavior in children with developmental disorders has had other benefits, including providing more effective treatment of other kinds of behavior problems For example, children (with and without developmental disorders) sometimes injure themselves to obtain a reward or escape an unpleasant task (Carr, 1977; Iwata et al., 1994; Lerman & Iwata, 1993). A child may, for example, hold his breath or slap his head to get attention (positive reinforcement) or to avoid taking a bath (negative reinforcement). Most of the time these episodes do no harm, but there are exceptions.

Edward Carr and Jack McDowell (1980) describe one such case in a normally developing, generally healthy 10-year-old boy. Jim began scratching following exposure to poison oak. The dermatitis cleared up after a few weeks, but Jim continued to scratch for *three years*. When Carr and McDowell finally saw Jim for treatment, his skin was covered with scars and sores, and he was the object of ridicule among his peers. Nearly all the scratching occurred at home and seemed to be maintained by parental attention. When Jim's parents saw him scratching, they would often make comments about it ("Jim, stop scratching") or attempt to restrain his hands. To be sure that attention was acting as a reinforcer, Carr and McDowell had the parents systematically withhold or provide attention for scratching. The results clearly showed that scratching depended on attention (see Figure 9-4).

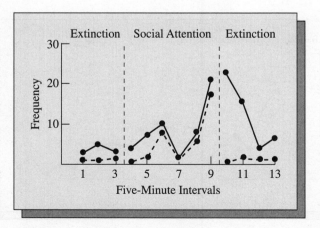

***Figure 9-4*** *Reinforcement of scratching. Scratching declined when ignored and increased when attended to. Note the high degree of correspondence between the frequency of attention (broken line) and scratching (solid line). (After "Social Control of Self-Injurious Behavior of Organic Etiology," by E. G. Carr and J. J. McDowell, 1980,* Behavior Therapy, *11, pp. 402–409. Copyright © 1980 by the Association for the Advancement of Behavior Therapy. Reprinted by permission of the publisher and author.)*

Jim's scratching might have been treated by having the parents simply ignore scratching entirely—that is, by putting the behavior on extinction. Unfortunately, the scratching so annoyed the boy's parents that they were unable to ignore it for long. Carr and McDowell recommended a combination of punishment and positive reinforcement. Punishment came in the form of Time Out (see Chapter 8): Each time the parents saw Jim scratch, they were to send him to a small, rather uninteresting room for several minutes. In other words, he was to be deprived of reinforcing activities whenever he scratched. Reinforcement came in the form of weekly rewards, such as a trip to a museum or a skating rink. Because it would be impossible to monitor Jim's scratching all the time, Jim earned rewards by reducing the number of sores on his body. This treatment resulted in a sharp reduction in the number of sores (see Figure 9-5). By the end of the study, Jim had only two sores, and these were almost completely healed.

Self-injurious behavior, once a potentially serious problem in otherwise healthy people and an absolute nightmare for some with developmental disorders, is now, thanks to operant procedures, usually eliminated in short order.

## Delusions

Delusions are false beliefs such as "Everyone is out to get me" or "There are little green men inside my stomach." Delusions can and often do have an organic basis: Schizophrenia, syphilis, Alzheimer's disease, traumatic brain injury, and other disorders can induce them. Delusions can also occur in people without any sort of disease. Regardless of the source of delusions, operant

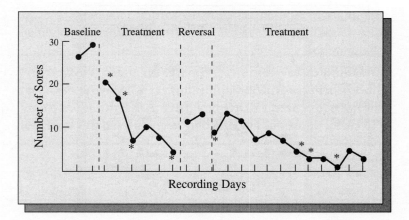

**Figure 9-5** *Reducing scratching. Number of body sores recorded over a nine-month period. Treatment consisted of positive reinforcement (indicated by asterisks) for a reduction in sores and punishment (in the form of time out) for scratching. (After "Social Control of Self-Injurious Behavior of Organic Etiology," by E. G. Carr and J. J. McDowell, 1980,* Behavior Therapy, *11, pp. 402–409. Copyright © 1980 by the Association for Advancement of Behavior Therapy. Reprinted by permission of the publisher and author.)*

procedures can play a role in their treatment (e.g., Liberman et al., 1973; Wincze, Lietenberg, & Agras, 1972).

Joe Layng and Paul Andronis (1984) provide the example of a psychiatric patient who complained that her head was falling off. She seemed quite frightened, so a member of the staff sat with her to calm her down. The delusion got worse. A discussion with the patient led to the discovery that she found it very difficult to engage the staff in conversation. Sometimes when she approached them, they responded with obvious annoyance. Her delusional behavior produced the desired effect (interaction with the staff) without the risk of hostile reactions. In other words, the delusion was reinforced. Once the woman learned how to approach the staff without incurring hostile reactions, the delusion disappeared, and her head remained securely attached.

Layng and Andronis also describe the case of a middle-aged man admitted to a locked hospital ward after he tried to pull a pair of clothesline poles out of the ground in his backyard. He shouted that the poles were blasphemous imitations of the cross and that Jesus had told him to tear them down. It turned out the man's efforts to involve his wife in his demanding business problems had been unsuccessful; she showed concern only when he behaved strangely. In other words, she inadvertently shaped increasingly pathological behavior until he finally behaved so bizarrely that he was hospitalized. When she learned to show concern for her husband's business problems instead of his bizarre behavior, his symptoms began to subside.

Another example is provided by Brad Alford (1986). He worked with a young schizophrenic patient in a psychiatric hospital. The man was greatly helped by medication but continued to complain that a "haggly old witch" followed him about. Alford asked the patient to keep a record of his feeling that he was being followed. The patient also indicated the strength of his belief, from 0 (certainty that the belief was just his imagination) to 100 (certainty that there really was a witch). During the treatment phases, Alford reinforced expressions of doubt about the witch. The result was that the patient's reported confidence in the delusion declined (see Figure 9-6).

One could argue, of course, that the patient believed in the witch as much as ever and merely learned not to admit it. To test this idea, Alford looked at the medication the patient received before and during the study. He found that the man received one kind of medication, a tranquilizer, only when he seemed agitated. If the patient remained convinced that the witch was real, then tranquilizer consumption should have remained constant. In fact, however, use of tranquilizers declined sharply.

**QUERY 5:** Alford's research demonstrates that _____ behavior can be modified by reinforcement.

These findings do not mean that delusions and other psychotic behaviors are entirely the product of learning; diseases of the brain, such as Alzheimer's and schizophrenia, *do* produce bizarre behavior. However, even when

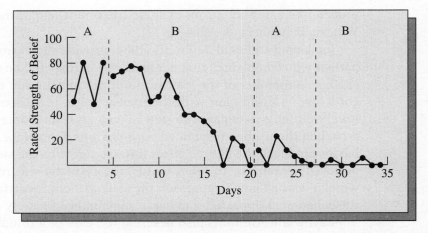

**Figure 9-6**   *Reinforcement and the strength of a delusion. During treatment (B) phases, expressions of doubt about a "haggly old witch" were reinforced, and the patient's confi-dence in the belief declined. (From "Behavioral Treatment of Schizophrenic Delu-sions: A Single-Case Experimental Analysis," by B. A. Alford, 1986,* Behavior Therapy, *17, pp. 637–644. Copyright © 1986 by the Association for Advancement of Behavior Therapy. Reprinted by permission of the publisher and author.)*

delusions or other abnormal behaviors arise from an organic disease, they may be modified by their consequences.

One objection to the operant interpretation of psychotic behavior is that such behavior often occurs even when it is not reinforced. Israel Goldiamond (1975a) describes a woman virtually paralyzed by fear of cockroaches. She remained in bed, too afraid to move about. Her husband was sympathetic and gave her the attention she had generally been denied. This attention was apparently the reinforcer that maintained her phobic behavior. But there seems to be a problem with this explanation because the woman stayed in bed even when her husband was not around to provide reinforcement. Why?

Goldiamond suggests that the answer is simple. If a person behaves bizarrely only when reinforcement for bizarre behavior is available, people catch on. And once they understand that the behavior is a way of obtaining reinforcers, they often stop providing those reinforcers. Bizarre behavior must therefore occur not only when reinforcement is available, *but also at times when reinforcement is unavailable.* "In other words," write Layng and Andronis (1984), "the apparent absence of maintaining consequences or the presence of aversive consequences on some occasions, may be requirements that must be met for reinforcement to be available on other occasions" (p. 142). I have dubbed this phenomenon **Goldiamond's Paradox.** The idea is familiar to every person who, as a child, got out of going to school by feigning illness: If you cheered with joy at being allowed to stay home, you were likely to be sent to school!

The traditional approach to delusions assumes that disordered thoughts reflect a disordered inner world. An analysis in terms of learning suggests that

*Some psychodynamic therapists claim that any problem behavior eliminated with learning procedures will be replaced by a new problem behavior, an idea called symptom substitution. There is no scientific support for symptom substitution (American Psychiatric Association, 1973; Baker, 1969; Cahoon, 1968; Garcia, 2003; Myers & Thyer, 1994; Yates, 1958).*

delusions often reflect a disordered *environment*; changing that environment can often change the "inner world."

## Paralysis

One amazing application of operant learning procedures is the restoration of function in apparently paralyzed limbs.

This story begins with laboratory research on loss of limb function in monkeys. Edward Taub of the University of Alabama (1977, 1980) found that monkeys failed to recover use of a limb following what should have been transient paralysis. He suspected that the failure was due to learning: Using the injured limb caused pain, loss of balance, and other problems, so the monkeys relied on the unaffected limb, and the affected limb remained useless. The monkey had learned *not* to use the affected limb. To test this idea Taub restricted movement of the normal limb, thereby increasing the reinforcing consequences of using the defective limb. The result was that the monkeys soon recovered use of the limb.

This led Taub and others to experiment with the same treatment, which came to be called **constraint-induced movement therapy (CIMT)**, with human stroke victims. In one study Taub and colleagues (Taub et al., 1994) worked with people who had suffered a stroke from 1 to 18 years earlier. The patients had very limited use of one of their upper limbs. Four patients received restraint treatment. This consisted of placing the *unaffected* hand in a splint and then putting that arm in a sling, thus rendering it essentially useless. The rest of the treatment consisted of having the patient repeatedly perform a variety of motor tasks. The treatment lasted only two weeks, yet produced a dramatic improvement in function of the "paralyzed" limb. One of the patients showed an 800% increase in the strength of the stroke-damaged limb. The patients showed improvement in feeding, dressing, and grooming themselves. A control group of five patients with similar stroke damage showed no significant progress. The benefits of CIMT were still apparent two years later.

**? QUERY 6:** CIMT reinforces _____ of a defective limb.

After this groundbreaking work, Taub modified the treatment to include shaping and detailed feedback about improvement, and this further improved CIMT benefits (see Figure 9-7). Therapists usually ignored any regression in performance, and instead focused on progress, however slight. CIMT has revolutionized rehabilitation treatment following stroke and spinal cord injury.

Taub and others have since applied CIMT to a variety of rehabilitation problems (see Taub, 2011; Taub & Uswatte, 2009), including multiple sclerosis (Mark et al., 2008), speech impediments (Pulvermuller et al., 2001), and cerebral palsy (Taub et al., 2004). Taub's work, which, remember, was a direct outgrowth of animal research, is now a model for translating basic research into practical applications (Huang et al., 2011).

*Taub's work shows that people planning a career in health care could find a good understanding of operant learning principles very useful.*

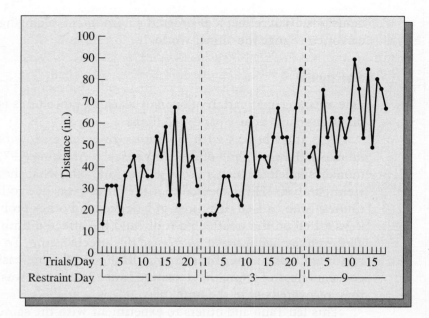

**Figure 9-7** *Shuffleboard performance. Distance a stroke patient propelled a shuffleboard disc using an affected limb on three days. The data reveal steady progress across practice sessions and over the two-week training period. (Adapted from "An Operant Approach to Rehabilitation Medicine: Overcoming Learned Nonuse by Shaping," by E. Taub, J. E. Crago, L. D. Burgio, T. E. Groomes, E. W. Cook, III, S. C. DeLuca, and N. E. Miller, 1994,* Journal of the Experimental Analysis of Behavior, *61[2], Figure 3, p. 287. Copyright © Society for the Experimental Analysis of Behavior, Inc. Reprinted with permission of the publisher and author.)*

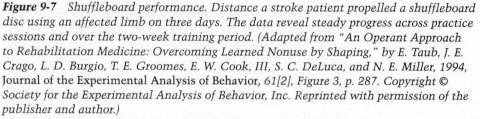

## OPERANT MEDICAL ASSESSMENT

Operant procedures may prove useful in assessing, as well as treating, certain medical conditions. For example, babies born prematurely often have various health problems and also tend to lag behind in cognitive development. Determining how severe their deficits are might help physicians determine what measures to take. A reliable assessment of an infant's learning ability might also help in assessing the effects of drugs and other treatments.

You will recall that infants with one foot tethered to a mobile soon learn to move the mobile by kicking (see Chapters 5 and 12). J. C. Heathcock and colleagues (2004) tested the idea of using this learning experience as a way of assessing the deficiencies of pre-term infants. The researchers compared ten pre-term infants with ten full-term infants when both were between the ages of three and four months. The result was that the rate of kicking increased in full-term babies but not in pre-term babies, suggesting that the latter were not learning normally. Periodic assessments would make it possible to determine whether a pre-term child were catching up or falling further behind normal development. Operant learning procedures may one day be considered essential tools for assessing certain medical problems and treatments.

CAPSULE **REVIEW**   Operant learning procedures are effective in the treatment of self-injurious behavior, delusions, and loss of motor function. They have also proved helpful in treating behavior problems associated with numerous other medical disorders, including anorexia (Bachmeyer, 2010; Kitfield & Masalsky, 2000), obesity (Finkelstein et al., 2007; Freedman, 2011), drug abuse (Silverman, Roll, & Higgins, 2008), and brain injury (Slifer & Amari, 2009), among others.

# WORK

Throughout much of history, the relationship between workers and employers has been adversarial. This seemed inevitable, since what benefits the worker (shorter hours, better working conditions, higher pay) would seem to reduce the benefits to the employer, and vice versa. But research on the application of operant learning, particularly reinforcement, suggests that contingencies might be arranged that would benefit both workers and their bosses.

One goal for the employer is to improve the performance of workers without adding to costs. In democratic countries, whipping people to get them to work harder or do better work is no longer an option, so how do you improve performance without reducing profits? Part of the answer seems to be providing simple feedback about performance. E. L. Thorndike demonstrated this a hundred years ago when he had  blindfolded  try to draw a 4-inch line (see Chapter 5). The feedback consisted of letting the person see what they had done or saying, "The line you drew was 3 inches"; "That line was 5¼ inches". Positive feedback was presumably reinforcing, and negative feedback punishing. Numerous experiments have shown that such feedback can also improve the performance of employees (Emmert, 1978; Feeney, 1972; Green et al., 2002). A master's thesis by David Harrison (2009), then a graduate student at Northeastern University, illustrates. He studied the effects of performance feedback on three managers who supervised staff providing services to people with developmental disabilities. All three managers used far too much overtime, presumably because of poor management skills. Harrison's intervention included providing periodic information about the amount of overtime paid, including a graph showing whether the amount had gone down or up. In the case of two managers, Harrison supplemented this factual feedback with praise if the overtime use went down, and a mild form of rebuke if the overtime went up. The result was that all three managers showed a reduction in overtime use of about 40% (see Figure 9-8).

Simple feedback by itself is, however, not always sufficient to improve worker performance (Alvero, Bucklin, & Austin, 2001; Balcazar, Hopkins, & Suarez, 1985/1986). Combining feedback with other consequences often produces greater and more consistent improvement (Bucklin & Dickinson, 2001; Redmon & Dickinson, 1990). For example, in a study of truck drivers, Jeanne Lamere and colleagues (1996) studied the effects of feedback combined with bonuses based

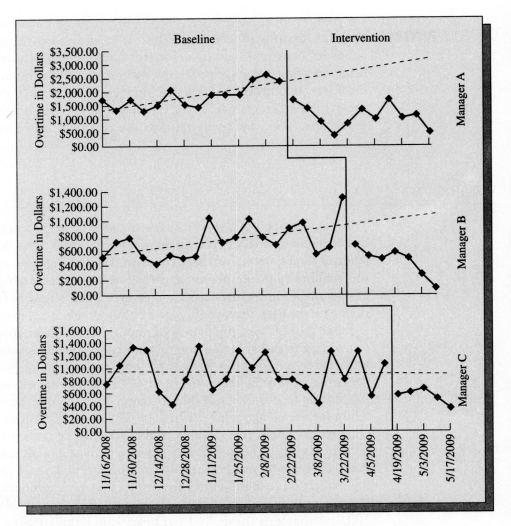

**Figure 9-8** *Overtime and feedback. Amount paid for overtime by three program managers during baseline and intervention. (From D. M. Harrison, "Performance Feedback: Its Effectiveness in the Management of Job Performance," unpublished master's thesis, Bouve College of Health Sciences, Northeastern University, 2009, Figure 1, p. 34. Reprinted with permission of the author.)*

on job performance. The size of bonuses varied from 0% to 9% of salary. The bonuses resulted in a substantial improvement in performance compared to salary alone. The employees received more money when the bonus plan was in effect, yet despite these additional payments the company *saved* an average of $5,000 a month in labor costs. In other words, both the employees and the company owners benefited. In a similar study, John Austin and co-researchers (1996) provided verbal and graphic feedback to roofers on their performance each day. The workers also received a bonus each week based on the reduction in labor costs from their efforts. The result was that the workers earned more, yet there was a 64% *reduction* in labor costs compared to the costs when the workers received no bonuses.

*Interestingly, while the bonuses in the Lamere study were effective, there was no difference between a 3% bonus and a 9% bonus.*

Another way that operant procedures can help both employers and employees is by reducing work-related accidents (Alavosius & Sulzer-Azaroff, 1985, 1990; DeVries, Burnette, & Redirion, 1991; Fitch, Herman, & Hopkins, 1976; Geller, 1984, 2005). On-the-job injuries and deaths are an important source of suffering for workers and their families (Sulzer-Azaroff, 1998) and a major expenditure for companies. Getting employees to follow safe practices is therefore an important goal. Austin and colleagues (1996) did a second study involving the same roofers mentioned above. In this study the researchers monitored the behavior of workers to determine their compliance with safety procedures. They provided daily feedback to the workers, and the workers who followed safe practices at least 80% of the time got time off. The result was a substantial improvement in safe practices.

CAPSULE **REVIEW**   Improving productivity and reducing accidents are two major ways of improving the quality of life for workers and the profitability of companies. Reinforcement plays a major role in achieving both goals. Success in these areas means that it may one day be possible to abandon the adversarial relationship between workers and their employers.

# ZOO

Operant principles are increasingly used in zoos to provide veterinary care and improve the quality of the animals' lives (Forthman & Ogden, 1991; Markowitz, 2012).

Providing veterinary care to captive wild animals, especially those that are large and aggressive, can be dangerous for both the animal and its caregivers. Not very long ago, such problems were dealt with using restraints or aversives, by anesthetizing the animal, or by simply not providing care. Operant procedures are not only more humane but also less risky for all concerned.

For instance, animal trainer Gary Wilkes (1994) describes the application of operant procedures to treat an aggressive elephant. Veterinary care of captive elephants includes periodically trimming calluses that build up on their feet. If the calluses are not removed, the animal eventually is unable to walk. An aggressive bull elephant at the San Diego Zoo had not had its calluses trimmed in almost ten years. Normally the job is done by going into a pen with the elephant and cutting away at the calluses with a sharp tool. Given this animal's history of aggressive behavior, there was not a lot of enthusiasm for this idea. Instead, the behavior specialist at the zoo, Gary Priest, had a large steel gate built at one end of an enclosure. The gate had a hole large enough to accommodate an elephant's foot (see Figure 9-9). "Now," writes Wilkes, "all that had to be done was to ask a violent bull elephant to daintily put his tootsies through a blank wall and let strange little creatures hack away at his feet with knives" (p. 32).

This was accomplished by shaping the desired behavior. Because shaping usually proceeds best with immediate reinforcement, the trainers established a clicking noise, made by a toy called a cricket, as a conditioned reinforcer (Skinner,

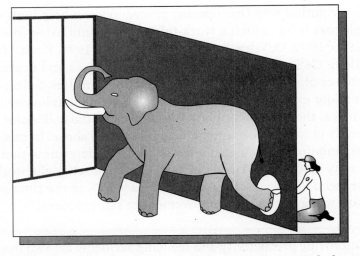

**Figure 9-9**   *How do you give an elephant a pedicure? With shaping. See text for explanation. (Drawing by Diane Chance)*

1951; Pryor, 1996). They did this by repeatedly making the clicking sound and then giving the elephant a piece of carrot. After this when the elephant approached the gate a trainer sounded the clicker and tossed the elephant a bit of carrot. When the animal was in front of the gate, the trainers reinforced lifting the left front foot off the ground, then reinforced raising the foot several inches, then reinforced moving it toward the hole, and so on. Wilkes writes that "soon the animal would voluntarily walk to the gate and put one foot after another into the mysterious hole. He would hold it there while the keeper trimmed the pads of his feet and groomed the animal's nails" (p. 33; see also Tresz & Wright, 2006).

**QUERY 7:**   The procedure used to modify the elephant's behavior was _____.

*An interesting but not unusual side effect of Wilke's manicure effort was that the elephant's temperament improved. He became far less aggressive and seemed to enjoy the training sessions.*

Operant procedures are used fairly routinely now in zoos and animal parks to provide veterinary care. But living well means more than keeping your toenails trimmed. It is difficult to say how captive animals feel about life in confinement, but zoo animals often appear to be very bored. Life in the wild is, as the English philosopher Thomas Hobbes said, "nasty, brutish, and short." Life in zoos usually can be described as easy, boring, and long. Many animals, especially bears and felines, can be seen pacing up and down in their small cages. Primates sit for long periods or swing in a desultory manner from one fake tree branch to another. Stereotypic behaviors seldom seen in animals in their natural habitat, such as swaying back and forth, are commonplace.

Zoo officials often put large balls or other toys in enclosures to entertain animals, but these items tend to lose their appeal in short order. Another tack has been to make enclosures larger and more natural. At the Wild Animal Park near San Diego, for example, many animals roam relatively large spaces freely in natural surroundings. Giraffes and antelope graze at their leisure in an open plain, while lions look harmlessly on. This makes for a more enjoyable experience for the human visitor, and it may make life more pleasant for the animals, but we can do better.

Hal Markowitz (1978, 1982, 2011), who pioneered the use of operant procedures to improve the quality of life of captive animals, noticed that the problem is that there is little for captive animals to do except eat and sleep. For many animals, life in the wild is a more or less constant search for food. Bears, for example, spend most of their waking time from spring to early winter foraging. They graze on berries, eat the carcasses of animals, and seek out and eat the caches of squirrels. Occasionally they kill and eat deer or other large animals. These activities are the substance of the bear's life in the wild. It isn't an easy life, but it isn't boring, either. But in zoos, even with large natural enclosures, food is provided daily "free of charge." There is no need for the bears to search for food, and there is little chance that they will find anything if they do. What is true of bears is true of many captive animals.

One of Markowitz's discoveries was that life becomes more interesting for captive animals (e.g., they spend less time in stereotypic behavior) when they obtain some of their food through their own efforts. For example, when Markowitz distributed food throughout a bear's enclosure, the animal spent part of its day turning over logs and stones, looking into tree cavities and the like, just as it would do in the wild. The bear now had a reason to be active. Markowitz used similar tactics for predatory birds, big cats, and other animals, thereby enriching life in zoos.

It is fair to say that animals, domestic and wild, have benefited greatly from the use of operant procedures in their care and treatment, and not just in zoos. Operant procedures are increasingly used to provide humane ways of training animals in a variety of settings to cooperate with essential veterinary procedures and to improve their quality of life. For example, researchers have successfully treated horses that resist boarding a trailer (Ferguson & Rosales-Ruiz, 2001) and have treated self-injurious behavior in animals in much the same way it is treated in people (Dorey et al., 2009). Operant procedures are also used to train animals in ways that benefit humans. You know about seeing eye dogs, but did you know that rats have been trained to detect landmines? This puts the rats at some risk, but it greatly reduces the risk of human injury (Poling et al., 2011; for more on this, see Chapter 11).

CAPSULE **REVIEW**

Operant principles are now being put to use to improve the lives of captive animals. Positive reinforcement, shaping, and chaining are almost taken for granted by many professional animal trainers and caretakers today, but 60 years ago people relied almost exclusively on negative reinforcement, punishment, and coercion. The strategies that have emerged from basic research, most of it with animals, have been of tremendous benefit to animals as well as to people.

# A FINAL WORD

One of my goals in this chapter was to show that operant learning has found wide application. I have barely scratched the surface, but I hope you can see that operant learning procedures have tremendous practical value. Despite the success of these efforts, there are those who oppose their use.

## REINFORCEMENT GOES TO THE DOGS

More dogs die each year because of behavior problems than from all diseases combined (reported in Jankowski, 1994). What often happens is that a dog develops a "bad habit" such as constantly barking, scratching at a door, or biting people. When efforts to change this behavior (usually with inappropriately applied aversives) fail, the dog is abandoned or taken to an animal shelter.

Sadly, even those dogs that make it to an animal shelter often face a grim fate because their behavior makes them unappealing. The history of exposure to inappropriately used aversives can produce a dog that behaves in an excessively shy, fearful, or aggressive manner. A dog that cowers in a corner with its tail between its legs and looks away from a visitor is unlikely to find a good home. It is fairly obvious that if such dogs were trained to behave in more attractive ways, fewer of them would be destroyed, but such training has not been available.

But that may be changing. Lauren Beck, the manager of an animal shelter, has used shaping to get dogs to make eye contact with people, to do a trick, and to display good canine manners (see Pryor, 1996). This change in behavior makes the animals far more appealing. When someone comes to the shelter hoping to adopt a dog, a member of the shelter staff points out the dog's virtues and invites the visitor to give the trick command and reinforce the behavior with a clicker. The usual reaction is something like, "This dog is brilliant!"

Of course, the dog is not brilliant. It has simply had good training for a change.

Some people resist the application of learning principles to real-world problems not because they don't work, but because they *do*. They fear a world in which behavioral engineers will control our every move. The fear is not entirely unwarranted: History is replete with examples of individuals and governments that manipulated their people like puppets on strings. However, they were successful not because they had a deep understanding of operant principles, but because their own behavior was shaped by its effects—they simply did what worked for them. The best defense against such abuses is an understanding of how behavior is affected by experience. We must learn about learning if we want to remain free.

## RECOMMENDED **READING**

1. Becker, W. (1971). *Parents are teachers*.

   This classic on child rearing has been in print for over 40 years. It is a simple, down-to-earth but research-based approach to child rearing.

2. Daniels, A. C. (1994). *Bringing out the best in people: How to apply the astonishing power of positive reinforcement*. New York: McGraw-Hill.

   Daniels, a successful management consultant, shows how reinforcement principles apply in the workplace. This is "must" reading for anyone planning a career in business.

3. Hart, B., & Risley, T. R. (1995). *Meaningful differences in the everyday experience of young American children*. Baltimore: Paul H. Brookes.

The research described makes it clear that parents and teachers play a profound role in the intellectual development of children. If you want your kids to be as smart as they can be, don't just read this book; study it.

4. Markowitz, H. (2011). *Enriching animal lives*. Pacifica, CA: Mauka Press.

   Markowitz's latest book is an entertaining read with delightful sketches. Anyone interested in working in a zoo should own this book.

5. Schreibman, L. (2007). *The science and fiction of autism*. Cambridge, MA: Harvard University Press.

   Laura Schreibman is one of the leading researchers and practitioners in the field of autism. Anyone who is the parent of a child with autism or other developmental disorder or who plans to teach special education classes should read this book.

# REVIEW **QUESTIONS**

1. Define the following terms in your own words:

   CITM                    Goldiamond's paradox

2. There is evidence that neglect in poor-quality orphanages interferes with normal brain development (Chugani et al., 2001). Could this be due in part to the lack of operant learning opportunities?

3. How could you train a child to be a quitter?

4. Research consistently shows that teachers typically reprimand students far more often than they praise them. Why do you suppose this is so?

5. What do you think is the key feature of the Headsprout program that makes it so successful?

6. Some people strenuously object to using punishment with children with developmental disorders, even to suppress behavior that poses serious risks to the child or others. "He does that because he's sick," they argue, "so he shouldn't be punished for it!" Assuming other efforts to reduce the behavior have failed, how would you respond to this argument?

7. Could delusions sometimes be a form of superstitious behavior (see Chapter 6)?

8. Do the benefits derived from CIMT justify the research on monkeys that led to this treatment? How would you have answered before CIMT proved to be effective?

9. How might a company improve the workplace environment of employees without significantly reducing their net profits?

10. How could you use operant learning to improve the life of lions in a zoo?

## PRACTICE **QUIZ**

1. Some people believe that a first language is acquired mainly without instruction and simply through _____ to the language.

2. Using extinction alone to eliminate tantrums is problematic. A better approach is to use extinction in conjunction with a form of _____ reinforcement.

3. The person who developed the first teaching machines was _____.

4. When teachers focus on reinforcing appropriate behavior rather than on punishing inappropriate behavior, disruptive behavior decreases and the rate of academic learning _____.

5. Ivar Lovaas was perhaps the first person to use punishment to suppress _____.

6. Self-injurious behavior is often maintained by attention or by _____.

7. The author of this text calls the tendency to engage in bizarre behavior even when no reinforcers are available for it _____.

8. To restore function in a limb damaged by a stroke, therapists use CIMT, which stands for _____.

9. CIMT was first used to treat stroke patients, but it has also been used to treat patients with _____.

10. In animal training, secondary reinforcement may be provided with a sound, such as that made by a toy called a _____.

## QUERY **ANSWERS**

Query 1. Madsen and colleagues asked teachers to shift their attention from *bad* behavior to *good* behavior.

Query 2. In Skinner's teaching machines, the reinforcer for correct answers was *the opportunity to go on to the next item.*

Query 3. The Headsprout reading program was designed so that most students will be *successful* most of the time.

Query 4. Once self-injurious behavior was thought to be due to an unconscious need to suffer, but if that were the case, the shocks given by Lovaas and Simmons should have *reinforced/strengthened/increased* self-injurious acts.

Query 5. Alford's research demonstrates that *delusional* behavior can be modified by reinforcement.

Query 6. CIMT reinforces *movement* of a defective limb.

Query 7. The procedure used to modify the elephant's behavior was *shaping.*

# CHAPTER

# 10 Observational Learning

*You can observe a lot by watching.*

—**Yogi Berra**

## PREVIEW

Behavior is an *individual* phenomenon. Learning is a change in behavior, so it is also an individual phenomenon. We learn a good deal by observing events around us, including the actions of other people and their conse-quences. Without such observational learning, advances in society would be much slower since we would not benefit much from what other people have learned.

# BEGINNINGS

Sometimes the history of science is the story of a steady progression, rather like the climb up a winding staircase. Progress requires effort, and occasionally the scientist is found panting on a landing, but movement is always forward and usually upward. The study of classical conditioning, for example, began with the brilliant experiments of Pavlov and his coworkers and progressed more or less steadily until today our understanding of this phenomenon is fairly sophisticated. The study of operant learning followed a similar course. But sometimes the history of science is more like a roller-coaster ride than the climb up a staircase: One moment we're plummeting toward ruin; the next we seem to be headed for the stars. Observational learning is a case in point.

The basic question originally posed by observational learning seems simple enough: Can one individual learn by observing the experience of another? The search for an answer to this question began with E. L. Thorndike. In Thorndike's day, it was widely believed that animals often learned by observing others. Everyone was convinced that the house cat watched people opening cabinet doors and then imitated their behavior. Could cats and other animals really learn this way? According to anecdotal evidence, the answer was yes.

Thorndike was not so sure, so he submitted the question to experimental test. His first subjects were chicks, cats, and dogs. In a typical experiment, Thorndike (1898) put one cat in a puzzle box and another cat in a nearby cage. The first cat had already learned how to escape from the box, and the second had only to observe its neighbor to learn the trick. But when Thorndike put this cat into the puzzle box, it did not imitate its more learned fellow. Instead, it went through the same sort of operant learning any other cat went through in learning to solve the problem. No matter how often one cat watched another escape, it seemed to learn nothing. Thorndike got similar results with chicks and dogs and concluded that "we should give up imitation as an *a priori* explanation of any novel intelligent performance" (p. 62). In other words, until someone demonstrates that animals learn by observing others, we ought not to assume that they do.

These experiments on observational learning, perhaps the first ever done, were published in 1898 as part of Thorndike's classic treatise on animal intelligence. Shortly thereafter, Thorndike (1901) conducted similar experiments with monkeys, but despite the popular belief that "monkey see, monkey do," Thorndike concluded that "nothing in my experience with these animals . . . favors the hypothesis that they have any general ability to learn to do things from seeing others do them" (p. 42). A few years after this, John B. Watson (1908) performed a similar series of experiments on monkeys with nearly identical results.

The negative findings seem to have had a devastating effect on research on observational learning, including observational learning in people. There was, in fact, almost no experimental investigation of this problem for a generation.

Then, in the 1930s, Carl Warden and his colleagues conducted a number of carefully controlled experiments and clearly demonstrated that monkeys can learn by observing others.

These studies should have prompted an upswing in research on observational learning, but it continued to receive little attention. Then, in the 1960s, research in this area began to take off. Much of the impetus for this change was the research of Albert Bandura and his colleagues on social learning, and the research of others on the use of modeling in the treatment of behavior disorders. This research showed the importance of observational learning in humans and spurred interest in the subject. After this spurt of interest, research once again lagged (Kymissis & Poulson, 1994; Robert, 1990), but since 2000 interest has once again picked up (Nielsen et al., 2012). The roller-coaster ride now seems to be headed upward.

# TYPES OF OBSERVATIONAL LEARNING

Learning is a change in behavior due to experience. Traditionally, observational learning is defined as learning from the experiences of a model. Recent research suggests that we should adopt a broader definition: **Observational learning** means learning by observing events and their consequences. This definition leads to recognition of two types of observational learning, which I will call social and asocial.

## Social Observational Learning

The **social** version of observational learning (which might also be called the **active model** type) is what has traditionally been considered observational learning. The experiments of Thorndike described above were of this type. It typically involves observing the behavior of another individual (usually of the same species as the observer) and the consequences of the model's behavior. The experience may be represented thus:

$$O[M_B \rightarrow S^{+/-}]$$

This is read: An observer (O) views a model's behavior ($M_B$) and its positive and/or negative consequences ($S^{+/-}$). If the consequences of the model's behavior strengthen the *observer's* tendency to behave in a similar way, we say the behavior has been **vicariously reinforced.** If the consequences of the model's behavior weaken the *observer's* tendency to behave in a similar way, the behavior is said to be **vicariously punished.** Usually the consequences that reinforce or punish the model's behavior have a similar effect on the observer's behavior. A hypothetical example may help.

Imagine that you have volunteered to participate in an experiment. You are seated in front of a window looking into a neighboring room. You see a woman seated in front of a table with a large box on it (Figure 10-1). The box has a sign that reads, "The Money Box. Take the Money and Run." The face of the box has a thin panel with rails above and below it. The woman slides

**Figure 10-1** *The money box. See text for explanation. (Drawing by Deborah Underwood.)*

the panel to the left, revealing a hole in the box. Inside the hole there is a shelf with an envelope on it. The woman takes the envelope and opens it, revealing numerous $20 bills. Next the experimenter enters the room, thanks the woman for her participation, and escorts her to the exit. The woman leaves clutching the envelope and smiling broadly. Now the experimenter enters the room you are in, and the next thing you know you are sitting in front of the box. What do you do? (Think about this for a moment before reading on.)

Chances are you push the sliding panel to the left and get the money. Your tendency to do what the model did has been vicariously reinforced.

As in this hypothetical experiment, many studies of the social version of observational learning involve problem solving. Carl Warden (Warden, Fjeld, & Koch, 1940; Warden & Jackson, 1935) was among the first to demonstrate experimentally that some animals can learn to solve problems by watching others do so. He began by constructing a special experimental environment with two compartments so that identical problems could be solved in each compartment. He put an observer monkey in one compartment and restrained it so that it could not get to the problem apparatus. Then he put another monkey, the model, in the other compartment. The model had already learned how to obtain reinforcement, so he demonstrated a skilled performance.

In one experiment (Warden & Jackson, 1935), the simplest problem involved pulling a chain that opened a door and revealed a raisin the model could retrieve and eat. After watching the model perform this act five times, the observer got a chance to tackle the same problem in its own chamber. If the observer did not solve the problem within 60 seconds, the experimenters pulled the monkey away from the apparatus and restrained it for about half a minute before letting it have a second trial. The results showed clearly that the observers benefited substantially from watching the model, often responding correctly on the very first trial. In fact, 47% of all observer solutions occurred within 10 seconds (almost as fast as the model's performance), and about 75% of the solutions occurred within 30 seconds.

**? QUERY 1:** This text identifies two types of observational learning. The kind being

discussed here is _____.

Marvin Herbert and Charles Harsh (1944) studied observational learning in cats using models. The researchers designed a structure that allowed as many as four cats at a time to watch a model as it worked at solving one of five problems (see Figure 10-2). In the turntable problem, a circular platform rotated on a bicycle axle (see Figure 10-3). By grasping the black cleats on the turntable, a cat could spin the platform so that a food dish came into its cage. On any given problem, the cat that served as model would have 30 learning trials while observer cats looked on. Some observers watched all 30 of a model's trials before tackling a problem; others watched only the last 15 trials. The results showed that the observer cats outperformed the models. Moreover, the more observing a cat did, the better it performed (see Figure 10-4). On the turntable problem, for instance, the models took an average of 62 seconds to solve the problem on the first trial. Cats that observed 15 trials took an average of 57 seconds, and those that observed 30 trials took an average of only 16 seconds.

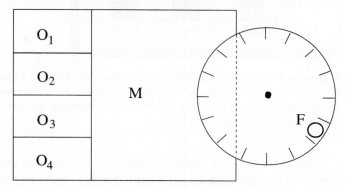

**Figure 10-2** *View from above the Herbert and Harsh apparatus with the turntable problem installed. Observers sat in chambers at $O_1$, $O_2$, $O_3$, and $O_4$ and watched as a model, at M, worked on the problem of getting the food at F. (After Herbert and Harsh, 1944.)*

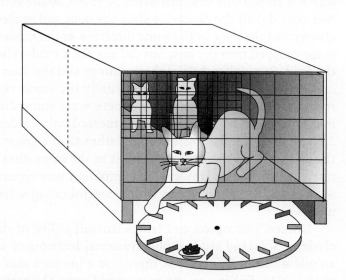

**Figure 10-3** *Miss White working at the turntable problem. (After Herbert and Harsh, 1944.)*

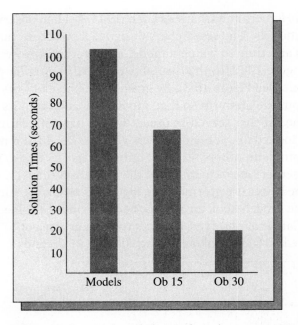

**Figure 10-4** *Number of observed reinforcements. Average solution times on fi rst trial of four problems by models and observers. Observers watched models perform on 15 or 30 trials. Data from one problem, failed by four observers, are not included. (Compiled from data in Herbert and Harsh, 1944.)*

Lydia Hopper, of Georgia State University, and her colleagues (2008) performed a study using an apparatus similar to the hypothetical money box described earlier. In one part of the research, a chimp saw a grape dropped into the box and looked on as a model slid the door either to the left or to the right, exposing an opening in the box, and then retrieved and ate the grape. The observer watched this demonstration 58 times before getting a chance at the box. Not only did all the observers slide the door and retrieve the fruit, they nearly always slid the door in the same direction as the model. A control group saw a grape dropped into the box, but did not see a model slide the door and retrieve the food. Fewer than half of these chimps slid the door and retrieved the grape.

The researchers performed virtually the same experiment with children roughly three to five years old. There were some differences in the experimental procedure: The children witnessed only 15 demonstrations instead of 58, and their reward was a sticker rather than a grape. Like the chimps, all of the children slid the door, and slid it in the same direction as the model, then retrieved the prize. However, the problem was apparently easy for children: Six out of the eight children in the control group solved it without viewing a model.

Doreen Thompson and James Russell (2004) of the University of Strathclyde in Scotland studied observational learning of a problem that required an odd solution. In one case there was a toy on a mat, but it was out of reach of the child. Pulling on the mat would seem the way to get the toy, but that did not work; pushing the mat *away* caused the toy to move *closer*. An adult model demonstrated the solution three times as the children, who were between 14 and 26 months old, looked on. Children who observed the demonstration were three times as likely to get the toy as children who tackled the problem on their own. Those who observed the model were also likely to solve the problem more quickly than those who worked on their own.

Not all studies of observational learning involve learning to solve a problem or perform a skill. Ellen Levy and her colleagues (1974), for example, studied the effects of model reinforcement and punishment on the picture preferences of children. In one experiment, children ranging from preschoolers to sixth graders looked on as a model went through a series of picture pairs, indicating which of each pair she preferred. Each of these choices resulted in approval, disapproval, or a neutral consequence from an adult. The observers then went through the picture pairs and indicated their own preferences. The results showed that the children were influenced by the consequences of the model's choices. Children tended to prefer pictures that won approval for the model, and to reject pictures that resulted in criticism of the model.

Similar influences have been demonstrated in adults. Frederick Kanfer and Albert Marston (1963) had college students sit in an experimental room alone and communicate with the experimenter by way of a microphone and earphones. Each time the experimenter signaled the student, he or she said the first word that came to mind. As the students waited for the signal, they could hear what seemed to be the responses of other students taking their turn. What the students really heard was a prerecorded tape. Over the course of the experiment, the people on the tape responded with more and more human nouns (presumably words such as *boy, woman,* and *hero*). Some of the

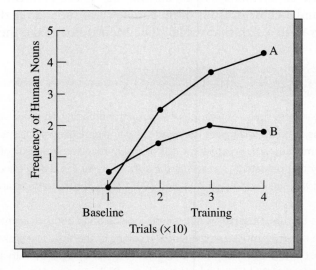

**Figure 10-5**   *Reinforcement of modeled verbal behavior. Group A heard people praised for saying human nouns; Group B did not. (Adapted from "Human Reinforcement: Vicarious and Direct," by Frederick Kanfer and Albert Marston, 1963,* Journal of Experimental Psychology, *65, p. 293, Figure 1. Copyright © 1963 by the American Psychological Association. Reprinted by permission.)*

students heard the experimenter say, "Good," each time a person on the tape responded with a human noun; others heard the experimenter say nothing. In neither case did the observer receive any direct reinforcement for saying human nouns. These two groups of students showed the same inclination to say human nouns during the baseline period, but the students who heard human nouns approved showed a marked increase in nouns compared to those who did not (see Figure 10-5).

These and other studies illustrate how observing a model influences people and animals. However, we can learn a great deal from observation even in the absence of models.

*Observational learning is usually thought to involve vision, but as Kanfer and Marston show, we can observe (and learn) through other senses.*

## Asocial Observational Learning

The **asocial** version of observational learning consists of learning from observed events in the absence of a model. It is not news to anyone that people learn from their surroundings in the absence of models, but this form of learning hasn't been thought of as observational. The experience involved may be represented thus:

$$O[E \rightarrow S^{+/-}]$$

This is read: An observer (O) views an event (E) and its positive and/or negative consequences ($S^{+/-}$). Note that since there is no model, there can be no *vicarious* reinforcement or punishment, yet the observer's behavior is influenced by the consequences of an event.

Consider again that you have volunteered to participate in an experiment. This time you are sitting in a room, looking through a window into the room where the experiment will be conducted. There is nothing in the room but a table and a chair in front of it. You see two men enter the room carrying a large box with a sign that reads, "The Money Box. Take the Money and Run."

## VICARIOUS PAVLOVIAN CONDITIONING?

Some learning researchers speak of vicarious Pavlovian conditioning. This involves an observer looking on as a model undergoes Pavlovian conditioning. Experiments have shown, for example, that a monkey with no apparent fear of snakes may acquire a fear of them by observing a monkey that repeatedly screams at the sight of a snake (Cook & Mineka, 1990; Mineka and Cook, 1988; see also Olsson & Phelps, 2007). This appears to be vicarious conditioning, but is it?

The problem is that the observer is not merely looking on as another animal displays a fear of snakes. The observer monkey experiences a pairing of the sight of a snake and the screaming of a monkey. Thus an initially neutral stimulus (the snake) is paired with a presumably fearful stimulus (screaming). This looks like ordinary Pavlovian conditioning. So, is the observer's acquired fear the product of vicarious conditioning or direct conditioning? It is a difficult question to answer, but it seems to be ordinary classical conditioning (see Venn & Short, 1973).

The face of the box has a thin panel with rails above and below it. One of the men is considerably taller than the other, and as they carry the box, the panel slides to the left, toward the shorter man, revealing a hole in the box. In the hole you see a shelf with a thick envelope on it. As the men set the box down on the table the panel slides to the right, covering the hole. Next, one of the experimenters escorts you to the room and signals that you should sit at the table, facing the box. He says, "You have one minute to solve the problem," then leaves the room. What do you do?

You may not "take the money and run," but it's likely that you will slide the door to the left and retrieve the envelope *even though you saw no model do this*. As this example suggests, we are capable of learning a great deal from observing events in the absence of models. One demonstration of this is provided by the sliding door study of Hopper et al. (2008) considered earlier. In that study, chimps watched a model slide a door and retrieve a desired item, then tackled the problem themselves. What I did not tell you earlier is that the researchers had other experimental groups. In one, there was no model to observe. Hopper attached a fishing line to the panel and then, out of sight of the observers, pulled the door to the left or right as the observer looked on. Thus, the door moved, exposing the opening in the box, but not because of a model's actions. This is often referred to as a **ghost condition** because, to the observer, it appears that no person causes the movement (Heyes, 1996). All eight chimps in the ghost condition solved the problem, whereas only three out of eight that tackled the problem without seeing the panel move did so.

The research by Thompson and Russell (2004) described above also included a ghost condition. In this case the experimenters moved the mat with hidden pulleys so that the child saw the mat and toy move, but did not see anyone move them. The children (remember, they were between 14 and 26 months old) moved the mat in the required direction to get the toy despite not seeing it demonstrated by a model. In fact, those who saw the mat move "on its own" were *more* successful than those who saw a model move it (see Figure 10-6; see also Huang & Charman, 2005). The time taken to solve the problem also suggests that the asocial observation was at least as effective as observing a model (Figure 10-7).

**? QUERY 2:** This text identifies two types of observational learning. The kind being

discussed here is _____.

One question that arises as a result of experiments on asocial observational learning is the extent to which social learning is truly social (Heyes, 2012). Michael Tomasello (1998) writes, "If a mother chimpanzee rolls a log and eats the insects underneath, her child will very likely follow suit . . . [but] the youngster would have learned the same thing if the wind, rather than the mother, had caused the log to roll over and expose the ants" (quoted in Whiten et al., 2009, p. 2422). The research reviewed here (see below) suggests that this statement goes too far, that there *are* differences in what is learned in

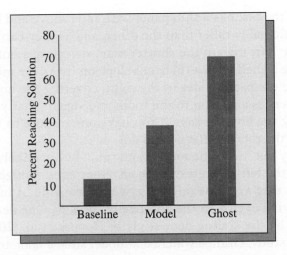

***Figure 10-6*** *Model vs. ghost. Percent of children who solved the sliding mat problem cold (baseline), after viewing a demonstration (model), or after watching the mat move as if on its own (ghost). (Compiled from data in Thompson and Russell, 2004. Drawn by illustrator.)*

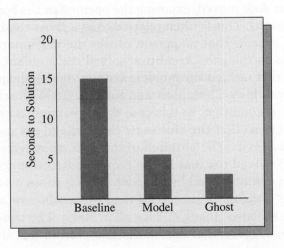

***Figure 10-7*** *Time to solution. Average number of seconds taken to solve the sliding mat problem. The difference between the model and ghost groups was not statistically significant, but clearly those in the ghost condition were not at a disadvantage. (Compiled from data in Thompson and Russell, 2004. Drawn by illustrator.)*

the presence and absence of a model. Yet we do have to wonder how much of the learning that occurs in observing a model is due to the action of the model, and how much is due to observing the physical events that occur. For example, did the observer cats in Herbert and Harsh's study (see Figure 10-4) benefit mostly from seeing a model pull on the wheel, or mostly from seeing the food approach the model when the wheel moved? This question has gotten considerable attention, particularly from primatologists (see Hopper, 2010, for a review), but the issue is unresolved. Another difference between social and asocial observational learning involves imitation.

Observational learning is usually defined as learning from observing a model. In this text it is defined as learning from observing environmental events and their consequences. Two types of observational learning are identified: social and asocial. The social type involves a model; the asocial type does not. People and some animals can learn from both kinds of observation.

# IMITATION

Traditionally, to **imitate** is to behave in a way that resembles the behavior of a model. We have seen that people and some animals reproduce events observed in the absence of a model: A child sees that when a mat moves away, a toy comes closer, and after this the child pushes the mat away even though he saw no model do this. This suggests that "to imitate" could be defined as "to perform an observed act, whether modeled or not." However, most research on imitation involves models, so I will focus on imitation as the performance of modeled behavior.

As you have seen, the modeled behaviors that are imitated tend to be those that have reinforcing consequences for the model. However, sometimes observers imitate acts that play little or no part in producing rewarding consequences. The door in the Hopper research, for example, could be slid left or right to get the prize, yet both chimps and children slid it in the same direction as the model.

*In the hypothetical money box, you could have slid the door to the left, as the model did, or to the right. Which did you do?*

You might argue that the observers slid the door in the modeled direction because sliding it in the opposite direction might not have worked. A model might turn a key to the left to unlock a door; if you turn the key to the right you will not gain entry. But people tend to imitate observed behavior even when it is clearly irrelevant to producing reinforcement. In fact, humans seem to be downright compulsive about imitating the details of modeled behavior.

Derek Lyons, Andrew Young, and Frank Keil (2007) demonstrated this in a series of experiments. In one experiment they trained 3- to 5-year-old children to identify actions that were irrelevant to the solution of problems. For example, they showed children a jar with a toy dinosaur inside, tapped the jar with a feather, unscrewed the lid, and removed the toy. Then they asked the child which acts had been necessary to get the dinosaur and which were silly. When the child answered correctly the experimenter heaped praise on the child; if the child answered incorrectly the experimenter provided corrective feedback. After training, the experimenter showed the child a new kind of container with a toy turtle inside and demonstrated how to get the turtle. The demonstration included irrelevant steps. The question was whether the child would imitate those steps. Since the child might feel some pressure to imitate the adult's irrelevant acts if he were present, the experimenter said he had to leave the room, but before leaving suggested that the child remove the turtle "however you want." Despite these efforts to discourage imitation of irrelevant acts, the children imitated them. Children who took on the task of removing the turtle without watching a model do it were successful and seldom engaged in unnecessary actions (see Figure 10-8).

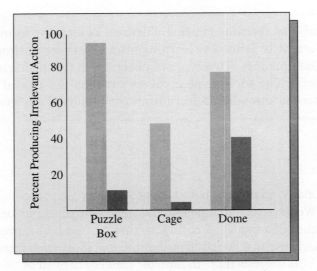

**Figure 10-8** *Over-imitation. Children who observed a model perform unnecessary acts (light bars) were far more likely to perform those acts than were children who did not observe a model (dark bars). Observers imitated irrelevant acts despite instructions* not *to do so. (Adapted from Lyons, Young, and Keil, 2007, Figure 2, p. 1975, Proceedings of the National Academy of Sciences, 2007, 104 (50), 19751-19756, Figure 2, p.19753.)*

In another experiment, after training a child in identifying unnecessary acts, the researchers explicitly urged the children *not* to include irrelevant acts. Just before demonstrating the solution to a new problem an experimenter said, "I want you to watch really carefully, because when I open this [puzzle box or dome], I might do something that's silly and extra, just like the feather." Then, after demonstrating a solution that included unnecessary acts, the experimenter said, "Remember, don't do anything silly and extra, okay? Only do the things you *have* to do." After this the experimenter left the room and the child worked on the problem. Despite these efforts to get the children to do only what was necessary, the majority of children performed superfluous acts modeled by the experimenter. The researchers dubbed this tendency to imitate irrelevant acts **over-imitation** (see also Nielsen & Blank, 2011; Nielsen & Tomaselli, 2010; Whiten et al., 2009).

It's tempting to dismiss over-imitation as the result of immaturity, but in fact it seems that in humans the tendency to over-imitate increases with age. Claudio Tennie, Josep Call, and Michael Tomasello (2006), primatologists at the Max Planck Institute in Leipzig, had children look on as a model obtained a toy in a box by opening a swinging door. The door could be opened by pushing or pulling. Some children saw a model open the door by pushing it, others saw a model pull the door open. The proportion of children who matched the model increased steadily with age from 12 to 24 months. Nicola McGuigan and colleagues (2007; McGuigan & Graham, 2010) found that 5-year-old children were *more* likely to over-imitate than 3-year-olds. McGuigan (2012) suggests that over-imitation progresses steadily into adulthood.

**? QUERY 3:** Over-imitation is the tendency to imitate behavior that is_____.

This tendency of humans to over-imitate is puzzling. Other primates are less inclined than humans to imitate irrelevant acts (e.g., Tennie, Call, & Tomasello, 2006). We are supposed to be the smartest apes on the planet (according to ourselves; the other apes have not yet voted); if that is so, why do chimps, gorillas, and orangutans imitate more sensibly than we do? One possibility is that the difference is an evolutionary fluke, the behavioral equivalent of the appendix.

A related idea is that the tendency to imitate evolved before the capacity for true observational learning. Thorndike (1911) reports that sheep were observed being boarded on a ship one at a time. At one point, the sheep had to jump over an obstacle. Someone removed the obstacle, but the next few sheep, having seen those before them jump the hurdle, also jumped at that point, even though there was no longer anything to jump. Although we humans are generally smarter than that, at times we, too, follow our leaders, however foolish they are.

Some researchers argue, however, that over-imitation is beneficial. Andrew Whiten and colleagues (2009) suggest that by over-imitating we ensure success, and if our performance includes irrelevant acts we can edit them out later on. Mark Nielsen of the University of Queensland and colleagues (2012) go a step further, arguing that over-imitation evolved because it facilitates the dissemination of new practices through a society, thereby improving the odds that the society will survive.

Another possibility is that the tendency is learned. Cecilia Heyes (2012) of the University of Oxford argues that from infancy on people are rewarded for imitating others. There is evidence to support this. In a classic study, Donald Baer and J. Sherman (1964) used a puppet to provide social reinforcers for imitative behavior in young children. The puppet modeled four acts: mouthing, head nodding, speaking nonsense, and pressing a lever. Whenever the children imitated any of the first three of these behaviors, the puppet provided reinforcement in the form of approving comments. The researchers discovered that as the tendency to imitate these acts increased, so did the tendency to imitate lever pressing, even though lever pressing never produced reinforcement. When the researchers stopped reinforcing imitative mouthing, head nodding, and nonsense talking, their frequency declined—and so did the frequency of lever pressing. When imitating the first three acts again resulted in praise, they increased—and so did lever pressing. Baer and Sherman concluded that it is possible not only to reinforce the imitation of *particular acts* but also to reinforce a general *tendency* to imitate. They called this tendency **generalized imitation.**

Numerous studies have replicated Baer and Sherman's findings (Baer & Deguchi, 1985; Baer, Peterson, & Sherman, 1967). Ivar Lovaas and his colleagues (1966), for example, established generalized imitation in two schizophrenic children. The researchers reinforced accurate imitation of English words and found that as performance improved, accurate imitation of Norwegian words increased as well, even though the researchers had never reinforced imitation of Norwegian words.

 QUERY 4:    Generalized imitation is the tendency to imitate modeled behavior even

when imitation of the behavior is not _____.

Some research suggests that this general tendency to imitate models occurs in humans in infancy (Poulson et al., 1991, 2002). Other research suggests that it seldom occurs in children under the age of two (Erjavec, Lovett, & Horne, 2009; Horne & Erjavec, 2007). Nevertheless, the general tendency to imitate others is at least partly the product of learning experiences (Steinman, 1970). So, it seems, is the tendency to imitate acts that are not required to obtain reinforcement, such as stroking a bottle with a feather to retrieve a toy from it.

CAPSULE **REVIEW**    Imitation of observed events, especially those performed by a model, is a strong tendency in a number of animals, especially primates. In humans, it sometimes includes the tendency to imitate acts that are irrelevant to achieving success. Some believe such over-imitation is an evolved characteristic, but another possibility is that it is learned. Generalized imitation is the learned tendency to imitate modeled behavior, even when the modeled behavior is not reinforced, so it might account for the imitation of irrelevant acts in over-imitation.

## VARIABLES AFFECTING OBSERVATIONAL LEARNING

The variables that are important in operant procedures seem to affect observational learning in a similar manner, but there are some additional tweaks and complications. We have considered two kinds of observational learning, social and asocial, but most of the research deals with variables affecting observation of modeled behavior, so that will be my focus.

### Difficulty of the Task

It is no surprise that the more difficult a task, the less learning is likely to occur during observation (Hirakawa & Nakazawa, 1977; Richman & Gholson, 1978). However, observing a model perform a difficult task improves the likelihood of success. In the Thompson and Russell (2004) study in which children had to push a mat away to get a toy, there was a second, more complicated problem. In this case there were two mats, one of which had a toy. To get the toy, the child had to pull on the mat that did *not* have the toy. Some children saw a model demonstrate this; others saw the mats and toy move on their own. In the one-mat study, the presence of a model actually resulted in *less* learning than watching the mat and toy move. In the more complicated two-mats study, observing a model got better results. In fact, observers who saw

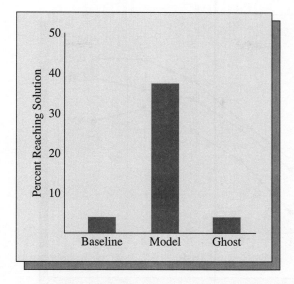

***Figure 10-9*** *Problem difficulty and model vs. ghost. Percent of children in each group who solved the difficult two-mat problem. (Compiled from data in Thompson and Russell, 2004. Drawn by illustrator.)*

a model did just as well on the two-mat problem as they had on the one-mat problem, whereas those who saw the mats move on their own did no better than those who saw nothing (Figure 10-9). Thus, the data suggest that models are most likely to be helpful when the task is difficult (Hopper, 2010; Hopper et al., 2008; Whiten et al., 2009).

## Skilled vs. Unskilled Model

Models demonstrating a skill or the solution to a problem tend to fall into one of two categories, skilled and unskilled (also called a **learning model**). In the skilled variation, the model demonstrates the proper performance of a task. For example, to learn to shoot foul shots in basketball, you might watch a video of a professional basketball player demonstrating the shot. The model repeatedly throws the ball and it falls through the net with the reinforcing "whoosh" sound every basketball player loves to hear. The logic of expert modeling is that the observer sees just what is required for positive results. In the unskilled variation the model is a novice and is observed as he or she learns to perform the task. A person who has never played basketball may attempt to shoot foul shots over and over again; some shots are good, many miss. The logic in using unskilled models is that the observer then sees both what works and what does not and will learn from the model's mistakes as well as her successes.

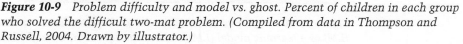

QUERY **5:**     An unskilled model is also called a _____ model.

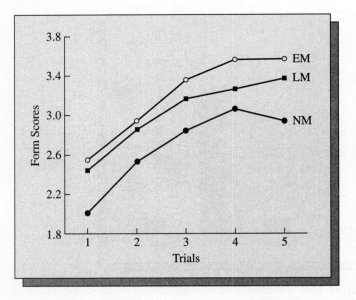

**Figure 10-10**  *Expert vs. learning model. College students watched either an expert model (EM) or a learning model (LM) perform the squat lift, a weight-lifting exercise, or practiced it without viewing a model (NM). Viewing a model helped, but the skill of the model made little difference. (Compiled from data in McCullagh and Meyer, 1997.)*

Which is more effective, observing a skilled or an unskilled model? I am not sure that the question has a definite answer. Some researchers got better results with skilled models (Landers & Landers, 1973; Lirgg & Feltz, 1991; Weir & Leavitt, 1990); others found that observers did just as well watching a learning model (Lee & White, 1990; McCullagh & Meyer, 1997; Pollock & Lee, 1992; see Figure 10-10). It seems likely that the skill level of the model is important, but researchers haven't yet worked out the factors that determine which will work better in a particular situation. For example, the number of observations of a model might interact with the skill level of the model. If you were trying to learn how to do heart bypass surgery, watching a medical resident practice on 30 cadavers might be very useful, but if you could watch only a few demonstrations, chances are you would get more out of watching a skilled heart surgeon.

## Characteristics of the Model

Numerous studies have demonstrated that human observers tend to learn more from models who are attractive, likable, and prestigious than from models who lack these characteristics. A study by Berger (1971), in which college students participated in what was ostensibly an investigation of extrasensory perception (ESP), will serve as an example. The experimenter introduced the model to the observer either as a fellow subject or as an assistant to the experimenter. Later on, those observers who thought they had watched a fellow student showed less evidence of learning than did those who thought they had observed the experimenter's assistant. The model was actually the same person in each case and behaved in the same way, so the difference in the observer's behavior apparently was due to the model's status. Studies of this sort raise an interesting question: Why should model characteristics such as status, attractiveness, competence, and so on have any effect on what an observer learns?

Research by Judith Fisher and Mary Harris (1976) provides one plausible answer. Fisher and Harris approached people in a shopping center or on a college campus and asked them to guess the prices of certain items. An experimenter would appear to approach two subjects simultaneously, but one of the people approached was actually a confederate of the researchers who served as a model. In one experiment, the model sometimes wore an eye patch. The model would guess at the price of an item, and then the observer would make a guess. Later, when the observers tried to remember the answers the model had given, the ones who were generally more accurate were those who had seen the model with an eye patch.

In a second experiment, the researchers manipulated the mood of the model. In one condition, the model smiled and nodded her head as the experimenter asked her questions. In another condition, the model frowned and shook her head. In a third condition, the model behaved in a neutral manner. In other respects, this experiment was similar to the first. The results showed that observers who witnessed one of the more expressive models recalled her behavior better than did observers who saw an impassive model. It made no difference whether the model's mood was positive or negative, as long as it was not neutral.

Fisher and Harris suggest the eye patch and mood affected the observer's learning because they attracted attention. Thus, status, likability, age, sex, competence, and other model characteristics affect observational learning apparently because they influence the observer's tendency to look at the model. The more attentive an observer, the more likely he or she is to learn from a model's behavior.

 QUERY 6: Model characteristics are important because they can induce the observer to

_____.

Model characteristics also have a strong effect on the tendency to imitate. Models who are attractive, powerful, or very popular are much more likely to be imitated than models who are not. Celebrities seem especially likely to be imitated. The hairstyles, clothing, language, and social behavior of popular figures in the entertainment field are likely to appear among their fans. If Jennifer Lopez has her hair dyed pink, chances are that within a short time pink hair will be a much more common sight (Stack, 1987, 2000; Wasserman, 1984).

Even fictional celebrities can be influential. Angie, a character in a televised soap opera called *East Enders* broadcast by the BBC (British Broadcasting Corporation), took a drug overdose to get attention. (Note that the actress playing the part did not take an overdose; the character she played did.) After this, cases of self-poisoning shot up at certain hospitals (Fowler, 1986; see also Stack, 1987, 2000). The phenomenon is not new. *The Sorrows of Young Werther*, by Johann Wolfgang von Goethe, describes a depressed young man who commits suicide. The book was widely read throughout Europe in the 18th century, and suicide rates in a country shot up as the book gained popularity.

## Characteristics of the Observer

Perhaps the most powerful variable affecting observational learning is the species of the observer. Overall, humans get the most out of observation; the other apes generally come in second. Studies comparing the observational learning of apes with humans typically compare adult apes with human children, sometimes children under two years of age—and the kids typically surpass their hairy cousins (e.g., Hopper et al., 2008; Tennie, Call, & Tomasello, 2006, 2009).

There are also important differences within species. Learning history is especially important (Williams & Meltzoff, 2011). Chimps that have had language training, for example, get more from observing models than those that have not (Williams, Whiten, & Singh, 2004). Language skill is important to observational learning in people as well (Taylor & Hoch, 2008). As noted above, the difficulty of a task is a factor in observational learning, but task difficulty is itself a function of learning history. The student who has mastered basic arithmetic is likely to get more out of a demonstration on solving algebraic equations than is the student who cannot add 3 and 5.

Age is sometimes a factor in observational learning. Young monkeys, for example, are more likely to imitate a model than are old monkeys (Adams-Curtiss & Fragaszy, 1995). The study by Levy and others (1974) described earlier found that children tended to imitate the picture choices of a model. The results were different with adult observers: The consequences of the model's behavior had no effect on their choices. These findings nicely demonstrate that observational experiences may have different effects with different age groups.

The influence of age may vary with gender. Primatologist Elizabeth Lonsdorf (2005) reports that, in the wild, young female chimps watch carefully as their mothers retrieve termites from a mound with a stick and quickly pick up the art of "termite fishing." Young male chimps, on the other hand, spend their time roughhousing and spinning in circles and, as a result, learn termite fishing about two years later than do females. This observation shows the advantage that observational learning bestows, but it also shows that one learns little from it if one fails to observe.

While the young seem more likely to imitate a model, the more mature usually get more from observing one. For example, Brian Coates and Willard Hartup (1969) had young children watch a film in which a model performed various novel acts. The older observers recalled more of the model's behavior than did the younger children (see also Yando, Seitz, & Zigler, 1978).

Those advanced in years, however, often are slower to benefit from the experiences of others than are the young (Kawamura, 1963).

Developmental age is even more important than chronological age. People who have developmental disabilities, such as mental retardation and autism, are less likely to benefit from observing a model than are those who do not have these problems (Delgado & Greer, 2009; Sallows & Graupner, 2005; Taylor, 2012).

Sensory handicaps, particularly poor vision and hearing, are also going to make learning from observation more difficult.

## Consequences of Observed Acts

The consequences of modeled acts are clearly critical. A study by Mary Rosekrans and Willard Hartup (1967) demonstrates this nicely. The researchers had nursery school children watch an adult model as she played with some toys, at times beating a large inflated doll on the head with a mallet and poking a clay figure with a fork. As she played, the model made comments such as, "Wham, bam, I'll knock your head off" and "Punch him, punch him, punch his legs full of holes." Some children saw another adult praise these aggressive acts, saying things such as, "Good for you! I guess you really fixed him that time." Other children saw an adult repeatedly criticize aggressive acts, saying things such as, "Now look what you've done; you've ruined it." Still other children saw the model's aggression praised on some occasions and criticized on others. After watching the model, the observer got a chance to play with the toys. The result was that children who always saw aggressive behavior praised tended to play aggressively; those who always saw the behavior criticized were far less aggressive; and those who saw aggressive acts produce mixed results fell in between (see Figure 10-11).

The consequences of observed events that are *not* modeled are also critical. If you saw a panel on a box slide to the left but it revealed nothing of any interest, you would surely be less likely to slide the panel than if you saw money.

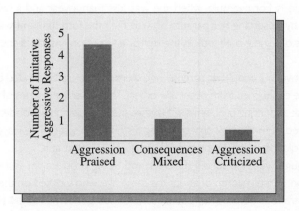

***Figure 10-11*** *Imitation and the consequences of the model's behavior. Mean number of imitative aggressive acts by observers who saw a model's aggression praised, criticized, or both. (Compiled from data in Rosekrans and Hartup, 1967.)*

## Consequences of the Observer's Behavior

If observing others pays off, we tend to spend more time observing others. Japanese researchers Satoshi Hirata and Naurki Morimura (2000) noticed this in chimpanzees. They paired chimps and gave them a problem that required using a tool. Once an animal had solved a problem, it never observed its partner's efforts. On the other hand, if a chimp attempted the problem and failed, it then watched as its neighbor struggled with the problem.

The consequences of imitating a model's behavior are also powerful. If a given behavior produces one kind of consequence for a model and a very different kind of consequence for an observer, the latter consequences will eventually win out. Neal Miller and John Dollard (1941) performed an experiment that demonstrates this. Children could get candy from a machine if they manipulated the handle the right way. A model used the machine just before the child. In one condition, if the child imitated the model's behavior, the machine provided candy. In another condition, the machine provided candy only if the child did *not* imitate the model. The children learned to imitate the model when imitating worked, and they learned *not* to imitate the model when *not* imitating worked (see also Ollendick, Dailey, & Shapiro, 1983; Ollendick, Shapiro & Barrett, 1982). Ultimately, observers do what works for them—regardless of whether it worked for a model.

**QUERY 7:** Two important variables in social observational learning are the _____

of the model's behavior and the _____ of the observer's behavior.

## OBSERVATIONAL LEARNING AND HUMAN NATURE

Viki had no memory of her natural parents. After all, she was only a few days old when Keith and Catherine Hayes (1952) adopted her and took her home. The Hayeses reared their adopted daughter with great care and affection. Their devotion paid off, for Viki proved to be extraordinarily precocious. For example, when she was less than a year and a half old, she began to learn, simply by observing her parents, how to dust the furniture and wash dishes. Before she was 2 years old, she would look in the mirror and put on lipstick as she had seen Catherine do.

When Viki was between 2 and 3, her parents, who were psychologists, decided to test her to see just how well she could learn from observing others. They gave her a series of problems. For instance, in the Stick and String problem the Hayeses put an object in a wooden box. The object could be retrieved from the box only by hitting a string with a stick. The Hayeses demonstrated the correct solution to the problem and then gave Viki a shot at it.

Overall, Viki did quite well. She solved the Stick and String problem, for instance, after only one demonstration. Some children of about the same age who worked on the problem required four demonstrations before they could solve it. Viki's performance did more than demonstrate observational learning, however. It raised all sorts of questions about human nature. Viki, you see, wasn't like the children with whom she competed on those problems.

Viki was a chimpanzee.

## CROSS-SPECIES OBSERVATIONAL LEARNING

People learn all sorts of things by observing other people. However, sometimes they learn important things by observing other species. Edward Maurice (2005), in his book *The Last Gentleman Adventurer,* describes one example. Maurice lived among the Inuit (Eskimos) in the Canadian Arctic in the early 1900s. He reports that polar bears would capture a seal pup in its den, then dangle it in the water through a hole in the ice. If the pup's mother tried to rescue the pup, the bear would grab the mother seal. The Inuit learned to imitate this practice, except that they used spears and hooks to kill the adult seal. Although the practice may strike us as inhumane and unsporting, life in the Arctic was harsh and tenuous for both people and bears, and it's clear that those who learn from the experiences of others, including different species, stand a better chance of surviving than those who do not.

CAPSULE **REVIEW**    As with Pavlovian and operant learning, the effectiveness of observational experiences depends on many variables. Some of the more important are task difficulty, the consequences of the model's behavior, the consequences of the observer's behavior, characteristics of the model, and characteristics of the observer.

## THEORIES OF OBSERVATIONAL LEARNING

The two main theories of observational learning are the social cognitive theory of Albert Bandura and the operant learning model. Both theories focus on the social form of observational learning, though the operant model applies as well to both forms of observational learning.

### Bandura's Social Cognitive Theory

Albert Bandura (1965, 1971a, 1971b, 1971c, 1977, 1986), the most prominent figure in social observational learning, developed a theory that focuses on cognitive processes. He does not deny that environmental and biological events influence behavior, but in his view it is cognitive processes—things going on inside the person—that account for learning from models. His theory identifies four kinds of cognitive processes: attentional, retentional, motor-reproductive, and motivational.

**Attentional processes** have to do with the individual directing his attention to the relevant aspects of the model's behavior and its consequences. Bandura writes that attention "involves self-directed exploration of the environment and construction of meaningful perception from ongoing modeled events" (1983/2004, p. 34). The term *self-directed* is critical because it suggests that what determines where we look and what we listen to originates inside us. The word *construction* likewise indicates that what we derive from the things we observe is less the product of those things than of something going on inside of us.

**Retentional processes** involve representing the model's behavior in some way, typically in words or images, to aid recall. "After modeling stimuli have been coded with images or words for memory representation they function as mediators for response retrieval and reproduction" (1969, p. 220). He gives the example of observing a model who follows a certain route to get to a particular location. The model's movements can be "encoded" in images (scenes of objects passed along the way) or as a sequence of right and left turns such as RRLRLL. Retentional processes also include covert rehearsal, such as silently saying the RRLRLL sequence repeatedly.

**Motor-reproductive** processes consist of using the symbolic representations stored during retentional processes to guide action. Or, as Bandura phrases it, "It is assumed that reinstatement of representational schemes provides a basis for self-instruction on how component responses must be combined and sequenced to produce new patterns of behavior" (1969, p. 223). Thus, we recall the images or words produced during the retentional process, and use them to guide us as we attempt to perform the observed acts.

**Motivational processes** have to do with evaluating the consequences of imitating modeled behavior. "When favorable incentives are introduced," Bandura writes, "observational learning promptly emerges in action" (1969, p. 225). However, in Bandura's theory, consequences are important because of their effects on our expectations about the outcomes of our behavior; it is the *expectations* that matter, not the actual consequences.

QUERY **8:**  According to Bandura's theory, we imitate successful models because we

_____ rewarding consequences.

These hypothetical cognitive processes can be illustrated at least in part. (Some of the processes presumably take place unconsciously and so cannot be described.) Suppose your aunt points to a wall safe and says, "I'm going to open that safe and then lock it again. If you can open it, you can keep whatever you find inside." Your aunt then proceeds to open the safe. She turns the dial clockwise to 20, counterclockwise to 40, clockwise to 20. She pulls down the handle and swings open the door, then immediately closes it.

Now, as you watch your aunt work, you direct your attention to which way she turns the safe dial and the numbers at which she stops. You may also represent her behavior by picturing a little pot-bellied Santa Claus whose measurements are 20–40–20. More likely, however, you repeat to yourself (or perhaps aloud), "Right 20; left 40; right 20." After Auntie has demonstrated how to open the safe, you covertly practice the motor skills necessary for opening it, using the Santa Claus image or the code, "Right 20, left 40, right 20," to guide you. But whether you imitate your aunt's behavior will depend, according to Bandura, on whether you expect to receive something of value after opening the safe.

Bandura's theory has tremendous intuitive appeal. It seems to capture the experience of observational learning as humans know it. The theory is not, however, without its problems.

We might question, for example, the explanatory value of unobservable and unmeasurable hypothetical processes. What does it mean, for example, to say that attention is self-directed? And if the source of attention is inside the person (where, exactly, is unclear: in the mind? in the brain?), why do people attend more to a model with an eye patch than to one without a patch? Similarly, motivation is important, but does the expectation of reward explain why people imitate a model? If you know that your aunt is rich and that rich people often keep valuable things in safes, then you might very well expect that opening the safe will be reinforced. But is it the *expectation* of reward that explains your behavior or the learning experiences that led to that expectation?

Because of such problems, some researchers prefer explanations that view observational learning as a form of operant learning.

## Operant Learning Model

It is possible to treat observational learning as a variation of operant learning (e.g., Deguchi, 1984; Gewirtz, 1971a, 1971b; Masia & Chase, 1997; Miller & Dollard, 1941; Skinner, 1969). In this approach, modeled behavior and consequences serve as cues that similar behavior will be reinforced or punished in the observer. We learn to attend to environmental events (modeled or not) because doing so pays off. We learn to imitate acts that have positive consequences and to avoid those that have negative consequences because doing so pays off.

Miller and Dollard (1941) offer this example: A boy hears his father returning from work and runs to greet him. The boy's younger brother follows him to the door. If the father greets both boys cheerfully and gives them pieces of candy, what behavior has he reinforced? In the case of the elder boy, the reinforced behavior is the act of running to the door when his father comes home. In the case of the younger boy, the reinforced behavior is the act of imitating his elder brother in going to the door. Put another way, the younger boy learns that going to the door when big brother does will have positive consequences.

The operant learning approach does not deny the importance of what Bandura calls attentional, retentional, motor-reproductive, and motivational processes, but it views these things very differently.

In the operant learning model, attention is not a thing in our head that we "self-direct" like someone watering a garden with a hose. On the contrary, it is the influence exerted by environmental events on our behavior. Often it can be measured in terms of overt behavior: making eye contact, following the shift in the gaze of a model, looking in the direction that a model points. Frederick Shic and others (2011) used eye-tracking technology to determine what children with autism look at, and found that they tend to focus on background items rather than people. Measuring what sounds a person attends to is more difficult, but not impossible. A person listening to a speaker typically turns toward the speaker, smiles or laughs at humorous lines, displays a wrinkled brow when the message is confusing, asks relevant questions, and starts to nod off when the speaker is as boring as a textbook. (Not *this* textbook, of course.) To attend to something is to come under the influence of that something (more on this in Chapter 11).

 QUERY 9: According to the operant learning model, attention refers to the influence of

_____ events on behavior.

Similarly, what Bandura calls retentional processes are, in the operant learning model, acts the observer performs, covertly or overtly, that can improve performance. If someone provides the instructions for reaching their house, we can repeatedly say, aloud or silently, "RRLRLL," as Bandura suggests. We can also write down the directions or record them on our cell phone. All of these "retentional activities" are things people *do* to help their performance. However, environmental events are again important. If you look up at the sky one night and see an image advertising a movie on the face of the moon, you are probably more likely to recall that ad than if you saw the same ad in a newspaper. If, however, moon ads become commonplace, remembering them will not be so easy.

Imitating behavior involves overt performance—what Bandura calls motor reproduction. Rules of thumb ("Keep your eyes on the ball"; "When turning the kayak to the left, lean to the right"; "Begin the report with a clear statement of the major findings") can help, but these are things we say silently or aloud, so once again they are behavior, and they help by providing cues about what we are to do in imitating a model. Like other behavior, they can be traced to environmental events, past or present.

Motivation is important, but the operant learning model points again to the environment. If we imitate behavior that is reinforced in a model, it is because experience has taught us that if a model's behavior is reinforced, our imitation of that behavior is likely to be reinforced. We may expect to obtain a reward for our imitative act, but our expectation and our imitation are both products of prior environmental events.

Learning is a change in behavior due to experience, so the operant approach to observational learning looks to the environmental events that comprise experience, not to hypothetical and unobservable mental processes.

The great weakness of the operant learning model is its lack of intuitive appeal. It takes the natural science approach to behavior (see Chapter 2), which is foreign to most people. It does not deny that people think and feel, but it sees those as behavior, not as explanations of behavior. That runs counter to the way most people (including Bandura) explain behavior.

While there is little consensus about the best explanation of observational learning, there is general agreement that observational learning has some practical applications. We will consider two of them: education and social change.

CAPSULE **REVIEW**   There are two prominent theories of observational learning. Bandura's social cognitive theory argues that mental processes are central to explaining observational learning. The operant learning model takes a natural science approach; it focuses on observable events, particularly those in the individual's current and past environments.

## APPLICATIONS OF OBSERVATIONAL LEARNING

### Education

Observational learning plays a major role in education starting in infancy. We can see this in a study by Rachel Barr, Anne Dowden, and Harlene Hayne (1996) in which an experimenter displayed a hand puppet to babies between the ages of 6 months and 2 years. The researchers held the puppet outside the child's reach and removed a mitten on one of the puppet's hands, disclosing a bell, which the experimenter then rang. The question was whether the child would try to remove the mitten when he or she next saw the puppet. Children as young as 6 months of age did so, thus demonstrating that they had learned from watching the experimenter. Children who had not seen the mitten removed did not attempt to remove it.

Observational learning is also clearly important in acquiring a first language. Jennifer Sweeney (2010) gives the example of a mother and child looking at a fish tank. The child, a toddler, points at a fish in the tank and looks at the mother, who says, "Fish." The child then imitates the mother, saying, "Fish." The mother may then smile at the child or say, "That's right! Fish," thereby reinforcing the child's effort. Thus, the child observes the mother's behavior, imitates it, and receives reinforcement for that imitation.

Observational learning also plays a major role in classroom learning (Delgado & Greer, 2009). Most classroom instruction is necessarily group-directed. The instructor lectures, demonstrates, or leads a discussion; in each case her efforts are usually directed at the entire class, not just one student. This means that much of the learning that occurs in group instruction is through observation. A teacher explains how to divide 74 by 3 as she demonstrates the procedure on the chalkboard. Then she has a student work a similar problem on the chalkboard. In both cases, most students must learn by observing a model.

*Academic skills are often picked up more readily by observing models than they are through explanation (Pollock & Lee, 1992). As the Dodo Bird in Alice and Wonderland reminds us, sometimes "the best way to explain it is to do it."*

Of course, how much students get out of observing a teacher's behavior depends on how attentive they are. A student staring out the window or chatting with a neighbor will learn little from a teacher demonstrating long division. One way to increase the attentiveness of a student is by praising or otherwise reinforcing attentiveness. Another way is by reinforcing attentiveness in *another* student. Alan Kazdin paired two boys and two girls between the ages of 8 and 12. A teacher praised one student in each pair when the child

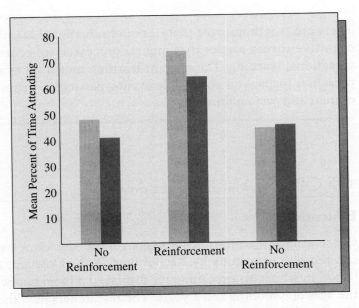

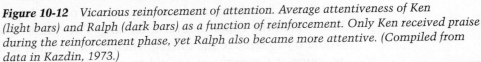

***Figure 10-12*** *Vicarious reinforcement of attention. Average attentiveness of Ken (light bars) and Ralph (dark bars) as a function of reinforcement. Only Ken received praise during the reinforcement phase, yet Ralph also became more attentive. (Compiled from data in Kazdin, 1973.)*

was attentive—that is, sitting in his or her seat, working on an assignment, and not talking to a neighbor without permission. The teacher did not praise the other child in the pair when he or she was attentive. It was expected that attentiveness would increase in the praised child, but would it also increase in the nearby peer? The answer was *yes* (see Figure 10-12; see also Broden et al., 1970). The child who did not receive praise for paying attention showed about as much improvement as the child who did. The children in this study were mentally retarded, but children of normal intelligence show the same effect (Ollendick, Shapiro, & Barrett, 1982). Of course, as noted earlier, the consequences of the observer's behavior will eventually overrule those of the model, so consistently reinforcing attentive behavior in one student and ignoring it in others is not going to result in an attentive class.

**QUERY 10:** Kazdin's research shows that attentiveness can be _____ reinforced.

Observational learning is put to good use in teaching practical skills in or out of school. In one study, Ann Griffen, Mark Wolery, and John Schuster (1992) taught three children with Down syndrome (a form of mental retardation) how to prepare scrambled eggs, pudding, and milkshakes. They did this by instructing one of the students directly while the other two looked on. The researchers provided reinforcement when the observers attended to the models. The result was that the observers' performance improved about as dramatically as did that of the individually instructed students (see also Werts, Caldwell, & Wolery, 1996).

Learning through observation requires certain behaviors, in particular attending to models and the consequences of their behavior, and imitating behavior that has positive consequences. In people with developmental disabilities these tendencies are often weak (Ledford et al., 2008; Taylor & DeQuinzio, 2012). Put such children in a regular classroom and they are likely to get little from group instruction (Sweeney, 2010). This means that the many things that normally developing children learn in and outside of school through observation must be explicitly taught to them, often one-on-one. Such instruction can be quite effective (Eikeseth, et al, 2002; Lovaas, 1987; Lovaas et al., 1981; Smith, 1999), but it is time-consuming and costly and requires that instructors undergo special training. The social and academic education of such children could be drastically improved if they could learn through observation.

Fortunately, many of these children can acquire the skills required for observational learning (Brown, Peace, & Parsons, 2009; Browder, Schoen, & Lentz, 1986; Ledford & Wolery, 2011; Loveland & Landry, 1986; Sundberg & Partington, 1998/2010; Sweeney, 2010; Taubman et al., 2001; Whalen & Schreibman, 2003). For example, Jo Ann Delgado and Douglas Greer (2009, experiment 1) taught two 5-year-old boys with autism to monitor the behavior of a peer learning to read words, such as *asked* and *every*, or to name items, such as a cantaloupe and avocado, shown in pictures. An instructor praised the model for correct answers and required correction of errors; the observing child earned praise and tokens not by imitating the model, but by indicating whether the model answered correctly. For example, if the observer indicated that the model answered *incorrectly*, and this was true, then the observer earned praise and a token. The result was that the participants came to monitor the model and the consequences of his or her behavior more closely, essential ingredients of observational learning. Once students can learn by observing a model, they have a powerful tool for advancing in school and out.

## Social Change

Imagine that you survive a shipwreck and find yourself alone on an island. You soon realize that you have a number of problems: How will you get water, food, and shelter? How can you attract the attention of people on a passing ship and thereby be rescued? You will need to solve each of these and other problems on your own. Now suppose that other victims of the shipwreck join you. Have your odds of surviving improved?

More than likely they have. One reason is that you can benefit from the learning of other people. John finds a spring with potable water and shows everyone where it is. Mary is a dedicated scuba diver. She has no scuba equipment, of course, but she makes a spear from a small bamboo tree found on the beech and demonstrates how to find and spear fish. Harry is a carpenter, and he draws a diagram in the sand to show the group what they need to do to build a sturdy shelter. This is the way society works. Learning is an individual phenomenon, but we do not solve every problem that confronts us on our own; we learn from others. If one person solves a problem, millions of others can benefit.

We can see examples of such social change in non human societies. In one experiment, biologists Kevin Laland and Kerry Williams (1997) trained guppies to follow a particular course to find food. The researchers then introduced untrained guppies and observed their behavior. Fish have an apparently innate tendency to shoal—to travel in groups—and the naïve fish joined their trained peers as they made their way to food. As the researchers gradually replaced trained guppies with naïve ones, the practice continued, thus becoming a self-perpetuating practice.

Perhaps the most famous case of such "social transmission" in animals is that of Imo, a monkey that learned that washing sand-covered sweet potatoes made them more palatable (Kawai, 1963). Imo's exercise spread through her community and became standard practice within about ten years. It is not clear just how the transmission occurred, but it seems likely that observational learning played a part.

More recently, researchers have seen evidence of the social transmission of flossing in a troop of free-ranging monkeys in Thailand. Researchers first observed nine adult female monkeys using human hair to floss their teeth (Watanabe, Urasopon, & Malaivitimond, 2007). (The monkeys are believed to have pulled the hair from the heads of women tourists.) Flossing has since become widespread in the community. As with the potato washing, there is no clear documentation of how this behavior spread. However, Nobuo Masataka, a primatologist at Kyoto University in Japan, and his colleagues (2009) found evidence that mother monkeys attempt to teach flossing to their offspring through modeling. The researchers videotaped the behavior of seven free-ranging female macaques when they were flossing and compared their behavior when their infant was nearby and when it was not. The results revealed that when an infant was present, the mother paused more often, repeated flossing more often, and flossed for a longer time than when the youngster was not around (see Figure 10-13). The researchers acknowledge that there is no direct evidence that the infants imitated their mother's behavior, but the behavior of the mothers suggests that modeling played a part in the spread of flossing through the community.

Chimps seem to rely even more on observational learning for the spread of new skills. Earlier I mentioned that chimps that could not solve a problem on their own observed a model work on it (Hirata & Morimura, 2000), and that young chimps learned from their mothers how to "fish" for ants by dipping a stick into an ant nest (Lonsdorf, 2005). Other research suggests social transmission of tool use, self-medication, grooming, and courtship in chimpanzees (Gruber et al., 2009; Luncz, Mundry, & Boesch, 2012; Whiten, 2006; Whiten et al., 2001).

Observational learning is particularly important in changes in human society. New tools spread throughout an entire country with the speed of an epidemic. Believe it or not, when I was a youngster there was no refrigerator in our house. Foods were kept cool in an icebox—literally a box with ice. There was also no TV, no microwave oven, no computer. To use a telephone you did not punch numbers on a keypad; you picked up the receiver and told

## With Infant

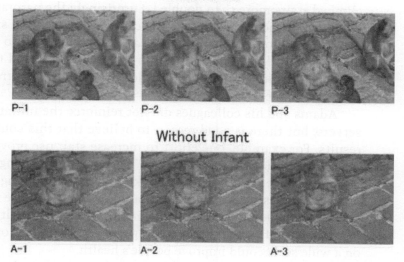

P-1    P-2    P-3

## Without Infant

A-1    A-2    A-3

**Figure 10-13**  *A monkey flossing when her infant was present (upper photos) and when the infant was absent (lower photos). See text for explanation. (Masataka, N., Koda, H., Urasopon, N., and Watanabe, K. (2009). Free-Ranging Macaque Mothers Exaggerate Tool-Using Behavior when Observed by Offspring. PLOS ONE 4(3): e4768.doi:10.1371/ journal.pone.0004768. Images courtesy of Nobuo Masataka. Photographs © 2009 Masataka et al.)*

an operator the number you wanted to call. Observational learning plays an important role in the adoption of new tools, and also of social practices.

Observational learning can also play a part in helping societies deal with various problems. The availability of cheap, high-calorie food and a sedentary lifestyle have led to an obesity epidemic in the United States (Ogden et al., 2012). There are two basic things people can do to maintain a healthy weight. One is to eat a healthier diet; the other is to exercise more. Research has shown that modeling can induce people to eat more sensibly. In some studies, when student models ate more fruit, their classmates tended to do likewise (Horne et al., 2011; Lowe et al., 2006).

Modeling can also influence exercise. An exploratory study by Marc Adams of Arizona State University and his colleagues (2006) provides an example. The researchers found that the vast majority of people at San Diego International Airport took an escalator rather than climb the nearby stairs. Climbing stairs is good exercise and can help to maintain a healthy weight. The question was, were people more likely to climb the stairs if they saw someone else do so? The researchers studied the effects of two kinds of models, confederates and "natural" models. The confederates were people involved in the study; they not only climbed the stairs but in some cases made comments to a fellow confederate such as, "Let's take the stairs!" or "It's faster to take the stairs." The "natural" models were not part of the study; they were passersby who simply elected to climb the stairs, thereby serving as models for others. The models were influential. The proportion of women who climbed the stairs during the study increased by about 68%, while the proportion of men who climbed stairs more than doubled. Surprisingly the natural models got better results than the confederates. The climbers were still a small minority, but the study demonstrates that if we can get *some* people to engage in exercise, others will follow. Adams suggests that this could lead to a cascade effect, since each person who follows the lead of a model in turn becomes a model, who then induces others to follow.

Adams and his colleagues did not reinforce the imitative behavior of observers, but there is good reason to believe that this could further improve results. For example, one effort to increase stair use provided music and art in a stairwell (Boutelle et al., 2001). The researchers changed the music every day and replaced the art once a week. Both made climbing the stairs more appealing. The result was a 40% increase in stair use. Those who used the stairs rather than an elevator were still a minority, but the results of these two studies suggest that combining modeling and reinforcement of imitative exercise on a wide scale could improve people's health.

Another possibility for influencing behavior on a large scale is through fictional models. You may recall that Goethe's book, *The Sorrows of Young Werther*, apparently inspired an epidemic of suicides in Europe. What if admired fictional characters displayed desirable forms of behavior? Would people adopt them?

An organization called Population Communications International (PCI) says the answer is *yes*. They create television and radio programs that combine education and entertainment (Singhal & Rogers, 1999; Singhal et al., 2004). They have created 75 such **edutainment** programs that have aired in over 40 countries and reached more than a billion people (Singhal, 2010). The programs are intended to change social practices while entertaining. For example, in parts of India, girls and boys are treated very differently. A boy's birthday is celebrated, for instance; a girl's is not. In a radio soap opera a popular female character asks, "Why don't I have a birthday?" The story line pursues the question and the girl eventually enjoys a birthday celebration. Following this, there were anecdotal reports that girls in the area where the program aired began celebrating their birthdays.

 QUERY 11: _____ uses fiction to model socially helpful behavior.

Other PCI programs have dealt with gender equality, sexual slavery, and other social problems. Unfortunately, thus far there seems to be little hard evidence that these efforts have had much impact. In one case, for example, researchers claim that a program aired in Tanzania, where AIDS is a major problem, resulted in people having fewer sexual partners, using condoms more often, and sharing needles and razors less (Vaughan et al., 2000). However, these claims are based on self-reports in surveys and interviews. As far as I could determine, no one has yet demonstrated a connection between the PCI program and a reduction in the rate of new HIV infections.

One problem with the edutainment approach is that it assumes that imitated behavior will be naturally reinforced, but naturally occurring reinforcers are often insufficient to maintain new behavior. It may be necessary to provide contrived reinforcers until the new behavior is well established. If this problem is dealt with, one day edutainment, a way of producing observational learning, might play an important part in helping societies advance. Unfortunately, edutainment can also help societies change for the worse (see *The Down Side of Observational Learning*).

CAPSULE **REVIEW**     Basic research on observational learning has led to research on ways it can help us deal with practical problems. Two areas that have received a fair amount of attention are education and social change. Observational learning is very important in instruction, both in and out of the classroom, and researchers have found that some of those who lack the skills necessary for learning from observation can acquire them. Observational learning also plays an important role in social change, and has the potential for helping societies advance.

## THE DOWN SIDE OF OBSERVATIONAL LEARNING

Observational learning is an important mechanism in helping societies advance, but not everything we learn through observation is helpful to us or to society. Numerous studies suggest, for example, that observational learning can result in individuals and societies becoming more aggressive.

People acquire aggressive behavior not only by observing those around them (Bandura, Ross, & Ross, 1961; Bandura, 1973; Bandura & Walters, 1959; Rosekrans and Hartup, 1967), but also by watching television and film (Huesmann & Miller, 1994; Huesmann, et al., 2003; Wyatt, 2001), playing video games (Anderson et al., 2010; Bushman & Gibson, 2010), and reading fictional stories (Coyne, et al., 2012).

A panel of experts, including members of the American Academy of Pediatricians, American Psychological Association, American Academy of Child and Adolescent Psychiatry, and American Medical Association, reviewed more than a thousand studies conducted over a 30-year period on the effect of violence on television and in films on the aggressive behavior of children (Wyatt, 2001). The panel concluded that the evidence for a causal connection was "overwhelming."

Criminal behavior can also be learned through observation. Bandura (1973) noted long ago that, thanks to television, children and adults have unlimited opportunities to learn "the whole gamut of felonious behavior within the comfort of their homes" (p. 1101). And they do. Viewing violent and criminal acts on television and other media leads people to perform such acts (e.g., Council on Communications and Media, 2009; Johnson et al., 2002; Kuntsche et al., 2006; Linz, Donnerstein, & Penrod, 1988). It is not surprising, then, that a longitudinal study found that the more time children spend watching television at age 8, the more likely they are at age 30 to have been convicted of a serious crime (reported in DeAngelis, 1992).

The point of all this is that observational learning can lead to desirable or undesirable changes in us, in our children, and in society. The question is, What sort of changes do we want?

## A FINAL WORD

Observational learning is historically the least studied form of learning, but it is important, particularly among the more social animals. Humans are especially adept at learning from observation, and there is little doubt that it has contributed greatly to our species' survival. We do not *all* need to eat poisonous food or be bitten by venomous snakes and spiders to learn to avoid them; we learn from seeing their effects on others. Similarly, if one person finds that boiling certain plants makes them tastier, others will soon follow his lead. We live at a time when our species faces major threats—the depletion of natural resources, climate change, pandemics, pollution. To deal effectively with such problems, we must learn from one another.

## RECOMMENDED **READING**

1. Bandura, A., Ross, D., & Ross, S. A. (1963). Vicarious reinforcement and imitative learning. *Journal of Abnormal and Social Psychology, 67,* 601–607.

   This study is a classic in the area of observational learning and should be read by all students majoring in psychology, social work, and education.

2. Lyons, D. E., Young, A. G., & Keil, F. C. (2007). The hidden structure of over-imitation. *Proceedings of the National Academy of Science, 104*(19), 751–756. doi:10.1073/pnas.0704452104.

   This article describes fascinating experiments on the tendency of children to imitate frivolous aspects of a model's behavior, despite instructions not to do so.

3. Masia, C. C., & Chase, P. N. (1997). Vicarious learning revisited: A contemporary behavior analytic interpretation. *Journal of Behavior Therapy and Experimental Psychiatry, 28,* 41–51.

   The authors provide a look at the operant learning approach toward observational learning.

4. Special Issue: Social learning in humans and nonhuman animals: Theoretical and empirical dissections. (2012). *Journal of Comparative Psychology, 126*(2).

   This special edition covers recent research on observational learning in animals and humans. The work is fascinating and, by science journal standards, surprisingly readable.

5. Taylor, B. A. (2012). Do this, but don't do that: Teaching children with autism to learn by observation. In W. L. Heward, ed., *Exceptional children: An introduction to special education* (10th ed., pp. 240–242). Upper Saddle River, NJ: Pearson.

   This brief, highly readable article provides an introduction to the role of observational learning in treating people with autism.

## REVIEW **QUESTIONS**

1. Define the following terms in your own words:

   | | |
   |---|---|
   | observational learning | learning model |
   | social observational learning | Bandura's social cognitive theory |
   | asocial observational learning | attentional processes |
   | vicarious reinforcement | retentional processes |
   | vicarious punishment | motor-reproductive |
   | ghost condition | processes |
   | imitation | motivational processes |
   | over-imitation | operant learning model |
   | generalized imitation | edutainment |

2. How might you use observational procedures to create a fad on a college campus?

3. Is vicarious reinforcement involved in asocial observational learning?

4. How could you teach a child to tie her shoes *without* using modeling?

5. Some researchers say that imitation is a form of learning. Do you agree?

6. Is over-imitation a strength or a weakness?

7. What is the chief difference between Bandura's social cognitive theory and the operant learning model?

8. Has edutainment been used for nefarious purposes?

9. How does Bandura's view of attention differ from that of the operant learning model? Which is more scientific? Which do you prefer?

10. How might the lack of research on observational learning have itself been due to observational learning?

## PRACTICE **QUIZ**

1. Observational learning can be defined as a change in behavior due to observing _____.

2. This text identifies two types of observational learning, _____ and _____.

3. There are two kinds of consequences of a model's behavior, _____ and _____.

4. Generally, the ability to learn from models _____ (increases/decreases) with age.

5. The tendency to imitate models even when the modeled behavior is not reinforced is called _____ imitation.

6. Imitating irrelevant aspects of a model's behavior is called _____.

7. Viki was a _____.

8. Bandura's theory relies on four processes. These include _____ and _____ processes.

9. The operant learning model says that observational learning is a variation of _____.

10. Some researchers use a _____ condition to study asocial observational learning.

## QUERY **ANSWERS**

Query 1. This text identifies two types of observational learning. The kind being discussed here is *social*.

Query 2. This text identifies two types of observational learning. The kind being discussed here is *asocial*.

Query 3. Over-imitation is the tendency to imitate behavior that is *irrelevant/superfluous/unnecessary*.

Query 4. Generalized imitation is the tendency to imitate modeled behavior even when imitation of the behavior is not *reinforced*.

Query 5. An unskilled model is also called a *learning* model.

Query 6. Model characteristics are important because they can induce the observer to *attend to the model's behavior*.

Query 7. Two important variables in social observational learning are the *consequences* of the model's behavior and the *consequences* of the observer's behavior.

Query 8. According to Bandura's theory, we imitate successful models because we *expect* rewarding consequences.

Query 9. According to the operant learning model, attention refers to the influence of *environmental* events on behavior.

Query 10. Kazdin's research shows that attentiveness can be *vicariously* reinforced.

Query 11. *Edutainment* uses fiction to model socially helpful behavior.

# Generalization, Discrimination, and Stimulus Control

*When you've seen one redwood tree, you've seen them all.*

—**Ronald Reagan**

*Like—but oh! How different!*

—**William Wordsworth**

## PREVIEW

Operant learning is often said to involve responding to a specific stimulus with a specific response. If this were the case, its value would be very limited. Every traffic light, for example, would have to be exactly like every other traffic light in size, shape, color, and location, or they would be useless. Fortunately, what we learn in one situation tends to carry over to similar situations. This is essential to our survival, but sometimes such "carry over" can be problematic: We need to respond differently to a red traffic light than to a green one. This chapter aims to help you understand these phenomena and how they apply to everyday behavior.

## BEGINNINGS

In the harsh, icy land of the Canadian Arctic, hunting seals was a basic survival skill for the Inuit people. Before the arrival of Europeans and their rifles, the Inuit hunted with spears. To make a kill, they had to get close to their prey, which was not easy because there is little cover in the Arctic. Seals could see a man long before he posed a threat and easily slip down an ice hole or off the edge of an ice sheet and disappear into the ocean. The hunter's solution was to approach while imitating the seals. The hunter crouched low and crept forward, occasionally raising his head as the seals themselves do. Proceeding slowly, if the hunter were lucky he got close enough to a seal to drive home his spear.

Edward Maurice (2005), who lived among the Inuit in the early days of the 20th century, tells us that one day a little Inuit boy was playing in the village. He pretended to be a hunter in pursuit of seals. He lay on the ground and crept along, now and then raising his head to look around, just as a hunter would do in imitation of a seal. Unfortunately, his play-hunting adventure ended tragically: The village sled dogs saw the boy and, evidently taking him for a seal, attacked and killed him.

This sad story illustrates three important learning concepts: generalization, discrimination, and stimulus control. Much of the research on these topics is done with pigeons and rats and involves pecking discs and pressing levers. Such experiments are essential to understanding these basic phenomena, but to students they often seem remote from everyday experience. As you read about these experiments, keep in mind the Inuit hunters, the seals, and the tragic story of the boy on the ice.

## GENERALIZATION

**Generalization** is the tendency for the effects of a learning experience to spread. It is sometimes called **transfer,** since the effects of a learning experience "move." (You get on bus 39, then *transfer* to bus 42.) Researchers have identified four kinds of generalization (Cooper, Heron, & Heward, 2007), depending on where the learning moves:

- Generalization across people (which might be called vicarious generalization; see Chapter 10)
- Generalization across time (also called response maintenance) could be considered the opposite of forgetting (see Chapter 12)
- Generalization across behaviors (known as response generalization)
- Generalization across situations (known as stimulus generalization)

A good deal of Chapter 10, on observational learning, was devoted to the first kind of generalization, the generalization of the learning experiences of a model to those of an observer. The following chapter, on forgetting, will deal largely with the second kind of generalization, the generalization of behavior over time. The third type, **response generalization,** is the tendency for changes in one behavior to spread to other behaviors. If a rat receives food after pressing a lever with its right front foot, it might then press the lever with its left front foot, or with its chin. Similarly, if a child is rewarded for expressing a *willingness* to share a toy, she is then more likely to actually *share* a toy (Barton & Ascione, 1979). All three of these kinds of generalization are important, but the one that gets the most attention from both basic and applied researchers is stimulus generalization so we will consider it in some detail. From now on, when I use the term generalization, I mean stimulus generalization.

**Stimulus generalization** is the tendency for changes in behavior in one situation to spread to other situations. It is often defined as the tendency to respond to stimuli not present during training. This definition is perhaps a better fit with laboratory measures of generalization, where the environment is made constant except for one or two features, such as a light or a tone. But stimuli never really occur alone; they are always part of a context, a situation. So it is fair to say that with generalization, what we learn in one situation carries over, or transfers to, a different situation. We could say that in generalization the behavior "travels" from one place to another.

**QUERY 1:** When the effects of learning spread across situations, it is called

_____ generalization.

Some examples may clarify the phenomenon. In Pavlovian conditioning, a dog may learn to salivate to the sound of a tuning fork vibrating at 1,000 cycles per second (cps). After this training, the dog may then salivate to the sound of a tuning fork vibrating at, say, 900 cps to 1,100 cps, even though it was never exposed to these stimuli. The conditional response spreads, or generalizes, to stimuli different from the CS.

The famous Watson and Rayner (1920) study (see Chapter 4) provides another example of the generalization of a conditional response. You will recall that Little Albert learned to fear a white rat. After establishing this fear, Watson and Rayner tested Albert to see whether other stimuli would frighten him. They presented Albert with a white rabbit, raw cotton, and a Santa Claus mask. None of these stimuli had been around when Albert learned to fear the rat, yet Albert was afraid of them, too. Albert's fear had spread, or generalized, from the white rat to other white, furry objects.

Carl Hovland (1937) studied the generalization of fear conditioning in college students. He began by pairing a tone of a particular pitch with a mild electric shock; the UR was the galvanic skin response, or GSR (a measure of emotional arousal). After 16 pairings of the CS and US, Hovland then presented four tones, including the CS. The results showed that the GSR spread from the original tone to the others; the less a stimulus resembled the CS, the weaker the CR was. When data on stimulus generalization are plotted on a graph, they yield a figure called a **generalization gradient** (Figure 11-1).

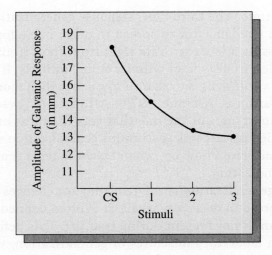

**Figure 11-1** *Generalization gradient. Average strength of conditional response (GSR) to the CS, and to other tones of decreasing similarity to the CS (1, 2, 3). (From "The Generalization of Conditioned Responses: 1. The Sensory Generalization of Conditioned Responses with Varying Frequencies of Tone," by Carl Hovland, 1937,* Journal of General Psychology, *17, p. 136, Figure 2. Copyright © 1937 by the Journal Press.)*

 **QUERY 2:** A generalization gradient shows the tendency for a behavior to occur in situations that differ systematically from _____.

Perhaps the first report of generalization following reinforcement came from Thorndike (1898). He observed that "a cat that has learned to escape from [box] A by clawing has, when put into [box] C or G, a greater tendency to claw at things than it instinctively had at the start" (p. 14). In other words, clawing generalized from box A to boxes C and G.

Those who followed Thorndike studied generalization in a more rigorous manner. In a classic study, Norman Guttman and Harry Kalish (1956) trained pigeons to peck a disc of a particular color and later gave them the opportunity to peck the disc when it was various colors, including the color used in training, for 30 seconds each. Pigeons pecked the disc most frequently when it was the color used during training, but they also pecked the disc when it was other colors. As the generalization gradient reveals, the more closely the disc resembled the training disc, the more often the birds pecked it. If a disc was almost the same color as the training disc, the birds pecked at it almost as much as if it were the training disc; if the disc was a very different color, the pigeons seldom touched it (see Figure 11-2).

Generalization is not restricted to highly specific acts such as disc pecking. Broader behavioral tendencies also generalize. You might recall from Chapter 6 that Robert Eisenberger and his colleagues found that rewarding

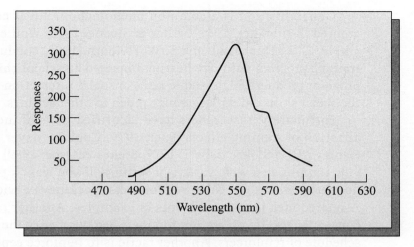

**Figure 11-2**  *Generalization gradient. When pecking a disc of a particular color (in this case a wavelength of 550 nanometers) had been reinforced, pigeons were likely to peck that disc at a high rate. However, they would also peck discs that were similar to the original disc. (After Guttman and Kalish, 1956.)*

people for making a strong effort on one task increases the level of effort made on *other* tasks, a phenomenon they call learned industriousness. This means that trying hard, if reinforced in one situation, may generalize to another situation, even though "trying hard" is not a specific act.

Studies of generalization usually involve the effects of reinforcement, but changes in behavior produced by extinction also spread beyond the learning situation. For example, R. E. P. Youtz (reported in Skinner, 1938) trained rats to press a horizontal lever for food and then put the behavior on extinction. After this, he tested the rats in a chamber with a vertical lever. He found that the effects of the extinction procedure reduced the rats' tendency to press the new lever. Youtz trained other rats to press the vertical lever, then put the behavior on extinction and tested them on the horizontal lever. Again, he found that the effects of extinction spread to the new situation. Overall, the extinction procedure reduced the tendency to perform in a similar situation by 63%.

The suppression of behavior produced by punishment spreads in much the same way as the effects of reinforcement and extinction. Werner Honig and Robert Slivka (1964) trained pigeons to peck discs of various colors. When the birds were pecking all the colors at the same rate, the experimenters continued reinforcing disc pecks but also punished pecking whenever the disc was a particular color. The tendency to peck the disc when it was that color declined, of course, but so did the tendency to peck when the disc was other colors. The frequency of pecking varied systematically with the similarity of the disc to the punished color. Thus, the effects of punishment formed a generalization gradient like those seen following reinforcement and extinction. Essentially the same phenomenon has been demonstrated in humans (O'Donnell & Crosbie, 1998).

*You saw an example of a behavioral tendency that generalizes in the chapter on observational learning. Now you know why it is called generalized imitation.*

Generalization is a common phenomenon, but it cannot be taken for granted (Birnbrauer, 1968; Miller & Sloane, 1976; Wolf et al., 1987). For example, D. E. Ducharme and S. W. Holborn (1997) conducted a social skills training program with five hearing-impaired preschool children. The training program produced high, stable rates of social interaction in that setting, but the social skills did *not* generalize much to other settings.

Fortunately, researchers have identified ways of increasing the generalization of training effects (Baer, 1999; Cook & Mayer, 1988; Francisco & Hanley, 2012; Stokes & Baer, 1977; Stokes & Osne, 1989). One way is to provide training in a wide variety of settings. If you want a pigeon to peck discs no matter what their color, reinforce disc pecking of a wide variety of colors. A related idea is to provide lots of examples. Another tactic is to vary the consequences. If you are reinforcing a behavior, vary the kind, amount, and schedule of reinforcers. Another tactic is to reinforce generalization when it occurs (see *Generalized Therapy*).

**QUERY 3:** Name one way of increasing generalization across situations.

The research on generalization and its enhancement has important implications in a variety of practical situations. Many educators assume that once a student understands a principle, such as the Pythagorean theorem or the refraction of light by water, the student should then be able to apply it in any situation. But the fact that a student can apply the Pythagorean theorem to a geometry problem posed by a teacher in a math class does not mean that he or she will apply it when constructing a toolbox in a garage. Managers make the same mistake when instructing workers in the operation of equipment or in following safety procedures. Parents also need to understand that just because their child has learned to look both ways before crossing a street does not mean they will do this when chasing a ball that rolls into the street (Miltenberger, 2009).

Doing things to increase the generalization of learning is important, but generalization is not always a desirable thing. A behavior that is useful in one situation is not always helpful in another. Thorndike (1898) noticed, for example, that a cat that had learned to escape from a box by pulling on a loop would later paw at the same spot—even though the loop had been removed! In the same way, a college student whose off-color jokes get big laughs in the dormitory may find that the same jokes are not appreciated at the family dinner table.

Carol Dweck and Dickon Repucci (1973) showed how generalization can work against a teacher and her students. Teachers first gave students unsolvable problems. Later these teachers gave the students problems that *could* be solved, but the students failed to solve them. The tendency to give up seems to have generalized from the first situation to the second. When a *different* teacher gave the students solvable problems, they were successful.

Generalization can also make problem behaviors more troublesome than they would otherwise be. For instance, if punching a large inflated doll is reinforced, children later tend to be more aggressive when interacting with other children (Walters & Brown, 1963). There is a substantial difference between an inflated doll and a child, yet the behavior generalized from one to the other.

Sometimes the results of generalization are tragic. Every year in America's national parks people are injured by bears. Most of these cases probably involve generalization. For example, bears will sometimes attack people when the people get near a blueberry patch or other source of food. The bear may have driven off bears and deer that compete with it for food, and this behavior may then generalize to people, though people are not usually competing for the bear's food. The dogs that attacked the Inuit boy mentioned earlier were also generalizing. These dogs would readily attack a real seal and kill it, and this behavior generalized to the boy who pretended to be a seal. Humans also make tragic generalization errors. Many bear attacks occur when people approach wild bears as though they were pets. One man wanted to get a photograph of his young daughter with a bear, so he urged her to go up to the bear with some food. The girl was lucky that she lost only a finger. Several years ago I read a newspaper item about the death of a skydiver. His parachute did not open, but there was nothing wrong with it. It turned out that he was using a new parachute, and the release cord was not on the same side as it was on his old chute. As he fell to his death he tore at the chute in the area where the pull cord *used to be*. His behavior had generalized from the old suit to the new one.

Generalization also appears to be involved in some hate crimes. Following the horrific attacks against the United States by Arab extremists on September 11, 2001, many people of Arab descent living in the United States were assaulted. No doubt in most instances the victim's only crime was physically resembling those who had committed crimes. Their attackers likely would have preferred to assault those involved in the 9/11 attacks, but those people were not available, so they attacked those who resembled them. Neal Miller (1948b) long ago provided evidence that such displaced aggression is due to stimulus generalization.

You can see that generalization is an important phenomenon, but it is only one side of a coin. The other side is discrimination.

**?) QUERY 4:** Sigmund Freud talked about displaced aggression. Displaced aggression is an

example of _____.

CAPSULE **REVIEW** Generalization is the tendency for the effects of learning to spread. They can spread to other behaviors, other people, and other times, but probably the most important form of generalization involves the spread to other situations. Without this stimulus generalization, learning would be far less helpful in adapting to a changing environment.

## GENERALIZED THERAPY

The patient was a 37-year-old woman who stood 5 feet 4 inches and weighed 47 pounds. She looked like a survivor of a concentration camp, but the emaciation that threatened to kill her was due to self-starvation. She had a mysterious aversion to eating called anorexia.

Arthur Bachrach and his colleagues (1965) took on the task of ending this woman's self-destructive refusal to eat. They used shaping and reinforcement principles to get her to eat more. The strategy worked, and she gained enough weight to be released from the hospital. But what would happen when she went home? Would she go back to starving herself again, or would the effects of the therapy generalize to the new situation?

The problem of generalization is critical for therapists: There is little value in changing behavior in a hospital or clinic if those changes do not carry over to the home and workplace. One way to attack the problem of generalization is to try to alter the natural environment so that appropriate behavior continues to be reinforced at a high rate. Bachrach and his coworkers used this approach. They asked the patient's family to cooperate in various ways. Among other things, they asked the family to avoid reinforcing invalidism, to reinforce maintenance of weight by, for example, complimenting the patient's appearance, and to encourage her to eat with other people under pleasant circumstances.

With reinforcement of appropriate behavior in the home, the behavior might then generalize to other settings. The reinforcement that naturally occurs in these settings would, it was hoped, maintain the desired behavior. The hope seems to have been fulfilled. For instance, the patient attended a social function at which refreshments were served. It had always been the woman's custom to refuse food on such occasions, but she surprised everyone by asking for a doughnut. All eyes were on her as she devoured the snack, and she later admitted that she got considerable pleasure from all the attention.

Generalization is not always established this easily (Holland, 1978; Miller & Sloane, 1976; Wolf et al., 1987). The juvenile delinquent who acquires cooperative social skills in a special rehabilitation center and then returns to a home and community where aggressive, antisocial acts are reinforced and cooperative behavior is punished is apt to revert to old habits. The chain-smoker who quits while on a vacation with nonsmokers must return to a world of smoke-filled rooms where smoking is reinforced . The rehabilitated and repentant child abuser returns to a neighborhood filled with naïve and easily seduced children. The problem of getting therapeutic gains to generalize to the natural environment is one of the most difficult the therapist faces, but understanding generalization helps.

## DISCRIMINATION

**Stimulus discrimination** is the tendency for behavior to occur in certain situations but not in others. It is often defined more narrowly as the tendency for behavior to occur in the presence of certain stimuli, but not in their absence. However, as mentioned earlier, stimuli are always part of a context, so the word *situation* is appropriate.

**? QUERY 5:** Discrimination is the opposite of _____.

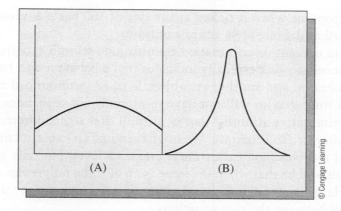

**Figure 11-3** *Discrimination and the generalization gradient. A relatively flat gradient (A) indicates little discrimination; a steep gradient (B) indicates considerable discrimination. (Hypothetical data.)*

You can see that discrimination and generalization are inversely related: The more discrimination, the less generalization, and vice versa. Generalization gradients therefore reflect the degree of discrimination. A relatively flat generalization gradient indicates little or no discrimination; a steep gradient indicates considerable discrimination (see Figure 11-3).

We saw earlier that the more a stimulus resembles the training stimulus, the greater will be the degree of generalization. It is therefore clear that the less similar a stimulus is to the training stimulus, the greater will be the degree of discrimination. A pigeon that has learned to peck a yellow disc for food is very likely to peck discs of similar color, but not so likely to peck a black disc. It is often possible, however, to establish a discrimination between very similar stimuli through discrimination training.

Any procedure for establishing a discrimination is called **discrimination training.** Discrimination can be established through both Pavlovian and operant procedures. In Pavlovian discrimination training, one conditional stimulus (designated **CS⁺**) is regularly paired with a US, and another (designated **CS⁻**) regularly appears alone. For example, we might put food into a dog's mouth each time a buzzer sounds and give the dog nothing when a bell rings. The result will be that the dog salivates at the sound of the buzzer (the CS⁺) but not at the sound of the bell (CS⁻). At this point, we say that the dog discriminates between the buzzer and the bell—that is, it behaves differently in the two situations.

Pavlov (1927) conducted many experiments on discrimination training. In one, a dog saw a rotating object. Whenever the object rotated in a clockwise direction, the dog received food; when it rotated in the opposite direction, the dog got nothing. The dog soon discriminated: It salivated at the CS⁺ (clockwise rotation) but not at the CS⁻ (counterclockwise rotation). Other experiments yielded similar results. Pavlov's dogs learned to discriminate between different volumes of a particular sound, different pitches of a tone, different geometric forms, different temperatures, and so on. Sometimes the level of discrimination achieved was remarkable. One dog learned to salivate at the sound of a metronome when it ticked at the rate of 100 beats a minute but not when it ticked at the rate of 96 times a minute.

In operant discrimination training, one stimulus, designated $S^+$ or $S^D$ (pronounced *ess-dee*) typically indicates that a behavior will have reinforcing consequences, and another stimulus, $S^-$ or $S^\Delta$ (pronounced *ess-delta*) indicates that the behavior will not have reinforcing consequences. $S^D$ and $S^\Delta$ are both **discriminative stimuli**—that is, stimuli that signal different consequences for a behavior. To illustrate: We might arrange an experimental chamber so that a rat receives food each time it presses a lever, but only if a lamp is on. The result will be that when the lamp is on ($S^D$), the rat presses the lever, and when the lamp is off ($S^\Delta$) it does not press. At this point, we say that the rat discriminates between the two situations.

**?** QUERY 6: An $S^-$ is the same as an S _____.

Discrimination training can take various forms. In **simultaneous discrimination training,** the discriminative stimuli are presented at the same time. In a classic experiment, Karl Lashley (1930) put a rat on a small platform before two cards, placed side by side (see Figure 11-4). The cards are distinguishable

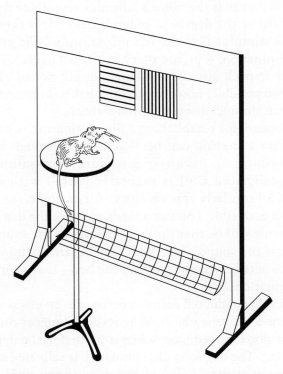

**Figure 11-4**  *Discrimination training. In the Lashley jumping stand, a rat could jump toward either of two doors that differed in design. If the rat jumped toward one, the door fell open, and it received food. The other door was locked; the rat that jumped toward it fell into a net below and received no food. (After Lashley, 1930.)*

in some way; for example, one may have horizontal stripes, the other vertical. One of the cards is locked in place; if the rat jumps at that card, it will then fall to the net below. The other card is not locked, so if the rat jumps toward it the card gives way and the rat lands on the other side. Whichever choice the rat makes, it is not hurt and is returned to the jumping stand for another trial. The difference is that if it jumps toward the correct card, it receives food. The position of the cards varies randomly so that the correct card will sometimes be on the right and sometimes on the left. The rat soon learns to jump toward the card that results in food.

In **successive discrimination training,** the $S^D$ and $S^\Delta$ alternate, usually randomly. When the $S^D$ appears, the behavior is reinforced; when the $S^\Delta$ appears, the behavior is not reinforced. Donald Dougherty and Paul Lewis (1991) used the successive procedure in doing one of the few discrimination training studies in horses. The horses learned to press a lever (the same kind used with rats) using their lip. The researchers projected images of circles, one at a time, in front of the horses. One circle was 2.5 inches in diameter, the other 1.5 inches. Lever pressing when the larger circle appeared resulted in grain; pressing when the smaller circle appeared got the horse nothing. The horses learned to discriminate between the two circles. One horse, Lady Bay, learned to discriminate very quickly (see Figure 11-5).

In a procedure called **matching to sample (MTS),** the task is to select from two or more alternatives (called *comparison stimuli*) the stimulus that matches a standard (the *sample*). The comparison stimuli include the $S^D$ —the stimulus that matches the sample—and one or more $S^\Delta$. For example, a sample disc on one wall of an experimental chamber may be illuminated by either a red or a green light. On some trials the disc will be red, on some trials green. After a short time the sample disc goes dark, and two comparison discs, one

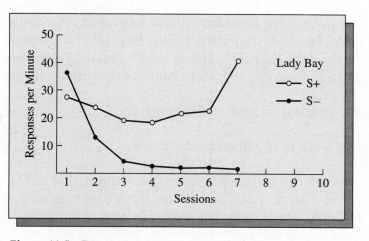

**Figure 11-5**  *Discrimination training in Lady Bay, a horse. Lever pressing when a 2.5-inch circle appeared resulted in food; pressing when the circle was 1.5 inches did not. (Adapted from "Stimulus Generalization, Discrimination Learning, and Peak Shift in Horses," by D. M. Dougherty and P. Lewis,* Journal of the Experimental Analysis of Behavior, *1991, 56, p. 102, Figure 2. Copyright © 1991 by the Society for the Experimental Analysis of Behavior, Inc. Reprinted by permission of the publisher and author.)*

red and one green, are illuminated. The $S^{D+}$ is the disc of the same color as the sample. If a pigeon pecks the comparison disc matching the sample, it receives food; if it pecks the other disc, it receives nothing. To obtain reinforcement, the bird must successfully discriminate between the disc that matches the sample (the $S^D$) and the one that does not (the $S^\Delta$).

The example of MTS just given is very simple, but the procedure can be more complicated. For example, a bird may be required to peck a disc that is *different from* the sample, a variation of MTS called **oddity matching** or **mismatching.** Increasing the number of variations in the sample and/or the comparison discs also may complicate the MTS procedure. For example, the sample may alternate among red, green, and blue, and the comparison discs may be red, green, blue, and yellow.

In the procedures described thus far, the animal or person undergoing training inevitably makes a number of mistakes. If you think about being a rat on Lashley's jumping stand, you can see that there is no way you can tell which card to jump toward on your first trial. No matter how clever you are, you have a 50% chance of being wrong. Moreover, you could easily be wrong on the second trial as well because the correct choice could be the card with the horizontal lines or it could be the card on the left. Even a simple discrimination can take some time to develop, and dozens of errors may be made along the way.

Herbert Terrace (1963a, 1963b, 1964, 1972) found that errors can be reduced through **errorless discrimination training.** In this procedure the $S^\Delta$ is presented in very weak form and for short periods. For example, in training a pigeon to discriminate between a red disc (the $S^D$) and a green disc (the $S^\Delta$), Terrace (1963a) presented the red disc at full strength for three minutes at a time, but presented an unlit green disc for only five seconds. Pigeons are less likely to peck a dark disc than a bright one, and the shorter the time the disc is available, the less likely it is to be pecked. The result was that the $S^\Delta$ was seldom pecked. Gradually, Terrace increased the duration and strength of the $S^\Delta$ while reinforcing pecking at the $S^D$. Finally, Terrace was able to present the green disc brightly lit for a prolonged time without the bird pecking it.

**?** **QUERY 7:** In errorless discrimination training, the _____ is presented in

very weak form and gradually "faded in."

With the Terrace procedure, a discrimination can be developed with few errors. This is important because errors tend to arouse undesirable emotional reactions. Birds trained in the traditional manner, for example, often stamp their feet or flap their wings when presented with the $S^\Delta$. Birds trained with the errorless procedure merely watch the disc calmly until the $S^D$ reappears.

Errorless discrimination training has been put to good use outside the laboratory. Richard Powers and his colleagues (1970) found, for instance, that preschoolers learned a subtle color discrimination more quickly and with fewer errors when trained with the Terrace procedure. Children trained in the usual way also became emotionally upset during the S$^\Delta$ periods: They banged hard on the lever and wandered around the room. In contrast, those who learned through the errorless procedure sat quietly when the S$^\Delta$ was present, patiently waiting for the S$^D$ to appear.

Another way to improve the rate of discrimination learning is to vary the consequences. In an experiment by M. A. Trapold (1970), rats could press either of two levers. When a light came on, pressing the lever on the left was reinforced, but when a tone sounded, pressing the lever on the right paid off. However, in this experiment Trapold provided different consequences for the two responses. The reinforcer for pressing on the left lever was food; the reinforcer for pressing on the right lever was sugar water. The result was that the rats learned to make the appropriate discrimination more quickly and achieved a higher level of accuracy than when reinforcers were the same for each response. This finding—improved performance in discrimination training as a result of different consequences—is called the **differential outcomes effect** (**DOE**) (Miyashita, Nakajima, & Imada, 2000; Peterson & Trapold, 1980; Goeters et al., 1992).

Normally, training is more effective if reinforcers follow behavior immediately than if they are delayed. But what if we provide immediate reinforcement for one correct behavior and delayed reinforcement for another correct behavior? Will the DOE still hold? J. G. Carlson and Richard Wielkiewicz (1972) performed just such an experiment and found that the DOE *did* hold. Animals receiving immediate reinforcement for one behavior and delayed reinforcement for the other learned the discrimination faster than animals receiving immediate reinforcement for both behaviors. Thus, the way discrimination training is conducted can have pronounced effects on learning.

**?** QUERY 8: The DOE implies that discrimination training can be improved by providing

different _____ for different _____.

The training procedures described are fairly simple, but the discriminations that can be produced with them are amazing. For example, in one experiment by Debra Porter (then an undergraduate student!) and Allen Neuringer (1984), two pigeons heard an excerpt from Bach's *Prelude in C Minor* for flute and Hindemith's *Sonata,* Opus 25, Number 1 for viola. When Bach was playing, pecking a disc resulted in food; when Hindemith played, pecking produced no food. By the end of the experiment, both birds responded correctly over 80% of the time (see Figure 11-6). In a second experiment, the researchers provided two discs and randomly alternated excerpts from Bach and Stravinsky. When the birds heard Bach, pecking the disc on the left resulted in food; when they heard Stravinsky, pecking the disc on the right got food. If a bird pecked the wrong disc (e.g., the left disc when Stravinsky aired), the result was no food and a penalty period when no music played and pecking had no effect. Four of the five pigeons in the study responded correctly over 70% of the time. Other research showed that fish can learn to discriminate between classical and blues music (Chase, 2001).

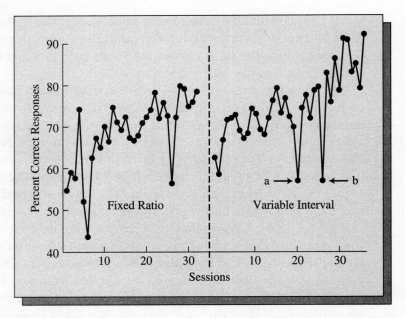

**Figure 11-6**  *Pigeon learns to tell Bach from Hindemith. Percent of correct responses (pecking when Bach was played but not Hindemith) by pigeon #25 increased steadily with training. (Adapted from Porter & Neuringer, 1984, Figure 1, p. 140. Journal of Experimental Psychology, 1984, 10 (2), 138–148.)*

In similar research, Shigeru Watanabe, Junko Sakamoto, and Masumi Wakita (1995) trained pigeons to discriminate between paintings by Picasso and those of Monet. Pecking on a disc resulted in access to grain, but only if a painting by the right artist was visible. For four birds this meant pecking when there was a Monet painting present; for four other birds, it meant pecking when there was a painting by Picasso. If a bird pecked when the wrong kind of painting was visible, it got nothing. The training continued until the birds responded correctly more than 90% of the time. After this the researchers ran tests using new pictures by the artists to determine the basis on which the birds discriminated between them. One possibility was differences in color: The two artists might have had different color preferences, and that might have been what the birds were responding to. To test this idea the researchers presented monochromatic paintings by both artists. It made little difference: Although the overall success rate declined slightly, all of the birds continued to discriminate between Picasso and Monet. Another idea was that the birds responded to differences in contour. Picasso's paintings tend to have sharp edges, whereas those of Monet, like all impressionist paintings, have a softer look. To rule out contour as the basis for discrimination, the researchers presented the images out of focus. Again, there was an overall decline in the accuracy level, but all of the birds continued to discriminate even when the images were blurred. The researchers tested other possible cues, but it does not appear that the birds responded to a single feature of either kind of painting. How they could tell Picasso from Monet is not clear, but they did.

In other experiments, pigeons learned to discriminate between different locations on a university campus (Honig & Stewart, 1988) and among the letters of the English alphabet (Blough, 1982), and rats learned to discriminate between spoken Dutch and Japanese (Toro, Trobalon, & Sebastian-Galles, 2005).

Discrimination learning is not merely an interesting laboratory phenomenon; it has important practical applications. Learning a second language in adulthood can be difficult because of differences in the sounds of the two languages. To the Japanese, for example, the English *L* sounds like the Japanese *R*. James McClelland, Julia Fiez, and Bruce McCandliss (2002) provided discrimination training to Japanese adults living in the United States. Training consisted of listening to an audiotape and indicating which of two words, one starting with L, the other with R, they heard. For some participants the two words were *rock* and *lock*; for others the words were *road* and *load*. Some participants got immediate feedback after each effort; others did not. The training consisted of only three 20-minute sessions, yet the participants showed marked improvement. (Those who did not get feedback showed far less progress.) This research and other work on discrimination training have important implications not only for second-language learning, but for education and training in general. Being an auto mechanic, for example, requires knowing the parts of an engine and how they relate to one another. Achieving that involves learning to discriminate among the various parts.

Discrimination training has also proved useful in training animals to help humans with a variety of tasks. For a dog to sniff out illegal drugs, for instance, requires discriminating among various fragrances. Animals with a keen sense of smell can also locate landmines. Alan Poling and others affiliated with APOPO (an organization devoted to the removal of landmines; Poling et al., 2011) describe how the African pouched rat, a large rodent, is trained to do this. The explosive most often present in landmines is TNT, so a key part of the rodent's training involves discrimination between that explosive and other substances. The training begins in a lab, then goes to field training before the real work begins. The animals learn to detect TNT and to indicate its presence by scratching at the ground for five seconds.

When discrimination training is highly effective, the $S^D$ reliably predicts the appearance of the reinforced behavior. At that point, the behavior is said to be under stimulus control, our next topic.

CAPSULE **REVIEW**  Discrimination means behaving differently in the presence of different stimuli. The standard procedure for establishing a discrimination is called discrimination training. It can take a variety of forms, including successive, simultaneous, matching to sample, and errorless. In each case, a behavior is reinforced in the presence of one stimulus, the $S^D$, but not in the presence of other stimuli, the $S^\Delta$.

# STIMULUS CONTROL

Consider a rat that has learned to press a lever when a light is on but not when the light is off. In a sense, you can control the rat's lever pressing with the light switch: Turn it on, and the rat presses the lever; turn it off, and the pressing stops. When discrimination training brings behavior under the influence of discriminative stimuli, the behavior is said to be under **stimulus control** (for a review, see Thomas, 1991).

Rats are not the only creatures, of course, that have behavior under stimulus control. While you are driving, if you approach an intersection and the traffic light turns red, you move your foot to the brake pedal. When the light turns green, you move your foot to the gas pedal. Your behavior has, as the result of discrimination training, come under the influence of the traffic signal. Similarly, you tend to enter stores that have signs that say "Open" and walk past stores that are marked "Closed." People respond to signs that say "Sale," "Reduced Prices," "Clearance," "Going Out of Business," and the like. Retailers know the influence exerted by such signs and use them to attract shoppers. You may have noticed that some retail stores are constantly "going out of business."

Sometimes (perhaps always) stimulus control is exerted not by a single stimulus but by a complex array of stimuli. We behave differently at a formal ball than we do at a square dance, and some behavior that would be acceptable at a beach party is unacceptable at a dinner party. The differential control exerted by such situations probably has to do with a number of stimuli including attire, furniture, food, and the behavior of other people present. When a youngster misbehaves, he often defends his actions by saying, "Well, everyone else was doing it!" This explanation is partly an appeal to the stimulus control exerted by the behavior of one's peers.

The term *stimulus control* suggests that we are manipulated by our environment, but there is another way of looking at it: The discriminative stimuli involved actually give us a kind of power. Consider the rat that learns to press a lever when a light is on but not when it is off. The light is said to control the rat's behavior, but the rat has also gained control: It no longer wastes time and energy pressing a lever when doing so is useless. Similarly, the behavior of motorists comes under the control of traffic lights and signs. But it is this stimulus control that enables us to travel more or less safely and efficiently. Without stimulus control, traffic jams would be routine and our highways would be deadly gauntlets. In fact, many traffic accidents are attributed to inattentive driving—and what is inattentive driving but a failure of driving behaviors to be under the control of appropriate stimuli?

An understanding of the control exerted by our immediate environment can also give us the power to change that environment in helpful ways. People who are overweight typically find it difficult to turn down delicious food; the items exert a measure of control over their behavior. But understanding this can help them avoid situations in which tempting foods are present. Many people who are overweight have dishes of candy about their homes; if they get rid of the candy, it has less opportunity to influence their behavior. Our environment exerts control over our behavior. Paradoxically, that can *increase* the control we have over our lives.

Now that you understand the basics of generalization, discrimination, and stimulus control, let us see how they can account for some important phenomena.

CAPSULE **REVIEW**   When a discrimination has been well established, the behavior is said to be under stimulus control. Generally that means that the behavior is orderly and efficient, that it enables us to obtain desirable consequences and avoid undesirable ones. Stimulus control can work against us, but we can also use it to our advantage.

# GENERALIZATION, DISCRIMINATION AND STIMULUS CONTROL IN THE ANALYSIS OF BEHAVIOR

Research on generalization, discrimination, and stimulus control has changed the way we think about many aspects of our lives. We will consider three examples.

## Mental Rotation as Generalization

Roger Shepard is a psychologist who has studied what he calls "mental rotation." In a typical experiment (Cooper & Shepard, 1973), people were shown letters that had been rotated varying degrees from their normal, upright position and were asked whether the letters were backward (that is, mirror images of the original) or not. The result was that the greater the rotation, the longer it took people to answer. Shepard concludes from such data that people mentally rotate an "internal representation" or image of the letter until it is in its normal, upright position and then decide whether it is backward.

Although Shepard refers to the mental rotation of images, his data consist of the time it takes to react to rotated figures. It is interesting that when these data are plotted graphically, the resulting curve looks remarkably like a generalization gradient (Figure 11-7). Participants respond most quickly to the "training stimulus" (the letter they were trained in school to recognize); the less the stimulus resembles the training stimulus, the slower is the response.

In one experiment, Donna Reit and Brady Phelps (1996) used a computer program to train college students to discriminate between geometric shapes that did and did not match a sample. The items were rotated from the sample position by 0, 60, 120, 180, 240, or 300 degrees. The students received feedback after each trial. When the researchers plotted the data for reaction times, the results formed a fairly typical generalization gradient (see Figure 11-8).

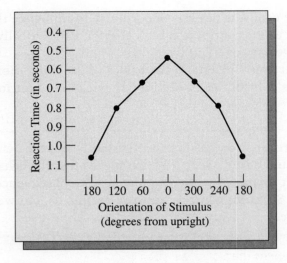

**Figure 11-7** *Mental rotation as generalization. Mean reaction time to a familiar stimulus is a function of the orientation of the stimulus. The shortest reaction times occurred when the stimulus was in its normal position (0 degrees from upright). The less the stimulus resembled the normal position, the longer the reaction time. (Compiled from data in Cooper and Shepard, 1973; see also Hollard & Delius, 1982.) (Note: Subjects were tested only once at 180 degrees; the point is plotted twice to show the symmetrical nature of the gradient.)*

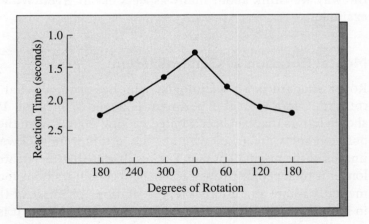

**Figure 11-8** *Mental rotation as generalization. Average reaction times to a figure in its normal, upright position (0 rotation) and to varying degrees of rotation. (Adapted from "Mental Rotation Reconceptualized as Stimulus Generalization," by D. J. Reit and B. J. Phelps, Figure 1. Paper presented at the 22nd annual convention of the Association for Behavior Analysis, San Francisco, CA, May 1996. Reprinted by permission of the authors.)*

In a second experiment, Phelps and Reit (1997) got nearly identical results, except that with continued training the generalization gradients flattened. This is probably because students continued to receive feedback during testing and therefore improved their reaction times to rotated items. (They could not improve their performance on unrotated items much because they were already reacting to those items quite quickly.) In any case, these data clearly suggest that "mental rotation" data are generalization data.

Phelps and Reit note that most of their students, like Shepard's, reported that they solved the problems by "mentally rotating" the test stimuli. As Phelps and Reit point out, however, the subjective experience of mental rotation does not explain the differences in reaction times. A scientific explanation must point to physical features of the situation and to the learning history of the participant. The expression "mental rotation" at best identifies the covert behavior involved; it does not explain the participant's performance.

## Concept Formation as Discrimination Learning

The word **concept** usually refers to any class the members of which share one or more defining features. The defining features allow us to discriminate the members of one class from the members of another. For example, all spiders have eight legs; this distinguishes them from other animals, including insects, which have fewer than or more than eight legs.

A concept is not a thing, however, but, as Fred Keller and William Schoenfeld (1950) put it, "only a name for a kind of behavior." They explain: "Strictly speaking, one does not *have* a concept, just as one does not *have* extinction—rather, one demonstrates conceptual behavior by acting in a certain way" (p. 154). Concepts require both generalization and discrimination. One must generalize within the conceptual class and discriminate between that and other classes. So, for example, to understand the concept, spider, one must both recognize a variety of spiders when one sees them, including spiders one has never seen before, and distinguish between spiders and other critters, such as ants and aphids. As Keller and Schoenfeld put it, "Generalization *within* classes and discrimination *between* classes—this is the essence of concepts" (p. 154f).

One way concepts are learned is through discrimination training. In one study, Kenneth Spence (1937) trained chimpanzees to find food under one of two white metal covers that differed only in size. One chimp got a choice between covers that were 160 and 100 square centimeters. Whenever it chose the larger cover, it found food; whenever it chose the smaller cover, it found nothing. After the chimp had learned to choose the larger cover reliably, Spence presented it with new covers, identical to the first set except that the choice was now between covers that were 320 and 200 square centimeters. We might expect that the chimp would select the 200 square centimeter cover because that one more closely resembled the cover that previously hid food. Instead, the chimp chose the larger cover. It had learned the concept "larger than."

In a similar experiment, Wolfgang Kohler (1939) trained chickens to select the lighter of two gray squares. After training, he tested them with the light gray square that had always led to food and with a still lighter gray square they had never seen before. Again, we might expect the animals to select the original gray stimulus because that had previously led to food. In fact, the birds chose the new, lighter square. In this case, the concept is "lighter than."

Richard and Maria Malott (1970) used discrimination to teach pigeons the concept of sameness. In this study, two halves of a key were illuminated independently and could therefore have different colors. When both halves were the same color (either all red or all violet), pecking the key produced food; when the two halves were different colors (one half red, the other violet), pecking did not produce food. After the pigeons had learned this discrimination, the researchers tested the birds on four new patterns: blue–blue, yellow–yellow, blue–yellow, and yellow–blue. Three out of the four pigeons pecked more often when the key halves were the same color than when they were different.

These results are impressive, but the kinds of concepts involved are far simpler than concepts such as house, boat, insect, and human. These concepts are large classes with tremendous variability within the class. Houses, for example, take a great many different forms. Can animals acquire such concepts through discrimination training?

Richard Herrnstein and his colleagues performed a series of brilliant experiments aimed at answering this question. In the first of these, Herrnstein and D. H. Loveland (1964) projected photographic images within a pigeon's chamber. The images included countryside, cities, bodies of water, lawn, meadow, and so on. About half of the photographs included at least one person, while the others did not. If the bird pecked a disc when an image included a person, it received food; if it pecked when there was no person, it received nothing. The people in the photos were sometimes partly hidden by other objects. Sometimes there was one person, sometimes a group of people. Some of the humans were clothed, some partly clothed, some nude. They included males and females, adults and children, and people of different races. Thus, to get food for pecking, the birds had to respond to a wide variety of human images. Any normally functioning adult could easily perform the task, but could a pigeon? The answer was a clear, *Yes*.

Herrnstein and Loveland next manipulated variables to see if the pigeons might be discriminating on the basis of some stimulus that happened to be correlated with humans, such as color. These efforts supported the idea "that the pigeons were, in fact, looking for, and reacting to, images of people" (p. 551). Additional support for this idea came from the mistakes the birds made. They sometimes failed to peck when the human being in the photo was largely hidden, and they occasionally pecked when the picture contained items commonly associated with people, such as cars, boats, and houses. It seems likely that these are the same kinds of errors people would make in performing the same task. "The evidence for a concept," the researchers conclude, "is incontrovertible" (p. 551). A replication of this study got similar results (Herrnstein, Loveland, & Cable, 1976).

Some people were skeptical that pigeons grasped such complex concepts. S. L. Greene (1983) suggested that the pigeons might simply memorize the figures associated with reinforcement. If this were the case, the birds should fail to discriminate accurately when tested on pictures they had not seen before. Herrnstein (1979) did an experiment in which the task was to respond when a photograph included one or more trees or parts of trees. In this case, the birds appeared to learn the concept "tree." Contrary to Greene's prediction, the birds pecked even when shown slides they had never seen before if those slides included trees (see also Edwards & Honig, 1987). The birds apparently responded to features that define the category, which is the essence of a concept.

An experiment by Robert Allan (1990; see also Allan, 1993) adds support to the idea that pigeons can learn concepts. Allan trained birds to peck a panel on which photographs could be projected, and he provided equipment to record the segment of the panel the bird pecked. His reasoning was that if birds were discriminating on the basis of a conceptual feature, they would peck at the part of the photograph that contained the conceptual item. He projected 40 slides, 20 of which included pictures of humans, the concept to be learned. Birds received food periodically if they pecked when a human figure appeared. The result was that the birds not only learned to make the appropriate discrimination, they also tended to peck *the part of the slide that included a human figure* (see Figure 11-9). Allan writes that "as the position of the human form changes from one segment to another, the pigeons track this movement by pecking in the same segment." In a sense, the bird points

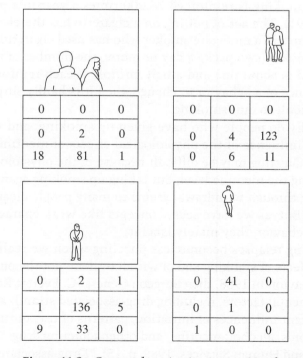

**Figure 11-9**  *Concept learning in pigeons. Numbers of responses occurring in each of nine equal-area segments of a slide as measured by an infrared touch device. The diagrams immediately above each accumulation set indicate the relative position of the human form in that particular slide. (From "Control of Pecking Response Topography by Stimulus-Reinforcer and Response-Reinforcer Contingencies," by R. W. Allan, 1993, in H. P. Zeigler and H. Bischof,* Vision, Brain, and Behavior in Birds, *p. 291, Figure 16.3. Copyright © 1993 The MIT Press. Reprinted with permission.)*

to the object in the concept category. In considering this finding, it is important to note that reinforcement was not contingent on pecking the part of the panel in which human figures appeared, yet that is what the birds did.

Researchers have demonstrated that pigeons and primates can master the concepts *fish, cats, flowers, ships, oak leaves, cars, letters*, and *chairs*, among others. Fifty years ago that idea would have been dismissed as absurd. The point of this is not that people are no better at grasping concepts than other animals. (So far as I know, no animal has yet mastered the concepts *justice, entropy*, or *concept*.) The point is that by viewing concepts as learned behavior, rather than "mental representations" (the phrase commonly used by philosophers [e.g., Carey, 2011] and some psychologists [e.g., Laurence & Margolis, 1999]), we are able to study them experimentally, learn how they are acquired, and put our improved understanding of them to practical use.

## Smoking Relapse as Stimulus Control

Mark Twain, a lifelong cigar smoker, once quipped: "It's easy to quit smoking. I've done it hundreds of times." It is not hard to understand why people who have become addicted to nicotine continue to smoke. By some estimates, cigarette smoking is reinforced 73,000 times a year in a pack-a-day smoker (Lyons, 1991). The act of puffing on a cigarette has therefore been reinforced 730,000 times in a moderate smoker who has used cigarettes for ten years. For a heavy smoker (two packs a day or more), the number of reinforcements for that period is about one-and-a-half *million*. If each reinforcement increases the resistance of a behavior to change, then it is hardly surprising that people find it difficult to quit smoking.

But why do people who have given up smoking, and who are no longer under the influence of the physiological effects of nicotine, so often resume smoking? Quitting may be difficult because of the physiological effects of not maintaining the nicotine level, but taking up smoking again weeks or months after going through withdrawal seems to many people clear evidence of weak character. But, as we have seen, concepts like weak character do not explain puzzling behavior; they merely label it.

Smoking relapses become less puzzling when we realize that the physiological effects of smoking and of withdrawal are not the only factors involved in this behavior. In 1988, then Surgeon General C. Everett Koop concluded that "environmental factors, including drug-associated stimuli and social pressure, are important influences of initiation, patterns of use, quitting, and relapse to use of opioids, alcohol, nicotine, and other addicting drugs" (U.S. Department of Health and Human Services, 1988, p. 15). "Drug-associated stimuli" include environmental events that, because they have preceded tobacco use in the past, have acquired some degree of stimulus control over tobacco use. In other words, drug abuse, including smoking, is under stimulus control.

Ask smokers when they are most likely to smoke, and you are likely to be told on arising from bed in the morning, while having coffee, after eating, during work breaks (including the interval between classes), during or after stress (such as an exam or city driving), after physical exertion, when social-izing with friends, and so on (Buckalew & Gibson, 1984; Smith & Delprato, 1976). Because the use of tobacco and the reinforcing effects of nicotine have frequently occurred together in these situations, they have become discrimi-native stimuli for lighting a cigarette. And because smokers typically smoke throughout the day, many different situations become discriminative stimuli for smoking. Charles Lyons (1991) writes that "few other activities are so con-sistently and powerfully strengthened in such a wide range of temporal, situ-ational, and physical settings" (p. 218).

Most people have witnessed stimulus control in smokers, although they may not have realized it at the time. Imagine a moderate smoker who has just joined a group of people in casual conversation. A member of the group lights a cigarette. This act is a discriminative stimulus for smoking by others so even if our hypothetical smoker has recently smoked a cigarette, he may light up after seeing someone else do so. The smoker may explain this behavior by saying, "When I see someone else smoke, it makes me think of smoking, and then I have to have a cigarette." Sometimes smokers report that cues that "remind them" of cigarettes also induce feelings of physiological deprivation or "craving." But these thoughts and feelings do not explain the behavior of smoking any better than a lack of willpower does. The tendency for certain kinds of events to elicit smoking is explained by the history of reinforcement for smoking in the presence of those events.

Smoking in situations previously associated with smoking seems particu-larly likely to lead to an abrupt return to regular smoking. T. H. Brandon and colleagues (reported in Lyons, 1991) studied people who had quit smoking and who then had a single cigarette in a situation previously associated with smok-ing. Ninety-one percent of them soon became regular smokers again, nearly half within a day of the single cigarette. In another study, R. E. Bliss and colleagues (1989) found the presence of other people smoking commonly led to relapse.

The research on the role of stimulus control in smoking has important implications for those who would like to quit. It would appear that there are two basic approaches to preventing relapse. The former smoker can avoid sit-uations in which he or she often smoked in the past, thereby avoiding the ability of these situations to elicit smoking. Or the smoker can undergo train-ing to reduce the control these situations have over his or her behavior. It is extremely difficult, if not impossible, for a smoker to avoid all situations in which he or she has smoked; therefore, the best bet may be to undergo train-ing that will undermine the power of those situations. This might be done, for example, by gradually exposing the smoker to those situations while prevent-ing him or her from smoking. For example, a smoker who typically lights up after drinking coffee may have coffee in a therapist's office without smoking. When this situation no longer arouses the urge to smoke, the same training might be repeated in the nonsmoking section of a restaurant. The training might continue with having a meal in the restaurant, with the therapist (or other supportive person) along to ensure that the smoker does not light up. The person who would quit smoking may need to undergo the same sort of treatment in each kind of situation in which he or she has often smoked in the past. Giving up smoking for good requires overcoming stimulus control.

The same may be said of many other habitual behaviors. We saw in an earlier chapter the role that the schedule of reinforcement exerts on gambling. But gambling is also a behavior that occurs in certain kinds of settings, and those settings and associated cues exert power over behavior. The same thing is true of overeating. Brian Wansink (2006), a marketing professor at Cornell University, talks about the effects of "hidden persuaders," environmental cues for eating. He describes an experiment in which people ate soup from a bowl that automatically refilled as they ate. Normally an empty soup bowl is a cue to stop eating, but in this case there was no such cue. People tended to eat more than one bowl of soup, but some people ate much more—in some cases, more than a quart of soup. If an empty bowl or an empty plate is a discriminative stimulus to stop eating, then limiting the amount of food we serve ourselves can help reduce calorie consumption.

Whether it's smoking, gambling, overeating, or some other behavior in which we participate to excess, the solution is not a matter of strengthening willpower; it is a matter of weakening the power of environmental cues.

CAPSULE **REVIEW**    Generalization, discrimination, and stimulus control are basic concepts in learning, and they add greatly to our understanding of how experience changes behavior. Studies of mental rotation, concept learning, and habits such as smoking illustrate this.

# THEORIES OF GENERALIZATION AND DISCRIMINATION

Three theories of generalization and discrimination have dominated the field: those of Pavlov, Spence, and Lashley and Wade.

## Pavlov's Theory

Pavlov's theory is physiological. He believed that discrimination training produces physiological changes in the brain. Specifically, it establishes an area of excitation associated with the CS+ and an area of inhibition associated with the CS-. If a novel stimulus is similar to the CS+, it will excite an area of the brain near the CS+ area. The excitation will irradiate to the CS+ area and elicit the CR. Similarly, if a novel stimulus resembles the CS-, it will excite an area of the brain near the CS- area. The excitation of this area will irradiate to the CS- area and inhibit the CR. A similar explanation could be applied to generalization and discrimination following operant learning.

Pavlov's theory provides an intuitively appealing explanation and, wrapped as it is in physiology, it has the smell of science. Unfortunately, the physiological events were merely inferred from observed behavior. Pavlov presumed that irradiation of excitation occurred because generalization occurred, but there was no independent validation of its happening. The theory therefore suffered from circularity. Other theorists, most notably Kenneth Spence, have modified Pavlov's ideas.

## Spence's Theory

Kenneth Spence (1936, 1937, 1960) put Pavlov's physiology aside but kept the notions of excitation and inhibition.

Pairing a CS⁺ with a US results in an increased tendency to respond to the CS⁺ and to stimuli resembling the CS⁺. Similarly, in operant learning, reinforcement for responding in the presence of an S^D results in an increased tendency to respond not only to the S^D but to similar stimuli. The generalization gradient that results is called an **excitatory gradient.** In the same way, presenting a CS⁻ without the US results in a *decreased* tendency to respond to the CS⁻ and to stimuli resembling the CS⁻. Likewise, withholding reinforcement when operant behavior occurs in the presence of an S^Δ results in a decreased tendency to respond to that stimulus and to similar stimuli. The generalization gradient that results is called an **inhibitory gradient.**

Spence proposed that the tendency to respond to any given stimulus was the result of the interaction of the increased and decreased tendencies to respond, as reflected in gradients of excitation and inhibition. Consider a dog that is trained to salivate at the sound of a high-pitched tone, and another that is trained *not* to salivate at the sound of a low-pitched tone. The first dog will show generalization of excitation around CS⁺; the second will show generalization of inhibition around CS⁻. We can plot the excitatory and inhibitory gradients that result and place them next to one another, as depicted in Figure 11-10. Notice that the two curves overlap.

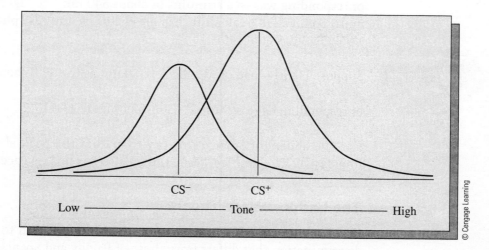

**Figure 11-10** *Spence's theory of generalization and discrimination. CS⁺ training produces a gradient of excitation; CS⁻ training produces a gradient of inhibition. The tendency to respond to a stimulus near the CS⁺ is reduced to the extent that it resembles the CS⁻. The tendency not to respond to a stimulus near the CS⁻ is reduced to the extent that it resembles the CS⁺.*

Discrimination training produces much the same effect within an individual. That is, the increased tendency to respond to stimuli resembling the CS+ (or S$^D$) overlaps with the decreased tendency to respond to stimuli resembling CS- (or S$^\Delta$). What Spence proposed was that the tendency to respond to a novel stimulus following discrimination training would be equal to the net difference between the excitatory and inhibitory tendencies. In other words, the tendency *to* respond to a novel stimulus will be reduced by the tendency *not* to respond to that stimulus.

Consider a hypothetical experiment in which a pigeon is trained to peck an orange disc but not a red one. After training, we give the bird the opportunity to peck the disc when it is a variety of colors, from pale yellow to deep red. What color disc will it peck most often? We know that if the bird had merely received food for pecking the orange disc, it would peck that same color most often. But discrimination training, according to Spence, should result in inhibition of the tendency to peck stimuli resembling the S$^\Delta$. Spence's theory therefore predicts that the peak of responding will not occur at the S$^D$ but at a stimulus further away from the S$^\Delta$. In other words, the peak of responding will not be on the orange disc but on one that is even less reddish.

This prediction, made in the 1930s, was actually confirmed in the 1950s in an experiment much like that just described. H. M. Hanson (1959) trained pigeons to peck a yellowish-green disc (550 nm, or nanometers, a measure of wavelength) and not to peck a slightly more yellowish (560 nm) disc.[1] A control group of birds did not undergo discrimination training but did receive food for pecking the yellowish-green disc. After training, Hanson let the birds peck discs of various colors, from yellow to green. The control group showed a peak of responding to the discriminative stimulus. Birds that had received discrimination training, however, showed a shift away from the S$^\Delta$; their peak of responding was to a stimulus of about 540 nm (see Figure 11-11). This phenomenon, called **peak shift,** has proved to be a robust phenomenon (Purtle, 1973; Thomas et al., 1991).

**QUERY 9:** Suppose Hanson had used a disc of 530 nm as the S$^D$. Where would the peak of responding have occurred? (Consider Figure 11-11.)

The ability of Spence's theory to predict the peak shift phenomenon is impressive. The Lashley–Wade theory also has had its successes.

## The Lashley-Wade Theory

Karl Lashley and M. Wade (1946) proposed an approach to generalization and discrimination that differs from those of Pavlov and Spence. These researchers argued that generalization gradients depend on prior experience with stimuli similar to those used in testing. Discrimination training increases the steepness

---

[1]A nanometer is 1 billionth of a meter, so a bird that can discriminate between discs of 550 nm and 540 nm is making a very fine discrimination indeed.

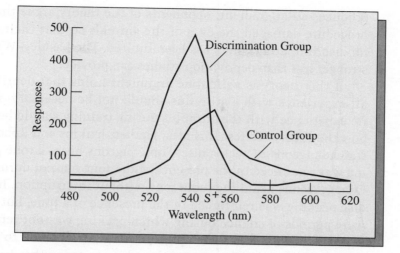

**Figure 11-11** *Peak shift. Pigeons trained to discriminate between an S⁺ (550 nm) and an S⁻ (560 nm) responded more often to a 540 nm stimulus than to the S⁺. Birds that had been trained only on the S⁻ did not show this peak shift. (After Hanson, 1959.)*

of the generalization gradient because it teaches the animal to tell the difference between the $S^D$ and other stimuli. But the generalization gradient is not usually flat even in the absence of training. Why is this so if the gradient depends on training? The answer Lashley and Wade give is that the animal has undergone a kind of discrimination training in the course of its everyday life. A pigeon, for example, learns to discriminate colors long before a researcher trains it to peck a red disc. The more experience a pigeon has had with colors, especially those resembling the $S^D$, the steeper its generalization gradient will be; the less experience the bird has had, the flatter the gradient will be.

The theory implies that if an animal is prevented from having any experience with a certain kind of stimulus, such as color, its behavior following training will be affected. If such a color-naïve animal is trained to respond in the presence of a red disc, for example, it will later respond just as frequently to a green disc. In other words, its gradient of generalization will be flat.

Several researchers attempted to test this hypothesis. In a typical experiment, animals were reared from birth in the dark to deprive them of experiences with color. Then they were trained to respond to a stimulus such as a green disc. After this, the animals were tested for generalization by presenting them with discs of other colors and noting the extent to which they discriminated. The results were then compared to those obtained from animals that had been reared normally. If the gradients of the color-deprived animals were flatter, the Lashley–Wade theory was supported; if rearing in the dark made no difference in the shape of the gradient, this argued against the theory.

Unfortunately, the results of such experiments have been ambiguous, with one study tending to support the theory and another tending to undermine it. Moreover, interpretation of the results is subject to argument. When there is no difference in the gradients of deprived and normally reared animals, proponents of the Lashley–Wade theory argue that the rearing procedure did not entirely preclude experience with the relevant stimuli. When deprivation produces a flat gradient, opponents of the theory argue that the deprivation procedure damaged the eyes of the animals so that their physical capacity for discriminating colors has been limited. The Lashley–Wade theory needs a stronger test than deprivation studies can provide.

If the theory is valid, one argument holds that depriving an animal of all experience with a stimulus should not be necessary; merely restricting its experience with the stimulus during training should be sufficient to support the theory. To test this idea, Herbert Jenkins and Robert Harrison (1960) trained pigeons to peck a disc. Some pigeons heard a tone periodically; pecking was reinforced in the presence of the tone but not during periods of quiet. Other pigeons heard the same tone without interruption. In both cases, then, disc pecking was reinforced in the presence of a tone; but in one case, there were periods of silence during which pecking was not reinforced. Next, the experimenters tested all the pigeons for generalization to other tones and to periods of silence. They found that those pigeons that had been exposed to periodic tone were much *less* likely to peck the disc during periods of silence than when the tone sounded. The other pigeons pecked the disc just as much when the tone was on as when it was off. This much is to be expected because the birds that heard the tone constantly had no opportunity to discriminate, whereas those that heard the tone periodically did. But what happened when the pigeons were exposed to different tones, sounds that neither group had heard before? The pigeons that had learned to discriminate between periods of tone and periods of silence also discriminated between the original tone and other tones. Pigeons that had received reinforcement during constant sound did not discriminate between tones (see Figure 11-12). These results are just what the Lashley–Wade theory predicts.

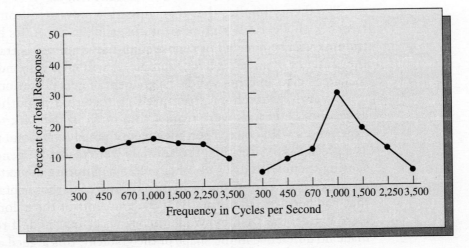

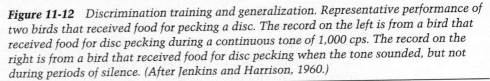

**Figure 11-12** *Discrimination training and generalization. Representative performance of two birds that received food for pecking a disc. The record on the left is from a bird that received food for disc pecking during a continuous tone of 1,000 cps. The record on the right is from a bird that received food for disc pecking when the tone sounded, but not during periods of silence. (After Jenkins and Harrison, 1960.)*

Not all tests of the Lashley–Wade theory have yielded positive results, but it is now generally acknowledged that the steepness of a generalization gradient depends to some extent on the experience the participant has had with the relevant stimuli before training.

No theory of discrimination and generalization has won universal support, but they have all spurred basic research. Some of this research has provided insights into problems of theoretical and practical importance.

---

CAPSULE **REVIEW**   Various theories have been proposed to account for generalization and discrimination. Pavlov explained the phenomena in terms of the irradiation of excitation. In his view, generalization occurs because a stimulus has excited an area of the brain near the area affected by the CS⁺. Spence believed that the net difference between gradients of excitation and inhibition predicts the response to novel stimuli. His theory accurately predicted the peak shift phenomenon. The Lashley–Wade theory maintains that generalization occurs because the animal has had too little experience with the stimuli involved to be able to discriminate among them.

---

# A FINAL WORD

The tendency to generalize is a blessing bestowed on us by natural selection because it has survival value. Conditioned taste aversion (see Chapter 4) offers a powerful illustration of this: Animals and people made sick by a food with a particular odor or taste then refuse to eat not only that food but others that resemble it. We can see the same sort of benefit from the generalization of food-gathering skills. In hunter-gatherer societies, young boys practice the skills of the hunt by shooting arrows at leaves. The survival of the group depends not on the boy's ability to shoot a leaf but on his ability to shoot a bird. The mastery of archery skills in the training situation generalizes to hunting situations. Academic education also would be of little value if what we learned did not generalize. Schoolchildren do not write essays about their summer vacations so they can later write similar essays for an employer; they do it so that they can write memos and reports.

Discrimination also plays an important role in survival. The blue jay that eats a monarch butterfly develops a conditioned taste aversion and thereafter avoids them (see Chapter 4). But the blue jay has to eat to survive, and it is not helped if it avoids eating all kinds of butterflies. It continues to eat butterflies, but not the monarch. In hunter-gatherer societies, girls learn to collect fruits and vegetables for food. They must be able to tell the difference between an edible and an inedible plant. They also learn to collect medicinal plants, and again discriminating is important: While some plants heal, others kill. Discrimination is also important in industrialized societies. The doctor who does not discriminate accurately between the symptoms of appendicitis and those of indigestion is in serious trouble—and so is her patient.

Discrimination learning leads to the tendency to respond, often more or less automatically, to events and situations where the behavior has been reinforced. This stimulus control also aids our survival by increasing our efficiency.

We see, then, that for both humans and animals, generalization and discrimination play major roles in adaptation. These phenomena greatly enhance—and complicate—the role of learning in survival.

## RECOMMENDED **READING**

1. Harlow, H. F. (1949). The formation of learning sets. *Psychological Review, 56,* 51–65.

   Harlow showed that through discrimination training, animals and people could "learn to learn." That is, they could become better at learning new things.

2. Skinner, B. F. (1953). *Science and human behavior.* New York: Free Press.

   See especially Chapter 7, "Operant Discrimination," and Chapter 8, "The Controlling Environment."

3. Staats, A. W., Staats, C. K., & Heard, W. G. (1959). Language conditioning of meaning using semantic generalization paradigm. *Journal of Experimental Psychology, 57,* 187–192.

   Most studies of generalization are based on the physical properties of stimuli (color, size, shape, pitch, etc.), but learned behavior sometimes generalizes on the basis of the conditioned meaning of the stimulus. This article describes some classic research on this topic.

4. Thomas, D. R. (1991). Stimulus control: Principles and procedures. In W. Ishaq (Ed.), *Human behavior in today's world* (pp. 191–203). New York: Praeger.

   In an overview of generalization, discrimination, and stimulus control, Thomas discusses many of the topics covered elsewhere in this text (e.g., overshadowing, state-dependent learning) under the heading of stimulus control.

5. Tumlinson, J. H., Lewis, W. J., & Vet, L. E. M. (1993, March). How parasitic wasps find their hosts. *Scientific American,* 100–106.

   This interesting study involves the interaction of innate tendencies and discrimination learning in the natural environment.

## REVIEW **QUESTIONS**

1. Define the following terms:

   | | |
   |---|---|
   | concept | inhibitory gradient |
   | CS⁻ | matching to sample (MTS) |

CS⁺
differential outcomes
effect (DOE)
discrimination
discrimination training
discriminative stimulus
errorless discrimination
training
excitatory gradient
generalization
generalization gradient

mismatching
oddity matching
peak shift
S⁺
S⁻
Sᴰ
Sᐃ
simultaneous discrimination training
stimulus control
successive discrimination training

2. Describe the relationship between generalization and discrimination.

3. There is a saying that goes, "He who has been bitten by a snake fears a rope." What phenomenon does this proverb implicitly recognize?

4. B. F. Skinner (1951) once taught pigeons to "read." They would peck a disc when a sign read, "Peck," and would not peck when a sign read, "Don't peck." Describe how Skinner might have accomplished this.

5. How might you use discrimination training to make someone capable of recognizing, from facial expression and other "body language," when people were lying?

6. What might be the role of discrimination training in racial prejudice?

7. How does Spence's theory differ from Pavlov's?

8. Explain why a stimulus that becomes an Sᴰ also becomes a secondary reinforcer.

9. Explain why a person who is red-green color blind (that is, red and green objects look gray) is at a disadvantage compared to his or her peers.

10. You see an American alone talking on a cell phone and notice she is gesturing with her free hand as she talks. Later you see an Oriental person alone talking on a cell phone and notice that she nods her head and occasionally bends forward from the hip. Explain these acts.

## PRACTICE **QUIZ**

1. One of the first reports of generalization came from _____ in 1898.

2. Arthur Bachrach and others got generalization of therapy in a young woman who would not _____.

3. Generalization across different behaviors is called _____ generalization.

4. Richard Herrnstein used discrimination training to teach the concepts "tree" and "human being" to _____ .

5. The peak shift phenomenon supports the theory of generalization and discrimination proposed by _____.

6. If a smoker nearly always lights a cigarette after a meal, lighting a cigarette is under _____.

7. Camouflage rests on the inability of a predator to _____ between the prey animal and other stimuli.

8. When generalization data are plotted on a curve, the result is a generalization _____.

9. One kind of discrimination training procedure is abbreviated MTS. This stands for _____.

10. The effects of learning can spread across _____, _____, _____, and situations.

## QUERY ANSWERS

Query 1. When the effects of learning spread across situations, it is called *stimulus* generalization.

Query 2. A generalization gradient shows the tendency for a behavior to occur in situations that differ systematically from *the training situation/ stimulus.*

Query 3. The paragraph preceding the query lists four tactics, including training in a variety of situations and using multiple examples.

Query 4. Sigmund Freud talked about displaced aggression. Displaced aggression is an example of *stimulus generalization.*

Query 5. Discrimination is the opposite of *generalization.*

Query 6: *An $S^-$ is the same as an $S^\Delta$.*

Query 7. In errorless discrimination training, the $S^-/S^\Delta$ is presented in very weak form and gradually "faded in."

Query 8. The DOE implies that discrimination training can be improved by providing different *outcomes* for different *behaviors.*

Query 9. Suppose Hanson had used a disc of 530 nm as the $S^D$. Where would the peak of responding have occurred? (Consider Figure 11-11.) *It would have shifted in the opposite direction, possibly to around 560 nm.*

# CHAPTER

# 12 Forgetting

*In a world of constantly changing environment, literal recall is extraordinarily unimportant.*

—**F. C. Bartlett**

## PREVIEW

This text is devoted to the changes in behavior produced by experience. One thing that experience has taught you is that those changes in behavior fade with time. This chapter deals with that "fading"—with how it can be measured, what causes it, and how an understanding of it can be put to practical use. It also deals with another topic that might make your teeth ache: Could it be that what we call forgetting is learning?

## BEGINNINGS

In the animated film *Monsters, Inc.* the inhabitants of a parallel universe generate electricity from the screams of human children. The monsters gain access to our world by means of closet doors. The doors are stored in a huge warehouse, and are retrieved by an electronically controlled system of conveyor belts. Once a door is retrieved and a few buttons are pressed, a monster can go through the door into our world, terrify a slumbering child, and capture the energy produced by the child's screams.

Memory is like that—according to some people. Like the closet doors, memories are stored in a warehouse and retrieved when needed to provide access to another world—the world of the past. The theory, like the film, is a little vague on the details, but it provides an appealing metaphor for explaining why learning persists.

There have been many variations of the storage metaphor over the ages. In ancient times, experiences were impressed on the mind like marks on a wax tablet. To remember an experience, one had only to look at one's mental tablet. In the Renaissance, experience wrote on a blank slate, which could be read so long as the message was not wiped off. In the Industrial Age, the blank slate gave way to memos and snapshots stored in mental filing cabinets. Experiences were "filed away" and retrieved by searching through the appropriate file when the need arose. The development of high-speed computers provides the current metaphor for memory storage.

However, there is evidence that the storage metaphor may be losing ground. There seems to be growing doubt that the storage metaphor is consistent with the changes in behavior we call forgetting. For one thing, it is clear that our recollections of an event are highly malleable. To use the *Monsters, Inc.* metaphor, it's as if we store away a large blue door with a round doorknob and shiny brass hinges and later find that it has become a small pink door with a lever handle and dark iron hinges. How can we speak of experiences being stored and retrieved when they undergo such drastic changes, particularly when the changes seem to be products of environmental, not physiological, events? As you read this chapter, you will be obliged to wrestle with this question.

## DEFINING FORGETTING

Learning is a marvelous invention of natural selection, but the changes in behavior that we call learning are not immutable. Once the experiences that produce learning end, the behavior may then change, and often does. You have, I hope, learned a lot about learning from this text and from your instructor and will do well on your final exam. But would you do just as well on the same exam a year from now? Similarly, if you take a drawing class and show a lot of progress in your ability to sketch human portraits, but stop doing so once the course ends, will your skill remain the same when you try to draw someone a year later? You know the answer in both cases is almost certainly, *No.*

It is such changes that people refer to when they speak of **forgetting,** so a common definition of forgetting is deterioration in performance of learned behavior following a retention interval. The phrase **retention interval** means a period during which learning or practice of the behavior does not occur.

Here's a simple laboratory example: You put a pigeon into an experimental chamber. There is a disc on one wall of the chamber, and you train the bird to peck the disc when it is illuminated, but not when it is dark. When you have established a high, steady rate of pecking the illuminated disc, you transfer the bird to another location where it serves as a breeder. You follow the same procedure with 19 other birds, and after various lengths of time you return the birds, one at a time, to the experimental chamber to see how they respond. You test four of the birds after a period of four years. You put the birds into the experimental chamber, but with the food mechanism disconnected so that pecking is now on extinction. What do they do?

B. F. Skinner (1950) carried out an experiment like this. When he put the birds in the chamber, the disc was not illuminated and the birds did not peck. Then when Skinner illuminated it, the birds began pecking. In short, they

## LEARNING FOR THE FUTURE

We have seen again and again that learning has tremendous survival value. Like camouflage, flying, and razor-sharp fangs, learning ability evolved because it helped individuals survive and reproduce. The ability to retain what is learned over long periods also aids survival.

In the wild, the availability of food is variable. One way to deal with this problem is to store food when it is plentiful and draw on these caches when food runs short. Many animals do exactly that. The Clark's nutcracker, a year-round resident of North America's Rocky Mountains, provides an example (Kamil & Balda, 1985, 1990a, 1990b). It feeds on pine seeds and can store more than 30,000 seeds in over 6,000 caches, but does it find the 2,000 caches needed to make it through the winter or does it simply stumble on its own and other birds' caches as it forages? A. C. Kamil and Russell Balda (1990b) conducted an experiment in which nutcrackers stored seeds and were then allowed to recover them one week, three months, and six months later. There was some decline in the ability to find caches after prolonged periods, but even after six months the birds found seeds with a level of success that could not be attributed to chance.

Further evidence supports the notion that learning accounts for the nutcracker's ability to find caches. In one study, Stephen Vander Wall (1982) allowed two Clark's nutcrackers to store seeds in an aviary and later retrieve them. Each bird found many of its own caches but seldom found caches of the other bird. This suggests that the birds did not find seeds simply by searching likely cache sites or by "sniffing out" the seeds.

Other studies show similar evidence of the ability of animals to retrieve caches after prolonged periods, including chipmunks (Vander Wall, 1991), gray squirrels (Jacobs & Liman, 1991), kangaroo rats (Jacobs, 1992), and monkeys (Menzel, 1991). Learning is important not only because it enables us and other animals to adapt to current challenges, but because it helps us meet the challenges of the future, sometimes the distant future.

behaved just as they had four years earlier, as though there had been no gap since their training ended. However, there was a difference: Skinner noted that pecking extinguished much more rapidly after four years than it had in other birds after a shorter period. This subtle deterioration in performance during extinction is an example of forgetting.

Some researchers argue that *deterioration* is the wrong word. The behavior doesn't deteriorate, they insist, it merely changes. As you saw in Chapter 11, through discrimination learning behavior can come under stimulus control. Since all behavior occurs in the presence of certain stimuli and not others, it can be argued that all behavior is under some degree of stimulus control. The control is not exerted by a single stimulus, but by a complex of stimuli present when the behavior is reinforced. If some of these stimuli are not present later, the behavior may not be elicited, and we say forgetting has occurred. There is no such thing as forgetting, the argument goes, there are just changes in behavior due to changes in the environment from the time of training to the time of testing (Branch, 1977; Capaldi & Neath, 1995; Palmer, 1991; Schlinger, pers. comm.; see also Jasnow, Cullen, & Riccio, 2012; Riccio, Rabinowitz, & Axelrod, 1994). This leads to a paradoxical conclusion: If forgetting is a change in behavior due to experience, and learning is a change in behavior due to experience, then forgetting is learning!

To say that forgetting is learning seems an absurd position, but you will soon see that there is actually empirical support for the idea. However, to equate forgetting with learning is problematic since it implies that there are no right or wrong answers, no standards of quality. To most people, a student who spells *Mississippi* correctly on Monday and then on Friday's test spells it *Misisipi* has shown a deterioration in performance. So in this text we will stick with the idea that forgetting means deterioration in performance after a retention interval.

Often the deterioration in forgetting is seen as a decline in the probability of some behavior, but this is not always the case. Sometimes forgetting means that a behavior becomes *more* likely to occur (Riccio, Rabinowitz, & Axelrod, 1994). For example, in the experiment by Skinner described above, the birds learned *not* to peck the disc when it was dark. If, four years later, they had done so this increase in pecking would qualify as forgetting.

In considering forgetting, it is important to realize that we are concerned with deterioration in measurable behavior, not the deterioration of neurological structures. No one disputes that learning experiences produce physical changes in the nervous system (Kandel, 2007; Steinmetz & Lindquist, 2009), and presumably something happens to these structures when forgetting occurs, but our subject matter is the effects of experience on *behavior*, not on the nervous system. When we ask whether an individual has forgotten something, then, we are asking whether the changes in behavior produced by experience persist. "Have you forgotten how to ride a bicycle?" is another way of saying, "Can you still ride a bike?" "Do you remember the algebra you learned in high school?" is a way of asking, "Can you solve the algebra problems you could solve in high school?" "Do you remember where you parked the car?" means,

"Can you find the car?" The corresponding physiological changes are certainly important, but they are the subject matter for a different text.

Not all deterioration in learned behavior following a retention interval is due to forgetting. If a dog is trained to jump through hoops when it is one year old and is retested after 12 years without practice, the deterioration in performance may have more to do with arthritic joints than with forgetting. Similarly, a person who learns to recite the alphabet may lose that ability as a result of a stroke. For our purposes, then, deteriorations in performance due to aging, injury, or disease do not qualify as forgetting.

You can see that forgetting is not as simple a topic as it seems. It is further complicated by the fact that it is typically incomplete. An individual's performance following a retention interval may be abysmal, yet some learning lingers. You might, for example, have learned the name of the capital of Montana, but now find you have no idea what it is, or even the first letter of the name or how many syllables the word has. Yet, though your "mind is blank," it is certain that the forgetting is not complete. Thus, there are degrees of forgetting. There are several ways that these degrees of forgetting can be measured, and we will consider some of them next.

 QUERY 1:   Forgetting is the deterioration in performance following _____.

CAPSULE **REVIEW**   In this text forgetting is defined as the deterioration of learned behavior following a retention interval. It often involves a decrease in the probability of a behavior, but it can also mean an increase in probability. Today, some researchers dismiss the idea of deterioration and argue that forgetting means that behavior has changed because of changes in the environment.

## A TAXONOMY OF KNOWLEDGE

Researchers who accept the storage metaphor of learning devote a good deal of time to identifying the kinds of memories that get cached. Here are some of the more common types of memories proposed:

**Declarative** memories involve things that can be expressed, usually in words but sometimes in pictures and gestures. The philosopher Gilbert Ryle (1949) called such knowledge *knowing that.* You know that biology is the study of living things, that there are 365 days in a year, that an elephant is bigger than a flea. You also know that your name is not Monty Python, that the earth is not flat, and that Mickey Mouse is not a real mouse. Declarative memories are said to be records of *explicit knowledge.*

Cognitive psychologist Endel Tulving (1972) suggested that declarative memories can be subdivided into semantic and episodic memories. He defined **semantic memory** as "knowledge of the world," and **episodic memory** as our memory for personally

*(Continued)*

experienced events. Episodic memories are sometimes called **autobiographical** or **event memories** (Tulving, 1983).

**Nondeclarative memories** are the records of learning that cannot be expressed. With declarative knowledge, you know *that* you know something; with nondeclarative knowledge you know, but you do not know that you know. Or, at least, you cannot express what you know. Nondeclarative memories are said to be records of *implicit knowledge* (Roediger, 1990; Schacter, 1987).

There are, according to some memory experts, various kinds of nondeclarative memories. Perhaps the most important is **procedural** memory (Tulving, 1985). As the name implies, procedural memory is memory for procedures. Gilbert Ryle (1949) called such knowledge *knowing how*. You know how to walk, how to cut your food with a knife and fork, how to read and write, how to do long division, how to peel a banana. The defining characteristic of procedural knowledge is that you can perform some procedure. It isn't your knowledge *about* the procedure (that's explicit knowledge); it is your ability to *perform* the procedure.

This classification of memories is widely accepted among memory researchers. Interestingly, it is as much a taxonomy of knowledge—of the kinds of things we learn—as it is a classification of stored experiences.

# MEASURING FORGETTING

In measuring forgetting, researchers test in various ways for evidence that the learned behavior has changed following a retention interval.

In **free recall,** the individual is given the opportunity to perform a previously learned behavior. An example is the student who is required to learn a poem by heart and then is asked to recite it again after a period of time. Or you might have someone learn a finger maze (a small maze that is "run" with a finger or stylus) and then have him run the maze after a period without practice. If the performance takes longer or there are more errors, forgetting has occurred.

The free recall method can also be used to study animal forgetting. A pigeon may learn to peck a disc for food. After training, the bird is removed from the experimental chamber and returned to its home cage. A month passes, during which time the bird has no opportunity to obtain food by pecking on a disc, and then the bird is returned to the training cage. If it pecks the disc just as it did in the last training session, little or no forgetting has occurred.

Although free recall is what most of us think of when we think of measuring forgetting, it is a rather crude yardstick. The student who cannot recall a French word he studied earlier has not necessarily forgotten everything about the missing word. He may be able to say that the word has three syllables, that the emphasis is on the middle syllable, that the word starts with the letter *f*, that it means window. Clearly the effects of the learning experience have not been entirely lost, but the free recall method does not recognize this fact.

A variation of the free recall technique is sometimes used to get at these more subtle remnants of learning. Known as **prompted** or **cued recall**, it consists of presenting hints, or prompts, to increase the likelihood that the behavior will be produced. The prompts are stimuli that were not present during training. A person who has studied a list of French words, for example, may be given a list of anagrams of the words; the participant's task would then be to unscramble the letters. Failure to do so correctly indicates forgetting. It's also possible to provide a series of prompts and measure the degree of forgetting by the number of prompts required to produce the behavior. You might, for instance, give a person the first letter of a French word learned earlier. If she does not answer correctly, you provide the second letter. If that does not prompt the correct word, you provide the third letter, and so on until the word is recalled.

Animal forgetting can also be studied with prompted recall. A chimp will learn to get fruit from a vending machine by inserting tokens into a slot (Cowles, 1937). If it fails to do so after a retention interval, we might prompt the behavior by offering the chimp a token. If the animal uses it correctly, then the effects of the previous learning experience have not been completely lost.

The **relearning method** measures forgetting in terms of the amount of training required to reach the previous level of performance. There is usually a savings compared to the original training program, so this is also called the **savings method.** Hermann Ebbinghaus (1885), the German psychologist who conducted the first experiments on forgetting, used the relearning method. He memorized lists of nonsense syllables, such as ZAK, KYL, and BOF, until he could produce the list twice without error. Then, after a retention interval, he relearned the list. If it took fewer trials to learn the list the second time, this savings provided a measure of forgetting. The greater the savings, the less the forgetting.

Relearning can be used to study forgetting in animals. If a rat takes 30 trials to learn to run a maze without errors, and requires 20 trials to reach that same criterion after a retention interval, there has been a savings of 10 trials. If another rat has a savings of 15 trials, this second rat has forgotten less.

**② QUERY 2:** The relearning method is also called the _____ method.

Another way of measuring forgetting is called **recognition.** In this case, the participant has only to identify the material previously learned. Typically this is done by presenting the participant with the original learning materials as well as some new material, sometimes called distractors. A person might be shown a list of Navajo words and asked to memorize them. Later the person is shown a list of words and asked to say which ones were on the list studied earlier. Thus, the person is asked to recognize words seen before. Some people might say this example looks like prompted recall since the Navajo words are there on the list, but the words were seen during the learning session so they are not additional hints. The words that were not part of training are not prompts either; they are distractors. The most familiar example of the recognition method is the multiple-choice test, although not all multiple-choice items involve simply recognizing the correct answer.

Another kind of recognition procedure is often used to study forgetting in animals, particularly pigeons. The procedure is called **delayed matching to sample (DMTS)** (Blough, 1959; D'Amato, 1973). DMTS is similar to the matching to sample procedure introduced in Chapter 11, except that the animal is prevented from performing following presentation of the sample—the stimulus to be "matched." In a typical experiment, a pigeon is presented with a row of three discs. The middle disc is illuminated for a brief period by either a yellow or a blue light. After this, the two discs on either side are illuminated, one with a yellow light, the other with a blue one. If the bird pecks the disc that matches the sample (the middle disc), it receives food. Once the bird has learned to match the sample, the experimenter introduces a delay between the offset of the sample and the illumination of the two alternative discs. This is the retention interval. Failure to peck the matching disc is forgetting. DMTS can, of course, be used to measure forgetting in humans, but it is more often used in animal research.

Another measure of forgetting that is often used with animals is the **extinction method.** In Skinner's study of forgetting, the birds learned to press a disc when it was illuminated. To test for forgetting, Skinner put this behavior on extinction after a retention interval. When extinction proceeds more rapidly than it would have immediately after training, forgetting has occurred. Note that extinction is not synonymous with forgetting; in fact, it is quite different. In extinction, a behavior is not reinforced, and the person or animal learns not to perform it. In forgetting, the behavior is not performed, often because there is no opportunity to perform it.

Forgetting may also be measured as a flattening of a generalization gradient, a method sometimes called **gradient degradation.** To the extent that training establishes stimulus control, any decline in the steepness of the generalization gradient indicates forgetting. For example, a pigeon may be trained to peck a disc that is a medium yellow. If, immediately after training, the bird is tested with discs that vary from dark yellow to very pale yellow, we would expect to see a steep generalization gradient, with the highest rate of pecking at the disc when it is medium yellow. If the bird is again tested a month later, it might have a greater tendency to peck discs that are lighter or darker than the training disc. This will yield a flatter generalization gradient, a measure of forgetting (Perkins & Weyant, 1958; Thomas, 1981; Thomas & Burr, 1969).

The procedures described here are the most common ways of measuring forgetting. These and other methods have allowed researchers to tackle the problem of identifying the sources of forgetting, our next topic.

CAPSULE **REVIEW**   Forgetting may be measured in various ways, including free recall, prompted recall, recognition, delayed matching to sample, relearning, and extinction. There are other ways of measuring forgetting, mainly variations on the methods just described. They make the study of forgetting and its causes possible.

## SOURCES OF FORGETTING

A famous musician once said that if he went without practicing the piano for one day, only he knew it; if he skipped two days, only he and his tutor knew it; if he skipped three days, everyone knew it. He was talking about forgetting. He recognized that even after mastering a skill at a very high level, that mastery deteriorates if the skill is neglected. But why? Why do we forget anything?

*In a previous edition I identified the musician mentioned here as Chopin, but then I received emails saying it wasn't Chopin, it was Louis Armstrong or Igor Stravinsky or Ringo Starr or Fats Waller or somebody else, so I now say vaguely, "a famous musician." (But it was really Chopin.)*

Very likely the musician believed that the passage of time since his last practice session caused forgetting. This is what most people think: The neurological "record" of learning breaks down or decays, like a rotting tomato, with the passage of time. It can't be denied that there is a strong relationship between the length of the retention interval and forgetting. Ebbinghaus (1885) found, for instance, that it took him longer to relearn lists of nonsense syllables after a long retention interval than after a short one. More carefully designed research with animals has shown the same thing. Robert M. Gagné (1941) trained rats to run down an alley to find food. After the training, Gagné tested the rats using the relearning method. Some rats relearned after an interval of 3 days, others after 7 days, 14 days, and 28 days. The results showed clearly that the longer the interval between training and relearning, the greater the forgetting (see Figure 12-1).

In another study, Henry Gleitman and J. W. Bernheim (1963) trained rats to press a lever on an FI schedule and then removed the animals from the training cage for either 24 hours or 24 days. The cumulative records from

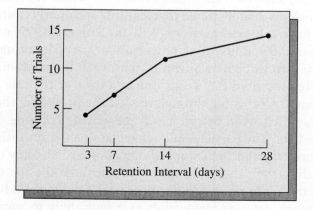

**Figure 12-1**  *Retention interval and forgetting. Average number of trials required to relearn a response increased with the length of the retention interval. (After Gagné, 1941.)*

these sessions showed that there was less of the scalloping associated with FI schedules (see Chapter 7) after the longer interval. After a period of 24 hours, rats were likely to pause following reinforcement; after a period of 24 days, they continued to press the lever. This failure to pause after reinforcement indicated greater forgetting.

Such studies clearly show that forgetting increases with the passage of time. The question is whether the passage of time *causes* the forgetting. John McGeoch (1932) argued that it does not. Time cannot explain forgetting, McGeoch said, because time itself is not an event. Time is not something that occurs but rather an invention for talking about the occurrence of events. An hour, for example, is 1/24 of earth's rotation on its axis; a week is seven complete rotations of the planet; a year is one complete revolution of earth around the sun, and so on. Time itself is not an event and can therefore not be said to cause other events.

Thus, the image on a piece of film fades with time, but it is the action of sunlight, not time, that causes the fading. People develop illnesses over time, but it is bacteria and viruses and toxins that cause disease, not time. Intellectual skills decline as people get old, but it is mini-strokes, the accumulation of neurotoxins, arteriosclerosis, and the like that cause the decline, not time. Learning occurs in time, but it is certain kinds of experiences, not time, that change behavior. Likewise, forgetting occurs in time, but time does not cause it. "Time, in and of itself," wrote McGeoch, "does nothing" (p. 359).

To explain forgetting, then, we must identify the events that account for its occurrence. We will now turn our attention to some of the more important of those events.

## Degree of Learning

The better something is learned, the more slowly it is forgotten. Ebbinghaus (1885) demonstrated this long ago. He found a systematic correlation between the number of learning trials and the amount of forgetting. When he practiced a list eight times, for example, the next day he could recall very little; when he practiced a list 64 times, the next day his recall was nearly perfect.

Ebbinghaus demonstrated that learning apparently continues even after we seem to have achieved mastery. William Krueger (1929) performed a famous study that showed just how powerful such **overlearning** can be. He asked adults to learn three lists of words, with each list containing 12 one-syllable nouns. He presented the words one at a time at the rate of one word every two seconds. After going through the list the first time, the participant's task was to say each word before it was presented. Training differed for each of the three lists. The participants worked at one list until they produced all 12 words correctly and then stopped. On another list, they continued working beyond this level; this time they went through the list half again as many times as it took to reach one errorless trial. On the third list, the participants went through twice as many trials as it took them to learn the list. Suppose, for example, that a given participant took 14 trials to get all 12 words correct on each of the three lists. On one of the lists, he would be allowed to quit (zero

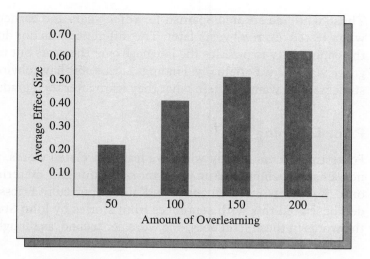

***Figure 12-2*** *Benefits of overlearning. Average effect sizes from numerous studies expressed in Z scores; the higher the score, the better the recall. (Compiled from data in Driskell et al., 1992, Table 3, p. 619)*

overlearning); on another he would do seven more trials (50% overlearning); and on the third he would do another 14 trials (100% overlearning). After this training, Krueger had his participants relearn the lists after a retention interval 1, 2, 4, 7, 14, or 28 days. The results clearly showed that the greater the amount of overlearning, the less forgetting. Other research confirms that overlearning reduces forgetting (Cascio, 1991; Schendel & Hagman, 1982; Underwood, 1957; for a review, see Driskell, Willis, & Copper, 1992; see Figure 12-2), though it is not without limitations (Driskell, Willis, & Copper, 1992).

Ebbinghaus and Krueger measured the degree of learning in terms of the number of practice trials. In recent years, some researchers have measured degree of learning in terms of the number of correct responses per minute. This measure is referred to as fluency (Binder, Haughton, & Van Eyk, 1990; see Chapter 2). Suppose two students are learning the English synonyms for a list of German words. They might do this by going through a series of flash cards, turning each card over as they go to see whether each answer is correct. Suppose that after ten trials, both students can go through a stack of 20 cards without error in 1 minute. This is their degree of fluency. One student stops at this point, while the other continues practicing until she can go through those 20 cards in 30 seconds without error. Her rate of fluency (40 correct per minute) is now twice that of her classmate. There is evidence that higher rates of fluency produce lower rates of forgetting (Johnson & Layng, 1992).

The benefits of overlearning may endure well beyond the final exam. Harry Bahrick (1984) found that a good indication of how well a person remembered Spanish 20, 30, or even 50 years after studying it in high school was how thoroughly he or she had learned it. People who had studied Spanish for only a year and earned a grade of C remembered little of what they once knew.

*Fluency is typically used as a measure of learning, but a decline in fluency can also serve as a measure of forgetting.*

Those who had studied Spanish for three years and earned A's did very well when tested, even 50 years later. The difference was not due to differences in the opportunity to practice the language over the years but to how well the language was learned originally. Findings of this sort have obvious implications for students who want to retain what they learn after their graduation ceremony.

## Prior Learning

Forgetting occurs rapidly when we learn unrelated words, random digits, and nonsense syllables. Fortunately, more meaningful material is easier to hold onto. K. Anders Ericsson and John Karat (reported in Ericsson & Chase, 1982) demonstrated this with sentences from stories by John Steinbeck. They read the words in these sentences, one word per second, as though they were reading

### THE MAN WHO COULDN'T FORGET

One day, around 1920, a young man named S. V. Shereshevski walked into the office of the now famous Russian neuropsychologist Aleksandr Luria. He had come to have his memory tested.

Testing a person's memory is ordinarily one of the easier tasks a neuropsychologist performs. But in the case of S, as Luria called him, it was quite difficult. Luria read off long strings of words or numbers, only to have S recite them with ease, as though he were reading over Luria's shoulder. Even lists of 70 items caused no problem, and S would repeat them without error as presented or, if Luria wished, in reverse order. And S could still repeat what he had learned a day later, a week later, a month later, a year later—even, it turned out, 15 or more years later; the man never seemed to forget.

Luria tried to discover how S accomplished his amazing feats. He found that S used a combination of mnemonic techniques. But he also experienced synesthesia, a synthesis of different senses. A sound, for example, may produce an experience of light, color, taste, odor, and touch. For S, a rainbow was not merely an array of colors, it was a shower of sensations. These experiences evidently helped make every experience memorable.

Students who hear of S's talent are sure to envy him. For him, there was no need to spend hours struggling to learn formulas, historical dates and events, passages of poetry, the periodic table, or the principles of learning. All such material could be learned with ease and recalled years later as if reading from an invisible book.

Yet the story of S is a rather sad one. It is sad, not in spite of his extraordinary talent, but in large measure because of it. You see, S's talent so preoccupied him that it interfered with his ability to do ordinary things. Sometimes S would interrupt a story Luria was telling. "This is too much," he would say. "Each word calls up images; they collide with one another, and the result is chaos. I can't make anything out of this" (Luria, 1968, p. 65). The least little thing could trigger a whole series of experiences, along with all sorts of sensations.

Most people struggle to remember, but S never stopped remembering. For him, the problem was not how to remember, but how to forget.

digits or nonsense syllables. Sometimes the words were in their correct order, sometimes the words were presented randomly. Not surprisingly, the original sentences were recalled far better than the same words in scrambled order. Most people could recall only about six words correctly when the words were in scrambled order. But people could recall complete sentences of 12 or 14 words when presented in their Steinbeckian splendor. Two of the 20 participants even recalled this 28-word sentence: "She brushed a cloud of hair out of her eyes with the back of her glove and left a smudge of earth on her cheek in doing it."

To say that the rate of forgetting varies with the meaningfulness of the material learned raises a question: What determines whether something is meaningful? We may get an idea by asking ourselves what would happen if we repeated the Ericsson and Karat study using sentences in a language the participants did not understand. It is likely that in this case there would be little difference in recall between the original sentences and a random arrangement of words. Thus, when people speak of the meaningfulness of what is learned, they are really talking about the importance of prior learning.

We can see the benefit of previous learning in studies of forgetting and expertise. In one study, Adriaan de Groot (1966) arranged pieces on a chessboard as though a game were in progress. He allowed chess players to study the boards for five seconds and then asked them to reproduce the arrangement of pieces on a cleared board. Some of de Groot's participants were chess masters, while others were members of a chess club. When he compared the two kinds of players, he found that the chess masters were right 90% of the time; club players were right only 40% of the time.

De Groot's data argue for the influence of previous learning on forgetting. But there is another possibility: Perhaps chess masters simply forget less than other people. To test this hypothesis, William Chase and Herbert Simon (1973) arranged chess pieces on the board in a random fashion and then showed it to chess masters and ordinary players. If the chess masters had fantastic ability to recall, the arrangement of pieces would make no difference; the experts would still come out on top. But Chase and Simon found that the chess masters' superb recall disappeared. In fact, under these conditions, they could recall no better than ordinary players. Their spectacular memories, it turns out, apply only when the chess pieces are placed on the board in "patterns that have become familiar with years of practice" (Ericsson & Chase, 1982, p. 608). Other studies show that past learning plays an important role in recall for contract bridge (Charness, 1979), circuit diagrams (Egan & Schwartz, 1979), and architectural drawings (Akin, 1983).

It is clear, then, that previous learning can reduce forgetting. Under some circumstances, however, previous learning can interfere with recall, a phenomenon called **proactive interference.**

Proactive interference is often studied in people by means of **paired associate learning,** a technique invented by Mary Calkins near the end of the 19th century (Calkins, 1894, 1896; see Madigan & O'Hara, 1992). Typically, the object is for the person to learn a list of word pairs, such as *hungry-beautiful,* so that when given the first word (*hungry*), the participant produces the second (*beautiful*). Usually, the researcher repeatedly presents

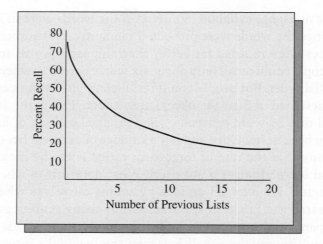

**Figure 12-3**   *Interference and forgetting. Underwood plotted data from a number of studies and found that forgetting increased with the number of previously learned lists. (After Underwood, 1957.)*

the participant with the first word in each pair, asks for the word that goes with it, and then presents the correct word. Typically in these studies all participants learn an A-C list (e.g., *hungry-beautiful*), but some participants first learn an A-B list (e.g., *hungry-fortunate*). Then, after a period of time without practice, all participants try to recall the A-C list. These studies reliably show that learning the A-B list interferes with recall of items later learned on the A-C list. Moreover, the more lists one learns before the test list, the more interference there will be (Underwood, 1957; see Figure 12-3).

 **QUERY 3:**   What sort of learning procedure (Pavlovian, operant, observational) is paired

associate learning?

Interference from previous learning accounts for forgetting in more complicated situations than paired associate learning. Consider, for example, the findings of a classic study by the famous British psychologist, Sir Frederick Bartlett (1932). He had people read a Native American folktale called *The War of the Ghosts*. Although the story runs well under 400 words, it is, by contemporary Western standards, disjointed and confusing. Bartlett had people read the story through twice and then, 15 minutes later, reproduce the story as accurately as they could. Bartlett also had the participants recall the story on other occasions over the coming weeks and months "as opportunity offered." When Bartlett examined the successive recollections, he found that the story became simpler, more coherent, and more modern. This finding can be understood partly in terms of proactive interference: Previous learning about how stories are constructed interfered with recalling a different sort of story.

Social psychologists Jerome Levine and Gardner Murphy (1943) studied the effects of proactive interference in a different way. They had college students read a passage and then, 15 minutes later, reproduce it as accurately as possible. The students then read a second passage and, 15 minutes later, tried to reproduce it. The students read and attempted to reproduce the two passages each week for four weeks. Both passages were on what was then a very controversial topic: communism. One of the passages expressed anticommunist sentiments; the other was favorable to communism. Some of the students were strongly disposed toward communism while others were strongly opposed to it. The researchers were interested in whether these personal inclinations would affect recollection.

They did. The results clearly showed that students who were procommunist forgot more of the anticommunist passage, while students who were anticommunist forgot more of the procommunist passage. Such findings are usually interpreted in terms of the effects of attitude or belief on forgetting, but since no one is born with particular inclinations concerning communism (or capitalism, fascism, democracy, homosexuality, or other topics), we have to assume that such views are learned. Thus, studies showing that attitudes affect recall are really studies of proactive interference.

Prior learning can have a profound effect on recall; so, we shall now see, can subsequent learning.

## Subsequent Learning

In a classic study by John Jenkins and Karl Dallenbach (1924), two college students learned lists of ten nonsense syllables. The researchers tested the students for forgetting after one, two, four, or eight hours of either sleep or wakefulness. The results showed that they forgot less after a period of sleep than after a similar interval of activity (see Figure 12-4; see also Gaias, Lucas, & Born, 2006).

Other studies showed that periods of inactivity produce less forgetting than comparable periods of activity. In one study, immobilized cockroaches forgot less than those allowed to move about (Minami & Dallenbach, 1946). These and similar studies suggest that forgetting is partly due to subsequent learning. As Jenkins and Dallenbach (1924) put it, forgetting is "a matter of interference, inhibition, or obliteration of the old by the new" (p. 612). Or, as another psychologist phrases it, "We forget because we keep on learning" (Gleitman, 1971, p. 20).

When what we learn increases forgetting of previous learning, the phenomenon is called **retroactive interference**. Like proactive interference, retroactive interference is often studied by having people learn two or more lists of paired associates. First, the A-B list is learned to a given criterion. Then, some participants learn an A-C list. After a period of time without practice, all participants try to recall the A-B list. These studies show that learning the A-C list interferes with recall of items learned earlier on the A-B list.

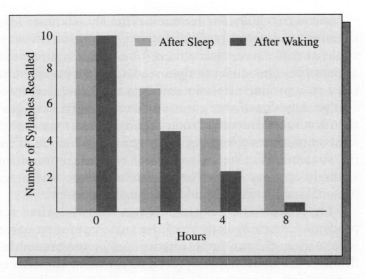

**Figure 12-4**  *Forgetting and sleep. Number of syllables recalled by one student after intervals of sleep and waking. (Compiled from data in Jenkins and Dallenbach, 1924.)*

Learning the A-C pair, *hungry-virtuous*, for example, results in errors on the A-B pair, *hungry-beautiful*.

Benton Underwood and his colleagues did a number of experiments with paired associates to study the interference effects of learning. In one experiment, he and Leland Thune (Thune & Underwood, 1943) had college students learn lists of ten paired associates made up of adjectives. Each participant learned an A-B list, then relearned the list after a 20-minute delay. During the delay period, some students just rested, while others had from 2 to 20 trials on an A-C list. Notice that the time lapse was the same for all participants; the difference was in the learning that took place during the retention interval. The results showed that learning the A-C list interfered with recall of the A-B list. Moreover, the better the A-C list was learned, the more it interfered with recall of the A-B list.

**QUERY 4:**  Thune and Underwood used the _____ method of studying

forgetting.

You experience much the same thing in your everyday life when, for example, you find that after learning your new license plate number, you can no longer recall the old one. Similarly, teachers often find it difficult to remember the names of previous students after learning the names of new students. And when an accountant learns new tax regulations, the old regulations slip away. New learning often pushes out old learning.

Interference from subsequent and prior learning is an important factor in forgetting. A related factor is the context in which learning and recall occur.

## Changes in Context

**Context** refers to stimuli present during learning that are not directly relevant to what is learned (Baddeley, 1982; McGeoch, 1932). For example, you are reading this text in a particular environment, and most of the stimuli that make up that environment (e.g., the color of the walls, the height of the ceiling, the hardness of the seat you are sitting on, the music or other sounds in the background, the presence of people) are largely irrelevant to what you learn from your reading. They and other stimuli constitute the context in which you are learning.

McGeoch (1932) suggested that changes in the context in which learning occurs affects forgetting. The idea is that learning inevitably occurs within a particular context—that is, in the presence of a given pattern of stimuli. These stimuli then act as cues that evoke the behavior learned in that context. If, later on, these cues are absent, performance suffers. This is sometimes called **cue-dependent forgetting** since it is due to the absence of stimuli that were present during learning (Tulving, 1974). Consider the case of a person who learns a list of words in the morning and then is tested on those words in the afternoon. Both sessions occur in a research cubicle with a chair, a table, and a window; the walls are painted a uniform off-white, and there are no decorations. The two environments seem identical, but wait: In the morning the window looked out on a foggy landscape, but by afternoon the sun was shining; the researcher (who had not yet had his morning coffee) was rather abrupt and sour in the morning, but by afternoon he was all smiles; in the morning, the heating system blew warm air on the participant from a heat vent; by afternoon it was warm enough that the heat was off. Can such insignificant differences in the two situations affect forgetting?

A number of experiments suggest that they can, and routinely do. In one study Joel Greenspoon and R. Ranyard (1957) had students learn lists of words under two different conditions, standing up or sitting down. After this, some students tried remembering the lists while standing up, others while sitting down. The results showed that students performed better when tested under conditions similar to those under which they had learned: Those who had learned the lists standing up remembered them better when standing up; those who had learned the lists while sitting down remembered them better while sitting down.

Duncan Godden and Alan Baddeley (1975) performed another imaginative study on the effects of context. In this case, some adults learned a list of words on dry land; others learned the list under water! After training, the experimenters tested some participants under the same conditions under which they learned, and others under the opposite conditions. For example, some students who learned words on dry land tried to recall those words under water. The results showed that recall suffered when the testing situation was different from the training situation.

Carolyn Rovee-Collier of Rutgers University and her colleagues have conducted a number of fascinating experiments on the role of context in infant forgetting. You may recall from Chapter 5 that the researchers tie one end of a ribbon or cord to a baby's foot and the other end to a mobile suspended above the baby's crib. When the baby moves the foot connected to the mobile, the mobile moves. Exerting control over the environment is a powerful reinforcer, even for infants, so the frequency of kicking rises until the baby is kicking like a soccer player and the mobile is bouncing around like a ship in heavy seas. (I am exaggerating slightly, of course.) This "training" is followed by a retention interval and then the baby is put back into the crib and researchers monitor the level of kicking. Sometimes a baby is tested under the same conditions as the training; in others, some aspect of the baby's environment (e.g., a feature of the crib or the mobile) is altered to determine the effects of context.

In one experiment (Rovee-Collier, Griesler, & Early, 1985) the crib included a distinctive bumper, a pad that lined the crib's rails. One week after training, the researchers tested the 3-month-old infants under the same circumstances except that in some cases the bumper was different. The result was that when the bumper was the same as in training, the infant resumed kicking as if there had been no retention interval, but when the bumper was different the baby did not kick. The bumper had nothing to do with the contingency between kicking and the mobile, yet the babies did not kick when the bumper was different. There was, in other words, no sign of forgetting when the context was the same, and no evidence of learning when the context was different!

An experiment by Dianne Borovsky and Rovee-Collier (1990) got similar results with 6-month-old infants after a two-week retention interval. In this study, the babies underwent mobile training and testing in their own playpen, in a playpen with a nylon mesh, or in the mesh playpen draped with a cloth liner. The only difference between testing and training conditions was that for some babies the mobile was different from the one used during training. The researchers measured retention as a ratio of the amount of kicking at two weeks compared to the amount at the end of training. Thus, a score of 100% would indicate that there was no change in the rate of kicking. The results showed that being trained in different playpens made no difference, but being tested with a different mobile made a substantial difference (see Figure 12-5).

Other researchers have followed Rovee-Collier's lead and replicated her findings. In a study by Melissa Schroers, Joyce Prigot, and Jeffrey Fagen (2007), 3-month-old infants learned to move a mobile in the presence of either a coconut or cherry fragrance. One or five days after training, the researchers tested the babies in the presence of the same fragrance that was present during training, the other fragrance, or no fragrance at all. There was little evidence of forgetting when the fragrance was the same, and no evidence of learning when there was no fragrance or the fragrance was different.

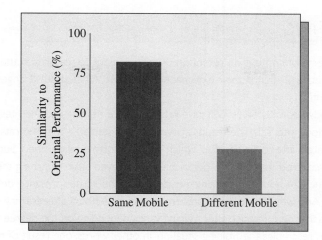

**Figure 12-5** *Context and recall in infants. Babies underwent mobile kicking training and testing in one of three kinds of playpens. Those tested with a different mobile than used in training (light bar) showed a marked decline in the rate of kicking. (Adapted from Figure 1 in "Contextual Constraints on Memory Retrieval at Six Months," by D. Borovsky and C. Rovee–Collier, Child Development, 1990, 61, pp.1569–1583.)*

The effects of changes in context varies with infant age (Borovsky & Rovee-Collier, 1990; Herbert & Hayne, 2000; Rovee-Collier & Cuevas, 2006); nevertheless, it is clear that it is a powerful influence even in the performance of babies.

The influence of context on recall can be illustrated from everyday experience. For instance, you may know the name of the person who sits next to you in your learning class, yet find you are unable to think of it when you run into him in a shopping mall. You may learn a speech to perfection at home, only to stumble over it when in front of an audience. And most of us have had the experience of studying until we have the material ""down pat"" and then ""draw a blank"" when taking a test in the classroom.

Where does all this research on the role of context in forgetting take us? Back to the definition of forgetting. You will recall (I hope) that some psychologists argue that there is no such thing as forgetting (see *Defining Forgetting*, above). The influence that learning experiences have on our future behavior depends in part on the similarity of the situation during learning and those future situations. If the two situations are identical, we are likely to behave in much the same way; if the two situations are markedly different, we will behave differently. Thus, there is a case to be made for the view that there is no such thing as forgetting, that our behavior is simply modified by changes in our environment. In which case, as proposed earlier, what we call forgetting is really learning!

That idea may give you a headache, so let us now turn to a simpler topic, the application of forgetting research to two practical problems.

*Thomas Wolfe's book, You Can't Go Home Again, is partly a recognition of the effects that changes in context have on behavior. You "can't go home" after a long absence because the home that once triggered so many responses in you is no longer there.*

## THE STATE OF LEARNING

Studies on the effects of context on retention usually manipulate features in the animal's or person's surroundings—that is, their external environment. What about changes in their *internal* environment?

In a classic study, Leon Kamin (1957) gave rats avoidance training and then tested their retention after various intervals. The results showed—as expected—that the rats were at their best immediately after training, after which their performance declined. Surprisingly, however, Kamin discovered that the rats' performance improved again, matching their previous best performance 24 hours after training ended. Why should performance deteriorate and then improve? And why should the improvement occur 24 hours after training ended?

We have seen that performance after training varies depending on the degree to which the testing situation resembles the training situation. In other words, one result of training is that the stimuli present during training acquire a certain degree of stimulus control over the behavior. What cues could be available 24 hours after training that are not available, say, 12 hours after training?

The most likely explanation seems to be the physiological state of the individual. Physiological conditions, such as those associated with hunger, fatigue, and alertness, vary in a rhythmic fashion over the course of a day. Twelve hours after training, they may be very different from what they were like during training. After a 24-hour period, however, the animal's physiology may come full circle. This raises the possibility that the physiological state of the organism during learning acquires some degree of stimulus control over the learned behavior. In other words, context can include internal as well as external cues.

This idea is supported by research on the effects of drugs (Overton, 1991). In one study, Donald Overton (1964) gave rats a tranquilizing drug and then taught them to run a simple T-maze. Later, when the effects of the drug had worn off, Overton tested the rats and found that they appeared to have forgotten their earlier learning. There is nothing very startling about this; we might easily believe that the drug interfered in some way with the brain's functioning. But Overton took one more step. He tranquilized the rats again and put them back into the maze. This time they performed well! Thus, performance of learned behavior varies with the physiological state during learning and during retention, a phenomenon now called **state-dependent learning** (see also Girden & Culler, 1937; Ho, Richards, & Chute, 1978; Shulz et al., 2000).

Anecdotes abound of people who show state-dependent learning as a result of alcoholic intoxication. A person hides his car keys while sober and then cannot find them after drinking; when he sobers up, he knows right where to look. It appears, then, that the contextual cues that influence performance include the physiological state of the learner, as well as the state of the learner's surroundings.

CAPSULE **REVIEW**  Forgetting increases with the length of the retention interval, but the passage of time is not itself a cause of forgetting. Key influences on forgetting appear to be the amount of learning, retroactive interference, proactive interference, and changes in context, including the physiological state of the learner.

# APPLICATIONS

Research on forgetting has helped us understand both animal and human behavior. We will consider the analysis of eyewitness testimony and some of the things we can all do to reduce forgetting.

### Eyewitness Testimony

Elizabeth Loftus has conducted a number of studies illustrating the malleability of reports about observed events (e.g., Loftus, 1979, 2006). Her work has all sorts of implications for witness interrogation, jury deliberations, and other aspects of our judicial system.

In her best-known work, Loftus and her colleagues showed college students short films of traffic accidents and then asked them questions about what they saw. In a classic experiment (Loftus & Zanni, 1975), students watched a film in which a car makes a right-hand turn into a stream of traffic. The oncoming cars stop suddenly, and there is a five-car collision. After viewing the film, the students filled out a questionnaire about what they saw. One question asked about a broken headlight. For some students, the question was, "Did you see the broken headlight?" For other students, the question was, "Did you see a broken headlight?" The only difference in the question was the article *the* or *a*. The definite article *the* implies that the item was present, whereas the indefinite article *a* implies only that the item might have been present. If I say to you, "Did you see a spaceship?" the implication is that there *might* have been a spaceship. If I say, "Did you see the spaceship?" the implication is that there *was* a spaceship. Loftus found that the answers she got depended on the way questions were phrased. Students were twice as likely to answer "yes" when a question included the definite article than when it included the indefinite article. There was no broken headlight in the film, for example, yet students were far more likely to report seeing it if asked about *the* broken headlight than if asked about *a* broken headlight.

In another of Loftus's studies (Loftus & Palmer, 1974), students watched a film of a traffic accident and then estimated how fast the cars were traveling. Researchers asked some students, "About how fast were the cars going when they hit each other?" For other students, the researchers replaced the word *hit* with *smashed, collided, bumped,* or *contacted*. The estimated speeds varied with the word used in the question, with *contacted* resulting in the lowest speeds and *smashed* producing the highest. Loftus had the students return a week later. Without viewing the film again, they answered more questions about it. The critical question asked whether the students remembered seeing broken glass. In fact, the film showed no broken glass, but students who had been asked earlier about cars smashing together were now twice as likely to report seeing broken glass as were those who had been asked about cars hitting one another.

 **QUERY 5:** Loftus found that use of the word _____ resulted in higher

estimates of car speed than use of the word *hit*.

One thing that helps explain such findings is the participant's reinforcement history. For example, when you are asked, "Do you remember seeing the hat?" the definite article *the* indicates that there was a hat and therefore reporting that you saw a hat might be reinforced. On the other hand, if you are asked, "Do you remember seeing a hat?" the indefinite article *a* makes the existence of a hat less certain and therefore reporting seeing it less likely to be reinforced. Words such as *the* and *a* affect our behavior (our recall) because of our previous experiences with those words. A similar analysis can be applied to the differential effects of words such as *hit* and *smashed*. *Hit* is used when a relatively mild collision occurs, and *smashed* is used when a more severe collision occurs. Apparently this differential learning history means that the words are likely to produce different reports about observed events.

Loftus's research has had an important impact on our legal system. Trial lawyers and some law enforcement officers now know that eyewitness testimony is of questionable value. Gary Wells and Elizabeth Olson (2003) report that more than 100 people convicted of crimes have been exonerated by DNA evidence, and that more than three-fourths of them were convicted at least partly because of erroneous eyewitness testimony. One source of these errors is the lineup procedure used by police to identify suspects, and alternatives to that procedure are now being considered (Wells & Olson, 2003; Wells, Steblay, & Dysart, 2011).

Studies of eyewitness testimony teach us how frail learning can be. Most people would like to reduce their tendency to forget. Let us consider that problem now.

## Learning to Remember

There are, no doubt, genetic differences that affect how well people retain what they learn, but it is clear that the ability to remember is to some extent a learned skill. Can you improve your ability to remember? The answer is yes, but not without effort. Let us consider a few of the more important ways of reducing forgetting.

***Overlearn.*** You saw earlier that there is a strong inverse relationship between the degree of learning and the rate of forgetting (Driskell, Willis, & Copper, 1992; Krueger, 1929; Underwood, 1957). The implication is clear: To forget less, learn more.

Do not merely go through those German flash cards until you get all the words correct one time; keep at it until you reach a rate of fluency of, say, 40 cards a minute (see *Say All Fast . . .*). To give a good speech, continue practicing even after you are satisfied with your performance. To play a sonata brilliantly at the concert, continue practicing after you get through it without errors. To do a good job in a play, go to all the rehearsals and practice your lines until you know them as well as you know your home address. The more thoroughly you learn something, the more slowly you will forget it.

***Practice with Feedback.*** Overlearning is important, but what form should learning take? Some students read a chapter and then reread it repeatedly. Some read their class notes repeatedly. Some go through flash cards by reading one side and then reading the other. These are not optimal forms of studying. What you need to do is *perform* the behavior you want to recall, and get feedback on that performance.

Feedback comes in two basic forms, positive and negative. Positive feedback tells you what you got right, and tends to be reinforcing (e.g., Buzas & Ayllon, 1981; see Figure 12-6); negative feedback tells you what you got wrong and can be demoralizing, but can provide cues about what to do to improve. Practice without feedback is of limited value, particularly in the early stages of learning (Kuo & Hirshman, 1996).

So, if you want to improve your performance, arrange to get feedback. Sometimes you can provide feedback yourself. If you are trying to learn the symbols for the elements (O for oxygen, H for hydrogen, He for helium, etc.), you can create flash cards with the name of the element on one side and the symbol on the other. You read the first card, *oxygen,* and say aloud, *O, then* flip the card. The flip side of the card reveals the correct answer, thereby providing positive or negative feedback about your answer. (Incidentally, instead of saying *O* you might write it, and then flip the card.) If you cannot provide feedback for yourself, arrange to get it from others. This is a potential benefit of studying with another person: One of you, for example, can attempt to recall the features of impressionistic art provided by your instructor while the

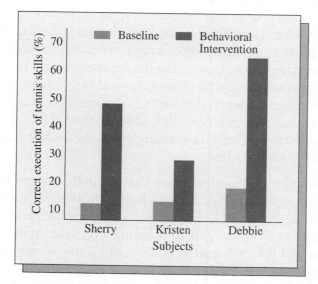

**Figure 12-6** *Tennis skills and feedback. Percentage of correct executions of tennis serves when the coach criticized faulty performance (baseline) and when the coach praised and recognized correct or nearly correct performance. Results for forehand and backhand were similar. (Compiled from data in Buzas and Ayllon, 1981.)*

other checks them off on a list. After one of you has been through the list, you trade places.

***Distribute Practice.*** The overlearning research suggests that the more study and practice sessions, the better. But when should those sessions take place? Many students tend to delay study sessions until shortly before an exam, when they pile up as predicted by FI schedules (see Figures 7-1c and 7-2); this amounts to what is called **massed practice**. A far better procedure is to spread the sessions out over time, called **distributed** or **spaced practice.**

Distributing practice does not mean spending more time learning. Studies comparing massed and distributed practice typically compare the same amount of study time; the difference is whether it is lumped together or spread out. For example, Bahrick and Elizabeth Phelps (1987) had college students study 50 English–Spanish synonyms in seven practice sessions. Some students had all seven sessions on the same day, some had one session a day for seven consecutive days, and some had one session a month for seven months. *Eight years* after their final practice session, the students took a test. Those who had studied once a month recalled nearly twice as many words as those who studied once a day, and those who studied once a day recalled more than those who did all their studying in one day.

How far apart should practice sessions be distributed? That is not yet clear (compare, for example, Bahrick, 1984, and Rovee-Collier, 1995). One potential problem with longer intervals is that there will be more errors and that the errors will interfere with learning, but there is some evidence that this need not be a concern (Pashler, Zarow, & Triplett, 2003). Oddly enough, students tend to think massed practice works better than spaced (Kornell, 2009), but over the long term spaced practice is definitely more effective (Bjork, 1979; Caple, 1996; Cepeda et al., 2006; Dempster, 1988; Ebbinghaus, 1885; Kerfoot et al., 2007; Kornell, 2009).

Students tend to think of study sessions, massed or distributed, as something that takes place during the duration of a course. No one is surprised to learn that a person who plays a musical instrument continues to practice after training ends since this helps maintain what was learned. Continuing to study and practice any skill, including the skill of using learning terms and procedures correctly, is ultimately the only way we can ensure indefinite retention of what we learn.

***Test yourself.*** There is evidence that periodic testing improves retention (Roediger & Karpicke, 2006a; Bjork, Storm, & deWinstanley, 2010; Karpicke & Blunt, 2011). In fact, some evidence suggests that testing can be more effective than studying in reducing forgetting. In one experiment, Henry Roediger and Jeffrey Karpicke (2006b) had some students study a passage for four 5-minute sessions, reading it an average of about 14 times; other students studied the passage for only one 5-minute session and then took three tests on it, reading the passage only a few times. When tested one week later, the students who had taken practice tests remembered almost *four times* as much as those who had spent more time studying.

*The queries, chapter quizzes, and review questions in this text are opportunities for distributed practice.*

***Use Mnemonics.*** A **mnemonic** is any device for aiding recall. Typically, these devices involve learning cues that will later prompt the desired behavior.

One common mnemonic is rhyme. Perhaps the best-known example is the little ditty we all memorize to help us remember the spelling of certain words: "Use i before e, except after c, and when sounding like a, as in *neighbor* and *weigh*." Another is the rhyme that reminds us how many days are in each month: "Thirty days hath September, April, June, and November. . . ." In the musical play *My Fair Lady*, Professor Higgins has Eliza Doolittle learn pronunciation and enunciation by repeating the line "The rain in Spain falls mainly in the plain." If the plains of Spain *do* get most of the country's rain, this bit of rhyme would help us remember that fact.

Some mnemonics combine rhyme with other prompts. For example, the first letter of each word to be learned may be the first letter of a word in the rhyme. Medical students learn the names of the 12 cranial nerves by memorizing the following doggerel:

On Old Olympus's towering top,

a Finn and German

vault and hop.

The first letter of each word provides the first letter of each cranial nerve (optic, otolaryngeal, etc.), and this helps prompt the wanted terms.

Sometimes we can get by with a sentence that does not rhyme. Can't remember the value of pi? British psychologist and memory researcher Alan Baddeley (1976) points out that all you need to do is say, "Pie. I wish I could remember pi." The number of letters in each word gives you the answer to six places: 3.141582.

A similar mnemonic device is the acronym, a set of letters forming a pronounceable set; each letter provides the first letter of a word. NATO, for example, is the North Atlantic Treaty Organization. The colors of the prism in their right order are remembered as Roy G. Biv, for red, orange, yellow, green, blue, indigo, and violet. And it is relatively easy to recall the names of the Great Lakes (Huron, Ontario, Michigan, Erie, and Superior) once you have learned that their first letters spell HOMES. So one thing you can do to aid recall is to create an acronym that will provide prompts.

***Use Context Cues.*** You saw earlier that we remember better when the same stimuli present during learning are present during recall. It follows that we can improve performance by identifying cues that will be present during recall and then learn in the presence of those or similar cues.

Students typically do exactly the opposite: They study in their room, often while lying on a bed and eating a snack. When they take a test on what they have studied, they are not lying on their bed eating a snack; they are in a classroom, seated in a rather uncomfortable chair, in the presence of a number of other students with whom they cannot converse. The two situations, learning and testing, are very different, and these differences in context account for some forgetting. Students find themselves unable to recall facts that they "knew cold" before they walked into the classroom. The clear implication is that students should study under conditions that closely resemble the conditions under which testing will take place. A student studying for a paper-and-pencil exam might even do well to spend some time studying in the classroom where the test will take place or in a similar room.

A less obvious implication of the work on context is that if you want to re-member what you learn well after the final exam, you should study in a variety of situations. Why? Because what you learn is apt to be needed in a wide variety of situations. If you are to be an engineer, the mathematics you study today may be needed at a construction site, on a factory floor, or in an executive's office, not in your dormitory room. If you are to be a historian, the history you study today may be needed not only in classrooms, but also at historical sites, in li-braries, and at meetings of historical societies. Or, to take an example of more immediate relevance, if you are trying to learn principles of learning that will re-duce forgetting, then you should keep in mind that you will need to recall those principles not only where you usually study but anywhere that you are likely to learn. Because what you learn is apt to be needed in many different situations, the best practice may be to study in many different situations: at home, in a classroom, on a bus, in coffee shops, while walking across campus or relaxing on the beach—any place and every place is a good place to learn so long as you are not engaged in a dangerous activity such as driving a car, flying a plane, or defus-ing a bomb.

***Take a Problem-Solving Approach.*** The suggestions made thus far focus on the things you can do during learning to reduce later forgetting. There are also things you can do when you are struggling to recall what you once knew. The essence of this is to take a problem-solving approach to remembering (Barlett, 1932; Palmer, 1991). As Palmer (1991) phrases it, "The behavior of a person asked to recall an incident in the past is the same, except in content, as the behavior of a person asked to solve a problem in his head" (p. 273). He gives the example of solving a mathematical problem: What is the square root of 1764? Chances are you never learned the answer, so you have to do things to figure it out. Remembering sometimes requires the same sort of effort. Palmer gives the example, "What did you have for breakfast three days ago?" Your first response might be, "Three days ago? How could I remember that!" But if you take a prob-lem solving approach, you might come up with the answer. One person replied to Palmer's question like this:

> Let's see . . . today's Monday . . . Sunday . . . Saturday . . . Friday. That was the day I went to Springfield. Hmm. . . . Oh yeah—I just had a glass of orange juice before I left.

Basically what the person is doing is emitting prompts—cues that may evoke behavior related to the solution. Consider the problem of trying to recall someone's name. You might recall things about the person, such as the circumstances under which you met, the nature of conversations you had with him, his occupation, where he works, what others have said about him. You may also recall things about the name itself that will prove helpful: that it is Anglo-Saxon, two syllables, with hard consonants. Perhaps now you recall that the name starts with B, and you say aloud or to yourself, "I think it starts with *Ba. Bah . . . Barns, Barnaby, Baker, Bantry, Battry.* Aha! It's Batman!"

You can also try to prompt a forgotten name by practicing an introduction covertly: "This is Mr. . . ." "I'd like you to meet. . . ." In doing so you create an unpleasant situation from which you can escape only by producing the person's name (Skinner, 1953).

If, during a paper-and-pencil test on computer keyboard commands, you are unable to recall the command to begin an electronic search of a document, try putting your hands on the keyboard and typing the command. The keys may prompt the appropriate action. If a keyboard is not available, it may suffice to pretend that you are at the keyboard. Arrange your hands as you would if the keyboard were present and try typing the wanted command. Closing your eyes may help by blocking out the empty desk in front of you, a scene that provides cues for *other* behavior.

The point is that when the cues that are present are not sufficient to evoke the needed behavior, you can often provide new cues that will prompt the behavior. Take a problem-solving approach and figure out what those cues are.

 **QUERY 6:**   Name three tactics for reducing forgetting.

CAPSULE **REVIEW**   Research on forgetting has important practical implications. It has shown, for example, that how a person describes a witnessed event depends in part on how we ask about the event. This finding has obvious implications for police inquiries, suspect identification procedures, and juries weighing the merits of eyewitness testimony. Education is another area in which forgetting studies have relevance. People can improve their ability to retain what they learn by, for example, overlearning, spacing practice sessions, using mnemonics, and taking a problem-solving approach to remembering.

## SAY ALL FAST MINUTE EACH DAY SHUFFLE

Almost everyone considers flash cards a bit old-fashioned today, but Ogden Lindsley believed that, old-fashioned or not, they work—if they are used properly. How should they be used? Lindsley and Stephen Graf (see Potts, Eshleman, and Cooper, 1993; McGreevy, 1983) answered with an acronym to help you remember: SAFMEDS.

SAFMEDS stands for "Say All Fast Minute Each Day Shuffle." *Say* the answer *before* you turn a flash card over. Go through *All* of the cards, or as many as you can, as *Fast* as you can, in one *Minute.* Do this *Each Day.* After you go through the cards, *Shuffle* them.

*(Continued)*

This use of flash cards is very different from what most students do, and the differences are important. Saying the answer, preferably aloud, ensures that you actually practice the behavior, rather than simply read. The one-minute time limit puts pressure on you to work quickly. It also provides a convenient measure of fluency. Each time you make an error, put that card aside. At the end of a minute, count the number of cards you got right. At first, you may get only 10 correct answers in a minute, but with practice you may get 30, 40, or even more. This means you can easily assess your degree of learning and the likelihood that you will forget. Going through the cards every day is a convenient way of spacing practice. Shuffling the cards precludes clues to answers from the position of the cards.

A lot of students who use flash cards do so in a way that makes the word *flash* silly. They have a word or question on one side, and a paragraph or long list on the other; you cannot go through such cards quickly. If you are learning basic anatomical terms, for example, one side of a card might say *heart chambers* and the other side, *atria & ventricles*. There's lots more to learn about the heart's chambers, but in using flash cards, keep it short. If you want to learn ten things about heart chambers, make ten cards.

Another thing many students fail to do is use the cards in both directions. Don't just go through the cards looking at side A and trying to remember what's on side B. Go through them in A-B order, then in B-A order. If you speak English and are studying Spanish, you need to learn both the Spanish word for *house* and the English word for *casa*.

Flash cards are out of favor with many educators today. Fortunately, this does not prevent them from working.

## A FINAL WORD

The public at large and some psychologists look on forgetting as deterioration in performance caused by the decay of a neurological or mental "snapshot" of an event. Increasingly, learning researchers take a very different view, arguing that forgetting is the deterioration (some would say change) in performance due to experience. Either way, there is no denying that many of the things we can do immediately after a learning experience we cannot do, or cannot do as well, later.

In general, humans and other animals seem to operate on the basis of a simple, practical rule: Keep what you need. If you accept that our capacity for learning is the product of evolution, then you will realize that for hundreds of thousands of years our ability to retain what we learned was important only insofar as it contributed to our survival. Survival depended, for example, on our ability to find our way to the strawberry patch and back, to be wary of bears when picking strawberries, to treat an injury, to make simple tools, to hunt and fish, to discriminate between nourishing and toxic plants, to recognize people and tell friend from foe. Only very recently, in evolutionary terms, has anyone ever asked us to name the months of the year, to conjugate verbs in a foreign language, to name the elements in the periodic table, to describe an event that happened in another country long before we were born, to solve algebra word problems, or to spell *Massachusetts*. None of these or countless other things that we now learn ever played any part in the survival of our species. We are, in other words, not designed by evolution to be the carbon equivalent of computer hard drives. We are living things, not machines.

Admittedly, sometimes the speed with which we forget is demoralizing. A comic (whose name I cannot recall!) suggests that what the typical college student remembers from a one-year course in American history is, "North wore blue; South wore gray." That is an exaggeration, of course, but it is an exaggeration that reveals a basic truth: We *do* forget a great deal of what we learn. So why bother learning? In particular, why spend years in school learning if much of that learning is bound to slip away from us?

Part of the answer is to be found in the realization that to learn is to change. We are, in a very real sense, different people each time we learn something. When college freshmen are told that college will change them, some angrily reject the idea. "I am who I am! College is not going to change me!" But it does. Every learning experience changes you. The changes are typically too small to detect, but they accumulate over time. You looked at yourself in the mirror this morning and saw the same person you saw yesterday—or did you? Look at a photograph of yourself taken five years ago and you are likely to notice a difference. The same is true of learning experiences: The changes are usually small, but they accumulate. The white, middle-class student who reads *The Autobiography of Malcolm X* may recall little about the book, or about Malcolm X, years later. But despite all the student has forgotten, she may behave differently toward African Americans as a result of having read the book. And if years from now you find you remember very little of what you now know about learning, you may still view behavior differently from the way you did before you studied learning.

We are bound to forget a great deal of what we learn, but that learning still leaves its mark on us. That is a point I hope you will *not* forget.

## RECOMMENDED **READING**

1. Ebbinghaus, H. (1885/1964). *Memory* (H. A. Ruger & C. E. Bussenius, Trans.). New York: Dover.

   Probably the first true experimental research on forgetting, this is the origin of the nonsense syllable and the famous "forgetting curve."

2. Ericsson, K. A., & Chase, W. G. (1982). Exceptional memory. *American Scientist, 70,* 607–615.

   The authors review cases of extraordinary memory and then argue that such feats are well within the range of ordinary people.

3. Loftus, E. (2003). Our changeable memories: Legal and practical implications. *Nature Reviews: Neuroscience, 4,* 231–234.

4. Lorayne, H., & Lucas, J. (2000). *The memory book: The classic guide to improving your memory at work, at school, and at play.* New York: Ballantine.

   There are many popular memory books. This one makes standard recommendations for reducing forgetting in a more entertaining style than most.

In this brief article, Loftus talks about the ways that experience changes our recollections of events, including events that never happened, and the implications of this for our legal system. Any student contemplating a career in law enforcement or legal work should read this article.

5. Luria, A. (1968). *The mind of a mnemonist*. New York: Avon.

Luria offers a fascinating look at someone whose compulsive use of mnemonics interfered with his ability to enjoy life.

# REVIEW **QUESTIONS**

1. Define the following terms:

| | |
|---|---|
| autobiographical, or event, memory | nondeclarative memory |
| context | overlearning |
| cue-dependent forgetting | massed practice |
| declarative memory | paired associate learning |
| delayed matching to sample | proactive interference |
| distributed practice | procedural memory |
| episodic memory | prompted, or cued, recall |
| extinction method | recognition |
| fluency | relearning method |
| forgetting | retention interval |
| free recall | retroactive interference |
| gradient degradation | SAFMEDS |
| massed practice | savings method |
| mnemonic | state-dependent learning |

2. Why do some teachers ask their students to take the same seat at each class meeting, particularly at the beginning of the year?

3. How could you use fluency to measure forgetting?

4. Hilda and Ethel work together to train a rat to press a lever. When they are satisfied that the behavior has been well learned, Hilda suggests that they remove the lever from the cage for a while and then reinstall it to see what happens. Ethel proposes that they leave the lever in place but disconnect the feeding mechanism. Then they begin to wonder whether they would be studying different phenomena or the same thing. What do you think?

5. In paired associate learning, what is the reinforcer?

6. The amount of forgetting varies directly with the length of the retention interval. Why, then, is time not a cause of forgetting?

7. What is wrong with defining *forgetting* as the loss of behavior?

8. What is the defining difference between free recall and prompted recall?

9. Some psychologists maintain that spontaneous recovery (Chapters 3 and 7) is a form of forgetting. Explain this.

10. What kinds of prompts could you use to remember the name of the sea captain in *Moby Dick*?

## PRACTICE **QUIZ**

1. The period between training and testing for forgetting is called the _____ interval.

2. _____ knowledge is said to be *implicit* because it cannot be expressed.

3. In his studies of nonsense syllables, Ebbinghaus used the _____ method.

4. DMTS stands for _____.

5. John McGeoch argued that _____ does *not* cause forgetting.

6. Practicing a skill even after it is performed without errors is an example of _____.

7. When experiences after training interfere with performance, the effect is called _____ interference.

8. Some researchers argue that forgetting is due to a failure of _____ control.

9. The research of Elizabeth Loftus and her colleagues raises doubts about the trustworthiness of _____ testimony.

10. The Russian neuropsychologist Aleksandr Luria studied the man who could not seem to _____.

## QUERY **ANSWERS**

Query 1. Forgetting is the deterioration in performance following *a period without practice.*

Query 2. The relearning method is also called the *savings* method.

Query 3. Paired associate learning is probably best viewed as an operant procedure. A behavior is followed by either a reinforcing or punishing consequence (the correct word).

Query 4. Thune and Underwood used the *relearning/savings* method of studying forgetting.

Query 5. Loftus found that use of the word *smashed* resulted in higher estimates of car speed than use of the word *hit*.

Query 6. Answers should include three of the following: overlearn; practice with feedback; distribute practice sessions; test yourself; use mnemonics; make use of context cues; take a problem-solving approach to remembering.

*We cannot command nature except by obeying her.*

**—Francis Bacon**

## PREVIEW

In the preceding chapters, you saw that learning plays a vital role in the behavior of animals and humans. It is clear, then, that to understand human nature—or the nature of chimpanzees, monkeys, giraffes, rats, pigeons, and many other animals—we must understand how behavior is changed by experience: We must understand learning. But we must also understand the limits of learning. For while learning contributes to the differences in behavior that distinguish a person from a chimpanzee, and one person from another person, there are limits to what people and chimpanzees can learn. In this chapter, we will consider some of these limitations.

## PHYSICAL CHARACTERISTICS

Fish can't jump rope, humans can't breathe under water, cows can't coil up like snakes. The very structure of an animal's body makes certain kinds of behavior possible and other kinds of behavior impossible. What an individual can learn to do is therefore limited by what it is physically capable of doing. This is such an obvious fact that one might think it goes without saying. Indeed, it is seldom, if ever, mentioned in other learning texts. But obvious generalizations are sometimes worth making because the particulars that lead to the generalization are not always so obvious.

For instance, a dog's keen sense of smell enables it to find objects hidden from sight. Similarly, a hawk's superb vision allows it to distinguish between heads and tails on a quarter at a great distance, whereas a person would be unable to see the coin at all. Under certain circumstances, then, dogs and hawks would learn faster than people. All sorts of physical characteristics set limits on what individuals can learn (see Figure 13-1).

Several decades ago, some people tried to teach chimpanzees to talk (Hayes, 1951; Kellogg, 1968). These efforts were almost wholly unsuccessful and convinced many people that chimpanzees could not acquire language. It seemed that language was the one thing that set us off from furrier creatures. But then Allen and Beatrice Gardner (1969) began teaching Washoe, a young female chimpanzee, the sign language of the deaf. In less than two years, Washoe had a vocabulary of over 30 signs, and by the time she was 7, her vocabulary approached 200 signs. Since the Gardners' first efforts, a number of other researchers have taught sign language to chimps (e.g., Fouts & Mills, 1998; Gardner, 2012). Researchers have also attempted to teach sign language to a gorilla (Patterson, 1978; Patterson, Patterson, & Brentari, 1987) and to an orangutan (Shapiro, 1982). Whether any of these animals has really learned to communicate in the human sense is

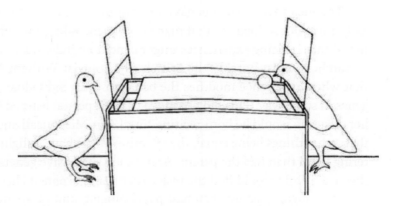

***Figure 13-1*** *Physical characteristics and learning. Pigeons cannot learn to play ping-pong in the usual manner, but these two have learned to play a variation of the game. (From "Two Synthetic Social Relations," by B. F. Skinner, 1962,* Journal of the Experimental Analysis of Behavior, *5, p. 531. Copyright © 1962 by the Society for the Experimental Analysis of Behavior, Inc. Reprinted by permission.)*

subject to debate (see, e.g., Petitto & Seidenberg, 1979; Terrace, 1979; Wallman, 1992). The point, however, is not that chimps and other animals are as adept as humans at learning language (they clearly are not) but rather that their difficulty in learning to *speak* is due at least partly to inadequate anatomical structures. People would also have a difficult time learning to speak if they had the kind of vocal equipment that other animals have.

 QUERY I:    Gardner and Gardner showed that the failure of chimpanzees to learn to speak

may be due more to differences in _____ than in learning ability.

CAPSULE **REVIEW**    The physical structure of an individual or species sets limits on what it can learn. Chimpanzees, for example, are apparently incapable of learning to speak because of the nature of their vocal equipment. Physical characteristics set important, but not always obvious, limits on what an individual can learn.

## NONHERITABILITY OF LEARNED BEHAVIOR

Another severe limitation of learning is that learned behavior is not inherited. Reflexes and fixed action patterns are passed on from generation to generation, but behavior that is acquired through learning dies with the individual. This places a serious limitation on the ability of a species to benefit from experience because it means that every individual is as ignorant at birth as its parents were when they were born. The lion cub must learn to stalk antelope just as its parents did; the rat must learn to avoid poisonous water; the child must learn to look for traffic before crossing streets.

The idea that learned behavior is not inherited was not always obvious. In fact, it was not so long ago that many people, including a number of scientists, believed that learning experiences might benefit an individual's offspring. But some researchers, most notably the British psychologist William McDougall, argued that when experience modifies the behavior of an individual, it also modifies its genes in some way. This did not mean that if a person learned to read Latin, his or her offspring would be born reciting Virgil. But McDougall and others did believe that, other things being equal, the offspring might have a slightly easier time mastering Latin than had the parent. And if each successive generation learned Latin, then each child would find the task easier than his parents had.

McDougall was no armchair psychologist, and he spent years performing experiments to test his theory. In a typical experiment, McDougall (1927, 1938) trained rats to avoid electric shocks. Then he trained the offspring of these rats on the same task, and then their offspring, and so on for several generations. The idea was that each generation should inherit more and more skill until, after many generations, the offspring would learn to avoid shock much more easily than their progenitors had. McDougall's research convinced him that his hypothesis held true.

Others were unconvinced. They ran similar experiments with better controls than McDougall had used and found no evidence that succeeding generations of animals learned a task any more readily than their forebears (see, e.g., Agar et al., 1954). Today, few behavior scientists or biologists believe that learning is inherited, though the issue is not dead (see Landman, 1991).

The nonheritability of learning is one of the severest of all its limitations. Certainly, anyone who has had a difficult time mastering parallel parking or memorizing the forms of the French verb *être* will agree that being able to benefit from the learning experiences of one's parents would be helpful. It is possible, however, that if we did inherit learned behavior, we would not be entirely happy with the results. Had our ancestors been born expert hunters and gatherers, for example, they might never have invented agriculture, probably the most important development in human history. In the past 60 years, there have been dramatic changes in the social roles of men and women in Western societies. It seems unlikely that such changes would have occurred if, over the past million years, men and women had inherited the roles of their parents. Inherited learning might also have slowed the advance of science. Had Copernicus been born believing that the earth is the center of the universe, he might not have developed the view that earth revolves about the sun.

The value of learning is that it enables us to adapt to changes in our environment. If we inherited learned behavior that was no longer adaptive, learning might be more of a hindrance than a help. Yet we must admit that the nonheritability of learning limits what any individual can learn in a lifetime.

> Research shows that the 18th-century poet John Gay was right: "Learning by study must be won/'Twas ne'er entail'd from sire to son."

CAPSULE **REVIEW**  Learned behavior is not passed on to future generations, which means that each individual must learn many of the same skills acquired by its parents. This limits what any one individual can learn in its lifetime.

## HEREDITY AND LEARNING ABILITY

There is nothing about the gross anatomy of the chimpanzee (e.g., the way its arms and legs are put together) that keeps it from learning calculus. Yet it seems extremely unlikely that anyone will ever succeed in training a chimpanzee, or any other animal, to perform so sophisticated a skill. Clearly there are genetic differences among species in the capacity for learning (Fuller & Scott, 1954).

Even animals that are genetically very similar show important differences in learning ability. For instance, Harry and Martha Frank (1982) compared the problem-solving abilities of wolves and dogs. They placed wolf pups on one side of a barrier from which they could see but not reach food. To get the food, they had to go around the barrier. The Franks counted the number of errors the wolf pups made and compared these data with similar data obtained by other researchers with dog pups. On three different tests, the wolves did far better than the dogs

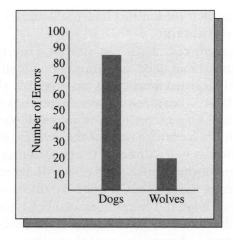

**Figure 13-2** *Barrier learning in dogs and wolves. Average number of daily errors in wolves and dogs on three problems. (Compiled from data in Frank and Frank, 1982.)*

(see Figure 13-2). Dogs and wolves are genetically almost identical, yet they performed differently (Pennisi, 2006; Topal et al., 2009). The Franks suggest that domestication has relieved pressure toward intelligence in the dog. In other words, because of dogs' association with humans, they are no longer naturally selected for intelligence, whereas wolves live by their wits or die.

It is also clear that there are differences in learning abilities within a given species, and these differences are also partly due to heredity. Robert Tryon (1940) demonstrated this in rats many years ago. He ran a large number of rats through a maze and recorded the number of errors each rat made on a series of trials. There was a great deal of variability among the rats, with some making over 20 times as many errors as others. Tryon then bred the rats that made the fewest errors with each other, and those that made the most errors with each other. Next, Tryon tested the offspring of these rats on the maze and again bred the brightest of the bright with each other and the dullest of the dull with each other. He repeated this procedure for 18 generations, all the while keeping the environments of the two strains as much alike as possible. The average number of errors in maze running for the two groups got farther and farther apart with each generation (see Figure 13-3), thus suggesting that heredity has an important impact on learning ability. Heredity also plays a role in human learning ability (e.g., Jacobs et al., 2007; Lynn & Hattori, 1990).

To say that heredity plays a role in learning ability does not mean, of course, that it is the sole determinant. In the case of both rats (e.g., Cooper & Zubek, 1958) and people (e.g., Cassidy, Roche, & Hayes, 2011; Hart & Risley, 1995; Turkheimer et al., 2003), learning history has a powerful effect on learning ability (see *Recipe for Genius*). The point is that there are biological limits on what we or any other species can learn.

**QUERY 2:** How does the breeding of dogs differ from Tryon's work? Could this

difference account for the findings of the Franks' research?

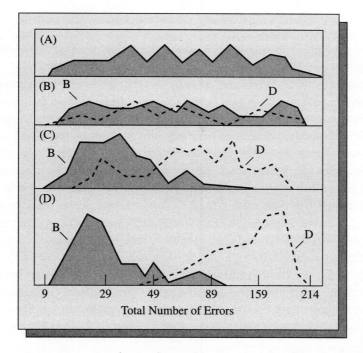

*Figure 13-3* *Heredity and maze learning. Tryon's original sample of rats (A) showed wide variation in maze learning. The first generation of selectively bred rats (B) showed considerable overlap between maze-bright B and maze-dull D rats, but the second generation (C) showed clear differences in maze-learning ability. By the seventh generation (D) there was a substantial difference in the average number of errors made by the two groups. (Copyright © 1940 by the National Society for the Study of Education. Reprinted by permission of the publisher.)*

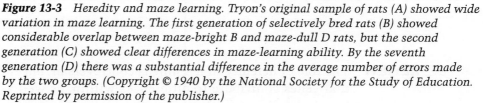

## RECIPE FOR GENIUS

Many of the world's geniuses have had unusually enriched early environments (Albert, 1980; Simonton, 1987). In fact, the childhoods of eminent figures such as Ludwig van Beethoven and Francis Galton are seldom ordinary. Could it be that we could create more geniuses by providing certain kinds of experiences in childhood? No one has performed an experiment that would answer this question with certainty. However, there is some very intriguing anecdotal evidence to support the idea.

The 19th-century British philosopher and historian James Mill could be said to have performed a kind of enrichment experiment with his first-born son, John Stuart Mill. The boy's father began tutoring him when he was still in the cradle. John was reading by age 3 and routinely answered questions from his father about what he had read. By the time John was 8 years old, he had already read most of the Greek classics (in Greek, incidentally); as an adult, he went on to outdistance his father as a philosopher. James Mill was unable to

*(Continued)*

devote the same effort to educating his other children, and none of them matched the achievements of their elder brother.

A more recent effort to improve ability by providing an enriched environment came from a man named Aaron Stern (1971). Too ill to work, Stern decided that he would devote his time toward the education of his daughter. When Edith was still an infant, Stern played classical music for her, showed her cards with numbers on them, read to her, and made a point of speaking to her slowly and in complete sentences. When she was 18 months old, Stern taught Edith math with an abacus, showed her words on cards, and taught her to read street signs. By age 2, Edith was reading books intended for children of 6 and 8; by age 4, she was reading *The New York Times* and playing chess; by age 5, she had read much of the *Encyclopaedia Britannica*; by age 6, she was reading Dostoevsky and Tolstoy; and by age 15, Edith had graduated from college and begun graduate work at Michigan State University.

Of course, it is possible that the remarkable achievements of John Stuart Mill and Edith Stern had little to do with the special environments in which they were reared. Nevertheless, these and other cases leave open the possibility that a rich intellectual environment in early childhood can have important effects on the ability to learn.

CAPSULE **REVIEW**    The role of heredity in learning is controversial, but there is strong evidence that genes contribute to differences within, as well as between, species in learning ability.

# NEUROLOGICAL DAMAGE AND LEARNING

The biological equipment with which we learn is not determined solely by heredity. The environment may limit learning ability, and therefore what we learn, by damaging the nervous system.

Prenatal exposure to alcohol and other drugs can interfere with neurological development, resulting in limited learning ability (Hawkins, 1983). Often the damage is not apparent at birth and may be revealed only when the child goes to school. It is even possible that children judged to be perfectly normal have somewhat less learning ability than would have been the case had they never been exposed prenatally to drugs.

**Neurotoxins**, substances that damage nerve tissues, are also a threat to learning ability after birth, particularly in infancy and early childhood. One of the most pervasive neurotoxins is lead, commonly found in old paint and in drinking water. Poor children often live in buildings with peeling paint, which they eat. The damage is not usually immediately obvious, but it is cumulative; over a period of months, it can make an important difference in the individual's ability to learn. Neurotoxins are also found in pesticides, herbicides, solvents, medications (including folk medicines), recreational drugs, and certain foods and food supplements (Costa et al., 2008; Hartman, 1995).

**?** **QUERY 3:** Substances that damage neural tissues are called _____.

Head injury can also diminish learning ability (Joseph, 2011). This may seem an insignificant factor, but child abuse is fairly widespread and often involves blows to the head or shaking of the child. The "punch drunk" boxer provides anecdotal evidence of the cumulative effects of repeated closed head injuries. Violently shaking a child causes the brain to bounce back and forth within the skull and can cause serious damage. Traffic accidents are probably the single most important source of serious head injuries among teens and young adults, but certain sports also result in significant brain damage (Carroll & Rosner, 2012).

Malnutrition, especially during fetal development and early childhood, can also prevent normal neurological development and result in reduced learning (Lieberman, Kanarek, & Prasad, 2005). The brain is not the *source* of learning—the environment is—but learning in humans and other complex animals is dependent on the brain, so anything that damages it is likely to affect the course of learning.

CAPSULE **REVIEW**    Neurological damage due to disease, malnutrition, head trauma, and exposure to neurotoxins can have a profound effect on learning. Unfortunately, anything that damages the brain is likely to reduce the ability to benefit from experience.

# CRITICAL PERIODS

Sometimes animals are especially likely to learn a particular kind of behavior at one point in their lives; these stages for optimum learning are referred to as **critical periods.**

For example, many animals are especially likely to form an attachment to their mothers during a critical period soon after birth. If the mother is unavailable, the youngster will become attached to any moving object that happens to pass by, whether another animal of the same species, a mechanical object, or a human being. Konrad Lorenz (1952) was one of the first to study this phenomenon, which he called **imprinting.** He discovered that if you remove a newly hatched goose chick from an incubator, you will have inadvertently become a parent; the chick will follow you about and ignore its mother:

> If one quickly places such an orphan amongst a brood which is following its parents in the normal way, the gosling shows not the slightest

tendency to regard the old birds as members of its own species. Peeping loudly, it runs away and, should a human being happen to pass, it immediately follows this person; it simply looks upon human beings as its parents. (quoted in Thorpe, 1963, p. 405)

Imprinting has been demonstrated in coots, moorhens, turkeys, ravens, partridges, ducks, chickens, deer, sheep, buffalo, zebras, guinea pigs, baboons, and other animals (Sluckin, 2007). Young animals have been imprinted to species different from themselves, including humans, and to objects such as wooden decoys and electric trains. All that is necessary for imprinting to take place is that the young animal be able to view the "mother" and that the mother-object move.

Imprinting is not the only evidence for critical periods. John Paul Scott (1958) has shown that social behavior in the dog depends on its experiences during certain critical periods. He points out, for example, that if a puppy is to become a good house pet, it must have contact with people when it is between 3 and 12 weeks old. Dogs deprived of human contact during this period behave like wild animals, ever fearful of humans.

Maternal behavior also may have to be learned during critical periods. Scott (1962) once bottle-fed a lamb for the first ten days of its life and then put the lamb in with a flock of sheep. The lamb cared little for the sheep, preferring to be with people. And when this lamb gave birth, it was a poor mother: It allowed its offspring to nurse, but took no particular interest in other motherly activities.

Harry and Margaret Harlow (Harlow, 1958; Harlow & Harlow, 1962a, 1962b) obtained similar results when they reared rhesus monkeys in isolation. In the Harlows' experiments, a surrogate mother, a terry cloth–covered object with fake eyes, did nothing but provide food and warmth to young monkeys. The infants became very attached to these cloth mothers and clung to them for hours. If a monkey were exploring about the cage and became frightened, it would run to "mother" for protection. Later, when these monkeys were placed in cages with normally reared monkeys, they were terrified. They would run to a corner of the cage and roll up into a ball. As adults, these monkeys did not play or mate or rear young the way normally reared monkeys do. Although these animals acquired some social skills as adults, they always seemed to be socially retarded. Apparently, the early part of their lives, when they ordinarily would have interacted with their mothers and young monkeys, was a critical period for acquiring social skills.

It is not clear whether there are critical periods for learning in humans. It is possible that there is a critical period in infancy or early childhood for learning to care about others (David et al., 1988). And there is evidence that the first 12 years of life may be a critical period for learning language (Harley & Wang, 1997; Patkowski, 1994). But the evidence for critical periods in people is generally far weaker than the evidence for such periods in animals.

*Although imprinting seems to be the product of genetics, there is evidence that learning may be involved (Hoffman & Ratner, 1973; Suzuki & Moriyama, 1999).*

CAPSULE **REVIEW**    Animals may be prepared to learn certain things at certain stages in their development. Such critical periods appear to play an important role in imprinting and other forms of social behavior. It is not clear whether there are critical periods for learning in human development. When critical periods do occur, they place severe limits on learning. Certain opportunities for learning may occur but once in a lifetime.

## PREPAREDNESS AND LEARNING

In the 1960s, researchers began to notice that the ease with which learning occurs varies not only across time, as the work on critical periods shows, but also across situations. Whereas a given animal might learn quite readily in one situation, it might seem downright stupid in a slightly different situation.

Keller and Marion Breland (1961) were among the first to report this phenomenon. They used operant procedures to train hundreds of animals to perform in TV commercials and films and in shopping center promotions. For example, "Priscilla the Pig" turned on a radio, ate breakfast at a table, picked up dirty clothes and put them in a hamper, ran a vacuum cleaner, and chose the sponsor's brand of animal feed. The Brelands were expert animal trainers, yet they sometimes had great difficulty getting an animal to perform what seemed to be a simple task. In a classic article entitled "The Misbehavior of Organisms," they described some of the peculiar problems they encountered in their work.

For instance, the Brelands wanted to train a raccoon to pick up some coins and put them in a metal box that served as a bank. The raccoon quickly learned to pick up a coin and carry it to the box, but it "seemed to have a great deal of trouble letting go of the coin. He would rub it up against the inside of the container, pull it back out, and clutch it firmly for several seconds" (p. 682). When the Brelands tried to teach the animal to pick up two coins and put them in the box, the raccoon became even more of a dunce. Instead of dropping the coins into the box, it would rub them together "in a most miserly fashion" (p. 682) and dip them in and out of the box. None of this behavior was reinforced by trainers. It might seem reasonable to conclude that the task was simply too difficult for the raccoon to master, but the raccoon had no trouble learning other, equally complex tasks.

Time and again, the Brelands had trouble getting animals to perform acts that should have been easy. In some cases, the Brelands managed to teach an animal to perform the desired behavior, only to find that the act later broke down. For example, they taught a pig to make bank deposits in a manner similar to that of the raccoon. But after a time, the pig began to behave oddly. Instead of picking up the large wooden coin and carrying it to the bank, the pig would drop the coin to the ground, push at it with its snout, toss it in the air, and nudge it again with its snout. None of this behavior produced reinforcement from the trainer.

Why did such "misbehavior" occur? The Brelands theorized that innate tendencies interfered with learning (Bihn, Gillaspy, Abbott et al., 2010). In the wild, raccoons dip their prey into the water and then rub it between their paws, as if washing it. Some biologists speculate that this serves to break away the outer shell of the crayfish that often form an important part of the raccoon's diet. In any case, it appears that this behavior interfered with teaching the raccoon to drop coins into a bank. Similarly, pigs dig their snouts into the ground to uncover edible roots, and this rooting behavior interfered with their learning to carry coins.

**?** QUERY 4:   The Brelands showed that _____ might facilitate learning in one situation and inhibit it in another.

This tendency of an animal to revert to a fixed action pattern, a phenomenon called **instinctive drift,** sets limits on learning. If a particular act conflicts with a fixed action pattern, the animal will have trouble learning it. After the Brelands' discoveries, other researchers began to report evidence that animals show peculiar talents for learning some things but are peculiarly resistant toward learning others. The limitations that the latter oddities place on learning were nicely illustrated in a study of taste aversion in rats.

John Garcia and Robert Koelling (1966) set up four classical conditioning experiments in which they paired water with aversive stimuli. The water was flavored, and a light and a clicking noise came on whenever the rat drank. Thus, in one experiment, rats drank water that was bright, noisy, and tasty, and later they became sick from exposure to X-radiation. In another experiment, rats drank water that was bright, noisy, and tasty, and later they received an electric shock. After training, the experimenters gave the rats a choice between bright-noisy water and tasty water. Rats that had been made sick were more likely to avoid the *tasty* water; those that had been shocked were more likely to avoid the *bright-noisy* water (see Figure 13-4). The rats had an apparently innate bias toward learning one thing rather than another.

The facility with which animals learn certain acts is illustrated by a classic experiment conducted by Paul Brown and Herbert Jenkins (1968). These researchers put pigeons into experimental chambers rigged so that periodically a disc would be illuminated. The disc remained lit for a few seconds, and when the light went off a food tray provided the pigeon with grain. The birds did not have to do anything to receive food, yet all the birds began pecking the disc. The researchers called the procedure **autoshaping** since the behavior was "shaped" without reinforcement (see Schwartz & Gamzu, 1979).

Robert Epstein and Skinner (1980; see also Skinner, 1983a) got similar results with a slightly different procedure. They shone a spot of light on a screen and made it move. When it reached the edge of the screen, the bird received some food. The bird did not have to do anything to receive food, nor did anything it did speed up delivery of the food, yet the bird pecked at the moving spot of light as if driving it across the screen.

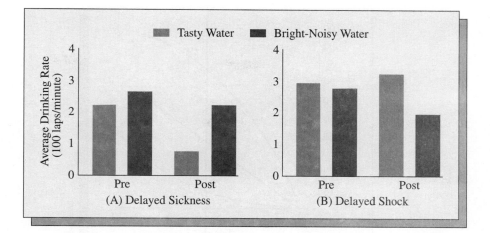

**Figure 13-4**  *Preparedness and taste aversion. Rats were given the opportunity to drink bright-noisy and tasty water before and after conditioning. When drinking preceded sickness, rats later tended to avoid tasty water (A); when drinking preceded shock, the rats learned to avoid bright-noisy water (B). ("Relation of Cue to Consequence in Avoidance Learning," by John Garcia and Robert Koelling, 1966,* Psychonomic Science, 4, *p. 124, Figure 1. Copyright 1966 by the Psychonomic Society. Reprinted by permission of the publisher and authors.)*

These and other studies show that animals have an inclination to behave in certain ways, and this means they will learn some things with ease while learning other things with difficulty. Martin Seligman (1970) proposed that such tendencies can be characterized as a **continuum of preparedness:** An animal comes to a learning situation genetically prepared to learn (in which case learning proceeds quickly), unprepared (in which case learning proceeds steadily but more slowly), or contraprepared (in which case the course of learning is slow and irregular; see Figure 13-5).

According to Seligman's theory, the raccoon's innate tendency to pick up its food and wash it may make it prepared to learn to pick up and carry coins to a bank, but its innate tendency to hold on to food it has dipped into a stream makes it contraprepared to learn to drop coins into a bank. Similarly, Garcia and Koelling's rats are genetically prepared to learn to avoid water that makes them sick if the water has a distinct taste, but not if it has a distinct look and sound. And Brown and Jenkins's pigeons pecked a lighted disk because pigeons are genetically prepared to peck bright objects.

Being prepared to acquire a fear of dangerous objects, such as snakes, could be very helpful. Monkeys seem to be particularly adept at acquiring a fear of snakes. In one experiment, Michael Cook and Susan Mineka (1990) had rhesus monkeys watch videotapes of monkeys reacting fearfully either to snakes or to flowers. The observers acquired a fear of snakes but not of flowers.

Seligman (1970, 1971) proposed that humans are also prepared to acquire certain fears. He points out that people are far more likely to fear sharks,

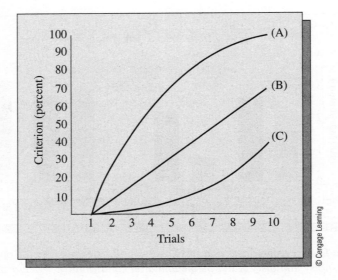

**Figure 13-5**   *Preparedness and learning. Hypothetical learning curves for a task an organism is prepared to learn (A), unprepared to learn (B), and contraprepared to learn (C).*

spiders, snakes, and dogs than they are lambs, trees, houses, and cars. Seligman and Joanne Hager (1972) tell the story of a 7-year-old girl who saw a snake while playing in the park. Sometime later, the girl accidentally slammed a car door on her hand, after which she developed a fear of snakes. Obviously, the snake did not hurt her hand. The implication is that people are biologically prepared to acquire a fear of snakes but not a fear of cars, although in this case a car phobia would have made more sense.

The idea that people have an innate disposition to fear certain kinds of stimuli is supported by research (for reviews, see McNally, 1987, and Öhman & Mineka, 2001, 2003). For example, Arne Öhman and his colleagues (2001) paired various images with brief electric shocks to the hand. The images included neutral objects, such as geometric forms and flowers, but also snakes and spiders. The result was that there was much greater conditioning to the potentially dangerous animals. In another experiment, researchers showed people an array of images and asked them to find the spider or the snake. They did so more quickly than when asked to find less hazardous items. Because the bite of some snakes and spiders can be lethal, this preparedness has obvious benefits.

**QUERY 5:**   Who proposed the continuum of preparedness?

The focus of work on preparedness has been on hazardous objects, but Seligman (1970) observes that people are far more likely to form strong attachments to some objects than to others. He notes that the cartoon character, Linus, carries a security blanket, not a security shoe.

Yet the case for preparedness in humans is not clear-cut. Joseph Wolpe and Joseph Plaud (1997) point out that objects that are seldom feared, such as flowers and triangles, are those to which we have been exposed many times without adverse effects. Flowers are normally paired with positive or neutral stimuli, and work on latent inhibition leads us to predict that such preexposure should make it difficult to establish flowers as a CS for fear. On the other hand, commonly feared objects such as snakes are encountered less frequently and are more likely to be paired with unpleasant stimuli, such as a person screaming.

CAPSULE **REVIEW**  It seems clear that in most animals, learning depends partly on whether the animal is genetically prepared, unprepared, or contraprepared to learn the task in question. Such genetic preparation sets limits on what is learned from a given experience.

## LEARNING AND HUMANITY

A common misconception about evolution is that it is a form of progress, as though each species were aimed at a distant goal and evolution were its means of reaching it. In fact, there is no evolutionary goal. Characteristics arise merely because those individuals that possess them tend to survive and pass on their genes.

Learning, as we have seen, is a kind of individual evolution: New behavior appears and either "survives" or "dies out." And like evolution, it has no ultimate goal. What we learn depends on the experiences we have, not on some scheme of nature.

We forget this. We tend to speak of learning as if it were necessarily a good thing, and use the term almost as a synonym for improvement. It is true that love, compassion, tenderness, cooperativeness, sharing, musical composition, and great literature are largely the products of learning. But so are the most despicable acts of which we are capable. Consider this report of one survivor of the concentration camp in Dachau, Germany:

> It was common practice to remove the skin from dead prisoners. . . . It was chemically treated and placed in the sun to dry. After that it was cut into various sizes for use as saddles, riding breeches, gloves, house slippers and ladies' handbags. Tattooed skin was especially valued by SS men. (Blaha, 1946, in Carey, 1988, pp. 557f)

This excerpt reveals that learning does not always mean progress. You may also see the undesirable effects of learning in your own reaction to the passage above. There was a time, not so very long ago, when reading such material would have made some students physically ill. Today's students have viewed so much brutality on television, and sometimes in the streets, that many can read Blaha's account without discomfort.

Learning defines our humanity. For better, and for worse.

## THE LAST FINAL WORD

I have concluded this introduction to learning by examining some of its limits. Those limits make learning appear to be a feeble weapon with which to battle the problems that threaten civilization. The world is faced with war, famine, crime, disease, pollution, climate change, the exhaustion of natural resources, and the grandfather of all problems, overpopulation. What good is an understanding of learning in dealing with problems of such magnitude?

The answer becomes obvious once we realize that the serious problems confronting us are fundamentally behavior problems. War is a fight between nations. Famine is at least partly the result of mismanaged resources. Crime is the performance of socially prohibited acts. Most diseases are at least partly the product of unhealthy lifestyles. Pollution and climate change are largely the result of fossil fuel use and the inappropriate disposal of industrial wastes. The exhaustion of natural resources is the result of excessive consumption and overpopulation. Overpopulation is partly a poor person's way of preparing for his or her care in old age.

Once we recognize that most of the problems facing society are essentially behavior problems, not technological or natural, we realize that we can prevent, solve, or at least ameliorate them *by changing behavior* (Heward & Chance, 2010). Learning is a change in behavior due to experience, so an understanding of learning is critically important to solving the problems that confront us.

To suggest that we can draw on learning research in dealing with societal problems does not mean that the problems will be easily solved (Chance, 2007). Human behavior is extremely complicated, and solutions to social problems are apt to come slowly. But there is reason to hope that through the application of scientific method to behavior problems, solutions will come.

Indeed, it may be our only hope.

## RECOMMENDED **READING**

1. Breland, K., & Breland, M. (1961). The misbehavior of organisms. *American Psychologist, 16,* 681–684.

   This classic paper discusses instinctive drift and individual differences among species in learning.

2. Hayes, C. (1951). *The ape in our house.* New York: Harper & Row.

   The Hayeses brought an infant chimpanzee into their home to see what it could accomplish if reared as a human.

3. Heward, W. L., & Chance, P. (Guest Eds.) (2010). Special section: The human response to climate change: Ideas from behavior analysis. *The Behavior Analyst, 33,* 145–206.

   This special section is devoted to ways that learning principles can be applied to coping with climate change.

4. Seligman, M. E. P., & Hager, J. L. (Eds.). (1972). *Biological boundaries of learning*. New York: Appleton-Century-Crofts.

  This is one of the classic works on the limits of learning.

5. Wilson, E. O. (1975). *Sociobiology: The new synthesis*. Cambridge, MA: Harvard University Press.

  Wilson stirred considerable controversy with this treatise on the role of evolution and heredity in human affairs.

## REVIEW **QUESTIONS**

1. Define the following terms:

   | | |
   |---|---|
   | autoshaping | imprinting |
   | continuum of preparedness | instinctive drift |
   | critical period | neurotoxins |

2. Sally buys a high-frequency whistle at a discount store. She attempts to train her dog to come on command using the whistle as a signal. She follows the correct training procedures but is unsuccessful. What is the likely cause of the failure?

3. Design a study to determine the effects of prenatal exposure to tobacco on subsequent learning ability.

4. Could variability in learning ability be useful to the survival of our species?

5. Suppose you had inherited everything your parents and grandparents knew. How would you be different?

6. Identify a social problem and explain how it might be dealt with through the application of learning principles you have learned in this text.

7. How would you go about creating a genius?

8. A visitor to New York complained about the noise of the city. Her host replied, "Oh, you get used to it." Does this demonstrate that learning is helpful or harmful?

9. Roger McIntire (1973) recommends that people be required to undergo training in child rearing before being allowed to have children. What support for his position can you provide?

10. What protection could the public have against the abuse of learning principles by political leaders?

## PRACTICE **QUIZ**

1. An example of the role of physical characteristics in learning is provided by the difficulty apes had in learning _____.

2. Harry and Martha Frank found that _____ solved certain problems better than dogs.

3. William _____ mistakenly believed that learned behavior could be inherited.

4. Substances that damage neural tissues are called _____.

5. A _____ is a stage in development during which an animal is particularly likely to learn a particular behavior.

6. Soon after hatching, ducklings become _____ on an object that moves, usually their mother.

7. _____ drift is the tendency of an animal to revert to innate patterns of behavior.

8. Garcia and Koelling found that when rats became sick after drinking water that was tasty and noisy, they were more likely to drink water that was _____ than water that was _____.

9. According to Martin Seligman, all behavior falls along a continuum of _____.

10. Rhesus monkeys can acquire a fear by observing a fearful model, but Cook and Mineka found that they are more likely to acquire a fear of snakes than of _____.

## QUERY ANSWERS

Query 1. Gardner and Gardner showed that the failure of chimpanzees to learn to speak may be due more to differences in *anatomy* than in learning ability.

Query 2. Dogs are typically bred ("selected") by breeders based on physical appearance and temperament, not learning ability. Wolves are products of natural selection, and learning ability likely contributes to their survival.

Query 3. Substances that damage neural tissues are called *neurotoxins*.

Query 4. The Brelands showed that *heredity/genetic factors* might facilitate learning in one situation and inhibit it in another.

Query 5: Martin Seligman proposed the continuum of preparedness.

# Glossary

**ABA reversal design** A type of within-subject experiment in which behavior is observed in the absence of the independent variable (A), in the presence of the independent variable (B), and then again in the absence of the independent variable (A). Sometimes the B condition is restored, thereby creating an ABAB design. The experimental manipulation is often referred to as an intervention.

**Abolishing operation** A motivating operation that decreases the effectiveness of a consequence (a reinforcer or punisher).

**Anecdote** First- or secondhand reports of personal experience. Anecdotes are notoriously unreliable, so they are not a good source of evidence; however, they can generate useful hypotheses about variables influencing behavior.

**Asocial observational learning** Learning from the observation of events and their consequences in the absence of a model. Note: The term is introduced in this edition, and is not part of the standard lexicon of learning. (*Cf.* social observational learning.)

**Autobiographical memory** *See* episodic memory.

**Autoshaping** The innate tendency of a pigeon to peck an object associated with food even though pecking is not required for the food to appear. Also called *sign tracking*.

**Aversion therapy** A form of counterconditioning in which a CS is paired with an aversive US, often a nausea-inducing drug.

**Aversive** (n.) Any stimulus an animal or person will avoid, given the opportunity to do so; any stimulus the removal of which is reinforcing; (adj.) characterizing an event that is likely to be avoided. Note that the word is aversive, not *ad*versive.

**Backward chaining** A chaining procedure in which training begins with the last link in the chain and adds preceding links in reverse order. (*Cf.* forward chaining.)

**Backward conditioning** A Pavlovian conditioning procedure in which the US precedes the CS.

**Baseline period** In a within-subject experiment, a period of observation (often designated "A") during which no attempt is made to modify the behavior under study.

**Behavior** Anything a person or other animal does that can be measured. In practice, the term usually refers to publicly observable overt behavior. However, behavior that is available only to the person performing it (such as thinking) may be included if it can be reliably measured.

**Behavior chain** A series of related behaviors, the last of which produces reinforcement.

**Behavioral momentum** A term used to refer to the strength of a reinforced behavior.

**Between-subjects experiment** An experimental design in which the independent variable is made to vary across two or more groups of subjects. (Subjects are now often called participants.) Also called *between-treatment* or *group experiment*. (*Cf.* within-subject experiment.)

**Blocking** Failure of a stimulus to become a CS when it is part of a compound stimulus that includes an effective CS. The effective CS is said to block the formation of a new CS. (*Cf.* overshadowing.)

**Break point** In a progressive reinforcement schedule, the point at which the rate of behavior falls off dramatically or stops entirely.

**Case study** Detailed study and description of a single case, such as a person who is a compulsive hand washer. Case studies are often used in clinical settings in an attempt to identify the sources of a disorder and/or its effective treatment. While case studies are a step above anecdotal evidence, they are also problematic.

**Chaining** The procedure of establishing a behavior chain. (*Cf.* behavior chain; forward chaining; backward chaining.)

**Chain schedule** A compound reinforcement schedule that consists of a series of simple schedules, each of which is associated with a particular stimulus, with reinforcement delivered only on completion of the last schedule in the series. (*Cf.* tandem schedule.)

**Classical conditioning** Another name for Pavlovian conditioning, which see.

**Compensatory response theory** A variation of the preparatory response theory that proposes that the CR prepares the organism for the US by compensating for its effects.

**Compound stimulus** Two or more stimuli presented simultaneously, often as a CS.

**Concept** Any class (i.e., group, category) the members of which share one or more defining features.

**Concurrent schedule** A compound reinforcement schedule in which two or more simple schedules are available at the same time.

**Conditional reflex** A reflex acquired through Pavlovian conditioning consisting of a conditional stimulus and a conditional response. (*Cf.* unconditional reflex.)

**Conditional response** The response part of a conditional reflex; the response elicited by a conditional stimulus. Often called *conditioned response*. Abbreviated CR.

**Conditional stimulus** The stimulus part of a conditional reflex; the stimulus that elicits a conditional response. Often called *conditioned stimulus.* Abbreviated CS.

**Conditioned emotional response** An emotional response to a stimulus that is acquired through Pavlovian conditioning. Abbreviated CER.

**Conditioned food avoidance** *See* conditioned taste aversion.

**Conditioned reinforcer** *See* secondary reinforcer.

**Conditioned taste aversion** An aversion, acquired through Pavlovian conditioning, to foods with a particular flavor. Also called *conditioned food avoidance.*

**Constraint-induced movement therapy** A reinforcement-based treatment of loss of limb function that involves restricting a normally functioning limb. Abbreviated CIMT.

**Contiguity** Nearness of events in time (temporal contiguity) or space (spatial contiguity).

**Contingency** A dependency between events. An event may be stimulus-contingent (dependent on the appearance of a stimulus) or response-contingent (dependent on the appearance of a behavior).

**Continuous reinforcement** A reinforcement schedule in which a behavior is reinforced each time it occurs. Abbreviated CRF. (*Cf.* intermittent schedule.)

**Continuum of preparedness** The idea that organisms are genetically disposed to learn some things but not others.

**Contrived reinforcer** Any reinforcer that is provided by someone for the purpose of changing behavior. (*Cf.* natural reinforcer.)

**Control group** In a between-subjects experiment, those subjects not exposed to the independent variable. (*Cf.* experimental group.)

**Cooperative schedule** A reinforcement schedule in which reinforcement is contingent on the behavior of two or more individuals.

**Counterconditioning** The use of Pavlovian conditioning to reverse the unwanted effects of prior conditioning. Typically takes the form of aversion therapy or exposure therapy, which see.

**CR** *See* conditional response.

**CRF** *See* continuous reinforcement.

**Critical period** A period in the development of an organism during which it is especially likely to learn a particular kind of behavior.

**CS** *See* conditional stimulus.

**CS⁺** In Pavlovian discrimination training, the stimulus that is regularly paired with a US. (*Cf.* CS⁻.)

**CS⁻** In Pavlovian discrimination training, the stimulus that regularly appears in the absence of the US. (*Cf.* CS⁺.)

**Cue-dependent forgetting** Forgetting that results from the absence of cues that were present during learning.

**Cued recall** *See* prompted recall.

**Cumulative record** A graphic record of behavior, each point of which reflects the total number of times a behavior has been performed as of that time. (*Cf.* cumulative recorder.)

**Cumulative recorder** An apparatus (or software) that records every occurrence of a behavior, thereby producing a cumulative record. (*Cf.* cumulative record.)

**Declarative memory** Memory of events that can be expressed, usually in words. Includes semantic and episodic memory. Also called *explicit memory*. (*Cf.* nondeclarative memory.)

**Delay conditioning** A Pavlovian conditioning procedure in which the CS and US overlap. The CS is presented before the US, but continues after the US appears.

**Delayed matching to sample** A method of measuring forgetting in which the opportunity to match a sample follows a retention interval. Abbreviated DMTS. (*Cf.* matching to sample.)

**Dependent variable** The variable by which the outcome of an experiment is measured. It is not manipulated by the researcher but is expected to vary with (to depend on) the independent variable.

**Descriptive study** A study in which the researcher attempts to describe a group by obtaining data from its members. In behavioral research the data often consists of replies to surveys or questionnaires.

**Differential outcomes effect** The finding that discrimination training proceeds more rapidly when different behaviors produce different reinforcers. Abbreviated DOE.

**Differential reinforcement** Any operant training procedure in which certain kinds of behavior are systematically reinforced and others are not.

**Differential reinforcement of alternative behavior** A form of differential reinforcement in which a behavior that is different from an undesired behavior is systematically reinforced. The procedure provides an alternative way of obtaining reinforcement. Abbreviated DRA.

**Differential reinforcement of incompatible behavior** A form of differential reinforcement in which a behavior that is incompatible with an unwanted behavior is systematically reinforced. Abbreviated DRI.

**Differential reinforcement of low rate** A form of differential reinforcement in which a behavior is reinforced only if it occurs no more than a specified number of times in a given period. Abbreviated DRL.

**Discrimination** The tendency for a behavior to occur in one situation, but not another. It is also defined as the tendency for a behavior to occur in the presence of certain stimuli, but not in their absence. (*Cf.* generalization.)

**Discrimination hypothesis** The idea that the partial reinforcement effect occurs because it is harder to discriminate between intermittent reinforcement and extinction than between continuous reinforcement and extinction.

**Discrimination training** Any procedure for establishing a discrimination. Discriminations can be established through both Pavlovian and operant procedures. Operant procedures include simultaneous and successive discrimination training, which see.

**Discriminative stimulus** In operant discrimination training, any stimulus that signals either that a behavior will be reinforced (an $S^D$) or will not be reinforced (an $S^\Delta$).

**Distributed practice** Learning or practice sessions spread out over time. Also called *spaced practice*. (*Cf.* massed practice.)

**DMTS** *See* delayed matching to sample.

**DOE** *See* differential outcomes effect.

**Dopamine** A neurotransmitter that produces a natural "high" and is thought to play a major role in reinforcement.

**DRA** *See* differential reinforcement of alternative behavior.

**DRI** *See* differential reinforcement of incompatible behavior.

**Drive** In Hull's theory of reinforcement, a motivational state (such as hunger) caused by a period of deprivation (as of food).

**Drive-reduction theory** The theory of reinforcement that attributes a reinforcer's effectiveness to the reduction of a drive.

**DRL** *See* differential reinforcement of low rate.

**Edutainment** Materials (books, videos, radio programs, etc.) that attempt to educate and entertain the public simultaneously.

**Episodic memory** Memory of life events. Also called *autobiographical* or *event memory*. (*Cf.* semantic memory.)

**Equilibrium theory** *See* response deprivation theory.

**Errorless discrimination training** A form of operant discrimination training in which the $S^\Delta$ is introduced in very weak form and gradually strengthened. The usual result is that discrimination is achieved with few or no errors. Also called the *Terrace procedure*.

**Escape-avoidance learning** A form of negative reinforcement in which the subject first learns to escape, and then to avoid, an aversive.

**Escape learning** *See* negative reinforcement.

**Establishing operation** A motivating operation that increases the effectiveness of a consequence (a reinforcer or punisher).

**Event memory** *See* episodic memory.

**Excitatory gradient** In Spence's theory of generalization and discrimination, a generalization gradient showing an increased tendency to respond to the $S^D$ or $CS^+$ and stimuli resembling them. (*Cf.* inhibitory gradient.)

**Experiment** A study in which the researcher measures the effects of one or more independent variables on one or more dependent variables.

**Experimental group** In a between-subjects experiment, those subjects exposed to the independent variable. *Cf.* control group.

**Exposure therapy** *See* counterconditioning.

**Extinction** (1) In Pavlovian conditioning, the regular appearance of the CS alone—i.e., without the US. (2) In operant learning, the regular appearance of a behavior alone—i.e., not followed by a reinforcer. (*Cf.* forgetting.)

**Extinction burst** A sudden increase in the rate of behavior during the early stages of extinction.

**Extinction method** A method of measuring forgetting by comparing the rate of extinction after a retention interval with the rate of extinction immediately after training.

**FD schedule** *See* fixed duration schedule.

**FI schedule** *See* fixed interval schedule.

**Fixed action pattern** *See* modal action patter.

**Fixed duration schedule** A reinforcement schedule in which reinforcement is contingent on the continuous performance of a behavior for a fixed period of time. Abbreviated FD. (*Cf.* variable duration schedule.)

**Fixed interval schedule** A reinforcement schedule in which a behavior is reinforced the first time it occurs following a specified interval since the last reinforcement. Abbreviated FI. (*Cf.* variable interval schedule.)

**Fixed ratio schedule** A reinforcement schedule in which every $n$th performance of a behavior is reinforced. Abbreviated FR. (*Cf.* variable ratio schedule.)

**Fixed time schedule** A reinforcement schedule in which reinforcement is delivered independently of behavior at fixed intervals. Abbreviated FT. (*Cf.* variable time schedule.)

**Fluency** A measure of learning consisting of the number of correct responses per minute. Fluency is a factor in forgetting: The higher the level of fluency, the lower the rate of forgetting. A decline in fluency following a retention interval can also serve as a measure of forgetting.

**Forgetting** Deterioration in learned behavior following a retention interval. Increasingly, learning researchers look on forgetting as changes in learned behavior due to differences in the environment during learning and during testing. (*Cf.* extinction.)

**Forward chaining** A chaining procedure in which training begins with the first link in the chain and adds subsequent links in order. (*Cf.* backward chaining.)

**Free recall** A method of measuring forgetting that consists of providing the opportunity to perform the learned behavior. (*Cf.* prompted recall.)

**FR schedule** *See* fixed ratio schedule.

**Frustration hypothesis** The idea that the partial reinforcement effect occurs because nonreinforcement is frustrating and during intermittent reinforcement responding while frustrated is reinforced, so frustration becomes a signal for responding.

**FT schedule** *See* fixed time schedule.

**General behavior trait** Any general behavioral tendency that is strongly influenced by genes. Examples include introversion and general anxiety. (*Cf.* modal action pattern.)

**Generalization** The tendency for the effects of a learning experience to spread. There are various kinds of generalization, but the two most researched types are called stimulus generalization and response generalization, which see. (*Cf.* discrimination.)

**Generalization gradient** Any graphic representation of generalization data.

**Generalized imitation** The tendency to imitate modeled behavior even though the imitative behavior is not reinforced.

**Generalized reinforcer** Any secondary reinforcer that has been paired with several different reinforcers and is effective in a wide variety of situations.

**Ghost condition** An experimental procedure in which an event normally performed by a model appears to occur without a model. The condition is used in studies of asocial observational learning.

**Gradient degradation** A method of measuring forgetting in which a behavior is tested for generalization before and after a retention interval. A flattening of the generalization gradient indicates forgetting.

**Group experiment** *See* between-subjects experiment.

**Habituation** A decrease in the intensity or probability of a reflex response resulting from repeated exposure to a stimulus that evokes that response. Habituation is perhaps the simplest form of learning.

**Higher-order conditioning** A variation of Pavlovian conditioning in which a neutral stimulus is paired, not with a US, but with a well-established CS.

**Hybridization** The cross-breeding of closely related species. For example, a wolf and dog may mate, producing a hybrid animal that is neither a wolf nor a dog. Hybridization may contribute to the evolution of new species.

**Imitate** To behave in a manner resembling the behavior of a model.

**Imprinting** The tendency of some animals, particularly birds, to follow the first moving object they see after birth, usually (but not necessarily) their mother.

**Independent variable** In an experiment, the variable that the researcher manipulates. The independent variable is usually expected to affect the dependent variable.

**Inhibitory gradient** In Spence's theory of generalization and discrimination, a gradient showing a decreased tendency to respond to the $S^\Delta$ or CS⁻ and stimuli resembling them. (*Cf.* excitatory gradient.)

**Instinct** *See* modal action pattern.

**Instinctive drift** The tendency for behavior to "drift toward" a modal action pattern.

**Instrumental learning** *See* operant learning.

**Intermittent schedule** Any of several reinforcement schedules in which a behavior is sometimes reinforced. Also called *partial reinforcement*. (*Cf.* continuous reinforcement.)

**Interstimulus interval (ISI)** The time between the appearance of the CS and the US.

**Intertrial interval** In Pavlovian conditioning, the interval between the pairings of a CS and US. In operant learning, the interval between the pairings of a behavior and its consequences.

**Latency** The time that passes between an event and a behavior.

**Latent inhibition** In Pavlovian conditioning, the failure of a CR to appear as a result of prior presentation of the CS in the absence of the US.

**Law of effect** The statement that behavior is a function of its consequences. So called because the strength of a behavior depends on its past *effects* on the environment. Implicit in the law is the notion that operant learning is an active process, since it is usually the behavior of the organism that, directly or indirectly, produces the effect.

**Learned helplessness** The tendency to give up on a problem as a result of previous exposure to insoluble problems. In experiments the problem typically involves escape learning. (*Cf.* learned industriousness.)

**Learned industriousness** The tendency to persist at a problem as a result of previous reinforcement of persistence at difficult problems. (*Cf.* learned helplessness.)

**Learning** A change in behavior due to experience.

**Learning model** In social observational learning, a model who is observed as he or she learns to perform a task. Also called an *unskilled model*.

**Massed practice** Learning or practice sessions separated by little or no time. (*Cf.* distributed practice.)

**Matched sampling** A procedure for reducing extraneous differences among subjects in between-subjects experiments by matching those in the experimental and control groups on specified characteristics, such as age, sex, and weight.

**Matching law** The principle that, given the opportunity to respond on two or more reinforcement schedules, the rate of responding on each schedule will match the reinforcement available on each schedule.

**Matching to sample** A discrimination training procedure in which the task is to select from two or more comparison stimuli the one that matches a sample. Abbreviated MTS.

**Mismatching** A variation of matching to sample in which reinforcement is available for selecting the comparison stimulus that is different from the sample. Also called *oddity matching*.

**Mixed schedule** A compound reinforcement schedule in which two or more simple schedules, neither associated with a particular stimulus, alternate. (*Cf.* multiple schedule.)

**Mnemonic** Any device for aiding recall. Typically they involve learning cues that will later prompt recall.

**Modal action pattern (MAP)** A series of related acts found in all or nearly all members of a species. Also called *fixed action pattern*. Formerly called instinct. (*Cf.* general behavior trait.)

**Motivating operation** Anything that changes the effectiveness of a consequence. There are two kinds of motivating operations, establishing and abolishing, which see.

**MTS** *See* matching to sample.

**Multiple schedule** A compound reinforcement schedule in which two or more simple schedules alternate, with each schedule associated with a particular stimulus. (*Cf.* mixed schedule.)

**Mutation** Any abrupt change in a gene. When the modified gene occurs in a reproductive cell, the mutation may be passed on to offspring.

**Natural reinforcer** Any reinforcer that is the spontaneous consequence of a behavior. Also called *automatic reinforcer*. (*Cf.* contrived reinforcer.)

**Natural science approach** This is the approach to studying natural phenomena that is based on certain assumptions, such as the idea that natural events, including human behavior, are caused by natural phenomena, not by mysterious forces such as willpower or the mind.

**Negative punishment** A punishment procedure or experience in which a behavior is followed by the removal of, or a decrease in the intensity of, a stimulus. Also called *type 2 punishment* or *penalty training*. (*Cf.* positive punishment.)

**Negative reinforcement** A reinforcement procedure or experience in which a behavior is followed by the removal of, or a decrease in the intensity of, a stimulus. Sometimes called escape learning. (*Cf.* positive reinforcement; punishment.)

**Negative reinforcer** Any stimulus which, when removed following a behavior, increases or maintains the strength of that behavior.

**Neurotoxin** Any substance capable of damaging neural tissues. Neurotoxins can interfere with learning.

**Noncontingent reinforcement schedule** A reinforcement schedule in which reinforcers are delivered independently of behavior. Abbreviated NCR.

**Nondeclarative memory** Memory of things that cannot be expressed, at least not in words. Includes procedural memory. Also called *implicit memory*. (*Cf.* declarative memory.)

**Observational learning** Learning by observing events and their consequences. This text identifies two kinds of observational learning, *social* and *asocial*, which see.

**Oddity matching** *See* mismatching.

**One-process theory** The view that avoidance and punishment involve only one procedure—operant learning. (*Cf.* two-process theory.)

**Operant learning** Any procedure or experience in which a behavior becomes stronger or weaker (e.g., more or less likely to occur), depending on its consequences. Also called *instrumental learning*. (*Cf.* Pavlovian conditioning.)

**Over-imitation** The tendency of observers to imitate acts by a model that are irrelevant to obtaining reinforcement. Also spelled overimitation.

**Overlearning** The continuation of training beyond the point required to produce one errorless performance.

**Overshadowing** Failure of a stimulus that is part of a compound stimulus to become a CS. The stimulus is said to be overshadowed by the stimulus that does become a CS. (*Cf.* blocking.)

**Paired associate learning** A learning task involving pairs of words or other stimuli in which the subject is presented with the first item of a pair and is expected to produce the second item.

**Partial reinforcement effect** The tendency of a behavior to be more resistant to extinction following intermittent reinforcement than following continuous reinforcement. Abbreviated PRE. (Also often referred to as the partial reinforcement extinction effect, or PREE.)

**Pavlovian conditioning** The procedure of pairing a neutral stimulus (one that does *not* elicit a reflex response) with a US, a stimulus that *does* elicit a reflex response. Also called *classical* or *respondent conditioning*. The neutral stimulus is often referred to as a CS, though strictly speaking it becomes a CS only after being paired with a US. (*Cf.* operant learning.)

**Peak shift** The tendency following discrimination training for the peak of responding in a generalization gradient to shift away from the CS⁻ or S^Δ.

**Positive punishment** A punishment procedure or experience in which a behavior is followed by the presentation of, or an increase in the intensity of, a stimulus. Also called *type 1 punishment*. (*Cf.* negative punishment.)

**Positive reinforcement** A reinforcement procedure or experience in which a behavior is followed by the presentation of, or an increase in the intensity of, a stimulus. Sometimes called reward learning, although the term *reward* is problematic. (*Cf.* negative reinforcement.)

**Positive reinforcer** Any stimulus which, when presented following a behavior, increases or maintains the strength of that behavior.

**Post-reinforcement pause** A pause in responding following reinforcement; associated primarily with FI and FR schedules. Also called *pre-ratio pause* or *between-ratio pause*.

**PRE** *See* partial reinforcement effect.

**Premack principle** The observation that high-probability behavior reinforces low-probability behavior.

**Preparatory response theory** Theory of Pavlovian conditioning that proposes that the CR prepares the organism for the appearance of the US.

**Preparedness** *See* continuum of preparedness.

**Primary reinforcer** Any reinforcer that is innately reinforcing; i.e., not dependent on its association with other reinforcers. Also called *unconditioned reinforcers*. (*Cf.* secondary reinforcer.)

**Proactive interference** Forgetting caused by learning that occurred prior to the behavior in question. (*Cf.* retroactive interference.)

**Problem** A situation in which reinforcement is available but the behavior necessary to produce it is not.

**Procedural memory** Memory for procedures; the ability to perform a set of actions. (*Cf.* nondeclarative memory.)

**Progressive ratio schedule** A reinforcement schedule in which the requirement for reinforcement typically increases in a predetermined way, often immediately following each reinforcement.

**Progressive schedule** A reinforcement schedule in which the requirements for reinforcement increase systematically. (*See* progressive ratio schedule.)

**Prompted recall** A method of measuring forgetting in which hints (prompts) about the behavior to be performed are provided. Also called *cued recall*. (*Cf.* free recall.)

**Pseudoconditioning** The tendency of a neutral stimulus to elicit a CR when presented after a US has elicited a reflex response.

**Punisher** Any consequence of a behavior that decreases the strength of that behavior. (*Cf.* reinforcer.)

**Punishment** A decrease in the strength of a behavior due to its consequences. As a procedure, it means providing consequences for a behavior that decrease the strength of that behavior. (*Cf.* positive punishment; negative punishment; reinforcement.)

**Ratio strain** Disruption of the pattern of responding due to stretching the ratio of reinforcement too abruptly or too much. Though called ratio strain, the same idea applies to interval schedules.

**Recognition** A method of measuring forgetting in which the subject is required to identify stimuli (e.g., images, words) experienced earlier.

**Reflex** A relationship between a specific event and a simple, response to that event. The term usually refers to an unconditional reflex. (*Cf.* unconditional reflex; conditional reflex.)

**Reinforcement** An increase in the strength of a behavior due to its consequences. As a procedure, it means providing consequences for a behavior that increase or maintain the strength of that behavior. (*Cf.* positive reinforcement; negative reinforcement; punishment.)

**Relative value theory** Theory of reinforcement that considers reinforcers to be behaviors rather than stimuli and that attributes a reinforcer's effectiveness to its probability relative to other behaviors.

**Relearning method** A method of measuring forgetting in which a behavior is learned to criterion before and after a retention interval. The less training required compared to the initial training, the less forgetting has occurred. Also called the *savings method*.

**Releaser** Any stimulus that reliably elicits a modal action pattern.

**Respondent conditioning** *See* Pavlovian conditioning.

**Response-deprivation theory** The theory of reinforcement that says a behavior is reinforcing to the extent that the organism has been deprived (relative to its baseline frequency) of performing that behavior. Also called *equilibrium theory* or *response-restriction theory*.

**Response generalization** The tendency for changes in one behavior to spread to other behaviors. (*Cf.* stimulus generalization.)

**Response prevention** The procedure of altering the environment to prevent unwanted behavior from occurring.

**Response unit hypothesis** The idea that the partial reinforcement effect is due to differences in the definition of a behavior during intermittent and continuous reinforcement.

**Resurgence** The reappearance during extinction of a previously reinforced behavior.

**Retention interval** A period during which learning or practice of a behavior does not occur. In research on forgetting, the retention interval is often the time between the end of training and testing for forgetting.

**Retroactive interference** Forgetting caused by learning that occurred subsequent to the behavior in question. (*Cf.* proactive interference.)

**Reward learning** *See* positive reinforcement.

**Reward pathway** An area of the brain that, when stimulated, reinforces behavior. Also called *reward center* or *reward circuit*. It is thought to be key to the neurological basis of reinforcement.

**Run rate** The rate at which a behavior occurs once it has resumed following reinforcement.

$S^D$ A stimulus in the presence of which a behavior will be reinforced. Pronounced *ess-dee*. Sometimes represented as $S^+$ (*Cf.* $S^\Delta$.)

$S^\Delta$ A stimulus in the presence of which a behavior will *not* be reinforced. Pronounced *ess-delta*. Sometimes represented as $S^-$. (*Cf.* $S^D$.)

**Satiation** The loss of effectiveness of primary reinforcers due to their repeated use.

**Savings method** *See* relearning method.

**Schedule effects** The distinctive rate and pattern of behavior associated with a particular reinforcement schedule.

**Schedule of reinforcement** A rule describing the delivery of reinforcers for a behavior.

**Secondary reinforcer** Any reinforcer that has acquired its reinforcing properties through its association with other reinforcers. Also called *conditioned reinforcer*. (*Cf.* primary reinforcer.)

**Semantic memory** Memory of facts about the world. (*Cf.* episodic memory.)

**Sensory preconditioning** A procedure in which two neutral stimuli are paired, after which one is repeatedly paired with a US. If the other stimulus is then presented alone, it may elicit a CR even though it was never paired with the US.

**Sequential hypothesis** The idea that the partial reinforcement effect occurs because the sequence of reinforced and nonreinforced behaviors during intermittent reinforcement becomes a signal for responding during extinction.

**Shaping** The reinforcement of successive approximations of a desired behavior.

**Sidman avoidance procedure** An escape-avoidance training procedure in which no stimulus regularly precedes the aversive stimulus. Also called *unsignaled avoidance*.

**Simultaneous conditioning** A Pavlovian conditioning procedure in which the CS and US coincide exactly. That is, the CS and US begin and end at the same time.

**Simultaneous discrimination training** An operant discrimination training procedure in which the $S^D$ and $S^\Delta$ are presented at the same time. (*Cf.* successive discrimination training.)

**Single-case experiment** *See* within-subject experiment.

**Single-subject experiment** *See* within-subject experiment.

**Social observational learning** Learning from the observation of a model and the consequences of the model's behavior. This form of observational learning is also called *vicarious learning*. Note: The term is introduced in this edition, and is not part of the standard lexicon of learning. (*Cf.* asocial observational learning.)

**Spaced practice** *See* distributed practice.

**Spontaneous recovery** The sudden reappearance of a behavior following its extinction.

**State-dependent learning** Learning that occurs during a particular physiological state (such as alcoholic intoxication), is lost when that physiological state passes, and reemerges when the state recurs.

**Stimulus** Any event that affects, or is capable of affecting, behavior.

**Stimulus control** The tendency for a behavior to occur in the presence of an $S^D$ but not in the presence of an $S^\Delta$. (*Cf.* discrimination.) Some researchers now consider forgetting, which see, a product of stimulus control.

**Stimulus generalization** The tendency for changes in behavior in one situation to spread to other situations. It is also defined as the tendency for a behavior that occurs in the presence of one stimulus to occur in the presence of another stimulus.

**Stimulus substitution theory** In Pavlovian conditioning, the theory that the CS substitutes for the US. It assumes that the CR is essentially the same as the UR.

**Stretching the ratio** The procedure of gradually increasing the number of responses required for reinforcement. The concept can be applied to interval as well as ratio schedules. (*Cf.* ratio strain.)

**Successive discrimination training** An operant discrimination training procedure in which the $S^D$ and $S^\Delta$ are presented one after the other in random sequence. (*Cf.* simultaneous discrimination training.)

**Superstitious behavior** Any behavior that occurs repeatedly even though it does not produce the reinforcers that maintain it.

**Systematic desensitization** A form of counterconditioning (which see) in which a patient imagines progressively troubling scenes while relaxed.

**Tandem schedule** A compound reinforcement schedule that consists of a series of simple schedules, with reinforcement delivered only on completion of the last schedule in the series. In a tandem schedule, the simple schedules are not associated with different stimuli. (*Cf.* chain schedule.)

**Task analysis** The procedure of identifying the component elements of a behavior chain. This is the first step in chaining, which see.

**Test trial** In Pavlovian conditioning, the procedure of presenting the CS on some occasions without the US to determine whether learning has occurred. Also called *probe trial*.

**Trace conditioning** A Pavlovian conditioning procedure in which the CS begins and ends before the US is presented.

**Two-process theory** The view that avoidance and punishment involve two procedures—Pavlovian and operant learning. (*Cf.* one-process theory.)

**Type 1 punishment** *See* positive punishment.

**Type 2 punishment** *See* negative punishment.

**Unconditional reflex** A reflex that is largely innate (i.e., not the product of experience). An unconditional reflex consists of an unconditional stimulus and an unconditional response. (*See* reflex; conditional reflex.)

**Unconditional response** The reflex response elicited by an unconditional stimulus. Often called an unconditioned response. Abbreviated UR. (*Cf.* conditional response.)

**Unconditional stimulus** A stimulus that elicits an unconditional response. Often called an unconditioned stimulus. Abbreviated US. (*Cf.* conditional stimulus.)

**Unsignaled avoidance** *See* Sidman avoidance procedure.

**UR** *See* unconditional response.

**US** *See* unconditional stimulus.

**Variable duration schedule** A reinforcement schedule in which reinforcement is contingent on the continuous performance of a behavior for a period of time, with the length of the time varying around an average. Abbreviated VD. (*Cf.* fixed duration schedule.)

**Variable interval schedule** A reinforcement schedule in which a behavior is reinforced the first time it occurs following an interval since the last reinforcement, with the interval varying around a specified average. Abbreviated VI. (*Cf.* fixed interval schedule.)

**Variable ratio schedule** A reinforcement schedule in which, on average, every *n*th performance of a behavior is reinforced. Abbreviated VR. (*Cf.* fixed ratio schedule.)

**Variable time schedule** A reinforcement schedule in which reinforcement is delivered independently of behavior at varying intervals. Abbreviated VT. (*Cf.* fixed time schedule.)

**VI schedule** *See* variable interval schedule.

**Vicarious learning** *See* social observational learning.

**Vicarious punishment** A decrease in the strength of an observed behavior following punishment of that behavior in a model. (*Cf.* vicarious reinforcement.)

**Vicarious reinforcement** An increase in the strength of an observed behavior following reinforcement of that behavior in a model. (*Cf.* vicarious punishment.)

**Virtual reality exposure therapy** A form of exposure therapy (which see) that relies on technology that creates simulated scenes that arouse anxiety. Abbreviated VRET.

**VRET** *See* virtual reality exposure therapy.

**VR schedule** *See* variable ratio schedule.

**VT schedule** *See* variable time schedule.

**Within-subject experiment** A research design in which the independent variable is made to vary at different times for the same subject. Thus, each subject serves as both an experimental and control subject. Also called *single-subject* or *single-case experiment*. (*Cf.* between-subjects experiment.)

# References

Abraham, A. D., Cunningham, C. L., & Lattal, K. M. (2012). Methylphenidate enhances extinction of contextual fear. *Learning & Memory*, 19, 67–72.

Abramowitz, A. J., & O'Leary, S. G. (1990). Effectiveness of delayed punishment in an applied setting. *Behavior Therapy*, 21, 231–239.

Abramowitz, A. J., O'Leary, S. G., & Rosen, L. A. (1987). Reducing off-task behavior in the classroom: A comparison of encouragement and reprimands. *Journal of Abnormal Child Psychology*, 15, 153–163.

Adams, M. A., Hovell, M. F., Irvin, V., Sallis, J. F., Coleman, K. J., & Liles, S. (2006). Promoting stair use by modeling: An experimental application of the behavioral ecological model. *American Journal of Health Promotion*, 21(2), 101–109.

Adams-Curtiss, L., & Fragaszy, D. M. (1995). Influence of a skilled model on the behavior of conspecific observers in tufted capuchin monkeys (*Cebus apella*). *American Journal of Primatology*, 37, 65–71.

Ader, R., & Cohen, N. (1975). Behaviorally conditioned immunosuppression. *Psychosomatic Medicine*, 37, 333–340.

Ader, R., & Cohen, N. (1993). Psychoneuroimmunology: Conditioning and stress. *Annual Review of Psychology*, 33, 53–86.

Agar, W. E., Drummond, F. H., Tiegs, O. W., & Gunson, M. M. (1954). Fourth (final) report on a test of McDougall's Lamarckian experiment on the training of rats. *Journal of Experimental Biology*, 31, 307–321.

Agnew, J. L., & Daniels, A. (2010). *Safe by accident?* Atlanta, GA: Performance Management Publications.

Agras, S., Sylvestor, D., & Oliveau, D. (1969). The epidemiology of common fears and phobias. *Comprehensive Psychiatry*, 10, 151–156.

Akin, O. (1983). *The psychology of architectural design.* London: Pion.

Alavosius, M. P., & Sulzer-Azaroff, B. (1985). An on-the-job method to evaluate patient lifting technique. *Applied Ergonomics*, 16(4), 307–311.

Alavosius, M. P., & Sulzer-Azaroff, B. (1990). Acquisition and maintenance of health-care routines as a function of feedback density. *Journal of Applied Behavior Analysis*, 23, 151–162.

Albert, M., & Ayres, J. J. B. (1997). One-trial simultaneous and backward excitatory conditioning in rats: Lick suppression, freezing, and rearing to CS compounds and their elements. *Animal Learning and Behavior*, 25(2), 210–220.

Albert, R. S. (1980). Family positions and the attainment of eminence. *Gifted Child Quarterly*, 24, 87–95.

Alford, B. A. (1986). Behavioral treatment of schizophrenic delusions: A single-case experimental analysis. *Behavior Therapy*, 17, 637–644.

Allan, R. W. (1990). Concept learning and peck location in the pigeon. Paper presented at the 16th annual convention of the Association for Behavior Analysis, Nashville, TN.

Allan, R. W. (1993). Control of pecking response topography by stimulus-reinforcer and response-reinforcer contingencies. In H. Philip Zeigler & Hans-Joachim Bischof (Eds.), *Vision, brain, and behavior in birds* (pp. 285–300). Cambridge, MA: MIT Press.

Allan, R. W. (1998). Operant-respondent interactions. In W. T. O'Donohue (Ed.), *Learning and behavior therapy* (pp. 146–168). Boston, MA: Allyn & Bacon.

Allen, C. T., & Janiszewski, C. A. (1989). Assessing the role of contingency awareness in attitudinal conditioning with implications for advertising research. *Journal of Marketing Research*, 26, 30–43.

Alloway, T., Wilson, G., & Graham, J. (2011). *Sniffy the virtual rat: Pro (version 3).* Belmont, CA: Wadsworth.

Almeida, M. B., Schild, A. L., Brasil, N. D. A., Quevedo, P. S., Fiss, L., Pfister, J. A., & Riet-Correa, F. (2009). Conditioned aversion in sheep induced by *Baccharis coridifolia. Applied Animal Behaviour Science*, 117, 197–200.

Almeida, M. B., Schild, A. L., Pfister, J., Assis-Brasil, N. D., Pimentel, M., Forster, K. M., & Riet-Correa, F. Methods of inducing conditioned food aversion to *Baccharis coridifolia* (mio-mio) in cattle. Unpublished Manuscript.

Altevogt, B. M., Pankevich, D. E., Pope, A. M., & Kahn, J. P. (2011). Guiding limited use of chimpanzees in research. *Science*, 335(6064), 41–42. Available at http://www.sciencemag.org/cgi/content/summary/335/6064/41.

Alvero, A. M., Bucklin, B. R., & Austin, J. (2001). An objective review of the effectiveness and essential characteristics of performance feedback in organizational settings. *Journal of Organizational Behavior Management*, 2(1), 3–5.

Amabile, T. M. (1982). Children's artistic creativity: Detrimental effects of competition in a field setting. *Personality and Social Psychology Bulletin, 8*, 573–578.

Amabile, T. M. (1983). *The social psychology of creativity.* New York: Springer-Verlag.

American Psychiatric Association. (1973). *Behavior therapy in psychiatry.* New York: Aronson.

American Psychological Association Ethics Committee. (2010). Ethical principles of psychologists and code of conduct. *American Psychologist, 47*, 1597–1611.

Amsel, A. (1958). The role of frustrative nonreward in noncontinuous reward situations. *Psychological Bulletin, 55*, 102–119.

Amsel, A. (1962). Frustrative nonreward in partial reinforcement and discrimination learning: Some recent history and theoretical extension. *Psychological Review, 69*, 306–328.

Anderson, C. A., Shibuya, A., Ihori, N., Swing, E. L., Bushman, B. J., Sakamoto, A. et al. (2010). Violent video game effects on aggression, empathy, and prosocial behavior in Eastern and Western countries: A meta-analytic review. *Psychological Bulletin, 136*(2), 151–173.

Anderson, P., Rothbaum, B. O., & Hodges, L. F. (2000). Social phobia: Virtual reality exposure therapy for fear of public speaking. Paper presented at the annual meeting of the American Psychological Association, Washington, DC.

Anderson, P., Rothbaum, B. O., & Hodges, L. F. (2003). Virtual reality exposure in the treatment of social anxiety. *Cognitive and Behavioral Practice, 10*, 240–247.

Andreasen, N. C. (2010). A journey into chaos: Creativity and the unconscious. Seminar on Mind, Brain and Consciousness, Thane, India, January 14 and 15.

Anger, D. (1963). The role of temporal discrimination in the reinforcement of Sidman avoidance behavior. *Journal of the Experimental Analysis of Behavior, 6*, 477–506.

Angier, N. (2009, July 21). When "what animals do" doesn't seem to cover it. *New York Times*, p. D1.

Angoff, W. H. (1984). *Scales, norms, and equivalent scores.* Princeton, NJ: Educational Testing Service.

Anrep, G. V. (1920). Pitch discrimination in the dog. *Journal of Physiology, 53*, 367–385.

Aristotle. (1985). *The politics* (Carnes Lord, Trans.) Chicago: University of Chicago Press.

Aronson, E. (2011). *The social animal* (11th ed). New York: Worth Publishers.

Athens, E. S., & Vollmer, T. R. (2010). An investigation of differential reinforcement of alternative behavior without extinction. *Journal of Applied Behavior Analysis, 43*, 569–589.

Austin, J., Kessler, M. L., Riccobono, J. E., & Bailey, J. S. (1996). Using feedback and reinforcement to improve the performance and safety of a roofing crew. *Journal of Organizational Behavior Management, 16*(2), 49–75.

Austin, J. L., & Bevan, D. (2011). Using differential reinforcement of low rates to reduce children's requests for teacher attention. *Journal of Applied Behavior Analysis, 44*, 451–461.

Axelrod, S. (1983). Introduction. In S. Axelrod & J. Apsche (Eds.), *The effects of punishment on human behavior.* New York: Academic Press.

Ayres, J. J. B., Haddad, C., & Albert, M. (1987). One-trial excitatory backward conditioning as assessed by conditioned suppression of licking in rats: Concurrent observations of lick suppression and defensive behaviors. *Animal Learning and Behavior, 15*(2), 212–217.

Aziz-Zadeh, L., Cattaneo, L., & Rizzolatti, G. (2005). Covert speech arrest induced by rTMS over both motor and non-motor left hemisphere frontal sites. *Journal of Cognitive Neuroscience, 17*(6), 928–938.

Azrin, N. H. (1959). A technique for delivering shock to pigeons. *Journal of the Experimental Analysis of Behavior, 2*, 161–163.

Azrin, N. H. (1960). Effects of punishment intensity during variable-interval reinforcement. *Journal of the Experimental Analysis of Behavior, 3*(2), 123–142.

Azrin, N. H., & Holz, W. C. (1961). Punishment during fixed-interval reinforcement. *Journal of the Experimental Analysis of Behavior, 4*, 343–347.

Azrin, N. H., & Holz, W. C. (1966). Punishment. In W. K. Honig (Ed.), *Operant behavior: Areas of research and application* (pp. 380–447). New York: Appleton-Century-Crofts.

Azrin, N. H., Holz, W. C., & Hake, D. F. (1963). Fixed-ratio punishment. *Journal of the Experimental Analysis of Behavior, 6*, 141–148.

Azrin, N. H., Hutchinson, R. R., & Hake, D. F. (1966). Extinction-induced aggression. *Journal of the Experimental Analysis of Behavior, 9*, 191–204.

Azrin, N. H., Hutchinson, R. R., & McLaughlin, R. (1965). The opportunity for aggression as an operant reinforcer during aversive stimulation. *Journal of the Experimental Analysis of Behavior, 8*, 171–180.

Bachmeyer, M. H. (2010). An evaluation of motivating operations in the treatment of food refusal. Doctoral dissertation, University of Iowa, Iowa City, IA. Available at http://ir.uiowa.edu/etd/637.

Bachrach, A. J., Erwin, W. J., & Mohr, J. P. (1965). The control of eating behavior in an anorexic by operant conditioning techniques. In L. P. Ullmann & L. Krasner (Eds.), *Case studies in behavior modification* (pp. 153–163). New York: Holt, Rinehart & Winston.

Baddeley, A., Eysenck, M. W., & Anderson, M. (2009). *Memory.* New York: Psychology Press.

Baddeley, A. D. (1976). *The psychology of memory.* New York: Basic Books.

Baddeley A. D. (1982). Domains of recollection. *Psychological Review, 89*, 708–729.

Baer, D. M. (1999). *How to plan for generalization* (2nd ed.). Austin, TX: Pro-Ed.

Baer, D. M., & Deguchi, H. (1985). Generalized imitation from a radical-behavioral viewpoint. In S. Reiss & R. R. Bootzin (Eds.), *Theoretical issues in behavior therapy* (pp. 197–217). Orlando, FL: Academic Press.

Baer, D. M., Peterson, R. F., & Sherman, J. A. (1967). The development of imitation by reinforcing behavioral similarity to a model. *Journal of the Experimental Analysis of Behavior, 10,* 405–416.

Baer, D. M., & Sherman, J. A. (1964). Reinforcement control of generalized imitation in young children. *Journal of Experimental Child Psychology, 1,* 37–49.

Bahrick, H. P. (1984). Semantic memory content in permastore: Fifty years of memory for Spanish learned in school. *Journal of Experimental Psychology: General, 113,* 1–29.

Bahrick, H. P., & Phelps, E. (1987). Retention of Spanish vocabulary over 8 years. *Journal of Experimental Psychology: Learning, Memory, and Cognition, 13*(2), 344–349.

Baldwin, J. (2007). The value of studying behavior in everyday life. Lecture given at the annual meeting of the Association for Behavior Analysis, San Diego, CA, May 29.

Baker, B. L. (1969). Symptom treatment and symptom substitution in enuresis. *Journal of Abnormal Psychology, 74*(1), 42–49.

Baker, W. E., Honea, H., & Russell, C. A. (2004). Do not wait to reveal the brand name: The effect of brand-name placement on television advertising effectiveness. *Journal of Advertising, 33,* 77–85.

Balcazar, F. E., Hopkins, B. L., & Suarez, Y. (1985–1986). A critical, objective review of performance feedback. *Journal of Organizational Behavior Management, 7*(3–4), 65–89.

Balster, R. (1992, December). In defense of animal research. *APA Monitor,* p. 3.

Bandura, A. (1965). Vicarious processes: A case of no-trial learning. In L. Berkowitz (Ed.), *Advances in experimental social psychology,* Vol. 2 (pp. 1–55). New York: Academic Press.

Bandura, A. (1969). Social-learning theory of identificatory processes. In D. A. Goslin (Ed.), *Handbook of socialization theory and research* (pp. 213–262). Skokie, IL: Rand McNally & Co.

Bandura, A. (1971a). Analysis of modeling processes. In A. Bandura (Ed.), *Psychological modeling: Conflicting theories* (pp. 1–62). Chicago: Aldine-Atherton.

Bandura, A. (Ed.). (1971b). *Psychological modeling: Conflicting theories.* Chicago: Aldine-Atherton.

Bandura, A. (1971c). *Social learning theory.* New York: General Learning Press.

Bandura, A. (1973). *Aggression: A social learning analysis.* Englewood Cliffs, NJ: Prentice-Hall.

Bandura, A. (1977). *Social learning theory.* Englewood Cliffs, NJ: Prentice-Hall.

Bandura, A. (1983/2004). Model of causality in social learning theory. In A. Freeman, M. Mahoney, P. L. DeVito, & D. M. Martin (Eds.), *Cognition and psychotherapy* (2nd ed.) (pp. 25–44). New York: Springer.

Bandura, A. (1986). *Social foundations of thought and action.* Englewood Cliffs, NJ: Prentice-Hall.

Bandura, A., & Mischel, W. (1965). Modification of self-imposed delay of reward through exposure to live and symbolic models, *Journal of Personality and Social Psychology, 2,* 698–705.

Bandura, A., Ross, D., & Ross, S. A. (1961) Transmission of aggression through imitation of aggressive models. *Journal of Abnormal and Social Psychology, 63,* 575–582.

Bandura, A., & Walters, R. H. (1959). *Adolescent aggression.* New York: Ronald Press.

Baron, A., & Derenne, A. (2000). Progressive-ratio schedules: Effects of later schedule requirements on earlier performances. *Journal of the Experimental Analysis of Behavior, 73,* 291–304.

Baron, A., & Galizio, M. (2005). Positive and negative reinforcement: Should the distinction be preserved? *The Behavior Analyst, 28,* 85–98.

Baron, A., & Galizio, M. (2006). Distinguishing between positive and negative reinforcement: Responses to Nakajima (2006) and Staats (2006). *The Behavior Analyst, 29,* 273–277.

Barr, R., Dowden, A., & Hayne, H. (1996). Developmental changes in deferred imitation by 6- to 24-month-old infants. *Infant Behavior and Development, 19,* 159–170.

Bartlett, F. C. (1932). *Remembering: A study in experimental social psychology.* New York: Macmillan.

Barton, E. J., & Ascione F. R. (1979). Sharing in preschool children: Facilitation, stimulus generalization, response generalization, and maintenance. *Journal of Applied Behavior Analysis, 12,* 417–430.

Baum, W. M. (1974). Choice in free-ranging wild pigeons. *Science, 185,* 78–79.

Baum, W. M. (1975). Time allocation in human vigilance. *Journal of the Experimental Analysis of Behavior, 23,* 43–53.

Baum, W. M. (2007). Evolutionary theory is the proper framework for behavior analysis. Lecture presented at the annual meeting of the Association for Behavior Analysis, San Diego, CA, May 28.

Baum, W. M. (2010). Dynamics of choice: A tutorial. *Journal of the Experimental Analysis of Behavior, 94*(2), 161–174. doi: 10.1901/jeab.2010.94-161.

Baum, W. M. (2011). Why private events are a mistake. Address given at the annual meeting of the Association for Behavior Analysis, Denver, CO, May.

Baum, W. M., & Kraft, J. R. (1998). Group choice: Competition, travel, and the ideal free distribution. *Journal of the Experimental Analysis of Behavior, 69,* 227–245.

Baumann, S., Neff, C., Fetzick, S., Stangl, G., Basler, L., Vereneck, R., et al. (2003). A virtual reality system for neurobehavioral and functional MRI studies. *CyberPsychology & Behavior, 6*(3), 259–266. doi: 10.1089/109493103322011542.

Beaman, R., & Wheldall, K. (2000). Teachers' use of approval and disapproval in the classroom. *Educational Psychology, 20,* 431–446.

Bean, A. W., & Roberts, M. W. (1981). The effect of time-out release contingencies on changes in child noncompliance. *Journal of Abnormal Child Psychology, 9,* 95–105.

Bechara, A., Damasio, H., Tranel, D., & Damasio, A. R. (1997). Deciding advantageously before knowing the advantageous strategy. *Science, 275*(5304), 1293–1295.

Bechara, A., Tranel, D., Damasio, H., Adolphs, R., Rockland, C., & Damasio, A. R. (1995). Double dissociation of conditioning and declarative knowledge relative to the amygdala and hippocampus in humans. *Science, 269*(5227), 1115–1118.

Becker, J. V., & Hunter, J. A. (1992). Evaluation of treatment outcome for adult perpetrators of child sexual abuse. *Criminal Justice and Behavior, 19*(1), 74–92.

Becker, W. C. (1971). *Parents are teachers: A child management program*. Champaign, IL: Research Press.

Belke, T. W., & Dunbar, M. J. (2001). Effects of cocaine on fixed interval responding reinforced by the opportunity to run. *Journal of the Experimental Analysis of Behavior, 75*, 77–91.

Berger, S. M. (1971). Observer perseverance as related to a model's success: A social comparison analysis. *Journal of Personality and Social Psychology, 19*, 341–350.

Berkowitz, L. (1983). Aversively stimulated aggression: Some parallels and differences in research with animals and humans. *American Psychologist, 38*, 1135–1144.

Berkowitz, L., & Donnerstein, E. (1982). External validity is more than skin deep: Some answers to criticisms of laboratory experiments. *American Psychologist, 37*, 245–257.

Bernard, J., & Gilbert, R. W. (1941). The specificity of the effect of shock for error in maze learning with human subjects. *Journal of Experimental Psychology, 28*, 178–186.

Bierley, C., McSweeney, F. K., & Vannieuwkerk, R. (1985). Classical conditioning of preferences for stimuli. *Journal of Consumer Research, 12*, 316–323.

Bihm, E. M., Gillaspy, J. A., Jr., Abbott, H. J., & Lammers, W. J. (2010). More misbehavior of organisms: A Psi Chi Lecture by Marian and Robert Bailey. *The Psychological Record, 60*(3), 505–522.

Binder, C. (1988). Precision teaching: Measuring and attaining exemplary academic achievement. *Youth Policy, 10*(7), 12–15.

Binder, C., Haughton, E., & Van Eyk, D. (1990). Increasing endurance by building fluency: Precision teaching attention span. *Teaching Exceptional Children, 22*, 24–27.

Binder, C., & Watkins, C. L. (1990). Precision teaching and direct instruction: Measurably superior instructional technology in schools. *Performance Improvement Quarterly, 3*(4), 74–96.

Binmore, K. (1991). Rational choice theory: Necessary but not sufficient. *American Psychologist, 46*, 797–799.

Birnbrauer, J. S. (1968). Generalization of punishment—A case study. *Journal of Applied Behavior Analysis, 1*(3), 201–211.

Bishop, M. P., Elder, S. T., & Heath, R. G. (1963). Intracranial self-stimulation in man. *Science, 140*(3565), 394–396.

Bitterman, M. E. (1964). Classical conditioning in the goldfish as a function of the CS-US interval. *Journal of Comparative and Physiological Psychology, 58*, 359–366.

Bjork, E. L., Storm, B. C., & de Winstanley, P. A. (2010). Learning from the consequences of retrieval: Another test effect. In A. S. Benjamin (Ed.), *Successful remembering and successful forgetting: A festschrift in honor of Robert A. Bjork* (pp. 351–368). New York: Psychology Press.

Bjork, R. A. (1979). Improving processing analysis of college teaching. *Educational Psychology, 14*, 15–23.

Blaha, F. (1946). In trial of the major German war criminals. *Proceedings of the International Military Tribunal at Nuremberg*, HMSO. Reprinted in J. Carey (Ed.), *Eyewitness to history*. Cambridge, MA: Harvard University Press.

Blakely, E., & Schlinger, H. (1988). Determinants of pausing under variable-ratio schedules: Reinforcer magnitude, ratio size, and schedule configuration. *Journal of the Experimental Analysis of Behavior, 50*, 65–73.

Bliss, R. E., Garvey, A. J., Heinold, J. W., & Hitchcock, J. L. (1989). The influence of situation and coping on relapse crisis outcomes after smoking cessation. *Journal of Consulting and Clinical Psychology, 57*, 443–449.

Bloom, B. S. (1986, February). Automaticity: The hands and feet of genius. *Educational Leadership*, 70–76.

Blough, D. S. (1959). Delayed matching in the pigeon. *Journal of the Experimental Analysis of Behavior, 2*, 151–160.

Blough, D. S. (1982). Pigeon perception of letters of the alphabet. *Science, 218*, 397–398.

Boakes, R. (1977). Performance on learning to associate a stimulus with positive reinforcement in the rat. *Journal of the Experimental Analysis of Behavior, 29*, 115–134.

Boe, E. E., & Church, R. M. (1967). Permanent effects of punishment during extinction. *Journal of Comparative and Physiological Psychology, 63*, 486–492.

Bond, N. W., & Di Giusto, E. L. (1976). One-trial higher-order conditioning of a taste aversion. *Australian Journal of Psychology, 28*, 53–55.

Booth, R., & Rachman, S. (1992). The reduction of claustrophobia—1. *Behavior Research and Therapy, 30*(3), 207–221.

Bordnick, P. S., Copp, H. L., Traylor, A., Graap, K. M., Carter, B. L., Walton, A., & Ferrer, M. (2009). Reactivity to cannabis cues in virtual reality environments. *Journal of Psychoactive Drugs, 41*(2), 105–112.

Borovsky, D., & Rovee-Collier, C. (1990). Contextual constraints on memory retrieval at six months. *Child Development, 61*, 1569–1583.

Borrero, J. C., & Vollmer, T. R. (2002). An application of the matching law to severe problem behavior. *Journal of Applied Behavior Analysis, 35*, 13–27.

Boutelle, K. N., Jeffery, R. W., Murray, D. M., & Schmitz, M. K. H. (2001). Using signs, artwork, and music to promote stair use in a public building. *American Journal of Public Health, 91*(12), 2004–2006.

Bouton, M. E., Garcia-Gutierrez, A., Zilski, J., & Moody, E. W. (2006). Extinction in multiple contexts does not necessarily make extinction less vulnerable to relapse. *Behavioural Research and Therapy, 44*, 983–994.

Bouton, M. E., & Swartzentruber, D. (1991). Source of relapse after extinction in Pavlovian and instrumental learning. *Clinical Psychology Review, 11*, 123–140.

Bovbjerg, D. H., Redd, W. H., Maier, L. A., Holland, J. C., Lesko, L. M., Niedzwiecki, D., et al. (1990). Anticipatory immune suppression and nausea in women receiving cyclic chemotherapy for ovarian cancer. *Journal of Consulting and Clinical Psychology, 58*, 153–157.

Boyer, E., Miltenberger, R. G., Batsche, C., & Fogel, V. (2009). Video modeling by experts with video feedback to enhance gymnastics skills. *Journal of Applied Behavior Analysis, 42*, 855–860.

Branch, M. N. (1977). On the role of "memory" in the analysis of behavior. *Journal of the Experimental Analysis of Behavior, 28,* 171–179.

Braun, H. W., & Geiselhart, R. (1959). Age differences in the acquisition and extinction of the conditioned eyelid response. *Journal of Experimental Psychology, 57,* 386–388.

Breland, K., & Breland, M. (1961). The misbehavior of organisms. *American Psychologist, 16,* 681–684.

Bridger, W. H. (1961). Sensory habituation and discrimination in the human neonate. *American Journal of Psychiatry, 117,* 991–996.

Broden, M., Bruce, C., Mitchell, M. A., Carter, V., & Hall, R. V. (1970). Effects of teacher attention on attending behavior of two boys at adjacent desks. *Journal of Applied Behavior Analysis, 3*(3), 199–203.

Brogden, W. J. (1939a). Higher order conditioning. *American Journal of Psychology, 52*(4), 579–591.

Brogden, W. J. (1939b). Sensory pre-conditioning. *Journal of Experimental Psychology, 25,* 323–332.

Browder, D. M., Schoen, S. F., & Lentz, F. E. (1986). Learning to learn through observation. *Journal of Special Education, 20*(4), 447–461.

Brown, F. J., Peace, N., & Parsons, R. (2009). Teaching children generalized imitation skills: A case study. *Journal of Intellectual Disabilities, 13,* 9–17.

Brown, P. L., & Jenkins, H. M. (1968). Auto-shaping of the pigeon's key-peck. *Journal of the Experimental Analysis of Behavior, 11,* 1–8.

Brown, R. I. (2007). Galen: Developer of the reversal design? *The Behavior Analyst, 30,* 31–35.

Bruchey, A. K., & Gonzalez-Lima, F. (2006). Brain activity associated with fear renewal. *European Journal of Neuroscience, 24*(12), 3567–3577.

Bruner, J. S. (1983). *In search of mind: Essays in autobiography.* New York: Harper/Collins.

Bryan, W. L., & Harter, N. (1899). Studies on the telegraphic language. The acquisition of a hierarchy of habits. *Psychological Review, 6,* 345–375.

Buckalew, L. W., & Gibson, G. S. (1984). Antecedent and attendant stimuli in smoking: Implications for behavioral maintenance and modification. *Journal of Clinical Psychology, 40,* 1101–1106.

Bucklin, B. R., & Dickinson, A. M. (2001). Individual monetary incentives: A review of different types of arrangements between performance and pay. *Journal of Organizational Behavior Management, 21*(3), 45–137.

Burdick, A. (1991, November/December). Spin doctors. *The Sciences,* 54.

Bushman, B. J., & Gibson, B. (2010). Violent video games cause an increase in aggression long after the game has been turned off. *Social Psychological and Personality Science, 2*(1), 29–32.

Buzas, H. P., & Ayllon, T. (1981). Differential reinforcement in coaching tennis skills. *Behavior Modification, 5,* 372–385.

Cahoon, D. D. (1968). Symptom substitution and the behavior therapies: A reappraisal. *Psychological Bulletin, 69*(3), 149–156.

Calkins, M. W. (1894). Association: I. *Psychological Review, 1,* 476–483.

Calkins, M. W. (1896). Association: II. *Psychological Review, 3,* 32–49.

Camp, D. S., Raymond, G. A., & Church, R. M. (1967). Temporal relationship between response and punishment. *Journal of Experimental Psychology, 74,* 114–123.

Cannon, D. S., Baker, G. A., & Nathan, P. E. (1986). Alcohol aversion therapy: Relation between strength of aversion and abstinence. *Journal of Consulting and Clinical Psychology, 54*(6), 825–830.

Capaldi, E. J. (1966). Partial reinforcement: A hypothesis of sequential effects. *Psychological Review, 73,* 459–477.

Capaldi, E. J. (1967). A sequential hypothesis of instrumental learning. In K. W. Spence & J. T. Spence (Eds.), *The psychology of learning and motivation,* Vol. 1 (pp. 67–156). New York: Academic Press.

Capaldi, E. J., & Neath, I. (1995). Remembering and forgetting as contextual discrimination. *Learning & Memory, 2,* 107–132.

Capehart, J., Viney, W., & Hulicka, I. M. (1958). The effect of effort upon extinction. *Journal of Consulting and Clinical Psychology, 51,* 505–507.

Caple, C. (1996). *The effects of spaced practice and review on recall and retention using computer assisted instruction.* Ann Arbor, MI: UMI.

Carey, J. (Ed.). (1988). *Eyewitness to history.* Cambridge, MA: Harvard University Press.

Carey, S. (2011). *The origin of concepts.* New York: Oxford University Press.

Carlin, A. S., Hoffman, H. G., & Weghorst, S. (1997). Virtual reality and tactile augmentation in the treatment of spider phobia: A case study. *Behavior Research and Therapy, 35,* 153–158.

Carlson, J. G., & Wielkiewicz, R. M. (1972). Delay of reinforcement in instrumental discrimination learning of rats. *Journal of Comparative and Physiological Psychology, 81,* 365–370.

Carr, A. (1967). Adaptive aspects of the scheduled travel of Chelonia. In R. M. Storm (Ed.), *Animal orientation and navigation* (pp. 35–52). Corvallis: Oregon State University Press.

Carr, E. G. (1977). The motivation of self-injurious behavior: A review of some hypotheses. *Psychological Bulletin, 84,* 800–816.

Carr, E. G., & McDowell, J. J. (1980). Social control of self-injurious behavior of organic etiology. *Behavior Therapy, 11,* 402–409.

Carr, E. G., Robinson, S., & Palumbo, L. W. (1990a). The wrong issue: Aversive versus nonaversive treatment. The right issue: Functional versus nonfunctional treatment.

In A. Rapp & N. Singh (Eds.), *Perspectives on the use of nonaversive and aversive interventions for persons with developmental disabilities* (pp. 361–379). Sycamore, IL: Sycamore Press.

Carroll, L., & Rosner, D. (2012). The concussion crisis: Anatomy of a silent epidemic. New York, NY: Simon & Schuster.

Carroll, S. (2010, September 14). Hybrids may thrive where parents fear to tread. *New York Times*, p. D2.

Carter, N., Homstrom, A., Simpanen, M., & Melin, L. (1988). Theft reduction in a grocery store through product identification and graphing of losses for employees. *Journal of Applied Behavior Analysis, 21*(4), 385–389.

Cascio, W. F. (1991). Applied psychology in personnel management. Englewood Cliffs, NJ: Prentice Hall.

Cassidy, S., Roche, B., & Hayes, S. (2011). A relational frame training intervention to raise intelligence quotients: A pilot study. *The Psychological Record, 61*, 173–198.

Catania, A. C. (1966). Concurrent operants. In W. K. Honig (Ed.), *Operant behavior: Areas of research and application* (pp. 213–230). New York: Appleton-Century-Crofts.

Catania, A. C. (2006). *Learning* (4th interim ed.). Cornwall-on-Hudson, NY: Sloan Publishing.

Ceci, S. J., & Bronfenbrenner, U. (1985). Don't forget to take the cupcakes out of the oven: Prospective memory, strategic time-monitoring, and context. *Child Development, 56*(1), 152–164.

Cepeda, N. J., Pashler, H., Vul, E., Wixted, J. T., & Rohrer, D. (2006). Distributed practice in verbal recall tasks: A review and quantitative synthesis. *Psychological Bulletin, 132*(3), 354–380.

Chall, J. S. (1995). *Learning to read: The great debate.* New York: Harcourt Brace.

Chambers, K., Goldman, L., & Kovesdy, P. (1977). Effects of positive reinforcement on creativity. *Perceptual and Motor Skills, 44*, 322.

Chance, P. (1974, January). After you hit a child, you can't just get up and leave him; you are hooked to that kid: An interview with Ivar Lovaas. *Psychology Today*, 76–84.

Chance, P. (1975, December). Facts that liberated the gay community: An interview with Evelyn Hooker. *Psychology Today*, 52–55, 101.

Chance, P. (1997). Speaking of differences. *Phi Delta Kappan, 78*(7), 506–507.

Chance, P. (1999). Thorndike's puzzle boxes and the origins of the experimental analysis of behavior. *Journal of the Experimental Analysis of Behavior, 72*(3), 433–440.

Chance, P. (2007). The ultimate challenge: Prove B. F. Skinner wrong. *The Behavior Analyst, 30*, 153–160.

Chance, P. (2008). *The teacher's craft: The 10 essential skills of effective teaching.* Long Grove, IL: Waveland Press.

Charness, N. (1979). Components of skill in bridge. *Canadian Journal of Psychology, 33*, 1–50.

Chase, A. R. (2001). Music discrimination by carp (*Cyprinus carpio*). *Animal Behavior, 29*, 336–353.

Chase, P. N. (2006). Teaching the distinction between positive and negative reinforcement. *The Behavior Analyst, 29*, 113–115.

Chase, W. G., & Simon, H. A. (1973). Perception in chess. *Cognitive Psychology, 4*, 55–81.

Christopher, A. B. (1988). *Predisposition versus experiential models of compulsive gambling: An experimental analysis using pigeons.* Unpublished Ph.D. dissertation, West Virginia University, Morgantown, WV.

Chugani, H. T., Behen, M. E., Muzik, O., Csaba, J., Nagy, F., & Chugani, D. C. (2001). Local brain function activity following early deprivation: A study of postinstitutionalized Romanian orphans. *NeuroImage, 14*, 1290–1301.

Cipani, E. (1999). *Helping parents help their kids: A clinical guide to six child problem behaviors.* Philadelphia, PA: Bruner-Mazel.

Cipani, E. (2004). *Punishment on trial: A resource guide to child discipline.* Available at ecipni.com/PoT.pdf.

Clark, R. E., & Squire, L. R. (1998). Classical conditioning and brain systems: The role of awareness. *Science, 280*(5360), 77–81.

Coates, B., & Hartup, W. (1969). Age and verbalization in observational learning. *Developmental Psychology, 1*, 556–562.

Cohen, J. Y., Haesler, S., Linh, V., Lowell, B. B., & Uchida, N. (2012). Neuro-type-specific signals for reward and punishment in the ventral tegmental area. *Nature, 482*, 85–88.

Conklin, C. A., & Tiffany, S. (2002). Applying extinction research and theory to cue-exposure addiction treatments. *Addiction, 97*(2), 155–167.

Cook, L. K., & Mayer, R. E. (1988). Teaching readers about the structure of scientific text. *Journal of Educational Psychology, 80*(4), 448–456.

Cook, M., & Mineka, S. (1990). Selective associations in the observational conditioning of fear in rhesus monkeys. *Journal of Experimental Psychology: Animal Behavior Processes, 16*, 372–389.

Cooper, J. O., Heron, T. E., & Heward, W. L. (2007). *Applied Behavior Analysis* (2nd ed.). Upper Saddle River, NJ: Pearson.

Cooper, L. A., & Shepard, R. N. (1973). Chronometric studies of the rotation of mental images. In W. G. Chase (Ed.), *Visual information processing* (pp. 75–176). New York: Academic Press.

Cooper, R. M., & Zubek, J. P. (1958). Effects of enriched and restricted early environment on the learning ability of bright and dull rats. *Canadian Journal of Psychology, 12*(3), 159–164.

Cordoba, O. A., & Chapel, J. L. (1983). Medroxyproesterone acetate antiandrogen treatment of hypersexuality in a pedophiliac sex offender. *American Journal of Psychiatry, 140*(8), 1036–1039.

Corte, H. E., Wolf, M. M., & Locke, B. J. (1971). A comparison of procedures for eliminating self-injurious behavior of retarded adolescents. *Journal of Applied Behavior Analysis, 4,* 201–213.

Costa, L. G., Giordano, G., Guizzetti, M., & Vitalone, A. (2008). Neurotoxicity of pesticides: A brief review. *Frontiers in Bioscience, 13,* 1240–1249.

Cotton, J. W. (1953). Running time as a function of amount of food deprivation. *Journal of Experimental Psychology, 46,* 188–198.

Council on Communications and Media. (2009). Media violence. *Pediatrics, 124*(5), 1495–1503.

Cowles, J. T. (1937). Food-tokens as incentives for learning by chimpanzees. *Comparative Psychology Monographs, 14*(5), 1–96.

Coyne, S. M., Ridge, R., Stevens, M., Callister, M., & Stockdale, L. (2012). Backbiting and bloodshed in books: Short-term effects of reading physical and relational aggression in literature. *British Journal of Social Psychology, 51*(1), 188–196.

Critchfield, T. S., Haley, R., Sabo, B., Colbert, J., & Macropoulis, G. (2003). A half century of scalloping in the work habits of the United States Congress. *Journal of Applied Behavior Analysis, 36,* 465–486.

Cronk, L. (1992, January/February). On human nature: Old dogs, old tricks. *The Sciences,* 13–15.

Crossman, E. K. (1991). Schedules of reinforcement. In W. Ishaq (Ed.), *Human behavior in today's world* (pp. 133–138). New York: Praeger.

Cuny, H. (1962). *Ivan Pavlov: The man and his theories* (P. Evans, Trans.). Greenwich, CT: Fawcett World Library.

D'Amato, M. R. (1973). Delayed matching to sample and short-term memory in monkeys. In G. H. Bower (Ed.), *The psychology of learning and motivation: Advances in research and theory,* Vol. 7 (pp. 227–269). New York: Academic Press.

Darwin, C. (1859). *On the origin of species.* London: J. Murray.

Darwin, C. (1874). *The descent of man* (2nd ed.). New York: Thomas Y. Crowell & Co.

Davey, G. C. L. (1994). Is evaluative conditioning a qualitatively distinct form of classical conditioning? *Behavior Research and Therapy, 32*(3), 291–299.

David, H. P., Dytrych, Z., Matejcek, Z., & Schuller, V. (Eds.). (1988). *Born unwanted: Developmental effects of denied abortion.* New York: Springer.

Davis, H., & Hurwitz, H. M. (Eds.). (1977). *Operant- Pavlovian interactions.* Hillsdale, NJ: Erlbaum.

Davis, W. M., & Smith, S. G. (1976). Role of conditioned reinforcers in the initiation, maintenance and extinction of drug-seeking behavior. *Pavlovian Journal of Biological Science, 11,* 222–236.

Davison, M., & McCarthy, D. (1988). *The matching law: A research review.* Hillsdale, NJ: Erlbaum.

Dawkins, R. (1986). *The blind watchmaker.* New York: Norton.

Dawkins, R. (1995, November). God's utility function. *Scientific American,* 80–86.

DeAngelis, T. (1992, May). Senate seeking answers to rising tide of violence. *APA Monitor,* 11.

Deci, E. L., & Ryan, R. M. (1985). *Intrinsic motivation and self-determination in human behavior.* New York: Plenum.

de Groot, A. D. (1966). Perception and memory versus thought: Some old ideas and recent findings. In B. Kleinmuntz (Ed.), *Problem solving: Research, method and theory* (pp. 19–50). New York: Wiley.

Deguchi, H. (1984). Observational learning from a radical-behavioristic viewpoint. *The Behavior Analyst, 7,* 83–95.

De Houwer, J. (2011). Evaluative conditioning: A review of functional knowledge and mental process theories. In T. R. Schachtman & S. S. Reilly (Eds.), *Associative learning and conditioning theory: Human and non-human applications* (pp. 399–416). Oxford, UK: Oxford University Press.

De Houwer, J., Hendrickx, H., & Baeyens, F. (1997). Evaluative learning with "subliminally" presented stimuli. *Consciousness and Cognition, 6,* 87–107.

De Houwer, J., Thomas, S., & Baeyens, F. (2001). Associative learning of likes and dislikes: A review of 25 years of research on human evaluative conditioning. *Psychological Bulletin, 127,* 853–869.

Deitz, S. M., & Repp, A. C. (1973). Decreasing classroom misbehavior through the use of DRL schedules of reinforcement. *Journal of Applied Behavior Analysis, 6,* 457–463.

Delgado, J. A. P., & Greer, R. D. (2009). The effects of peer monitoring training on the emergence of the capability to learn from observing instruction received by peers. *Psychological Record, 59,* 407–434.

Dempster, F. N. (1988). The spacing effect: A case study in the failure to apply the results of psychological research. *American Psychologist, 43*(8), 627–634.

Derenne, A., & Baron, A. (2002). Preratio pausing: Effects of an alternative reinforcer on fixed- and variable-ratio responding. *Journal of the Experimental Analysis of Behavior, 77*(3), 273–282.

Derenne, A., Richardson, J. V., & Baron, A. (2006). Long-term effects of suppressing the preratio pause. *Behavioral Processes, 72*(1), 32–37.

Dermer, M. L., Lopez, S. L., & Messling, P. A. (2009). Fluency training a writing skill: Editing for concision. *The Psychological Record, 59,* 3–20.

Descartes, R. (1637/2000). *Discourse on the method of rightly conducting the reason, and seeking truth in the sciences.* London: Penguin Books.

Descartes, R. (1641/2011). *Meditations on first philosophy.* Hollywood, FL: Simon & Brown.

deVilliers, P. A. (1977). Choice in concurrent schedules and a quantitative formulation of the law of effect. In W. K. Honig & J. E. R. Staddon (Eds.), *Handbook of operant behavior* (pp. 233–287). Englewood Cliffs, NJ: Prentice-Hall.

deVries, J. E., Burnette, M. M., & Redirion, W. K. (1991). AIDS prevention: Improving nurses' compliance with glove wearing through performance feedback. *Journal of Applied Behavior Analysis, 24*(4), 705–711.

Dickinson, A., & Brown, K. J. (2007). Flavor-evaluative conditioning is unaffected by contingency knowledge during training with color-flavored compounds. *Learning & Behavior, 35*(1), 36–42.

Dickinson, A., Watt, A., & Griffiths, W. J. H. (1992). Free-operant acquisition with delayed reinforcement. *Quarterly Journal of Experimental Psychology, 45B,* 241–258.

Dierick, H. A., & Greenspan, R. J. (2006). Molecular analysis of flies selected for aggressive behavior. *Nature Genetics, 38,* 1023–1031. Published online August 13, 2006. doi: 10.1038/ng1864.

Difede, J., & Hoffman, H. G. (2002). Virtual reality exposure therapy for World Trade Center post-traumatic stress disorder: A case report. *CyberPsychology & Behavior, 5,* 529–535. Downloaded from www.hitl.washington.edu/people/hunter/wtcbrenda.pdf.

Dinsmoor, J. A. (1954). Punishment: I: The avoidance hypothesis. *Psychological Review, 61,* 34–46.

Dinsmoor, J. A. (1955). Punishment: II: An interpretation of empirical findings. *Psychological Review, 62,* 96–105.

Dinsmoor, J. A. (2001). Stimuli inevitably generated by behavior that avoids electric shock are inherently reinforcing. *Journal of the Experimental Analysis of Behavior, 75,* 311–333.

Diven, K. (1937). Certain determinants in the conditioning of anxiety reactions. *Journal of Psychology, 3,* 291–308.

Dixon, M. (2006, Spring). Beating the odds. *Perspectives.* Retrieved on September 7, 2007, from www.siu.edu/ ~perspect/06_sp/gambling.html.

Donahoe, J. W., & Palmer, D. C. (1994). *Learning and complex behavior.* Boston, MA: Allyn & Bacon.

Dorey, N. R., Rosales-Ruiz, J., Smith, R., & Lovelace, B. (2009). Functional analysis and treatment of self-injury in a captive olive baboon. *Journal of Applied Behavior Analysis, 42,* 785–794.

Dougherty, D. M., Cherek, D. R., & Roache, J. D. (1994). The effects of smoked marijuana on progressive-interval schedule performance in humans. *Journal of the Experimental Analysis of Behavior, 62,* 73–87.

Dougherty, D. M., & Lewis, P. (1991). Stimulus generalization, discrimination learning, and peak shift in horses. *Journal of the Experimental Analysis of Behavior, 56*(1), 97–104.

Doughty, A. H., Cirino, S., Mayfield, K. H., Da Silva, S. P., Okouchi, H., & Lattal, K. A. (2005). Effects of behavioral history on resistance to change. *The Psychological Record, 55,* 315–330.

Doughty, A. H., Galuska, C. M., Dawson, A. E., & Brierley, K. P. (2012). Effects of reinforcer magnitude on response acquisition with unsignaled delayed reinforcement. *Behavioral Processes, 90,* 287–290.

Driskell, J. E., Willis, R. P., & Copper, C. (1992). Effect of overlearning on retention. *Journal of Applied Psychology, 77*(5), 615–622.

Ducharme, D. E., & Holborn, S. W. (1997). Programmed generalization of social skills in preschool children with hearing impairments. *Journal of Applied Behavior Analysis, 30*(4), 639–651.

Durlach, P. J. (1982). Pavlovian learning and performance when CS and US are uncorrelated. In M. L. Commons, R. J. Herrnstein, & A. R. Wagner (Eds.), *Quantitative analysis of behavior,* Vol. 3: *Acquisition* (pp. 173–193). Cambridge, MA: Ballinger.

Dweck, C. S., & Repucci, N. D. (1973). Learned helplessness and reinforcement responsibility in children. *Journal of Personality and Social Psychology, 25,* 109–116.

Dworkin, B. R., & Miller, N. E. (1986). Failure to replicate visceral learning in the acute curarized rat preparation. *Behavioral Neuroscience, 100,* 299–314.

Ebbinghaus, H. (1885). *Memory, a contribution to experimental psychology* (H. A. Ruger, Trans., 1913). New York: Columbia University Press.

Edwards, C. A., & Honig, W. K. (1987). Memorization and "feature selection" in the acquisition of natural concepts in pigeons. *Learning and Motivation, 18,* 235–260.

Egan, D. E., & Schwartz, B. J. (1979). Chunking in recall of symbolic drawings. *Memory and Cognition, 7,* 149–158.

Egan, S. (1981). Reduction of anxiety in aquaphobics. *Canadian Journal of Applied Sport Sciences, 6,* 68–71.

Eikelboom, R., & Stewart, J. (1982). Conditioning of drug-induced physiological responses. *Psychological Review, 89,* 507–528.

Eikeseth, S., Smith, T., Jahr, E., & Eledevik, S. (2002). Intensive behavioral treatment at school for 4-7-year-old children with autism: A one-year comparative controlled study. *Behavior Modification, 26,* 49–68.

Eisenberger, R. (1992). Learned industriousness. *Psychological Review, 99*(2), 248–267.

Eisenberger, R., & Armeli, S. (1997). Can salient rewards increase creative performance without reducing intrinsic creative interest? *Journal of Personality and Social Psychology, 72,* 652–663.

Eisenberger, R., Armeli, S., & Pretz, J. (1998). Can the promise of reward increase creativity? *Journal of Personality and Social Psychology, 74,* 704–714.

Eisenberger, R., & Cameron, J. (1996). Detrimental effects of reward: Reality or myth? *American Psychologist, 51,* 115–166.

Eisenberger, R., Karpman, M., & Trattner, J. (1967). What is the necessary and sufficient condition in the contingency situation? *Journal of Experimental Psychology, 74,* 342–350.

Eisenberger, R., Masterson, F. A., & McDermott, M. (1982). Effects of task variety on generalized effort. *Journal of Educational Psychology, 74*(4), 499–505.

Eisenberger, R., & Rhoades, L. (2001). Incremental effects of reward on creativity. *Journal of Personality and Social Psychology, 81*(4), 728–741.

Eisenberger, R., & Selbst, M. (1994). Does reward increase or decrease creativity? *Journal of Personality and Social Psychology, 66,* 1116–1127.

Eisler, R. M., Hersen, M., & Agras, W. S. (1973). Effects of video tape and instructional feedback on nonverbal marital interaction: An analog study. *Behavior Therapy, 4,* 551–558.

Elkins, R. L. (1991). An appraisal of chemical aversion (emetic therapy) approaches to alcoholism treatment. *Behavioral Research and Therapy, 29*(5), 387–413.

Elliott, M. H. (1928). The effect of change of reward on the maze performance of rats. *University of California Publications in Psychology, 4,* 19–30.

Emmert, G. D. (1978). Measuring the impact of group performance feedback versus individual performance feedback in an industrial setting. *Journal of Organization Behavior Management, 1,* 134–141.

Epstein, R. (1983). Resurgence of previously reinforced behavior during extinction. *The Behavior Analyst Letters, 3,* 391–397.

Epstein, R. (1984). Simulation research in the analysis of behavior. *Behaviorism, 12,* 41–59.

Epstein, R. (1985). Extinction-induced resurgence: Preliminary investigation and possible application. *Psychological Record, 35,* 143–153.

Epstein, R. (1999). Generativity theory. In M. Runco (Ed.), *Encyclopedia of creativity* (pp. 759–766). New York: Academic Press.

Epstein, R., Kirshnit, C., Lanza, R., & Rubin, L. (1984). Insight in the pigeon: Antecedents and determinants of an intelligent performance. *Nature, 308,* 61–62.

Epstein, R., & Skinner, B. F. (1980). Resurgence of responding after the cessation of response-independent reinforcement. *Proceedings of the National Academy of Sciences, 77,* 6251–6253.

Erickson, L. M., Tiffany, S. T., Martin, E. M., & Baker, T. B. (1983). Aversive smoking therapies: A conditioning analysis of therapeutic effectiveness. *Behavior Research and Therapy, 21*(6), 595–611.

Ericsson, K. A., & Chase, W. G. (1982). Exceptional memory. *American Scientist, 70,* 607–615.

Erjavec, M., Lovett, V. E., & Horne, P. J. (2009). Do infants show generalized imitation of gestures? II: The effects of skills training and multiple exemplar matching training. *Journal of the Experimental Analysis of Behavior, 91,* 355–376.

Escobar, R., & Bruner, C. A. (2007). Response induction during the acquisition and maintenance of lever pressing with delayed reinforcement. *Journal of the Experimental Analysis of Behavior, 88,* 29–49.

Estes, W. K. (1944). An experimental study of punishment. *Psychological Monographs, 57*(3), 1–40.

Esteves, F., Parra, C., Dimberg, U., & Öhman, A. (1994). Nonconscious associative learning: Pavlovian conditioning of skin conductance responses to masked fear-relevant facial stimuli. *Psychophysiology, 31,* 375–385.

Evans, M. J., Duvel, M. L., Funk, M. L., Lehman, B., Sparrow, J., Watson, N. T., et al. (1994). Social reinforcement of operant behavior in rats: A methodological note. *Journal of the Experimental Analysis of Behavior, 62,* 149–156.

Fanselow, M. S. (1989). The adaptive function of conditioned defensive behavior: An ecological approach to Pavlovian stimulus substitution theory. In R. J. Blanchard, P. F. Brain, D. C. Blanchard, & S. Parmigiani (Eds.), *Etho-experimental approaches to the study of behavior* (pp. 151–166). Dordrecht: Kluwer Academic.

Fanselow, M. S. (1990). Factors governing one-trial contextual conditioning. *Animal Learning & Behavior, 18*(3), 264–270.

Feeney, E. J. (1972). Performance audit, feedback and positive reinforcement. *Training and Development Journal, 26,* 8–13.

Feierman, J. R., & Feierman, L. A. (2000). Paraphilias. In L. T. Szuchman & F. Muscarella (Eds.), *Psychological perspectives on human sexuality* (pp. 480–518). New York: Wiley.

Ferguson, D. L., & Rosales-Ruiz, J. (2001). Loading the problem loader: The effects of target training and shaping on trailer-loading behavior of horses. *Journal of Applied Behavior Analysis, 34,* 409–424.

Ferster, C. B., & Skinner, B. F. (1957). *Schedules of reinforcement.* New York: Appleton-Century-Crofts.

Field, D. P., Tonneau, F., Ahearn, W., & Hineline, P. N. (1996). Preference between variable-ratio schedules: Local and extended relations. *Journal of the Experimental Analysis of Behavior, 66,* 283–295.

Field, L., & Nevin, J. A. (Eds.). (1993). *Stimulus equivalence. A special issue. The Psychological Record, 43*(4).

Finch, G., & Culler, E. (1934). Higher order conditioning with constant motivation. *American Journal of Psychology, 46,* 596–602.

Finkelstein, E. A., Linnan, L. A., Tate, D. F., & Birken, B. E. (2007). A pilot study testing the effect of different levels of financial incentives on weight loss among overweight employees. *Journal of Occupational & Environmental Medicine, 49*(9), 981–989.

Finlayson, C. (2010). *The humans who went extinct: Why Neanderthals died out and we survived.* New York: Oxford University Press.

Fiore, M. C., Jaen, C. R., Baker, T. B., Bailey, W. C., Benowitz, N. L., Curry, S. J., et al. (2008). Treating tobacco use and dependence: 2008 update. Rockville, MD: U. S. Department of Health and Human Services, U.S. Public Health Service.

Fisher, J. L., & Harris, M. B. (1976). The effects of three model characteristics on imitation and learning. *Journal of Social Psychology, 98,* 183–199.

Fitch, H. G., Herman, J., & Hopkins, B. L. (1976). Safe and unsafe behavior and its modification. *Journal of Occupational Safety Medicine, 18,* 618–622.

Flora, S. R. (2004). *The power of reinforcement.* Albany, NY: State University of New York Press.

Forthman, D. L., & Ogden, J. L. (1991). The role of applied behavior analysis in zoo management: Today and tomorrow. Talk presented at the annual meeting of the

Association for Behavior Analysis. Available at www.be-havior.org.

Fouts, R., & Mills, S. T. (1998). *Next of kin: My conversations with chimpanzees.* New York: William Morrow.

Fowler, B. P. (1986). Emotional crisis imitating television. *Lancet, 1*(8488), 1036–1037.

Foxx, R. M. (2001). Behavioral treatment of aggression, self-injury, and other severe behaviors: Methods, strategies, and skill building interventions. Address given at the annual meeting of the Association for Science in Autism Treatment, San Diego, CA, March 8.

Francisco, M. T., & Hanley, G. P. (2012). An evaluation of progressively increasing intertrial intervals on the acquisition and generalization of three social skills. *Journal of Applied Behavior Analysis, 45*(1), 137–142.

Frank, H., & Frank, M. G. (1982). Comparison of problem-solving performance in six-week-old wolves and dogs. *Animal Behavior, 30,* 95–98.

Freedman, D. H. (2011, February). How to fix the obesity crisis. *Scientific American,* 40–47.

Freud, S. (1958/2009). *On creativity and the unconscious: Papers on the psychology of art, literature, love and religion.* New York: HarperCollins, 2009.

Frisch, C. J., & Dickinson, A. M. (1990). Work productivity as a function of the percentage of monetary incentives to base pay. *Journal of Organizational Behavior Management, 11,* 13–33.

Fuller, J. L., & Scott, J. P. (1954). Heredity and learning ability in infrahuman mammals. *Eugenics Quarterly, 1,* 28–43.

Furedy, J. J., & Kristjansson, M. (1996). Human Pavlovian autonomic conditioning and its relation to awareness of the CS/US contingency: Focus on the phenomenon and some forgotten facts. *Behavioral and Brain Sciences, 19,* 555–556, 558.

Gage, F. H., & Muotri, A. R. (2012, March). What makes each brain unique. *Scientific American,* 26–31.

Gagné, R. M. (1941). The retention of a conditioned operant response. *Journal of Experimental Psychology, 29,* 296–305.

Gais, S., Lucus, B., & Born, J. (2006). Sleep after learning aids memory, recall. *Learning and Memory, 13,* 259–262.

Gallistel, C. R., & Gibbon, J. (2000). Time, rate, and conditioning. *Psychological Review, 107*(2), 289–344.

Gallistel, C. R., & Gibbon, J. (2002). *The symbolic foundations of conditioned behavior.* New York: Erlbaum.

Gantt, W. H. (1941). Introduction. In I. P. Pavlov, *Lectures on conditioned reflexes and psychiatry,* Vol. 2 (W. H. Gantt, Trans.). New York: International Publishers.

Gantt, W. H. (1966). Conditional or conditioned, reflex or response. *Conditioned Reflex, 1,* 69–74.

Garcia, J., Kimeldorf, D. J., & Koelling, R. A. (1955). A conditioned aversion towards saccharin resulting from exposure to gamma radiation. *Science, 122*(3160), 157–158.

Garcia, J., & Koelling, R. A. (1966). Relation of cue to consequence in avoidance learning. *Psychonomic Science, 4,* 123–124.

Garcia, V. (2003). Signalization and stimulus-substitution in Pavlov's theory of conditioning. *The Spanish Journal of Psychology, 6*(2), 168–176.

Garcia-Palacios, A., Hoffman, H., Carlin, A., Furness, T. A., III, & Botella, C. (2002). Virtual reality in the treatment of spider phobia: A controlled study. *Behaviour Research and Therapy, 40,* 983–993.

Gardner, R. A. (2012). *Teaching sign language to chimpanzees.* New York: SUNY Press.

Gardner, R. A., & Gardner, B. T. (1969). Teaching sign language to a chimpanzee. *Science, 165*(3894), 664–672.

Garfield, A. S., Cowley, M., Smith, F. M., Moorwood, K., & Stewart-Cox, J. E. (2011). Distinct physiological and behavioural functions for parental alleles of imprinted Grb10. *Nature, 469,* 534–538.

Garland, T., Jr., Kelly, S. A., Malisch, J. L., Kolb, E. M., Hannon, R. M., Keeney, B. K., et al. (2011). How to run far: Multiple solutions and sex-specific responses to selective breeding for high voluntary activity levels. *Proceedings of the Royal Society: Biological Sciences, 278*(1705), 574–581.

Garrett, L. (1995). *The coming plague: Newly emerging diseases in a world of of balance.* New York: Penguin.

Gawronski, B., & Walther, E. (2012). What do memory data tell us about the role of contingency awareness in evaluative conditioning? *Journal of Experimental Social Psychology, 48,* 617–623. doi: 10.1016/j. jesp.2012.01.002.

Geller, E. S. (1984). A delayed reward strategy for large-scale motivation of safety belt use: A test of long-term impact. *Accident Analysis and Prevention, 16*(5/6), 457–463.

Geller, E. S. (2005). Behavior-based safety and occupational risk management. *Behavior Modification, 29*(3), 539–561.

Gewirtz, J. L. (1971a). Conditional responding as a paradigm for observational, imitative learning, and vicarious learning. In H. W. Reese (Ed.), *Advances in child development and behavior,* Vol. 6 (pp. 273–304). New York: Academic Press.

Gewirtz, J. L. (1971b). The roles of overt responding and extrinsic reinforcement in "self-" and "vicarious-reinforcement" phenomena and in "observational learning" and imitation. In R. Glaser (Ed.), *The nature of reinforcement* (pp. 279–309). New York: Academic Press.

Gibson, B. (2008). Can evaluative conditioning change attitudes toward mature brands? New evidence from the Implicit Association Test. *Journal of Consumer Research, 35,* 178–188.

Girden, E., & Culler, E. A. (1937). Conditioned responses in curarized striate muscle in dogs. *Journal of Comparative Psychology, 23,* 261–274.

Gleeson, S., Lattal, K. A., & Williams, K. S. (1989). Superstitious conditioning: A replication and extension of Neuringer (1970). *Psychological Record, 39,* 563–571.

Gleitman, H. (1971). Forgetting of long-term memories in animals. In W. K. Honig & P. H. R. James (Eds.), *Animal memory* (pp. 2–46). New York: Academic Press.

Gleitman, H., & Bernheim, J. W. (1963). Retention of fixed-interval performance in rats. *Journal of Comparative and Physiological Psychology, 56,* 839–841.

Glover, J. A., & Gary, A. L. (1976). Procedures to increase some aspects of creativity. *Journal of Applied Behavior Analysis, 9,* 79–84.

Godden, D. B., & Baddeley, A. D. (1975). Context-dependent memory in two natural environments: On land and under water. *British Journal of Psychology, 66,* 325–331.

Goeters, S., Blakely, E., & Poling, A. (1992). The differential outcomes effect. *Psychological Record, 42,* 389–411.

Goetz, E. M. (1982). A review of functional analysis of preschool children's creative behavior. *Education and Treatment of Children, 5,* 157–177.

Goetz, E. M., & Baer, D. M. (1973). Social control of form diversity and the emergence of new forms in children's blockbuilding. *Journal of Applied Behavior Analysis, 6,* 209–217.

Goldberg, S. R., Spealman, R. D., & Goldberg, D. M. (1981). Persistent behavior at high rates maintained by intravenous self-administration of nicotine. *Science, 214*(4520), 573–575.

Goldiamond, I. (1975a). A constructional approach to self-control. In A. Schwartz & I. Goldiamond (Eds.), *Social casework: A behavioral approach* (pp. 67–130). New York: Columbia University Press.

Goldiamond, I. (1975b). Insider-outsider problems: A constructional approach. *Rehabilitation Psychology, 22,* 103–116.

Goldman, J. G. (2010, September). Man's new best friend? A forgotten Russian experiment in fox domestication. *Scientific American,* 35.

Goleman, D. (2006). *Emotional intelligence.* New York: Bantam Books.

Goodlad, J. I. (1984). *A place called school.* New York: McGraw-Hill.

Gordon, S. P., Reznick, D. N., Kinnison, M. R., Bryant, M. J., Weese, D. J., Rasanen, K., et al. (2009). Adaptive changes in life history and survival following a new guppy introduction. *The American Naturalist, 174*(1), 34–45.

Gormezano, I. (2000). Learning: Conditioning approach. In A. Kazdin (Ed.), *Encyclopedia of psychology,* Vol. 5 (pp. 5–8). Washington, DC: American Psychological Association and Oxford University Press.

Gormezano, I., & Moore, J. W. (1969). Classical conditioning. In M. H. Marx (Ed.), *Learning: Processes* (pp. 119–203). London: MacMillan.

Gorn, G. J. (1982). The effects of music in advertising on choice behavior: A classical conditioning approach. *Journal of Marketing, 46,* 94–101.

Grace, R. C., Bedell, M. A., & Nevin, J. A. (2002). Preference and resistance to change with constant- and variable-duration terminal links: Independence of reinforcement rate and magnitude. *Journal of the Experimental Analysis of Behavior, 77,* 233–255.

Graham, J. M., & Desjardins, C. (1980). Classical conditioning: Induction of luteinizing hormone and testosterone secretion in anticipation of sexual activity. *Science, 210,* 1039–1041.

Green, C. H., Rollyson, J. H., Passante, S. C., & Reid, D. H. (2002). Maintaining proficient supervisor performance with direct support personnel: An analysis of two management approaches. *Journal of Applied Behavior Analysis, 35,* 205–208.

Green, G. R., Linsk, N. L., & Pinkston, E. M. (1986). Modification of verbal behavior of the mentally impaired elderly by their spouses. *Journal of Applied Behavior Analysis, 19,* 329–336.

Greene, S. L. (1983). Feature memorization in pigeon concept formation. In M. L. Commons, R. J. Herrnstein, & A. R. Wagner (Eds.), *Quantitative analysis of behavior, Vol. 4: Discrimination processes* (pp. 209–229). Cambridge, MA: Ballinger.

Greenspoon, J., & Ranyard, R. (1957). Stimulus conditions and retroactive inhibition. *Journal of Experimental Psychology, 53,* 55–59.

Gregg, L., & Tarrier, N. (2007). Virtual reality in mental health: A review of the literature. *Social Psychiatry and Psychiatric Epidemiology, 42*(5), 343–354.

Grether, W. F. (1938). Pseudoconditioning without paired stimulation encountered in attempted backward conditioning. *Journal of Comparative Psychology, 25,* 91–96.

Griffen, A. K., Wolery, M., & Schuster, J. W. (1992). Triadic instruction of chained food preparations responses: Acquisition and observational learning. *Journal of Applied Behavior Analysis, 25,* 193–204.

Groenland, E. A. G., & Schoormans, J. P. L. (1994). Comparing mood-induction and affective conditioning as mechanisms influencing product evaluation and product choice. *Psychology & Marketing, 11,* 183–197.

Grossman, R. P. (1997). Co-branding in advertising: Developing effective associations. *Journal of Product and Brand Management, 6,* 191–201.

Gruber, H. (1981). *Darwin on man: A psychological study of scientific creativity* (2nd ed.). Chicago: University of Chicago Press.

Gruber, T., Muller, M. N., Strimling, P., Wrangham, R., Zuberbuhler, K. (2009). Wild chimpanzees rely on cultural knowledge to solve an experimental honey acquisition task. *Current Biology, 19*(21), 1806–1810.

Guthrie, E. R. (1952). *The psychology of learning* (rev. ed.). Gloucester, MA: Smith.

Guttman, N., & Kalish, H. I. (1956). Discriminability and stimulus generalization. *Journal of Experimental Psychology, 51,* 79–88.

Hajek, P., & Stead, L. F. (2001). Aversive smoking for smoking cessation. *Cochrane Database of Systematic Reviews,* Issue 3. Article No. CD000546. doi: 1002/14651858.

Haley, W. E. (1983). A family-behavioral approach to the treatment of the cognitively impaired elderly. *The Gerontologist, 23*(1), 18–20.

Hall, C. S. (1951). The genetics of behavior. In S. S. Stevens (Ed.), *Handbook of experimental psychology* (pp. 304–329). New York: Wiley.

Hall, G., & Pearce, J. M. (1979). Latent inhibition of a CS during CS-US pairings. *Journal of Experimental Psychology: Animal Behavior Processes, 5,* 31–42.

Hall, G. C. N. (1995). Sexual offender recidivism revisited: A meta-analysis of recent treatment studies. *Journal of Consulting and Clinical Psychology, 63,* 802–809.

Hall, J. F. (1984). Backward conditioning in Pavlovian-type studies: Reevaluation and present status. *Pavlovian Journal of Biological Sciences, 19,* 163–168.

Hall, R. V., Lund, D., & Jackson, D. (1968). Effects of teacher attention on study behavior. *Journal of Applied Behavior Analysis, 1,* 1–12.

Hall-Johnson, E., & Poling, A. (1984). Preference in pigeons given a choice between sequences of fixed-ratio schedules: Effects of ratio values and duration of food delivery. *Journal of the Experimental Analysis of Behavior, 42,* 127–135.

Hammond, L. J. (1980). The effect of contingency upon the appetitive conditioning of free-operant behavior. *Journal of the Experimental Analysis of Behavior, 34*(3), 297–304.

Hanley, G. P., Iwata, B. A., & Thompson, R. H. (2001). Reinforcement schedule thinning following treatment with functional communication training. *Journal of Applied Behavior Analysis, 34,* 17–38.

Hanson, G. R., Leshner, A. I., & Tai, B. (2002). Putting drug abuse research to use in real-life settings. *Journal of Substance Abuse Treatment, 23,* 69–70.

Hanson, H. M. (1959). Effects of discrimination training on stimulus generalization. *Journal of Experimental Psychology, 58,* 321–334.

Hanson, P. K., Gordon, A., Harris, A. J. R., Marques, J. K., Murphy, W., Quinsey, V. L., et al. (2002). First report of the collaborative outcome data project on the effectiveness of psychological treatment for sex offenders. *Sexual Abuse: A Journal of Research and Treatment, 14*(2), 169–194.

Harley, B., & Wang, W. (1997). The critical period hypothesis: Where are we now? In A. M. E. de Groot & J. F. Kroll (Eds.), *Tutorials in bilingualism: Psycholinguistic perspective.* (pp. 19–51). Mahwah, NJ: Erlbaum.

Harlow, H. F. (1949). The formation of learning sets. *Psychological Review, 56,* 51–65.

Harlow, H. F. (1958). The nature of love. *American Psychologist, 13,* 673–685.

Harlow, H. F., & Harlow, M. K. (1962a). The effect of rearing conditions on behavior. *Bulletin of the Menninger Clinic, 26,* 213–224.

Harlow, H. F., & Harlow, M. K. (1962b, November) Social deprivation in monkeys. *Scientific American, 207,* 136–146.

Harrison, D. M. (2009). Performance feedback: Its effectiveness in the management of job performance. Unpublished master's thesis, Bouvé College of Health Sciences, Norhteastern University, Boston, MA. Available at http://hdl.handle.net/2047/d10019443.

Hart, B., & Risley, T. R. (1995). *Meaningful differences in the everyday experience of young American children.* Baltimore, MD: Paul H. Brookes.

Hart, B. M., Allen, K. E., Buell, J. S., Harris, F. R., & Wolf, M. M. (1964). Effects of social reinforcement on operant crying. *Journal of Experimental Child Psychology, 1,* 145–153.

Hartman, D. E. (1995). *Neuropsychological toxicology: Identification and assessment of human neurotoxic syndromes* (2nd ed.). New York: Springer.

Hawkins, D. F. (Ed.). (1983). *Drugs and pregnancy.* Edinburgh: Churchill Livingston.

Hayes, C. (1951). *The ape in our house.* New York: Harper & Row.

Hayes, K. J., & Hayes, C. (1952). Imitation in a home-raised chimpanzee. *Journal of Comparative and Physiological Psychology, 45,* 450–459.

Heathcock, J. C., Bhat, A. N., Lobo, M. A., & Galloway, J. C. (2004). The performance of infants born preterm and full-term in the mobile paradigm: Learning and memory. *Physical Therapy, 84*(9), 808–821.

Hennessey, B., & Amabile, T. (1998). Reward, intrinsic motivation, and creativity. *American Psychologist, 53,* 674–675.

Herbert, J., & Hayne, H. (2000). Memory retrieval by 18–30-month-olds: Age-related changes in representation flexibility. *Developmental Psychology, 36*(4), 473–484.

Herbert, M. J., & Harsh, C. M. (1944). Observational learning by cats. *Journal of Comparative Psychology, 37,* 81–95.

Herman, R. L., & Azrin, N. H. (1964). Punishment by noise in an alternative response situation. *Journal of the Experimental Analysis of Behavior, 7,* 185–188.

Hernandez, R. D., Kelley, J. L., Elyashiv, E., Melton, S. C., Auton, A., McVean, G., et al. (2011). Classic selective sweeps were rare in recent human evolution. *Science, 331*(6019), 920–924. doi: 10.1126/science.1198878.

Herrnstein, R. J. (1961). Relative and absolute strength of response as a function of frequency of reinforcement. *Journal of the Experimental Analysis of Behavior, 4,* 267–272.

Herrnstein, R. J. (1966). Superstition: A corollary of the principle of operant conditioning. In W. K. Honig (Ed.), *Operant behavior: Areas of research and application.* New York: Appleton-Century-Crofts.

Herrnstein, R. J. (1969). Method and theory in the study of avoidance. *Psychological Review, 76,* 49–69.

Herrnstein, R. J. (1970). On the law of effect. *Journal of the Experimental Analysis of Behavior, 13,* 243–266.

Herrnstein, R. J. (1979). Acquisition, generalization, and discrimination reversal of a natural concept. *Journal of Experimental Psychology: Animal Behavior Processes, 5,* 116–129.

Herrnstein, R. J. (2000). *The matching law: Papers in psychology and economics* (H. Rachlin & D. I. Laibson, Eds.). Cambridge, MA: Harvard University Press.

Herrnstein, R. J., & Hineline, P. N. (1966). Negative reinforcement as shock-frequency reduction. *Journal of the Experimental Analysis of Behavior, 9,* 421–430.

Herrnstein, R. J., & Loveland, D. H. (1964). Complex visual concepts in the pigeon. *Science, 146*(3643), 549–551.

Herrnstein, R. J., Loveland, D. H., & Cable, C. (1976). Natural concepts in pigeons. *Journal of Experimental Psychology: Animal Behavior Processes, 2*, 285–311.

Herrnstein, R. J., & Mazur, J. E. (1987, November/December). Making up our minds. *The Sciences*, 40–47.

Heth, C. D. (1976). Simultaneous and backward fear conditioning as a function of number of CS-US pairings. *Journal of Experimental Psychology: Animal Behavior Processes, 2*, 117–129.

Hettema, J. M., Annas, P., Neale, M. C., Kendler, K. S., Fredrikson, M. (2003). A twin study of the genetics of fear conditioning. *Archives of General Psychiatry, 60*, 702–708.

Heward, W. L. (2012). *Exceptional children: An introduction to special education* (10th ed.). New York: Pearson.

Heward, W. L., & Chance, P. (2010). Introduction: Dealing with what is. *The Behavior Analyst, 33*, 145–151.

Heyes, C. (2012). What's social about social learning? *Journal of Comparative Psychology, 126*(2), 193–202. doi: 10.1037/a0025180.

Heyes, C. M. (1996). Genuine imitation. In C. M. Heyes & B. G. Galef, Jr. (Eds.), *Social learning in animals: The roots of culture* (pp. 371–389). New York: Academic Press.

Higgins, S. T., Rush, C. R., Hughes, J. R., Bickel, W. K., Lynn, M., & Capeless, M. A. (1992). Effects of cocaine and alcohol, alone and in combination, on human learning and performance. *Journal of the Experimental Analysis of Behavior, 58*, 87–105.

Hilgard, E. R. (1936). The nature of the conditioned response, I: The case for and against stimulus substitution. *Psychological Review, 43*, 366–385.

Hirakawa, T., & Nakazawa, J. (1977). Observational learning in children: Effects of vicarious reinforcement on discrimination shift behaviors in simple and complex tasks. *Japanese Journal of Educational Psychology, 25*, 254–257.

Hirata, S., & Morimura, N. (2000). Naive chaimpanzees' (*Pan troglotytes*) observation of experienced conspecifics in a tool-using task. *Journal of Comparative Psychology, 114*(3), 291–296.

Hiroto, D. S. (1974). Locus of control and learned helplessness. *Journal of Experimental Psychology, 102*, 187–193.

Hiroto, D. S., & Seligman, M. E. P. (1974). Generality of learned helplessness in man. *Journal of Personality and Social Psychology, 102*, 187–193.

Ho, B. T., Richards, D. W., & Chute, D. L., (Eds.). (1978). *Drug discrimination and state dependent learning.* New York: Academic Press.

Hodos, W. (1961). Progressive ratio as a measure of reward strength. *Science, 134*(3483), 943–944.

Hoffman, H. (2011). Hot and bothered: Classical conditioning of sexual incentives in humans. In T. R. Schachtman & S. Reilly (Eds.), *Associative learning and conditioning theory: Human and non-human applications (Kindle locations, 11,271-11,656).* Oxford, UK: Oxford University Press.

Hoffman, H. G. (2004, August). Virtual reality therapy. *Scientific American*, 58–65.

Hoffman, H. S., & Ratner, A. M. (1973). A reinforcement model of imprinting. *Psychological Review, 80*, 527–544.

Hofman, W., De Houwer, J., Perugini, M., Baeyens, F., & Crombez, G. (2010). Evaluative conditioning in humans: A meta-analysis. *Psychological Bulletin, 136*, 390–421.

Hogg, C., Neveu, M., Stokkan, K., Folkow, L., Cottrill, P., Douglas, R., et al. (2011). Artic reindeer extend their visual range into the ultraviolet. *Journal of Experimental Biology, 214*, 2014–2019. doi: 10.1242/jeb.053553.

Holechek, J. L. (2002). Do most livestock losses to poisonous plants result from "poor" range management? *Journal of Range Management, 55*(3), 270–276.

Holland, J. G. (1978). Behaviorism: Part of the problem or part of the solution? *Journal of Applied Behavior Analysis, 11*, 163–174.

Hollard, V. D., & Delius, J. D. (1982). Rotational invariance in visual pattern recognition by pigeons and humans. *Science, 218*(4574), 804–806.

Hollerman, J. R., & Schultz, W. (1998). Dopamine neurons report an error in the temporal prediction of reward during learning. *Nature Neuroscience, 1*, 304–309.

Holmes, R. M. (1991). *Sex crimes.* Beverly Hills, CA: Sage.

Holy, T. E. (2012). Neuroscience: Reward alters specific connections. *Nature, 482*, 39–41.

Honig, W. K., & Slivka, R. M. (1964). Stimulus generalization of the effects of punishment. *Journal of the Experimental Analysis of Behavior, 7*, 21–25.

Honig, W. K., & Stewart, K. E. (1988). Pigeons can discriminate locations presented in pictures. *Journal of the Experimental Analysis of Behavior, 50*, 541–551.

Hopkins, B. L., & Conard, R. J. (1975). Putting it all together: Superschool. In N. G. Haring & R. L. Schiefelbusch (Eds.), *Teaching special children* (pp. 342–385). New York: McGraw-Hill.

Hopper, L. M. (2010). "Ghost" experiments and the dissection of social learning in humans and animals. *Biological Reviews, 85*(4), 685–701.

Hopper, L. M., Lambeth, S. P., Schapiro, S. J., & Whiten, A. (2008). Observational learning in chimpanzees and children studied through "ghost" conditions. *Proceedings of the Royal Society of London Series B, 275*, 835–840.

Horne, P. J., & Erjavec, M. (2007). Do infants show generalized imitation of gestures? *Journal of the Experimental Analysis of Behavior, 87*, 63–87.

Horne, P. J., Greenhalgh, J., Erjavec, M., Lowe, C. F., Viktor, S., & Whitaker, C. J. (2011). Increasing pre-school children's consumption of fruit and vegetables: A modeling and rewards intervention. *Appetite, 56*(2), 375–385.

Horowitz, E. L. (1936). The development of attitude toward the Negro. *Archives of Psychology, 28*, 510–511.

Hovland, C. I. (1937). The generalization of conditioned responses, I: The sensory generalization of conditioned responses with varying frequencies of tone. *Journal of General Psychology, 17,* 125–148.

Huang, C., & Charman, T. (2005). Gradations of emulation learning in infants' imitation of actions on objects. *Journal of Experimental Child Psychology, 92,* 276–302.

Huang, J., Carr, T. H., & Cao, Y. (2001). Comparing cortical activations for silent and overt speech using event-related fMRI. *Human Brain Mapping, 15,* 39–53.

Huang, W., Chen, J., Chien, C., & Kashima, H., & Lin, K. (2011). Constraint-induced movement therapy as a paradigm of translational research in neurorehabilitation: Reviews and prospects. *American Journal of Translational Research, 3*(1), 48–60.

Huesmann, L. R., & Miller, L. S. (1994). Long-term effects of repeated exposure to media violence in childhood. In L. R. Huesmann (Ed.), *Aggressive behavior: Current perspectives* (pp. 153–186). New York: Plenum.

Huesmann, L. R., Moise-Titus, J., Podolski, C., & Eron, L. D. (2003). Longitudinal relations between children's exposure to TV violence and their aggressive and violent behavior in young adulthood: 1977–1992. *Developmental Psychology, 39,* 201–221.

Hugdahl, K. (1995/2001). *Psychophysiology: The mind-body perspective.* Cambridge, MA: Harvard University Press.

Hull, C. L. (1943). *Principles of behavior.* New York: Appleton-Century-Crofts.

Hull, C. L. (1951). *Essentials of behavior.* New Haven, CT: Yale University Press.

Hull, C. L. (1952). *A behavior system.* New Haven, CT: Yale University Press.

Hummel, J. H., Abercrombie, C., & Koepsel, P. (1991). Teaching students to analyze examples of classical conditioning. *The Behavior Analyst, 14,* 241–246.

Hundt, A. G., & Premack, D. (1963). Running as both a positive and negative reinforcer. *Science, 142*(3595), 1087–1088.

Hunter, W. S. (1913). The delayed reaction in animals and children. *Behavior Monographs, 2*(1), 1–86.

Ito, M., & Nakamura, K. (1998). Humans' choice in a self-control choice situation: Sensitivity to reinforcer amount, reinforcer delay, and overall reinforcement density. *Journal of the Experimental Analysis of Behavior, 69,* 87–102.

Ito, M., Saeki, D., & Green, L. (2011). Sharing, discounting, and selfishness: A Japanese-American comparison. *The Psychological Record, 60,* 59–76.

Iwata, B. A. (1987). Negative reinforcement in applied behavior analysis: An emerging technology. *Journal of Applied Behavior Analysis, 20*(4), 361–378.

Iwata, B. A. (2006). On the distinction between positive and negative reinforcement. *Journal of Applied Behavior Analysis, 29*(1), 121–123.

Iwata, B. A., Dorsey, M. F., Slifer, K. J., Bauman, K. E., & Richman, G. S. (1994). Toward a functional analysis of self-injury. *Journal of Applied Behavior Analysis, 27*(2), 197–209.

Iwata, B. A., Smith, R. G., & Michael, J. (2000). Current research on the influence of establishing operations on behavior in applied settings. *Journal of Applied Behavior Analysis, 33,* 411–418.

Jacobs, L. F. (1992). Memory for cache locations in Merriam's kangaroo rats. *Animal Behavior, 43,* 585–593.

Jacobs, L. F., & Liman, E. R. (1991). Grey squirrels remember the locations of buried nuts. *Animal Behavior, 41,* 103–110.

Jacobs, N., van Os, J., Derom, C., & Thiery, E. (2007). Heritability of intelligence. *Twin Research and Human Intelligence, 10,* 11–14.

Jankowski, C. (1994). Foreword. In G. Wilkes, *A behavior sampler.* North Bend, WA: Sunshine Books.

Jasnow, A. M., Cullen, P. K., & Riccio, D. C. (2012). Remembering another aspect of forgetting. *Frontiers in Psychology, 3*(175). Available at frontiersin.org. doi: 10.3389/fpsyg.2012.00175.

Jenkins, H. M. (1962). Resistance to extinction when partial reinforcement is followed by regular reinforcement. *Journal of Experimental Psychology, 64,* 441–450.

Jenkins, H. M., & Harrison, R. H. (1960). Effect of discrimination training on auditory generalization. *Journal of Experimental Psychology, 59,* 246–253.

Jenkins, H. M., & Moore, B. R. (1973). The form of the auto-shaped response with food or water reinforcers. *Journal of the Experimental Analysis of Behavior, 20,* 163–181.

Jenkins, J. C., & Dallenbach, K. M. (1924). Obliviscence during sleep and waking. *American Journal of Psychology, 35,* 605–612.

Johnson, J. G., Cohen, P., Smailes, E. M., Kasen, S., Brook. J. S. (2002). Television viewing and aggressive behavior during adolescence and adulthood. *Science, 295*(5564), 2468–2471.

Johnson, K. R., & Layng, T. V. J. (1992). Breaking the structuralist barrier: Literacy and numeracy with fluency. *American Psychologist, 47,* 1475–1490.

Jonas, I., Schubert, K. A., Reijne, A. C., Scholte, J., Garland, T., Jr., Gerkema, M. P. et al. (2010). Behavior traits are affected by selective breeding for increased wheel-running behavior in mice. *Behavioral Genetics, 40*(4), 542–550.

Joncich, G. (1968). *The sane positivist: A biography of Edward L. Thorndike.* Middleton, CT: Wesleyan University Press.

Jones, M. C. (1924a). The elimination of children's fears. *Journal of Experimental Psychology, 7,* 382–390.

Jones, M. C. (1924b). A laboratory study of fear: The case of Peter. *Pedagogical Seminary, 31,* 308–315.

Joseph, R. (2011). *Head injuries, concussions and brain damage: Cerebral and cranial trauma, skull fractures, contusions, hemorrhage, loss of consciousness, coma.* Cambridge, UK: Cambridge University Press.

Justice, T. C., & Looney, T. A. (1990). Another look at "superstitions" in pigeons. *Bulletin of the Psychonomic Society, 28*(1), 64–66.

Kalnins, I. V., & Bruner, J. S. (1973). The coordination of visual observation and instrumental behavior in early infancy. *Perception, 2(3),* 307–314.

Kamil, A. C., & Balda, R. P. (1985). Cache recovery and spatial memory in Clark's nutcrackers. *Journal of Experimental Psychology: Animal Behavior Processes, 11,* 95–111.

Kamil, A. C., & Balda, R. P. (1990a). Differential memory for cache cites in Clark's nutcrackers. *Journal of Experimental Psychology: Animal Behavior Processes, 16,* 162–168.

Kamil, A. C., & Balda, R. P. (1990b). Spatial memory in seed-caching corvids. In G. H. Bower (Ed.), *Psychology of learning and motivation,* Vol. 26 (pp.1–25). New York: Academic Press.

Kamin, L. J. (1957). The retention of an incompletely learned avoidance response. *Journal of Comparative and Physiological Psychology, 50,* 457–460.

Kamin, L. J. (1969). Predictability, surprise, attention and conditioning. In B. A. Campbell & R. M. Church (Eds.), *Punishment and aversive behavior* (pp. 279–296). New York: Appleton-Century-Crofts.

Kamin, L. J., Brimer, C. J., & Black, A. H. (1963). Conditioned suppression as a monitor of fear of the CS in the course of avoidance training. *Journal of Comparative and Physiological Psychology, 56,* 497–501.

Kandel, E. R. (1970, July). Nerve cells and behavior. *Scientific American, 223,* 57–70. doi: 10.10.1038/scientificamerican0770-57.

Kandel, E. R. (2007). *In search of memory.* New York: Norton.

Kanfer, F. H., & Marston, A. R. (1963). Human reinforcement: Vicarious and direct. *Journal of Experimental Psychology, 65,* 292–296.

Kang, N., Brinkman, W. P., van Riemsdijk, M. B., Neerincx, M. A. (2011). Internet-delivered multi-patient virtual reality exposure therapy system for the treatment of anxiety disorders. *Proceedings of ECCE2011,* 233–236.

Karpicke, J. D., & Blunt, J. R. (2011). Retrieval practice produces more learning than elaborative studying with concept mapping. *Science, 331,* 772–775.

Kassinove, J. I., & Schare, M. L. (2001). Effects of the "near miss" and the "big win" on persistence at slot machine gambling. *Psychology of Addictive Behavior, 15*(2), 155–158.

Kawai, M. (1963). On the newly-acquired behaviors of the natural troop of Japanese monkeys on Koshima Island. *Primates, 4*(1), 113–115.

Kawamura, S. (1963). The process of sub-cultural propagation among Japanese macaques. In C. H. Southwick (Ed.), *Primate social behavior* (pp. 82–90). New York: Van Nostrand.

Kazdin, A. E. (1973). The effect of vicarious reinforcement on attentive behavior in the classroom. *Journal of Applied Behavior Analysis, 6,* 71–78.

Kazdin, A. E. (1980). Acceptability of alternative treatments for deviant child behavior. *Journal of Applied Behavior Analysis, 13,* 259–273.

Kazdin, A. E. (1982). *Single-case research designs: Methods for clinical and applied settings.* New York: Oxford University Press.

Kazdin, A. E., & Rotella, C. (2009). Like a rat: Animal research and your child`s behavior. *Slate* Posted November 12, 2009. Available at http://www.slate.com/articles/life/family/2009/11/like_a_rat.html.

Keith-Lucas, T., & Guttman, N. (1975). Robust single-trial delayed backward conditioning. *Journal of Comparative and Physiological Psychology, 88,* 468–476.

Keller, F. S., & Schoenfeld, W. N. (1950). *Principles of psychology.* New York: Appleton-Century-Crofts.

Kellogg, W. N. (1968). Communication and language in the home-raised chimpanzee. *Science, 162,* 423–427.

Kerfoot, B. P., DeWolf, W. C., Masser, B. A., Church, P. A., & Federman, D. D. (2007). Spaced education improves the retention of clinical knowledge by medical students: A randomized controlled trial. *Medical Education, 41*(1), 23–31.

Kerr, S. (1975). On the folly of rewarding A, while hoping for B. *Academy of Management Journal, 18,* 769–783.

Kessler, R. C. Berglund, P. A., Demier, O., Jin, R., & Waleters, E. E. (2005). Lifetime prevalence and age of onset distributions of DSM-IV disorders in the National Comorbidity Survey Replication (NCS-R). *Archives of General Psychiatry, 62*(6), 593–602.

Kettlewell, H. B. D. (1959, March). Darwin's missing evidence. *Scientific American,* 48–53.

Killeen, P. R., Cate, H., & Tran, T. (1993). Scaling pigeons' choice of feeds: Bigger is better. *Journal of the Experimental Analysis of Behavior, 60,* 203–217.

Killeen, P. R., Posadas-Sanchez, D., Johansen, E. B., & Thraikill, E. A. (2009). Progressive ratio schedules of reinforcement. *Journal of Experimental Psychology: Animal Behavior Processes, 35*(1), 35–50.

Kilmann, P. R., Sabalis, R. F., Gearing, M. L., II, Bukstel, L. H., & Scovern, M. L. (1982). The treatment of sexual paraphilias: A review of the outcome research. *Journal of Sex Research, 18*(3), 193–252.

Kimble, G. A. (1947). Conditioning as a function of the time between conditioned and unconditioned stimuli. *Journal of Experimental Psychology, 37,* 1–15.

Kimble, G. A. (1961). *Hilgard and Marguis' conditioning and learning* (2nd ed.). London: Methuen.

Kimble, G. A. (1967). *Foundations of conditioning and learning.* New York: Irvington Press.

King, G. D., Schaeffer, R. W., & Pierson, S. C. (1974). Reinforcement schedule preference of a raccoon (*Procyon lotor*). *Bulletin of the Psychonomic Society, 4,* 97–99.

Kingsley, H. L., & Garry, B. (1962). *The nature and conditions of learning* (2nd ed.). New York: Prentice-Hall.

Kinloch, J. M., Foster, T. M., & McEwan, J. S. A. (2009). Extinction-induced variability in human behavior. *The Psychological Record*, 59(3), Article 3. Available at http://opensiuc.lib.siu.edu/tpr/vol50/iss3/3.

Kirsch, I., & Boucsein, W. (1994). Electrodermal Pavlovian conditioning with prepared and unprepared stimuli. *Integrative Physiological and Behavioral Science*, 29(2), 134–140.

Kitfield, E. B., & Masalsky, C. J. (2000). Negative reinforcement-based treatment to increase food intake. *Behavior Modification*, 24(4), 600–608.

Kiviat, B. (2007, August 16). Why we buy the products we buy. *Time Magazine*. Available at www.time.com/time/magazine/article/0,9171,1653,659,00.html

Klinkenborg, V. (2005, November 21). The grandeur of evolution. *International Herald Tribune*, p. A14.

Knafo, A., Israel, S., Darvasi, A., Bachner-Melman, R., Uzefovsky, F., Cohen, L., et al. (2008). Individual differences in allocation of funds in the Dictator Game associated with length of the arginine vasopressin 1a receptor RS3 promoter region and correlation between RS3 length and hippocampal mRNA. *Genes, Brain, & Behavior*, 7(3), 266–275.

Knox, D., George, S. A., Fitszaptrick, C. J., Raninak, C. A., Maren, S., & Liberzon, I. (2012). Single prolonged stress disrupts retention of extinguished fear in rats. *Learning & Memory*, 19, 43–49.

Kohler, W. (1927/1973). *The mentality of apes* (2nd ed.). New York: Liveright.

Kohler, W. (1939). Simple structural function in the chimpanzee and the chicken. In W. A. Ellis (Ed.), *A sourcebook of Gestalt psychology* (pp. 217–227). New York: Harcourt Brace.

Kornell, N. (2009). Optimising learning using flashcards: Spacing is more effective than cramming. *Applied Cognitive Psychology*, 23, 1297–1317.

Kraft, J. R., & Baum, W. M. (2001). Group choice: The ideal free distribution of human social behavior. *Journal of the Experimental Analysis of Behavior*, 76(1), 21–42.

Kreek, M. J., Nielsen, D. A., Butelman, E. R., & LaForge, K. S. (2005). Genetic influences on impulsivity, risk taking, stress responsivity and vulnerability to drug abuse and addiction. *Nature Neuroscience*, 8(11), 1450–1457. Published online October 26, 2005. doi: 10.1038/nn1583.

Krueger, T. H. C., Schedlowski, M., & Meyer, G. (2005). Cortisol and heart rate measures during casino gambling in relation to impulsivity. *Neuropsychobiology*, 52, 206–211.

Krueger, W. C. F. (1929). The effects of overlearning on retention. *Journal of Experimental Psychology*, 12, 71–78.

Kruglanski, A. W., Friedman, I., & Zeevi, G. (1971). The effects of extrinsic incentive on some qualitative aspects of task performance. *Journal of Personality*, 39, 606–617.

Kuhnen, C. M., & Chiao, J. Y. (2009). Genetic determinants of financial risk taking. *PLoS ONE*, 4(2), e4362. doi: 10.1371/journal.pone.0004362.

Kukekova, A., & Trut, L. N. (2007). Domestication of the silver fox and its research findings. Address presented at the annual meeting of the Association for Behavior Analysis, San Diego, CA, May 27.

Kuntsche E., Pickett, W., Overpeck, M., Craig, W., Boyce, W., & Gaspar de Matos, M. (2006). Television viewing and forms of bullying among adolescents from eight countries. *Journal of Adolescent Health*, 39(6), 908–915.

Kuo, T., & Hirshman, E. (1996). Investigations of the testing effects. *American Journal of Psychology*, 109, 451–464.

Kuo, Z. Y. (1930). The genesis of the cat's response to the rat. *Journal of Comparative Psychology*, 11, 1–36.

Kuo, Z. Y. (1967). *The dynamics of behavior development: An epigenetic view*. New York: Random House.

Kymissis, E., & Poulson, C. L. (1990). The history of imitation in learning theory: The language acquisition process. *Journal of the Experimental Analysis of Behavior*, 54, 113–127.

Kymissis, E., & Poulson, C. L. (1994). Generalized imitation in preschool boys. *Journal of Experimental Child Psychology*, 58, 389–404.

Lachter, G. D., Cole, B. K., & Schoenfeld, W. N. (1971). Response rate under varying frequency of non-contingent reinforcement. *Journal of the Experimental Analysis of Behavior*, 15, 233–236.

Lafferty, K. D., & Morris, A. K. (1996). Altered behavior of a parasitized Killifish increases suspectibility to predation by bird final hosts. *Ecology*, 77(5), 1390–1397.

Laland, K. N., & Williams, K. (1997). Shoaling generates social learning of foraging information in guppies. *Animal Behaviour*, 53, 1161–1169.

Lamb, T. D. (2011, July). Evolution of the eye. *Scientific American*, 64–69.

Lamere, J. M., Dickinson, A. M., Henry, M., Henry, G., Poling, A. (1996). Effects of a multicomponent incentive program on the performance of truck drivers: A longitudinal study. *Behavior Modification*, 20(4), 385–405.

Lancioni, G. E., & Hoogland, G. A. (1980). Hearing assessment in young infants by means of a classical conditioning procedure. *International Journal of Pediatric Otorhinolaryngology*, 2(3), 193–200.

Landers, D. M., & Landers, D. M. (1973). Teacher versus peer models: Effects of model's presence and performance level on motor behavior. *Journal of Motor Behavior*, 5, 129–139.

Landman, O. E. (1991). The inheritance of acquired characteristics. *Annual Review of Genetics*, 25, 1–20.

Lane, H. L., & Shinkman, P. G. (1963). Methods and findings in an analysis of a vocal operant. *Journal of the Experimental Analysis of Behavior*, 6, 179–188.

Laraway, S., Snycerski, S., Michael, J., & Poling, A. (2003). Motivating operations and terms to describe them: Some further refinements. *Journal of Applied Behavior Analysis*, 36, 407–414.

Larson, J. D., Calamari, J. E., West, J. G., & Frevent, T. A. (1998). Aggression-management with disruptive adolescents in the residential setting: Integration of a cognitive-behavioral component. *Residential Treatment for Children and Youth*, 15, 1–9.

Lashley, K. S. (1930). The mechanism of vision, I: A method of rapid analysis of pattern-vision in the rat. *Journal of Genetic Psychology*, 37, 453–640.

Lashley, K. S., & Wade, M. (1946). The Pavlovian theory of generalization. *Psychological Review, 53*, 72–87.

Latham, G. (1997). *Behind the schoolhouse door*. Logan: Utah State University Press.

Lattal, K. A. (2010). Delayed reinforcement of operant behavior. *Journal of the Experimental Analysis of Behavior, 93*, 129–139.

Lattal, K. A., & Gleeson, S. (1990). Response acquisition with delayed reinforcement. *Journal of Experimental Psychology: Animal Behavior Processes, 16*, 27–39.

Lattal, K. A., & Neef, N. A. (1996). Recent reinforcement-schedule research and applied behavior analysis. *Journal of Applied Behavior Analysis, 29*, 213–230.

Lattal, M. (2007, December). Extinction and the erasures of memory. *Psychological Science Agenda.* Available at www.apa.org/science/about/psa/d007/12/lattal.aspx.

Lavigna, G. W., & Donnellan, A. M. (1986). *Alternatives to punishment: Solving behavior problems with non-aversive strategies*. New York: Irvington.

Lavin, N. I., Thorpe, J. G., Barker, J. C., Blakemore, C. B., & Conway, C. G. (1961). Behavior therapy in a case of transvestism. *Journal of Nervous and Mental Disorders, 133*, 346–353.

Lavond, D. G., & Steinmetz, J. E. (2003). *Handbook of classical conditioning*. New York: Springer.

Laws, D. R., & Marshall, W. L. (1991) Masturbatory reconditioning with sexual deviates: An evaluation review. *Advances in Behaviour Research and Therapy, 13*, 13–25.

Layng, T. V. J., & Andronis, P. T. (1984). Toward a functional analysis of delusional speech and hallucinatory behavior. *The Behavior Analyst, 7*, 139–156.

Layng, T. V. J., Twyman, J. S., & Stikeleather, G. (2003). Headsprout early reading : Reliably teaching child to read. *Behavioral Technology Today, 3*, 7–20.

Layng, T. V. J., Twyman, J. S., & Stikeleather, G. (2004). Engineering discovery learning: The contingency adduction of some precursors of textual responding in a beginning reading program. *Analysis of Verbal Behavior, 20*, 99–109.

Leader, L. R. (1995). The potential value of habituation in the prenate. In J.-P. Lecanuet, W. P. Fifer, N. A. Krasnegor, & W. P. Smotherman (Eds.), *Fetal development: A psychobiological perspective* (pp. 383–404). Hillsdale, NJ: Erlbaum.

Ledford, J. R., & Wolery, M. (2011). Teaching imitation to young children with disabilities: A review of the literature. *Topics in Early Childhood Special Education, 30*(4), 245–255.

Lee, T. D., & White, M. A. (1990). Influence of an unskilled model's practice schedule on observational motor learning. *Human Movement Science, 9*, 349–344.

Lerman, D. C., & Iwata, B. A. (1993). Descriptive and experimental analyses of variables maintaining self-injurious behavior. *Journal of Applied Behavior Analysis, 26*(3), 293–319.

Lerman, D. C., Iwata, B. A., Shore, B. A., & De Leon, I. G. (1997). Effects of intermittent punishment on self-injurious behavior: An evaluation of schedule thinning. *Journal of Applied Behavior Analysis, 30*, 187–201.

Leshner, A. I. (1997). Addiction is a brain disease, and it matters. *Science, 278*(5335), 45–47.

Levine, J. M., & Murphy, G. (1943). The learning and forgetting of controversial material. *Journal of Abnormal and Social Psychology, 38*, 507–517.

Levitt, S. D., & Dubner, S. J. (2005). *Freakonomics: A rogue economist explores the hidden side of everything*. New York: Harper.

Levy, E. A., McClinton, B. S., Rabinowitz, F. M., & Wolkin, J. R. (1974). Effects of vicarious consequences on imitation and recall: Some developmental findings. *Journal of Experimental Child Psychology, 17*, 115–132.

Li, M. D., & Burmeister, M. (2009). New insights into the genetics of addiction. *Nature Reviews Genetics, 10*, 225–231.

Liberman, R. P., Teigen, J., Patterson, R., & Baker, V. (1973). Reducing delusional speech in chronic paranoid schizophrenics. *Journal of Applied Behavior Analysis, 6*, 57–64.

Libet, B. (2005). *The temporal factor in consciousness*. Cambridge, MA: Harvard University Press.

Libet, B., Gleason, C. A., Wright, E. W., Pearl, D. K. (1983). Time of conscious intention to act in relation to onset of cerebral activity (readiness-potential). The unconscious initiation of a freely voluntary act. *Brain, 106*, 623–642.

Libet, B., Sinnott-Armstrong, W., & Nadel, L. (Eds.). (2010). *Conscious will and responsibility: A tribute to Benjamin Libet*. New York: Oxford University Press.

Lichstein, K. L., & Schreibman, L. (1976). Employing electric shock in autistic children: A review of the side effects. *Journal of Autism and Childhood Schizophrenia, 6*, 1163–1173.

Lieberman, H. R., Kanarek, R. B., & Prasad, C. (Eds.). (2005). *Nutritional neuroscience*. Boca Raton, FL: CRC Press.

Lightfoot, L. O. (1980). *Behavioral tolerance to low doses of alcohol in social drinkers*. Unpublished Ph.D. dissertation, Waterloo University, Ontario, Canada.

Lindsley, O. R. (1963). Direct measurement and functional definition of vocal hallucinatory symptoms. *Journal of Nervous and Mental Disease, 136*, 293–297.

Linz, D. G., Donnerstein, E., & Penrod, S. (1988). Effects of long-term exposure to violent and sexually degrading depictions of women. *Journal of Personality and Social Psychology, 55*(5), 758–768.

Lirgg, C. D., & Feltz, D. L. (1991). Teacher versus peer models revisited: Effects on motor performance and self-efficacy. *Research Quarterly for Exercise Sport, 62*(2), 217–224.

Lockhart, L. L., Saunders, B. E., & Cleveland, P. (1989). Adult male sexual offenders: An overview of treatment techniques. In J. S. Wodarski & D. L. Whitaker (Eds.), *Treatment of sex offenders in social work and mental health settings* (pp. 1–32). New York: Haworth Press.

Loftus, E. F. (1979). *Eyewitness testimony*. Cambridge, MA: Harvard University Press.

Loftus, E. F. (2006). What's the matter with memory? Presidential scholar's address. Presented at the 32nd annual convention of the Association for Behavior Analysis, Atlanta, GA, May.

Loftus, E. F., & Palmer, J. C. (1974). Reconstruction of automobile destruction: An examination of the interaction between language and memory. *Journal of Verbal Learning and Verbal Behavior, 13*, 585–589.

Loftus, E. F., & Zanni, G. (1975). Eyewitness testimony: The influence of the wording of a question. *Bulletin of the Psychonomic Society, 5*, 86–88.

Lonsdorf, E. V. (2005). Sex differences in the development of termite-fishing skills in wild chimpanzees (*Pan troglodytes schweinfurthii*) of Gombe National Park, Tanzania. *Animal Behaviour, 70*, 673–683.

Lorenz, K. (1952). *King Solomon's ring*. New York: Crowell.

Lovaas, O. I., Ackerman, A., Alexander, D., Firestone, P., Perkins, M., & Young, D. B. (1981). *Teaching developmentally disabled children: The me book*. Austin, TX: Pro Ed.

Lovaas, O. I. (1987). Behavioral treatment and normal educational and intellectual functioning in young autistic children. *Journal of Consulting and Clinical Psychology, 55*, 3–9.

Lovaas, O. I. (1993). The development of a treatment-research project for developmentally disabled and autistic children. *Journal of Applied Behavior Analysis, 26*, 617–630.

Lovaas, O. I., Berberich, J. P., Perloff, B. F., & Schaeffer, B. (1966). Acquisition of imitative speech by schizophrenic children. *Science, 151*(3711), 705–707.

Lovaas, O. I., Schaeffer, B., & Simmons, J. Q. (1965). Building social behavior in autistic children by use of electric shock. *Journal of Experimental Research in Personality, 1*, 99–109.

Lovaas, O. I., & Simmons, J. Q. (1969). Manipulation of self-destruction in three retarded children. *Journal of Applied Behavior Analysis, 2*, 143–157.

Loveland, K. A., & Landry, S. H. (1986). Joint attention and language in autism and developmental language delay. *Journal of Autism and Developmental Disorders, 16*, 335–349.

Lovibond, P. F., & Shanks, D. R. (2002). The role of awareness in Pavlovian conditioning: Empirical evidence and theoretical implications. *Journal of Experimental Psychology: Animal Behavior Processes, 28*(1), 3–26.

Lowe, C. F., Horne, P. J., Hardman, C. A., & Tapper, K. (2006). A peer-modeling and rewards-based intervention is effective in increasing fruit and vegetable consumption in children. *Preventive Medicine, 43*(4), 351–352.

Lowe, C. F., Horne, P. J., Tapper, K., Bowdery, M., & Egerton, C. (2004). Effects of a peer modelling and rewards-based intervention to increase fruit and vegetable consumption in children. *Europena Journal of Clinical Nutrition, 58*, 510–522.

Lubow, R. E., & Moore, A. V. (1959). Latent inhibition: The effect of nonreinforced pre-exposure to the conditional stimulus. *Journal of Consulting and Clinical Psychology, 52*, 415–419.

Ludvig, E. A., Conover, K., & Shizgal, P. (2007). The effects of reinforcer magnitude on timing in rats. *Journal of the Experimental Analysis of Behavior, 87*, 201–218.

Luiselli, J. K., & Reed, D. D. (Eds.). (2011). *Behavioral sports psychology: Evidence-based approaches to performance enhancement*. New York, NY: Springer.

Luncz, L. V., Mundry, R., & Boesch, C. (2012). Evidence for cultural differences between neighboring chimpanzee communities. *Current Biology, 22*(10), 922–926.

Luria, A. R. (1968). *The mind of a mnemonist: A little book about a vast memory* (L. Solotaroff, Trans.). New York: Basic.

Lynn, R., & Hattori, K. (1990). The heritability of intelligence in Japan. *Behavior Genetics, 20*(4), 545–546.

Lyons, C. (1991). Application: Smoking. In Waris Ishaq (Ed.), *Human behavior in today's world* (pp. 217–230). New York: Praeger.

Lyons, D. E., Young, A. G., & Keil, F. S. (2007). The hidden structure of overimitation. *Proceedings of the National Academy of Science, 104*(19), 751–756. doi: 10.1073/pnas.0704452104.

Mace, F. C., Mauro, B. C., Boyojian, A. E., & Eckert, T. L. (1997). Effects of reinforcer quality on behavioral momentum: Coordinated applied and basic research. *Journal of Applied Behavior Analysis, 30*, 1–20.

Mackintosh, N. J. (1974). *The psychology of animal learning*. Oxford, UK: Oxford University Press.

Macklin, M. C. (1996). Preschoolers' learning of brand names from visual cues. *Journal of Consumer Research, 23*, 251–261.

MacRae, J. R., & Siegel, S. (1997). The role of self-administration in morphine withdrawal in rats. *Psychobiology, 25*(1), 77–82.

Madigan, S., & O'Hara, R. (1992). Short-term memory at the turn of the century. *American Psychologist, 47*(2), 170–174.

Madsen, C. H., Jr., Becker, W. C., & Thomas, D. R. (1968). Rules, praise, and ignoring: Elements of elementary classroom control. *Journal of Applied Behavior Analysis, 1*, 139–150.

Maier, S. F., Albin, R. W., & Testa, T. J. (1973). Failure to learn to escape in rats previously exposed to inescapable shock depends on the nature of the escape response. *Journal of Comparative and Physiological Psychology, 85*, 581–592.

Maletzky, B. M. (1980). Assisted covert sensitization. In D. J. Cox & R. J. Daitzman (Eds.), *Exhibitionism: Description, assessment, and treatment* (pp. 187–251). New York: Garland.

Maloney, S. K., Fuller, A., & Mitchell, D. (2010). A warming climate remains a plausible hypothesis for the decrease in dark Soay sheep. *Biological Letters, 6*, 680–681. doi: 10.1098/rsbl.2010.0253.

Malott, R. W., & Malott, M. K. (1970). Perception and stimulus generalization. In W. C. Stebbins (Ed.), *Animal psychophysics: The design and conduct of sensory experiments* (pp. 363–400). New York: Appleton-Century-Crofts.

Malthus, T. (1798). *An essay on the principle of population.* Available at www.gutenberg.org and at www.amazon.com.

Mansfield, R. J. W., & Rachlin, H. C. (1970). The effect of punishment, extinction, and satiation on response chains. *Learning and Motivation, 1*, 27–36.

Marcus, G. (2009). *Kluge: The haphazard evolution of the human mind.* Boston: Mariner Books.

Marcus-Newhall, A., Pedersen, W. C., Carlson, M., & Miller, N. (2000). Displaced aggression is alive and well: A meta-analytic review. *Journal of Personality and Social Psychology, 78*(4), 670–689.

Marenco, S., Weinberger, D. R., & Schreurs, B. G. (2003). Single-cue delay and trace conditioning in schizophrenia. *Biological Psychiatry, 53*(5), 390–402.

Margolis, E., & Laurence, S. (1999). *Concepts: Core readings.* Cambridge, MA: MIT Press.

Mark, V., Taub, E., Bashir, K., Uswatte, G., Delgado, A., Bowman, M. H., et al. (2008). Constraint-induced movement therapy can improve hemiparetic progressive multiple sclerosis: Preliminary findings. *Multiple Sclerosis, 14*(7), 992–994.

Markowitz, H. (1978). *Behavior of captive wild animals.* Chicago: Burnham, Inc.

Markowitz, H. (1982). *Behavioral enrichment in the zoo.* New York: Van Nostrand Reinhold.

Markowitz, H. (2011). *Enriching animal lives.* Pacifica, CA: Mauka Press.

Marks, I. M. (1986). Genetics of fear and anxiety disorders. *British Journal of Psychiatry, 149*, 406–418.

Marschall, L. A. (1993, March/April). Books in brief. *The Sciences,* 45.

Marshall, W. L., & Eccles, A. (1991). Issues in clinical practice with sex offenders. *Journal of Interpersonal Violence, 6*, 69–93.

Martins, B. K., & Collier, S. R. (2011). Developing fluent, efficient and automatic repertoires of athletic performance. In J. K. Luiselli & D. D. Reed (Eds.), *Behavioral sports psychology: Evidence-based approaches to performance enhancement* (pp. 159–176). New York: Springer.

Masataka, N., Koda, H., Urasopon, N., & Watanabe, K. (2009). Free-ranging Macaque mothers exaggerate tool-using behavior when observed by offspring. *PLOS One, 4*(3), e4768. doi: 10.1371/journal.pone.0004768.

Masia, C. L., & Chase, P. N. (1997). Vicarious learning revisited: A contemporary behavior analytic interpretation. *Journal of Behavior Therapy & Experimental Psychiatry, 28*, 41–51.

Masserman, J. H. (1943). *Behavior and neurosis: An experimental-psychoanalytic approach to psychobiologic principles.* New York: Hafner.

Masserman, J. H. (1946). *Principles of dynamic psychiatry.* Philadelphia, PA: Saunders.

Matson, L. M., & Grahame, N. J. (2011). Pharmacologically relevant intake during chronic, free-choice drinking rhythms in selectively bred high alcohol-preferring mice. *Addiction Biology.* Published online November 29. doi: 10.1111/j.1369-1600.2011.00412.x.

Maurice, E. B. (2005). *The last gentleman adventurer: Coming of age in the Arctic.* Boston, MA: Houghton Mifflin.

Max, L. W. (1937). Experimental study of the motor theory of consciousness, IV: Action—current responses in the deaf during awakening, kinaesthetic imagery, and abstract thinking. *Journal of Comparative Psychology, 42*(2), 301–344.

Mazur, J. E. (1975). The matching law and quantifications related to Premack's principle. *Journal of Experimental Psychology: Animal Behavior Processes, 1*, 374–386.

Mazur, J. E., & Wagner, A. R. (1982). An episodic model of associative learning. In M. Commons, R. Herrnstein, & A. R. Wagner (Eds.), *Quantitative analyses of behavior: Acquisition,* Vol. 3 (pp. 3–39). Cambridge, MA: Ballinger.

McCarthy, D. E., Baker, T. B., Minami, H. M., & Yeh, V. M. (2011). Applications of contemporary learning theory in the treatment of drug abuse. In T. Schachtman & S. Reilly (Eds.), *Applications of Learning and Conditioning* (pp. 235–269). Oxford, UK: Oxford University Press.

McCarty, R. (1998, November). Making the case for animal research. *APA Monitor,* 18.

McClelland, J. L., Fiez, J. A., & McCandliss, B. D. (2002). Teaching the /r/-/l/ discrimination to Japanese adults: Behavioral and neural aspects. *Physiology and Behavior, 77*, 657–662.

McCullagh, P., & Meyer, K. N. (1997). Learning versus correct models: Influence of model type on the learning of a free-weight squat lift. *Research Quarterly for Exercise and Sport, 68*(1), 56–61.

McDougall, W. (1908). *An introduction to social psychology.* London: Methuen.

McDougall, W. (1927). An experiment for the testing of the hypothesis of Lamarck. *British Journal of Psychology, 17*, 267–304.

McDougall, W. (1938). Fourth report on a Lamarckian experiment. *British Journal of Psychology, 28*, 321–345.

McDowell, J. J. (1982). The importance of Herrnstein's mathematical statement of the law of effect for behavior therapy. *American Psychologist, 37*, 771–779.

McGeoch, J. A. (1932). Forgetting and the law of disuse. *Psychological Review, 39*, 352–370.

McGlynn, F. D. (2010). Systematic desensitization. In I. Weiner & W. E. Craighead (Eds.), *The Corsini Encyclopedia of Psychology*. Wiley Online Library. Published online January 30, 2010. doi: 10.1002/9780470479216.corpsy0972.

McGreevy, P. (1983). *Teaching and learning in plain English* (2nd ed.). Kansas City, MO: Plain English Publications.

McGuigan, F. J. (1966). Covert oral behavior and auditory hallucinations. *Psychophysiology, 3*(1), 73–80.

McGuigan, N. (2012). The role of transmission biases in the cultural diffusion of irrelevant actions. *Journal of Comparative Psychology, 126*(2), 150–160.

McGuigan, N., & Graham, M. (2010). Cultural transmission of irrelevant tool actions in diffusion chains of 3- and 5-year-old children. *European Journal of Developmental Psychology, 7,* 561–577.

McGuigan, N., Whiten, A., Flynn, E., Horner, V. (2007). Imitation of causally opaque versus causally transparent tool use by 3- and 5-year old children. *Cognitive Development, 22*(3), 353–364.

McNally, R. J. (1987). Preparedness and phobias: A review. *Psychological Bulletin, 101,* 283–303.

McNamara, E. (1987). Behavioural approaches in the secondary school. In K. Wheldall (Ed.), *The behaviourist in the classroom* (pp. 50–68). London: Allen & Unwin.

McPhee, J. E., Rauhut, A. S., & Ayres, J. J. B. (2001). Evidence for learning-deficit vs. performance-deficit theories of latent inhibition in Pavlovian fear conditioning. *Learning and Motivation, 32,* 1–32.

Mello, N. K., & Mendelson, J. H. (1970). Experimentally induced intoxication in alcoholics: A comparison between programmed and spontaneous drinking. *Journal of Pharmacology and Experimental Therapeutics, 173,* 101–116.

Menzel, C. R. (1991). Cognitive aspects of foraging in Japanese monkeys. *Animal Behavior, 41,* 397–402.

Metzgar, L. H. (1967). An experimental comparison of screech owl predation on resident and transient white-footed mice (*Peromyscus leucopus*). *Journal of Mammology, 48,* 387–391.

Michael, J. (1975). Positive and negative reinforcement: A distinction that is no longer necessary; or, a better way to talk about bad things. *Behaviorism, 3,* 33–44.

Michael, J. (1982). Distinguishing between discriminative and motivational functions of stimuli. *Journal of the Experimental Analysis of Behavior, 37,* 149–155.

Michael, J. (1983). Evocative and repertoire-altering effects of an environmental event. *The Analysis of Verbal Behavior, 2,* 19–21.

Michael, J. (1991). A behavioral perspective on college teaching. *The Behavior Analyst, 14,* 229–239.

Michael, J. (1993). Establishing operations. *The Behavior Analyst, 16,* 191–206.

Michael, J. (2006). Comment on Baron and Galizio (2005). *The Behavior Analyst, 29,* 117–119.

Midgley, B. D. (1987). Instincts—Who needs them? *The Behavior Analyst, 10,* 313–314.

Miller, N. E. (1948a). Studies of fear as an acquired drive, I: Fear as a motivation and fear-reduction as reinforcement in learning of new responses. *Journal of Experimental Psychology, 38,* 89–101.

Miller, N. E. (1948b). Theory and experiment relating psychoanalytic displacement to stimulus-response generalization. *Journal of Abnormal Psychology, 43*(2), 155–178.

Miller, N. E. (1960). Learning resistance to pain and fear: Effects of overlearning, exposure, and rewarded exposure in context. *Journal of Experimental Psychology, 60,* 137–145.

Miller, N. E. (1978). Biofeedback and visceral learning. *Annual Review of Psychology, 29,* 373–404.

Miller, N. E. (1985). The value of behavioral research on animals. *American Psychologist, 40,* 423–440.

Miller, N. E., & DiCara, L. (1967). Instrumental learning of heart rate changes in curarized rats: Shaping and specificity to discriminative stimulus. *Journal of Comparative and Physiological Psychology, 63,* 12–19.

Miller, N. E., & Dollard, J. (1941). *Social learning and imitation.* New Haven, CT: Yale University Press.

Miller, R. R., Barnet, R. C., & Grahame, N. J. (1995). Assessment of the Rescorla-Wagner model. *Psychological Bulletin, 117*(3), 363–386.

Miller, S. J., & Sloane, H. N. (1976). The generalization effects of parent training across stimulus settings. *Journal of Applied Behavior Analysis, 9,* 355–370.

Mills, H. L., Agras, W. S., Barlow, D. H., & Mills, J. R. (1973). Compulsive rituals treated by response prevention: An experimental analysis. *Archives of General Psychiatry, 28*(4), 524–529.

Miltenberger, R. G., & Gross, A. (2011). Teaching safety skills to children. In W. Fisher, C. Piazza, & H. Roane (Eds.), *Handbook of Applied Behavior Analysis* (pp. 417–432). New York, NY: Guilford Press.

Minami, H., & Dallenbach, K. M. (1946). The effect of activity upon learning and retention in the cockroach (*Periplaneta americana*). *American Journal of Psychology, 59,* 1–58.

Mineka, S., & Cook, M. (1988). Social learning and the acquisition of snake fear in monkeys. In T. Zentall & B. Galef (Eds.), *Social learning: Psychological and biological perspectives* (pp. 51–73). Hillsdale, NJ: Erlbaum.

Miyashita, Y., Nakajima, S., & Imada, H. (2000). Differential outcome effect in the horse. *Journal of the Experimental Analysis of Behavior, 74,* 245–253.

Mock, D. W. (2006). *More than kin and less than kind: The evolution of family conflict.* Cambridge, MA: Belknap Press.

Money, J. (1987). Masochism: On the childhood origin of paraphilia, opponent-process theory, and antiandrogen therapy. *Journal of Sex Research, 23*(2), 273–275.

Moore, D. S. (2001). *The dependent gene: The fallacy of nature vs. nurture.* New York: W. H. Freeman.

Moore, J. (2010). What do mental terms mean? *Psychological Record, 60,* 699–714.

Moore, J. (2011). The case for private behavioral events. Address given at the annual meeting of the Association for Behavior Analysis, Denver, CO, May 30.

Morgan, D. H. (2010). Schedules of reinforcement at 50: A retrospective appreciation. *The Psychological Record, 60,* 151–172.

Morgan, D. L., & Morgan, R. L. (2008). *Single-case research methods for the behavioral and health sciences.* New York: Sage.

Morris, E. K. (2001). B. F. Skinner. In B. J. Zimmerman & D. H. Schunk (Eds.), *Educational psychology: A century of contributions* (pp. 229–250). Hillsdale, NJ: Erlbaum.

Morris, E. K., Lazo, J. F., & Smith, N. G. (2004). Whether, when and why Skinner published on biological participation in behavior. *The Behavior Analyst, 27,* 153–169.

Morse, W. H. (1966). Intermittent reinforcement. In W. H. Honig (Ed.), *Operant behavior: Areas of research and application* (pp. 52–108). New York: Appleton-Century-Crofts.

Morse, W. H., & Kelleher, R. T. (1977). Determinants of reinforcement and punishment. In W. K. Honig & J. E. R. Staddon (Eds.), *Handbook of operant behavior* (pp. 174–200). Englewood Cliffs, NJ: Prentice-Hall.

Mowrer, O. H. (1940). An experimental analysis of "regression" with incidental observations on "reaction-formation." *Journal of Abnormal and Social Psychology, 35,* 56–87.

Mowrer, O. H. (1947). On the dual nature of learning: A reinterpretation of "conditioning" and "problem solving." *Harvard Educational Review, 17,* 102–150.

Mowrer, O. H., & Jones, H. (1945). Habit strength as a function of the pattern of reinforcement. *Journal of Experimental Psychology, 35,* 293–311.

Myers, L. L., & Thyer, B. A. (1994). Behavioral therapy: Popular misconceptions. *Scandinavian Journal of Behavior Therapy, 23*(2), 99–107.

Nakajima, S. (2006). Speculation and explicit identification as judgmental standards for positive or negative reinforcement: A comment on Baron and Galizio (2005). *The Behavior Analyst, 29,* 269–270.

National Center on Addiction and Substance Abuse. (2009). *Shoveling up II: The impact of substance abuse on federal, state and local budgets.* New York: Columbia University Press.

National Highway Traffic Safety Administration. (2009). *Traffic safety facts.* Washington, DC: NHTSA.

National Research Council. (2011). *Chimpanzees in biomedical and behavioral research: Assessing the necessity.* Washington, DC: The National Academies Press.

Nelson, C. A., Furtago, E. A., Fox, N. A., & Zeanah, C. H., Jr. (2009, May/June). The deprived human brain. *American Scientist,* 222–229.

Neuringer, A. (1970). Superstitious key-pecking after three peck-produced reinforcements. *Journal of the Experimental Analysis of Behavior, 13,* 127–134.

Neuringer, A. (1986). Can people behave "randomly"? The role of feedback. *Journal of Experimental Psychology: General, 115,* 62–75.

Neuringer, A. (2002). Operant variability: Evidence, functions, and theory. *Psychonomic Bulletin and Review, 9,* 672–705.

Neuringer, A. (2003). Creativity and reinforced variability. In K. A. Lattal & P. N. Chase (Eds.), *Behavior theory and philosophy* (pp. 323–338). New York: Springer.

Neuringer, A. (2004). Reinforced variability in animals and people: Implications for adaptive action. *American Psychologist, 59*(9), 891–906.

Nevin, J. A. (1992). An integrative model for the study of behavioral momentum. *Journal of the Experimental Analysis of Behavior, 57,* 301–316.

Nevin, J. A. (2003). Retaliating against terrorists. *Behavior and Social Issues, 12,* 109–128.

Nevin, J. A. (2004). Retaliating against terrorists: Erratum, reanalysis, and update. *Behavior and Social Issues, 13,* 155–159.

Nevin, J. A. (2012). Resistance to extinction and behavioral momentum. *Behavioural Processes, 90,* 89–97.

Nevin, J. A., & Grace, R. C. (2000). Behavioral momentum and the law of effect. *Behavioral and Brain Sciences, 23,* 73–130.

Newport, F. (2010, December 17). Four in 10 Americans believe in strict creationism. Available at http://www.gallup.com/poll/145286/four-americans-believe-strict-creationism.aspx.

Newsom, C., Flavall, J. E., & Rincover, A. (1983). Side effects of punishment. In S. Axelrod & J. Apsche (Eds.), *The effects of punishment on human behavior* (pp. 285–316). New York: Academic Press.

Nielsen, D. A., Ji, F., Yuferov, V., Ho, A., Chen, A., Levran, O., et al. (2008). Genotype patterns that contribute to increased risk for or protection from developing heroin addiction. *Molecular Psychiatry, 13,* 417–428.

Nielsen, M., & Blank, C. (2011). Imitation in young children: When who gets copied is more important than what gets copied. *Developmental Psychology, 47,* 1050–1053.

Nielsen, M., Subiaul, F., Whiten, A., Galef, B., & Zentall, T. (2012). Social learning in humans and nonhuman animals: Theoretical and empirical dissections. *Journal of Comparative Psychology.* doi: 10.1037/a0027758y.

Nielsen, M., & Tomaselli, K. (2010). Over-imitation in Kalahari Bushman children and the origins of human cultural cognition. *Psychological Science, 21,* 729–736.

Nisbett, R. E. (1990). The anti-creativity letters: Advice from a senior tempter to a junior tempter. *American Psychologist, 45,* 1078–1082.

Northrop, J., Fusilier, I., Swanson, V., Roane, H., & Borrero, J. (1997). An evaluation of methylphenidate as a potential establishing operation for some common classroom reinforcers. *Journal of Applied Behavio Analysis, 30,* 615–625.

Obhi, S. S., & Haggard, P. (2004, July/August). Free will and free won't. *American Scientist,* 358–365.

O'Brien, S. J., Wildt, D. E., & Bush, M. E. (1986, May). The cheetah in genetic peril. *Scientific American*, 84–92.

O'Donnell, J., & Crosbie, J. (1998). Punishment gradients with humans. *Psychological Record, 48*(2), 211–233.

O'Donohue, W., & Plaud, J. J. (1994). The conditioning of human sexual arousal. *Archives of Sexual Behavior, 23*(3), 321–344.

Odum, A. L. (2011). Delay discounting: Trait variable? *Behavioural Processes, 87*, 1–9.

Ogden, C. L., Carroll, M. D., Kit, B. K., & Flegal, K. M. (2012). *Prevalence of obesity in the United States, 2009–2010*. NCHS Data Bbrief No.82. Hyattsville, MD: National Center for Health Statistics.

Öhman, A., Esteves, F., & Soares, J. J. F. (1995). Preparedness and preattentive associative learning: Electrodermal conditioning to masked stimuli. *Journal of Psychophysiology, 9*, 99–108.

Öhman, A., Flykt, A., & Esteves, F. (2001). Emotion drives attention: Detecting the snake in the grass. *Journal of Experimental Psychology: General, 130*(3), 466–478.

Öhman, A., Fredrikson, M., Hugdahl, K., & Rimmo, P. A. (1976). The premise of equipotentiality in human classical conditioning: Conditioned electrodermal responses to potentially phobic stimuli. *Journal of Experimental Psychology: General, 103*, 313–337.

Öhman, A., & Mineka, S. (2001). Fears, phobias, and preparedness: Toward an evolved module of fear and learning. *Psychological Review, 108*(3), 483–522.

Öhman, A., & Mineka, S. (2003). The malicious serpent: Snakes as a prototypical stimulus for an evolved module of fear. *Current Directions in Psychological Science, 12*, 5–9.

Öhman, A., & Soares, J. J. F. (1994). "Unconscious anxiety": Phobic responses to masked stimuli. *Journal of Abnormal Psychology, 103*, 231–240.

Öhman, A., & Soares, J. J. F. (1998). Emotional conditioning to masked stimuli: Expectancies for aversive outcomes following nonecognized fear-relevant stimuli. *Journal of Experimental Psychology, 127*, 69–82.

Okouchi, H. (2007). An exploration of remote history effects in humans. *The Psychological Record, 57*, 241–263.

Okouchi, H. (2009). Response acquisition with humans with delayed reinforcement. *Journal of the Experimental Analysis of Behavior, 91*, 377–390.

Olds, J. (1969). The central nervous system and reinforcement of behavior. *American Psychologist, 24*, 114–132.

Olds, J., & Milner, P. M. (1954). Positive reinforcement produced by electrical stimulation of the septal area and other regions of the rat brain. *Journal of Comparative and Physiological Psychology, 47*, 419–427.

Ollendick, T. H., Dailey, D., & Shapiro, E. S. (1983). Vicarious reinforcement: Expected annd unexpected effects. *Journal of Applied Behavior Analysis, 16*, 485–491.

Ollendick, T. H., Shapiro, E. S., & Barrett, R. P. (1982). Effects of vicarious reinforcement in normal and severely disturbed children. *Journal of Consulting and Clinical Psychology, 50*, 63–70.

Olshansky, S. J. (2009, July). Why haven't we humans evolved eyes in the backs of our heads? *Scientific American*, 88. doi: 10.1038/scientificamerican0709-88.

Olsson, A., & Phelps, E. A. (2007). Social learning of fear. *Naure Neuroscience, 10*, 1095–1102.

Olsson, M. A., & Fazio, R. H. (2002). Implicit acquisition and manifestation of classically conditioned attitudes. *Social Cognition, 20*, 89–103.

Olsson, M. A., & Fazio, R. H. (2006). Reducing automatically activated racial prejudice through implicit evaluative conditioning. *Personality and Social Psychology Bulletin, 32*, 421–433.

Ono, K. (1987). Superstitious behavior in humans. *Journal of the Experimental Analysis of Behavior, 47*, 261–271.

Ost, L., & Hugdahl, K. (1985). Acquisition of blood and dental phobia and anxiety response patterns in clinical patients. *Behavior Research and Therapy, 23*, 27–34.

Overmier, J. B., & Seligman, M. E. P. (1967). Effects of inescapable shock upon subsequent escape and avoidance learning. *Journal of Comparative and Physiological Psychology, 63*, 23–33.

Overton, D. A. (1964). State-dependent or "dissociated" learning produced by pentobarbital. *Journal of Comparative and Physiological Psychology, 57*, 3–12.

Overton, D. A. (1991). Historical context of state dependent learning and discriminative drug effects. *Behavioural Pharmacology, 2*(4–5), 253–264.

Ozgul, A., Tuljapurkar, S., Benton, T. G., Pemberton, J. M., Clutton-Brock, T. H., & Coulson, T. (2009). The dynamics of phenotypic change and the shrinking sheep of St. Kilda. *Science, 325*, 464–467. doi: 10.1126/science.1173668.

Padilla, A. M., Padilla, C., Ketterer, T., & Giacalone, D. (1970). Inescapable shocks and subsequent avoidance conditioning in goldfish (*Carrasius auratus*). *Psychonomic Science, 20*, 295–296.

Page, S., & Neuringer, A. (1985). Variability is an operant. *Journal of Experimental Psychology: Animal Behavior Processes, 11*, 429–452.

Palmer, D. (1991). A behavioral interpretation of memory. In L. J. Hayes & P. N. Chase (Eds.), *Dialogues on verbal behavior* (pp. 261–279). Reno, NV: Context Press.

Palmer, D. (2003). Cognition. In K. A. Lattal & P. N. Chase (Eds.), *Behavior theory and philosophy* (pp. 167–185). New York: Springer.

Palmer, D. (2007). On Chomsky's appraisal of Skinner's *Verbal Behavior*: A half century of misunderstanding. *The Behavior Analyst, 29*, 253–267.

Papini, M. R., & Bitterman, M. E. (1990). The role of contingency in classical conditioning. *Psychological Review, 97*, 396–403.

Papka, M., Ivry, R. B., & Woodruff-Pak, D. S. (1997). Eyeblink classical conditioning and awareness revisited. *Psychological Science, 8*, 404–408.

Parish, T. S., & Fleetwood, R. S. (1975). Amount of conditioning and subsequent change in racial attitudes of children. *Perceptual and Motor Skills, 40,* 79–86.

Parish, T. S., Shirazi, A., & Lambert, F. (1976). Conditioning away prejudicial attitudes in children. *Perceptual and Motor Skills, 43,* 907–912.

Parsons, M. B., & Reid, D. H. (1990). Assessing food preferences among persons with profound mental retardation. *Journal of Applied Behavior Analysis, 23,* 183–195.

Parsons, T. D., and Rizzo, A. A. (2008). Affective outcomes of virtual reality exposure therapy for anxiety and specific phobias: a meta-analysis. *Journal of Behavior Therapy and Experimental Psychiatry, 39*(3), 250–261.

Pashler, H., Zarow, G., & Triplett, B. (2003). Is temporal spacing of tests helpful even when it inflates error rates? *Journal of Experimental Psychology: Learning, Memory, and Cognition, 29*(6), 1051–1057.

Patkowski, M. S. (1994). The critical age hypothesis and interlanguage phonology. In M. S. Yavas (Ed.), *First and second language phonology* (pp. 267–282). San Diego, CA: Singular Publications Group.

Patterson, C. J., & Mischel, W. (1976). Effects of temptation-inhibiting and task-facilitating plans on self-control. *Journal of Personality and Social Psychology, 33,* 209–217.

Patterson, F. P. (1978). The gesture of a gorilla: Language acquisition in another pongid. *Brain and Language, 5,* 72–97.

Patterson, F. P., Patterson, C. H., & Brentari, D. K. (1987). Language in child, chimp and gorilla. *American Psychologist, 42,* 270–272.

Paul, G. L. (1969). Outcome of systematic desensitization I & II. In C. M. Franks (Ed.), *Behavior therapy: Appraisal and status* (pp. 63–159). New York: McGraw-Hill.

Pavlov, I. P. (1927). *Conditioned reflexes* (G. V. Anrep, Ed. & Trans.). London: Oxford University Press.

Pear, J. J., & Chan, W. S. (2001). Video tracking of male Siamese fighting fish (*Betta splendens*). Poster presented at the annual meeting of the Association for Behavior Analysis, New Orleans, LA, May 25–29.

Pear, J. J., & Legris, J. A. (1987). Shaping by automated tracking of an arbitrary operant response. *Journal of the Experimental Analysis of Behavior, 47,* 241–247.

Pearce, J. M., & Hall, G. (1980). A model of Pavlovian learning: Variations in the effectiveness of conditioned but not of unconditioned stimuli. *Psychological Review, 87,* 532–552.

Peckstein, L. A., & Brown, F. D. (1939). An experimental analysis of the alleged criteria of insightful learning. *Journal of Educational Psychology, 30,* 38–52.

Peiris, J. S. M., Poon, L. L. M., & Guan, Y. (2012). Suveillance of animal influenza for pandemic preparedness. *Science, 335*(6073), 1173–1174.

Pellicciari, M. C., Domenica, V., Marzano, C., Moroni, F., Pirulli, C., Curcio, G., et al. (2009). Heritability of intracortical inhibition and facilitation. *Journal of Neuroscience, 29*(28), 8897–8900. doi: 10.1523/JNEUROSCI.2112-09.2009.

Pennisi, E. (2006). Man's best friends(s) reveal the possible roots of social intelligence. *Science, 312*(5781), 1734–1738.

Perkins, C. C., Jr., & Weyant, R. G. (1958). The interval between training and test trials as determiner of the slope of generalization gradients. *Journal of Comparative and Physiological Psychology, 51,* 596–600.

Perkins, D., Hammond, S., Coles, D., & Bishop, D. (1998, November). Review of sex offender treatment programmes. Paper prepared for the High Security Psychiatric Services Commissioning Board. Downloaded April 17, 2012, from http://www.ramas.co.uk/report4.pdf.

Perone, M. (2003). Negative effects of positive reinforcement. *The Behavior Analyst, 26,* 1–14.

Perusse, L., Tremblay, A., LeBlanc, C., & Bouchard, C. (1989). Genetic and environmental influences on level of habitual physical activity and exercise participation. *American Journal of Epidemiology, 129*(5), 1012–1022.

Peterson, G. B., & Trapold, M. A. (1980). Effects of altering outcome expectancies on pigeons' delayed conditional discrimination performance. *Learning and Motivation, 11,* 267–288.

Petitto, L. A., & Seidenberg, M. S. (1979). On the evidence for linguistic abilities in signing apes. *Brain and Language, 8,* 162–183.

Petscher, E. S., Rey, C., & Bailey, J. S. (2009). A review of empirical support for differential reinforcement of alternative behavior. *Research in Developmental Disabilities, 30*(3), 409–425.

Pfaus, J. G., Kippin, T. E., & Centeno, S. (2001). Conditioning and sexual behavior. *Hormones and Behavior, 40,* 291–321.

Pfister, J. A. (2000). Food aversion learning to eliminate cattle consumption of pine needles. *Journal of Range Management, 53,* 655–659.

Pfister, J. A., Stegelmeier, B. L., Cheney, C. D., Ralphs, M. H., & Gardner, D. R. (2002). Conditioning taste aversions to locoweed (*Oxytropis serices*) in horses. *Journal of Animal Science, 80,* 79–83.

Phelps, B. J., & Reit, D. J. (1997). The steepening of generalization gradients from "mentally rotated" stimuli. Paper presented at the 23rd annual convention of the Association for Behavior Analysis, Chicago, IL.

Piazza, C. C., Bowman, L. G., Contrucci, S. A., Delia, M. D., Adelinis, J. D., & Goh, H. (1999). An evaluation of the properties of attention as reinforcement for destructive and appropriate behavior. *Journal of Applied Behavior Analysis, 32,* 437–499.

Pierce, W. D., & Epling, W. F. (1983). Choice, matching, and human behavior: A review of the literature. *The Behavior Analyst, 6,* 57–76.

Pipitone, A. (1985, April 23). Jury to decide if sex obsession pushed man over edge. *The* (Baltimore) *Evening Sun,* pp. D1–D2.

Pipkin, C. St. P., & Vollmer, T. R. (2009). Applied implications of reinforcement history effects. *Journal of Applied Behavior Analysis, 42*(1), 83–103. doi: 10.1901/.

Pithers, W. D. (1994). Process evaluation of a group therapy component designed to enhance sex offenders' empathy for sexual abuse survivors. *Behavioural Research Therapy*, 32, 365–570.

Pittenger, D. J., & Pavlik, W. B. (1989). Analysis of the partial reinforcement extinction effect in humans using absolute and relative comparisons of schedules. *American Journal of Psychology*, 101(1), 1–14.

Polenchar, B. E., Romano, A. G., Steinmetz, J. E., & Patterson, M. M. (1984). Effects of US parameters on classical conditioning of cat hindlimb flexion. *Animal Learning and Behavior*, 12, 69–72.

Poling, A., Edwards, T. L., Weeden, M., & Foster, T. M. (2011). The matching law. *The Psychological Record*, 61, 313–322.

Poling, A., Weetjens, B., Cox, C., Beyene, N. W., Bach, H., & Sully, A. (2011). Using trained pouched rats to detect land mines: Another victory for operant conditioning. *Journal of Applied Behavior Analysis*, 44, 351–355.

Pollock, B. J., & Lee, T. D. (1992). Effects of the model's skill level on observational motor learning. *Research Quarterly for Exercise and Sport*, 63(1), 25–29.

Poon, L., & Halpern, J. (1971). A small-trials PREE with adult humans: Resistance to extinction as a function of number of N-R transitions. *Journal of Experimental Psychology*, 91(1), 124–128.

Porter, D., & Neuringer, A. (1984). Music discrimination by pigeons. *Journal of Experimental Psychology: Animal Behavior Processes*, 10, 138–148.

Potts, L., Eshleman, J. W., & Cooper, J. O. (1993). Ogden R. Lindsley and the historical development of precision teaching. *The Behavior Analyst*, 16(2), 177–189.

Poulson, C. L., Kyparissos, N., Andreatos, M., Kymissis, E., & Parnes, M. (2002). Generalized imitation within three response classes in typically developing infants. *Journal of Experimental Child Psychology*, 81, 341–357.

Poulson, C. L., Kymissis, E., Reeve, K. F., Andreatos, M., & Reeve, L. (1991). Generalized vocal imitation in infants. *Journal of Experimental Child Psychology*, 51, 267–279.

Powers, M. B., & Emmelkamp, P. M. (2008). Virtual reality exposure therapy for anxiety disorders: A meta-analysis. *Journal of Anxiety Disorders*, 22(3), 561–569.

Powers, R. B., Cheney, C. D., & Agostino, N. R. (1970). Errorless training of a visual discrimination in preschool children. *Psychological Record*, 20, 45–50.

Premack, D. (1959). Toward empirical behavioral laws, I: Positive reinforcement. *Psychological Review*, 66, 219–233.

Premack, D. (1962). Reversibility of the reinforcement relation. *Science*, 136(3512), 255–257.

Premack, D. (1965). Reinforcement theory. In D. Levine (Ed.), *Nebraska Symposium on Motivation*, Vol. 13 (pp. 189–282). Lincoln: University of Nebraska Press.

Premack, D. (1971). Catching up with common sense, or two sides of a generalization: Reinforcement and punishment. In R. Glaser (Ed.), *The nature of reinforcement* (pp. 121–150). New York: Academic Press.

Prokasy, W. F., & Whaley, F. L. (1963). Inter-trial interval range shift in classical eyelid conditioning. *Psychological Reports*, 12, 55–88.

Provenza, F. D. (1996). Acquired aversions as the basis for varied diets of ruminantes foraging on rangelands. *Journal of Animal Science*, 74, 2010–2020.

Provenza, F. D., Burrit, E. A., Clausen, T. P., Bryant, J. P., Reichardt, P. B., Distel, R. A. (1990). Conditioned flavor aversion: a mechanism for goats to avoid condensed tannins in blackbrush. *The American Naturalist*, 136(6), 810–828.

Provenza, F. D., Lynch, J. J., & Nolan, J. U. (1993). Temporal contiguity between food ingestion and toxicosis affects the acquisition of food aversions in sheep. *Applied Animal Behavior Science*, 38, 269–281.

Pryor, K. (1991). *Lads before the wind* (2nd ed.). North Bend, WA: Sunshine Books.

Pryor, K. (1996). Clicker training aids shelter adoption rates. *Don't Shoot the Dog! News*, 1(2), 2.

Pryor, K. (1999). *Don't shoot the dog* (rev. ed.). New York: Bantam.

Pryor, K., Haag, R., & O'Reilly, J. (1969). The creative porpoise: Training for novel behavior. *Journal of the Experimental Analysis of Behavior*, 12, 653–661.

Pulvermuller, F., Neininger, B., Elbert, T., Mohr, B., Rockstroh, B., Kobbel, P., et al. (2001). Constraint-induced therapy of chronic aphasia following stroke. *Stroke*, 32, 1621–1626.

Purtle, R. B. (1973). Peak shift: A review. *Psychological Bulletin*, 80, 408–421.

Quinton, D., Rutter, M., & Liddle, C. (1984). Institutional rearing, parenting difficulties, and marital support. *Psychological Medicine*, 14, 107–124.

Ralphs, M. H. (1997). Persistence of aversions to larkspur in naïve and native cattle. *Journal of Range Management*, 50, 367–370.

Ralphs, M. H., & Provenza, F. D. (1999). Conditioned food aversions: Principles and practices, with special reference to social facilitation. *Proceedings of Nutrition Society*, 58, 813–820.

Razran, G. (1956). Extinction re-examined and re-analyzed: A new theory. *Psychological Review*, 63, 39–52.

Reber, A. S. (1995). *Penguin dictionary of psychology*. New York: Penguin.

Redelmeier, D. A., & Tibshirani, R. T. (1997). Association between cellular telephone calls and motor vehicle collisions. *New England Journal of Medicine*, 336, 453–458.

Redker, C., & Gibson, G. (2009). Music as an unconditioned stimulus: Positive and negative effects of country music on implicit attitudes, explicit attitudes, and product choice. *Journal of Applied Social Psychology*, 39(11), 2689–2705.

Reed, D. D., Critchfield, T. S., & Martens, B. K. (2006). The generalized matching law in elite sport competition: Football play calling as operant choice. *Journal of Applied Behavior Analysis, 39,* 281–297.

Reed, P. (1991). Multiple determinants of the effects of reinforcement magnitude on free-operant response rates. *Journal of the Experimental Analysis of Behavior, 55,* 109–123.

Reed, P., & Yoshino, T. (2001). The effect of response-dependent tones on the acquisition of concurrent behavior in rats. *Learning & Motivation.* Electronic edition published March 20, 2001.

Reed, T. (1980). Challenging some "common wisdom" on drug abuse. *International Journal of Addiction, 15,* 359–373.

Reger, G., & Gahm, G. (2008). Virtual reality exposure therapy for active duty soldiers. *Journal of Clinical Psychology, 64,* 940–946.

Reger, G. M., Holloway, K. M., Candy, C., Rothbaum, B. O., Difede, J., Rizzo, A. A., et al. (2011). Effectiveness of virtual reality exposure therapy for active duty soldiers in a military mental health clinic. *Journal of Traumatic Stress, 24*(1), 93–96.

Reiss, S. (2000). *Who am I: The 16 basic desires that motivate our actions and define our personality.* New York: Tarcher/Putnam.

Reit, D. J., & Phelps, B. J. (1996). Mental rotation reconceptualized as stimulus generalization. Paper presented at the 22nd annual convention of the Association for Behavior Analysis, San Francisco, CA, May 24–28.

Remoser, M. R. E., & Fisher, D. L. (2009). The effect of active versus passive training strategies on improving older drivers' scanning in intersections. *Human Factors, 51*(5), 652–668.

Rescorla, R. A. (1967). Pavlovian conditioning and its proper control procedures. *Psychological Review, 74,* 71–80.

Rescorla, R. A. (1968). Probability of shock in the presence and absence of CS in fear conditioning. *Journal of Comparative and Physiological Psychology, 66,* 1–5.

Rescorla, R. A. (1972). "Configural" conditioning in discrete-trial bar pressing. *Journal of Comparative and Physiological Psychology, 79,* 307–317.

Rescorla, R. A. (1973). Evidence of "unique stimulus" account of configural conditioning. *Journal of Comparative and Physiological Psychology, 85,* 331–338.

Rescorla, R. A. (1980). *Pavlovian second-order conditioning: Studies in associative learning.* Hillsdale, NJ: Erlbaum.

Rescorla, R. A., & Wagner, A. R. (1972). A theory of Pavlovian conditioning: Variations in the effectiveness of reinforcement and nonreinforcement. In A. H. Black & W. F. Prokasy (Eds.), *Classical conditioning, II: Current research and theory* (pp. 151–160). New York: Appleton-Century-Crofts.

Revusky, S. H., & Garcia, J. (1970). Learned associations over long delays. In G. H. Bower & J. T. Spence (Eds.), *The psychology of learning and motivation,* Vol. 4 (pp. 53–58). New York: Academic Press.

Reynolds, W. F., & Pavlik, W. B. (1960). Running speed as a function of deprivation period and reward magnitude. *Journal of Comparative and Physiological Psychology, 53,* 615–618.

Rhee, S. H., & Waldman, I. D. (2002). Genetic and environmental influences on antisocial behavior: A meta-analysis of twin and adoption studies. *Psychological Bulletin, 128,* 490–529.

Riccio, D. C., Rabinowitz, V. C., & Axelrod, S. (1994). Memory: When less is more. *American Journal of Psychology, 49,* 917–926.

Richman, S., & Gholson, B. (1978). Strategy modeling, age, and information-processing efficiency. *Journal of Experimental Child Psychology, 26,* 58–70.

Rickard, J. F., Body, S., Zhang, Z., Bradshaw, C. M., & Szabadi, E. (2009). Effect of reinforcer magnitude on performance maintained by progressive-ratio schedules. *Journal of the Experimental Analysis of Behavior, 91,* 75–87.

Ridley, M. (2003). *Nature via nurture: Genes, experience, and what makes us human.* New York: HarperCollins.

Rilling, M., & Caplan, H. J. (1973). Extinction-induced aggression during errorless discrimination learning. *Journal of the Experimental Analysis of Behavior, 20,* 85–91.

Risley, T. R. (1968). The effects and side-effects of punishing the autistic behaviors of a deviant child. *Journal of Applied Behavior Analysis, 1,* 21–34.

Rizzo, A., Parsons, T. D., Lange, B., Kenny, P., Buckwalter, J. G., Rothbaum, B. O., et al. (2011). Virtual reality goes to war: A brief review of the future of military behavioral healthcare. *Journal of Clinical Psychology in Medical Settings, 18,* 176–187.

Rizzo, H. S., Buckwalter, J. G., John, B., Newman, B., Parsons, T., Kenny, P., et al. (2012). STRIVE: Stress resilience in virtual environments: A pre-deployment VR system for training emotional coping skills and assessing chronic and acute stress responses. In J. D. Westwood et al., (Eds.), *Medicine meets virtual reality,* 19: *NextMed* (pp. 379–385). Amsterdam: IOS Press.

Roane, H. S. (2008). On the applied uses of progressive ratio schedules of reinforcement. *Journal of Applied Behavior Analysis, 41*(2), 155–161.

Robert, M. (1990). Observational learning in fish, birds, and mammals: A classified bibliography spanning over 100 years of research. *The Psychological Record, 40,* 289–311.

Roberts, M. W., & Powers, S. W. (1990). Adjusting chair timeout enforcement procedures for oppositional children. *Behavior Therapy, 21,* 257–271.

Rodriguez, G., Alonso, G., & Lombas, S. (2006). Previous blocking trials impede learning about the added CS during compound conditioning trials with an intensified US. *International Journal of Psychology and Psychological Therapy, 6*(3), 301–312.

Roediger, H. L. (1990). Implicit memory: Retention without remembering. *American Psychologist, 45*(9), 1043–1056.

Roediger, H. L., & Karpicke, J. D. (2006a). The power of testing memory: Basic research and implications for educational practice. *Perspectives on Psychological Science, 1,* 181–210.

Roediger, H. L., & Karpicke, J. D. (2006b). Test-enhanced learning: Taking memory tests improves long-term retention. *Psychological Science, 17,* 249–255.

Roediger, H. L., & Meade, M. L. (2000). Cognitive approach for humans. In A. E. Kazdin (Ed.), *Encyclopedia of Psychology,* Vol. 5 (pp. 8–11). New York: Oxford University Press.

Romanowich, P., Bourret, J., & Vollmer, T. R. (2007). Further analysis of the matching law to describe two- and three-point shot selection by professional basketball players. *Journal of the Experimental Analysis of Behavior, 40,* 311–315.

Rosenblum, E. B., Rompler, H., Schoneberg, T., & Hoekstra, H. E. (2010). Molecular and functional basis of phenotypic convergence in white lizards at White Sands. *Proceedings of the National Academy of Sciences, 107*(5), 2113–2117.

Rosenkrans, M. A., & Hartup, W. W. (1967). Imitative influences of consistent and inconsistent response consequences to a model on aggressive behavior in children. *Journal of Personality and Social Psychology, 7,* 429–434.

Rosenthal, M. Z., Lynch, T. R., Strong, D., & Baumann, S. B. (2010). Exposure therapy with portable reminders in substance abuse counseling for crack cocaine dependence. Paper presented at the Association for Behavioral and Cognitive Therapies, San Francisco, CA.

Rothbaum, B. O., Hodges, L. F., Kooper, R., Opdyke, D., Williford, J. S., & North, M. (1995). Virtual reality graded exposure in the treatment of acrophobia: A case report. *Behavior Therapy, 26,* 547–554.

Rothbaum, B. O., Hodges, L. F., Ready, D., Graap, K., & Alarcon, R. (2001). Virtual reality exposure therapy for Vietnam veterans with posttraumatic stress disorder. *Journal of Clinical Psychiatry, 62,* 617–622.

Rothbaum, B. O., Hodges, L. F., Smith, S., Lee, J. H., & Price, L. (2000). A controlled study of virtual reality exposure therapy for the fear of flying. Paper presented at the annual meeting of the American Psychological Association, Washington, DC.

Rothbaum, B. O., Rizzo, A., Difede, J., Reger, G. (2012). Virtual reality exposure therapy for PTSD. In C. Figley (Ed.), *Encyclopedia of trauma: An interdisciplinary guide* (2nd ed.). New York: Sage.

Rovee, C. K., & Rovee, D. T. (1969). Conjugate reinforcement of infant exploratory behavior. *Journal of Experimental Child Psychology, 8,* 33–39.

Rovee-Collier, C. (1995). Time windows in cognitive development. *Developmental Psychology, 51,* 1–23.

Rovee-Collier, C. (1999). The development of infant memory. *Current Directions in Psychological Science, 8*(3), 80–85.

Rovee-Collier, C., & Cuevas, K. (2006). Contextual control of infant retention. *The Behavior Analyst Today, 7,* 121–132.

Rovee-Collier, C., Griesler, P. C., & Earley, L. A. (1985). Contextual determinants of retrieval in three-month-old infants. *Learning and Motivation, 16,* 139–157.

Russell, M., Dark, K. A., Cummins, R. W., Ellman, G., Callaway, E., & Peeke, H. V. S. (1984). Learned histamine release. *Science, 225,* 733–734.

Ryle, G. (1949). *The concept of mind.* London: Hutchinson.

Sallows, G. O., & Graupner, T. D. (2005). Intensive behavioral treatment for children with autism: Four-year outcome and predictors. *American Journal for Mental Retardation, 110,* 417–438.

Salzinger, K. (1996). Reinforcement history: A concept underutilized by behavior analysts. *Journal of Behavior Therapy and Experimental Psychiatry, 27,* 199–207.

Salzinger, K. (2011). Reinforcement gone wrong. Address given at the annual meeting of the Association for Behavior Analysis, Denver, CO, May.

Savory, T. (1974). *Introduction to arachnology.* London: Muller.

Schachtman, T., Walker, J., & Fowler, S. (2011). Effects of conditioning in advertising. In T. Schachtman & S. Reilly (Eds.), *Associative learning and conditioning theory: Human and non-human applications* (pp. 481–506). Oxford, UK: Oxford University Press.

Schacter, D. L. (1987). Implicit memory: History and current status. *Journal of Experimental Psychology: Learning, Memory, and Cognition, 13,* 501–518.

Schall, D. W. (2005). Naming our concerns about neuroscience: A review of Bennett and Hacker's *Philosophical Foundations sof Neuroscience. Journal of the Experimental Analysis of Behavior, 4,* 683–692.

Schendel, J. D., & Hagman, J. D. (1982). On sustaining procedural skills over a prolonged retention interval. *Journal of Applied Psychology, 67,* 605–610.

Schiffman, K., & Furedy, J. J. (1977). The effect of CS-US contingency variation on GSR and on subjective CS-US relational awareness. *Memory and Cognition, 5,* 273–277.

Schlinger, H. D. (2008). Listening is behaving verbally. *The Behavior Analyst, 31,* 145–161.

Schlinger, H. D. (2009). Some clarifications on the role of inner speech in consciousness. *Consciousness and Cognition, 18,* 530–531.

Schlinger, H. D., & Blakely, E. (1994). The effects of delayed reinforcement and a response-produced auditory stimulus on the acquisition of operant behavior in rats. *The Psychological Record, 44,* 391–409.

Schlinger, H. D., Blakely, E., & Kaczor, T. (1990). Pausing under variable-ratio schedules: Interaction of reinforcer magnitude, variable-ratio size, and lowest ratio. *Journal of the Experimental Analysis of Behavior, 53,* 133–139.

Schlinger, H. D., Derenne, A., & Baron, A. (2008). What 50 years of research tell us about pausing under ratio schedules of reinforcement. *The Behavior Analyst, 31,* 39–60.

Schneider, J. W. (1973). Reinforcer effectiveness as a function of reinforcer rate and magnitude: A comparison of concurrent performance. *Journal of the Experimental Analysis of Behavior, 20*, 461–471.

Schneider, S. M. (2003). Evolution, behavior principles, and developmental systems: A review of Gottlieb's Synthesizing nature: Prenatal roots of instinctive behavior. *Journal of the Experimental Analysis of Behavior, 79*, 137–152.

Schneirla, T. C. (1944). A unique case of circular milling in ants, considered in relation to trail following and the general problem of orientation. *American Museum Novitiates, 1253*, 1–26.

Schroers, M., Prigot, J., & Fagen, J. (2007). The effect of a salient odor context on memory retrieval in young infants. *Infant Behavioral Development, 30*(4), 685–689.

Schwab, I. R. (2011). *Evolution's witness: How eyes have evolved.* New York: Oxford University Press.

Schwartz, B., & Gamzu, E. (1979). Pavlovian control of operant behavior: An analysis of autoshaping and its implication for operant conditioning. In W. K. Honig & J. E. R. Staddon (Eds.), *Handbook of operant behavior* (pp. 53–97). Englewood Cliffs, NJ: Prentice Hall.

Schwartz, B., & Lacey, H. (1982). *Behaviorism, science, and human nature.* New York: Norton.

Schwartz, B., Schuldenfrei, R., & Lacey, H. (1978). Operant psychology as factor psychology. *Behaviorism, 6*, 229–254.

Scott, J. P. (1958). *Animal behavior.* Chicago: University of Chicago Press.

Scott, J. P. (1962). Critical periods in behavioral development. *Science, 138*, 949–958.

Sears, R. R., Maccoby, E. E., & Levin, H. (1957) *Patterns of child rearing.* Evanston, IL: Row, Peterson.

Seely, H. (2007, March 23). *If you want the Yankees to win, the key plays are at home.* Available at www.travel.nytimes.com/2007/03/23/travel/escapes/23Ritual.html.

Seligman, M. E. P. (1970). On the generality of the laws of learning. *Psychological Review, 77*, 406–418.

Seligman, M. E. P. (1971). Phobias and preparedness. *Behavior Therapy, 2*, 307–321.

Seligman, M. E. P. (1975). *Helplessness: On depression, development, and death.* San Francisco, CA: Freeman.

Seligman, M. E. P., & Hager, J. L. (1972, August). Biological boundaries of learning: The sauce-bearnaise syndrome. *Psychology Today*, 59–61, 84–87.

Seligman, M. E. P., & Maier, S. F. (1967). Failure to escape traumatic shock. *Journal of Experimental Psychology, 74*, 1–9.

Servatius, R. J., Brennan, F. X., Beck, K. D., Beldowicz, D., & Coyle-Di Norcia, K. (2001). Stress facilitates acquisition of the classically conditioned eyeblink response at both long and short interstimulus intervals. *Learning and Motivation, 32*(2), 178–192.

Shahan, T. A., & Podlesnik, C. A. (2005). Rate of conditioned reinforcement affects observing rate but not resistance to change. *Journal of the Experimental Analysis of Behavior, 84*, 1–17.

Shanks, D. R., & St. Johns, M. F. (1994) Characteristics of dissociable human learning systems. *Behavioral and Brain Sciences, 17*, 367–447.

Shapiro, G. L. (1982). Sign acquisition in a home-reared, free-ranging orangutan: Comparisons with other signing apes. *American Journal of Primatology, 3*, 121–129.

Shapiro, K. J. (1991a, July). Rebuttal by Shapiro: Practices must change. *APA Monitor*, 4.

Shapiro, K. J. (1991b, July). Use morality as a basis for animal treatment. *APA Monitor*, 5.

Sharpless, S. K., & Jasper, H. H. (1956). Habituation of the arousal reaction. *Brain, 79*, 655–680.

Sheffield, F. D., Roby, T. B., & Campbell, B. A. (1954). Drive reduction versus consummatory behavior as determinants of reinforcement. *Journal of Comparative and Physiological Psychology, 47*, 349–354.

Sheffield, F. D., Wulff, J. J., & Barker, R. (1951). Reward value of copulation without sex drive reduction. *Journal of Comparative and Physiological Psychology, 44*, 3–8.

Shermer, M. (2002). Why people believe weird things: Pseudoscience, superstition, and other confusions of our time. New York, NY: Owl Books.

Shic, F., Bradshaw, J., Klin, A., Scassellati, B., & Chawarska, K. (2011). Limited activity monitoring in toddlers with autism spectrum disorder. *Brain Research, 1380*, 246–254. doi: 10.1016/j.brainres.2010.11.074.

Shulz, D. E., Sosnik, R., Ego, V., Haidarliu, S., & Ahissar, E. (2000). A neuronal analogue of state-dependent learning. *Nature, 403*, 549–553.

Shumyatsky, G. P., Malleret, G., Shin, R. M., Takizawa, S., Tully, K., Tsvetkov, E., et al. (2005). Stathmin, a gene enriched in the amygdala, controls both learned and innate fear. *Cell, 123*, 697–709.

Sidman, M. (1953). Avoidance conditioning with brief shock and no exteroceptive warning signal. *Science, 118*(3508), 157–158.

Sidman, M. (1960/1988). *Tactics of scientific research.* Boston, MA: Authors Cooperative.

Sidman, M. (1962). Reduction of shock frequency as reinforcement for avoidance behavior. *Journal of the Experimental Analysis of Behavior, 5*, 247–257.

Sidman, M. (1966). Avoidance behavior. In W. K. Honig (Ed.), *Operant behavior* (pp. 448–498). New York: Appleton-Century-Crofts.

Sidman, M. (1989a). Avoidance at Columbia. *The Behavior Analyst, 12*, 191–195.

Sidman, M. (1989b). *Coercion and its fallout.* Boston, MA: Authors Cooperative.

Siegel, S. (1972). Conditioning of insulin-induced glycemia. *Journal of Comparative and Physiological Psychology, 78*, 233–241.

Siegel, S. (1975). Evidence from rats that morphine tolerance is a learned response. *Journal of Comparative and Physiological Psychology, 89*, 498–506.

Siegel, S. (1984). Pavlovian conditioning and heroin overdose: Reports by overdose victims. *Bulletin of the Psychonomic Society, 22*, 428–430.

Siegel, S. (2005). Drug tolerance, drug addiction, and drug anticipation. *Current Directions in Psychological Science, 14*(6), 296–300.

Siegel, S., Hinson, R. E., Krank, M. D., & McCully, J. (1982). Heroin "overdose" death: Contribution of drug-associated environmental cues. *Science, 216*(4544), 436–437.

Silberman, S. (2006, January). Don't even think about lying: How brain scans are reinventing the science of lie detection. *Wired,* 142.

Silverman, K., Roll, J. M., & Higgins, S. T. (2008). Introduction to the special issue on the behavior analysis and treatment of drug addiction. *Journal of Applied Behavior Analysis, 41*(4), 471–480.

Simmons, R. (1924). The relative effectiveness of certain incentives in animal learning. *Comparative Psychology Monographs,* No. 7.

Simonton, D. K. (1987). Developmental antecedents of achieved eminence. *Annals of Child Development, 5,* 131–169.

Singhal, A. (2010). *Riding high on Taru fever: Entertainment-education broadcasts, ground mobilization, and service delivery in rural India.* Available at www.oxfamnovib.nl.

Singhal, A., Cody, M. J., Rogers, E. M., Sabido, M. (Eds.). (2004). *Entertainment-education and social change: History, research, and practice.* Mahwah, NJ: Erlbaum.

Singhal, A., & Rogers, E. M. (1999). *Entertainment-education: A strategy for social change.* Mahwah, NJ: Erlbaum.

Siqueland, E., & Delucia, C. A. (1969). Visual reinforcement on non-nutritive sucking in human infants. *Science, 165*(3898), 1144–1146.

Skaggs, K. J., Dickinson, A. M., & O'Connor, K. A. (1992). The use of concurrent schedules to evaluate the effects of extrinsic rewards on "intrinsic motivation": A replication. *Journal of Organizational Behavior Management, 12,* 45–83.

Skinner, B. F. (1938). *The behavior of organisms: An experimental analysis.* New York: Appleton-Century-Crofts.

Skinner, B. F. (1948). Superstition in the pigeon. *Journal of Experimental Psychology, 38,* 168–172.

Skinner, B. F. (1950). Are theories of learning necessary? *Psychological Review, 57,* 193–216.

Skinner, B. F. (1951, December). How to teach animals. *Scientific American, 185,* 26–29.

Skinner, B. F. (1953). *Science and human behavior.* New York: Free Press.

Skinner, B. F. (1958a). Reinforcement today. *American Psychologist, 13,* 94–99.

Skinner, B. F. (1958b). Teaching machines. *Science, 128*(3330), 969–977.

Skinner, B. F. (1966). The phylogeny and ontogeny of behavior. *Science, 153*(3741), 1205–1213.

Skinner, B. F. (1968). *The technology of teaching.* Englewood Cliffs, NJ: Prentice-Hall.

Skinner, B. F. (1969). *Contingencies of reinforcement: A theoretical analysis.* New York: Appleton-Century-Crofts.

Skinner, B. F. (1975). The shaping of phylogenetic behavior. *Acta Neurobiologiae Experimentalis, 35,* 409–415.

Skinner, B. F. (1977). *The shaping of a behaviorist.* New York: Knopf.

Skinner, B. F. (1981). Selection by consequences. *Science, 213*(4507), 501–504.

Skinner, B. F. (1984). The evolution of behavior. *Journal of the Experimental Analysis of Behavior, 41,* 217–221.

Skinner, B. F. (1987). Antecedents. *Journal of the Experimental Analysis of Behavior, 48,* 447–448.

Slade, P. D. (1974). The external control of auditory hallucinations: An information theory analysis. *British Journal of Social and Clinical Psychology, 13,* 73–79.

Slifer. K. J., & Amari, A. (2009). Behavior management for children and adolescents with acquired brain injury. *Developmental Disabilities Research Reviews, 15*(2), 144–151.

Sloane, H. N. (1979). *The good kid book' How to solve the 16 most common behavior problems.* Champaign, IL: Research Press.

Sloane, H. N., Endo, G. T., & Della-Piana, G. (1980). Creative behavior. *The Behavior Analyst, 3,* 11–22.

Slonaker, J. R. (1912). The normal activity of the albino rat from birth to natural death, its rate of growth and the duration of life. *Journal of Animal Behavior, 2*(1), 20–42.

Sluckin, W. (2007). *Imprinting and early learning* (2nd ed.) Piscataway, NJ: Aldine Transactions.

Smith, G. S., & Delprato, D. J. (1976). Stimulus control of covert behaviors (urges). *The Psychological Record, 26,* 461–466.

Smith, K. (1984). "Drive": In defense of a concept. *Behaviorism, 12,* 71–114.

Smith, K. M., Anthony, S. J., Switzer, W. M., Epstein, J. H., Seimon, T., Jia, H., et al. (2012). Zoonotic viruses associated with illegally imported wildlife products. *PLoS ONE, 7*(1), e29505. doi: 10.1371/journal.pone.0029505.

Smith, M. D. (1987). Treatment of pica in an adult disabled by autism by differential reinforcement of incompatible behavior. *Journal of Behavior Therapy and Experimental Psychiatry, 18*(3), 285–288.

Smith, T. (1999). Outcome of early intervention for children with autism. *Clinical Psychology: Science and Practice, 6,* 33–49.

Soares, J. J. F., & Öhman, A. (1993). Backward masking and skin conductance responses after conditioning to non-feared but fear-relevant stimuli in fearful subjects. *Psychophysiology, 30,* 460–466.

Solomon, P. R., Levine, E., Bein, R., & Pendlebury, W. W. (1991). Disruption of classical conditioning in patients with Alzheimer's disease. *Neurobiology of Aging, 12*(4), 283–287.

Solomon, R. L., & Corbet, J. D. (1974). An opponent-process theory of motivation: I. Temporal dynamics of affect. *Psychological Review, 81,* 119–143.

Solomon, R. L., & Wynne, L. C. (1953). Traumatic avoidance learning: Acquisition in normal dogs. *Psychological Monographs, 67*(4), 1–19.

Soon, C. S., Brass, M., Heinze, H., & Haynes, J. (2008). Unconscious determinants of free decisions in the human brain. *Nature Neuroscience, 11,* 543–545. doi: 10.1038/nn.2112.

Sosa, J. J. S. (1982). Behavior analysis in marriage counseling: A methodological review of the research literature. *Revista Mexicana de Analisis de la Conducta, 8*(2), 149–156.

Spector, N. H. (2009). A tribute to Elena Korneva: Reversal of aging and cancer by Pavlovian conditioning: Neuroimmunomodulation—some history. *Neuroscience and Behavioral Physiology, 41*(1), 102–116.

Spence, D. P. (2001). Dangers of anecdotal reports. *Journal of Clinical Psychology, 57,* 37–41.

Spence, K. W. (1936). The nature of discrimination learning in animals. *Psychological Review, 43,* 427–449.

Spence, K. W. (1937). The differential response in animals to stimuli varying within a single dimension. *Psychological Review, 44,* 430–444.

Spence, K. W. (1953). Learning and performance in eyelid conditioning as a function of intensity of the UCS. *Journal of Experimental Psychology, 45,* 57–63.

Spence, K. W. (1960). *Behavior theory and learning.* Englewood Cliffs, NJ: Prentice-Hall.

Spetch, M. L., Wilkie, D. M., & Pinel, J. P. J. (1981). Backward conditioning: A reevaluation of the empirical evidence. *Psychological Bulletin, 89,* 163–175.

Staats, A. W. (2006). Positive and negative reinforcers: How about the second and third functions? *The Behavior Analyst, 29,* 271–272.

Staats, A. W., & Staats, C. K. (1958). Attitudes established by classical conditioning. *Journal of Abnormal and Social Psychology, 57,* 37–40.

Staats, C. K., & Staats, A. W. (1957). Meaning established by classical conditioning. *Journal of Experimental Psychology, 54,* 74–80.

Stack, S. (1987). Celebrities and suicide: A taxonomy and analysis, 1948–1983. *American Sociological Review, 52*(3), 401–412.

Stack, S. (2000). Media impacts on suicide: A quantitative review of 293 findings. *Social Science Quarterly, 81*(4), 957–971.

Staddon, J. E. R. (1991). Selective choice: A commentary on Herrnstein (1990). *American Psychologist, 46,* 793–797.

Staddon, J. E. R. (2001). *The new behaviorism: Mind, mechanism, and society.* Philadelphia, PA: Psychology Press.

Staddon, J. E. R., & Simmelhag, V. L. (1971). The "superstition" experiment: A reexamination of its implications for the principles of adaptive behavior. *Psychological Review, 78,* 3–43.

Stanton, M. E., & Gallagher, M. (1998). Use of Pavlovian conditioning techniques to study disorders of attention and learning. *Mental Retardation and Developmental Disabilities Research Reviews, 2,* 234–242.

Steinman, W. M. (1970). The social control of generalized imitation. *Journal of Applied Behavior Analysis, 3,* 159–167.

Steinmetz, J. E., & Lindquist, D. H. (2009). Neuronal basis of learning. *Handbook of Neuronal Science for the Behavioral Sciences.* doi: 10.1002/9780470478509.neubb00102.

Stephane, M., Barton, S., & Boutros, N. N. (2001). Auditory verbal hallucinations and dysfunction of the neural substrates of speech. *Schizophrenia Research, 50*(1), 61–78.

Stern, A. (1971, August). *The making of a genius.* Miami: Hurricane House.

Stewart, T., Ernstam, H. T., & Farmer-Dougan, V. (2001, May 25–29). Operant conditioning of reptiles: Conditioning two Galapagos and one African Spurred Tortoises to approach, follow and stand. Poster presented at the annual convention of the Association for Behavior Analysis, New Orleans.

Stewart, W. J. (1975). Progressive reinforcement schedules: A review and assessment. *Australian Journal of Psychology, 27*(1), 9–22.

Stix, G. (2010, October). Craving a cure. *Scientific American,* 32.

Stokes, T. F., & Baer, D. M. (1977). An implicit technology of generalization. *Journal of Applied Behavior Analysis, 10,* 349–367.

Stokes, T. F., & Osne, P. G. (1989). An operant pursuit of generalization. *Behavior Therapy, 20,* 337–355.

Stuart, E. W., Shimp, T. A., & Engle, R. W. (1987). Classical conditioning of consumer attitudes: Four experiments in an advertising context. *Journal of Consumer Research, 14,* 334–349.

Sugai, R., Azami, S., Shiga, H., Watanabe, T., Sadamoto, H., Kobayashi, S., et al. (2007). One-trial conditioned taste aversion in *Lymnaea*: Good and poor performers in long-term memory acquisition. *Journal of Experimental Biology, 210,* 1225–1237.

Sulzer-Azaroff, B. (1998). *Who killed my daddy?: A behavioral safety fable.* Beverly, MA: Cambridge Center for Behavioral Studies.

Sundberg, M. L., & Partington, J. W. (1998/2010). *Teaching language to children with autism or other developmental disabilities.* Concord, CA: AVB Press.

Sung, H. (2009, January 31). Father who used dog shock collar on his kids sentenced to prison. *The Examiner,* 5.

Suzuki, T., & Moriyama, T. (1999). Contingency of food reinforcement necessary for maintenance of imprinted responses in chicks. *Japanese Journal of Animal Psychology, 49,* 139–156.

Sweeney, J. J. (2010). A systematic replication of the effectiveness of group discrete trial teaching for students with autism. Unpublished Ph.D. dissertation, Kent State University, Kent, OH.

Sy, J. R., Borrero, J. C., Borrero, C. S. W. (2010). Characterizing response-reinforcer relations in the natural environment: Exploratory matching analyses. *The Psychological Record, 60,* 609–626.

Szcytkowski, J. L., & Lysle, D. T. (2011). Conditioned immunomodulation. In T. Schachtman & S. Reilly (Eds.), *Associative learning and conditioning theory: Human and non-human applications.* Oxford, UK: Oxford University Press.

Szyszka, P., Dimmler, C., Oemisch, M., Sommer, L., Biergans, S., Birnbach, B., et al. (2011). Mind the gap: Olfactory trace conditioning in honeybees. *The Journal of Neuroscience, 31*(20), 7229–7239.

Tabone, B. A., & de Belle, J. S. (2011). Second-order conditioning in Drosophilia. *Learning and Motivation, 18(4),* 250–253.

Talwar, S. J., Xu, S., Hawley, E. S., Weiss, S. A., Moxon, K. A., & Chapin, J. K. (2002). Behavioral neuroscience: Rat navigation guided by remote control. *Nature, 417,* 37–38.

Tanner, B. A., & Zeiler, M. (1975). Punishment of self-injurious behavior using aromatic ammonia as an aversive stimulus. *Journal of Applied Behavior Analysis, 8,* 53–57.

Tarpley, H. D., & Schroeder, S. R. (1979). Comparison of DRO and DRI on rate of suppression of self-injurious behavior. *American Journal of Mental Deficiency, 84,* 188–194.

Tate, B. G. (1972). Case study: Control of chronic self-injurious behavior by conditioning procedures. *Behavior Therapy, 3,* 72–82.

Tate, B. G., & Baroff, G. S. (1966). Aversive control of self-injurious behavior in a psychotic boy. *Behavior Research and Therapy, 4,* 281–287.

Taub, E. (1977). Movement in nonhuman primates deprived of somatosensory feedback. *Exercise and Sports Science Reviews, 4,* 335–374.

Taub, E. (1980). Somatosensory deafferentation research with monkeys: Implications for rehabilitation medicine. In L. P. Ince (Ed.), *Behavioral psychologyin rehabilitation medicine: Clinical applications* (pp. 371–401). New York: Williams & Wilkns.

Taub, E. (2011). Constraint-induced therapy: The use of operant training to produce new treatments in neuro-rehabilitation. Invited address, ABAI convention, Denver, CO, May.

Taub, E., Crago, J. E., Burgio, L. D., Groomes, T. E., Cook, E. W., III, DeLuca, S. C., et al. (1994). An operant approach to rehabilitation medicine: Overcoming learned nonuse by shaping. *Journal of the Experimental Analysis of Behavior, 61*(2), 281–293.

Taub, E., Ramey, S. L., DeLuca, S., & Echols, E. (2004). Efficacy of constraint-induced (CI) movement therapy for children with cerebral palsy with asymmetric motoar impairment. *Pediatrics, 113,* 305–312.

Taub, E., & Uswatte, G. (2009). Constraint-induced movement therapy: A paradigm for translating advances in behavioral neuroscience into rehabilitation treatments. In G. B. Berntson & J. T. Cacioppo (Eds.), *Handbook of neuroscience for the behavioral sciences* (pp. 1296–1319). Published online October 30, 2009. http://onlinelibrary.wiley.com/book/10.1002/9780470478509.

Taubman, M., Brierley, S., Wishner, J., McEachin, J., & Leaf, R. B. (2001). The effectiveness of a group discrete trial instructional approach for preschoolers with developmental disabilities. *Research in Developmental Disabilities, 22,* 205–219.

Taylor, B. A. (2012). Do this, but don't do that: Teaching children with autism to learn by observation. In W. L. Heward, *Exceptional children: An introduction to special education* (10th ed.) (pp. 240–242). Upper Saddle River, NJ: Pearson.

Taylor, B. A., & DeQuinzio, J. A. (2012). Observational learning and children with autism. *Behavior Modification, 36*(3), 341–360.

Taylor, B. A., & Hoch, H. (2008). Teaching children with autism to respond to and initiate bids for joint attention. *Journal of Applied Behavior Analysis, 41,* 377–391.

Taylor, J. A. (1951). The relationship of anxiety to the conditioned eyelid response. *Journal of Experimental Psychology, 41,* 81–92.

Taylor, J. B. (2008). *My stroke of insight.* New York: Viking.

Templeman, T. L., & Stinnett, R. D. (1991). Patterns of sexual arousal and history in a "normal" sample of young men. *Archives of Sexual Behavior, 20,* 137–150.

Tennie, C., Call, J., & Tomasello, M. (2006). Push or pull: Imitation vs. emulation in great apes and human children. *Ethology: International Journal of Behavioral Biology, 112*(12), 1159–1169.

Tennie, C., Call, J., & Tomasello, M. (2009). Racheting up the ratchet: On the evolution of cumulative culture. *Philosophical Transactions of the Royal Society Series B, 364,* 2405–2415. doi: 10.1098/rstb.2009.0052.

ter Heijden, N., & Brinkman, W. P. (2011). Design and evaluation of a virtual reality exposure therapy system with automatic free speech interaction. *Journal of CyberTherapy and Rehabilitation, 4*(1), 41–55.

Terrace, H. S. (1963a). Discrimination learning with and without "errors." *Journal of the Experimental Analysis of Behavior, 6,* 1–27.

Terrace, H. S. (1963b). Errorless transfer of a discrimination across two continua. *Journal of the Experimental Analysis of Behavior, 6,* 223–232.

Terrace, H. S. (1964). Wavelength generalization after discrimination learning with and without errors. *Science, 144,* 78–80.

Terrace, H. S. (1972). By-products of discrimination learning. In G. H. Bower (Ed.), *The psychology of learning and motivation,* Vol. 5 (pp. 195–266). New York: Academic Press.

Terrace, H. S. (1979). *Nim.* New York: Knopf.

30,000 obscene calls traced. (1991, July 7). *The* (Wilmington, DE) *News Journal,* p. A2.

This smart University of Minnesota rat works a slot machine for a living. (1937, May 31). *Life*, 80–81.

Thomas, D. R. (1981). Studies of long-term memory in the pigeon. In N. E. Spear & R. R. Miller (Eds.), *Information processing in animals: Memory mechanisms*. Hillsdale, NJ: Erlbaum.

Thomas, D. R. (1991). Stimulus control: Principles and procedures. In W. Ishaq (Ed.), *Human behavior in today's world* (pp. 191–203). New York: Praeger.

Thomas, D. R., Becker, W. C., & Armstrong, M. (1968). Production and elimination of disruptive classroom behavior by systematically varying teacher's behavior. *Journal of Applied Behavior Analysis, 1*, 35–45.

Thomas, D. R., & Burr, D. E. S. (1969). Stimulus generalization as a function of the delay between training and testing procedures: a reevaluation. *Journal of the Experimental Analysis of Behavior, 12*(1), 105–109.

Thomas, D. R., Mood, K., Morrison, S., & Wiertelak, E. (1991). Peak shift revisited: A test of alternative interpretations. *Journal of Experimental Psychology: Animal Behavior Processes, 17*, 130–140.

Thompson, D. E., & Russell, J. (2004). The ghost condition: Imitation versus emulation in young children's observational learning. *Developmental Psychology, 40*(5), 882–889.

Thompson, L. G. (in press). The greatest challenge of global climate change: An inconvenient truth meets the inconvenienced mind. *Inside Behavior Analysis*. This article will be available at www.abai.org.

Thompson, R. F. (2000). Habituation. In A. E. Kazdin (Ed.), *Encyclopedia of psychology* (pp. 47–50). New York: Oxford University Press.

Thompson, R. F. (2009). Habituation: A history. *Neurobiology of Learning and Memory, 92*, 127–134.

Thompson, T., Heistad, G. T., & Palermo, D. S. (1963). Effect of amount of training on rate and duration of responding during extinction. *Journal of the Experimental Analysis of Behavior, 6*(2), 155–161.

Thorndike, E. L. (1898). Animal intelligence. *Psychological Review Monographs, 2*(8).

Thorndike, E. L. (1901). The mental life of the monkeys. *Psychological Review Monographs, 3*(15).

Thorndike, E. L. (1911). *Animal intelligence: Experimental studies*. New York: Hafner.

Thorndike, E. L. (1927). The law of effect. *American Journal of Psychology, 39*, 212–222.

Thorndike, E. L. (1931/1968). *Human learning*. Cambridge, MA: MIT Press.

Thorndike, E. L. (1932). *Fundamentals of learning*. New York: Teachers College Press.

Thorndike, E. L. (1936). Autobiography. In C. Murchison (Ed.), *A history of psychology in autobiography*, Vol. 3 (pp. 263–270). Worcester, MA: Clark University Press.

Thornton, A., & McAuliffe, K. (2006). Teaching in wild meerkats. *Science, 313*(5784), 227–229.

Thorpe, W. H. (1963). *Learning and instinct in animals*. London: Methuen.

Thune, L. E., & Underwood, B. J. (1943). Retroactive inhibition as a function of degree of interpolated learning. *Journal of Experimental Psychology, 32*, 185–200.

Timberlake, W. (1980). A molar equilibrium theory of learned performance. In G. H. Bower (Ed.), *The psychology of learning and motivation*, Vol. 14 (pp. 1–58). New York: Academic Press.

Timberlake, W., & Allison, J. (1974). Response deprivation: An empirical approach to instrumental performance. *Psychological Review, 81*, 146–164.

Timberlake, W., & Lucas, G. A. (1985). The basis of superstitious behavior: Chance contingency, stimulus substitution, or appetitive behavior? *Journal of the Experimental Analysis of Behavior, 44*, 279–299.

Tinbergen, N. (1951). *The study of instinct*. Oxford, UK: Clarendon Press.

Tizard, B., & Hodges, J. (1978). The effect of early institutional rearing on the development of eight year old children. *Journal of Child Psychology and Psychiatry, 19*, 99–118.

Todd, D. E., Besko, G. T., & Pear, J. J. (1995). *Human shaping parameters: A 3-dimensional investigation*. Poster presented at the meeting of the Association for Behavior Analysis, San Francisco, CA, May 26–30.

Todd, J. T., & Morris, E. K. (1992). Case histories in the great power of steady misrepresentation. *American Psychologist, 47*, 1441–1453.

Todorov, J. C., Hanna, E. S., & Bittencourt de Sa, M. C. N. (1984). Frequency versus magnitude of reinforcement: New data with a different procedure. *Journal of the Experimental Analysis of Behavior, 4*, 157–167.

Tøien, Ø., Blake, J., Edgar, D. M., Grahn, D. A., Heller, H. C., & Barnes, B. M. (2011). Hibernation in black bears: Independence of metabolic suppression from body temperature. *Science, 331*(6019), 906–909.

Tolman, E. C., & Honzik, C. H. (1930). Introduction and removal of reward, and maze performance in rats. *University of California Publications in Psychology, 4*, 257–275.

Topal, J., Gergely, G., Erdohegy, A., Csibra, G., & Miklosi, A. (2009). Differential sensitivity to human communication in dogs, wolves, and human infants. *Science, 325*(5945), 1269–1272.

Toro, J. M., Trobalon, J. B., & Sebastian-Galles, N. (2005). Effects of backward speech and speaker variability in language discrimination in rats. *Journal of Experimental Psychology: Animal Behavior Processes, 31*(1), 95–100.

Towles-Schwen, T., & Fazio, R. H. (2001). On the origin of racial attitudes: Correlates of childhood experiences. *Personality and social psychology bulletin, 27*, 162–175.

Tracy, J. A., Ghose, S. S., Stecher, T., McFall, R. M., & Steinmetz, J. E. (1999). Classical conditioning in a nonclinical obsessive-compulsive population. *Psychological Science, 10*(1), 9–13.

Trained sheep graze vineyard weeds. (2007, June 11). Available at www.news.ucdavis.edu/search/printable_news.lasso?id-8200&table=news.

Trapold, M. A. (1970). Are expectancies based upon different positive reinforcing events discriminably different? *Learning and Motivation, 1,* 129–140.

Treiman, R. (2000). The foundations of literacy. *Current Directions in Psychological Science, 9(3),* 89–92.

Tresz, H., & Wright, H. (2006). Let them be elephants! How Phoenix Zoo integrated three "problem" animals. *International Zoo News, 53*(3), 154–160.

Trout, J. D. (2001). The biological basis of speech: What to infer from talking to the animals. *Psychological Review, 108,* 523–549.

Trut, L. N. (1999). Early canid domestication: The farm-fox experiment. *American Scientist, 87,* 160–169.

Tryon, R. C. (1940). Genetic differences in maze-learning ability in rats. In *Thirty-ninth yearbook of the National Society for the Study of Education. Intelligence: Its nature and nurture, Part I: Comparative and critical exposition.* Bloomington, IN: Public School Publishing Co.

Tulving, E. (1972). *Episodic and semantic memory.* New York: Oxford University Press.

Tulving, E. (1974). Cue-dependent forgetting. *American Scientist, 62*(1), 74–82.

Tulving, E. (1983). *Elements of episodic memory.* New York: Clarendon Press.

Tulving, E. (1985). How many memory systems are there? *American Psychologist, 40,* 38–398.

Turkheimer, E., Haley, A., Waldron, M., D'Onofrio, B., & Gottesman, I. (2003). Socioeconomic status modizfies heritability of IQ in young children. *Psychological Science, 14*(6), 623–628.

Turkkan, J. S. (1989). Classical conditioning: The new hegemony. *Behavioral and Brain Sciences, 12,* 121–179.

Twyman, J. S., Layng, T. V. J., & Layng, Z. R. (2011). The likelihood of instructionally beneficial, trivial, or negative results for kindergarten and first grade learners who complete at least half of Headsprout® *Early Reading. Behavioral Technology Today, 6,* 1–19.

Ulrich, R. E., & Azrin, N. A. (1962). Reflexive fighting in response to aversive stimuli. *Journal of the Experimental Analysis of Behavior, 5,* 511–520.

Ulrich, R. E., Hutchinson, R. R., & Azrin, N. H. (1965). Pain-elicited aggression. *The Psychological Record, 15,* 116–126.

Underwood, B. J. (1957). Interference and forgetting. *Psychological Review, 64,* 49–60.

U.S. Department of Health and Human Services. (1988). *The health consequences of smoking: Nicotine addiction. A report of the Surgeon General.* DHHS Publication No. (CDC) 88-8406. Washington, DC: U.S. Government Printing Office.

Valentine, C. W. (1930). The innate bases of fear. *Journal of Genetic Psychology, 37,* 394–420.

Van Damme, S., Crombez, G., Hermans, D., Koster, E. H. W., & Eccleston, C. (2006). The role of extinction and reinstatement in attentional bias to threat: A conditioning approach. *Behavior Research and Therapy, 44*(11), 1555–1563.

Vander Wall, S. B. (1982). An experimental analysis of cache recovery by Clark's nutcracker. *Animal Behavior, 30,* 80–94.

Vander Wall, S. B. (1991). Mechanisms of cache recovery by yellow pine chipmunks. *Animal Behavior, 41,* 851–863.

Van Houten, R. (1983). Punishment: From the animal laboratory to the applied setting. In S. Axelrod & J. Apsche (Eds.), *The effects of punishment on human behavior* (pp. 13–44). New York: Academic Press.

Vaughan, P. W., Rogers, E. M., Singhal, A., & Swalehe, R. M. (2000). Entertainment-education and HIV/AIDS prevention: A field experiment in Tanzania. *Journal of Health Communications, 5*(Suppl.), 81–100.

Venn, J. R., & Short, J. G. (1973). Vicarious classical conditioning of emotional responses in nursery school children. *Journal of Personality and Social Psychology, 28*(2), 249–255.

Verplanck, W. S. (1955). The operant, from rat to man: An introduction to some recent experiments on human behavior. *Transactions of the New York Academy of Sciences, 17,* 594–601.

Vollmer, T. R., & Bourret, J. (2000). An application of the matching law to evaluate the allocation of two- and three-point shots by college basketball players. *Journal of Applied Behavior Analysis, 33,* 137–150.

Volpicelli, J. R., Ulm, R. R., Altenor, A., & Seligman, M. E. P. (1983). Learned mastery in the rat. *Learning and Motivation, 14,* 204–222.

Vyse, S. A. (2000). *Believing in magic: The psychology of superstition.* New York: Oxford University Press.

Wagner, A. R. (1981). SOP: A model of automatic memory processing in animal behavior. In N. E. Spear & R. R. Miller (Eds.), *Information processing in animals: Memory mechanisms* (pp. 5–47). Hillsdale, NJ: Erlbaum.

Wagner, A. R., & Rescorla, R. A. (1972). Inhibition in Pavlovian conditioning: Application of a theory. In R. A. Boakes & M. S. Halliday (Eds.), *Inhibition and learning* (pp. 5–39). New York: Academic Press.

Wagner, G. A., & Morris, E. K. (1987). "Superstitious" behavior in children. *The Psychological Record, 37,* 471–488.

Wallace, K. J., & Rosen, J. B. (2000). Predator odor as an unconditional fear stimulus in rats: Elicitation of freezing by trimethylthiazoline, a component of fox feces. *Behavioral Neuroscience, 114*(5), 912–922.

Wallace, P. (1976). Animal behavior: The puzzle of flavor aversion. *Science, 193*(4257), 989–991.

Wallman, J. (1992). *Aping language*. Cambridge, UK: Cambridge University Press.

Walters, R. H., & Brown, M. (1963). Studies of reinforcement of aggression, III: Transfer of responses to an interpersonal situation. *Child Development, 34*, 563–571.

Walther, E., & Nagengast, B. (2006). Evaluative conditioning and the awareness issue: Assessing contingency awareness with the four-picture recognition test. *Journal of Experimental Psychology: Animal Behavior Processes, 32*, 454–459.

Wansink, B. (2006). *Mindless eating: Why we eat more than we think*. New York: Bantam.

Ward, P. (2011). Goal setting and performance feedback. In J. K. Luiselli & D. D. Reed (Eds.), *Behavioral sports psychology: Evidence-based approaches to performance enhancement* (pp. 99–112). New York: Springer.

Warden, C. J., & Aylesworth, M. (1927). The relative value of reward and punishment in the formation of a visual discrimination habit in the white rat. *Journal of Comparative Psychology, 7*, 117–128.

Warden, C. J., Fjeld, H. A., & Koch, A. M. (1940). Imitative behavior in cebus and rhesus monkeys. *Journal of Genetic Psychology, 56*, 311–322.

Warden, C. J., & Jackson, T. A. (1935). Imitative behavior in the rhesus monkey. *Journal of Genetic Psychology, 46*, 103–125.

Wasserman, E. (1989). Pavlovian conditioning: Is temporal contiguity irrelevant? *American Psychologist, 44*, 1550–1551.

Wasserman, I. M. (1984). Imitation and suicide: A reexamination of the Werther effect. *American Sociological Review, 49*(3), 427–436.

Watanabe, K., Urasopon, N., & Malaivitimond, S. (2007). Long-tailed macaques use human hair as dental floss. *American Journal of Primatology, 69*, 940–944.

Watanabe, S., Sakamoto, J., & Wakita, M. (1995). Pigeons' discrimination of paintings by Monet and Picasso. *Journal of the Experimental Analysis of Behavior, 63*, 165–174.

Watson, J. B. (1908). Imitation in monkeys. *Psychological Bulletin, 5*, 169–178.

Watson, J. B. (1920). Is thinking merely the action of language mechanisms? *British Journal of Psychology, 11*, 87–104.

Watson, J. B. (1930/1970). *Behaviorism*. New York: Norton & Co.

Watson, J. B., & Rayner, R. (1920). Conditioned emotional reactions. *Journal of Experimental Psychology, 3*, 1–4.

Watson, J. B., & Watson, R. R. (1921). Studies in infant psychology. *Scientific Monthly, 13*, 493–515.

Weatherly, J., & Dannewitz, H. (2005). Behavior analysis and illusion of control in gamblers. Talk presented at the annual meeting of the Association for Behavior Analysis–International, Beijing, China, November.

Weiner, J. (1994). The beak of the finch: A study of evolution in our time. New York, NY: Knopf.

Weir, P. L., & Leavitt, J. L. (1990). Effects of model's skill level and model's knowledge of results on the performance of a dart throwing task. *Human Movement Science, 9*, 369–383.

Weisberg, P., & Fink, E. (1966). Fixed ratio and extinction performance of infants in the second year of life. *Journal of the Experimental Analysis of Behavior, 9*(2), 105–109.

Weisberg, P., & Waldrop, P. B. (1972). Fixed-Interval work habits of Congress. *Journal of Applied Behavior Analysis, 5*(1), 93–97.

Wells, G. L., & Olson, E. A. (2003). Eyewitness testimony. *Annual review of psychology, 54*, 277–295.

Wells, G. L., Steblay, N. K., & Dysart, J. E. (2011). *A test of the simultaneous vs. sequential lineup methods: An initial report of the AJS national eyewitness identification field studies*. Des Moines, Iowa: American Judicature Society.

Wells, H. K. (1956). *Pavlov and Freud, I: Toward a scientific psychology and psychiatry*. London: Lawrence and Wishart.

Werts, M. G., Caldwell, N. K., & Wolery, M. (1996). Peer modeling of response chains: Observational learning by subjects with disabiliies. *Journal of Applied Behavior Analysis, 29*, 53–66.

Whalen, C., & Schreibman, L. (2003). Joint attention training for children with autism using behavior modification procedures. *Journal of Child Psychology and Psychiatry, 44*(3), 456–468.

Whiten, A. (2006). The significance of socially transmitted information for nutrition and health in the great ape clade. In J. C. K. Wells, K. Laland, & S. S. Strickland (Eds.), *Social information transmission and human biology* (pp. 118–134). London: CRC Press.

Whiten, A., Goodall, J., McGrew, W. C., Nishida, T., Reynolds, V., Sugiyama, Y., et al. (2001). Charting cultural variation in chimpanzees. *Behaviour, 138*(11/12), 1481–1516.

Whiten, A., McGuigan, N., Marshall-Pescini, S., & Hopper, L. M. (2009). Emulation, imitation, over-imitation and the scope of culture for child and chimpanzee. *Philosophical Transactions of the Royal Society Series B, 364*, 2417–2428.

Whitlock, J., & Eckenrode, J. (2006). Self-injurious behavior in a college population. *Pediatrics, 117*(6), 1939–1948.

Wilkenfield, J., Nickel, M., Blakely, E., & Poling, A. (1992). Acquisition of lever-press responding in rats with delayed reinforcement: A comparison of three procedures. *Journal of the Experimental Analysis of Behavior, 58*, 431–443.

Wilkes, G. (1994). *A behavior sampler*. North Bend, WA: Sunshine Books.

Williams, S. L., Turner, S. M., & Peer, D. F. (1985). Guided mastery and performance desensitization for severe acrophobia. *Journal of Counseling and Clinical Psychology, 53*, 237–247.

Williams, J. E. (1966). Connotations of racial concepts and color names. *Journal of Personality and Social Psychology, 3*, 531–540.

Williams, J. E., & Edwards, C. D. (1969). An exploratory study of the modification of color concepts and racial attitudes in preschool children. *Child Development, 40*, 737–750.

Williams, J. H. G., Whiten, A., & Singh, T. (2004). A systematic review of action imitation in autistic spectrum disorder. *Journal of Autism and Developmental Disorders, 34*(3), 285–299.

Williams, S. B. (1938). Resistance to extinction as a function of the number of reinforcements. *Journal of Experimental Psychology, 23*, 506–522.

Williamson, R. A., & Meltzoff, A. N. (2011). Own and others' prior experiences influence children's imitation of causal acts. *Cognitive Development, 26*(3), 260–268.

Wilson, E. O. (1978). *On human nature.* Cambridge, MA: Harvard University Press.

Wilson, K. G., & Blackledge, J. T. (1999). Recent developments in the behavioral analysis of language: Making sense of clinical phenomena. In M. J. Dougher (Ed.), *Clinical Behavior Analysis* (pp. 27–46). Reno, NV: Context Press.

Wincze, J. P., Leitenberg, H., & Agras, W. S. (1972). The effects of token reinforcement and feedback on the delusional verbal behavior of chronic paranoid schizophrenics. *Journal of Applied Behavior Analysis, 5*, 247–262.

Winston, A. S., & Baker, J. E. (1985). Behavior-analytic studies of creativity: A critical review. *The Behavior Analyst, 8*, 191–205.

Wolf, M. M., Birnbrauer, J. S., Williams, T., & Lawler, J. (1965). A note on apparent extinction of the vomiting behavior of a retarded child. In L. P. Ullmann & L. Krasner (Eds.), *Case studies in behavior modification* (pp. 364–366). New York: Holt, Rinehart, & Winston.

Wolf, M. M., Braukmann, C. J., & Ramp, K. A. (1987). Serious delinquent behavior as part of a significantly handicapping condition: Cures and supportive environments. *Journal of Applied Behavior Analysis, 20*, 347–359.

Wolfe, J. B. (1936). Effectiveness of token-rewards for chimpanzees. *Comparative Psychology Monographs, 12*(60).

Wolpe, J. (1973). *The practice of behavior therapy* (2nd ed.). New York: Pergamon.

Wolpe, J., & Plaud, J. J. (1997). Pavlov's contributions to behavior therapy: The obvious and the not so obvious. *American Psychologist, 52*, 966–972.

Woman pesters ex-lover with 1,000 calls a day. (2000, February 24). Reuters News Service on America Online.

Wong, K. (2000, April). Who were the Neandertals? *Scientific American*, 98–107.

Wong, K. (2002, January). Taking wing. *Scientific American*, 16–18.

Wood, S. M., & Craigen, L. M. (2011). Self-injurious behavior in gifted and talented youth: What every educator should know. *Journal for the Education of the Gifted, 34*(6), 839–859.

Woodruff-Pak, D. S. (2001). Eyeblink classical conditioning differentiates normal aging from Alzheimer's disease. *Integrative Physiological and Behavioral Science, 36*(2), 87–108.

Woodruff-Pak, D. S., Papka, M., Romano, S., & Li, Y. (1996). Eyeblink classical conditioning in Alzheimer disease and cerebrovascular dementia. *Neurobiology of Aging, 17*(4), 505–512.

Woods, P. J. (1974). A taxonomy of instrumental conditioning. *American Psychologist, 29*(8), 584–597.

Wyatt, W. J. (2001). TV, films, blamed for child violence. *Behavior Analysis Digest, 13*(2), 7.

Yando, R. M., Seitz, V., & Zigler, E. (1978). *Imitation: A developmental perspective.* Hillsdale, NJ: Erlbaum.

Yates, A. J. (1958). Symptom and symptom substitution. *Psychological Review, 65*(6), 371–374.

Yerkes, R. M., & Morgulis, S. (1909). The method of Pavlov in animal psychology. *Psychological Bulletin, 6*, 257–273.

Zane, J. P. (2012, March 8). Why the Fonz is back as TV pitchman. *New York Times*, p. F1.

Zeiler, M. D. (1968). Fixed and variable schedules of response-independent reinforcement. *Journal of the Experimental Analysis of Behavior, 11*, 405–414.

Zeiler, M. D. (1984). The sleeping giant: Reinforcement schedules. *Journal of the Experimental Analysis of Behavior, 42*, 485–493.

Zener, K. (1937). The significance of behavior accompanying conditioned salivary secretion for theories of the conditioned response. *American Journal of Psychology, 50*, 384–403.

Zentall, T. R., & Singer, R. A. (2007). Within-trial contrast: Pigeons prefer conditioned reinforcers that follow a relatively more rather than a less aversive event. *Journal of the Experimental Analysis of Behavior, 88*, 131–149.

Zettle, R. D. (2003). Acceptance and commitment therapy vs. systematic desensitization in treatment of mathematical anxiety. *The Psychological Record, 53*, 197–215.

Zimmerman, D. W. (1957). Durable secondary reinforcement: Method and theory. *Psychological Review, 64*, 373–383.

Zorawski, M., Cook, C. A., Kuhn, C. M., LaBar, K. S. (2005). Sex, Stress, and Fear: Individual differences in conditioned learning. *Cognitive, Affective and Behavioral Neuroscience, 5*(2), 191–201.

# Author Index

# Subject Index